World Cultures
AND
GEOGRAPHY
Western Hemisphere and Europe

McDOUGAL LITTELL

McDOUGAL LITTELL

World Cultures AND GEOGRAPHY

Western Hemisphere and Europe

Sarah Witham Bednarz

Inés M. Miyares

Mark C. Schug

Charles S. White

McDougal Littell

A DIVISION OF HOUGHTON MIFFLIN COMPANY

Senior Consultants

Sarah Witham Bednarz is associate professor of geography at Texas A&M University, where she has taught since 1988. She earned a Ph.D. in educational curriculum and instruction in 1992 from Texas A&M University and has written extensively about geography literacy and education. Dr. Bednarz was an author of *Geography for Life: National Geography Standards,* 1994. In 1997 she received the International Excellence Award from the Texas A&M University International Programs Office.

Inés M. Miyares is associate professor of geography at Hunter College–City University of New York. Born in Havana, Cuba, and fluent in Spanish, Dr. Miyares has focused much of her scholarship on Latin America, immigration and refugee policy, and urban ethnic geography. She holds a Ph.D. in geography from Arizona State University. In 1999 Dr. Miyares was the recipient of the Hunter College Performance Excellence Award for excellence in teaching, research, scholarly writing, and service.

Mark C. Schug is director of the University of Wisconsin–Milwaukee Center for Economic Education. A 30-year veteran of middle school, high school, and university classrooms, Dr. Schug has been cited for excellence in teaching by the University of Wisconsin–Milwaukee and the Minnesota Council on Economic Education. In addition to coauthoring eight national economics curriculum programs, Dr. Schug has spoken on economic issues to audiences throughout the world. Dr. Schug edited *The Senior Economist* for the National Council for Economics Education from 1986 to 1996.

Charles S. White is associate professor in the School of Education at Boston University, where he teaches methods of instruction in social studies. Dr. White has written and spoken extensively on the role of technology in social studies education. He has received numerous awards for his scholarship, including the 1995 Federal Design Achievement Award from the National Endowment for the Arts, for the Teaching with Historic Places project. In 1997, Dr. White taught his Models of Teaching doctoral course at the Universidad San Francisco de Quito, Ecuador.

Copyright © 2005 by McDougal Littell, a division of Houghton Mifflin Company. All rights reserved.

Maps on pages A1-A37 © Rand McNally & Company. All rights reserved.

Acknowledgments begin on page R53.

ISBN 0-618-37756-5

Printed in the United States of America

1 2 3 4 5 6 7 8 9 – VJM – 07 06 05 04 03

Consultants and Reviewers

Content Consultants

Charmarie Blaisdell
Department of History
Northeastern University
Boston, Massachusetts

David Buck, Ph.D.
Department of History
University of Wisconsin–Milwaukee
Milwaukee, Wisconsin

Erich Gruen, Ph.D.
Departments of Classics and History
University of California, Berkeley
Berkeley, California

Charles Haynes, Ph.D.
Senior Scholar for Religious Freedom
The Freedom Forum First
    Amendment Center
Arlington, Virginia

Alusine Jalloh, Ph.D.
The Africa Program
University of Texas at Arlington
Arlington, Texas

Shabbir Mansuri
Council on Islamic Education
Fountain Valley, California

Michelle Maskiell, Ph.D.
Department of History
Montana State University
Bozeman, Montana

Vasudha Narayanan, Ph.D.
Department of Religion
University of Florida
Gainesville, Florida

Amanda Porterfield, Ph.D.
Department of Religious Studies
University of Wyoming
Laramie, Wyoming

Mark Wasserman, Ph.D.
Department of History
Rutgers University
New Brunswick, New Jersey

Multicultural Advisory Board

Dr. Munir Bashshur
Education Department
American University of Beirut
Beirut, Lebanon

Stephen Fugita
Ethnic Studies Program
Santa Clara University
Santa Clara, California

Sharon Harley
Afro-American Studies Program
University of Maryland at
    College Park
College Park, Maryland

Doug Monroy
Department of Southwest Studies
Colorado College
Colorado Springs, Colorado

Cliff Trafzer
Departments of History and
    Ethnic Studies
University of California, Riverside
Riverside, California

Some scientists believe the continents were once joined, page 35.

A variety of people inhabit the world, page 14.

UNIT 1

Introduction to World Cultures and Geography

Satellite photographs of Earth, pages 2–3

UNIT 2

The United States and Canada

A bald eagle, page 71

Baseball is often called America's pastime, page 111.

Inuit build an iglo, page 124.

An Aztec stone carving,
page 162

Mount Popocatépetl in
Mexico is a volcano,
page 153.

A Quechua mother and
daughter, page 254

UNIT 3

Latin America

Europe, Russia, and the Independent Republics

A stained-glass window from the Middle Ages, page 294

A wealthy merchant family built this Renaissance palace, page 303.

These dogs helped fight World War I, page 335.

J.K. Rowling wrote the popular Harry Potter books, page 383.

UNIT 4 *continued from page ix*

The Brandenburg Gate in Berlin, page 347

A high-speed train rushes across France, pages 350–351.

Features

Interdisciplinary Challenge

Infographics, Time Lines, and Cartoons

Literature Connections

Linking Past and Present

DATELINE

SKILLBUILDER

Citizenship IN ACTION

Strange but TRUE

Connections To...

MAPS

CHARTS, DIAGRAMS, AND GRAPHS

STRATEGIES for TAKING STANDARDIZED TESTS

This section will help you develop and practice the skills you need to study social studies and to take standardized tests. Part 1, **Strategies for Studying Social Studies,** shows you the features of this book. It also shows you how to improve your reading and study skills.

   Part 2, **Test-Taking Strategies and Practice,** gives you strategies to help you answer the different kinds of questions that appear on standardized tests. Each strategy is followed by a set of questions you can use for practice.

CONTENTS

Part 1: Strategies for Studying Social Studies

Reading is important in the study of social studies or any other subject. You can improve your reading skills by practicing certain strategies. Good reading skills help you remember more when you read. The next four pages show how some of the features of *World Cultures and Geography: Western Hemisphere* can help you learn and understand social studies.

Preview Chapters Before You Read

Each chapter begins with a two-page chapter opener. Study these pages to help you get ready to read.

1 Read the chapter title. Read the section titles. These tell what topics will be covered in the chapter.

2 Look at the art and photographs. Use the illustrations to help you identify themes or messages of the chapter.

3 Study the **Focus on Geography** feature. Use the questions to help you think about the information you might find in the chapter.

CHAPTER 10

1 Western Europe: Its Land and Early History

SECTION 1   A Land of Varied Riches
SECTION 2   Ancient Greece
SECTION 3   Ancient Rome
SECTION 4   Time of Change: The Middle Ages

Region Many European cities show their history in their architecture. In Segovia, Spain, an ancient Roman aqueduct lies below the walls of a castle built in the Middle Ages.

3 FOCUS ON GEOGRAPHY

How does the Gulf Stream affect the climate of Europe?

Region • The Gulf Stream is a strong ocean current that flows from the Gulf of Mexico across the Atlantic Ocean to Europe. It carries warm water and warm, moist air, which contribute to Europe's mild climate. The Gulf Stream warms the water of some Northern European ports, allowing them to remain open in the winter when they might otherwise be frozen. Palm trees even grow in Scotland, which is as far north as southern Alaska!

What do you think?

♦ In what other ways, such as tourism, might Europe benefit from the Gulf Stream?

♦ How might a region's mild climate help its economy?

270

271

Preview Sections Before You Read

Each chapter has three, four, or five sections. These sections cover shorter time periods or certain themes.

1 Study the sentences under the headings **Main Idea** and **Why It Matters Now.** These headings tell what's important in the material you're about to read.

2 Look at the **Terms & Names** list. This list tells you what people and issues will be covered in the section.

3 Read the feature titled **Dateline.** It tells about a historical event as if it were happening today.

4 Skim the pages to see how the section is organized. Red headings are major topics. Blue headings are smaller topics or subtopics. The headings provide an outline of the section.

5 Skim the pages of the section to find key words. These words will often be in **boldface** type. Use the **Vocabulary** notes in the margin to help you with unfamiliar terms.

TERMS & NAMES
Mediterranean Sea
peninsula
fjord
Ural Mountains
plain

SECTION 1 — A Land of Varied Riches

2 TERMS & NAMES
Mediterranean Sea
peninsula
fjord
Ural Mountains
plain

1 MAIN IDEA
Europe is a continent with varied geographic features, abundant natural resources, and a climate that can support agriculture.

WHY IT MATTERS NOW
The development of Europe's diverse cultures has been shaped by the continent's diverse geography.

3 DATELINE EXTRA

LONDON, ENGLAND, MAY 6, 1994
Rough waters have always made the English Channel, which separates England and France, difficult to cross. Now, however, you can travel under the water! Today, a tunnel nicknamed "the Chunnel"

opens, allowing high-speed trains to travel between London and Paris in about three hours. The Chunnel—short for Channel Tunnel—was carved through chalky earth under the sea floor and took seven years to build. It is the largest European construction project of the 20th century.

Movement • Eurostar trains make the 31-mile trip under the English Channel in only 20 minutes. ▲

Location • The Channel Tunnel connects England and France. ▲

The Geography of Europe 4
Today, cars, airplanes, and trains are common forms of high-speed transportation across Europe. Before the 19th century, however, the fastest form of transportation was to travel by water—on top of it, rather than under it.

TAKING NOTES
Use your chart to take notes about Western Europe.

Time Period	Social Structure	Artistic Factors
Ancient Greece		
Ancient Rome		

Western Europe: Its Land and Early History **273**

Place • The Alps remain snowcapped year-round. ▶

Reading Social Studies

B. Clarifying What natural landform separates Europe from Asia?

Mountain ranges, including the towering Alps, also stretch across much of the continent. Along Europe's eastern border, the **Ural Mountains** (YUR•uhl) divide the continent from Asia. The many mountain ranges of Europe separated groups of people from one another as they settled the land thousands of years ago. This is one of the reasons why different cultures developed across the continent.

The Great European Plain Not all of Europe is mountainous. A vast region called the Great European Plain stretches from the coast of France to the Ural Mountains. A **plain** is a large, flat area of land, usually without many trees. The Great European Plain is the location of some of the world's richest farmland. Ancient trading centers attracted many people to this area, which today includes some of the largest cities in Europe—Paris, Berlin, Warsaw, and Moscow.

5 Vocabulary
Gulf Stream: a warm ocean current that flows northeast from the Gulf of Mexico through the Atlantic Ocean.

Climate
Although the Gulf Stream brings warm air and water to Europe, the winters are still severe in the mountains and in the far north. In some of these areas, cold winds blow southward from the Arctic Circle and make the average temperature fall below 0°F in January. The Alps and the Pyrenees, however, protect the European countries along the Mediterranean Sea from these chilling winds. In these warmer parts of southern Europe, the average temperature in January stays above 50°F.

Western Europe: Its Land and Early History **275**

Use Active Reading Strategies As You Read

Now you're ready to read the chapter. Read one section at a time, from beginning to end.

1 Begin by looking at the **Reading Social Studies** page. Consider the questions under the **Before You Read** heading. Think about what you know already about the chapter topic and what you'd like to learn.

2 Review the suggestions in the **Read and Take Notes** section. These will help you understand and remember the information in the chapter.

3 Ask and answer questions as you read. Look for the **Reading Social Studies** questions in the margin. Answering these questions will show whether you understand what you've just read.

4 Study the **Background** notes in the margin for additional information on people, places, events, or ideas discussed in the chapter.

Reading Social Studies

A. Clarifying Why were waterways important for the movement of people and goods?

CHAPTER 10

READING SOCIAL STUDIES

BEFORE YOU READ

►► What Do You Know?

Before you read the chapter, think about what you already know about Europe. What are some of its geographical features? What do you know about its early history? Have you ever read myths from ancient Greece or ancient Rome? Have you ever heard of Julius Caesar or Hercules? What do you know about knights and castles from the Middle Ages?

►► What Do You Want to Know?

Decide what you want to know about these early periods of European history. Record your questions in your notebook before you read this chapter.

2

READ AND TAKE NOTES

Reading Strategy: Categorizing One way to make sense of what you read is to categorize, or sort, information. Making a chart to categorize the information in this chapter will help you to understand the contributions made by early European cultures.

• Copy the chart below into your notebook.
• As you read, look for information relating to the categories of social structure, architecture, religion, and arts and sciences.
• Write your notes under the appropriate headings.

Region • Ancient Greece made important contributions in literature, philosophy, and architecture. ▼

Region • The Middle Ages saw the rise of the Catholic Church and the growth of a middle class. ▲

Region • Ancient Rome made its mark in government, law, and engineering. ▲

Time Period	Social Structure	Architecture	Religion	Arts and Sciences
Ancient Greece				
Ancient Rome				
Middle Ages				

272 CHAPTER 10

Waterways Look at the map of Europe on page 277. Water surrounds the continent to the north, south, and west. The southern coast of Europe borders the warm waters of the **Mediterranean Sea.** Europe also has many rivers. The highly traveled Rhine and Danube rivers are two of the most important. The Volga, which flows nearly 2,200 miles through western Russia, is the continent's longest. For hundreds of years, these and other waterways have been home to boats and barges carrying people and goods inland across great distances.

Landforms Several large **peninsulas,** or bodies of land surrounded by water on three sides, form the European continent. In Northern Europe, the Scandinavian Peninsula is home to Norway and Sweden. Along the jagged shoreline of this peninsula are beautiful fjords (fyawrdz). A **fjord** is a long, narrow deep inlet of the sea located between steep cliffs. In Western Europe, the Iberian Peninsula includes Portugal and Spain. The Iberian Peninsula is separated from the rest of the continent by a mountain range called the Pyrenees (PEER·uh·NEEZ). The entire continent of Europe, itself surrounded by water on three sides, is a giant peninsula.

Reading Social Studies

A. Clarifying Why were waterways important for the movement of people and goods? **3**

BACKGROUND **4**

Europe can be divided into four areas: Western Europe, Northern Europe, Eastern Europe, and Russia and its neighboring countries.

Place • The Scandinavian Peninsula is the location of many spectacular fjords, such as this one in Norway. ►

274 CHAPTER 10

BACKGROUND

Europe can be divided into four areas: Western Europe, Northern Europe, Eastern Europe, and Russia and its neighboring countries.

Review and Summarize What You Have Read

When you finish reading a section, review and summarize the information you have learned. Reread any information that is still unclear.

1 Look again at the red and blue headings for a quick summary of the section.

2 Study the photographs, maps, charts, graphs, and illustrated features in the section. Think about how these visuals relate to the information you've learned.

3 Answer the questions in the **Assessment** section. This will help you think critically about what you've just read.

The summers in the south are usually hot and dry, with an average July temperature around 80°F. This makes the Mediterranean coast a popular vacation spot. Elsewhere in Europe, in all but the coldest areas of the mountains and the far north, the average July temperature ranges from 50°F to 70°F.

1 Natural Resources

Europe has a large variety of natural resources, including minerals. The rich coal deposits of Germany's Ruhr (rur) Valley region have helped to make that area one of the world's major industrial centers. Russia and Ukraine have large deposits of iron ore, which is used to make iron for automobiles and countless other products.

Region • Western Europe benefits from a varied landscape rich in natural resources. ▼

2

Land Use in Europe Today

Forest
Orchards and vineyards
Dairy land and fodder crops
Rye and potatoes
Wheat
Upland grazing
Unused land
Urban and industrial

INTERACTIVE

ATLANTIC OCEAN

North Sea

Bay of Biscay

Black Sea

Mediterranean Sea

GEOGRAPHY SKILLBUILDER: Interpreting a Map
1. **Place** • What are the three most common uses of land in Europe?
2. **Location** • Where is the majority of unused land?

Vocabulary

precipitation: moisture, including rain, snow, and hail, that falls to the ground

Europe also has rich soil and plentiful rainfall. The average precipitation for the Great European Plain, for example, is between 20 and 40 inches per year. The map above shows the agricultural uses of the land, highlighting the major crops. Notice that few parts of the continent are too cold or too hot and dry to support some form of agriculture. These characteristics have made Europe a world leader in crop production.

3

SECTION 1 ASSESSMENT

Terms & Names
1. Explain the significance of:
   (a) Mediterranean Sea   (b) peninsula   (c) fjord
   (d) Ural Mountains   (e) plain

Using Graphics
2. Use a spider map like this one to list the different geographic features of Europe, and give a few specific examples of each.

Peninsula

Main Ideas
3. (a) How does the Gulf Stream affect the climate of Europe?
   (b) What separates Europe from Asia?
   (c) How do waterways, such as rivers and seas, strengthen trade in Europe?

Critical Thinking
4. Recognizing Effects

   How did Europe's many mountain ranges affect its development?

Think About
   • climate
   • trade and travel
   • the separation of groups of people

ACTIVITY -OPTION- Reread the information about the Chunnel. Write a **short story** in which you imagine what it might have been like to work on the Chunnel's construction.

Part 2: Test-Taking Strategies and Practice

Use the strategies in this section to improve your test-taking skills. First read the tips on the left page. Then use them to help you with the practice items on the right page.

Multiple Choice

A multiple-choice question is a question or incomplete sentence and a set of choices. One of the choices correctly answers the question or completes the sentence.

1 Read the question or incomplete sentence carefully. Try to answer the question before looking at the choices.

2 Read each choice with the question. Don't decide on your final answer until you have read all the choices.

3 Rule out any choices that you know are wrong.

4 Look for key words in the question. They may help you figure out the correct answer.

5 Sometimes the last choice is *All of the above*. Make sure that the other choices are all correct if you pick this answer.

6 Be careful with questions that include the word *not*.

❶ 1. Which of the following countries shares a border with the United States?

    A. Brazil

❷ choices   **B.** Canada

    C. Cuba

    D. Venezuela

> **❸** Since Cuba is an island, you know that it cannot share a border with the United States.

2. Which language is spoken by (most) of the people who live in Latin America and the Caribbean?

    A. English

    B. French

    C. Portuguese

    D. Spanish

> **❹** The word *most* is key here. All of the languages listed are spoken in Latin America and the Caribbean, but most people there speak Spanish.

3. The Andes mountains run through

    A. Colombia.

    B. Ecuador.

    C. Peru.

    D. all of the above

> **❺** Before selecting *All of the above*, make sure that all of the choices are, indeed, correct.

4. Which of the following is (not) an island in the Caribbean?

    A. Barbados

    B. Cuba

    C. Hawaii

    D. Jamaica

> **❻** First rule out all the choices that name islands in the Caribbean. The choice that remains is the correct answer.

answers: 1 (B); 2 (D); 3 (D); 4 (C)

Directions: Read each question carefully. Choose the *best* answer from the four choices.

1. Which of the following conquered the Inca?

    A. Francisco Pizarro

    B. Miguel Hidalgo

    C. Hernán Cortés

    D. Simón Bolívar

2. Until recent years, many Central American and Caribbean countries had single-product economies, depending on such crops as

    A. bananas.

    B. coffee.

    C. sugar cane.

    D. all of the above

3. Many Canadians are bilingual, which means that they speak

    A. French at home and English at work.

    B. English and their native language.

    C. two languages.

    D. several languages.

4. During the 1700s, England controlled which of the following?

    A. the sugar trade

    B. the Atlantic slave trade

    C. the cotton trade

    D. the coconut trade

Primary Sources

Sometimes you will need to look at a document to answer a question. Some documents are primary sources. Primary sources are written or made by people who either saw an event or were actually part of the event. A primary source can be a photograph, letter, diary, speech, or autobiography.

1 Look at the source line to learn about the document and its author. Consider how reliable the information might be.

2 Skim the article to get an idea of what it is about. As you read, look for the main idea. The main idea is the writer's most important point. Sometimes it is not directly stated.

3 Note any special punctuation. For example, ellipses (…) mean that words and sentences have been left out.

4 Ask yourself questions about the document as you read.

5 Review the questions. This will give your reading a purpose and also help you find the answers more easily. Then reread the document.

A Native American View of Nature

Plants are of different families… It is the same with animals… It is the same with human beings; there is some place which is best adapted to each. The seeds of the plants are blown about by the wind until they reach the place where they will grow best…and there they take **3** root and grow… In the early days the animals probably roamed over a very wide country until they found a proper place. An animal depends on the natural conditions around it. If the buffalo were here today, I think they would be different from the buffalo of the old days because all the natural conditions have changed. They would not find the same food, nor the same surroundings. We see the change in our ponies… Now… they have less endurance and must have constant care [unlike in the past]. It is the same with the Indians; they have less freedom and they fall an easy prey to disease.

—Okute, a Teton Sioux (1911)

The Sioux were a Native American people who lived on the Great Plains of North America. **1**

1. Okute thinks that horses and Indians now are different from those of the early days because

A. the buffalo are gone.

B. natural conditions have changed.

C. they cannot roam to find the best place to live.

D. there is no water.

2. Which sentence *best* expresses the main idea of this passage?

A. "Animals and humans must always roam."

B. "Each plant, animal, and human is different."

C. "Each plant, animal, and human thrives in a particular place."

D. "Plants and animals were created for humans to eat."

answers: 1 (B); 2 (C)

Directions: Read this passage from the English Bill of Rights. Use this document and your knowledge of world cultures and geography to answer questions 1 and 2.

> **A Declaration of English Rights**
>
> The… Lords… and Commons,… being now assembled in a full and free representative of this nation,… declare:
>
> 1. That the pretended power of suspending of laws, or the execution of laws, by [the King], without consent of Parliament, is illegal…
>
> 4. That [raising] money for or to the use of the [King], without grant of Parliament,… is illegal.
>
> 5. That it is the right of the subjects to petition the King, and all commitments and prosecutions for such petitioning are illegal.
>
> 6. That the raising or keeping a standing army within the kingdom in time of peace, unless it be with consent of parliament, is against the law…
>
> —*Declaration of Rights,* 1689
> (English Bill of Rights)

1. Which of the articles of the *Declaration of Rights* is concerned with taxation?

    A. Article 1
    B. Article 4
    C. Article 5
    D. Article 6

2. The *Declaration of Rights* was aimed at limiting the power of the

    A. Parliament.
    B. nobles and clergy.
    C. rising middle class.
    D. King.

Secondary Sources

A secondary source is an account of events by a person who did not actually experience them. The author often uses information from several primary sources to write about a person or event. Biographies, many newspaper articles, and history books are examples of secondary sources.

1 Read the title to get an idea of what the passage is about. (The title here indicates that the passage is about a person named Malinche about whom people have different opinions.)

2 Skim the paragraphs to find the main idea of the passage.

3 Look for words that help you understand the order in which events happen.

4 Ask yourself questions as you read. (You might ask yourself: Why did people's opinions about Malinche change over time?)

5 Review the questions to see what information you will need to find. Then reread the passage.

❶ Malinche—Heroine or Traitor?

No one knows much about Malinche's early life. People do know that in 1519 she met Hernán Cortés. The Spanish conquistador had landed in Mexico earlier that year. Malinche was only 15 years old. Even though she was very **❷** young, Malinche helped Cortés conquer the Aztecs. She spoke the languages of the Aztec and the Maya. Over time, she learned Spanish. She translated for Cortés and advised him on Native American politics.

The Spanish conquistadors admired Malinche, calling **❸** her Doña Marina. For many centuries, the Spanish people regarded her as a heroine. In the 1800s, however, Mexico won its independence from Spain. People rejected their Spanish rulers. Writers and artists started calling Malinche a traitor to her people. Today, however, she is seen as a heroine again. **❹**

1. Which of the following statements about Malinche is an (opinion)?

    A. She was very young when she met Cortés.

    B. She became a translator for Cortés.

    C. She was a traitor to her own people.

    D. She understood Native American politics.

> Remember that an opinion is a statement that cannot be proved. A fact is a statement that can be proved.

2. Based on this source, which person or group would view Malinche as a heroine?

    A. a fighter for Mexican independence from Spain

    B. the soldiers and officers in Cortés's army

    C. the Aztec ruler and his court in Mexico

    D. a historian writing about Mexico in the 1800s

answers: 1 (C); 2 (B)

Directions: Read this passage. Use the passage and your knowledge of world cultures and geography to answer questions 1 and 2.

Before World War I

In 1892, France and Russia had become military allies. Later, Germany signed an agreement to protect Austria. If any nation attacked Austria, Germany would fight on its side. France and Russia had to support each other as well. For instance, if France got into a war with Germany, Russia had to fight Germany, too. This meant that in any war, Germany would have to fight on two fronts: France on the west and Russia on the east.

If a war broke out, what part would Great Britain play? No one knew. It might remain neutral, like Belgium. It might, if given a reason, fight against Germany.

1. If Russia and Germany went to war, which country had to help Russia?

   A. Great Britain
   B. Belgium
   C. Austria
   D. France

2. When World War I broke out, what part did Great Britain play?

   A. It remained neutral, like Belgium.
   B. It sided with Germany and Austria.
   C. It joined France in fighting Germany.
   D. It fought Russia after its revolution.

Political Cartoons

Cartoonists who draw political cartoons use both words and art to express opinions about political issues.

1 Try to figure out what the cartoon is about. Titles and captions may give clues.

2 Use labels to help identify the people, places, and events represented in the cartoon.

3 Note when and where the cartoon was published.

4 Look for symbols—that is, people, places, or objects that stand for something else.

5 The cartoonist often exaggerates the physical features of people and objects. This technique will give you clues as to how the cartoonist feels about the subject.

6 Try to figure out the cartoonist's message and summarize it in a sentence.

1 NEXT!

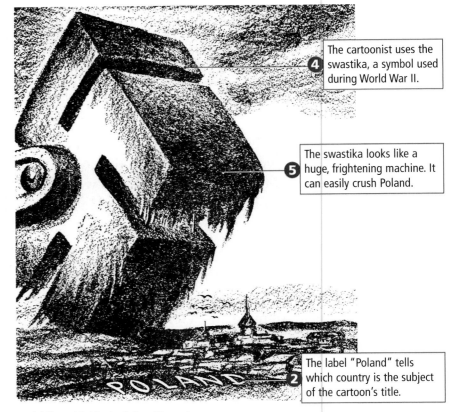

4 The cartoonist uses the swastika, a symbol used during World War II.

5 The swastika looks like a huge, frightening machine. It can easily crush Poland.

2 The label "Poland" tells which country is the subject of the cartoon's title.

Daniel Fitzpatrick / *St. Louis Post-Dispatch,* August 24, 1939.

3 The date is a clue that the cartoon refers to the beginning of World War II.

1. What does the swastika in the cartoon stand for?

  A. the Soviet Union
  B. Nazi Germany
  C. the Polish army
  D. Great Britain

6 2. Which sentence *best* summarizes the cartoonist's message?

  A. Germany will attack Poland next.
  B. Poland should stop Germany.
  C. Germany will lose this battle.
  D. Poland will fight a civil war.

answers: 1 (B); 2 (A)

Directions: Study this cartoon. Use the cartoon and your knowledge of world cultures and geography to answer questions 1 and 2.

The Granger Collection, New York

Benjamin Franklin (1754)

1. What do the sections of the snake in the cartoon represent?

    A. army units
    B. states
    C. Native American groups
    D. colonies

2. Which phrase *best* states the message of the cartoon?

    A. "East is East, and West is West, and never the twain shall meet."
    B. "Taxation without representation is tyranny."
    C. "United we stand, divided we fall."
    D. "Out of many, one."

Charts

Charts present facts in a visual form. History textbooks use several different types of charts. The chart that is most often found on standardized tests is the table. A table organizes information in columns and rows.

1 Read the title of the chart to find out what information is represented.

2 Read the headings at the top of each column. Then read the headings at the left of each row.

3 Notice how the information in the chart is organized.

4 Compare the information from column to column and row to row.

5 Try to draw conclusions from the information in the chart.

6 Read the questions and then study the chart again.

1 This chart is about the number of people who immigrated to different countries.

4 Notice that different years are used for different countries.

Immigration to Selected Countries

2 Country	Years	Number of Immigrants
Argentina	1856-1932	6,405,000
Australia	1861-1932	2,913,000
Brazil	1821-1932	4,431,000
British West Indies	1836-1932	1,587,000
Canada	1821-1932	5,206,000
Cuba	1901-1932	857,000
Mexico	1911-1931	226,000
New Zealand	1851-1932	594,000
South Africa	1881-1932	852,000
United States	1821-1932	34,244,000
Uruguay	1836-1932	713,000

Source: Alfred W. Crosby, Jr. *The Columbian Exchange: Biological and Cultural Consequences of 1492*

3 This chart lists countries in alphabetical order. Other charts organize information by years or by numbers.

5 Of all the countries listed, six received the most immigrants. Think about what these countries have in common.

6

1. The country that received the most immigrants was

   A. Canada.

   B. the British West Indies.

   C. the United States.

   D. Brazil.

2. Different countries received immigrants in different years. Which countries received immigrants the earliest?

   A. Argentina, New Zealand, and Canada

   B. Canada, Brazil, and United States

   C. Mexico, United States, and British West Indies

   D. Brazil, South Africa, and Cuba

answers: 1 (C); 2 (B)

Directions: Read the chart carefully. Use the chart and your knowledge of world cultures and geography to answer questions 1 and 2.

Mexico and the Nations of Central America				
Country	Capital	Area (sq. miles)	Population	Per Capita Gross Domestic Product (in U.S. dollars)
Belize	Belmopan	8,900	249,183	3,000
Costa Rica	San José	19,700	3,710,558	6,700
El Salvador	San Salvador	8,100	6,122,515	3,000
Guatemala	Guatemala City	42,000	12,639,939	3,800
Honduras	Tegucigalpa	43,300	6,249,598	2,400
Mexico	Mexico City	761,600	100,349,766	8,300
Nicaragua	Managua	49,998	4,812,569	2,500
Panama	Panama City	32,200	2,808,268	7,300

Source: *World Almanac and Book of Facts* (2001)

1. The largest country in terms of both area and population is
   A. Guatemala.
   B. Honduras.
   C. Mexico.
   D. Nicaragua.

2. Which correctly states the countries' rank from high to low in terms of per capita gross domestic product?
   A. Honduras, Nicaragua, Belize, Guatemala
   B. Mexico, Panama, El Salvador, Honduras
   C. Panama, Costa Rica, Mexico, Belize
   D. Mexico, Costa Rica, Panama, Guatemala

Line and Bar Graphs

Graphs are often used to show numbers. Line graphs often show changes over time. Bar graphs make it easy to compare numbers.

1 Read the title of the graph to find out what information is represented.

2 Study the labels on the graph.

3 Look at the source line that tells where the graph is from. Decide whether you can depend on the source to provide reliable information.

4 See if you can make any generalizations about the information in the graph. Note whether the numbers change over time.

5 Read the questions carefully and then study the graph again.

1 Exports of English Manufactured Goods, 1699–1774

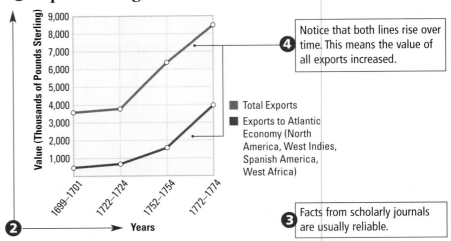

4 Notice that both lines rise over time. This means the value of all exports increased.

Total Exports

Exports to Atlantic Economy (North America, West Indies, Spanish America, West Africa)

3 Facts from scholarly journals are usually reliable.

Source: R. Davis, "English Foreign Trade, 1700–1774," *Economic History Review* (1962)

5 1. Which of the following is a true statement?

A. Exports to the New World declined over time.

B. Total exports stayed the same over time.

C. Total exports rose sharply after 1724.

D. Exports to the New World fell sharply after 1754.

1 Nations with High Foreign Debt, 2000

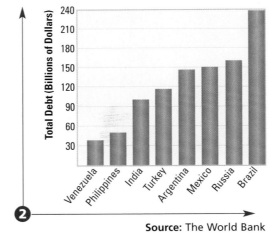

Source: The World Bank

3 Facts from major organizations, such as the World Bank, usually are reliable.

5 2. The nation with the largest foreign debt is

A. Brazil.

B. Argentina.

C. Mexico.

D. Venezuela.

answers: 1 (C); 2 (A)

Directions: Study the graphs carefully. Use the graphs and your knowledge of world cultures and geography to answer questions 1 and 2.

Canada: Imports and Exports, 1995–2000

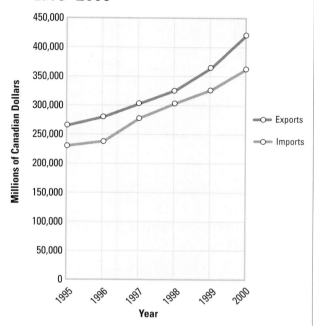

Source: *Statistics Canada*

Unemployment Rates for Selected Countries, 2000

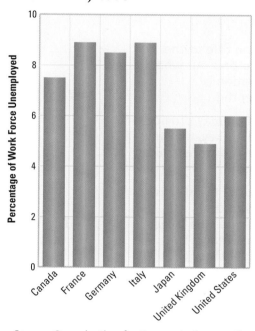

Source: Organization for Economic Cooperation and Development

1. In which year was the difference in the value of imports and exports the greatest?

   A. 1995

   B. 1996

   C. 1999

   D. 2000

2. Which country had the lowest unemployment rate in 2000?

   A. Canada

   B. Japan

   C. United Kingdom

   D. United States

Pie Graphs

A pie, or circle, graph shows the relationship among parts of a whole. These parts look like slices of a pie. Each slice is shown as a percentage of the whole pie.

1 Read the title of the chart to find out what information is represented.

2 The graph may provide a legend, or key, that tells you what different slices represent.

3 The size of the slice is related to the percentage. The larger the percentage, the larger the slice.

4 Look at the source line that tells where the graph is from. Ask yourself if you can depend on this source to provide reliable information.

5 Read the questions carefully, and study the graph again.

1 **World Population by Region, 2002**

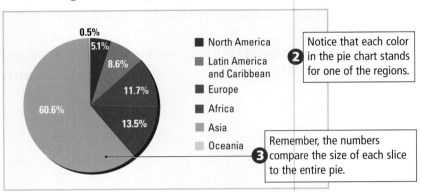

- North America
- Latin America and Caribbean
- Europe
- Africa
- Asia
- Oceania

2 Notice that each color in the pie chart stands for one of the regions.

3 Remember, the numbers compare the size of each slice to the entire pie.

The Population Reference Bureau studies population data for the United States and other countries.

4 **Source:** Population Reference Bureau

1. Which region accounts for nearly 5 percent of the world's population?

    A. Africa

    B. North America

    C. Europe

    D. Asia

2. About one-twelfth of the world's population lives in

    A. Africa.

    B. Europe.

    C. Latin America and Caribbean.

    D. North America.

answers: 1 (B); 2 (C)

Directions: Study the pie graph. Use the graph and your knowledge of world cultures and geography to answer questions 1 and 2.

World Energy Consumption by Region

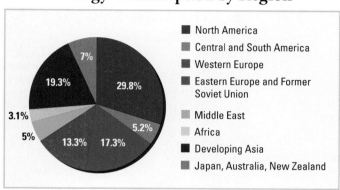

- ■ North America
- ■ Central and South America
- ■ Western Europe
- ■ Eastern Europe and Former Soviet Union
- ■ Middle East
- ■ Africa
- ■ Developing Asia
- ■ Japan, Australia, New Zealand

Source: "Earth Pulse," *National Geographic* (March 2001)

1. Which region uses the most energy?

   A. Western Europe
   B. Developing Asia
   C. North America
   D. Eastern Europe and Former Soviet Union

2. Two regions consumed nearly the same amount of the world's energy. They are Central and South America and

   A. Middle East.
   B. Western Europe.
   C. Developing Asia.
   D. North America.

Political Maps

Political maps show the divisions within countries. A country may be divided into states, provinces, etc. The maps also show where major cities are. They may also show mountains, oceans, seas, lakes, and rivers.

1 Read the title of the map. This will give you the subject and purpose of the map.

2 Read the labels on the map. They also give information about the map's subject and purpose.

3 Study the key or legend to help you understand the symbols in the map.

4 Use the scale to estimate distances between places shown on the map. Maps usually show the distance in both miles and kilometers.

5 Use the North arrow to figure out the direction of places on the map.

6 Read the questions. Carefully study the map to find the answers.

1 Canada and Its Provinces

The legend gives symbols for Canada's boundaries and major cities.

The labels identify Canada's provinces.

1. Which province or territory is the furthest west?

A. Northwest Territories

B. Yukon Territory

C. British Columbia

D. Alberta

2. About how many miles is the United States-Canada border from the Great Lakes west to Vancouver on the Pacific Ocean?

A. 1,000

B. 1,500

C. 2,000

D. 2,500

answers: 1 (B); 2 (B)

Directions: Study the map carefully. Use the map and your knowledge of world cultures and geography to answer questions 1 and 2.

The Roman Empire, A.D. 400

1. Which area was part of the Eastern Roman Empire?

   A. Spain

   B. Gaul

   C. Anatolia

   D. all of the above

2. The most northern country in the Western Roman Empire was

   A. Syria.

   B. Gaul.

   C. Spain.

   D. Britain.

Thematic Maps

Thematic maps focus on special topics. For example, a thematic map might show a country's natural resources or major battles in a war.

1 Read the title of the map. This will give you the subject and purpose of the map.

2 Read the labels on the map. They give information about the map's subject and purpose. (The labels identify the three European empires.)

3 Study the key or legend to help you understand the symbols and/or colors on the map. (The legend shows the colors that indicate the three European Empires.)

4 Try to make generalizations about information shown on the map.

5 Read the questions. Carefully study the map to find the answers.

1 **European Empires in North America, 1700**

French territory
English territory
Spanish territory

4 One generalization you might make is that the French and English empires occupied much of the central and northern areas of North America, while the Spanish Empire occupied much of the south.

1. The land around the Great Lakes was controlled by

A. England.

B. France.

C. Spain.

D. all of the above

2. Which of the following statements about the English colonial empire in North America is *not* true?

A. English lands shared borders with both French and Spanish lands.

B. English lands did not stretch as far west as those held by Spain.

C. England held no land on the Pacific Coast of North America.

D. England held no lands east of 60° W longitude.

answers: 1 (B); 2 (D)

Directions: Study the map carefully. Use the map and your knowledge of world cultures and geography to answer questions 1 and 2.

The Christian Conquest of Muslim Spain

1. By A.D. 1250, how much of Spain did Christians control?

   A. only a small portion
   B. about one third
   C. about one half
   D. almost all the land

2. When did Spain recover Granada?

   A. 1000
   B. 1150
   C. 1450
   D. 1492

Time Lines

A time line is a chart that lists events in the order in which they occurred. Time lines can be vertical or horizontal.

1 Read the title to learn what subject the time line covers.

2 Note the dates when the time line begins and ends.

3 Read the events in the order they occurred.

4 Think about what else was going on in the world on these dates. Try to make connections.

5 Read the questions. Then carefully study the time line to find the answers.

❶ The Struggle for Mexican Independence

❷ Vertical time lines show the earliest date at the top. Horizontal time lines show the earliest date on the far left.

1810
Father Miguel Hidalgo issues the "Cry of Dolores," launching the Mexican independence movement.

1811
Spanish forces capture Hidalgo and execute him. Father José María Morelos takes over leadership of the revolt.

1813
Morelos calls a congress of representatives from all of Mexico's provinces. The congress writes a constitution for a Mexican republic.

1815
Spanish forces capture and execute Morelos.

❹ Note that Mexico, like other Latin American countries, was deeply influenced by the revolutions in the United States and France.

1820
Spain sends large force, under the command of Agustín de Iturbide, to round up guerilla bands. Iturbide throws his support to the rebellion.

1815 to 1820
Vicente Guerrero, with a small band of followers, continues the rebellion against Spain.

1821
Iturbide and rebel leaders declare Mexico's independence.

1. In which year did Father José María Morelos become the leader of the Mexican independence movement?

A. 1810
B. 1811
C. 1813
D. 1815

2. Which of the following switched sides during the struggle for Mexican independence?

A. Vicente Guerrero
B. Father Miguel Hidalgo
C. Augustín de Iturbide
D. José María Morelos

answers: 1 (B); 2 (C)

Directions: Study the time line. Use the information shown and your knowledge of world cultures and geography to answer questions 1 and 2.

The Breakup of the Soviet Union

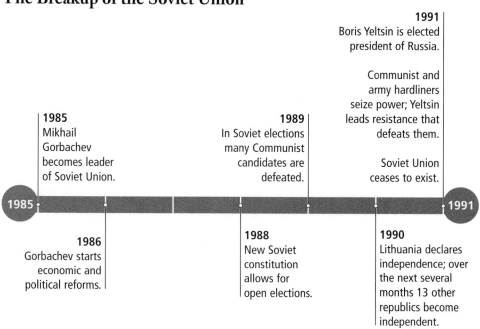

1991
Boris Yeltsin is elected president of Russia.

Communist and army hardliners seize power; Yeltsin leads resistance that defeats them.

Soviet Union ceases to exist.

1985
Mikhail Gorbachev becomes leader of Soviet Union.

1989
In Soviet elections many Communist candidates are defeated.

1985

1991

1986
Gorbachev starts economic and political reforms.

1988
New Soviet constitution allows for open elections.

1990
Lithuania declares independence; over the next several months 13 other republics become independent.

1. What happened after Lithuania became independent?

   A. Gorbachev started economic and political reforms.

   B. Many other republics became independent.

   C. A new constitution allowed for open elections.

   D. Gorbachev defeated Yeltsin in a new election.

2. In which year did Communist and army hardliners try to seize power?

   A. 1985

   B. 1988

   C. 1990

   D. 1991

Constructed Response

Constructed-response questions focus on a document, such as a photograph, cartoon, chart, graph, or time line. Instead of picking one answer from a set of choices, you write a short response. Sometimes, you can find the answer in the document. Other times, you will use what you already know about a subject to answer the question.

1 Read the title of the document to get an idea of what it is about.

2 Study the document.

3 Read the questions carefully. Study the document again to find the answers.

4 Write your answers. You don't need to use complete sentences unless the directions say so.

1 The Temple of Inscriptions, Palenque, Mexico

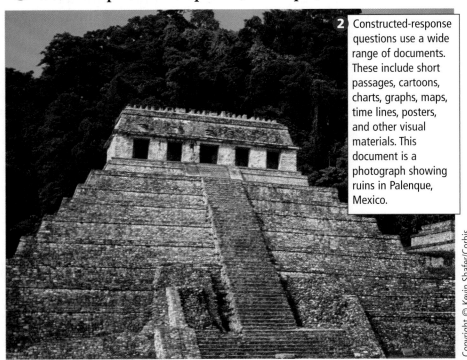

2 Constructed-response questions use a wide range of documents. These include short passages, cartoons, charts, graphs, maps, time lines, posters, and other visual materials. This document is a photograph showing ruins in Palenque, Mexico.

The Temple of Inscriptions stands over the tomb of Pakal, a great Maya king. The Maya used the temple for religious purposes. Such flat-topped, pyramid-like buildings are typical of Maya architecture.

3 1. Palenque, with its massive pyramid structures, was one of the city-states of what civilization?

4 *Maya*

2. For what purpose was this building used?

   religious purposes

3. This civilization went into decline around A.D. 900. Which great civilization arose in its place?

   Aztec civilization

Directions: Read the following passage from *Zlata's Diary.* Use the passage and your knowledge of world cultures and geography to answer questions 1 through 3. You do not need to use complete sentences.

Saturday, May 2, 1992

Dear Mimmy,

Today was truly, absolutely the worst day ever in Sarajevo. The shooting started around noon. Mommy and I moved into the hall. Daddy was in his office, under our apartment, at the time. We told him on the intercom to run quickly to the downstairs lobby where we'd meet him… The gunfire was getting worse, and we couldn't get over the wall to the Bobars', so we ran down to our own cellar.

The cellar is ugly, dark, smelly. Mommy, who's terrified of mice, had two fears to cope with. The three of us were in the same corner as the other day. We listened to the pounding shells, the shooting, the thundering noise overhead. We even heard planes. At one moment I realized that this awful cellar was the only place that could save our lives. Suddenly, it started to look almost warm and nice. It was the only way we could defend ourselves against all this terrible shooting. We heard glass shattering in our street. Horrible. I put my fingers in my ears to block out the terrible sounds. I was worried about Cicko. We had left him behind in the lobby. Would he catch cold there? Would something hit him? I was terribly hungry and thirsty. We had left our half-cooked lunch in the kitchen.

—Zlata Filipovic, *Zlata's Diary: A Child's Life in Sarajevo* (1994)

1. In the early 1990s, war broke out in the Balkans. Why were people fighting in Bosnia and Herzegovina?

2. What does Zlata say is happening in the city of Sarajevo?

3. How does the war affect Zlata and her family?

Extended Response

3 Read the column heads carefully. They offer important clues about the subject of the chart. For instance, the column head "Impact" is a clue about why these inventions were so important.

Extended-response questions, like constructed-response questions, focus on a document of some kind. However, they are more complicated and require more time to complete. Some extended-response questions ask you to present the information in the document in a different form. You might be asked to present the information in a chart in graph form, for example. Other questions ask you to complete a document such as a chart or graph. Still others require you to apply your knowledge to information in the document to write an essay.

1 Read the title of the document to get an idea of what it is about.

2 Carefully read directions and questions.

3 Study the document.

4 Sometimes the question may give you part of the answer. (The answer given tells how inventions were used and what effects they had on society. Your answers should have the same kind of information.)

5 The question may require you to write an essay. Write down some ideas to use in an outline. Then use your outline to write the essay. (A good essay will contain the ideas shown in the rubric to the right.)

1 **Inventions of the Industrial Revolution**

Invention	Impact
Flying shuttle, spinning jenny, water frame, spinning mule, power loom	Spun thread and wove cloth faster; **4** more factories were built and more people were hired
Cotton gin	Cleaned seeds faster from cotton; companies produced more cotton
Macadam road, steamboat, locomotive	Made travel over land and water faster; could carry larger, heavier loads; railroads needed more coal and iron
Mechanical reaper	Made harvesting easier; increased wheat production

2 **1.** Read the list of inventions in the left-hand column. Then in the right-hand column briefly state what the inventions meant to industry. The first item has been filled in for you.

2. The chart shows how some inventions helped create the Industrial Revolution. Write a short essay describing how the Industrial Revolution changed people's lives.

5 **Sample Response** The best essays will point out that progress in agriculture meant that fewer people were needed to work the farms. As a result, many farm workers went to the city looking for work in factories. As cities grew, poor sanitation and poor housing made them unhealthy and dangerous places to live. Life for factory workers was hard. They worked long hours under very bad conditions. At first, the Industrial Revolution produced three classes of people: an upper class of landowners and aristocrats; a middle class of merchants and factory owners; and a large lower class of poor people. Over the long term, though, working and living conditions improved, even for the lower class. This was partly because factory goods could be sold at a lower cost. In time, even lower classes could afford to buy many goods and services.

Directions: Use the drawing and passage below and your knowledge of world cultures and geography to answer question 1.

Smallpox Spreads Among the Aztecs

The Granger Collection, New York.

European diseases were like a second "army" of conquerors. Native people had no way to treat diseases like smallpox, typhoid fever, or measles. This "army" was more deadly than swords or guns.

— Based on P. M. Ashburn, *The Ranks of Death* (1947)

1. What role did disease play in the Spanish conquest of the Aztecs and Inca?

Document-Based Questions

To answer a document-based question, you have to study more than one document. First you answer questions about each document. Then you use those answers and information from the documents as well as your own knowledge of world cultures and geography to write an essay.

1 Read the "Context" section. It will give you an idea of the topic that will be covered in the question.

2 Read the "Task" section carefully. It tells you what you will need to write about in your essay.

3 Study each document. Think about the connection the documents have to the topic in the "Task" section.

4 Read and answer the questions about each document. Think about how your answers connect to the "Task" section.

Introduction

1 **Context:** South America is made up of 12 very different countries. However, these countries have many features in common. The ways of living in these countries are quite similar. The challenges they face are similar, too.

Task: Identify and discuss the common features that make the countries of South America a culture region.

2 ## Part 1: Short Answers

Study each document carefully. Answer the questions that follow.

3 ## Document 1: The Countries of South America

Country	Main Language	Major Religion	Colonized by	Date Became Independent
Argentina	Spanish	Catholic	Spain	1816
Bolivia	Spanish	Catholic	Spain	1825
Brazil	Portuguese	Catholic	Portugal	1822
Chile	Spanish	Catholic	Spain	1818
Colombia	Spanish	Catholic	Spain	1819
Ecuador	Spanish	Catholic	Spain	1830
Guyana	English	Christian	Great Britain	1966
Paraguay	Spanish, Guarani	Catholic	Spain	1811
Peru	Spanish	Catholic	Spain	1821
Suriname	Dutch	Christian	Netherlands	1975
Uruguay	Spanish	Catholic	Spain	1828
Venezuela	Spanish	Catholic	Spain	1830

4 **What are the dominant language and religion in South America?**

Spanish, Catholicism

Document 2: Government in South America

Oligarchy (government by the few) and military rule have characterized the governments of many of the countries of South America since they won their independence…

Although many South American nations gained freedom in the 1800s, hundreds of years of colonialism had its effects. Strong militaries, underdeveloped economies, and social class divisions still exist in the region today.

—Daniel D. Arreola, et al., *World Geography*

What kinds of governments have ruled in South America for much of the time since independence?

Oligarchies and military governments

Document 3: Crowded São Paulo

Over the last 60 years, many South Americans have moved to the cities. Today, nearly 80 percent of the people live in cities. Close to 18 million people live in the Brazilian city of São Paulo.

What is one of the major challenges facing the countries of South America today?

rapid urbanization and overcrowding of cities

❺ Part 2: Essay

Using information from the documents, your answers to the questions in Part 1, and your knowledge of world cultures and geography, write an essay identifying and discussing the features that make South America a culture region. ❻

---

❺ Read the essay question carefully. Then write a brief outline for your essay.

❻ Write your essay. The first paragraph should introduce your topic. The middle paragraphs should explain it. The closing paragraph should restate the topic and your conclusion. Support your ideas with quotations or details from the documents. Add other supporting facts or details from your knowledge of world history.

❼ A good essay will contain the ideas in the sample response below.

Sample Response The best essays will begin by noting that a culture region is a large geographic area marked by a common culture. Essays will go on to discuss the common historical and cultural background of the countries of South America (Document 1). Essays also will note that most South American countries share similar experiences in political and economic development (Document 2). Finally, essays will point out that the major challenges that South American countries face today are alike (Document 3).

Introduction

Historical Context: For many centuries, kings and queens ruled the countries of Europe. Their power was supported by nobles and armies. European society began to change. In the late 1700s, those changes produced a violent revolution in France.

Task: Discuss how social conflict and new ideas contributed to the French Revolution and why the Revolution turned radical.

Part 1: Short Answers

Study each document carefully. Answer the questions that follow.

Document 1: Social Classes in Pre-Revolutionary France

LE GRAND ABUS

This cartoon shows a peasant woman carrying women of nobility and the Church. What does the cartoon say about the lives of the poor before the revolution?

Engraving: *Le Grand Abus.* Engraving of a cartoon held in the collection of M. de baron de Vinck d'Orp of Brussels/Mary Evans Picture Library, London.

Document 2: A Declaration of Rights

1. Men are born and remain free and equal in rights…

2. The aim of all political association is the preservation of the natural and [unlimited] rights of man. These rights are liberty, property, security, and resistance to oppression…

— Declaration of the Rights of Man and of the Citizen (1789)

According to this document, which rights belong to all people?

Document 3: The French Revolution — Major Events

July 1789
Crowd storms the Bastille.

Aug. 1789
National Assembly abolishes feudalism, approves *Declaration of the Rights of Man and of the Citizen.*

Nov. 1789
National Assembly seizes lands of Catholic Church.

Aug. 1792
Paris mob captures King Louis XVI.

Sep. 1792
Crowds kill priests, nobles in September Massacres; monarchy is abolished.

July 1794
Robespierre is executed, Reign of Terror ends.

1789 — 1794

July 1790
Church is put under control of government; France is made a constitutional monarchy.

June 1791
Royal family is arrested in escape attempt.

Jan. 1793
King is executed by guillotine.

Spring 1793
Robespierre and allies gain control of government, begin to arrest rivals.

1793–1794
Reign of Terror: about 300,000 are arrested and 17,000 are executed.

Over time, the revolution became more violent. How does the information in the timeline show this?

Part 2: Essay

Write an essay discussing how social conflict and new ideas led to the French Revolution and why it became so violent. Use information from the documents, your short answers, and your knowledge of world cultures and geography.

RAND McNALLY
World Atlas

Contents

Complete Legend for Physical and Political Maps

Symbols

 Lake

 Salt Lake

 Seasonal Lake

 River

 Waterfall

 Canal

△ Mountain Peak

▲ Highest Mountain Peak

Cities

■ **Los Angeles** City over 1,000,000 population

▣ **Calgary** City of 250,000 to 1,000,000 population

• Haifa City under 250,000 population

✪ *Paris* National Capital

★ **Vancouver** Secondary Capital (State, Province, or Territory)

Type Styles Used to Name Features

CHINA Country

O N T A R I O State, Province, or Territory

PUERTO RICO (U.S.) Possession

A T L A N T I C O C E A N Ocean or Sea

A l p s Physical Feature

Borneo Island

Boundaries

 International Boundary

 Secondary Boundary

Land Elevation and Water Depths

Land Elevation

Meters		Feet
3,000 and over --		-- 9,840 and over
2,000 - 3,000 --		-- 6,560 - 9,840
500 - 2,000 --		-- 1,640 - 6,560
200 - 500 --		-- 656 - 1,640
0 - 200 --		-- 0 - 656

Water Depth

Less than 200 --		-- Less than 656
200 - 2,000 --		-- 656 - 6,560
Over 2,000 --		-- Over 6,560

ARCTIC OCEAN

Greenland

Jan Mayen

Baffin
Bay

Baffin
Island

Arctic Circle

Iceland

Hudson
Bay

Faroe Is.

British
Isles

Mt. McKinley △
20,320 Ft.
6,194m

Yukon

Mackenzie

Canadian Shield

NORTH

AMERICA

Rocky Mountains

Great Plains

St. Lawrence

Newfoundland

London

Vancouver

Appalachian Mts.

Azores

Iberian
Peninsula

Los Angeles

Colorado

Mississippi

Washington D.C.

Cape Hatteras

ATLANTIC

Canary
Islands

Atlas
Mts.

Aleutian Islands

Midway Is.

Tropic of Cancer

Baja
California

Gulf of Mexico

Hawaiian
Islands

Yucatan
Peninsula

Cuba

Hispaniola

Puerto Rico

Cape
Verde
Islands

PACIFIC

Jamaica

Caribbean
Sea

Trinidad

Cape Verde

Niger

OCEAN

Palmyra

Orinoco

Amazon

Equator

Kiribati

OCEAN

Galapagos Islands

Amazon
Basin

SOUTH

Marquesas Is.

AMERICA

Andes

Samoa
Islands

Mato Grosso
Plateau

St. Helena

Tonga
Is.

Cook
Islands

Tahiti

Tropic of Capricorn

Rio de Janeiro

Easter Island

Andes

Paraná

Chatham Is.

△ Mt. Aconcagua
22,831 Ft.
6,959m

Buenos Aires

N

Archipiélago
Juan Fernández

Patagonia

0   1000   2000 Miles

0   1000   2000   3000 Kilometers

Copyright by Rand McNally & Co.
Robinson Projection

Falkland Is.

South
Georgia

Tierra del Fuego

South
Sandwich Is.

Cape Horn

South
Orkney Is.

South
Shetland Is.

Antarctic Circle

Antarctic
Peninsula

Weddell
Sea

Ross
Sea

Marie
Byrd
Land

△ Vinson Massif
16,066 Ft.
4,897m

A2

ARCTIC OCEAN

Spitsbergen
Franz Josef
Land
North Cape
Novaya
Zemlya
Scandinavian
Peninsula
North
Sea
EUROPE
Moscow
Volga
Alps
Don
Balkan
Peninsula
Black Sea
Caucasus
Sardinia
Mt. Elbrus
18,510 Ft.
5,642m
Sicily
Crete
Cyprus
Mediterranean
Cairo
Zagros Mts.
Sahara Desert
AFRICA
Sahel
Red Sea
Arabian
Peninsula
Nile
Socotra
Ethiopian
Plateau
Congo
Congo
Basin
Rift Valley
Gulf
of Guinea
Kilimanjaro
19,340 Ft.
5,895m
Seychelles
Zambezi
Kalahari
Desert
Madagascar
Mauritius
Reunion
Cape Town
Cape of Good Hope

Yenisey
Ob'
Ural Mts.
Siberia
Lena
Aral
Altai Mts.
ASIA
Pamir
Plateau
of
Tibet
Himalayas
Ganges
Indus
Mt. Everest
29,035 Ft.
8,850m
Mumbai
(Bombay)
Arabian
Sea
Deccan
Plateau
Lakshadweep
Bay of
Bengal
Sri Lanka
Mekong
Maldive
Islands
Sumatra
Java
INDIAN
Cocos
Island
OCEAN

Gobi Desert
Beijing
Huang
Yangtze
Amur
Sea of Okhotsk
Sakhalin
Kamchatka
Peninsula
Bering
Sea
Hokkaidō
Sea of Japan
Honshū
Kyūshū
East
China
Sea
Taiwan
Hainan
Island
South China
Sea
Luzon
Mindanao
Malay
Peninsula
Borneo
Celebes
Timor
New Guinea
Palau
Islands

PACIFIC
Tropic of Cancer
Mariana
Islands
Wake
Island
Guam
OCEAN
Caroline
Islands
Marshall
Islands
Equator
Solomon
Islands
New
Hebrides
Coral Sea
New Caledonia
Fiji
Is.

Great
Sandy
Desert
AUSTRALIA
Cape Leeuwin
Darling
Great Dividing Range
Sydney
North Island
Aoraki
(Mt. Cook)
12,316 Ft.
3,754m
Tasmania
South Island
Tropic of Capricorn

Kerguelen
Islands

Queen Maud
Land
Enderby
Land
Wilkes Land
Victoria Land
ANTARCTICA
Antarctic Circle

Land Elevation	
Meters	Feet
3,000	9,840
2,000	6,560
500	1,640
200	656
0	0

Water Depth	
0	0
200	656
2,000	6,560

RAND MCNALLY

A3

ARCTIC OCEAN

GREENLAND
(Den.)

Baffin
Bay

Arctic Circle

ICELAND

FAROE IS.
(Den.)

ALASKA

RUSSIA

Yukon (U.S)

Anchorage

Aleutian Islands

UNITED
KINGDOM

IRELAND

London

FRANCE

C A N A D A

Hudson
Bay

Newfoundland

Vancouver

Montréal

Ottawa

Chicago

Missouri

New York

Washington D.C.

Madrid

PORTUGAL

SPAIN

Azores
(Port.)

UNITED STATES

Colorado

Los Angeles

Mississippi

ATLANTIC

Casablanca

Houston

Canary
Islands
(Sp.)

MOROCCO

MIDWAY IS.
(U.S)

Tropic of Cancer

MEXICO

Gulf of Mexico

BAHAMAS

W. SAHARA

Hawaiian
Islands
(U.S)

CUBA

DOM. REP.

MAURITANIA

MALI

Mexico City

HAITI

PUERTO RICO (U.S.)

BELIZE

PACIFIC

JAMAICA

Caribbean
Sea

SENEGAL

Niger

GUAT.

HOND.

CAPE
VERDE

GAMBIA

BURK.
FASO

EL. SAL.

NIC.

GUINEA-BISSAU

GUINEA

COSTA
RICA

Caracas

TRINIDAD AND TOBAGO

SIERRA LEONE

COTE
D'IVOIRE

GHANA

PANAMA

VENEZUELA

GUYANA

LIBERIA

COLOMBIA

SURINAME

FRENCH GUIANA

Galapagos Islands
(Ecuador)

ECUADOR

Amazon

OCEAN

Equator

KIRIBATI

PERU

B R A Z I L

OCEAN

Lima

SAMOA

AMERICAN
SAMOA

COOK
ISLANDS (N.Z.)

BOLIVIA

ST. HELENA
(U.K.)

TONGA

FRENCH POLYNESIA

Tropic of Capricorn

PARAGUAY

Rio de Janeiro

Easter Island
(Chile)

ARGENTINA

URUGUAY

Santiago

Buenos
Aires

CHILE

N

0   1000   2000 Miles

0   1000   2000   3000 Kilometers

Copyright by Rand McNally & Co.
Robinson Projection

FALKLAND IS.
(U.K.)

South
Georgia
(U.K.)

South
Orkney Is.
(U.K.)

Antarctic Circle

South
Shetland Is.
(U.K.)

Weddell
Sea

A4

ATLAS

ARCTIC OCEAN

Spitsbergen
(Nor.)

Franz Josef
Land

Novaya
Zemlya

Yenisey

Lena

NORWAY   FINLAND

SWEDEN   EST.
                    LAT.
North   LITH.
Sea   DEN.
       GERMANY BELARUS
NETH. POLAND
BEL.
SWITZ. CZ. SLVK.
       AUS. HUNG. UKRAINE
ITALY CRO. ROM. MOLD.
       BOS. YUG.
Rome✹ ALB. BUL.
       GREECE

R U S S I A

•Novosibirsk

Volga
✹Moscow

KAZAKHSTAN

MONGOLIA

Bering
Sea

Sea of Okhotsk

Black Sea

Mediterranean Sea

Crete

TUNISIA

ALGERIA

LIBYA   EGYPT

NIGER

CHAD   SUDAN

BENIN
NIGERIA
Lagos•

CAMEROON

EQUATORIAL
GUINEA

GABON

REP. OF
CONGO

DEM. REP.
OF CONGO

ANGOLA

NAMIBIA

BOTSWANA

SOUTH
AFRICA

Cape Town✹

TURKEY
CYPRUS LEB.
        SYRIA
ISRAEL
JORDAN IRAQ

GEO.
ARM. AZER.
        TURKMENISTAN

UZBEKISTAN

KYRG.

TAJIK.

IRAN   AFGHANISTAN

KUWAIT

QATAR
SAUDI
U.A.E.
ARABIA

OMAN

YEMEN

ERITREA
DJIBOUTI

Addis
Ababa•

ETHIOPIA

UGANDA
RWANDA
BURUNDI

KENYA

SOMALIA

TANZANIA

Nile

Red Sea

Cairo•✹

PAKISTAN

NEPAL
Ganges
BHU.
Kolkata•
(Calcutta)

INDIA

Mumbai•
(Bombay)
Arabian
Sea

BNGL.

MYANMAR

SRI LANKA

MALDIVES

CHINA

Beijing✹

NORTH
KOREA

SOUTH
KOREA

Sea of Japan

JAPAN
✹Tokyo

Chang Jiang
(Yangtze)

•Shanghai

Guangzhou•

TAIWAN

PACIFIC

Tropic of Cancer

LAOS

THAILAND

Bangkok•✹
CAMBODIA

VIETNAM

South China
Sea

PHILIPPINES

NORTHERN
MARIANA ISLANDS
(U.S.)

GUAM (U.S.)

WAKE ISLAND
(U.S.)

O C E A N

Bay of
Bengal

BRUNEI

MALAYSIA

SINGAPORE

Borneo

PALAU

FED. STATES OF
MICRONESIA

MARSHALL
ISLANDS

Equator

SEYCHELLES

COMOROS

Sumatra

Java

✹Jakarta

I N D O N E S I A

EAST TIMOR

New Guinea

PAPUA
NEW GUINEA

SOLOMON
ISLANDS

•Darwin

Coral Sea

VANUATU

NEW CALEDONIA
(Fr.)

FIJI

I N D I A N

MADAGASCAR

MAURITIUS

REUNION
(Fr.)

ZAMBIA

ZIMBABWE

SWAZILAND

LESOTHO

MALAWI
MOZAMBIQUE

CENTRAL
AFRICAN
REPUBLIC

Congo

Tropic of Capricorn

A U S T R A L I A

Perth•

Darling

•Sydney

O C E A N

Melbourne•

Tasmania

NEW ZEALAND
Wellington✹

Kerguelen
Islands
(Fr.)

A N T A R C T I C A

Antarctic Circle

| ✹ | National Capital |
| • | Major Cities |

✹ RAND M⊆NALLY

A5

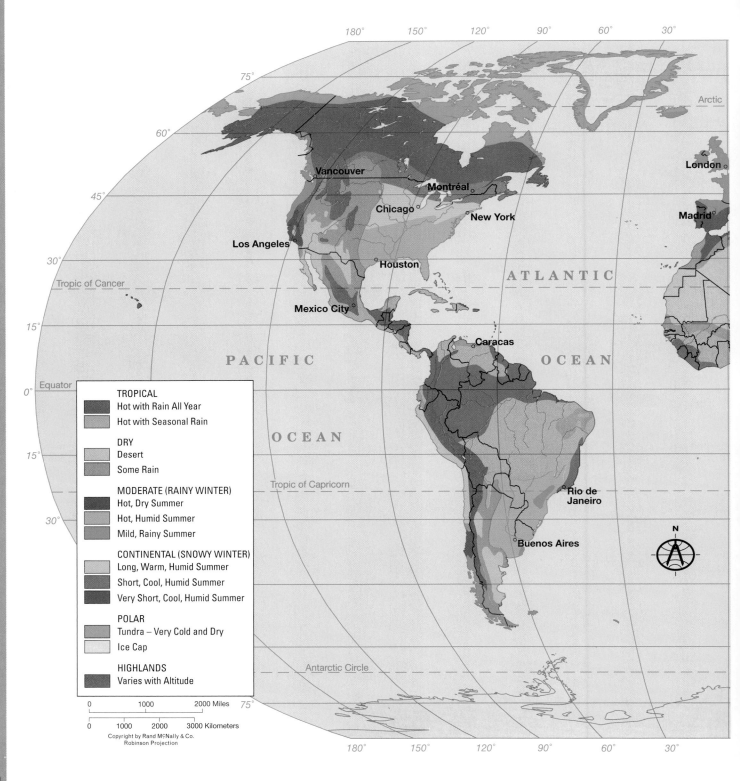

TROPICAL
Hot with Rain All Year
Hot with Seasonal Rain

DRY
Desert
Some Rain

MODERATE (RAINY WINTER)
Hot, Dry Summer
Hot, Humid Summer
Mild, Rainy Summer

CONTINENTAL (SNOWY WINTER)
Long, Warm, Humid Summer
Short, Cool, Humid Summer
Very Short, Cool, Humid Summer

POLAR
Tundra – Very Cold and Dry
Ice Cap

HIGHLANDS
Varies with Altitude

0   1000   2000 Miles

0   1000   2000   3000 Kilometers

Copyright by Rand McNally & Co.
Robinson Projection

Vancouver
Montréal
Chicago
New York
Los Angeles
Houston
Mexico City
Caracas
Rio de Janeiro
Buenos Aires
London
Madrid

ATLANTIC OCEAN
PACIFIC OCEAN

Arctic
Tropic of Cancer
Equator
Tropic of Capricorn
Antarctic Circle

N

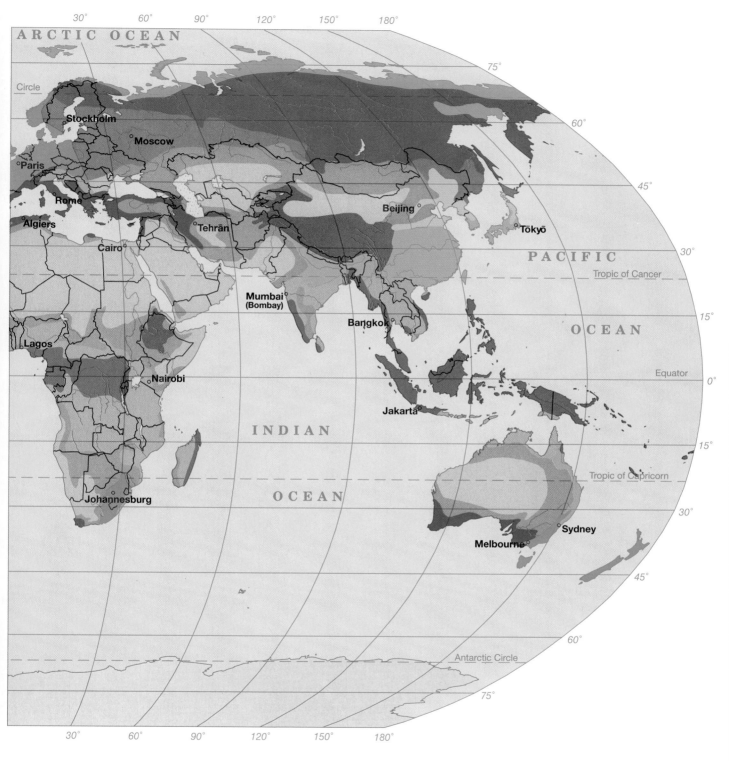

ARCTIC OCEAN

Circle

Stockholm

Moscow

Paris

Rome

Algiers

Tehrān

Cairo

Beijing

Tōkyō

PACIFIC

Tropic of Cancer

Mumbai
(Bombay)

Bangkok

OCEAN

Lagos

Nairobi

Jakarta

Equator

INDIAN

OCEAN

Johannesburg

Tropic of Capricorn

Sydney

Melbourne

Antarctic Circle

75°

60°

45°

30°

15°

0°

15°

30°

45°

60°

75°

30° 60° 90° 120° 150° 180°

30° 60° 90° 120° 150° 180°

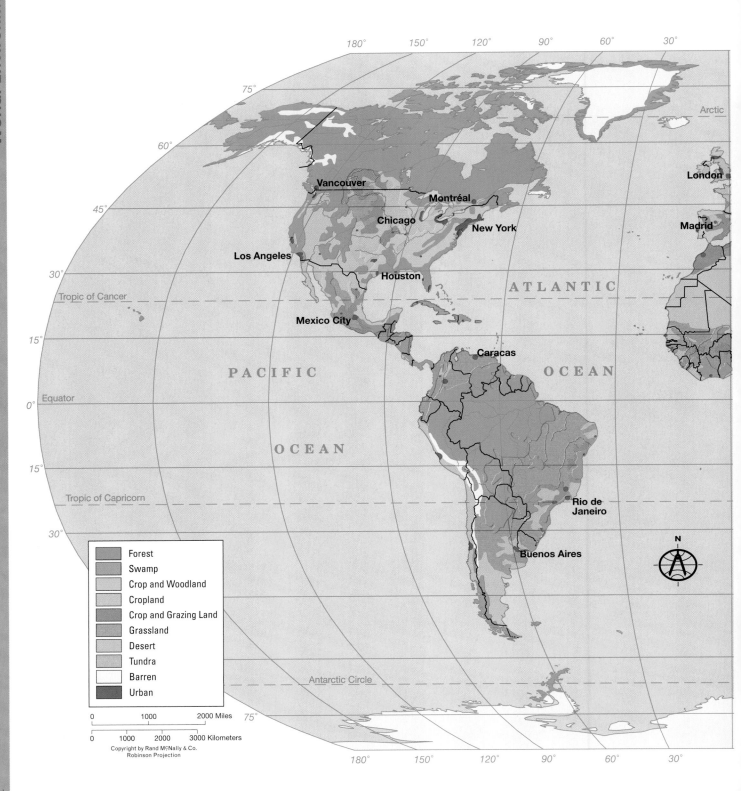

Forest
Swamp
Crop and Woodland
Cropland
Crop and Grazing Land
Grassland
Desert
Tundra
Barren
Urban

PACIFIC

OCEAN

ATLANTIC

OCEAN

Tropic of Cancer

Equator

Tropic of Capricorn

Antarctic Circle

Arctic

London

Madrid

Vancouver

Montréal

Chicago

New York

Los Angeles

Houston

Mexico City

Caracas

Rio de Janeiro

Buenos Aires

N

0   1000   2000 Miles
0   1000   2000   3000 Kilometers
Copyright by Rand McNally & Co.
Robinson Projection

RAND McNALLY

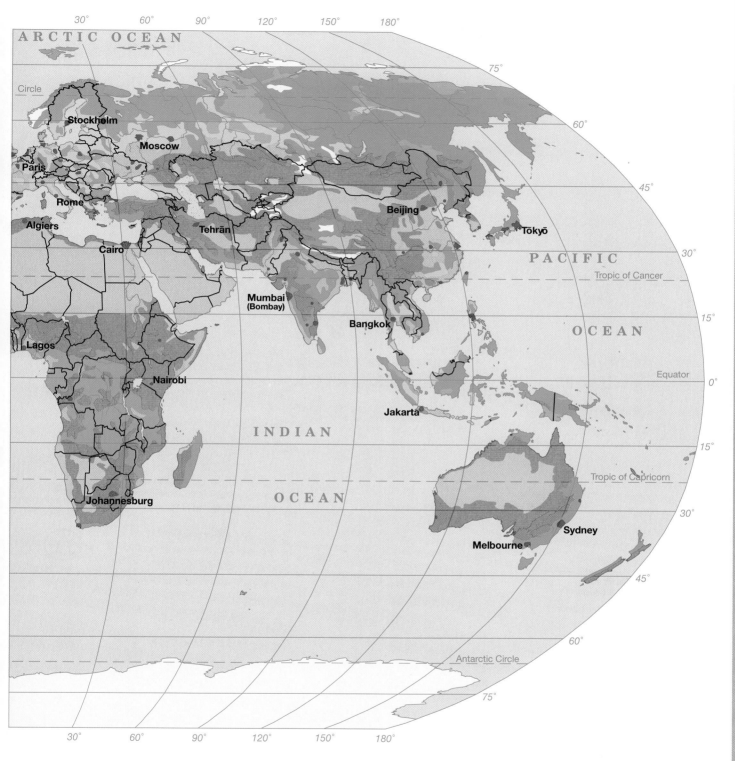

ARCTIC OCEAN

Circle

Stockholm

Moscow

Paris

Rome

Algiers

Cairo

Tehrān

Beijing

Tōkyō

Mumbai
(Bombay)

Bangkok

PACIFIC

Tropic of Cancer

OCEAN

Lagos

Nairobi

Equator

Jakarta

INDIAN

Tropic of Capricorn

OCEAN

Johannesburg

Sydney

Melbourne

Antarctic Circle

30° 60° 90° 120° 150° 180°

75°

60°

45°

30°

15°

0°

15°

30°

45°

60°

75°

Per square mile
(per square kilometer)

- Under 2 *(Under 1)*
- 2-60 *(1-25)*
- 60-125 *(25-50)*
- 125-250 *(50-100)*
- Over 250 *(Over 100)*

0   1000   2000 Miles

0   1000   2000   3000 Kilometers

Copyright by Rand McNally & Co.
Robinson Projection

Vancouver
Montréal
Chicago
New York
Los Angeles
Houston
Mexico City
Caracas
Rio de Janeiro
Buenos Aires
London
Madrid

ATLANTIC
OCEAN
PACIFIC
OCEAN
OCEAN

Arctic
75°
60°
45°
Tropic of Cancer
30°
15°
Equator
15°
Tropic of Capricorn
30°
Antarctic Circle
75°

180°   150°   120°   90°   60°   30°

N

RAND McNALLY

ARCTIC OCEAN

Circle

Stockholm

Moscow

Yekaterinburg

Paris

Rome

Algiers

Cairo

Tehrān

Beijing

Tōkyō

PACIFIC

Tropic of Cancer

Mumbai
(Bombay)

Bangkok

OCEAN

Lagos

15°

Nairobi

Equator

Jakarta

INDIAN

15°

OCEAN

Tropic of Capricorn

Johannesburg

Sydney

Melbourne

Antarctic Circle

30° 60° 90° 120° 150° 180°

75°

60°

45°

30°

15°

0°

15°

30°

45°

60°

75°

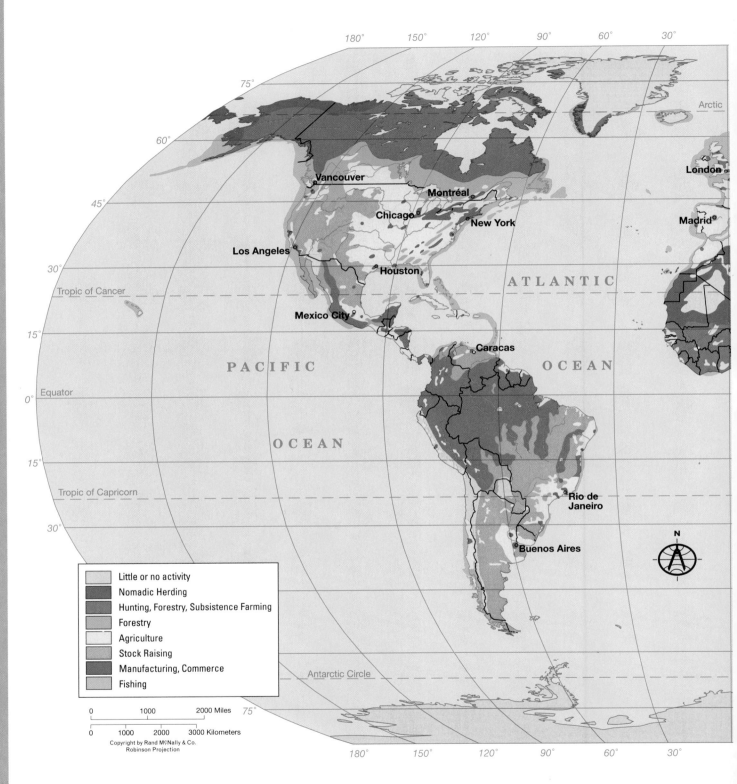

Little or no activity
Nomadic Herding
Hunting, Forestry, Subsistence Farming
Forestry
Agriculture
Stock Raising
Manufacturing, Commerce
Fishing

0   1000   2000 Miles

0   1000   2000   3000 Kilometers

Copyright by Rand McNally & Co.
Robinson Projection

RAND McNALLY

A12

ARCTIC OCEAN

Circle

Stockholm

Moscow

Paris

Rome

Algiers

Cairo

Tehrān

Beijing

Tōkyō

PACIFIC

Tropic of Cancer

Mumbai
(Bombay)

Bangkok

OCEAN

15°

Lagos

Nairobi

Equator

Jakarta

INDIAN

Johannesburg

OCEAN

Tropic of Capricorn

Sydney

Melbourne

Antarctic Circle

30°   60°   90°   120°   150°   180°

75°

60°

45°

30°

15°

0°

15°

30°

45°

60°

75°

30°   60°   90°   120°   150°   180°

Eurasian Plate

North America Plate

Juan de Fuca Plate

Philippine Plate

Pacific Plate

Cocos Plate

Indo-Australian Plate

Nazca Plate

N

Scale at Equator

| 0 | 500 | 1000 | 1500 | 2000 | 2500 Miles |

| 0 | 1000 | 2000 | 3000 | 4000 Kilometers |

Copyright by Rand McNally & Co.
Miller Cylindrical Projection

Antarctic Plate

	Volcanic eruptions since 1900
•	Earthquakes of 7.7 magnitude and above since 10 A.D.
→	Directions of plate movement

Eurasian Plate

Caribbean Plate

Arabian Plate

African Plate

Indo-Australian Plate

South American Plate

Antarctic Plate

Scotia Plate

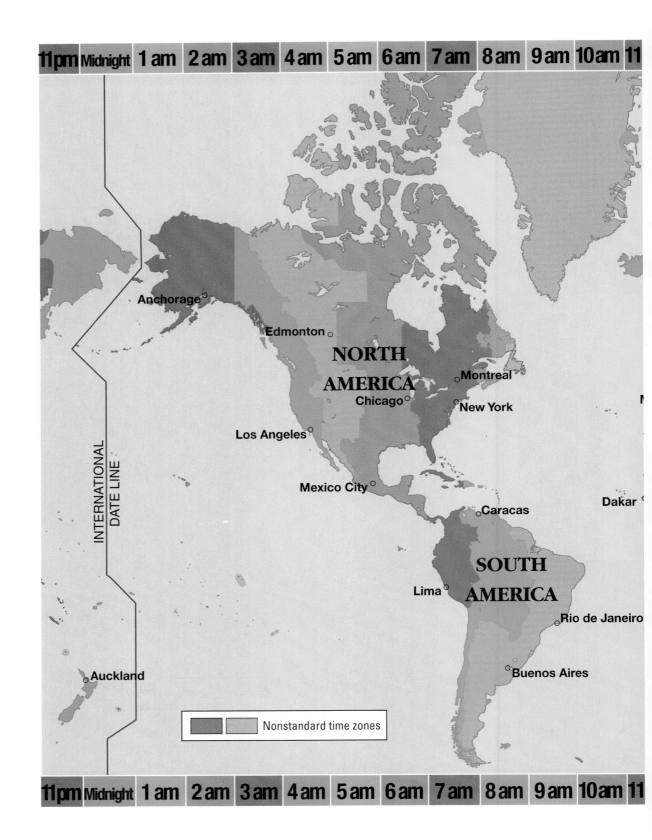

11pm Midnight 1 am 2 am 3 am 4 am 5 am 6 am 7 am 8 am 9 am 10 am 11

Anchorage

Edmonton

NORTH
AMERICA

Montreal

Chicago

New York

Los Angeles

INTERNATIONAL
DATE LINE

Mexico City

Caracas

Dakar

SOUTH
AMERICA

Lima

Rio de Janeiro

Buenos Aires

Auckland

Nonstandard time zones

11pm Midnight 1 am 2 am 3 am 4 am 5 am 6 am 7 am 8 am 9 am 10 am 11

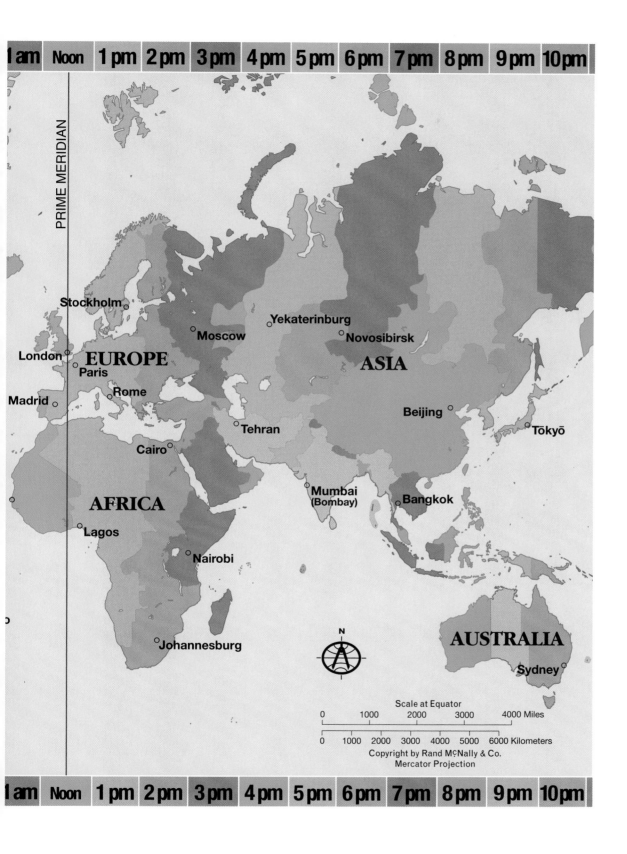

| 1 am | Noon | 1 pm | 2 pm | 3 pm | 4 pm | 5 pm | 6 pm | 7 pm | 8 pm | 9 pm | 10 pm |

PRIME MERIDIAN

Stockholm

Yekaterinburg

Moscow

Novosibirsk

London

EUROPE

Paris

ASIA

Rome

Madrid

Beijing

Tehran

Tōkyō

Cairo

Mumbai (Bombay)

Bangkok

AFRICA

Lagos

Nairobi

Johannesburg

AUSTRALIA

N

Sydney

Scale at Equator

| 0 | 1000 | 2000 | 3000 | 4000 Miles |

| 0 | 1000 | 2000 | 3000 | 4000 | 5000 | 6000 Kilometers |

Copyright by Rand McNally & Co.
Mercator Projection

| 1 am | Noon | 1 pm | 2 pm | 3 pm | 4 pm | 5 pm | 6 pm | 7 pm | 8 pm | 9 pm | 10 pm |

ATLAS

RAND McNALLY

A17

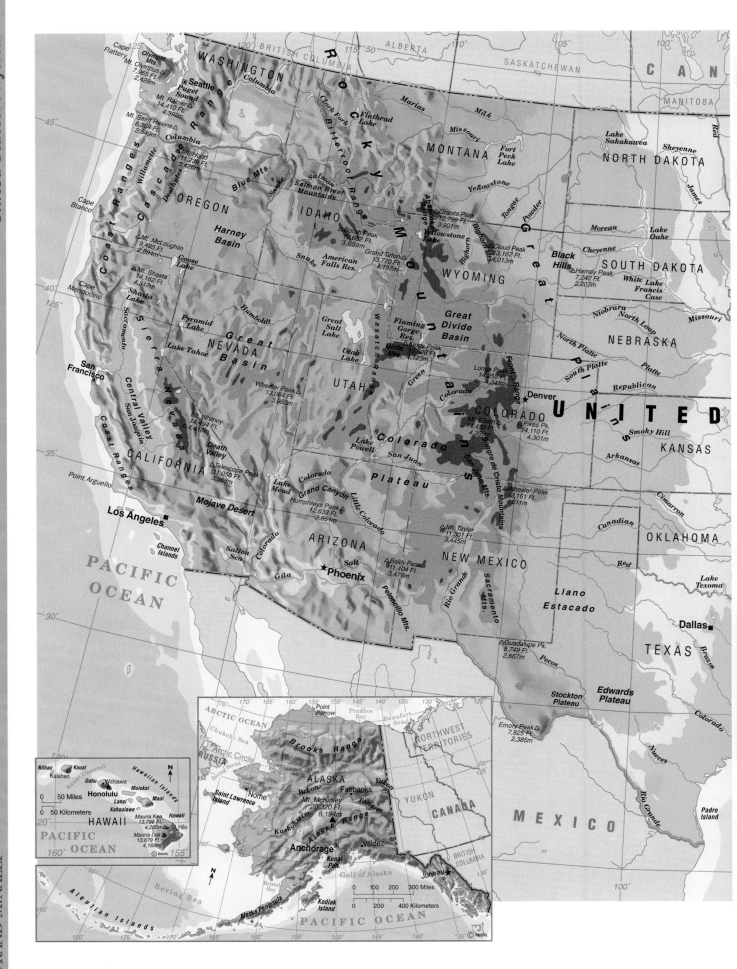

PACIFIC OCEAN

WASHINGTON

Cape Flattery
Mt. Olympus 7,965 Ft. 2,428m
Olympic Mts.
Seattle
Puget Sound
Mt. Rainier 14,410 Ft. 4,392m
Cascade Ranges
Columbia
Mt. Saint Helens 8,364 Ft. 2,549m
Cape Blanco
Coast Ranges
Willamette
OREGON
Deschutes
Mt. Hood 11,239 Ft. 3,426m
Blue Mts.
Harney Basin
Mt. McLoughlin 9,495 Ft. 2,894m
Goose Lake
Mt. Shasta 14,162 Ft. 4,317m
Cape Mendocino
Shasta Lake
Sacramento
Pyramid Lake
Humboldt
Lake Tahoe
Sierra Nevada
Great NEVADA Basin
San Francisco
Wheeler Peak 13,064 Ft. 3,982m
Central Valley
San Joaquin
Mt. Whitney 14,494 Ft. 4,418m
CALIFORNIA
Death Valley
Telescope Peak 11,050 Ft. 3,368m
Point Arguello
Mojave Desert
Los Angeles
Channel Islands
Salton Sea
Colorado
Lake Mead
Colorado
Grand Canyon
Humphreys Peak 12,633 Ft. 3,851m
Little Colorado
ARIZONA
Gila
Salt
Phoenix
Baldy Peak 11,404 Ft. 3,476m
Peloncillo Mts.

IDAHO
Snake
Clark Fork
Flathead Lake
Bitterroot Range
Salmon River Mountains
Salmon
Borah Peak 12,662 Ft. 3,859m
American Falls Res.
Grand Teton 13,770 Ft. 4,197m
Snake
ROCKY MOUNTAINS
Absaroka Range
Granite Peak 12,799 Ft. 3,901m
Yellowstone Lake
WYOMING
Cloud Peak 13,167 Ft. 4,013m
Bighorn Mts.
Bighorn
Great Salt Lake
Wasatch Range
Flaming Gorge Res.
Kings Peak
Uinta Mts. 13,528 Ft. 4,123m
Great Divide Basin
Utah Lake
Green
UTAH
Colorado
Lake Powell
San Juan
Plateau
San Juan Mts.
Longs Peak 14,255 Ft. 4,345m
Front Range
Denver
Mt. Elbert 14,433 Ft. 4,399m
COLORADO
Pikes Pk. 14,110 Ft. 4,301m
Sangre de Cristo Mountains
Wheeler Peak 13,161 Ft. 4,011m
Mt. Taylor 11,301 Ft. 3,445m
Rio Grande
NEW MEXICO
Sacramento Mts.

BRITISH COLUMBIA
ALBERTA
SASKATCHEWAN
MANITOBA
CANADA
MONTANA
Columbia
Marias
Milk
Missouri
Fort Peck Lake
Yellowstone
Tongue
Powder
Great Plains
Moreau
Cheyenne
Black Hills
Harney Peak 7,242 Ft. 2,207m
NORTH DAKOTA
Lake Sakakawea
Sheyenne
Red
James
Missouri
Lake Oahe
SOUTH DAKOTA
White
Lake Francis Case
Niobrara
North Loup
North Platte
NEBRASKA
South Platte
Platte
Republican
UNITED
Smoky Hill
KANSAS
Arkansas
Cimarron
Canadian
OKLAHOMA
Red
Lake Texoma
Llano Estacado
Pecos
TEXAS
Stockton Plateau
Edwards Plateau
Guadalupe Pk. 8,749 Ft. 2,667m
Emory Peak 7,825 Ft. 2,385m
MEXICO
Colorado
Nueces
Brazos
Rio Grande
Padre Island
Dallas

PACIFIC OCEAN

ARCTIC OCEAN
Point Barrow
Prudhoe Bay
Beaufort Sea
Chukchi Sea
Arctic Circle
RUSSIA
Bering Strait
Brooks Range
NORTHWEST TERRITORIES
ALASKA
Yukon
Fairbanks
Yukon
Tanana
Saint Lawrence Island
Nome
Mt. McKinley 20,320 Ft. 6,194m
Alaska Range
YUKON
CANADA
Kuskokwim
Kuskokwim
Anchorage
Kenai Pen.
Valdez
BRITISH COLUMBIA
Juneau
Bristol Bay
Gulf of Alaska
Bering Sea
Kodiak Island
Alaska Peninsula
Aleutian Islands
PACIFIC OCEAN
0 100 200 300 Miles
0 200 400 Kilometers

Niihau
Kauai
Kalaheo
Oahu
Wahiawa
Honolulu
Molokai
Lanai
Maui
Kahoolawe
Hawaiian Islands
Mauna Kea 13,796 Ft. 4,205m
Hawaii
Mauna Loa 13,679 Ft. 4,169m
Hilo
HAWAII
0 50 Miles
0 50 Kilometers
PACIFIC OCEAN

A18

A19

Map Labels

A D A

ONTARIO

QUEBEC

NEW BRUNSWICK

Lake Winnipeg

Lake of the Woods

Lake Nipigon

Isle Royale

Lake Superior

Great Lakes

Keweenaw Peninsula

Whitefish Point

St. Lawrence

Mt. Katahdin 5,268 Ft △1,606m

MINNESOTA

Upper Peninsula

MICHIGAN

Bruce Peninsula

Georgian Bay

Lake Huron

Montréal

MAINE

Moosehead Lake

Kennebec

Minneapolis

Chippewa

WISCONSIN

Lake Winnebago

Wisconsin

Saginaw Bay

Lower Peninsula

Lake Michigan

Muskegon

Grand

Toronto ★

Lake Ontario

Niagara Falls

VERMONT

Lake Champlain

Adirondack Mountains

NEW YORK

White Mts.

Mt. Washington 6,288 Ft △1,917m

NEW HAMPSHIRE

Green Mts.

Connecticut

MASS. ★ Boston

Gulf of Maine

Cape Cod

Minnesota

Detroit

Lake Erie

Allegheny Plateau

Catskill Mts.

Hudson

CONNECTICUT R.I.

Nantucket Island

IOWA

Iowa

Des Moines

Chicago

INDIANA

OHIO

Maumee

Scioto

PENNSYLVANIA

Appalachian Mountains

Susquehanna

Long Island

New York

Philadelphia

NEW JERSEY

ATLANTIC OCEAN

Kansas

S T A T E S

ILLINOIS

Illinois

White

Wabash

Ohio

WEST VIRGINIA

Washington D.C.

Delaware Bay

DELAWARE

MARYLAND

Mississippi

St. Louis

Lake of the Ozarks

Missouri

MISSOURI

Flint Hills

Neosho

Ozark Plateau

Boston Mts.

White

Arkansas

Ouachita Mts.

ARKANSAS

KENTUCKY

Green

Lake Cumberland

Cumberland

Kentucky Lake

TENNESSEE

Tennessee

Mt. Mitchell 6,684 Ft △2,087m

Cumberland Plateau

Blue Ridge

Piedmont

VIRGINIA

James

Roanoke

Chesapeake Bay

Albemarle Sound

Cape Hatteras

Pamlico Sound

NORTH CAROLINA

Cape Lookout

Cape Fear

Yazoo

Ouachita

Sabine

Sam Rayburn Res.

Toledo Bend Res.

Red

MISSISSIPPI

Pearl

ALABAMA

Tombigbee

Alabama

Chattahoochee

Flint

GEORGIA

Altamaha

Clarks Hill Lake

Atlanta ★

SOUTH CAROLINA

Santee

Pee Dee

Savannah

Sea Islands

Coastal Plain

Cape Fear

Trinity

LOUISIANA

Houston

New Orleans

Atchafalaya Bay

Cape San Blas

Apalachee Bay

Suwannee

Cape Canaveral

Mississippi Delta

GULF OF MEXICO

Tampa Bay

FLORIDA

Lake Okeechobee

The Everglades

Miami

Cape Sable

Florida Keys

Land Elevation

Meters		Feet
3,000		9,840
2,000		6,560
500		1,640
200		656
0		0

Water Depth

0		0
200		656
2,000		6,560

N

| 0 | 100 | 200 | 300 Miles |
| 0 | 100 | 200 | 300 | 400 Kilometers |

Copyright by Rand McNally & Co.
Alber's Conic Equal Area Projection

PUERTO RICO (U.S.)

ATLANTIC OCEAN

N

San Juan

Arecibo

Mayagüez

Ponce

Caguas

Caribbean Sea

| 0 | 25 | 50 Miles |
| 0 | 25 | 50 Kilometers |

© RMcN

United States: Political

ATLAS

National Capital
★ Secondary Capital (State, Province, or Territory)
■ City over 1,000,000 population
▣ City of 250,000 to 1,000,000 population
• City under 250,000 population

Copyright by Rand McNally & Co.
Alber's Conic Equal Area Projection

0 100 200 300 Miles
0 100 200 300 400 Kilometers

ATLANTIC OCEAN
San Juan
Arecibo
Mayagüez   Caguas
Ponce
PUERTO RICO (U.S.)
Caribbean Sea
0 25 50 Miles
0 25 50 Kilometers

RAND McNALLY

A21

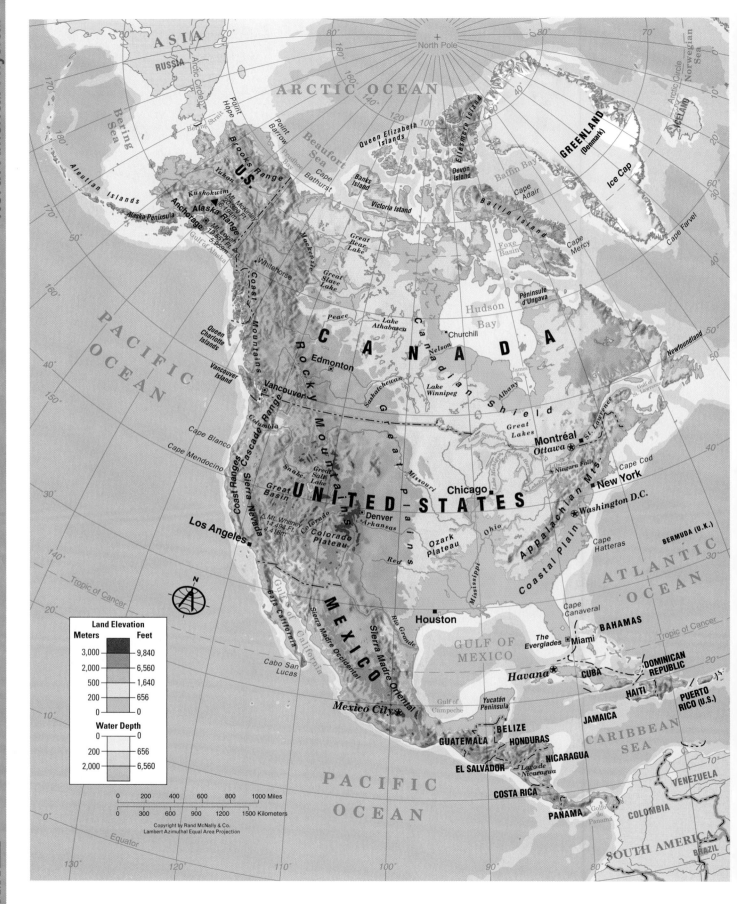

ASIA

RUSSIA

Arctic Circle

North Pole

ARCTIC OCEAN

Point Hope
Point Barrow
Brooks Range
U.S.
Yukon
Kuskokwim
Mt. McKinley 20,320 Ft. 6,194 m
Alaska Range
Anchorage
Mt. Logan 19,551 Ft. 5,959 m
Gulf of Alaska
Aleutian Islands
Alaska Peninsula
Bering Sea
Bering Strait

Queen Elizabeth Islands
Ellesmere Island
Devon Island
Cape Bathurst
Banks Island
Victoria Island
Beaufort Sea
Baffin Bay
Cape Adair
Baffin Island
Cape Mercy

GREENLAND (Denmark)
Ice Cap
ICELAND
Arctic Circle
Norwegian Sea
Cape Farvel

Mackenzie
Great Bear Lake
Whitehorse
Great Slave Lake
Peace
Lake Athabasca
Churchill
Hudson Bay
Foxe Basin
Péninsule d'Ungava

CANADA

PACIFIC OCEAN

Queen Charlotte Islands
Vancouver Island
Vancouver
Coast Mountains
Rocky Mountains
Columbia
Edmonton
Saskatchewan
Nelson
Lake Winnipeg
Canadian Shield
James Bay
Albany
Great Lakes
Lake Superior
Newfoundland
Gulf of St. Lawrence

Cape Blanco
Cape Mendocino
Coast Ranges
Cascade Range
Sierra Nevada
Great Basin
Snake
Great Salt Lake
Colorado
Mt. Whitney 14,494 Ft. 4,418 m
Colorado Plateau
Los Angeles

Great Plains
Missouri
Chicago
Denver
Arkansas
Ozark Plateau
Ohio
Red
Mississippi
Lake Michigan
Lake Huron
Lake Erie
Lake Ontario
Niagara Falls
Montréal
Ottawa
St. Lawrence
Appalachian Mts.
Cape Cod
New York
Washington D.C.
Coastal plain
Cape Hatteras

UNITED STATES

BERMUDA (U.K.)

ATLANTIC OCEAN

Tropic of Cancer
Baja California
Gulf of California
Cabo San Lucas
Sierra Madre Occidental
Houston
Rio Grande
Sierra Madre Oriental
Gulf of Campeche
Yucatán Peninsula

MEXICO

Mexico City

GULF OF MEXICO
The Everglades
Cape Canaveral
Miami
Havana
CUBA
BAHAMAS
Tropic of Cancer

HAITI
DOMINICAN REPUBLIC
PUERTO RICO (U.S.)
JAMAICA
CARIBBEAN SEA

BELIZE
GUATEMALA
HONDURAS
EL SALVADOR
NICARAGUA
Lago de Nicaragua
COSTA RICA
PANAMA
Golfo de Panamá

VENEZUELA
COLOMBIA

PACIFIC OCEAN

SOUTH AMERICA
BRAZIL

Equator

Land Elevation

Meters		Feet
3,000		9,840
2,000		6,560
500		1,640
200		656
0		0

Water Depth

0		0
200		656
2,000		6,560

N

0   200   400   600   800   1000 Miles
0   300   600   900   1200   1500 Kilometers

Copyright by Rand McNally & Co.
Lambert Azimuthal Equal Area Projection

ASIA

RUSSIA

Arctic Circle

Bering
Sea

Aleutian Islands

ARCTIC OCEAN

North Pole

Beaufort
Sea

Prudhoe Bay

U.S.

Anchorage
Fairbanks
Valdez
Gulf of Alaska

Whitehorse

Juneau

Yukon

Mackenzie

Queen Elizabeth
Islands

Banks
Island

Victoria Island

Great
Bear
Lake

Yellowknife

Great
Slave
Lake

Ellesmere Island

Devon
Island

Baffin Bay

Baffin Island

GREENLAND
(Denmark)

Godthåb

ICELAND
Reykjavik

Arctic Circle

PACIFIC

OCEAN

Edmonton

Calgary

Victoria
Vancouver
Seattle

Portland

Columbia

Spokane

Saskatoon

Regina

Peace

C A N A D A

Nelson

Saskatchewan

Lake
Winnipeg

Winnipeg

Missouri

Billings

Hudson

Bay

Thunder Bay

Lake Superior

Newfoundland

St. John's

Gulf of
St. Lawrence

Quebec
St. Lawrence

Montréal
Ottawa
Toronto

Saint John

Halifax

ATLANTIC

OCEAN

BERMUDA (U.K.)

Sacramento
San Francisco

Las Vegas

UNITED STATES

Great
Salt
Lake

Denver

Colorado

Arkansas

Minneapolis

Omaha

Milwaukee
Chicago

Kansas City

St. Louis

Ohio

Detroit

Indianapolis

Cleveland

Cincinnati

Nashville

New York

Philadelphia
Washington D.C.

Norfolk

Los Angeles
San Diego
Tijuana

Phoenix

Albuquerque

Oklahoma
City

Red

Memphis

Charlotte

Atlanta

Hermosillo

Ciudad
Juárez

MEXICO

Chihuahua

Rio Grande

Gulf of California

Culiacán

Torreón

Monterrey

Dallas

Houston

Mississippi

San Antonio

New Orleans

Jacksonville

Tampa

GULF OF
MEXICO

Miami

Nassau

BAHAMAS

Tropic of Cancer

Havana

CUBA

DOMINICAN
REPUBLIC

PUERTO
RICO
(U.S.)

Guadalajara

San Luis Potosí

León

Mérida

Cancún

JAMAICA

Kingston

HAITI

Port-au-
Prince

Santo
Domingo

Mexico City
Puebla

Veracruz

Acapulco

GUATEMALA

BELIZE

Belmopan

CARIBBEAN

SEA

Guatemala City

HONDURAS

Tegucigalpa

San Salvador

EL SALVADOR

Managua

NICARAGUA

Lago de
Nicaragua

Panama
City

VENEZUELA

Caracas

COSTA RICA

San José

PANAMA

Golfo
de
Panamá

COLOMBIA

Bogotá

PACIFIC

OCEAN

SOUTH AMERICA

BRAZIL

Equator

Legend

- ✪ National Capital
- ★ Secondary Capital (State, Province, or Territory)
- ■ City over 1,000,000 population
- ▣ City of 250,000 to 1,000,000 population
- • City under 250,000 population

Scale:
0 200 400 600 800 1000 Miles
0 300 600 900 1200 1500 Kilometers

Copyright by Rand McNally & Co.
Lambert Azimuthal Equal Area Projection

RAND McNALLY

A23

GULF OF MEXICO

NORTH AMERICA

CUBA

Greater Antilles

HAITI DOMINICAN REPUBLIC

PUERTO RICO (U.S.)

JAMAICA

BELIZE

MEXICO

GUATEMALA HONDURAS Gulf of Honduras

EL SALVADOR NICARAGUA

COSTA RICA

PANAMA Gulf of Panama

CARIBBEAN SEA

Lesser Antilles

ATLANTIC OCEAN

Cristóbal Colón Peak 18,948 Ft. 5,775m

Caracas

TRINIDAD AND TOBAGO

Llanos Orinoco

VENEZUELA

GUYANA

SURINAME FRENCH GUIANA

Cape Orange

Bogotá

COLOMBIA

Galapagos Islands (Ec.)

ECUADOR Chimborazo 20,703 Ft. 6,310m

Putumayo

Japurá

Negro

Amazon

Manaus

Ilha de Marajó Belém

Equator

Amazon

Juruá

Amazon Basin

Madeira

Tapajós

BRAZIL

Tocantins

Selvas

Ucayali

PERU

Mt. Huascarán 22,133 Ft. 6,746m

Lima

Andes

Lake Titicaca

Mt. Illampu 21,066 Ft. 6,421m

Cordillera Oriental

BOLIVIA

Recife

Mato Grosso Plateau

São Francisco

Brasília

Serra do Espinhaço

Mt. Sajama 21,463 Ft. 6,542m

Atacama Desert

Gran Chaco

PARAGUAY

Paraná

São Paulo

Rio de Janeiro

Tropic of Capricorn

Isla San Ambrosio (Chile)

Mt. Ojos del Salado 22,615 Ft. 6,893m

Isla San Felix (Chile)

Andes

Paraná

Tropic of Capricorn

PACIFIC OCEAN

Archipiélago Juan Fernández (Chile)

CHILE

Mt. Aconcagua 22,831 Ft. 6,959m

Santiago

ARGENTINA

Buenos Aires

URUGUAY

Río de la Plata

Pampas

N

Chiloé

San Matías Gulf

Península Valdés

Land Elevation

Meters		Feet
3,000		9,840
2,000		6,560
500		1,640
200		656
0		0

Water Depth

0		0
200		656
2,000		6,560

Patagonia

San Jorge Gulf

Point Medanoso

ATLANTIC OCEAN

Grand Bay

West Falkland

FALKLAND ISLANDS (U.K.)

East Falkland

Strait of Magellan

Tierra del Fuego

Cape Horn

South Georgia (U.K.)

0	200	400	600	800	1000 Miles
0	300	600	900	1200	1500 Kilometers

Copyright by Rand McNally & Co.
Lambert Azimuthal Equal Area Projection

Drake Passage

South Shetland Islands (U.K.)

South Orkney Islands (U.K.)

South Sandwich Islands (U.K.)

ATLAS

National Capital

★ Secondary Capital
(State, Province, or Territory)

■ City over 1,000,000 population

▣ City of 250,000 to 1,000,000 population

• City under 250,000 population

0   200   400   600   800   1000 Miles

0   300   600   900   1200   1500 Kilometers

Copyright by Rand McNally & Co.
Lambert Azimuthal Equal Area Projection

RAND McNALLY

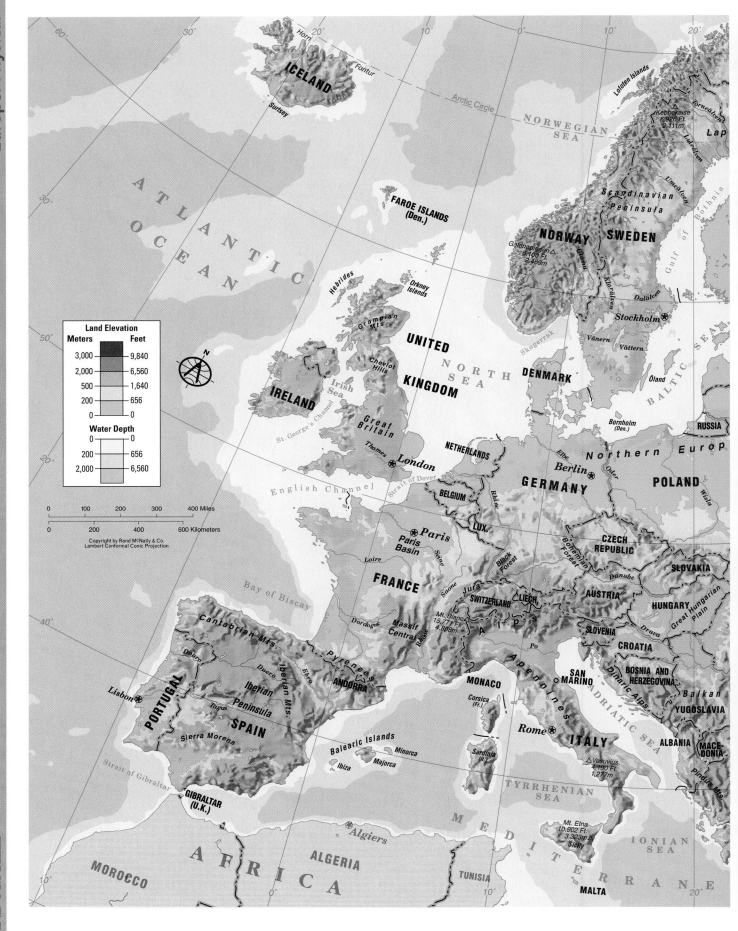

Land Elevation

Meters		Feet
3,000		9,840
2,000		6,560
500		1,640
200		656
0		0

Water Depth

0		0
200		656
2,000		6,560

0   100   200   300   400 Miles
0   200   400   600 Kilometers

Copyright by Rand McNally & Co.
Lambert Conformal Conic Projection

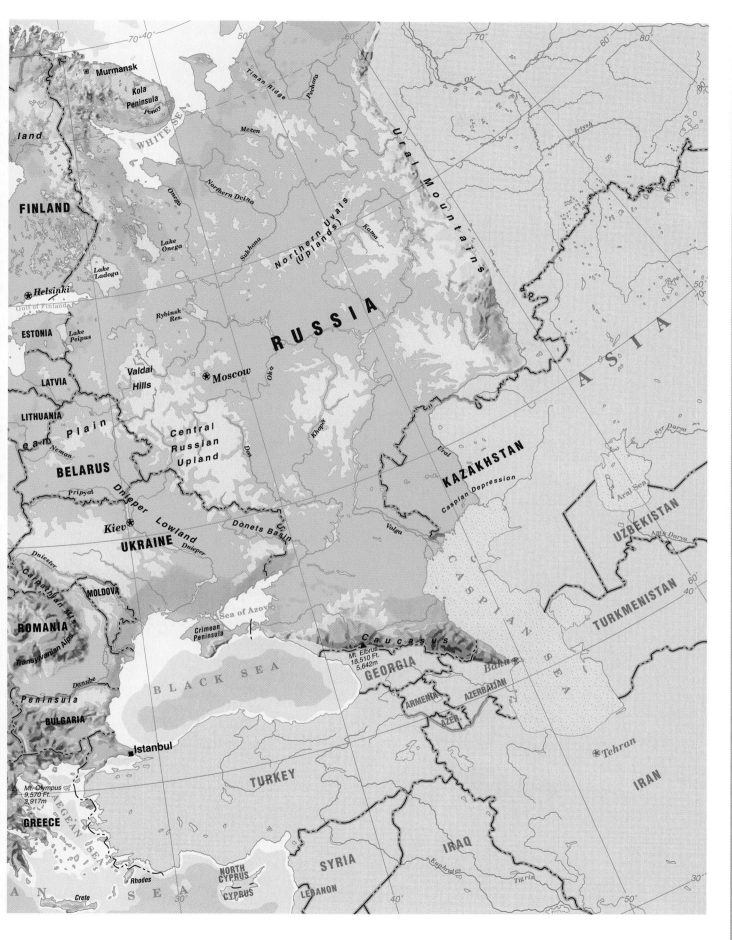

Murmansk

Kola
Peninsula
Ponoy

land

WHITE SEA

Timan Ridge

Pechora

Mezen

Ural Mountains

Ob'

Irtysh

FINLAND

Northern Dvina

Onega

Lake
Onega

Sukhona

Northern Uvals
(Uplands)

Kama

Lake
Ladoga

☆ Helsinki

Gulf of Finland

RUSSIA

ASIA

ESTONIA

Lake
Peipus

Rybinsk
Res.

Oka

☆ Moscow

50°

70°

LATVIA

Valdai
Hills

Sır Darya

Aral Sea

LITHUANIA

e a n

Plain

Neman

Central
Russian
Upland

Don

Khopër

KAZAKHSTAN

BELARUS

Pripyat

Dnieper

Caspian Depression

UZBEKISTAN

Amu Darya

Kiev ☆

Lowland

Donets Basin

Volga

Ural

UKRAINE

Dnieper

60°

40°

Dniester

Carpathian Mts.

MOLDOVA

Sea of Azov

C
A
S
P
I
A
N

S
E
A

TURKMENISTAN

ROMANIA

Crimean
Peninsula

Transylvanian Alps

Caucasus

▲ Mt. Elbrus
18,510 Ft.
5,642m

Baku ☆

Danube

Peninsula

GEORGIA

AZERBAIJAN

BULGARIA

BLACK   SEA

ARMENIA

AZER.

Istanbul ■

☆ Tehran

Mt. Olympus
9,570 Ft.
2,917m

TURKEY

IRAN

GREECE

AEGEAN SEA

SYRIA

IRAQ

Euphrates

Tigris

30°

50°

A
N

S
E
A

Rhodes

Crete

30°

NORTH
CYPRUS

CYPRUS

LEBANON

40°

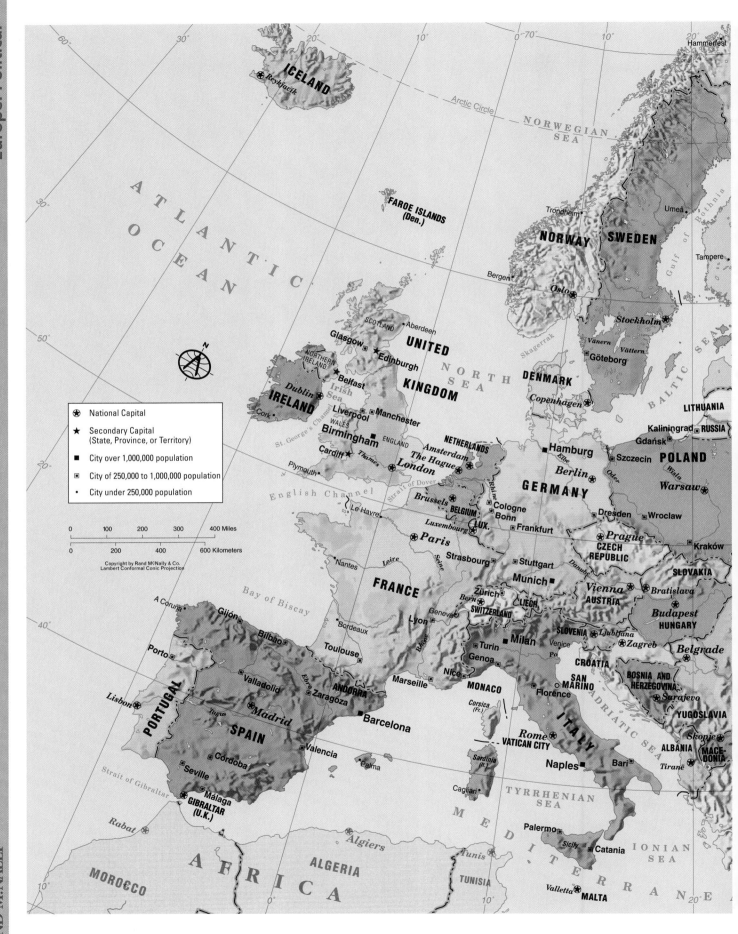

Legend

- ⊛ National Capital
- ★ Secondary Capital (State, Province, or Territory)
- ■ City over 1,000,000 population
- ▣ City of 250,000 to 1,000,000 population
- • City under 250,000 population

```
0    100   200   300    400 Miles
0      200       400     600 Kilometers
```

Copyright by Rand M°Nally & Co.
Lambert Conformal Conic Projection

RAND McNALLY

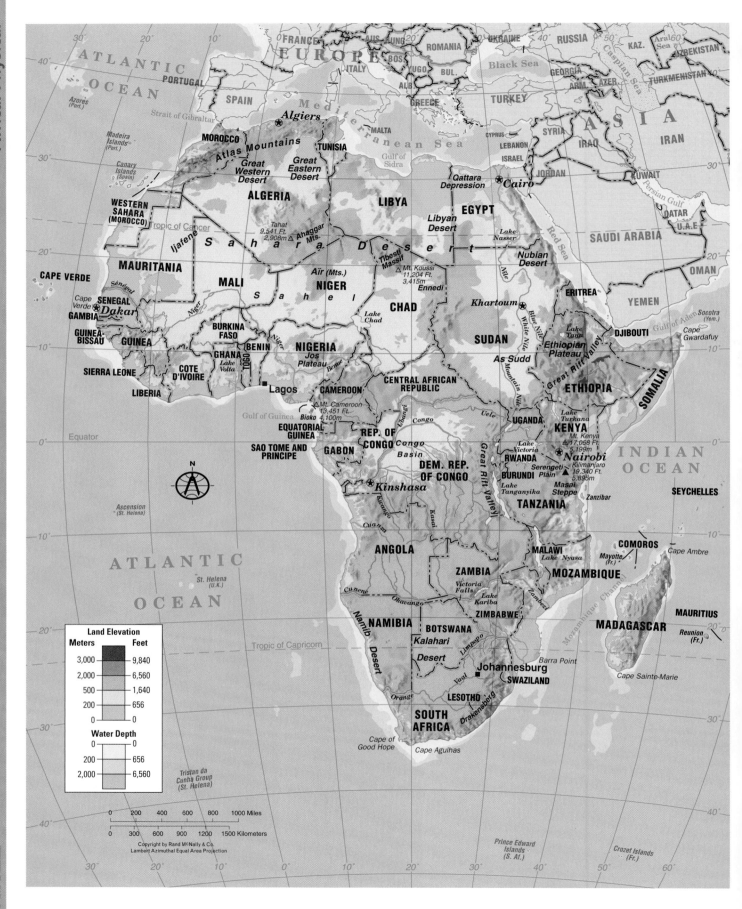

ATLANTIC
OCEAN

EUROPE

PORTUGAL
SPAIN

FRANCE

ITALY
BOS.
YUGO.
ALB.

ROMANIA
BUL.

UKRAINE

RUSSIA

KAZ.

Aral
Sea

UZBEKISTAN

Azores
(Port.)

Strait of Gibraltar

Mediterranean Sea

GREECE

MALTA

Black Sea

GEORGIA

ARM. AZER.

TURKEY

CYPRUS

SYRIA

LEBANON

Caspian Sea

TURKMENISTAN

ASIA

IRAN

Madeira
Islands
(Port.)

Algiers

MOROCCO

Atlas Mountains

TUNISIA

Gulf of
Sidra

IRAQ

JORDAN

ISRAEL

Cairo

KUWAIT

Persian Gulf

QATAR

U.A.E.

Canary
Islands
(Spain)

Tropic of Cancer

Great
Western
Desert

Great
Eastern
Desert

ALGERIA

LIBYA

EGYPT

SAUDI ARABIA

OMAN

WESTERN
SAHARA
(MOROCCO)

Ijafene

Tahat
9,541 Ft.
2,908m

Ahaggar
Mts.

Libyan
Desert

Qattara
Depression

Lake
Nasser

Red Sea

S   a   h   a   r   a   D   e   s   e   r   t

MAURITANIA

MALI

Aïr (Mts.)

NIGER

Tibesti
Massif

Mt. Koussi
11,204 Ft.
3,415m

Ennedi

Nubian
Desert

YEMEN

Gulf of Aden

Socotra
(Yem.)

CAPE VERDE

S   a   h   e   l

CHAD

Khartoum

ERITREA

DJIBOUTI

Cape
Gwardafuy

Cape
Verde

Sénégal

SENEGAL

Dakar

GAMBIA

Niger

BURKINA
FASO

Lake
Chad

SUDAN

White Nile

Blue Nile

Lake
Tana

Ethiopian
Plateau

GUINEA-
BISSAU

GUINEA

BENIN

NIGERIA

Jos
Plateau

As Sudd

Great Rift Valley

Mountain Nile

Niger

GHANA

TOGO

Lake
Volta

Benue

ETHIOPIA

SOMALIA

SIERRA LEONE

COTE
D'IVOIRE

CENTRAL AFRICAN
REPUBLIC

Nile

LIBERIA

Lagos

CAMEROON

Mt. Cameroon
13,451 Ft.
4,100m

UGANDA

KENYA

Lake
Turkana

Mt. Kenya
17,058 Ft.
5,199m

Gulf of Guinea

Bioko

Congo

Uele

Equator

EQUATORIAL
GUINEA

REP. OF
CONGO

Congo
Basin

Lake
Victoria

Nairobi

INDIAN

OCEAN

SAO TOME AND
PRINCIPE

GABON

Congo

DEM. REP.
OF CONGO

Ubangi

RWANDA

BURUNDI

Kilimanjaro
19,340 Ft.
5,895m

SEYCHELLES

Ascension
(St. Helena)

N

Kinshasa

Kwango

Kasai

Great Rift Valley

Serengeti
Plain

Lake
Tanganyika

Masai
Steppe

Zanzibar

TANZANIA

ATLANTIC

St. Helena
(U.K.)

OCEAN

Cuanza

Cuango

ANGOLA

MALAWI

Lake Nyasa

COMOROS

Mayotte
(Fr.)

Cape Ambre

ZAMBIA

MOZAMBIQUE

Cunene

Okavango

Victoria
Falls

Lake
Kariba

Zambezi

Mozambique Channel

MADAGASCAR

MAURITIUS

Reunion
(Fr.)

Namib

ZIMBABWE

NAMIBIA

BOTSWANA

Kalahari

Desert

Tropic of Capricorn

Barra Point

Cape Sainte-Marie

Desert

Limpopo

Johannesburg

SWAZILAND

Orange

Vaal

LESOTHO

Drakensberg

SOUTH
AFRICA

Cape of
Good Hope

Cape Agulhas

Land Elevation

Meters	Feet
3,000	9,840
2,000	6,560
500	1,640
200	656
0	0

Water Depth

0	0
200	656
2,000	6,560

Tristan da
Cunha Group
(St. Helena)

| 0 | 200 | 400 | 600 | 800 | 1000 Miles |

| 0 | 300 | 600 | 900 | 1200 | 1500 Kilometers |

Copyright by Rand McNally & Co.
Lambert Azimuthal Equal Area Projection

Prince Edward
Islands
(S. Af.)

Crozet Islands
(Fr.)

ATLAS

ATLANTIC OCEAN

30° 20° 10°

PORTUGAL

Azores (Port.)

Madeira Islands (Port.)

Canary Islands (Spain)

CAPE VERDE

EUROPE

FRANCE AUS. HUNG. 20° ROMANIA UKRAINE 40° RUSSIA KAZ. Aral 60 Sea UZBEKISTAN

ITALY YUGO. BOS. BUL. Black Sea GEORGIA Caspian Sea TURKMENISTAN

Madrid SPAIN Rome ALB. GREECE TURKEY ARM. AZER.

Strait of Gibraltar MALTA Athens CYPRUS SYRIA IRAN

Algiers Qacentina Tunis Mediterranean Sea LEBANON IRAQ

Oran TUNISIA Gulf of Sidra Banghāzī Alexandria ISRAEL JORDAN KUWAIT

Rabat Casablanca MOROCCO Ghardaia Tripoli Cairo Suez Persian Gulf QATAR

Marrakech ALGERIA LIBYA EGYPT Asyut Riyadh U.A.E.

Tropic of Cancer In Salah Sabhā Aswan Lake Nasser SAUDI ARABIA OMAN

El Aaiún WESTERN SAHARA (MOROCCO) Tamanrasset Red Sea Port Sudan

MAURITANIA MALI NIGER CHAD Abéché SUDAN ERITREA YEMEN Socotra (Yem.)

Nouakchott Timbuktu Gao Agadez Lake Chad N'Djamena Omdurman Khartoum Asmara Gulf of Aden

Sénégal Bamako Niamey Kano Waw Blue Nile Lake Tana DJIBOUTI

Dakar SENEGAL BURKINA FASO BENIN NIGERIA Benue Djibouti

GAMBIA Niger Ouagadougou Abuja CENTRAL AFRICAN REPUBLIC ETHIOPIA SOMALIA

GUINEA-BISSAU GHANA Lake Volta Cotonou Lagos CAMEROON Bangui Mountain Nile Addis Ababa Dire Dawa

Conakry GUINEA COTE D'IVOIRE Accra Douala Yaoundé Ubangi Uele UGANDA KENYA

Freetown SIERRA LEONE Malabo EQUATORIAL GUINEA Congo Kisangani Kampala Lake Turkana Mogadishu

Monrovia LIBERIA SAO TOME AND PRINCIPE GABON REP. OF CONGO DEM. REP. OF CONGO Kigali RWANDA Nairobi INDIAN OCEAN

Abidjan Libreville Brazzaville Kinshasa Bujumbura BURUNDI Mombasa

Equator Mbuji-Mayi Lake Tanganyika Dodoma SEYCHELLES

Luanda TANZANIA Dar es Salaam

Ascension (St. Helena) Kolwezi Lubumbashi COMOROS

St. Helena (U.K.) Lobito ANGOLA Ndola MALAWI Lake Nyasa Mayotte (Fr.) Antsiranana

Huambo ZAMBIA Lilongwe MOZAMBIQUE

Zambezi Lusaka Lake Kariba Antananarivo MAURITIUS

Okavango Harare Beira MADAGASCAR Reunion (Fr.)

NAMIBIA BOTSWANA ZIMBABWE Fianarantsoa

Windhoek Gaborone Limpopo Pretoria Maputo

Johannesburg SWAZILAND

Orange Maseru LESOTHO Durban

SOUTH AFRICA

Cape Town Port Elizabeth

ATLANTIC OCEAN

N

⊛	National Capital
★	Secondary Capital (State, Province, or Territory)
■	City over 1,000,000 population
⊡	City of 250,000 to 1,000,000 population
•	City under 250,000 population

Tristan da Cunha Group (St. Helena)

0 200 400 600 800 1000 Miles
0 300 600 900 1200 1500 Kilometers
Copyright by Rand McNally & Co.
Lambert Azimuthal Equal Area Projection

Prince Edward Islands (S. Af.)

Crozet Islands (Fr.)

30° 20° 10° 0° 10° 20° 30° 40° 50° 60°

RAND McNALLY

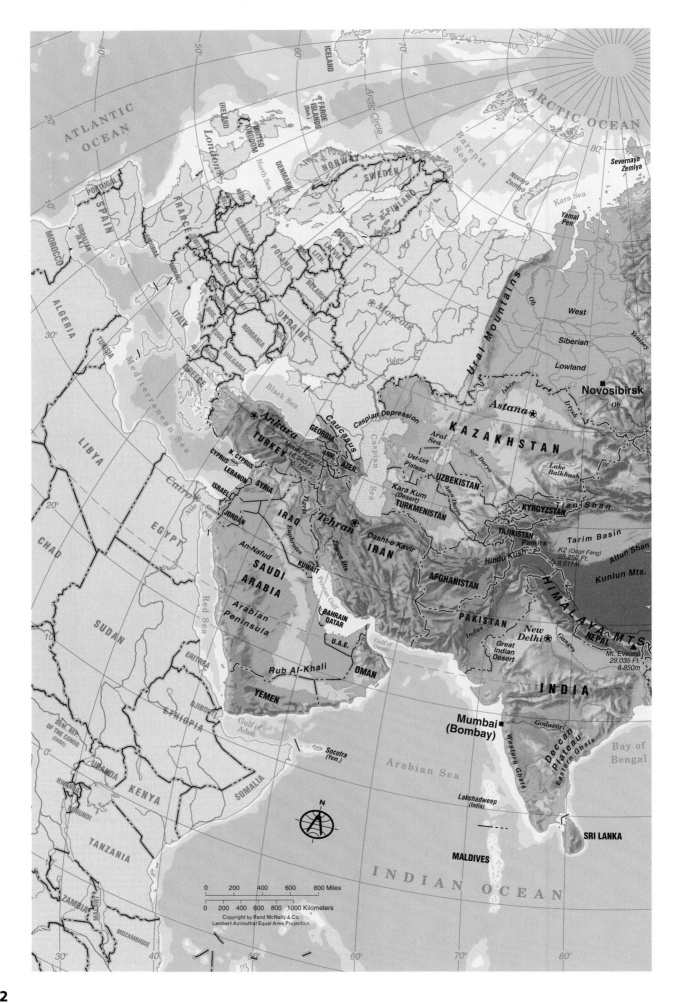

ATLANTIC OCEAN

ARCTIC OCEAN

ICELAND

IRELAND
FAEROE
ISLANDS
(Den.)

UNITED
KINGDOM

London

North Sea

NORWAY

SWEDEN

FINLAND

Barents
Sea

Novaya
Zemlya

Severnaya
Zemlya

Kara Sea

Yamal
Pen.

Arctic Circle

PORTUGAL

SPAIN

FRANCE

DENMARK

ESTONIA

LATVIA

LITH.

Moscow

Ural Mountains

West

Siberian

Lowland

Ob

Yenisey

Novosibirsk

MOROCCO

GIBRALTAR
(U.K.)

ANDORRA

MONACO

ITALY

GERMANY

POLAND

BELARUS

Volga

Ob

Irtysh

Ishim

Astana

KAZAKHSTAN

Lake
Balkhash

ALGERIA

TUNISIA

Mediterranean Sea

GREECE

ALB.
MAC.
BULGARIA

ROMANIA

UKRAINE

Black Sea

Caspian Depression

Aral
Sea

Syr Darya

Tian Shan

LIBYA

N. CYPRUS

CYPRUS

Ankara

TURKEY

Mount Ararat
16,940 Ft.
5,165m

GEORGIA

ARM.

AZER.

Caspian
Sea

Ust-Urt
Plateau

UZBEKISTAN

KYRGYZSTAN

EGYPT

Cairo

Nile

Sinai
Pen.

ISRAEL

LEBANON

SYRIA

JORDAN

Tigris

IRAQ

Euphrates

Tehran

Zagros Mts.

IRAN

Dasht-e Kavir

Amu Darya

TURKMENISTAN

Kara Kum
(Desert)

TAJIKISTAN

Pamirs

Tarim Basin

K2 (Qogir Feng)
28,250 Ft.
8,611m

Altun Shan

Kunlun Mts.

CHAD

SUDAN

Red Sea

An-Nafud

SAUDI
ARABIA

Arabian
Peninsula

KUWAIT

Persian Gulf

BAHRAIN
QATAR

U.A.E.

Gulf of
Oman

AFGHANISTAN

Hindu Kush

PAKISTAN

Indus

HIMALAYA MTS.

NEPAL

Mt. Everest
29,035 Ft.
8,850m

New
Delhi

Ganges

Great
Indian
Desert

Rub Al-Khali

OMAN

YEMEN

ERITREA

DJIBOUTI

ETHIOPIA

Gulf of
Aden

Socotra
(Yem.)

Arabian Sea

Mumbai
(Bombay)

Godavari

INDIA

Western Ghats

Deccan
Plateau

Eastern Ghats

Bay of
Bengal

DEM.
REP.
OF THE
CONGO
(ZAIRE)

UGANDA

RWANDA

BURUNDI

KENYA

SOMALIA

Lakshadweep
(India)

SRI LANKA

N

TANZANIA

MALDIVES

INDIAN OCEAN

ZAMBIA

MALAWI

MOZAMBIQUE

0   200   400   600   800 Miles

0   200 400 600 800 1000 Kilometers

Copyright by Rand McNally & Co.
Lambert Azimuthal Equal Area Projection

ATLAS

Land Elevation

Meters		Feet
3,000		9,840
2,000		6,560
500		1,640
200		656
0		0

Water Depth

0		0
200		656
2,000		6,560

Taymyr
Peninsula

New Siberian
Islands

East Siberian
Sea

Laptev Sea

Arctic Circle

Kolyma

Indigirka

Central
Siberian
Uplands

Verkhoyansk Mts.

Lena

RUSSIA

Siberia

Angara

Lake
Baikal

Stanovoy Range

Sayan Mountains

Altai Mts.

Greater Khingan Range

Amur

MONGOLIA

Gobi Desert

Qilian Shan

Beijing

CHINA

Qinling Shandi

Huang

Chang (Yangtze)

Xi

Bering
Sea

Aleutian Islands
(U.S.)

Kamchatka
Peninsula

Sea of
Okhotsk

Sakhalin

Kuril Islands

Sikhote Alin Mts.

Tatar Strait

Hokkaido

Sea of
Japan

Honshu

Tokyo

Mt. Fuji △
12,388 Ft.
3,776m

JAPAN

Shikoku

Kyushu

NORTH
KOREA

SOUTH
KOREA

Yellow
Sea

Shanghai

East
China
Sea

Taiwan Strait

TAIWAN

PACIFIC

OCEAN

Tropic of Cancer

NORTHERN MARIANA
ISLANDS (U.S.)

GUAM (U.S.)

Philippine
Sea

FEDERATED STATES OF
MICRONESIA

BHUTAN

Brahmaputra

BNGL.

MYANMAR

Irrawaddy

Salween

Chindwin

Mekong

LAOS

Red

Gulf of
Tonkin

Hainan Island

Luzon Strait

Luzon

PHILIPPINES

Manila

Mindanao

South

China

Sea

THAILAND

Bangkok

CAMBODIA

VIETNAM

Andaman
Islands
(India)

Andaman
Sea

Gulf of
Thailand

Sulu Sea

PALAU

Nicobar
Islands
(India)

MALAY   PENINSULA

MALAYSIA

Str. of Malacca

Singapore

BRUNEI

MALAYSIA

Borneo

Celebes
Sea

Celebes

Ceram

Moluccas

New
Guinea

PAPUA NEW
GUINEA

Sumatra

Greater Sunda

Islands

Java Sea

Jakarta   Java

INDONESIA

EAST TIMOR

Timor

Timor Sea

Banda Sea

Arafura Sea

Gulf
of
Carpentaria

AUSTRALIA

Coral
Sea

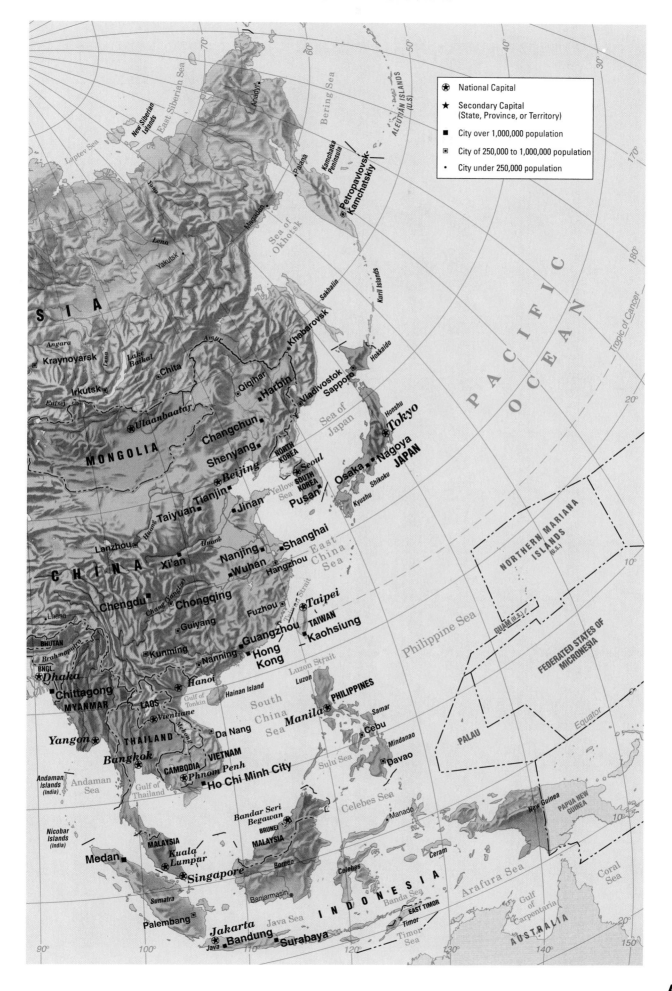

ATLAS

Legend:
- ✹ National Capital
- ★ Secondary Capital (State, Province, or Territory)
- ■ City over 1,000,000 population
- ▣ City of 250,000 to 1,000,000 population
- • City under 250,000 population

New Siberian Islands
East Siberian Sea
Laptev Sea
Anadyr
Pajana
Bering Sea
ALEUTIAN ISLANDS (U.S.)
Kamchatka Peninsula
Petropavlovsk-Kamchatskiy
Magadan
Sea of Okhotsk

A S I A

Angara
Kraynoyarsk
Lena
Lake Baikal
Yana
Yakutsk
Enisei
Irkutsk
Chita
Amur
Khabarovsk
Sakhalin
Kuril Islands

Ulaanbaatar
MONGOLIA
Qiqihar
Harbin
Vladivostok
Sapporo
Hokkaido

Changchun
Shenyang
NORTH KOREA
Sea of Japan
Honshu
Tokyo

Beijing
Seoul
SOUTH KOREA
Osaka
Nagoya
JAPAN

Tianjin
Yellow Sea
Pusan
Shikoku

Taiyuan
Jinan
Kyushu

Huang
Lanzhou
Huang
Shanghai
East China Sea

CHINA
Xi'an
Nanjing
Wuhan
Hangzhou

Chengdu
Chang (Yangtze)
Chongqing
Fuzhou
Taipei
TAIWAN

Lhasa
Guiyang
Guangzhou
Kaohsiung

BHUTAN
Brahmaputra
Kunming
Nanning
Hong Kong

BNGL
Dhaka
Hanoi
Hainan Island
Luzon Strait
Luzon

Chittagong
LAOS
Gulf of Tonkin
South China Sea
PHILIPPINES
Manila
Samar

MYANMAR
Vientiane
Da Nang
Cebu

Yangon
THAILAND
VIETNAM
Mindanao
Davao

Bangkok
CAMBODIA
Phnom Penh
Ho Chi Minh City
Sulu Sea

Andaman Islands (India)
Andaman Sea
Gulf of Thailand
Celebes Sea
Manado

PACIFIC OCEAN

Tropic of Cancer

NORTHERN MARIANA ISLANDS (U.S.)

GUAM (U.S.)

Philippine Sea

FEDERATED STATES OF MICRONESIA

PALAU

Equator

Nicobar Islands (India)
Bandar Seri Begawan
BRUNEI
MALAYSIA
Borneo
Ceram

New Guinea
PAPUA NEW GUINEA

MALAYSIA
Kuala Lumpur
Banjarmasin

Medan
Singapore
Celebes
INDONESIA
Banda Sea
Arafura Sea
Gulf of Carpentaria
Coral Sea

Sumatra
Palembang
Jakarta
Bandung
Java
Java Sea
Surabaya
Timor
EAST TIMOR
Timor Sea
AUSTRALIA

RAND McNALLY

RAND MCNALLY

ATLAS

RAND McNALLY

UNIT 1

Human-Environment Interaction
An orbiting satellite took these photographs of Earth after dark. They have been combined into one image. The glow of electric lights shows the locations of cities and towns.

INTRODUCTION TO WORLD CULTURES AND GEOGRAPHY

INTEGRATED TECHNOLOGY

eEdition
- Interactive Maps
- Interactive Visuals

INTERNET RESOURCES

Go to **classzone.com** for:
- Research Links
- Internet Activities
- Data Updates
- Unit Quiz
- Maps
- Test Practice
- Current Events
- Web Research Guide

Map Basics

Maps are an important tool for studying the use of space on Earth. This handbook covers the basic map skills and information that geographers rely on as they investigate the world—and the skills you will need as you study geography.

Mapmaking depends on surveying, or measuring and recording the features of Earth's surface. Until recently, this could be undertaken only on land or sea. Today, aerial photography and satellite imaging are the most popular ways to gather data.

Location • Magnetic compasses, introduced by the Chinese in the 1100s, help people accurately determine directions. ▲

Location • Determining a ship's location at sea was the purpose of this 1750 instrument, called a sextant. ▲

Location • An early example of a three-dimensional geographic grid. ▼

Human-Environment Interaction • Surveyors use a theodolite, which measures angles and distances on Earth. ▲

South America's Economic Activity

▶▶ Reading a Map
Most maps have these parts, which help you to read and understand the information presented.

TITLE The title indicates the subject of the map and tells you what information it contains.

ATLANTIC OCEAN

SYMBOLS Symbols may stand for capital cities, economic activities, or natural resources. Check the map legend for more details.

COLORS Colors show a variety of information on a map. The map legend tells what the colors mean.

LABELS Labels are words or phrases that name features on the map.

• Recife

AMAZON BASIN

Orinoco River

Amazon River

BRAZILIAN HIGHLANDS

Lima

La Paz

Paraguay River

PACIFIC OCEAN

LINES OF LONGITUDE These are imaginary lines that show distances east or west of the prime meridian.

LINES OF LATITUDE These are imaginary lines that show distances north or south of the equator.

LEGEND A legend or key lists and explains the symbols and colors used on the map.

20°S

M O U N T A I N S

Santiago

Buenos Aires

30°S

COMPASS ROSE The compass rose shows you north (N), south (S), east (E), and west (W) on the map. Sometimes only north is shown.

N

	Commercial fishing
	Farming
	Hunting and gathering
	Livestock ranching
	Limited economic activity
	Gold
	Hydroelectric power
	Natural gas
	Petroleum
	Silver
	Timber

40°S

SCALE A scale compares a unit of length on the map and a unit of distance on Earth.

| 0 | 250 | 500 miles |
| 0 | 250 | 500 kilometers |

50°S

Geography Skills Handbook **5**

Map Basics, cont.

Longitude Lines (Meridians)

Latitude Lines (Parallels)

▶▶ Longitude and Latitude Lines

Longitude and latitude lines appear together on a map and allow you to pinpoint the absolute locations of cities and other geographic features. You express these locations as coordinates of intersecting lines. These are measured in degrees.

Longitude lines are imaginary lines that run north and south; they are also known as meridians. They show distances in degrees east or west of the prime meridian. The prime meridian is a longitude line that runs from the North Pole to the South Pole through Greenwich, England. It marks 0° longitude.

Latitude lines are imaginary lines that run east to west around the globe; they are also known as parallels. They show distances in degrees north or south of the equator. The equator is a latitude line that circles Earth halfway between the north and south poles. It marks 0° latitude. The tropics of Cancer and Capricorn are parallels that form the boundaries of the tropical zone, a region that stays warm all year.

▶▶ Hemisphere

Hemisphere is a term for half the globe. The globe can be divided into northern and southern hemispheres (separated by the equator) or into eastern and western hemispheres. The United States is located in the northern and western hemispheres.

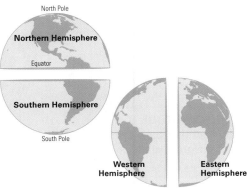

▶▶ Scale

A geographer decides what scale to use by determining how much detail to show. If many details are needed, a large scale is used. If fewer details are needed, a small scale is used.

Small scale used, without a lot of detail. ▼

WASHINGTON, D.C., METRO AREA
Scale: 1:4,500,000
1 inch = 70 miles

Larger scale used, with a lot of detail. ▼

WASHINGTON, D.C.
Scale: 1:88,700
1 inch = 1.4 miles

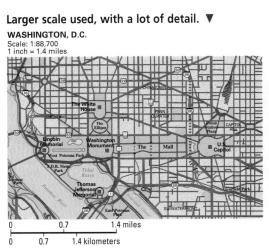

►► Projections

A projection is a way of showing the curved surface of Earth on a flat map. Flat maps cannot show sizes, shapes, and directions with total accuracy. As a result, all projections distort some aspect of Earth's surface. Below are four projections.

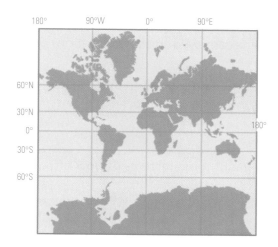

Mercator Projection • The Mercator projection shows most of the continents as they look on a globe. However, the projection stretches out the lands near the north and south poles. The Mercator projection is used for all kinds of navigation. ▲

Azimuthal Projection • An azimuthal projection shows Earth so that a straight line from the central point to any other point on the map corresponds to the shortest distance between the two points. Sizes and shapes of the continents are distorted. ▲

Homolosine Projection • This projection shows landmasses' shapes and sizes accurately, but distances are not correct. ▲

Robinson Projection • For textbook maps, the Robinson projection is commonly used. It shows the entire Earth, with continents and oceans having nearly their true sizes and shapes. However, the landmasses near the poles appear flattened. ▲

MAP PRACTICE

MAIN IDEAS

1. (a) What are the longitude and latitude of your city or town?

   (b) What information is provided by the legend in the map on page 5?

   (c) What is a projection? Compare and contrast the depictions of Antarctica in the Mercator and Robinson projections.

CRITICAL THINKING

2. **Making Inferences** Why do you think latitude and longitude are important to sailors?

Think About

- the landmarks you use to find your way around
- the landmarks available to sailors on the ocean

Different Types of Maps

►► Physical Maps

Physical maps help you see the landforms and bodies of water in specific areas. By studying a physical map, you can learn the relative locations and characteristics of places in a region.

On a physical map, color, shading, or contour lines are used to show elevations or altitudes, also called relief.

Ask these questions about the physical features shown on a physical map:

◆ Where on Earth's surface is this area located?

◆ What is its relative location?

◆ What is the shape of the region?

◆ In which directions do the rivers flow? How might the directions of flow affect travel and transportation in the region?

◆ Are there mountains or deserts? How might they affect the people living in the area?

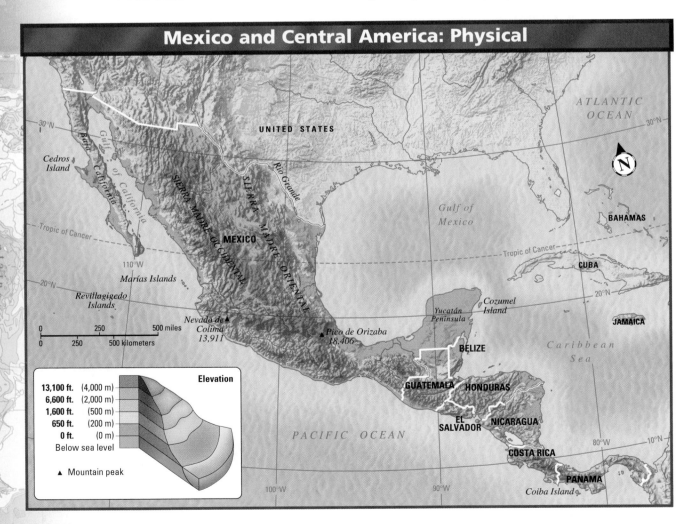

Mexico and Central America: Physical

▶▶ Political Maps

Political maps show features that humans have created on Earth's surface. Included on a political map may be cities, states, provinces, territories, and countries.

Ask these questions about the political features shown on a political map:

♦ Where on Earth's surface is this area located?

♦ What is its relative location? How might a country's location affect its economy and its relationships with other countries?

♦ What is the shape and size of the country? How might its shape and size affect the people living in the country?

♦ Who are the region's, country's, state's, or city's neighbors?

♦ How populated does the area seem to be? How might that affect activities there?

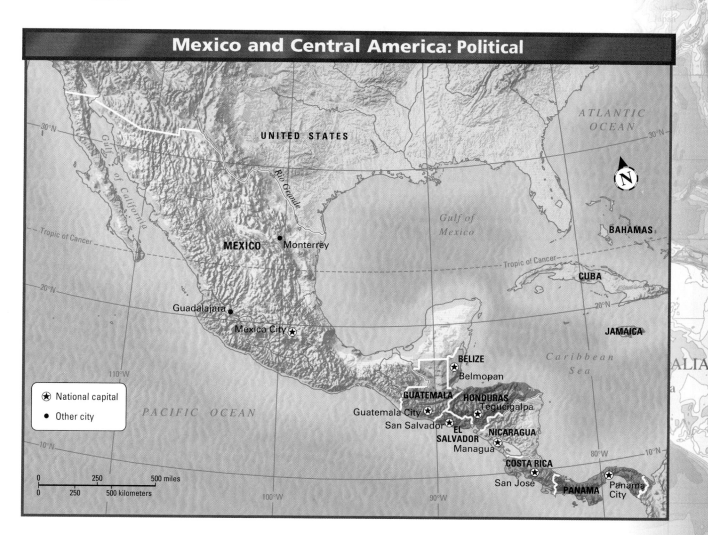

Mexico and Central America: Political

Different Types of Maps, cont.

▶▶ Thematic Maps

Geographers also rely on thematic maps, which focus on specific ideas. For example, in this textbook you will see thematic maps that show climates, types of vegetation, natural resources, population densities, and economic activities. Some thematic maps show historical trends; others may focus on movements of people or ideas. Thematic maps may be presented in a variety of ways.

Major Rain Forests of Latin America

Legend:
- Original rain forest
- Rain forest, 2000

Qualitative Maps On a qualitative map, colors, symbols, dots, or lines are used to help you see patterns related to a specific idea. The map shown here depicts the influence of the Roman Empire on Europe, North Africa, and Southwest Asia.

Use the suggestions below to help you interpret the map.

- Check the title to identify the theme and the data being presented.
- Carefully study the legend to understand the theme and the information presented.
- Look at the physical or political features of the area. How might the theme of the map affect them?
- What are the relationships among the data?

Oil Reserves in the Western Hemisphere Cartogram

Each square equals 1 billion barrels

Source: *World Oil 2002*

Cartograms A cartogram presents information about countries other than their shapes and sizes. The size of each country is determined by the data being presented, and not by its actual land size. On the cartogram shown here, the countries' sizes show the amounts of their oil reserves.

Use the suggestions below to help you interpret the map.

- Check the title and the legend to identify the data being presented.
- Look at the relative sizes of the countries shown. Which is the largest?
- Which countries are smallest?
- How do the sizes of these countries on a physical map differ from their sizes in the cartogram?
- What are the relationships among the data?

Flow-Line Maps Flow-line maps illustrate movements of people, goods, or ideas. The movements are usually shown by a series of arrows. Locations, directions, and scopes of movement can be seen. The width of an arrow may show how extensive a flow is. Often the information is related to a period of time. The map shown here portrays immigration to the United States during 2000.

Use the suggestions below to help you interpret the map.

♦ Check the title and the legend to identify the data being presented.

♦ Over what period of time did the movement occur?

♦ In what directions did the movement occur?

♦ How extensive was the movement?

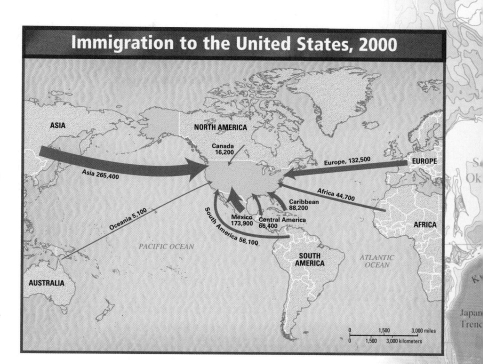

Immigration to the United States, 2000

ASIA
Asia 265,400
NORTH AMERICA
Canada 16,200
Europe, 132,500
EUROPE
Africa 44,700
Caribbean 88,200
Mexico 173,900
Central America 66,400
South America 56,100
Oceania 5,100
PACIFIC OCEAN
SOUTH AMERICA
ATLANTIC OCEAN
AFRICA
AUSTRALIA

0   1,500   3,000 miles
0   1,500   3,000 kilometers

MAP PRACTICE

Use pages 8–11 to help you answer these questions. Use the maps on pages 8–9 to answer questions 1–3.

1. What areas in Mexico are of lowest elevation?

2. Belmopan is the capital of which nation?

3. Which is the highest mountain on the physical map?

4. Why are only a few nations shown in the cartogram?

5. Which kind of thematic map would be best for showing the locations of climate zones?

GeoActivity

Exploring Local Geography Obtain a physical-political map of your state. Use the data on it to create **two separate maps.** One should show physical features only, and the other should show political features only.

Geographic Dictionary

SEA LEVEL
the level of the ocean's surface, used as a reference point when measuring heights and depths on Earth's surface

VOLCANO
an opening in Earth's surface through which gases and lava escape from Earth's interior

BAY
part of an ocean or a lake partially enclosed by land

(RIVER) MOUTH
the place where a river flows into a lake or an ocean

CAPE
a pointed piece of land extending into an ocean or a lake

HARBOR
a sheltered area of water, deep enough for docking ships

STRAIT
a narrow strip of water connecting two large bodies of water

MARSH
a soft, wet, low-lying, grassy area located between water and dry land

ISLAND
a body of land surrounded by water

DELTA
a triangular area of land formed from deposits at the mouth of a river

FLOOD PLAIN
flat land alongside a river, formed by mud and silt deposited by floods

SWAMP
an area of land that is saturated by water

DESERT
a dry area where few plants grow

OASIS
a spot of fertile land in a desert, supplied with water by a well or spring

BUTTE
a raised, flat area of land with steep sides, smaller than a mesa

MOUNTAIN
a natural elevation of Earth's surface with steep sides, higher than a hill

PRAIRIE
a large, level area of grassland with few or no trees

STEPPE
a wide, treeless plain

VALLEY
low land between hills or mountains

GLACIER
a large ice mass that moves slowly down a mountain or over land

CATARACT
a large, powerful waterfall

MESA
a wide, flat-topped mountain with steep sides, larger than a butte

CANYON
a deep, narrow valley with steep sides

CLIFF
the steep, almost vertical edge of a hill, mountain, or plain

PLATEAU
a broad, flat area of land higher than the surrounding land

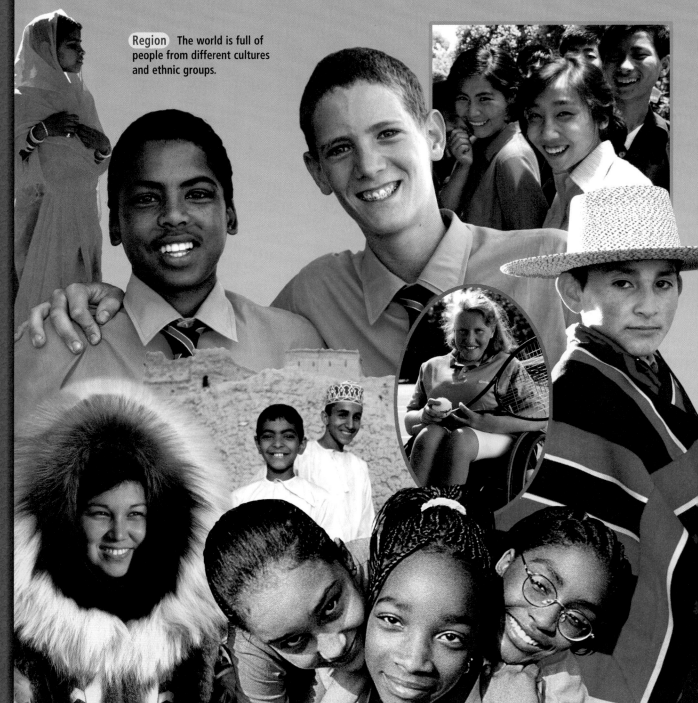

Welcome to the World

SECTION **1**   The World at Your Fingertips

SECTION **2**   Many Regions, Many Cultures

Region The world is full of people from different cultures and ethnic groups.

How have geographic features influenced settlement patterns?

Movement • People settle where they can most easily and comfortably meet their needs for clean water, food, work, communication, trade, and transportation. Before there were good roads, boats were the easiest way to travel or send and receive goods. As a result, people often settled near rivers, lakes, and oceans. They also often settled where the land was suitable for cultivation and the climate was comfortable. You will not find many cities in the frozen wastelands of Siberia.

What do you think?

♦ Why are there few settlements in the desert?

♦ Why is there often a city where two rivers meet?

BEFORE YOU READ

▶▶ *What Do You Know?*

You live in the world, but how much do you know about it? The best way to find out is through social studies. *Social studies* is an umbrella term. It covers history, geography, economics, government, and culture. History, as you probably know, is the study of the past. How clearly can you define the other terms? How do you think they can help you to learn about the world?

▶▶ *What Do You Want to Know?*

Think about what else you need to know before you can come up with clear, complete, and accurate definitions. Record any questions you have in a notebook before you read this chapter.

Region • Citizens have more rights under some governments than others. ▼

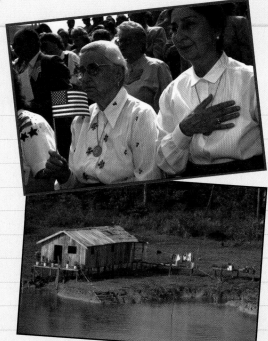

READ AND TAKE NOTES

Reading Strategy: Categorizing One way to make sense of information is to organize it in a chart. Writing your notes in a chart with categories can help you remember the most important parts of what you have read.

- Copy the chart below into your notebook.
- As you read the chapter, note the definition of each term listed on the chart.
- Write these definitions next to the appropriate heading.

Region •
Prepared for a flood,
this house was built to suit its environment. ▲

Term	Definition
history	
geography	
economics	
government	
culture	

The World at Your Fingertips

TERMS & NAMES
history
geography
government
citizen
economics
scarcity
culture
culture trait

MAIN IDEA

Social studies includes information from five fields of learning to provide a well-rounded picture of the world and its peoples.

WHY IT MATTERS NOW

Understanding your world is essential if you are to be an informed citizen of a global society.

DATELINE

EXTRA

SAN FRANCISCO, USA, JUNE 26, 1945

Fifty nations signed a charter today to establish a new organization called the United Nations. The organization will go into effect October 24.

The United Nations is a successor to the old League of Nations, founded after World War I to prevent another world war, which it failed to do.

The purpose of the new organization is to maintain peace and develop friendly relations among nations.

The member nations hope to cooperate to solve economic, social, cultural, and humanitarian problems and to promote respect for human rights and freedom.

Region • Flags of member countries fly in front of the United Nations headquarters in New York City. ▲

The Peoples of the World

For centuries, people in different parts of the world have been trying to get along with one another, not always with success. Part of the problem is a lack of understanding of other people's ways of life. Certain advances in communication and transportation, such as the Internet and high-speed planes, have brought people closer together. So have increased international trade and immigration. Knowledge of other societies can be a key to understanding them.

TAKING NOTES

Use your chart to take notes about these terms.

Term	Definition
history	
geography	

Learning About the World

Social studies is a way to learn about the world. It draws on information from five fields of learning—geography, history, economics, government, and culture. Each field looks at the world from a different angle. Consider the approaches you might use if you were starting at a new school. Figuring out how to get around would be learning your school's geography. Asking other students where they come from is learning their history. Making choices about which school supplies you can afford to buy is economics. Learning the school rules is learning about its government. Clubs, teams, styles of clothing, holidays, and even ways of saying things are part of the school's culture.

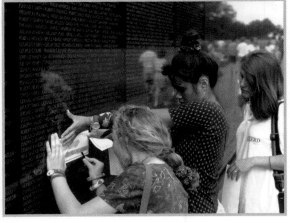

Place • The five fields of learning in social studies are well represented in daily life. ▲

History and Geography

Knowing history and geography helps orient you in time and space. **History** is a record of the past. The people and events of the past shaped the world as it is today. Historians search for primary sources, such as newspapers, letters, journals, and other documents, to find out about past events.

Connections to Science

Historians of the Earth
Geologists are scientists who study how Earth was formed and how it has changed over time. There are many kinds of geologists. Some geologists study the materials that make up Earth and processes, such as erosion, that change Earth. Other geologists are interested in the history of Earth. They study fossils, which are the remains of animals and plants that lived millions of years ago.

A VOICE FROM TODAY

How can we know who we are and where we are going if we don't know anything about where we have come from and what we have been through, the courage shown, the costs paid, to be where we are?

David McCullough, Historian

The Five Themes of Geography **Geography** is the study of people, places, and the environment. Geography deals with the world in spatial terms. The study of geography focuses on five themes: location, region, place, movement, and human-environment interaction.

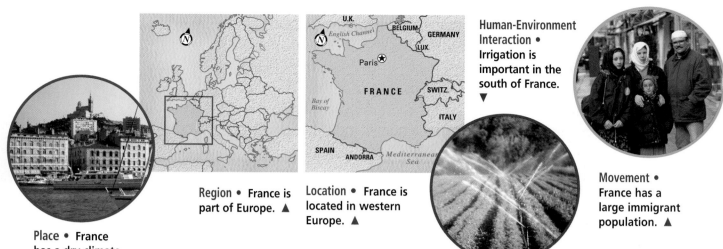

Place • France has a dry climate in the south, and a wetter climate in the north, with prosperous farms and thriving cities. ▲

Region • France is part of Europe. ▲

Location • France is located in western Europe. ▲

Human-Environment Interaction • Irrigation is important in the south of France. ▼

Movement • France has a large immigrant population. ▲

Location tells where a place is. Several countries that have features in common form a region. Place considers an area's distinguishing characteristics. Movement is a study of the migrations of people, animals, and even plants. Human-environment interaction considers how people change and are changed by the natural features of Earth.

Government

Every country has laws and a way to govern itself. Laws are the rules by which people live. **Government** is the people and groups within a society that have the authority to make laws, to make sure they are carried out, and to settle disagreements about them. The kind of government determines who has the authority to make the laws and see that they are carried out.

Limited and Unlimited Governments In a limited government, everyone, including those in charge, must obey the laws. Some of the laws tell the government what it cannot do. Democracies and republics are two forms of limited government. In a democracy, the people have the authority to make laws directly. In a republic, the people make laws through elected representatives. The governments of the United States, Mexico, and India are examples of republics.

Rulers in an unlimited government can do whatever they want without regard to the law. Totalitarianism is a form of unlimited government. In a totalitarian government the people have no say. Rulers have total control.

BACKGROUND

Local, state, and national governments provide needed services, such as schools, parks, electricity, and roads.

Vocabulary

totalitarian government: a government in which the rulers have total control

Citizenship A **citizen** is a legal member of a country. Citizens have rights, such as the right to vote in elections, and duties, such as paying taxes. Being born in a country can make you a citizen. Another way is to move to a country, complete certain requirements, and take part in a naturalization ceremony.

Vocabulary

naturalization: the process of becoming a citizen

Economics

Looking at the long list of flavors at the ice cream store, you have a decision to make. You have only enough money for one cone. Will it be mint chip or bubble gum flavor? You will have to choose. **Economics** is the study of how people manage their resources by producing, exchanging, and using goods and services. Economics is about choice.

Some economists claim that people's desires are unlimited. Resources to satisfy these desires, however, are limited. These economists refer to the conflict between people's desires and their limited resources as **scarcity**.

Resources Economists identify three types of resources: natural, human, and capital. Natural resources are gifts of nature, such as forests, fertile soil, and water. Human resources are skills people have to produce goods and services. Capital resources are the things people make, such as machines and equipment, to produce goods and services.

Movement • One way people become American citizens is by participating in a naturalization ceremony. ▲

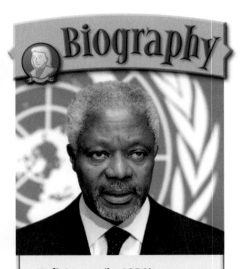

Biography

Kofi Annan (b. 1938)
Kofi Annan (KOH•fee AN•uhn) was born in Ghana, West Africa. He is the seventh Secretary-General of the United Nations (UN). Annan studied economics in the United States and Switzerland. In 1972, he earned a graduate degree in management from the Massachusetts Institute of Technology. Annan is a passionate reformer. He cares deeply about HIV/AIDS funding, conflict resolution, educational reform, and ending poverty. In 2001, Annan and the UN jointly received the Nobel Peace Prize.

Kinds of Economies

Blue jeans are a product. Who decides whether to make them and how many to make and what price to charge? In a command economy, the government decides. In a market economy, individual businesses decide, based on what they think consumers want.

Levels of Development Different countries and regions have different levels of economic development. In a country with a high level of development, most people are well educated, have good health, and earn decent salaries. Services such as clean running water, electricity, and transportation are plentiful. Technology is advanced, and businesses flourish.

Reading **Social Studies**

A. Contrasting How does a market economy differ from a command economy?

A country with a low level of development is marked by few jobs in industry, poor services, and low literacy rates. Life expectancy is low. These countries are often called developing countries.

Culture

Some people wear saris. Others wear T-shirts. Some people eat cereal and milk for breakfast. Others eat pickled fish. Some people go to church on Sunday morning. Others kneel and pray to Allah five times a day. All these differences are expressions of **culture**. Culture consists of the beliefs, customs, laws, art, and ways of living that a group of people share.

Religion is part of most cultures; so is a shared language. The ways people express themselves through music, dance, literature, and the visual arts are important parts of every culture; so are the technology and tools they use to accomplish various tasks. Each kind of food, clothing, or technology, each belief, language, or tool shared by a culture is called a **culture trait**. Taken together, the culture traits of a people shape their way of life.

Reading
Social Studies

B. Recognizing Important Details What are three characteristics that can define a culture?

Habitat for Humanity International Since 1984 former President Jimmy Carter, below, has worked with Habitat for Humanity International. Habitat is a charity that builds and restores homes for people in need. The houses have a low cost, and the new homeowners pay for them over time.

The homeowners also help build their own houses. Carter explains that taking part gives people self-respect: "The people who will live in the homes work side-by-side with the volunteers, so they feel very much that they are on an equal level."

SECTION 1 ASSESSMENT

Terms & Names
1. Explain the significance of:

   (a) history   (b) geography   (c) government   (d) citizen

   (e) economics   (f) scarcity   (g) culture   (h) culture trait

Using Graphics
2. Use a chart like this one to list the five themes of geography and their characteristics.

Theme	Characteristics

Main Ideas
3. (a) What five areas of learning does social studies include?

   (b) What are the three main kinds of resources, and how is each one defined?

   (c) What is the difference between limited and unlimited government?

Critical Thinking
4. **Making Inferences**

   Does the United States have a shared, or common, culture?

Think About
- what you eat and wear, where you live, how you spend your free time
- who else shares these activities with you

ACTIVITY -OPTION- Reread the section on citizenship. Make a **poster** showing the rights and responsibilities of a citizen.

Investigate Your World

Suppose that someone has given you a globe as a gift. What a great present! Unlike a flat map, your globe gives you a more accurate view of the world. Best of all, this new globe is programmable. You can input new information about different features and places on Earth. In fact, the manufacturer has set up a contest—the Global Game—giving prizes for the best and most creative approaches to programming the globe. Good luck!

COOPERATIVE LEARNING On these pages are challenges you will meet in trying to win the Global Game. Working with a small group, choose which one you want to solve. Divide the work among group members. Look for helpful information in the Data File. Keep in mind that you will present your solution to the class.

STATE CAPITOL

Austin

HISTORY/ECONOMICS CHALLENGE

". . . you want to know more about the world closer to home."

Now that your globe has shown you the worldwide picture, you want to know more about the world closer to home. How has geography influenced the history of your community? What features or resources brought settlers there? Choose one of these options. Look in the Data File for information.

ACTIVITIES

1. Make a time line of major events in the growth of your community. If possible, begin with the Native Americans who originally inhabited the area. Include the arrival of immigrants from various places.
2. Draw or trace an outline of your state. Then make a thematic map of its major products and industries. Use words or symbols (such as a cow, a factory, a computer) and create a map key to identify each product.

Ft. Worth ∙∙ Dallas

T E X A S

★ Austin

● San Antonio

Rio Grande

Gulf of Mexico

WORLD STATISTICS

- **Circumference** at Equator: 24,902 mi.
- **Earth's speed** of orbit: 18.5 mi./sec.
- **Total area:** 197,000,000 sq. mi.; land area: 57,900,000 sq. mi.
- **Highest point:** 29,035 ft.— Mt. Everest.
- **Lowest point:** 35,800 ft. below sea level—Marianas Trench, Pacific Ocean.
- **Lowest point on land:** 1,312 ft. below sea level, Dead Sea, Israel, and Jordan.

HIGHEST ELEVATIONS BY CONTINENT

- **Asia:** Mt. Everest, Nepal–Tibet, 29,035 ft.
- **South America:** Mt. Aconcagua, Argentina–Chile, 22,834 ft.
- **North America:** Mt. McKinley (Denali), Alaska, 20,320 ft.
- **Africa:** Mt. Kilimanjaro, Tanzania, 19,340 ft.
- **Europe:** Mt. Elbrus, Russia, 18,510 ft.
- **Antarctica:** Vinson Massif, 16,066 ft.
- **Western Europe:** Mont Blanc, France, 15,771 ft.
- **Australia:** Mt. Kosciusko, 7,310 ft.

SOME MAJOR RIVER SYSTEMS

- **Nile,** Africa: 4,160 mi.
- **Amazon,** South America: 4,080 mi.
- **Mississippi**–Missouri, North America (U.S.): 3,740 mi.
- **Chang Jiang** (Yangtze), China: 3,915 mi.
- **Yenisey,** Russia: 2,566 mi.
- **Plata,** South America: 3,030 mi.
- **Huang He** (Yellow), China: 3,010 mi.
- **Congo** (Zaire), Africa: 2,880 mi.

To learn more about Earth's geography, go to

RESEARCH LINKS
CLASSZONE.COM

". . . you are taken on an audio journey to new places."

Your new globe has built-in sensors activated by a laser wand. When you point the wand at a spot on the globe, you are taken on an audio journey to new places. The sound clip introduces you to a place's culture—the things that make it unique.

As part of the Global Game, the manufacturer is looking for new ways to present this information. What will you include in your approach? How can you add to the globe's popular appeal? Choose one of these options. Look in the Data File for help.

ACTIVITIES

1. Choose one continent and write a script about it for a seven-minute "audio journey." Remember to include information about geographic features as well as aspects of culture.
2. Design another geography game that the manufacturer can use to market its globe. The game should appeal to students of your age. Write a brief description of the game and its rules.

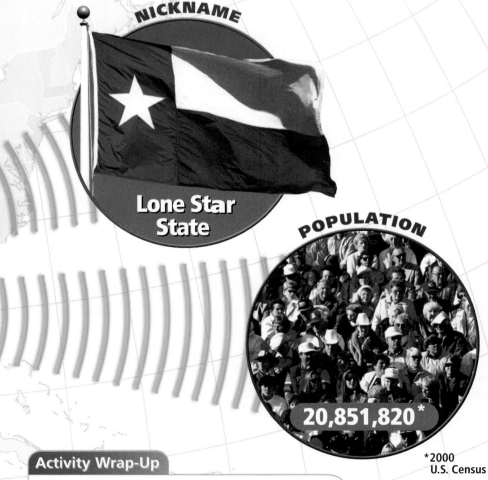

NICKNAME

Lone Star State

POPULATION

20,851,820*

*2000
U.S. Census

Activity Wrap-Up

As a group, review your solution to the challenge you selected. Then present your solution to the class.

Many Regions, Many Cultures

TERMS & NAMES
culture region
interdependence

MAIN IDEA

The world can be divided into regions according to culture.

WHY IT MATTERS NOW

Understanding other cultures can help you understand how people in other regions live and think.

DATELINE

TENOCHTITLÁN, AZTEC CAPITAL, A.D. 1519—Frightening news has arrived from the coast. Warriors from a land called "Spain" are marching toward the capital of our Aztec Empire. They are covered in metal armor and have thundering weapons. They have no respect for our gods, our temples, or our customs. Because we have never seen warriors like these, we do not know if they are men or gods. Nor do we know why are they coming toward our city. Some of our priests say these invaders have come to destroy our world.

Culture • The Aztecs had never seen horses and believed that Spanish soldiers rode giant deer. ▲

Different Places, Different Cultures

In 1519, one of the greatest culture clashes in history took place. That year, the Spanish invaded the powerful Aztec Empire, in what is now Mexico. The Spanish and the Aztecs were confused by each other's customs because they came from different culture regions. A **culture region** is an area of the world in which many people share similar beliefs, history, and languages. The people in a culture region may have religion, technology, and ways of earning a living in common as well. They may grow and eat similar foods, wear similar kinds of clothes, and build houses in similar styles.

TAKING NOTES

Use your chart to take notes about these terms.

Term	Definition
history	
geography	

INTER**ACTIVE**

Legend:
- United States and Canada
- Latin America
- Europe and former U.S.S.R.
- North Africa and Southwest Asia
- Africa south of the Sahara
- South Asia
- East Asia, Australia, and the Pacific Islands

GEOGRAPHY SKILLBUILDER:
Interpreting a Map

1. **Region** • How many culture regions are shown on this map?
2. **Location** • Name three culture regions in the Eastern Hemisphere.

The World's Culture Regions

The map above shows the major culture regions of the world. Latin America is one culture region. The Spanish and Portuguese languages help to tie its people together. So does its common history. Southwest Asia and North Africa is another culture region. Most countries in this region share a common desert climate and landscape. People have adapted to the desert in similar ways, thus creating a common culture. Islam, which is the major religion in this region, also helps shape a common culture.

Usually, not every person in a region belongs to the dominant, or mainstream, culture. Some regions are multicultural. For example, the United States and Canada contain other cultures besides the dominant one. Although most people in this region speak English, many people in eastern Canada speak French. Many people in the United States speak Spanish, especially in the Southwest. In both countries, Catholics, Protestants, Jews, Muslims, Buddhists, and members of other religions are free to worship.

Reading
Social Studies

A. Recognizing Important Details Name two characteristics that make the United States multicultural.

Strange ?? but TRUE

Children Invent Language In the late 1700s, most people in Hawaii spoke English or native Hawaiian. As people began immigrating to Hawaii to work on the sugar cane plantations, they brought their native languages with them: Japanese, Chinese, Korean, Spanish, and Portuguese.

At school, the children of these immigrants began speaking a form of English that was a blend of native Hawaiian, Pidgin English, Pidgin Hawaiian, and their native languages, especially Portuguese. Eventually, children began to learn this form of English as their native language. This was the beginning of Hawaii Creole English, and it soon became the language of the majority of Hawaiians.

Da kaet ste in da haus.

Culture Regions Change For thousands of years, culture regions have changed and evolved as they have borrowed culture traits from one another. They have also come to depend upon each other economically. Decisions and events in one part of the world affect other parts. Advances in transportation and communication have increased this **interdependence.** When oil-producing nations in the Middle East raise the price of oil, for example, the price of gasoline at the neighborhood gas station is likely to rise. If there is an especially abundant banana crop in parts of Latin America, the price of bananas may drop at the local grocery store. More and more, people of different countries are becoming part of one world.

Region • Home life can differ greatly in different culture regions, sometimes depending on a region's climate or natural resources. ▲

SECTION 2 ASSESSMENT

Terms & Names
1. Explain the significance of: (a) culture region   (b) interdependence

Using Graphics

2. Use a chart to list the major culture regions of the world.

Major Culture Regions of the World
1.
2.
3.
4.
5.
6.
7.

Main Ideas

3. (a) List at least three things people in a culture region may have in common.

   (b) Which continents have more than one culture region?

   (c) What is one cause of cultural change?

Critical Thinking

4. **Clarifying**

   Why might Brazilian coffee at your local supermarket suddenly cost more?

   Think About
   ◆ price setting
   ◆ coffee supplies

ACTIVITY -OPTION-   Write a **dialogue** between you and a visitor from another country in which you explain what makes the culture in your region different from others.

Reading a Time Zone Map

▶▶ Defining the Skill

A time zone map shows the 24 time zones of the world. The prime meridian runs through Greenwich (GREHN•ich), England. Each zone east of Greenwich is one hour later than the zone before. Each zone west of Greenwich is one hour earlier. The International Date Line runs through the Pacific Ocean. It is the location where each day begins. If it is Saturday to the east of the International Date Line, then it is Sunday to the west of it.

▶▶ Applying the Skill

Use the strategies listed below to help you find times and time differences on a time zone map.

How to Read a Time Zone Map

Strategy ❶ Read the title. It tells you what the map is intended to show.

Strategy ❷ Read the labels at the top of the map. They show the hours across the world when it is noon in Greenwich. The labels at the bottom show the number of hours earlier or later than the time in Greenwich.

Strategy ❸ Locate a place whose time you know. Locate the place where you want to know the time. Count the number of time zones between them. Then add or subtract that number of hours.

For example, if it is noon time on the west coast of Africa, you can see that it is 7:00 A.M. on the east coast of the United States. That is a difference of five hours.

❶ **WORLD TIME ZONES**

▶▶ Practicing the Skill

Practice determining the difference in hours between various time zones. For example, if you select the yellow zone in western Asia and you live in Texas, you will have a time difference of 11 hours. Now select one time zone in Africa, one in Europe, and one in Australia. For each location, determine the number of hours' difference with the time zone in which you live.

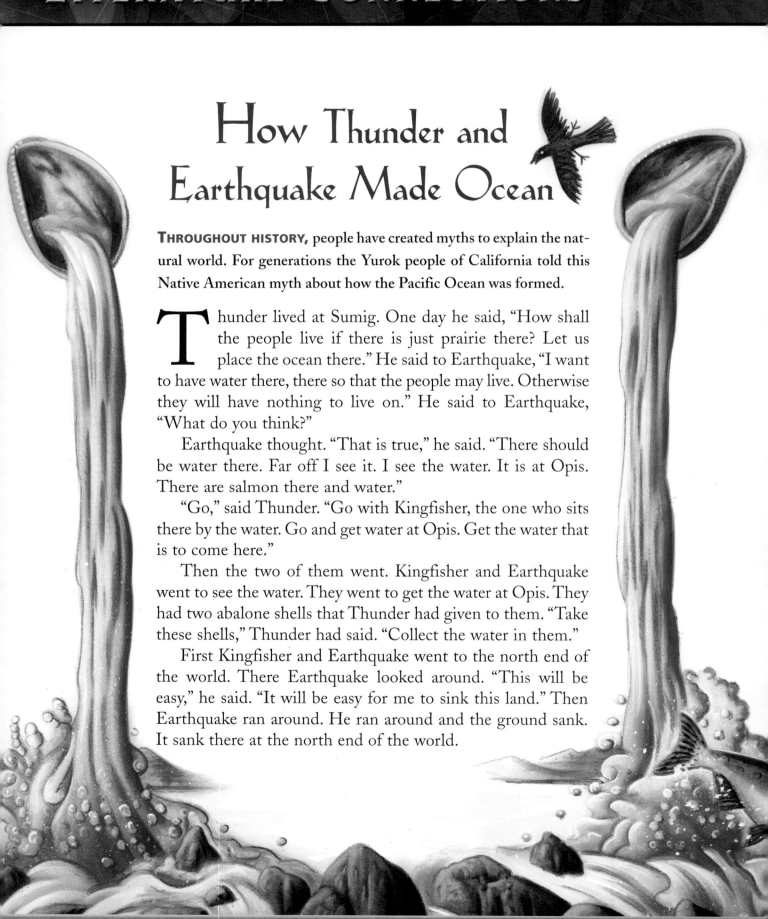

How Thunder and Earthquake Made Ocean

THROUGHOUT HISTORY, people have created myths to explain the natural world. For generations the Yurok people of California told this Native American myth about how the Pacific Ocean was formed.

Thunder lived at Sumig. One day he said, "How shall the people live if there is just prairie there? Let us place the ocean there." He said to Earthquake, "I want to have water there, there so that the people may live. Otherwise they will have nothing to live on." He said to Earthquake, "What do you think?"

Earthquake thought. "That is true," he said. "There should be water there. Far off I see it. I see the water. It is at Opis. There are salmon there and water."

"Go," said Thunder. "Go with Kingfisher, the one who sits there by the water. Go and get water at Opis. Get the water that is to come here."

Then the two of them went. Kingfisher and Earthquake went to see the water. They went to get the water at Opis. They had two abalone shells that Thunder had given to them. "Take these shells," Thunder had said. "Collect the water in them."

First Kingfisher and Earthquake went to the north end of the world. There Earthquake looked around. "This will be easy," he said. "It will be easy for me to sink this land." Then Earthquake ran around. He ran around and the ground sank. It sank there at the north end of the world.

Then Kingfisher and Earthquake started for Opis. They went to the place at the end of the water. They made the ground sink behind them as they went. At Opis they saw all kinds of seals and salmon. They saw all the kinds of animals and fish that could be eaten there in the water at Opis. Then they took water in the abalone shells.

"Now we will go to the south end of the world," said Earthquake. "We will go there and look at the water. Thunder, who is at Sumig, will help us by breaking down the trees. The water will extend all the way to the south end of the world. There will be salmon and fish of all kinds and seals in the water."

Now Kingfisher and Earthquake came back to Sumig. They saw that Thunder had broken down the trees. Together the three of them went north. As they went together they kept sinking the ground. The Earth quaked and quaked and water flowed over it as Kingfisher and Earthquake poured it from their abalone shells. Kingfisher emptied his shell and it filled the ocean halfway to the north end of the world. Earthquake emptied his shell and it filled the ocean the rest of the way.

As they filled in the ocean, the creatures which would be food swarmed into the water. The seals came as if they were thrown in in handfuls. Into the water they came, swimming toward shore. Earthquake sank the land deeper to make gullies and the whales came swimming through the gullies where that water was deep enough for them to travel. The salmon came running through the water.

Now all the land animals, the deer and elk, the foxes and mink, the bear and others had gone inland. Now the water creatures were there. Now Thunder and Kingfisher and Earthquake looked at the ocean. "This is enough," they said. "Now the people will have enough to live on. Everything that is needed is in the water."

So it is that the prairie became ocean. It is so because Thunder wished it so. It is so because Earthquake wished it so. All kinds of creatures are in the ocean before us because Thunder and Earthquake wished the people to live.

Reading THE LITERATURE

Before you read, examine the title. What kind of story might this be? What is the purpose of the story?

Thinking About THE LITERATURE

What does this myth suggest about the importance of the ocean in the lives of Native Americans? What does the myth reveal about Native American attitudes to the natural world?

Writing About THE LITERATURE

Write a continuation of the story, showing how the people reacted when they saw that an ocean had replaced the prairie.

Further Reading

Legends of Landforms by Carole G. Vogel explores Native American legends about the origins of many places in the United States.

Keepers of the Earth by Michael J. Caduto and Joseph Bruchac retells Native American stories.

TERMS & NAMES

Explain the significance of each of the following:

1. history	**2.** geography	**3.** government
6. scarcity	**7.** culture	**8.** culture trait

4. citizen   **5.** economics

9. culture region   **10.** interdependence

REVIEW QUESTIONS

The World at Your Fingertips *(pages 17–21)*

1. What are the five themes of geography?

2. What are the main differences between a limited and an unlimited government?

3. How can someone become a citizen of a country?

4. What is the difference between a command economy and a market economy?

5. What are some characteristics of a culture?

Many Regions, Many Cultures *(pages 24–26)*

6. How can decisions made in one part of the world affect people in another part of the world?

7. What aspects of daily life might people in the same culture region share?

8. What makes the United States and Canada a multicultural region?

CRITICAL THINKING

Remembering Definitions

1. Using your completed chart from Reading Social Studies, p. 16, tell how understanding the culture could help you make friends in a new country.

Making Inferences

2. Why might someone's life expectancy be low in a region with a low level of development?

Identifying Problems

3. If countries in the Middle East stopped producing oil, how might that affect the economy of the United States?

Visual Summary

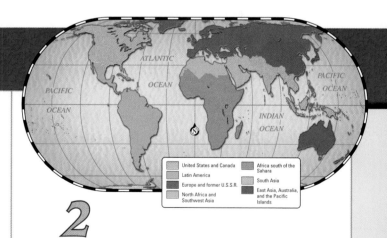

1

The World at Your Fingertips

- History, geography, government, economics, and culture are five ways to understand Earth and its peoples.

2

Many Regions, Many Cultures

- People live, dress, and think differently in each of the world's culture regions.

Use the map and your knowledge of world cultures and geography to answer questions 1 and 2.

Additional Test Practice, pp. S1–S33

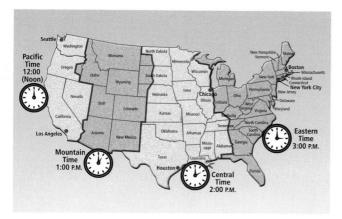

1. What is the time difference between Los Angeles and New York City?

A. one hour

B. two hours

C. three hours

D. four hours

2. If it is 2 P.M. in Houston, what time would it be in Chicago?

A. 1 P.M.

B. 2 P.M.

C. 3 P.M.

D. 4 P.M.

In the following quotation, writer Aime Cesair talks about culture. Use the quotation and your knowledge of world cultures and geography to answer question 3.

PRIMARY SOURCE

Culture is everything. Culture is the way we dress, the way we carry our heads, the way we walk, the way we tie our ties—it is not only the fact of writing books or building houses.

AIME CESAIR, speech to the World Congress of Black Writers and Artists in Paris

3. Which of the following statements would Cesair agree with most?

A. Culture refers to fine art, drama, and classical music.

B. Culture includes all the things that characterize a group.

C. Most people in the world do not take part in culture.

D. Some parts of culture are more important than others.

TEST PRACTICE
CLASSZONE.COM

ALTERNATIVE ASSESSMENT

1. **WRITING ABOUT HISTORY**

The United States and Canada share a culture region. Think about the elements that contribute to this culture region. Then write a script for a one-act play in which a person from another culture region experiences our culture for the first time. Focus on unique aspects of our language, technology, food, and clothing that a person might find surprising and strange.

2. COOPERATIVE LEARNING

With a group of three to five students, set up a peace conference to help two warring groups make peace. Choose two specific groups and a specific issue that caused the hostility, such as a conflict over the scarcity of water. Do research to understand each side's point of view in the conflict. Group members should take on specific roles, such as conference moderator and spokesperson for each side. Present your peace conference to the class as a skit.

INTEGRATED TECHNOLOGY

Doing Internet Research

Use the Internet to research a culture, such as the people of Lebanon or Hong Kong. Write a report of your findings. List the Web sites you used to prepare your report.

• Specifically find out about the daily life of the people, including what jobs they have, what foods they eat, what clothes they wear, and what their homes are like.

• Also, research what most people in the culture value, what governments they live under, and what common difficulties they face.

For Internet links to support this activity, go to

RESEARCH LINKS
CLASSZONE.COM

The Geographer's World

SECTION 1 The Five Themes of Geography

SECTION 2 The Geographer's Tools

Place In the 16th century, Nicolaus Copernicus, a Polish astronomer, suggested that the Earth and the other planets of the solar system revolved around the sun.

How has science broadened our understanding of Earth?

Human-Environment Interaction • People once believed that the Earth stood motionless at the center of the solar system, as shown in the drawing at the top of the page. In the centuries after the astronomer Nicholaus Copernicus first challenged this theory, scientists have developed sophisticated technology for studying the Earth. One such technological system is called *Terra,* the Earth Observing System [EOS] satellite. *Terra* was launched in 1999 and helps scientists study Earth's air, land, and water.

Terra helps to answer such questions as: Which environmental changes result from natural causes? Which are caused by humans? Satellites like *Terra* also help scientists study natural disasters such as hurricanes, volcanic eruptions, and floods. Today, several countries are working together in the Earth Observing System program to gather information about climate and environmental change on Earth.

What do you think?

♦ How can *Terra* benefit people?

♦ Why do countries work together to study climate and environmental change?

READING SOCIAL STUDIES

BEFORE YOU READ

▶▶ *What Do You Know?*

Do you know how to find important places in your town? Have you visited cities, towns, or rural areas and noticed what made these places special? Do you ever use terms like "up north" or "back east"? Have you ever moved from one neighborhood, town, or country to another? Do you know about the harmful effects of pollution on wildlife habitats? If you answered yes, then you know something about each of geography's five big themes—location, place, region, movement, and human-environment interaction.

▶▶ *What Do You Want to Know?*

Decide what more you want to learn about geography's five themes. Write your ideas, and any questions you may have, in your notebook before you read this chapter.

READ AND TAKE NOTES

Reading Strategy: Identifying Main Ideas One way to make sense of what you read is to look for main ideas and supporting details. Each paragraph, topic heading, and section in a chapter usually has a main idea. Supporting details help to explain the main idea. Use this spider map to write a main idea and its supporting details from this chapter.

- Copy the spider map in your notebook.
- As you read, look for information about the five themes of geography.
- Write a main idea in the center circle.
- Write details supporting the main idea in the other circles.

Place • Physical and human characteristics reveal patterns in places. ▲

The Five Themes of Geography

The Five Themes of Geography

TERMS & NAMES
continent
absolute location
latitude
longitude
relative location
migrate

MAIN IDEA

The five themes of geography are location, place, region, movement, and human-environment interaction.

WHY IT MATTERS NOW

The five themes enable you to discuss and explain people, places, and environments of the past and present.

DATELINE

EXTRA

FRANKFURT, GERMANY, JANUARY 6, 1912

Scientist Alfred Wegener sent out shock waves today when he proposed a radical new hypothesis. The continents were once joined together as one huge landmass. In time, he suggests, pieces of this landmass broke away and drifted apart.

Wegener calls this super-continent *Pangaea*. To support his theory, Wegener points out that the continents seem to fit together.

He notes, for example, that the east coast of South America fits snugly against the west coast of Africa. Mountain ranges continue across both continents as smoothly as the lines of print across torn pieces of a newspaper.

Other scientists reject Wegener's claim. They say that they know of no force strong enough to cause continents to move.

PANGAEA

Asia
Europe
North America
South America
Africa
Australia
Antarctica

Movement • Seven continents were once one continent. A <u>continent</u> is a landmass above water on earth. ▲

The Five Themes

Eventually, the scientific community accepted Alfred Wegener's theory. Scientists discovered that giant slabs of Earth's surface, called tectonic plates, move, causing the continents to drift. This creates earthquakes, volcanoes, and mountains. Geographers study the processes that cause changes like these. To help you understand how geographers think about the world, consider geography's five themes—location, place, region, movement, and human-environment interaction.

TAKING NOTES
Use your web to take notes about the five themes.

The Five Themes of Geography

Southeastern United States

GEOGRAPHY SKILLBUILDER:
Interpreting a Map
1. **Location** • Which states have borders that run along latitude 35°N?
2. **Location** • Which state extends south to longitude 80°W and latitude 25°N?

The WORLD'S HERITAGE

The Galápagos Islands The Galápagos Islands are an archipelago, or group of islands, 600 miles off the coast of South America. These islands, which contain many forms of plant and animal life found nowhere else in the world, are a unique "living museum."

Scientists and tourists are fascinated by the islands' creatures, such as Galápagos hawks, land iguanas, waved albatrosses, and blue-footed boobies. The islands are also home to giant tortoises, which can weigh up to 650 pounds and can live to be 200 years old. One of the 11 subspecies of giant tortoises has only one member left. Lonesome George, shown below, is about 80 years old.

Location

Often, the first thing you want to know about a place is where it is located in space. Geography helps you think about things spatially—where they are located and how they got there. Location allows you to discuss places in the world in terms everyone can understand.

Absolute Location If someone asks you where your school is, you might say, "At the corner of Fifth Street and Second Avenue." Ask a geographer where Melbourne, Australia, is located, and you may get the answer "38° south latitude, 145° east longitude." This is the absolute location of the city of Melbourne. **Absolute location** is the exact spot on Earth where a place can be found.

Using a system of imaginary lines drawn on its surface, geographers can locate any place on Earth. Lines that run parallel to the equator are called **latitude** lines. They show distance north and south of the equator. Lines that run between the North and South Poles are called **longitude** lines. They show distance east and west of the prime meridian.

Reading
Social Studies

A. Contrasting
Contrast absolute
location with
relative location.

Relative Location Another way to define the location of a place is to describe its relation to other places. You might say your school is "near the fire station" or "two blocks west of the pet store." If someone asks you where Canada is, you might say, "North of the United States." The location of one place in relation to other places is called its **relative location**.

Place • On the west coast of South America, the ancient Inca farmed the steep slopes of the Andes mountains by carving the slopes into terraces. ▲

Place

Another useful theme of geography is place. If you go to a new place, the first thing you want to know is what it is like. Is it crowded or is there a lot of open space? How is the climate? What language do people speak? Every place on Earth has a distinct group of physical features, such as its climate, landforms and bodies of water, and plant and animal life. Places can also have human characteristics, or features that human beings have created, such as cities and towns, governments, and cultural traditions.

Places Change If you could go back to the days when dinosaurs roamed Earth, you would see a world much different from the one you know. Much of Earth had a moist, warm climate, and the continents were not located where they are today. Rivers, forests, wetlands, glaciers, oceans—the physical features of Earth—continue to change. Some changes are dramatic, caused by erupting volcanoes, earthquakes, and hurricanes. Others happen slowly, such as the movement of glaciers or the formation of a delta.

Place • This satellite photo shows the Mississippi River delta. It was formed from sediment and mud carried by the river to its mouth. ▼

Region

Geographers group places into regions. A region is a group of places that have physical features or human characteristics, or both, in common. A geographer interested in languages, for example, might divide the world into language regions. All the countries where Spanish is the major language would form one Spanish-speaking language region. Geographers compare regions to understand the differences and similarities among them.

Natural Regions of the World

Region	Climate	Plant Life
Tropical Rain Forest	Hot and wet all year	Thick trees, broad leaves Trees stay green all year
Tropical Grassland	Hot all year Wet and dry seasons	Tall grasses Some trees
Mediterranean	Hot, dry summers Cool-to-mild winters	Open forests Some clumps of trees Many shrubs, herbs, grasses
Temperate Forest	Warm summers Cold-to-cool winters	Mixed forests; some trees lose leaves in winter, others stay green all year
Cool Forest	Cool-to-mild summers Long, cold winters	Mostly trees with needles; stay green all year; some trees lose leaves in winter
Cool Grassland	Warm summers Cool winters Drier than forest regions	Prairies: Tall, thick grass Higher lands: Shorter grass
Desert	Hot all year Very little rain	Sand or bare soil, few plants May have cactus, some grass and bushes
Tundra	Short, cool summers Long, cold winters Little rain or snow	Rolling plains: No trees Some patches of moss, short grass, flowering plants
Arctic	Very cold Covered in ice all year	None
High Mountain	Varies, depending on altitude	Varies, depending on altitude

SKILLBUILDER: Interpreting a Chart

1. **Region** • How are desert regions and tropical grasslands alike and how are they different?
2. **Region** • In which type of climate are trees most likely to stay green all year?

Natural Regions The world can be divided into ten natural regions. A natural region has its own unique combination of plant and animal life and climate. Tropical rain forest regions are in Central and South America, Africa south of the Sahara, Southeast Asia, Australia, and the Pacific Islands. Where are desert regions located?

Region • The tropical rain forest is one of the ten natural regions of the world. ▲

Movement

People, goods, and ideas move from one place to another. So do animals, plants, and other physical features of Earth. Movement is the fourth geographic theme. The Internet is a good tool for the movement of ideas. Sometimes people move within a country. For example, vast numbers of people have migrated from farms to cities. **Migrate** means to move from one area to settle in another. You may have ancestors who immigrated to the United States—perhaps from Africa, Europe, Latin America, or Asia. When people emigrate, they take their ideas and customs with them. They may also adopt new ideas from their new home.

Vocabulary

immigrate: to move to an area

emigrate: to move away from an area

Reasons for Moving Migration is a result of push and pull factors. Problems in one place push people out. Advantages in another place pull people in. Poverty, overcrowding, lack of jobs and schooling, prejudice, war, and political oppression are push factors. Pull factors include a higher standard of living, employment and educational opportunities, rights, freedom, peace, and safety.

Reading **Social Studies**

B. Synthesizing How do push and pull factors work together?

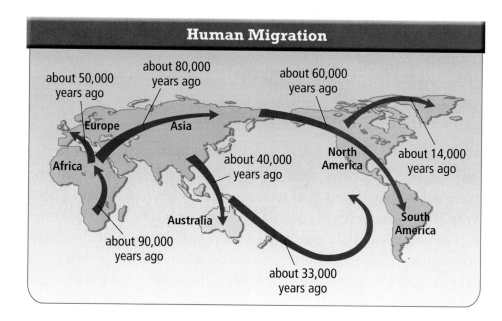

Human Migration

about 50,000 years ago

about 80,000 years ago

about 60,000 years ago

Europe

Asia

Africa

North America

about 14,000 years ago

about 40,000 years ago

Australia

South America

about 90,000 years ago

about 33,000 years ago

Movement • As you can see, people have been on the move for at least 90,000 years. ◄

Vocabulary

navigable: deep and wide enough for boats to travel on

Barriers to Movement Natural barriers, such as mountain ranges, canyons, and raging rivers, can make migration difficult. Oceans, lakes, navigable rivers, and flat land can make it easier. Modern forms of transportation have made it easier than ever for people to move back and forth between countries.

Human-Environment Interaction

Interaction between human beings and their environment is the fifth theme of geography. Human-environment interaction occurs because humans depend on, adapt to, and modify the world around them. Human society and the environment cannot be separated. Each shapes and is shaped by the other. Earth is a unified system.

Some places are the way they are because people have changed them. For example, if an area has a lot of open meadows, this may be because early settlers cleared the land for farming.

Saving Special Places Many of the most wonderful and special places on Earth may be destroyed or ruined over time unless they are protected. To prevent this, UNESCO (the United Nations Educational, Scientific, and Cultural Organization) set up the World Heritage Committee in 1972. This group identifies human-made and natural wonders all over the world and looks for ways to protect them for the benefit of the world community. So far, the list of World Heritage Sites numbers more than 690. The Grand Canyon (see photograph at right), the Galápagos Islands, the Roman Colosseum, and the Pyramids of Giza are just a few of the places protected for future generations.

Human changes may help or hurt the environment. Pollution is an example of a harmful effect. The environment can also harm people. For example, hurricanes wash away beaches and houses along the shore; earthquakes cause fire and destruction.

Adaptation Humans have often adapted their way of life to the natural resources that their local environment provided. In the past, people who lived near teeming oceans learned to fish. Those who lived near rich soil learned to farm. People built their homes out of local materials and ate the food easily grown in their surroundings. Cultural choices, such as what clothes to wear or which sports to participate in, often reflected the environment.

Because of technology, this close adaptation to the environment is not as common as it once was. Airplanes, for example, can quickly fly frozen fish from the coast to towns far inland. Even so, there are many more ice skaters in Canada and surfers in California than the other way around.

Interaction People and the environment continually interact. For example, when thousands of people in a city choose to use public transportation or ride bicycles rather than drive, less gasoline is burned. When less gasoline is burned, there is less air pollution. In other words, when the environment is healthy, the people who live in it are able to lead healthier lives.

SECTION 1 ASSESSMENT

Terms & Names
1. Explain the significance of: **(a)** continent   **(b)** absolute location   **(c)** latitude   **(d)** longitude   **(e)** relative location   **(f)** migrate

Using Graphics
2. Use a chart like this one to list and explain the five themes of geography.

Theme	Explanation

Main Ideas
3. **(a)** What physical processes can cause places to change over time?

   (b) How do push and pull factors cause migration?

   (c) What are some ways people have adapted to their environment?

Critical Thinking
4. **Making Inferences**
   What factors make your part of the United States a region?

   Think About
   - similar human geography
   - similar physical geography

ACTIVITY -OPTION-   Write and illustrate a **magazine advertisement** to persuade people to move to a new place. Include several pull factors for the place you are advertising.

Reading Latitude and Longitude

▶▶ Defining the Skill

To locate places, geographers use a global grid system (see the chart directly below). Imaginary lines of latitude, called parallels, circle the globe. The equator circles the middle of the globe at 0°. Parallels measure distance in degrees north and south of the equator.

Lines of longitude, called meridians, circle the globe from pole to pole. Meridians measure distance in degrees east and west of the prime meridian. The prime meridian is at 0°. It passes through Greenwich, England.

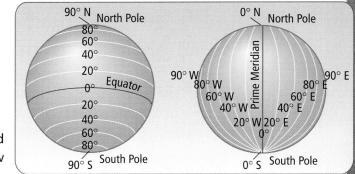

▶▶ Applying the Skill

The world map below shows lines of latitude and longitude. Use the strategies listed directly below to help you locate places on Earth.

How to Read Latitude and Longitude

Strategy ❶ Place a finger on the place you want to locate. With a finger from your other hand, find the nearest parallel. Write down its number. Be sure to include north or south. (You may have to guesstimate the actual number.)

Strategy ❷ Keep your finger on the place you want to locate. Now find the nearest meridian. Write down its number. Be sure to include east or west. (You may have to guesstimate the actual number.)

Strategy ❸ If you know the longitude and latitude of a place and want to find it on a map, put one finger on the line of longitude and another on the line of latitude. Bring your fingers together until they meet.

Write a Summary

Writing a summary will help you understand latitude and longitude. The paragraph below and to the right summarizes the information you have learned.

▶▶ Practicing the Skill

Turn to page 36 in Chapter 2, Section 1, "The Five Themes of Geography." Look at the map of Australia and write a paragraph summarizing how you located the city of Adelaide.

Use latitude and longitude to locate a place on a globe or map. Lines of latitude circle Earth. Lines of longitude run through the poles. The numbers of the lines at the place where two lines cross is the location of that place.

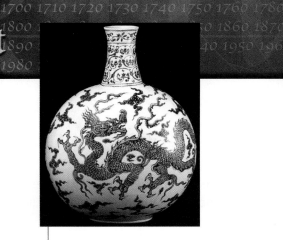

The Legacy of World Exploration

Movement of People

The Age of Exploration that began in the 1400s led to massive movements of peoples. Millions of Europeans settled in the Americas. Many Native Americans were forced to move as settlers took their lands. Europeans also brought large numbers of enslaved Africans to the Americas. The racial and ethnic mix of modern societies is a legacy of this period of world exploration.

Global Trade

The European demand for Eastern goods such as porcelain, silk, and spices encouraged explorers to seek a direct sea route to East Asia. Global trade increased—Europeans bought products in Asia, using gold and silver from Spanish colonies in the Americas to buy goods in India and China. In this way global trade encouraged contact between different cultures. It also helped prepare the way for today's multicultural societies.

Cultural Exchange

Explorers and settlers helped spread European languages, religions, and ideas around the globe. At the same time, Western culture was enriched by contact with foreign cultures. For example, as English speakers traveled, their vocabulary grew. English now includes words from India, such as *shampoo* and *pajamas,* as well as Native American words, such as *toboggan* and *barbecue.*

Exchange of Plants and Animals

Exploration encouraged not only the movement of people and goods, but also the exchange of plants and animals. From the Americas, Europeans transported tomatoes, corn, and potatoes to other continents. They brought wheat, rice, and sugarcane to the Americas. This exchange of plants and animals provided new food sources and improved many aspects of life. However, introduced species sometimes threatened and destroyed native species.

Spread of Disease

Europeans unknowingly brought a host of deadly new diseases to the Americas, including smallpox, malaria, and bubonic plague. With no natural defenses against these diseases, Native Americans died in large numbers. The spread of disease as a result of global trade and travel continues today. Medical organizations around the world are struggling to control the spread of diseases such as SARS.

Science and Technology

World exploration helped spread Western technology around the globe. However, Western technology had itself developed from the inventions of many different cultures. China had invented gunpowder and paper; Muslims had made many important mathematical and scientific discoveries. One particularly important invention was the astrolabe, which measured the sun's and stars' angles above the horizon. This instrument became essential to world explorers as it helped them to determine their ships' position at sea.

Find Out More About It!

Study the text and photos on these pages to learn about world exploration. Then choose the topic that interests you the most and research it in the library or on the Internet to learn more about it. Use the information you gather to write a short play that you and your classmates can perform.

RESEARCH LINKS
CLASSZONE.COM

A Map of Earth in 3-D

On February 11, 2000, the space shuttle *Endeavour* was launched into space on an 11-day mission to complete the most in-depth mapping project in history. The Shuttle Radar Topography Mission (SRTM) collected data on 80 percent of Earth's surface. This information was gathered by beaming radar waves at Earth and converting the echoes into images through a process known as interferometry (IHN•tuhr•fuh•RAHM•ih•tree).

With the aid of computers, the resulting information can be used to produce almost limitless numbers of three-dimensional (3-D) maps. These maps show the topography—rivers, forests, mountains, and valleys—of Earth's surface. It took one year to process the data into 3-D maps. These maps, the most accurate topographical maps ever, will help scientists to better study Earth's surface. The data will also be useful to the general public; for example, it can be used to find new locations for cellular-phone towers and to create maps for hikers.

The data collected on the 11-day SRTM mission can be used by many people—such as the military, the science community, and civic groups—and can be tailored to their needs.

The 200-foot mast is the longest structure used in space today.

Radar interferometry uses radar images taken from two different angles to produce a single 3-D image.

THINKING

Critically

1. Drawing Conclusions
How will new, sophisticated tools such as radar interferometry and computers change the study of Earth and the environment?

2. Making Predictions How will these topographical maps help the world?

The Geographer's Tools

TERMS & NAMES
cartographer
thematic map
map projection

MAIN IDEA

Geographers use maps, globes, charts, graphs, and new technology to learn about and display the features of Earth.

WHY IT MATTERS NOW

Knowing how to use the tools of geography adds to your ability to understand the world.

DATELINE

PARIS, 1650—The world looks very different today. A new map of North America has just been published by Nicolas Sanson, the famous French mapmaker. Sanson based his map on reports from explorers, missionaries, and other travelers. The map shows five great lakes. Two of these lakes, Lake Ontario and Lake Superior, have been named for the first time.

Certain regions to the north and west remain unknown. Could there be a northwest passage that will allow us to sail to China and the Far East? Only one thing is certain—our knowledge of this mysterious continent will grow with time.

Location • Nicolas Sanson created one of the most important 17th-century maps of North America. ▲

Maps and Globes

People have been drawing maps of their world for thousands of years. Geographers today have many tools, such as remote sensing and the Global Positioning System, to help them represent Earth. Increased knowledge and technology allows a **cartographer**, or mapmaker, to construct maps that give a much more detailed and accurate picture of the world. The "Linking Past and Present" and "Technology: 2004" features on pages 42–44 provide more information on modern mapmaking technology.

TAKING NOTES
Use your web to take notes about the five themes.

The Five Themes of Geography

Location • Draw a picture on the entire surface of an orange and then peel the orange in one continuous piece. After you lay the peel flat, your image will be distorted.

Differences Between Maps and Globes Both maps and globes represent Earth and its features. A globe is an accurate model of the world because it has three dimensions and can show its actual shape. Globes are difficult to carry around, however. Maps are more practical. They can be folded, carried, hung on a wall, or printed in a book or magazine. However, because maps show the world in only two dimensions, they are not perfectly accurate. Look at the pictures above to see why. When the orange peel is flattened out, the picture on the orange is distorted, or twisted out of shape. Cartographers have the same problem with maps.

Reading
Social Studies

A. Clarifying
Why does a globe represent Earth better than a map?

Three Kinds of Maps General reference maps, which show natural and human-made features, are used to locate a place. **Thematic maps** focus on one specific idea or theme. The population map on page 48 is an example of a thematic map. Pilots and sailors use nautical maps to find their way through air and over water. A nautical map is sometimes called a chart.

Location • A road map is a reference map that shows how to get from one place to another. ▼

Connections to Math

Measuring Earth In 230 B.C., the Greek scientist Eratosthenes used basic geometry to measure the circumference of Earth. Eratosthenes knew that at noon on June 21, the sun cast no shadow in the Egyptian city of Syene (now Aswan). (See the diagram below.) At the same time, the sun cast a shadow of 7°12′ in Alexandria, about 500 miles from Syene.

The circumference of a circle is 360°; 7°12′ is about 2 percent, or 1/50, of 360°. Therefore, he concluded, 500 miles must be about 2 percent of the distance around Earth, which at the equator would be about 25,000 miles.

7°12′ = 1/50 circumference

Road Map of Prince Edward Island, 2002

Mercator Projection

Robinson Projection

GEOGRAPHY SKILLBUILDER: Interpreting a Map

1. Location • Compare the size of Africa in relation to other continents on the two projections. How do they differ?
2. Location • What other differences do you notice between the Mercator projection and the Robinson projection?

Reading
Social Studies

B. Identifying Problems What are the main problems faced by cartographers?

Map Projections The different ways of showing Earth's curved surface on a flat map are called **map projections**. All projections distort Earth, but different projections distort it in different ways. Some make places look bigger or smaller than they really are in relation to other places. Other projections distort shapes. For more than 400 years, the Mercator projection was most often shown on maps of the world. Recently, the Robinson projection has come into common use because it gives a fairer and more accurate picture of the world.

Colonial Map This map of Boston was drawn by Jacques Nicolas Bellin and published in Paris around 1764. It shows the harbor and the bays surrounding Boston in the mid-18th century.

THINKING CRITICALLY

1. **Recognizing Important Details** How was it possible for travelers to enter Boston by land?

2. **Making Inferences** Why was Boston's site a good location for a colonial city?

For more on colonial maps, go to

RESEARCH LINKS
CLASSZONE.COM

World Population and Life Expectancy, 2000

Population

= 500,000 people

Life Expectancy

Life Expectancy in Years, 2000

- Less than 55
- 55–64
- 65–69
- 70–74
- 75 or more
- No data

GEOGRAPHY SKILLBUILDER: Interpreting a Map

1. Region • Which continent has the largest population? the smallest?

2. Region • What is the life expectancy in most parts of North America?

Comparing Maps, Charts, and Graphs

Along with maps, geographers use charts and graphs to display and compare information. The graphs on this page and the maps on page 48 contain related information about the world's population. Notice how each quickly and clearly presents facts that would otherwise take up many paragraphs of text.

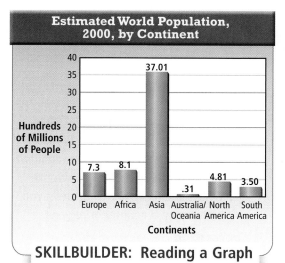

Estimated World Population, 2000, by Continent

SKILLBUILDER: Reading a Graph

1. How many people live in Europe?
2. Which continent has the smallest population?

World Population Growth, 1600–Present

SKILLBUILDER: Reading a Graph

1. How many people lived in the world in 1900?
2. How much did the world's population increase between 1600 and 1900? between 1900 and 2000?

SECTION 2 ASSESSMENT

Terms & Names

1. Explain the significance of: (a) cartographer   (b) thematic map   (c) map projection

Using Graphics

2. Use a chart like the one below to compare the advantages and disadvantages of maps and globes.

	Maps	Globes
Advantages		
Disadvantages		

Main Ideas

3. (a) What are the differences among the three main kinds of maps?
   (b) How have new tools and knowledge helped cartographers?
   (c) What kinds of information can be displayed in maps and graphs?

Critical Thinking

4. **Using Maps**

   What kind of map would show how many students are in each school in your district?

Think About

- the three kinds of maps
- what information different kinds of population maps show

ACTIVITY -OPTION- Draw a **map** of the route you take to and from school or some other familiar destination. Include the names of streets, landmarks such as shops and other buildings, and any other useful information.

TERMS & NAMES

Explain the significance of each of the following:

1. absolute location
2. latitude
3. longitude
4. relative location
5. cartographer
6. thematic map
7. map projection
8. migrate
9. continent

REVIEW QUESTIONS

The Five Themes of Geography *(pages 35–40)*

1. What system do geographers use to determine absolute location?
2. How is relative location different from absolute location?
3. What are some of the natural barriers that made migration difficult in the past?
4. How has technology changed the way humans adapt to their environment?

The Geographer's Tools *(pages 45–49)*

5. Why is a globe an accurate representation of the world?
6. Why would a pilot use a nautical map?
7. How has modern technology helped cartography?
8. Why do most modern cartographers prefer the Robinson projection to the Mercator projection?

CRITICAL THINKING

Drawing Conclusions

1. Using your completed spider map from Reading Social Studies, p. 34, draw a conclusion about which theme of geography is most useful in familiarizing you with an area of the world. Which details in your chart help you understand a country or region?

Contrasting

2. Maps and globes both represent Earth and its features. Contrast the advantages of a map with the advantages of a globe.

Clarifying

3. Why would the leaders of a country find a population density map of their country useful?

Visual Summary

The Five Themes of Geography *1*

- The five themes of geography are location, place, region, movement, and human-environment interaction.
- These themes are the keys to understanding the geography of the world.

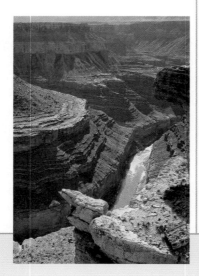

The Geographer's Tools *2*

- Maps, globes, charts, graphs, and other tools are available to geographers to help them understand the features of Earth.
- Geographers use these tools to organize and explain Earth's features.

Use the map and your knowledge of world cultures and geography to answer questions 1 and 2.

Additional Test Practice, pp. S1–S33

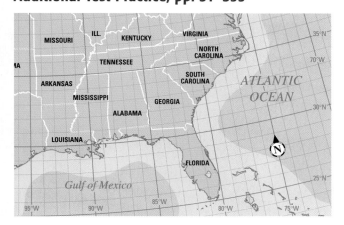

1. Which states have their northern border near latitude 35°N?

A. Arkansas, Tennessee, North Carolina

B. Louisiana, Mississippi, Alabama

C. Mississippi, Alabama, Georgia

D. Missouri, Kentucky, Virginia

2. Which state extends to about latitude 25°N and longitude 81°W?

A. Florida

B. Mississippi

C. North Carolina

D. South Carolina

In this quotation from a press release, a UNESCO spokesperson describes the archaeological site Mapungubwe. It was the center of the largest kingdom to exist in Africa south of the Sahara before the 14th century. Use the quotation and your knowledge of world cultures and geography to answer question 3.

PRIMARY SOURCE

What survives are the almost untouched remains of the palace sites and also the entire settlement area dependent upon them, as well as two earlier capital sites, the whole presenting an unrivalled picture of the development of social and political structures over some 400 years.

JASMINI SOPOVA, UNESCO spokesperson in *allAfrica.com*

3. Why is it so important that the archaeological remains are untouched?

A. They will be clean, not damaged by dirt and mud.

B. They will accurately show how people once lived.

C. They will make the person who found them famous.

D. They can be rearranged however the archaeologists want.

TEST PRACTICE
CLASSZONE.COM

ALTERNATIVE ASSESSMENT

1. **WRITING ABOUT HISTORY**

The world can be divided into ten natural regions. Find out what these ten regions are. Then choose one region and write a poem about it. In the poem, provide information about where the region is located, what plant life it has, what animal life it has, and what the climate is like in that particular region. Share your poem with the class.

2. COOPERATIVE LEARNING

With a small group of classmates, choose any country in the world and use the five themes of geography to describe it. Divide the tasks of answering these questions: Where is the country located? (location) What are its physical and human characteristics? (place) How can you classify the region? (region) What movement has occurred in the country? (movement) How have the people who live there adapted to the environment? (human-environment interaction) Arrange your findings on a poster board.

INTEGRATED TECHNOLOGY

Doing Internet Research

Use the Internet to research how technology can be used to study natural events. Write a report of your findings, including a list of the Web sites you used.

• Focus on one natural event, such as tropical rainfall or a hurricane. Look into how technology is helping us understand it.

• Include a prediction about the future uses of technology that involve these kinds of events.

For Internet links to support this activity, go to

RESEARCH LINKS
CLASSZONE.COM

Place Mount Rushmore is a monument located in the Black Hills of South Dakota. The 60-foot likenesses of (from left to right) George Washington, Thomas Jefferson, Theodore Roosevelt, and Abraham Lincoln took 14 years to carve into the granite cliff.

THE UNITED STATES AND CANADA

MOUNT RUSHMORE

THE UNITED STATES AND CANADA

N

PACIFIC OCEAN

ATLANTIC OCEAN

INDIAN OCEAN

PACIFIC OCEAN

INTEGRATED TECHNOLOGY

eEdition
- Interactive Maps
- Interactive Visuals

VIDEO
USA: Chris in Louisiana

INTERNET RESOURCES
Go to **classzone.com** for:
- Research Links
- Internet Activities
- Data Updates
- Unit Quiz
- Maps
- Test Practice
- Current Events
- Web Research Guide

The United States and Canada: Physical

N

Elevation

13,100 ft.	(4,000 m)
6,600 ft.	(2,000 m)
3,275 ft.	(1,000 m)
650 ft.	(200 m)
0 ft.	(0 m)
Below sea level	

▲ Mountain peak

180°   100°W   80°W   60°W

80°N

60°N

40°N

Tropic of Cancer

20°N

0°

20°S

Chukchi Sea

Beaufort Sea

Ellesmere Island

Queen Elizabeth Islands

Baffin Bay

Victoria Island

Baffin Island

Davis Strait

BROOKS RANGE

Yukon R.

Bering Strait

Bering Sea

ALASKA RANGE

Mt. McKinley 20,320 ft. (6,194 m)

MACKENZIE MTS.

Mackenzie R.

Great Bear Lake

Mt. Logan 19,551 ft. (5,959 m)

Kodiak Is.

Great Slave Lake

Hudson Bay

Aleutian Islands

Gulf of Alaska

Queen Charlotte Is.

COAST MOUNTAINS

Lake Athabasca

CANADA

CANADIAN SHIELD

James Bay

Vancouver I.

ROCKY MOUNTAINS

GREAT PLAINS

Lake Winnipeg

Great Lakes

St. Lawrence R.

Gulf of St. Lawrence

Newfoundland and Labrador

COAST RANGES

Columbia R.

GREAT BASIN

Sierra Nevada

Colorado R.

Missouri R.

Mississippi R.

UNITED STATES

Ohio R.

APPALACHIAN MTS.

Mt. Whitney 14,494 ft. (4,421 m)

Death Valley -282 ft. (-86 m)

Mississippi R.

COASTAL PLAIN

ATLANTIC OCEAN

Channel Is.

Rio Grande

Gulf of Mexico

Caribbean Sea

PACIFIC OCEAN

Equator

Hawaiian Islands

PACIFIC OCEAN

Tropic of Capricorn

HAWAII

22°N
Niihau Kauai Oahu
Molokai
Lanai Maui
Kahoolawe

20°N

Hawaii

| 0 | 75 | 150 miles |
| 0 | 75 | 150 kilometers |

160°W   158°W   156°W   154°W

| 0 | 600 | 1,200 miles |
| 0 | 600 | 1,200 kilometers |

Natural Hazards of the United States and Canada

Legend:
- ☐ Earthquakes in the 20th century
- ▲ Volcanoes in the 20th century
- 〰 Tsunamis
- ◀•• Tropical storm track
- Areas at high risk for tornadoes
- 〜 Selected rivers subject to flooding
- Areas subject to desertification

Canada–United States: Landmass and Population

Canada

United States

LANDMASS

Canada

3,851,809 square miles

Continental United States

3,165,630 square miles

POPULATION

Canada
30,750,100

United States
281,421,906

👤 = 50,000,000

FAST FACTS

HIGHEST TIDE:
The Bay of Fundy, between New Brunswick and Nova Scotia in Canada, has the highest tides in the world, sometimes running as high as 70 feet.

HIGHEST MOUNTAIN:
Mt. McKinley, 20,320 ft.

LONGEST RIVER:
Mississippi River, 2,357 mi.

HIGHEST RECORDED TEMPERATURE:
134°F, Death Valley, California, July 10, 1913

LOWEST RECORDED TEMPERATURE:
−81.4°F, Snag, Yukon, February 3, 1947

GEOGRAPHY SKILLBUILDER: Interpreting Maps and Visuals

1. **Location** • What is the elevation of the land along the Gulf of Mexico and Hudson Bay?
2. **Place** • Where are most of the volcanoes in the United States and Canada?

The United States and Canada: Political

Beaufort Sea

Chukchi Sea

Bering Strait

Bering Sea

AK (U.S.)

Anchorage

Yukon R.

Gulf of Alaska

NORTHWEST TERRITORIES

YUKON TERRITORY

Mackenzie R.

Great Bear Lake

Great Slave Lake

Lake Athabasca

NUNAVUT

Hudson Bay

Baffin Bay

Davis Strait

BRITISH COLUMBIA

Vancouver

Edmonton

Calgary

ALBERTA

SASKATCHEWAN

MANITOBA

Lake Winnipeg

CANADA

Winnipeg

James Bay

ONTARIO

QUEBEC

NEWFOUNDLAND AND LABRADOR

Gulf of St. Lawrence

PRINCE EDWARD ISLAND

NOVA SCOTIA

NEW BRUNSWICK

Montreal

Ottawa

Toronto

St. Lawrence R.

WA

Seattle

OR

Columbia R.

ID

MT

WY

ND

SD

Minneapolis

MN

WI

Mississippi R.

MI

Detroit

ME

NH

VT

NY

MA

RI

CT

Boston

NV

UT

Salt Lake City

CO

NE

Missouri R.

IA

Kansas City

IL

St. Louis

IN

OH

PA

NJ

MD

New York

Philadelphia

DE

Washington, D.C.

San Francisco

CA

Colorado R.

KS

MO

KY

WV

VA

Los Angeles

San Diego

AZ

Phoenix

NM

UNITED STATES

OK

Dallas

TX

Houston

AR

Mississippi R.

TN

NC

SC

Atlanta

GA

MS

AL

LA

New Orleans

Rio Grande

Gulf of Mexico

FL

Miami

ATLANTIC OCEAN

Caribbean Sea

PACIFIC OCEAN

Hawaiian Islands

Niihau

Kauai

Oahu

Honolulu

Molokai

Lanai

Kahoolawe

Maui

HAWAII

Hawaii

| 0 | 75 | 150 miles |
| 0 | 75 | 150 kilometers |

160°W 158°W 156°W 154°W

Tropic of Cancer

Equator

PACIFIC OCEAN

Tropic of Capricorn

| 0 | 600 | 1,200 miles |
| 0 | 600 | 1,200 kilometers |

★ National capital

● Other city

180° 100°W 80°W 60°W

80°N

60°N

40°N

22°N

20°N

20°N

0°

20°S

Population Density of the United States and Canada, 2001

Persons per sq. mi. / Persons per sq. km
- Over 520 / Over 200
- 260–520 / 100–200
- 130–259 / 50–99
- 25–129 / 10–49
- 1–24 / 1–9
- 0 / 0

◉ Metropolitan area greater than 2 million
• Other major metropolitan area

The United States and Canada: Selected Native Peoples, c. 1600

Major food source
- Animals and wild plants
- Cultivated plants
- Fish
- Animals
- Wild plants

Crow Native peoples

FAST FACTS

✔ **WORLD'S HIGHEST IMMIGRATION RATE:** Canada, with about 240,000 immigrants per year.

✔ **LOWEST POPULATION DENSITY:** Canada has only about 3.4 people per square kilometer. Nearly 90 percent of Canada's population lives within about 100 miles of the Canada–U.S. border.

✔ **LARGEST CITY:** New York City, 16,640,000 (2000)

GEOGRAPHY SKILLBUILDER: Interpreting Maps and Visuals

1. **Location** • Name the Canadian provinces and the U.S. states that lie along the border between the two countries.
2. **Location** • Which native peoples lived along the Pacific Coast circa 1600?

State Flag	State/ Capital	Population (2000)	Population Rank (2000)	Infant Mortality (per 1,000 live births) (1998)	Doctors (per 100,000 pop.) (1998–1999)
	Alabama (AL) Montgomery	4,447,100	23	10.2	198
	Alaska (AK) Juneau	626,900	48	5.9	167
	Arizona (AZ) Phoenix	5,130,600	20	7.5	202
	Arkansas (AR) Little Rock	2,673,400	33	8.9	190
	California (CA) Sacramento	33,871,600	1	5.8	247
	Colorado (CO) Denver	4,301,300	24	6.7	238
	Connecticut (CT) Hartford	3,405,600	29	7.0	354
	Delaware (DE) Dover	783,600	45	9.6	234
	*District of Columbia (DC)	572,100	—	12.5	737
	Florida (FL) Tallahassee	15,982,400	4	7.2	238
	Georgia (GA) Atlanta	8,186,500	10	8.5	211
	Hawaii (HI) Honolulu	1,211,500	42	6.9	265
	Idaho (ID) Boise	1,294,000	39	7.2	154
	Illinois (IL) Springfield	12,419,300	5	8.4	260
	Indiana (IN) Indianapolis	6,080,500	14	7.6	195
	Iowa (IA) Des Moines	2,926,300	30	6.6	173
	Kansas (KS) Topeka	2,688,400	32	7.0	203

*The federal district of Washington, D.C., is the capital city of the United States.

DATA FILE

Population Density (per square mile)	Per Capita Income ($) (1999)	High School Graduates (%) (1998)	Area Rank (2000)	Total Area (square miles)	Map (not to scale)
85.1	21,941	78.8	30	52,237	
1.0	27,274	90.6	1	615,230	
45.0	24,199	81.9	6	114,006	
50.3	21,146	76.8	28	53,182	
213.2	28,513	80.1	3	158,869	
41.3	30,291	89.6	8	104,100	
614.3	37,452	83.7	48	5,544	
327.0	29,341	85.2	49	2,396	
8,412.6	36,554	83.8	51	68	
266.7	26,796	81.9	23	59,928	
138.8	26,007	80.0	24	58,977	
187.6	26,623	84.6	47	6,459	
15.5	22,418	82.7	14	83,574	
214.4	29,908	84.2	25	57,918	
167.0	24,949	83.5	38	36,420	
51.9	24,600	87.7	26	56,276	
32.7	25,467	89.2	15	82,282	

State Flag	State/Capital	Population (2000)	Population Rank (2000)	Infant Mortality (per 1,000 live births) (1998)	Doctors (per 100,000 pop.) (1998–1999)
	Kentucky (KY) Frankfort	4,041,800	25	7.5	209
	Louisiana (LA) Baton Rouge	4,469,000	22	9.1	246
	Maine (ME) Augusta	1,274,900	40	6.3	223
	Maryland (MD) Annapolis	5,296,500	19	8.6	374
	Massachusetts (MA) Boston	6,349,100	13	5.1	412
	Michigan (MI) Lansing	9,938,400	8	8.2	224
	Minnesota (MN) St. Paul	4,919,500	21	5.9	249
	Mississippi (MS) Jackson	2,844,700	31	10.1	163
	Missouri (MO) Jefferson City	5,595,200	17	7.7	230
	Montana (MT) Helena	902,200	44	7.4	190
	Nebraska (NE) Lincoln	1,711,300	38	7.3	218
	Nevada (NV) Carson City	1,998,300	35	7.0	173
	New Hampshire (NH) Concord	1,235,800	41	4.4	237
	New Jersey (NJ) Trenton	8,414,400	9	6.4	295
	New Mexico (NM) Santa Fe	1,819,000	36	7.2	212
	New York (NY) Albany	18,976,500	3	6.3	387
	North Carolina (NC) Raleigh	8,049,300	11	9.3	232

DATA FILE

Population Density (per square mile)	Per Capita Income ($) (1999)	High School Graduates (%) (1998)	Area Rank (2000)	Total Area (square miles)	Map (not to scale)
100.0	22,147	77.9	37	40,411	
90.0	21,794	78.6	31	49,651	
37.8	23,867	86.7	39	33,741	
430.7	30,757	84.7	42	12,297	
687.1	34,168	85.6	45	9,241	
102.8	26,625	85.4	11	96,705	
56.6	29,281	89.4	12	86,943	
58.9	19,608	77.3	32	48,286	
80.3	25,040	82.9	21	69,709	
6.1	21,337	89.1	4	147,046	
22.1	26,235	87.7	16	77,358	
18.1	29,022	89.1	7	110,567	
133.1	29,552	84.0	44	9,283	
1,024.3	34,525	86.5	46	8,215	
15.0	21,097	79.6	5	121,598	
351.5	32,459	81.5	27	53,989	
153.0	25,072	81.4	29	52,672	

State Flag	State/Capital	Population (2000)	Population Rank (2000)	Infant Mortality (per 1,000 live births) (1998)	Doctors (per 100,000 pop.) (1998–1999)
	North Dakota (ND) Bismarck	642,200	47	8.6	222
	Ohio (OH) Columbus	11,353,100	7	8.0	235
	Oklahoma (OK) Oklahoma City	3,450,700	27	8.5	169
	Oregon (OR) Salem	3,421,400	28	5.4	225
	Pennsylvania (PA) Harrisburg	12,281,100	6	7.1	291
	Rhode Island (RI) Providence	1,048,300	43	7.0	338
	South Carolina (SC) Columbia	4,012,000	26	9.6	207
	South Dakota (SD) Pierre	754,800	46	9.1	184
	Tennessee (TN) Nashville	5,689,300	16	8.2	246
	Texas (TX) Austin	20,851,800	2	6.4	203
	Utah (UT) Salt Lake City	2,233,200	34	5.6	200
	Vermont (VT) Montpelier	608,800	49	7.0	305
	Virginia (VA) Richmond	7,078,500	12	7.7	241
	Washington (WA) Olympia	5,894,100	15	5.7	235
	West Virginia (WV) Charleston	1,808,300	37	8.0	215
	Wisconsin (WI) Madison	5,363,700	18	7.2	227
	Wyoming (WY) Cheyenne	493,800	50	7.2	171
	United States Washington, D.C.	281,422,000	3	7.0	251

DATA FILE

Population Density (per square mile)	Per Capita Income ($) (1999)	High School Graduates (%) (1998)	Area Rank (2000)	Total Area (square miles)	Map (not to scale)
9.1	22,488	84.3	18	70,704	
253.3	25,895	86.2	34	44,828	
49.4	21,802	84.6	20	69,903	
35.2	25,947	85.5	10	97,132	
266.6	27,420	84.1	33	46,058	
851.6	24,418	80.7	50	1,231	
128.6	22,467	78.6	40	31,189	
9.8	24,007	86.3	17	77,121	
135.0	24,461	76.9	36	42,146	
78.0	25,363	78.3	2	267,277	
26.3	22,333	89.3	13	84,904	
63.3	24,758	86.7	43	9,615	
167.2	28,193	82.6	35	42,326	
83.4	28,968	92.0	19	70,637	
74.6	19,973	76.4	41	24,231	
82.0	26,212	88.0	22	65,499	
5.0	24,864	90.0	9	97,818	
74.3	33,900	83.0	4	3,787,319	

Province or Territory Flag	Province or Territory/ Capital	Population (2000)	Population Rank (2000)	Infant Mortality (per 1,000 live births) (1998)	Doctors (per 100,000 pop.) (1998–1999)
	Alberta (AB) Edmonton	2,997,200	4	4.8	162
	British Columbia (BC) Victoria	4,063,800	3	4.7	193
	Manitoba (MB) Winnipeg	1,147,900	5	7.5	177
	New Brunswick (NB) Fredericton	756,600	8	5.7	153
	Newfoundland and Labrador (NF) St. John's	538,800	9	5.2	171
	Northwest Territories (NT) Yellowknife	42,100	11	10.9	92
	Nova Scotia (NS) Halifax	941,000	7	4.4	196
	Nunavut (NU) Iqaluit	27,700	13	N/A	N/A
	Ontario (ON) Toronto	11,669,300	1	5.5	178
	Prince Edward Island (PE) Charlottetown	138,900	10	4.4	128
	Quebec (QC) Quebec City	7,372,400	2	5.6	211
	Saskatchewan (SK) Regina	1,023,600	6	8.9	149
	Yukon Territory (YT) Whitehorse	30,700	12	8.4	149
	Canada Ottawa, Ontario	30,750,000	36	5.5	185

DATA FILE

Population Density (per square mile)	Per Capita Income ($) (1999)	High School Graduates (%) (1998)	Area Rank (2000)	Total Area (square miles)	Map (not to scale)
11.7	30,038	86	6	255,285	
11.1	31,592	87	5	366,255	
4.6	26,829	79	8	250,934	
26.7	26,607	78	11	28,345	
3.4	27,692	71	10	156,649	
0.08	33,738 (1994)	64 (1996)	3	503,951	
44.0	25,712	78	12	21,425	
0.03	27,421 (1994)	N/A	1	818,959	
28.3	32,537	84	4	412,582	
49.4	25,534	74	13	2,814	
12.4	28,826	78	2	594,860	
4.1	26,463	82	7	251,700	
0.2	36,130	67 (1996)	9	186,661	
8.0	23,000	82	3	3,850,420	

GEOGRAPHY SKILLBUILDER: Interpreting a Chart

1. **Place** • Which province or territory in Canada has the fewest people? How is it ranked in area? How do these two facts explain the population density?
2. **Place** • What is the highest percentage of high school graduates in a state? What is the lowest percentage?

The Physical Geography of the United States and Canada

Place The aurora borealis, or northern lights, is a natural phenomenon most commonly seen in the winter skies over Alaska and northern Canada.

How do Canada and the U.S. benefit from the variety of natural features?

Place • North America is a vast area with varied physical features and climates. A mountain range runs parallel to each coastline. Grasslands cover much of the land between the mountain ranges. One of the world's longest rivers runs from north to south through the east central portion of the United States. Oceans and seas almost completely surround the continent. In northern Canada, the ground is always frozen. In the southeastern United States, plants grow year round.

What do you think?

♦ How does the variety of types of land benefit the people of North America?

♦ How are some places in North America better to live in than others?

♦ Describe the landforms, climate, and vegetation where you live.

READING SOCIAL STUDIES

BEFORE YOU READ

▶▶ *What Do You Know?*

Before you read the chapter, reflect on what you already know about the United States and Canada. On which continent will you find these countries? Remember what you have read, seen, or learned in other classes about their physical features and natural resources. They are two of the wealthiest and most powerful countries in the modern world. What makes nations powerful in today's world?

▶▶ *What Do You Want to Know?*

Decide what you want to know about the United States and Canada. In your notebook, record what you hope to learn from this chapter.

Region • Water resources, such as the Mississippi River, contribute to the wealth of the United States and Canada and to their positions of leadership in the world. ▲

READ AND TAKE NOTES

Reading Strategy: Drawing Conclusions
As you read Chapter 3, think about how geographic factors support the strong economies of the United States and Canada. Use this chart to show how natural features have assisted in creating a strong economy. Notice that several geographic features may contribute to the same economic strength.

- Copy the chart into your notebook.
- On the chart, read the characteristics of the strong economies of the United States and Canada.
- As you read the chapter, identify the geographic features that contribute to each group of economic strengths. Note them on the chart.

Human-Environment Interaction • Rich soil and a moderate climate support a productive agricultural industry. ▲

Geographic Features	Contribute to	Economic Strengths/Benefits
	→	productive farmland, agricultural exports
	→	natural routes for travel to and trade with Canada and the United States, easy-to-defend location, fishing industry, recreation and tourism
	→	transportation by water for people and goods within North America, fishing industry, power source, recreation
	→	raw materials, sources of fuel and power for transportation, industry, and new technologies
	→	good trade and regulatory relations between Canada and the United States, tourism

From Coast to Coast

TERMS & NAMES
Sacagawea
landform
glacier
erosion
river system

MAIN IDEA

North America has varied regions and landforms.

WHY IT MATTERS NOW

North America's geography contributes to the prosperity of the people who live there.

DATELINE

EXTRA

MOUNT ST. HELENS, WASHINGTON, MAY 18, 1980

Mount St. Helens, an ancient volcano in Washington's Cascade Mountains, erupted this morning, killing 60 people and thousands of animals. An earthquake caused the mountain's north face to fall away. The debris from this landslide filled Spirit Lake. Hot air blasts traveling at 300 miles per hour threw both gas and volcanic ash 12 miles high and destroyed 10 million trees.

The avalanche and the mudslide that followed buried parts of the Toutle River Valley to a depth of almost 500 feet. The hot ash and rock started forest fires, ruined crops, and covered cities. Fortunately, the land around the volcano has begun to recover from the eruptions.

Place • Gas and volcanic ash from the eruption of Mount St. Helens vaporized trees and caused widespread devastation as far as 19 miles from the volcano. ▲

North America

Earth's geography changes continually. Sometimes change happens violently, as in the eruption of a volcano such as Mount St. Helens, or the jolt of an earthquake. At other times, change occurs very slowly, as when rain washes away soil, or weather wears down a mountain. All these natural processes affect the physical geography of North America.

TAKING NOTES
Use your chart to take notes about the United States and Canada.

Geographic Features → Economic Strengths/Benefits

productive farmland

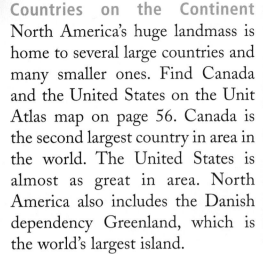

Countries on the Continent
North America's huge landmass is home to several large countries and many smaller ones. Find Canada and the United States on the Unit Atlas map on page 56. Canada is the second largest country in area in the world. The United States is almost as great in area. North America also includes the Danish dependency Greenland, which is the world's largest island.

Mexico, the Central American countries, and the Caribbean island nations, such as Cuba, the Dominican Republic, and Haiti, are part of the continent of North America. These countries, along with the South American nations, make up what is considered Latin America. Find these countries on the Unit 3 Atlas map on page 144. Their heritage differs from that of the United States and Canada. Historically, Latin America owes much of its culture to Spain and Portugal. The United States and Canada were greatly influenced by the British and French. Because of these different cultural heritages, geographers study the United States and Canada separately from Latin America.

GEOGRAPHY SKILLBUILDER:
Interpreting a Map

1. **Region** • Do you think Canada or the United States has the colder climate? Why?
2. **Location** • Where in Canada would you expect to find the most people living? Explain.

Middle Latitudes Most of the United States and Canada is located in the middle latitudes of the northern hemisphere of Earth. This area between the Arctic Circle and the Tropic of Cancer has a temperate climate. It is not as hot as land closer to the Equator. It is not as cold as regions near the North or South Poles. Many plants and animals thrive in this climate. Productive farming enables countries in the middle latitudes to feed large populations.

Human-Environment Interaction • Crops raised in the United States and Canada feed the people of these countries and are exported to other countries all over the world. ▼

A. Analyzing Effects Why do the middle latitudes have a moderate climate?

An Isolated Continent

North America is almost completely surrounded by water. Its landmass stretches from the Arctic Ocean to the Gulf of Mexico and from the Pacific Ocean to the Atlantic Ocean. Find these bodies of water on page 54 of the Unit Atlas.

At one time, these waters isolated North America, or kept it separate from the rest of the world. Unique plants, such as the giant sequoia and the saguaro cactus, and animals, such as the bald eagle and the American alligator, developed in North America.

Region • The bald eagle has been the national bird of the United States since 1782. ▲

The oceans and seas were also a barrier to people. The earliest settlers arrived 12,000 to 35,000 years ago. No other people reached this continent until thousands of years later.

Crossing the Barriers

As people learned more about shipbuilding and navigation, the oceans became a hazardous but passable travel route. Settlers arrived in North America with plants and animals from their home countries. Many of these plants and animals were new to the continent. In some places, these replaced the native plants and animals.

In the 20th century, the distance from other countries helped protect Canada and the United States mainland from attack during the two World Wars. Today, satellites, the Internet, modern transportation, and other technologies link people everywhere.

BACKGROUND

Hawaii, the 50th state of the United States, is a group of volcanic islands in the central Pacific Ocean.

Place • Sailors have used the sextant to navigate their ships since its invention in 1731. ▲

Sacagawea **Sacagawea** (SAK•uh•guh•WEE•uh) was a Shoshone woman who had a vital role in the exploration of what is now the northwestern United States. She guided explorers Meriwether Lewis and William Clark from what is now North Dakota into the Pacific Northwest. They had been sent to explore the newly purchased Louisiana Territory. Sacagawea's husband, French Canadian trapper Toussaint Charbonneau, and their baby son were also on the journey, which lasted from 1804 to 1806.

Sacagawea identified fruits and vegetables for the group to eat and helped the explorers communicate with the Native Americans whom they met along the trail. Historians believe that she was born around 1786 and probably died in 1812.

Regions of the United States and Canada

The United States and Canada share many geographic regions. Find these regions on the Unit Atlas map on page 54.

Atlantic Coastal Plain This region runs along the Gulf of Mexico and the east coast of North America. The region has much rich farmland and some swamps and wetlands.

Appalachian Mountains This 400-million-year-old mountain range lies west of the Atlantic Coastal Plain. These forest-covered mountains have weathered, or worn down, over time.

Central Lowlands West of the Appalachians are the Central Lowlands. They extend west to the Great Plains and are generally flat. The soil is rich, and many farms are located here.

Great Plains The Great Plains have grasslands and few trees. The land gradually rises from the Central Lowlands to the Rocky Mountains. Farmers grow crops and ranchers raise cattle in some areas.

The Rocky Mountains and Coastal Ranges North America's highest mountain ranges lie in the west. They include the Rocky Mountains, the Sierra Nevada and the Cascade ranges of the United States, and the Coast Mountains of Canada. These high, rugged, and heavily forested mountain ranges run along the western part of the continent from Mexico to Alaska.

Intermountain Region Located between the Rocky Mountains and the western coastal mountains, this region is dry and contains plateaus, basins, and deserts. Ranchers raise cattle and sheep in some areas. The Grand Canyon is found here.

Region • The Canadian Rocky Mountains are part of the rugged range that reaches from Mexico to Alaska in western North America. ▼

Region • The Grand Canyon in Arizona is one of the natural wonders of the world. ▼

Canadian Shield or Laurentian Plateau The Canadian Shield covers most of Greenland, curves around the Hudson Bay, and reaches into the United States along the Great Lakes. The central and northwestern part of this huge rocky region has flat plains with hills and lakes. The northeast has high mountains and the south is covered with forests. The shield is rich in minerals, such as iron, gold, copper, and uranium. Most of the land is not farmable and is sparsely populated.

Reading
Social Studies

B. Clarifying
Which regions of Canada and the United States have productive farmland?

Physical Processes That Shaped the Land

Natural processes have shaped North America. Some of the continent's most dramatic landforms were created by the action of wind, water, ice, and moving slabs of Earth's crust. **Landforms** are features of Earth's surface, such as mountains, valleys, and plateaus.

A **glacier** is a thick sheet of ice that moves slowly across land. Thousands of years ago, when Earth was much colder, glaciers covered much of North America. As they flowed across the land, they smoothed out rough surfaces, carved depressions and deep trenches, and piled up rock and dirt. When the ice melted, North America had new valleys, lakes, and hills.

Strange but TRUE

Quakes Shake Central U.S. Lands Usually, earthquakes shake up California and other parts of the western United States. But from December 1811 to February 1812, Mississippi River Valley residents were shocked by several powerful quakes.

The earthquakes changed the Mississippi River's path. Islands disappeared, riverbanks collapsed, and waves capsized boats and drowned people. Farmland was flooded, new lakes appeared, and forests were destroyed. Trees such as this one were uprooted.

Eyewitnesses saw "houses, gardens, and fields . . . swallowed up" in New Madrid, Missouri, in the final quake.

Formation of the Rocky Mountains

INTERACTIVE

Plates collide over millions of years

Main Ranges

Collision causes uplifting of rock layers

Front Ranges

Movement of plate under Pacific Ocean

Movement of North American plate

Region •
The Rocky Mountains were formed 40 to 70 million years ago as a result of a collision between the tectonic plate under the Pacific Ocean and the North American plate. ◄

The Physical Geography of the United States and Canada **73**

The WORLD'S HERITAGE

The St. Lawrence Seaway This seaway, completed in 1959 by Canada and the United States, is one of the largest civil engineering projects ever built. It enables ships to travel 2,340 miles inland from the Atlantic Ocean through locks such as this one, to the Great Lakes. As a result, trade between the United States and Canada and between North America and other continents has improved. Grain, iron ore, and coal are three vital goods shipped on the seaway.

Wind, rivers, and rain wear away soil and stone in a process called **erosion.** Erosion can create magnificent landforms. The Grand Canyon is at least partly the result of millions of years of erosion by the Colorado River. Volcanoes, such as Mount St. Helens, and earthquakes are other natural forces that change the land. All these mighty forces have created landforms across North America.

Waterways

North America has an extensive **river system**, or network of major rivers and their tributaries. The longest rivers are the Mississippi and Missouri rivers in the United States and the Mackenzie River in Canada. Find these rivers on the Unit Atlas map on page 54. When snow melts and rain falls, the water runs down into creeks that collect more water, becoming rivers. North America's rivers empty into bays, oceans, seas, gulfs, lakes, and other rivers.

Vocabulary

gulf: large area of a sea or ocean partially enclosed by land

---

SECTION 1 ASSESSMENT

Terms & Names

1. Explain the significance of:
   (a) Sacagawea
   (b) landform
   (c) glacier
   (d) erosion
   (e) river system

Using Graphics

2. Use a Venn diagram like the one shown, to compare two geographic regions of North America.

   Region 1   Both   Region 2

Main Ideas

3. (a) Describe North America's location on Earth and tell how this affects its climate and plant and animal life.

   (b) What barriers prevented plants, animals, and people from reaching North America? How were the barriers overcome?

   (c) What processes of nature help to shape the land?

Critical Thinking

4. **Making Inferences**

   What natural features of North America attracted people from other lands? Support your conclusion with details from the text.

   Think About
   • the natural resources
   • the climate

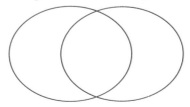
ACTIVITY -OPTION-

List two regions of North America. Describe in a few words the kinds of plants, animals, and jobs that are found in each.

74 CHAPTER 3

A Rich Diversity in Climate and Resources

TERMS & NAMES
weather
precipitation
climate
vegetation
economy

MAIN IDEA

A region's climate, vegetation, and natural resources are contributing factors to economic activities.

WHY IT MATTERS NOW

The prosperity of people living in the United States and Canada affects the prosperity of the modern global economy.

DATELINE

ST. LOUIS, MISSOURI, U.S.A., OCTOBER 7, 1993—The worst flood in United States history is finally over. Heavy, almost continuous rain fell on much of the upper Midwest. In St. Louis, where the Mississippi and Missouri rivers meet, the flooding began in April and continued for six months.

The disaster affected nine states. Tens of thousands of people had to leave their homes. More than 10,000 homes were destroyed, and 50 people lost their lives.

Human-Environment Interaction • At least 75 towns are under water as a result of the flooding. ▲

Climate and Vegetation

The flood of 1993 was caused by unusual **weather.** Weather is the state of the atmosphere near Earth at a given time and place. It includes temperature, wind, and **precipitation,** or moisture such as rain or snow that falls to Earth. **Climate** is the typical weather in a region over a long period of time. A region's climate helps determine what types of **vegetation**—trees, shrubs, grasses, and other plants—will grow there.

TAKING NOTES
Use your chart to take notes about the United States and Canada.

Geographic Features → Economic Strengths/ Benefits → productive farmland

The Dust Bowl Disaster From 1931 to 1939, the southern Great Plains suffered one of the worst droughts in U.S. history. In the 1920s, farmers used up the soil's natural nutrients, and cattle and sheep ranchers destroyed native grasses by overgrazing. When the drought began, crops died, and there were no plant root systems to hold the soil.

The southern Great Plains became known as the Dust Bowl. By 1934, dust storms of topsoil were causing serious damage in 27 states. Ships 300 miles off the Atlantic Coast were covered by blowing dirt. Thousands of people, like this boy, had to leave their farms.

Vegetation Zones

North America's vegetation zones are determined by the climate and physical geography of each area. It is usually warmer in the south and colder in the north, but physical features such as mountains and oceans also affect the climate. Find these vegetation zones on the map on page 77.

Polar and Tundra Northern Canada and Alaska have cool summers and very cold winters. It is usually above freezing (32°F/0°C) there for only two months each year. Precipitation varies from 4 to 20 inches a year. Much of the ground is frozen all year except for the surface, which thaws in summer.

Forest Forests of conifer (evergreen) and broadleaf trees cover much of Canada and the northwest, northeast, and southeast United States. Precipitation averages between 10 and 80 inches annually. Temperatures vary from mild to cold in different forested areas.

Rain Forest Along the Pacific Coast, precipitation can reach 167 inches each year. Rain forests with trees 300 feet tall grow in these areas. The ground is covered in bushes, small trees, and other plants. Moss and lichen are the smallest vegetation. One acre of rain forest might have 6,000 pounds of these tiny plants. The temperature is moderate even in the north, seldom falling below 32°F in winter.

Grassland The center of North America is covered by grasslands. The prairie in the Mississippi Valley may get 30 inches or more of precipitation each year. Grasses are tall and thick. Farther west, the land gets less rainfall—as little as 15 inches in Alberta, Canada—and the grass is shorter. People grow grain and raise cattle in these areas.

Desert The deserts of the American Southwest get less than 10 inches of precipitation a year. Plants in the deserts must be able to endure harsh sun, high temperatures, and little rain. Only the hardiest bushes, shrubs, a few small trees, and cacti survive there.

Vocabulary
lichen (LY•kuhn): organism that grows with algae on rocks or tree trunks

Reading
Social Studies

A. Recognizing Effects How do climate and geography influence the attraction of people to an area?

Vegetation Zones of Canada and the United States

INTERACTIVE

GEOGRAPHY SKILLBUILDER: Interpreting a Map

1. **Region** • What kind of vegetation zone covers most of Canada?
2. **Region** • What part of the United States is covered by temperate grassland?

ARCTIC OCEAN

ALASKA (U.S.)

Baffin Bay

Hudson Bay

CANADA

PACIFIC OCEAN

UNITED STATES

ATLANTIC OCEAN

Gulf of Mexico

Tropic of Cancer

MEXICO

Caribbean Sea

HAWAII (U.S.)

PACIFIC OCEAN

| 0 | 50 | 150 miles |
| 0 | 50 | 150 kilometers |

Legend

- Temperate rain forest
- Tropical rain forest
- Tropical grassland
- Desert and dry shrub
- Temperate grassland
- Mediterranean shrub
- Deciduous and mixed forest
- Coniferous forest
- Tundra
- Icecap

| 0 | 250 | 500 miles |
| 0 | 250 | 500 kilometers |

Natural Wealth

The United States and Canada are rich in natural resources. This wealth has influenced their economic development.

Land and Power Resources The farmlands of the midwestern United States and the prairies in the central provinces of Canada have rich soil. Forests are found in western Canada and the northwestern, northeastern, and southeastern United States. There are oil fields in Alberta, Canada; in Texas, California, Louisiana, Oklahoma, and Alaska; and in the Gulf of Mexico. Coal is in Canada's western provinces; in the Appalachian Mountains; and in Illinois, Indiana, and Wyoming.

Water Resources Water routes affect where people and industry are located. Settlers in North America followed rivers to areas where fresh water and good soil permitted farming and raising cattle. Businesses grew in new communities. People still use rivers to ship natural resources, such as timber and coal, and as trade and travel routes. Fishing is a food source and an industry. Rivers and lakes supply water and power, and offer recreational activities.

Region • The Mississippi River has been an important commercial shipping route for more than a century. ▼

BACKGROUND

The Mississippi River is the largest river in North America. From its source, Lake Itasca in Minnesota, to its mouth in the Gulf of Mexico, it flows for 2,350 miles. The name *Mississippi* is from the Native American Algonquian language and means "Big River."

Spotlight on CULTURE

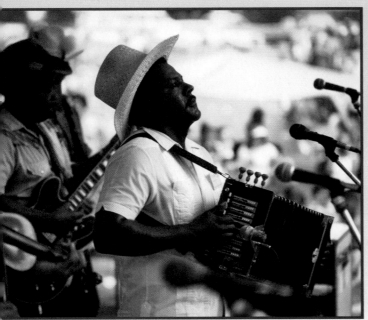

The Cajuns: Americans with Canadian Roots The French settled in Acadia, which is now Nova Scotia, Canada, in 1604. The British gained control of much of Nova Scotia, and in 1755, they expelled most French Acadians. Many of the displaced settlers relocated to southern Louisiana, which was under the rule of France at that time.

Known as Cajuns, the descendants of those French Canadians share a special cultural heritage. Their language has French, English, Spanish, German, and Native American influences. Their unique music is played with fiddles, accordions, and guitars. The man shown at left plays the accordion at a Cajun music festival in Louisiana.

THINKING CRITICALLY

1. **Recognizing Effects** What effect did Britain's rule over Nova Scotia have on the French in Acadia?

2. **Recognizing Important Details** What are some features of the Cajun culture?

For more on the Cajuns, go to ⓘ **RESEARCH LINKS** CLASSZONE.COM

Neighbors and Leaders

More than 200 million people cross the U.S.-Canadian border every year. Trade between the two countries exceeds $1 billion a day. They cooperate on issues as diverse as national security and defense, the environment, air traffic, and fishing regulations. A United States president described the relationship between these countries.

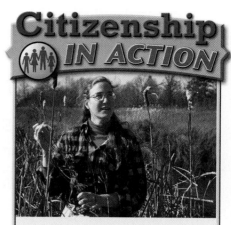

Citizenship IN ACTION

The Nature Conservancy The Conservancy works with communities to protect natural areas, plants, and animals. It has safeguarded 12 million acres and 1,400 land preserves, such as this one, in the United States. In its Great Lakes Program, and in Minnesota, the Conservancy is working with Canadian and U.S. groups to protect wildlife and 10,000 acres of the last tallgrass prairie on the U.S.-Canadian border.

A VOICE FROM THE UNITED STATES

Geography has made us neighbors, history has made us friends, economics has made us partners, and necessity has made us allies.

John F. Kennedy

Reading
Social Studies

B. Finding Causes
What common interests make the United States and Canada allies and partners?

Both countries have strong economies and are leaders in world trade. An **economy** is the way that business owners use resources to provide the goods and services that people want.

SECTION 2 ASSESSMENT

Terms & Names

1. Explain the significance of:
   (a) weather
   (b) precipitation
   (c) climate
   (d) vegetation
   (e) economy

Using Graphics

2. Make a chart such as this one to list details about vegetation zones of the United States and Canada.

Polar and Tundra	Forest	Rain Forest	Grassland	Desert

Main Ideas

3. (a) How do climate and geography affect vegetation?

   (b) What natural resources are found in North America?

   (c) How have waterways affected settlement and development in the United States and Canada?

Critical Thinking

4. **Drawing Conclusions**

   How does the variety of vegetation zones affect the economies of the United States and Canada?

Think About
   - crops and resources found in each vegetation zone
   - world economy

ACTIVITY -OPTION- Choose one of the vegetation zones discussed in the section. Draw a **picture** showing what the land looks like.

Reading a Physical Map

▶▶ Defining the Skill

Physical maps show the natural features of Earth's surface. These include landforms such as mountains, hills, and plains; and bodies of water such as rivers, lakes, bays, and oceans. Land elevation may be shown in a map key. National boundaries and major cities may also be included.

▶▶ Applying the Skill

The physical map below shows the natural features of Canada. Use these strategies to identify the information shown on the map.

How to Read a Physical Map

Strategy ❶ Read the title. It tells you which region's physical features are being represented.

Strategy ❷ Read the key. It tells you the elevation of land each color represents. A map key may also show boundaries between nations, national capitals, and other cities.

Strategy ❸ Read the scale. It tells you how many miles or kilometers each inch on the map represents.

Make a Chart

A chart can help you organize information given on maps. The chart below organizes information from the map on this page.

Canada	
Bodies of Water	Atlantic Ocean, Pacific Ocean, Arctic Ocean, Hudson Bay, Davis Strait, Baffin Bay, Labrador Sea, Beaufort Sea, Mackenzie River, Lake Winnipeg, Saskatchewan River, Lake Superior, Lake Huron, Lake Erie, Lake Ontario, St. Lawrence River, Gulf of St. Lawrence
Landforms	Rocky Mountains, Coast Ranges, Mackenzie Mountains, Canadian Shield, Interior Plains, Laurentian Highlands

▶▶ Practicing the Skill

Turn to page 54 in the Unit 2 Atlas. Study the physical map of North America. Make a chart listing major physical landforms of North America that you see on the map. You may also include a section in your chart labeled "Countries."

Technology: 1971

TER**ACTIVE**

IMAX

Although the IMAX system was first successfully demonstrated during Expo '70 (a world's fair) in Osaka, Japan, it has its roots in Expo '67 in Montreal, Canada. There people flocked to special motion-picture theaters, where they stood in the middle of circular auditoriums to watch images projected on the surrounding walls. What they saw was incredible. Hockey players seemed to skate right through them, and cars seemed to drive over them!

The first permanent IMAX theater was built in Toronto in 1971. Two years later, the first IMAX Dome (also called OMNIMAX) was built in San Diego. Since then, IMAX has developed three-dimensional and high-definition systems and incorporated the technology into amusement-park rides. Because of the size of its frames, an IMAX movie generally has a shorter running time than a standard movie. However, IMAX movies require more film. A typical 45-minute IMAX feature requires nearly 16,000 feet of film!

❶ Dome Early IMAX theaters had flat screens up to eight stories high, but most are now domes up to 100 feet in diameter. When large images are projected, they extend beyond normal peripheral vision—what a person can see without moving his or her eyes—and create the sensation of being in the middle of the action.

❷ Film IMAX movies use what is called the 15/70 format, in which the film has 15 perforations—little holes along the side—per frame and is 70 millimeters wide. This makes each frame ten times larger than conventional 35-millimeter film and accounts for the exceptional size and sharpness of IMAX images.

❸ Projector Because of its size, IMAX film is fed through the projector horizontally in a wavelike motion, or "rolling loop" movement. The newest IMAX systems project film at 48 frames per second, twice the rate of standard movie film, which results in even sharper images.

THINKING Critically

1. Recognizing Effects
How does IMAX make images appear three-dimensional?

2. Drawing Conclusions
Despite the system's technical advantages, IMAX theaters have not been as financially successful as standard movie theaters. Why do you think this is so?

TERMS & NAMES

Explain the significance of each of the following:

1. Sacagawea
2. landform
3. glacier
4. erosion
5. river system
6. weather
7. precipitation
8. climate
9. vegetation
10. economy

REVIEW QUESTIONS

From Coast to Coast *(pages 69–74)*

1. Describe the location of North America.
2. What effect did the oceans have on the settlement of North America?
3. What regions are best for farming and ranching? for mining? for lumber?
4. What natural processes have changed the geography of North America?

A Rich Diversity in Climate and Resources *(pages 75–79)*

5. Why are there different vegetation zones?
6. Which vegetation zones permit farming and ranching?
7. How do natural resources affect the economies of the United States and Canada?
8. How have waterways helped people in the past, and how do they help people today?

CRITICAL THINKING

Synthesizing

1. Using your completed chart from Reading Social Studies p. 68, list the geographic features that contribute to productive farmland and agricultural exports.

Drawing Conclusions

2. Choose one of the regions of the United States and Canada. Think about what you know about the region's natural resources and economics. What do you think are the economic advantages and disadvantages of the region?

Making Inferences

3. What industries that depend on natural resources might flourish in the United States and Canada? Why?

Visual Summary

From Coast to Coast

- North America is located in the middle latitudes and is surrounded on most sides by oceans.
- Various regions, each with its own characteristics, make up the United States and Canada.

A Rich Diversity in Climate and Resources

- The vegetation of North America is affected by both climate and geography.
- Natural resources contribute to the prosperous economies of the United States and Canada.

Use the map and your knowledge of world cultures and geography to answer questions 1 and 2.

Additional Test Practice, pp. S1–S33

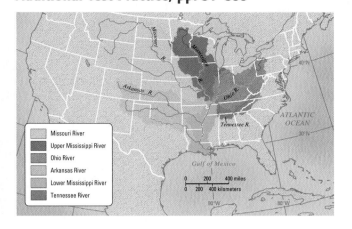

1. Into which body of water or bodies of water does the Mississippi River flow?

   A. Atlantic Ocean

   B. Great Lakes

   C. Gulf of Mexico

   D. Ohio River

2. Which of the following is a major tributary of the Mississippi River?

   A. Atlantic Ocean

   B. Gulf of Mexico

   C. Hudson River

   D. Missouri River

The following passage describes farmers' reactions to the Dust Bowl. Use the quotation and your knowledge of world cultures and geography to answer question 3.

PRIMARY SOURCE

The story of the dust bowl was the story of people—folks who had the courage and fortitude to endure the stress and strain . . . and to emerge scarred but victorious. . . . The vast majority of the residents had come when the land first opened for homesteading. . . . The pioneering days on subsistence farms provided the folks with the know-how to survive depressions and droughts.

PAUL BONNIFIELD, excerpt from *The Dust Bowl: Men, Dirt, and Depression*

3. This passage supports which of the following points of view?

   A. The pioneers should not have tried so hard to farm this land.

   B. The farmers were too weak to continue and would have to give up.

   C. The farmers needed government help to survive the hard times.

   D. The farmers' past experience enabled them to deal with the Dust Bowl.

TEST PRACTICE
CLASSZONE.COM

ALTERNATIVE ASSESSMENT

1. 📝 **WRITING ABOUT HISTORY**

   Jedediah Smith, John Jacob Astor, Alexander Mackenzie, and James McGill were fur traders who traveled across the United States and Canada. Write a journal entry that one of these men might have written about his experience.

   • Use the Internet or other library resources to learn about the journey of one of the fur traders.

   • Write your journal entry from the point of view of the fur trader. You might want to include a map illustrating an important trade route. Show and describe important landmarks along the way.

2. **COOPERATIVE LEARNING**

   With a small group of classmates, prepare and present a television news report on the Lewis and Clark Expedition. One group member can be the news anchor. Other group members can take the roles of reporters, Lewis, Clark, Sacagawea, or Native Americans. As a group, make a list of interview questions. Then share the responsibility of researching to find answers to the questions.

INTEGRATED TECHNOLOGY

Doing Internet Research

The climate and vegetation differ in the several regions of North America. Choose one region and do research to learn about its climate and vegetation. Then use your research to write a report.

• Research online or print encyclopedias, atlases, and almanacs. You might also find articles in periodicals or newspapers.

• Focus your research on how climate and vegetation affect people's lives, the economy, and the history of the region.

For Internet links to support this activity, go to

RESEARCH LINKS
CLASSZONE.COM

CHAPTER 4

The United States Today

Movement Between 1892 and 1943, 17 million immigrants arrived in the United States through Ellis Island in New York Harbor. Today, ferries bring tourists to the Ellis Island Immigration Museum, which commemorates the stories of these immigrants.

How do immigrants contribute to a country's culture?

Hakeem Olajuwon

Itzhak Perlman

Midori

Isabel Allende

Andy Garcia

I. M. Pei

Madeleine Albright

FOCUS ON **GEOGRAPHY**

Movement • In 1998, about 675,000 people immigrated to the United States from around the world. Of these immigrants, 33 percent came from Asia and 20 percent came from Mexico.

This country has been a land of immigrants from its earliest days. People have contributed customs, art, music, languages, foods, and ideas from their homelands to enrich U.S. culture. Violinist Itzhak Perlman, writer Isabel Allende, violinist Midori, actor Andy Garcia, architect I. M. Pei, basketball player Hakeem Olajuwon, and former Secretary of State Madeleine Albright are just a few famous U.S. immigrants.

What do you think?

♦ How do immigrants change and benefit the United States?

♦ What contributions by immigrants have influenced your life?

BEFORE YOU READ

▶▶ *What Do You Know?*

Before you read the chapter, think about how you would describe the United States to a person from another country. What do you and your classmates do for fun? What information could you give about U.S. history, government, economy, and culture? Reflect on your experience and what you have already read or learned about these aspects of the United States. How accurate and complete do you think your knowledge is?

▶▶ *What Do You Want to Know?*

Decide what you want to know about the characteristics of history, government, economy, and culture that make the United States unique. In your notebook, record what you hope to learn from this chapter.

Place • After years of campaigning, women won the right to vote in 1920 when the 19th Amendment to the Constitution was adopted. ▲

READ AND TAKE NOTES

Reading Strategy: Identifying Main Ideas Look for main ideas as you read to help you identify and remember important information. Record the main ideas of this chapter in the chart below.

- Copy the chart into your notebook.

- Notice that each section of Chapter 4 covers a different topic: history, government, economy, and culture.

- As you read each section, look for the main ideas. Use section titles and headings, and find the main idea of each paragraph.

- After you read each section, record what you think are the main ideas about aspects of the United States.

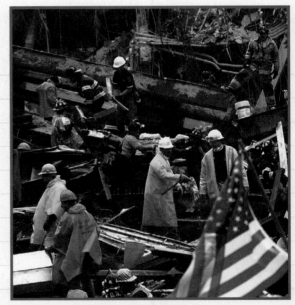

Place • Firefighters and rescue personnel rushed to the scene of the terrorist attacks on New York City's World Trade Center, on September 11, 2001. ▲

The United States Today	
History	
Government	
Economy	
Culture	

We the People

TERMS & NAMES
immigrant
Anasazi
equal opportunity
citizenship
democracy
republic
political process
patriotism

MAIN IDEA	WHY IT MATTERS NOW
Citizens of the United States come from many cultures and share the same rights and responsibilities.	The ideas and values of U.S. immigrants have helped shape the success of the country in the world today.

DATELINE

EXTRA

NEW YORK CITY, 1849

Ships docked today, bringing more people from their Irish homeland to live in the United States. These immigrants have suffered through four years of a deadly potato famine. A blight, or disease, has almost completely destroyed the potato crop every year since 1845. The Irish, especially those who are poor, depend on this crop to survive.

The failure of the potato crop has resulted in the deaths of more than 1 million people—12% of the population of Ireland—from starvation and disease. Today's arrivals join more than 1 million Irish people who are already in the United States.

Movement • Irish immigrants wait to board a ship that will bring them to the United States. ▲

One Country, Many Cultures

Immigrants, such as the Irish, have brought unique contributions to the United States from their homelands all over the world. The United States is sometimes called a "melting pot," a "salad bowl," or a "patchwork quilt" to illustrate how U.S. society combines aspects of many cultures. Some features may blend into the culture of the United States, while others retain their original characteristics.

TAKING NOTES
Use your chart to take notes about the United States today.

The United States Today	
History	
Government	

For example, settlers from Great Britain brought English, the most widely spoken language in the United States. Spanish is often spoken in the Southeast and the Southwest, where people from Spain and Mexico settled. French is heard in Louisiana, which was once held by France. People in the United States enjoy the influence of different groups on their foods, music, sports, and other areas of their lives.

Why People Immigrate An **immigrant** is someone who chooses to move to a new country. They come to the United States for different reasons. Some are escaping from discrimination, persecution, or war. Others leave their homelands because of drought, earthquake, or other natural disasters. Often, people come hoping to improve their economic or educational opportunities.

Reading
Social Studies

A. Summarizing Why have people immigrated to the United States?

People from Many Lands

Over the past 500 years, millions of immigrants have come to the land that is now the United States and Canada. However, this land was inhabited long before they arrived. In fact, people have lived in North America for thousands of years.

The First Americans Native Americans were the first people to inhabit the Western Hemisphere. They came to North America from Eastern Asia, 12,000 to 35,000 years ago. Some groups, such as the Mississippians and **Anasazi** (Navajo for "Ancient Ones"), developed complex civilizations.

The Anasazi civilization developed around A.D. 100 and reached its height in the 11th to 13th centuries. The Anasazi were experts at irrigation. They built homes called cliff dwellings that had from 20 to 1,000 rooms. Remains of these structures survive in the Mesa Verde National Park in Colorado and in other places in the Southwestern United States.

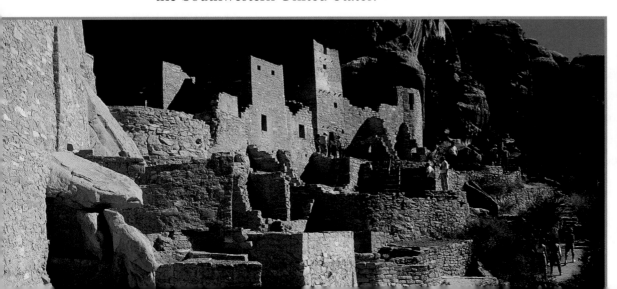

Human-Environment Interaction • **The remains of Anasazi cliff dwellings, such as Cliff Palace in Mesa Verde National Park, are found in the Southwestern United States.** ◄

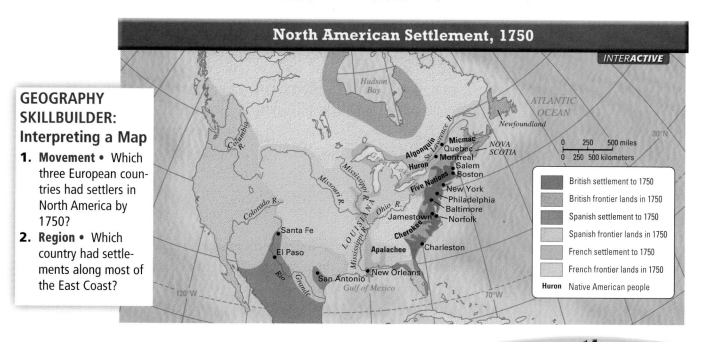

North American Settlement, 1750

INTERACTIVE

Hudson Bay

ATLANTIC OCEAN

Newfoundland

Columbia R.

St. Lawrence R.

Micmac

Algonquin • Quebec — NOVA SCOTIA

Huron • Montreal
• Salem
• Boston

Missouri R.

Five Nations
• New York
• Philadelphia
• Baltimore

Colorado R.

Ohio R.

Jamestown
• Norfolk

• Santa Fe

Cherokee

LOUISIANA

Apalachee • Charleston

Mississippi R.

• El Paso

Rio Grande

• San Antonio • New Orleans

Gulf of Mexico

120°W   70°W

0   250   500 miles
0 250 500 kilometers

British settlement to 1750
British frontier lands in 1750
Spanish settlement to 1750
Spanish frontier lands in 1750
French settlement to 1750
French frontier lands in 1750
Huron Native American people

GEOGRAPHY SKILLBUILDER: Interpreting a Map

1. **Movement** • Which three European countries had settlers in North America by 1750?
2. **Region** • Which country had settlements along most of the East Coast?

The Europeans Arrive European exploration of the Americas began in the late 1400s. Colonists soon followed the explorers. The British settled along the Atlantic coast, in what is now southeastern Canada and the Northeastern United States. Spaniards settled in Florida and came north from Mexico to build towns in the Southwest. Often, the settlers' ways of life and needs for resources conflicted with those of the Native Americans. As the European population grew, competition for land intensified. Europeans often took land from Native Americans. Cultural differences and land disputes led to distrust and war.

Slaves in the Colonies European settlers began to plant and harvest crops and started businesses and towns. This created a demand for cheap labor, so Europeans forced some people to migrate to America.

They had been buying people from slave traders in Africa since the 1500s. Beginning in 1619, enslaved Africans were shipped to the American colonies under such harsh conditions that many died during the journey. Those who survived were bought and sold as property and forced to work for free all their lives. Their children were born into slavery. Although these Africans did not arrive by choice, their labor helped build the country, and their influence is seen in our culture today.

Connections to History

Indentured Servants Indentured servants were immigrants who agreed to work in the colonies for a certain number of years in exchange for passage to America. Their indentures, or contracts, could be bought and sold by employers.

Indentured servants were often forced to work long hours and were sometimes treated very badly. Many did not live long enough to gain their freedom. Most, however, settled in the colonies after completing their contracts.

From Far and Near In the second half of the 1800s, many Chinese immigrants entered the United States. Some worked in mines, while others helped build the transcontinental railroad. In the 1880s and the 1920s, new laws limited the number of U.S. immigrants from various countries. In 1952, legislation again allowed immigrants of all nationalities to become citizens.

Rights of Citizens

Although the United States is among the world's leaders in protecting individual freedom, many U.S. citizens have struggled for their rights. Even after African Americans were freed from slavery in 1865 by the 13th Amendment to the Constitution, they were denied their rights. Women could not vote in the United States until 1920. Native Americans, as well as Hispanics, Asians, the Irish, and other immigrants, have fought against discrimination.

The guarantee of **equal opportunity** in education, employment, and other areas of life has expanded over the years. Today, it is illegal for the government or private institutions to discriminate because of race, gender, religion, age, or disability.

Responsibilities of Citizenship

U.S. citizens' rights come with responsibilities. Citizens should help decide who will run their government and what actions it will take.

Reading Social Studies

B. Making Inferences Do you think citizens of a democracy have greater responsibilities because they have more rights? Explain.

Citizenship IN ACTION

Americans Join Together On September 11, 2001, terrorists hijacked four U.S. planes. They flew two into the twin towers of the World Trade Center in New York City and one into the Pentagon in Washington, D.C. Both towers collapsed, and one wing of the Pentagon was damaged. Thousands of people were killed, and hundreds more were injured or trapped under debris. The fourth plane crashed in Pennsylvania after passengers struggled with the hijackers.

During the crisis, Americans like these rescue workers showed their patriotism and heroism. Hundreds of firefighters, police officers, and medical personnel worked tirelessly, risking their own lives to save others. Citizens and companies across the country donated time, blood, supplies, and millions of dollars to the victims and their families through organizations such as the Red Cross and the United Way. Americans came together in response to the attack on their nation.

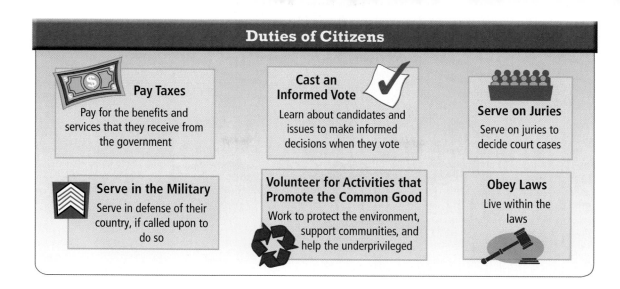

Duties of Citizens

Pay Taxes
Pay for the benefits and services that they receive from the government

Cast an Informed Vote
Learn about candidates and issues to make informed decisions when they vote

Serve on Juries
Serve on juries to decide court cases

Serve in the Military
Serve in defense of their country, if called upon to do so

Volunteer for Activities that Promote the Common Good
Work to protect the environment, support communities, and help the underprivileged

Obey Laws
Live within the laws

Citizenship is a combination of the duties and rights of a citizen. Good citizenship means doing more than the minimum required by law to secure the good of the people.

The Political Process in a Democracy and a Republic In a democracy, government receives its power from the people. **Democracy** is a Greek word that means "rule of the people." In a **republic**, the people also hold power, but they rule through elected representatives. The United States is a republic. The citizens of a democracy or a republic have the responsibility to take part in the political process. The **political process** refers to those legal activities through which citizens can change public policy. By becoming involved, citizens demonstrate their **patriotism,** or love for their country.

Vocabulary

public policy: Actions that a government takes to carry out its responsibilities, such as making laws and creating rules and regulations.

SECTION 1 ASSESSMENT

Terms & Names

1. Explain the significance of:
   (a) immigrant   (b) Anasazi   (c) equal opportunity   (d) citizenship
   (e) democracy   (f) republic   (g) political process   (h) patriotism

Using Graphics

2. Use a chart like this one to list five groups that immigrated to America. List the approximate date they began arriving.

Group	First Arrived

Main Ideas

3. (a) Why do people immigrate to the United States?

   (b) What are some of the rights guaranteed to U.S. citizens by the Constitution?

   (c) What are some responsibilities of U.S. citizens?

Critical Thinking

4. **Draw Conclusions**

   In what ways do the rights and duties of U.S. citizens reflect the ideas of the writers of the Constitution?

   Think About

   • reasons people immigrated to the colonies

   • the way a democracy works

ACTIVITY -OPTION- Think about one of the immigrant populations described. Write and illustrate a **magazine article** about the contributions this group has made to the culture of the United States.

Plan an Earth-Surveying Satellite Mission

Satellites supply scientists with information such as data about Earth's surface, the atmosphere, and the ocean floor. They carry instruments to analyze weather conditions and survey the ozone layer. Satellites measure heat radiation, plant growth, ocean conditions, and other features of our environment. They relay phone calls and TV programs. You and a team of scientists are getting ready to launch a new Earth-surveying satellite.

COOPERATIVE LEARNING On these pages are challenges you will face as you plan your mission. Working in a small group, choose one of the challenges. Divide the work among group members. You will find helpful information in the Data File. Keep in mind that you will present your solution to the class.

LANGUAGE ARTS CHALLENGE

"How can you find these talented people?"

As you plan, you find that you need new team members for several jobs. You need computer scientists and engineers who design instruments to measure data. Experts in forestry, geology, weather, and other fields will interpret the satellite data. How can you find these talented people? Choose one of these options. Use the Data File for help.

ACTIVITIES

1. As part of the satellite team, you give recruitment speeches to science students. Write and deliver a speech explaining what you do, what background and education you needed, and why your job is interesting.

2. Write help-wanted ads for three different jobs. Describe the education, technical background, and personality traits needed for each position.

Engineers working on the satellite. ▲

GEOGRAPHY CHALLENGE

The satellite "swoops around Earth from the North Pole to the South Pole."

An Earth-observation satellite usually follows a sun-synchronous polar orbit. That is, it swoops around Earth from the North Pole to the South Pole, then from the South Pole to the North Pole. How can you make the best use of this satellite path? How can you schedule your work? Choose one of these options. Look for information in the Data File.

ACTIVITIES

1. Your sun-synchronous satellite passes over the equator twice a day—at 10:00 A.M. traveling north to south, at 10:00 P.M. traveling south to north. At what time will the satellite pass over the South Pole? At about what time will the satellite pass over North America? Make a diagram to illustrate the satellite's movement.

2. Suppose you decide instead to put the satellite in orbit above the equator. Plot its course and list the countries and bodies of water it will fly over.

Integral satellite in orbit. ◀

SATELLITE ORBITS

- **High-altitude geosynchronous orbit:** The satellite travels above the equator at a height of about 22,300 miles. It moves at the same speed and in the same direction as Earth is turning. Because the satellite's orbit coordinates with Earth's movement, to an observer on the ground it seems to hover overhead at the same place in the sky.

- **Sun-synchronous polar orbit:** The satellite passes over the north and south poles, circling the globe north to south and south to north in a 24-hour day. As a result, the satellite always crosses the equator at the same local times—say, 2:00 A.M. and 2:00 P.M. As it circles Earth, it makes observations of lands at every latitude.

- **Low-altitude orbit:** The satellite travels within Earth's atmosphere, but in the highest layer, where friction is less because the air is thin.

TYPES OF ARTIFICIAL SATELLITES

- **Earth observation:** map and monitor physical changes on Earth.

- **Scientific research:** gather data for scientists to analyze.

- **Weather:** make local or worldwide observations, depending on orbit; measure cloud patterns, air pressure, air pollution, and air chemistry.

- **Communications:** relay radio, TV, and telephone signals.

- **Navigation:** provide location information.

- **Military:** gather information for military use.

To learn more about Earth-surveying satellites, go to

RESEARCH LINKS
CLASSZONE.COM

Activity Wrap-Up

As a group, review your solution to the challenge you selected. Then present your solution to the class.

A Constitutional Democracy

TERMS & NAMES
United States Constitution
limited government
unlimited government
constitutional amendment
Bill of Rights
federal government

MAIN IDEA

The founders of the United States drafted a constitution that protected the rights of citizens.

WHY IT MATTERS NOW

After more than 200 years, the Constitution continues to protect the freedoms of U.S. citizens.

DATELINE

U.S. SUPREME COURT, MAY 17, 1954—Oliver Brown, an African American, wanted his daughter to attend a nearby all-white school. When the Board of Education in Topeka, Kansas, refused to admit her, Brown went to court. Today, the U.S. Supreme Court ruled that separate schools for different races violate the equal protection guaranteed by the 14th Amendment to the U.S. Constitution.

In 1896, the Supreme Court had allowed states to provide "separate but equal" facilities for blacks and whites. The words in the Constitution remain the same, but changes in society have led to a new interpretation of those words.

Place • Soldiers and police escort students into a formerly all-white school following this Supreme Court ruling. ▲

The Law of the Land

The basis for U.S. law is the **United States Constitution,** written by the country's first leaders. Amazingly, this document remains the foundation for all laws and the framework for the U.S. government more than 200 years after its creation. The Supreme Court decides whether the actions of states, businesses, and individuals are in accordance with the ideas in the Constitution, as it did in this 1954 case.

TAKING NOTES
Use your chart to take notes about the United States today.

The United States Today	
History	
Government	

Forming a New Government American colonists living under British rule did not have the rights and the protections they wanted. After gaining independence from Great Britain in 1783, they established a nation called the United States of America. The writers of the Constitution designed a government that received its power from the people.

Reading
Social Studies

Making Inferences
What were two goals that the writers of the Constitution wanted to achieve?

The founders, or early American leaders, wanted to protect people's individual rights and freedoms from government interference. They also knew that a society needs strong laws and a stable government to ensure the common good. They wrote a constitution that achieved both goals. The U.S. Constitution describes and limits the power of the government and its leaders. It also defines the rights of citizens and their role in governing their country. In 1902, President Theodore Roosevelt explained the relationship between U.S. citizens and their government.

A VOICE FROM THE UNITED STATES

The government is us; we are the government, you and I.

Theodore Roosevelt

Limited and Unlimited Governments

The constitutional republic of the United States is one example of a **limited government.** In other types of government, called **unlimited governments,** the leaders have almost total power. For instance, dictators control their countries' laws and people.

The United States Constitution The U.S. Constitution is the oldest national constitution still in use. It was written in 1787 at the Constitutional Convention in Philadelphia and ratified in 1789. Ideas that shaped the U.S. Constitution came from many places and times, including Great Britain, France, and ancient Rome. Native American nations, such as the Iroquois Confederacy, may also have influenced political ideas at the time that the Constitution was drafted. This painting, *Scene at the Signing of the Constitution of the United States* by H. C. Christy, hangs in the Capitol in Washington, D.C.

Place • Women began the fight for suffrage, or the right to vote, in the early 1800s and continued until they succeeded in 1920. ▲

The Constitution Grows and Changes

The Constitution went into effect in 1789. A condition of ratifying, or approving, it in many states was the promise of a bill of rights. In 1791, the states adopted ten constitutional amendments proposed by Congress. A **constitutional amendment** is a change or addition to the Constitution. This **Bill of Rights** lists specific freedoms guaranteed to every U.S. citizen. Among them are freedom of speech and religion, the right to a fair trial, and the right to gather peaceably. In all, 27 amendments have adapted the Constitution to the country's changing needs. Some amendments passed after the Bill of Rights include ones that ended slavery, gave women the right to vote, and limited a president's terms to two.

Limiting Powers of Government

Leaders of the new country wanted to limit government power and to preserve each state's right to govern itself. To accomplish these goals, they created a federal system in which power is divided between the **federal government**, or national government, and the state governments. The federal government is a republic headed by the President.

Biography

Martin Luther King, Jr. (1929–1968) Reverend King was a civil rights leader in the 1950s and 1960s. A gifted speaker, he argued for voting rights, equal opportunities in education and jobs, and justice not based on the color of people's skin. He expressed these hopes in a famous 1963 speech in Washington, D.C., shown at right.

Influenced by his study of Christianity and his admiration for India's civil rights leader Mahatma Gandhi, Reverend King used nonviolent protest. He received the Nobel Peace Prize in 1964.

On April 4, 1968, he was assassinated. Since 1986, a U.S. holiday has been observed in January to honor him, and he is remembered around the country for his leadership in the civil rights movement.

Places of Interest in Washington, D.C.

GEOGRAPHY SKILLBUILDER:
Interpreting a Map

1. **Location** • On what river is Washington, D.C., located?
2. **Location** • What is the distance between the Capitol, where Congress meets, and the Supreme Court Building?

Federal and State Government The Constitution gives the federal government specific powers, including establishing an army, waging war, raising money through taxes, and making laws to carry out its duties. All other powers are held by the states. The Constitution does not refer to local government, so each state determines the form of town or county rule.

Checks and Balances Three branches share the powers of the U.S. government. Each branch checks the power of the other branches. The process by which a bill, or a proposal for a new law, becomes a law shows how this balance of power works.

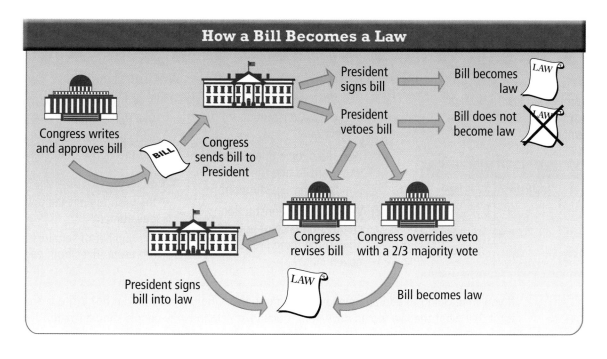

How a Bill Becomes a Law

Congress writes and approves bill → Congress sends bill to President → President signs bill → Bill becomes law

President vetoes bill → Bill does not become law

Congress revises bill → President signs bill into law → LAW

Congress overrides veto with a 2/3 majority vote → Bill becomes law

Three Branches of Government

The Constitution separates powers of government into the executive, legislative, and judicial branches. Each branch has its own job. All are located in the U.S. capital, Washington, D.C.

Executive Branch
Enforces the laws

The Executive Branch The President is elected to head the executive branch. He enforces the laws, serves as commander in chief of the armed forces, and conducts foreign affairs. The Vice-President is elected with the President. The President's cabinet includes the secretaries of the 14 executive departments and other key members of the executive branch.

Legislative Branch
Makes the laws and controls taxes and spending

The Legislative Branch Congress is made up of two houses—the Senate and the House of Representatives—and makes national laws. Two senators are elected from each of the 50 states. The House of Representatives has 435 members, elected from each state according to its population. The two houses have some shared responsibilities and some separate ones.

Judicial Branch
Decides if laws agree with the U.S. Constitution

The Judicial Branch The judicial branch is the system of federal courts that makes sure all laws and treaties are constitutional, or agree with the U.S. Constitution. The highest federal court, the Supreme Court, has nine justices, or judges, nominated by the President and approved by the Senate.

SECTION 2 ASSESSMENT

Terms & Names

1. Explain the significance of:
   (a) United States Constitution
   (b) limited government
   (c) unlimited government
   (d) constitutional amendment
   (e) Bill of Rights
   (f) federal government

Using Graphics

2. Use a diagram like this one to record the organization of the government.

Branches of Government		
Executive	Legislative	Judicial

Main Ideas

3. (a) What two goals did the writers of the U.S. Constitution try to achieve?

   (b) Why did people think it was important to add the Bill of Rights to the Constitution?

   (c) Why does the Constitution create a balance of powers among the three branches of government?

Critical Thinking

4. **Drawing Inferences**

   Why do you think Congress is made up of two parts, the Senate and the House of Representatives?

   Think About
   - the wish to limit the power of government
   - the number of senators and representatives from each state

---

ACTIVITY -OPTION- If you were going to add an amendment to the Constitution, what would it be? Write a **proposal** for it. Tell what the law would do, whom it would affect, and why people should support it.

Sequencing Events

▶▶ Defining the Skill

Sequence is the order in which events follow one another. If you learn to follow the sequence of events through history, you can better understand how events relate to each other.

▶▶ Applying the Skill

This passage at the right describes the sequence of events that improved the transportation of natural resources and goods in the United States. Use the strategies listed below to understand how transportation has improved.

How to Sequence Events

Strategy ❶ Look for time periods of events or discoveries. Some dates may be exact, and others may be indicated only by decades or centuries. Words such as *day, month, year,* or *century* may help you to sequence the events or discoveries.

Strategy ❷ Look for clues about time that allow you to order events according to sequence. Words such as *first, next, later,* and *finally* may help you order events that are not dated.

Make a Time Line

Making a time line can help you sequence events. This time line shows the sequence of events in the passage you just read.

RESOURCES, GOODS, AND PEOPLE

The United States could not have developed without new ways of transporting natural resources and goods. ❶ In the early 19th century, water provided the fastest way to transport goods. Canals linked some lakes and rivers, so places became more ❷ accessible. A little later, steamboats allowed river traffic to go upstream and downstream easily.

❶ By the middle of the century, steam-powered railroads had replaced steamboats because they could reach more places and carry larger loads. At the ❶ beginning of the 20th century, people and goods in many cities and towns were linked by railroad.

❶ In the early 1900s, automobiles and trucks began to move raw materials and goods. Airplanes ❶ began to transport goods in the 1930s. By the ❶ 1950s, paved roads connected much of the country. ❷ Today, fast jets also bring goods and people to many parts of the United States.

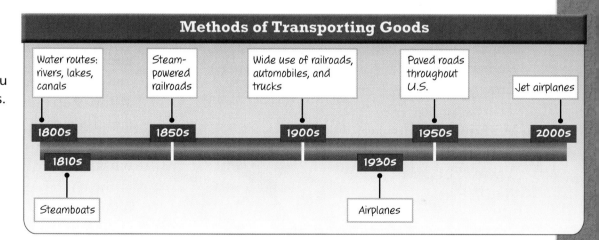

Methods of Transporting Goods

Water routes: rivers, lakes, canals	Steam-powered railroads	Wide use of railroads, automobiles, and trucks	Paved roads throughout U.S.	Jet airplanes
1800s	1850s	1900s	1950s	2000s
1810s			1930s	
Steamboats			Airplanes	

▶▶ Practicing the Skill

Turn to Chapter 4, Section 1, "We the People." Read about the different groups of people who settled the land that became the United States. Make a list showing the sequence of the arrival of different immigrant groups.

WITH A LAND AREA of over 3.7 million square miles and a population of more than 285 million, the United States is an amazingly varied country. From small towns, forests, and farmland to big cities like San Francisco and New York, the United States has a wealth of both human-made and natural features. The poems here celebrate this variety.

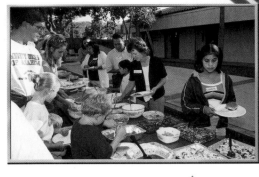

CONEY

By Virginia Schonborg

There's hot corn
And franks.
There's the boardwalk
With lots of games,
With chances
To win or lose.
There's the sun.
Underneath the boardwalk
It's cool,
And the sand is salty.
The beach is
Like a fruitstand of people,
Big and little,
Red and white,
Brown and yellow.
There's the sea
With high green waves.
And after,
There's hot corn
And franks.

KNOXVILLE, TENNESSEE

By Nikki Giovanni

I always like summer
best
you can eat fresh corn
from daddy's garden
and okra
and greens
and cabbage
and lots of
barbecue
and buttermilk
and homemade ice-cream
at the church picnic
and listen to
gospel music
outside
at the church
homecoming
and go to the mountains with
your grandmother
and go barefooted
and be warm
all the time
not only when you go to bed
and sleep

SCENIC ★

By John Updike

O when in San Francisco do
As natives do: they sit and stare
And smile and stare again. The view
Is visible from anywhere.

Here hills are white with houses whence,
Across a multitude of sills,
The owners, lucky residents,
See other houses, other hills.

The meanest[1] San Franciscan knows,
No matter what his past has been,
There are a thousand patios
Whose view he is included in.

The Golden Gate, the cable cars,
Twin Peaks, the Spreckles habitat,[2]
The local ocean, sun, and stars—
When fog falls, one admires *that*.

Here homes are stacked in such a way
That every picture window has
An unmarred prospect of the Bay
And, in its center, Alcatraz.[3]

1. Poorest.

2. In the late 1950s, Twin Peaks was a well-to-do residential neighborhood where a very wealthy family, the Spreckles, lived.

3. An island in San Francisco Bay, site of a former federal prison.

Reading THE LITERATURE

Pick out the words each poet uses to give a sense of place. How can you tell that some places are rural, some urban? What aspects of geography has each poet highlighted?

Thinking About THE LITERATURE

Imagine that you live in one of these places. What kinds of jobs might people have there? What might they do for fun? How does the place where you live influence your daily activities?

Writing About THE LITERATURE

Which of the poems creates the strongest image in your mind? Using examples from that poem, write a short paragraph explaining why.

About the Authors

Virginia Schonborg (b. 1913) was born in Rhode Island and is the author of *The Salt Marsh* and *Subway Swinger.*

Nikki Giovanni (b. 1943) was born in Tennessee and became well-known as a poet in the 1960s.

John Updike (b. 1932), born in Shillington, Pennsylvania, is the author of many short stories, novels, and poems.

Further Reading For more outstanding poems about the United States, read *My America: A Poetry Atlas of the United States*, edited by Lee Bennett Hopkins.

The United States Economy

factors of
production

GDP

free enterprise/
market economy

consumer

profit

competition

MAIN IDEA

The United States has an economy based on free enterprise. Consumers and business owners decide what goods and services to produce.

WHY IT MATTERS NOW

This economic system has made it possible for the United States to become a leader in the worldwide economy.

DATELINE

JUNE 2001, THE UNITED STATES—The collapse of many dot-coms has shaken consumer confidence. Internet-based companies, nicknamed "dot-coms" for the last part of their Web addresses, have been failing by the hundreds.

In the mid-1990s, investors backed dot-com companies in hopes of making a huge return on their investments. This ready money encouraged people with limited management experience, untested technologies, and experimental Web sales strategies to start companies. In 1999, more than 1,700 Internet start-ups were born.

When investors realized that many start-ups were losing money, they began to withdraw their support. Between January 2000 and May 2001, 435 Internet companies shut down. Over 31,000 people have lost their jobs.

Place • When companies fail, employees are often left without jobs and office equipment is sold. ▲

The Study of Economics

Business start-ups and shutdowns, the rise and fall of investor and consumer confidence, the increase and decrease in the number of people without jobs—all of these changes are part of the market economy of the United States. Investors, service providers, manufacturers, and consumers make choices each day, and these choices affect the state of the economy.

TAKING NOTES

Use your chart to take notes about the United States today.

The United States Today	
History	
Government	

102 CHAPTER 4

Goods and Services Suppose you want a CD recording just released by your favorite music group. To earn the money to pay for it, you might rake your neighbor's leaves or care for his or her child for a few hours. The CD is a good. A good is any object you can buy to satisfy a want. Raking leaves or baby-sitting is a service you provide. A service is an action that meets a want. Your neighbor buys your service to meet his or her want.

What to Buy People constantly decide which goods and services to buy. They usually satisfy basic needs such as food, clothing, housing, transportation, childcare, and medical treatment first. If there is money left over, they might choose to spend it on music CDs, in-line skates, a computer game, or a vacation.

A government must also make decisions. Tax dollars must be set aside to pay for police and fire protection, schools, roads, and military forces. Once these expenses have been determined, other choices can be made.

Reading
Social Studies

A. Synthesizing
After a government has set aside money for basic wants, what additional goods or services might it pay for?

A Growing Economy

A nation must produce goods and provide services to support a growing economy. In an expanding economy, citizens have better-paying jobs, so the government collects more tax money. Then people and the government can satisfy more wants.

To sustain a growing economy, business owners must keep production at a high level. Production is the making of goods and services. The four **factors of production** are the ingredients, or elements, needed for production to occur.

Culture • Christina Aguilera's critical contribution in the production of a CD is as one of the labor resources. ▼

Factors of Production for a Music CD

Entrepreneur
(owner of recording studio and factory)

Labor Resources
(musicians, sound technician, producer, factory manager, factory workers)

Natural Resources
(materials to manufacture CDs)

Capital Resources
(recording equipment, studio, factory and manufacturing equipment)

MUSIC CD

Natural Resources Raw materials are used to make goods. Examples include land, water, forests, minerals, soil, and climate.

Labor Resources Workers are needed with the appropriate knowledge, skills, and experience to make goods or provide services.

Capital Resources Machines, factories, and supplies are needed.

Entrepreneurs These are the people who bring natural resources, labor resources, and capital resources together to produce goods and services.

Strange but TRUE

The Value of Money The U.S. Department of the Treasury first issued paper money in 1861. During the Civil War, people hoarded coins. This caused a severe shortage of coins in circulation.

The Bureau of Engraving and Printing printed "fractional currency" bills of 3 cents, 5 cents, 10 cents, 25 cents, and 50 cents. These were the smallest bills ever printed in this country. The largest note was the $100,000 Gold Certificate printed in 1934 and 1935. These notes were used for bank transactions and were not available for the public to use.

The United States Economy

The U.S. economy is one of the wealthiest in the world. One way to measure a country's economy is to look at its **GDP**, or gross domestic product. This tells the total value of the goods and services that a country produces each year. The GDP is also a way to compare the economies of different countries.

U.S. industries include services, such as health care and legal services; communications, such as publishing, television and radio, telephone, and mail delivery; finance, such as banks and stock markets; manufacturing, such as food products, automobiles, and clothing; and electronics, such as televisions, computers, and sound equipment. The success of these industries helps make many Americans wealthier than people in other parts of the world.

BACKGROUND

In 2000, 2.8 billion of the world's 6 billion people lived on less than $2 a day.

Estimated 2000 Per Capita* GDP	
Country	**U.S. Dollars**
United States	36,200
China	3,600
India	2,200
Saudi Arabia	10,500
France	24,400
Zimbabwe	2,500

Per capita means for each person.
Source: *CIA World Factbook*

The Free Enterprise or Market Economy U.S. citizens and businesses make most economic decisions. Business owners control the factors of production. The government plays a limited role. It does not decide which or how many goods are produced. It does not set prices or tell people where to work. These are the qualities of a **free enterprise/market economy**. A market is a setting for exchanging goods and services. In a free enterprise economy, business owners compete in the market with little government interference. Other nations, such as Canada, many countries in Western Europe, Japan, and some Latin American countries, also have market economies.

Culture • The machines that make CDs are a capital resource, one of the four factors of production. ▲

Supply and Demand In a free enterprise or market economy, **consumers**—the people who use goods and services—help decide what will be produced. Prices affect how products are distributed to consumers. For example, suppose a music company produces 1,000 CDs priced at $16.95 each, but 1,100 people want to buy them. There are not enough CDs to satisfy the wants of these consumers. Because demand for the good is greater than the supply, the seller can increase the price to $17.95. He or she sells all the CDs and makes an extra $1.00 profit on each. The seller, like all entrepreneurs, wants to increase profit. **Profit** is the money that remains after all the costs of producing a product have been paid.

Now suppose the seller offers 1,000 more CDs at the original $16.95 price. One hundred sell right away, leaving 900 CDs that no one wants at this price. The seller then reduces the price to $15.95. Consumers who didn't want the CD at $16.95 may want it at this lower price. Because the supply of the good is greater than the demand, the seller must reduce the price.

Supply and Demand

8 Price increases and demand falls.

1 Price is high.

2 Producer wants to increase supply.

3 More goods push price down.

4 Demand increases.

5 Producer increases supply.

6 Price decreases again.

7 Producer supplies fewer goods.

Culture • Stores compete in malls and online to attract consumers. They use advertising and appealing store displays to catch the attention of potential customers. ▲

Supply and demand explain how price and availability are affected by how much consumers are willing to pay for an item and how much the seller decides to charge for it. The number of CDs offered at each price is the supply. The number of CDs that people will buy at each price is the demand.

Competition In a free enterprise or market economy, many businesses produce similar goods or services. There is competition to attract consumers. **Competition** is the rivalry among businesses to sell goods to consumers and make the greatest profit. To achieve these goals, a company may offer an improved product, manufacture it more cheaply, or sell it at a better price.

Other Economic Systems

Most countries combine features from three types of economic systems: market, command, and traditional economies.

Command Economy In this system, the government decides how many of which goods are produced and sets the prices. Countries, such as North Korea and Cuba with Communist governments, have command economies. China has elements of market and command economies.

Traditional Economy In this system, social roles and culture determine how goods and services are produced, what prices and individual incomes are, and which consumers are allowed to buy certain goods. For instance, a family's status may determine whether they can own a tractor. Farmers may give much of their produce to community leaders. India has features of both market and traditional economies.

Reading
Social Studies

B. Making Inferences Why might countries combine features of different economic systems?

The Global Economy

Today, more countries than ever before have market economies. Communication and transportation are fast and dependable, making trade easier among countries. The movement of people, goods, and ideas around the world has helped build a global, or worldwide, economy in which the United States is a leader. Expanding trade can open new markets and keep prices low and quality high for consumers. U.S. citizens buy many cars and clothes from other countries that take part in the global economy.

World Trade Partners of the United States, 2000

NAFTA – 32.9%
East Asia NICs* – 19.8%
European Union – 19.3%
Japan – 10.6%
Latin America – 7.8%
Middle East – 2.9%
Africa – 1.9%
East Europe and Former Soviet Union – 1.1%
India – 0.4%

* Newly industrialized countries:
China, Hong Kong, Indonesia,
Malaysia, Singapore, South Korea,
Taiwan, Thailand

Source: U.S. Dept. of Commerce,
International Trade Summary, 1998–2001

ATLANTIC OCEAN
PACIFIC OCEAN
PACIFIC OCEAN
INDIAN OCEAN

0   3,000 miles
0   3,000 kilometers

GEOGRAPHY SKILLBUILDER:
Interpreting a Map

1. **Movement** • Who are the largest U.S. trade partners?
2. **Movement** • With which countries or regions does the United States trade least?

Trade Barriers Sometimes countries establish barriers to restrict trade because they prefer to produce their own goods or services. Tariffs, or taxes on imported goods, raise the price to the consumer and make it more difficult for other countries to compete.

In 1994, NAFTA, the North American Free Trade Agreement, reduced trade barriers among the United States, Canada, and Mexico. There was concern that companies would move factories to Mexico, where workers earn less, and U.S. workers would lose jobs. However, many economists believe free trade benefits all three countries.

SECTION 3 ASSESSMENT

Terms & Names
1. Explain the significance of:
   (a) factors of production
   (b) GDP
   (c) free enterprise/market economy
   (d) consumer
   (e) profit
   (f) competition

Using Graphics
2. Use a chart like this one to take notes on the characteristics of free enterprise/market, command, and traditional economies.

Free Enterprise/ Market Economy	Command Economy	Traditional Economy

Main Ideas
3. (a) How is the price of goods decided in the U.S. economic system?

   (b) What are the four factors of production?

   (c) What role does government have in the U.S. market economy?

Critical Thinking
4. **Making Inferences**
   What effect will reducing trade barriers between countries have on the price of goods? Explain.

   Think About
   • the characteristics of a free enterprise/market economy
   • competition

ACTIVITY -OPTION- Write an **advertisement** for a new business showing the goods or services it will produce. Make a chart showing the type of materials, labor, and capital you will need to produce the product.

The Legacy of North America

Telephones

In 1876, the Scottish-born American Alexander Graham Bell (1847–1922) invented the telephone. Telephones have come a long way since Bell's day. Today, caller identification, automatic redialing, and call waiting are common telephone services. Cordless phones, mobile phones, and the Internet allow people throughout the world to communicate over great distances.

Lacrosse

Native peoples of North America played an early version of lacrosse long before Columbus landed. Players used a racket, now known as a crosse, to throw a hard ball down the field and into the opposing team's goal. Today, lacrosse is a popular sport not only in North America but also in Ireland, Australia, and South Africa. Men's teams play for the ILF World Championship, and women's teams compete for the World Cup.

Airplanes

In 1903, Wilbur (1867–1912) and Orville (1871–1948) Wright achieved the first powered, sustained flight near Kitty Hawk, N.C. The flight lasted 12 seconds and reached a height of 120 feet. By the 1920s, aviation had become a booming industry. Today, jumbo and supersonic jets allow people to travel around the world in just a day or two. More than 1.5 billion passengers land and take off at the world's 50 busiest airports every year.

Find Out More About It!

Study the text and photos on these pages to learn about inventions, creations, and contributions that have come from North America. Then choose the item that interests you the most and do research in the library or on the Internet to learn more about it. Use the information you gather to construct a model of the item you choose.

RESEARCH LINKS
CLASSZONE.COM

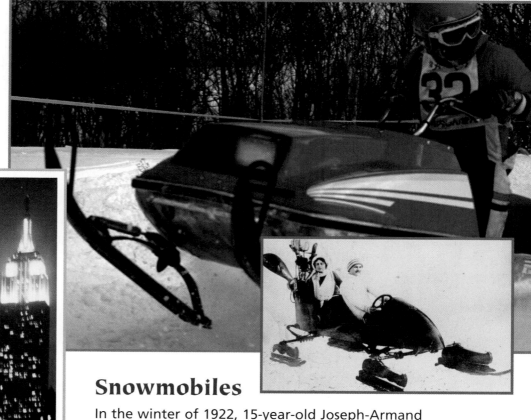

Skyscrapers

In the late 1800s, U.S. architects and engineers worked together to build the first skyscrapers in Chicago and New York City. Today, these enormous structures rise in cities all over the world. The tallest skyscrapers in the world are the Petronas Towers in Kuala Lumpur, Malaysia, which reach a height of 1,483 feet.

Snowmobiles

In the winter of 1922, 15-year-old Joseph-Armand Bombardier of Canada invented the first crude snowmobile by attaching a car engine to sleigh runners and adding a wooden propeller to the back. In 1935, he refined his invention after his young son died from appendicitis because they couldn't make it through the snow to the hospital in time. Today, people around the world use snowmobiles for winter fun, and people in the remote north depend on them for transportation when the snows are deep.

United States Culture: Crossing Borders

TERMS & NAMES
value
globalization
technology

MAIN IDEA

The American way of life reflects the cultures of people from many countries around the world.

WHY IT MATTERS NOW

People around the world are more closely connected than ever before.

DATELINE

NEW YORK CITY, 1905—Visit Gennaro Lombardi's pizzeria—the first in the United States—to try a pizza. This baked, flat pie has a bread crust covered with cheese, tomato sauce, and seasonings.

Lombardi's pizzas are not exactly like the pizzas made in Naples, Italy, because different seasonings, flour, and cheese are available here. Also, instead of using sliced tomatoes like those put on Italian pizzas, Lombardi adds a spicy homemade tomato sauce. Customers say this pizza is as good as any from Naples. Judging by the warm reception it has received so far, pizza may become a popular U.S. food.

Place • Pizza, brought here by Italian immigrants, is becoming a popular food. ▲

American Way of Life

People in the United States have brought diverse customs, traditions, and foods, like pizza, from their homelands, but they share many of the same values. **Values** are the principles and ideals by which people live. U.S. citizens care about individual freedoms; equal opportunities for jobs and education; fair treatment of people regardless of race, religion, or gender; and private ownership of property. Many of these values are part of the U.S. Constitution and help define American culture.

TAKING NOTES
Use your chart to take notes about the United States today.

The United States Today	
History	
Government	

Education U.S. citizens believe they can improve their lives through education. In 1647, Massachusetts established the first colonial public school system. Today, state laws require that all children attend school or be taught at home until they are at least 16. More than 99 percent of U.S. children finish elementary school, and more than 85 percent complete high school.

U.S. Religions About 70 percent of all U.S. citizens are members of religious groups. Many colonists, such as British Protestants and Catholics, settled in America so that they could worship as they wished. Since then, people with many different religious beliefs have come to the United States. Most Spanish, French, and Italian immigrants were Catholic. In the 1900s, many European Jews settled in the United States. Asian immigrants practice Buddhism and Hinduism. North Africans and Southwest Asians brought Islam. Many Native Americans continue to practice their ancestors' religions.

Reading
Social Studies

Drawing Conclusions
Why do you think values such as freedom of religion were written into the U.S. Constitution?

The Arts and Entertainment

Leisure activities in the United States reflect the influence of other cultures. For example, sports such as tennis, golf, soccer, and even baseball originated in other countries. Tennis came from France, golf from Scotland, and soccer from England. Baseball is probably based on rounders, a game played in Great Britain in the late 1700s. Basketball was invented in the United States by a Canadian and later spread to other countries. Football is played chiefly in the United States and Canada.

Culture • Baseball, often called America's national pastime, was probably adapted from a British game played in the 1700s. ▲

The movie and television industries and certain musical forms, such as rock 'n' roll, developed in the United States, although they were affected by other cultures. Jazz was greatly influenced by the blues, which is rooted in spirituals once sung by enslaved Africans. Today, artists and audiences around the world enjoy these American musical styles.

Place •
Americans eat foods from the traditions of many countries, such as Japanese sushi and sashimi. ▼

Globalization of Culture The international popularity of U.S. music is an example of the globalization of culture. **Globalization** means spreading around the world. Today, cultural influences often cross national boundaries. People around the world enjoy blue jeans, sodas, and fast food from the United States. McDonald's serves about 45 million people a day in 121 countries.

U.S. citizens eat Japanese sushi, listen to Italian operas, and drive South Korean cars. Literature from many nations is translated into different languages. Print and electronic communication, television, movies, and the Internet provide speedy ways to share the products and creations of different cultures.

U.S. Science and Technology

U.S. scientists are mapping DNA, discovering treatments and cures for diseases, and finding new energy sources for industry and homes. Once discoveries are made, inventors create **technology,** such as tools or equipment, to apply the new knowledge in practical ways. Modern technology enables U.S. scientists to work with other scientists from around the world.

Science and Technology Change the World Discoveries by U.S. scientists help people throughout the world. Polio, a disease that usually affects children, was widespread in the 1940s and 1950s.

BACKGROUND

DNA is the molecule that carries the information that determines the characteristics of every living thing. It was first identified by Francis Crick, James Watson, and others in 1953.

Spotlight on CULTURE

Skyscrapers The skyscraper originated in the United States in the 1870s and has caught on in other countries. Limited space in cities, plus materials and technology, such as steel and elevators, have inspired architects to design taller buildings.

The height of each building is measured from the ground-level main entrance to the structural top, including spires but not antennas or flagpoles. Today, many of the tallest buildings are located outside the United States in places such as Kuala Lumpur, Malaysia, and Hong Kong and Shanghai in China.

World's Tallest Skyscrapers

Height in Feet

Name	Petronas Towers	Sears Tower	Jin Mao Building	Plaza Rakyat	Empire State Building	Central Plaza	Bank of China
City	Kuala Lumpur	Chicago	Shanghai	Kuala Lumpur	New York	Hong Kong	Hong Kong
Year Built	1998	1974	1998	1999	1931	1992	1989

THINKING CRITICALLY

1. **Finding Causes**
   What were two factors that led architects to design skyscrapers?

2. **Recognizing Important Details**
   How is building height measured?

For more on skyscrapers, go to

RESEARCH LINKS
CLASSZONE.COM

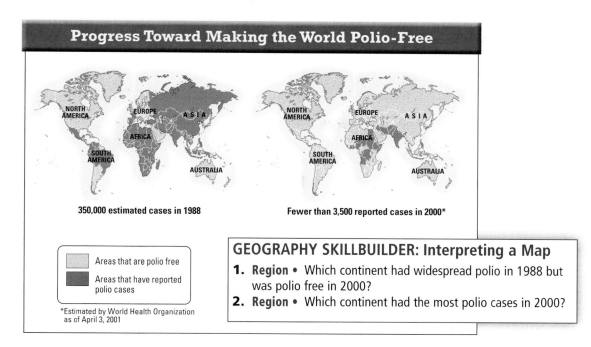

Progress Toward Making the World Polio-Free

350,000 estimated cases in 1988

Fewer than 3,500 reported cases in 2000*

Areas that are polio free

Areas that have reported polio cases

*Estimated by World Health Organization as of April 3, 2001

GEOGRAPHY SKILLBUILDER: Interpreting a Map

1. **Region** • Which continent had widespread polio in 1988 but was polio free in 2000?
2. **Region** • Which continent had the most polio cases in 2000?

Then, U.S. doctors Jonas Salk and Albert Sabin each developed a different vaccine. As a result, great progress has been made toward making the world free of polio.

Negative effects of technology include increased pollution of the environment and the loss of unique cultural features as countries share languages, foods, and customs. Poorer nations may lack the money and skilled labor needed to benefit from new applications of science.

SECTION 4 ASSESSMENT

Terms & Names

1. **Explain the significance of:** (a) value   (b) globalization   (c) technology

Using Graphics

2. Make a chart like the one below to show features of U.S. culture and science that have spread to other parts of the world.

U.S. Culture and Science Around the World	
Culture	Science and Technology

Main Ideas

3. (a) What are some values shared by people in the United States?

   (b) What are some examples of contributions from other cultures to the American way of life?

   (c) In what ways does American culture influence people in other countries?

Critical Thinking

4. **Forming and Supporting Opinions**

   Do you think globalization has a positive or a negative effect on the world? Support your opinion.

Think About

   ◆ the effects of globalization
   ◆ the changes caused by international trade and communication
   ◆ the effects of scientific discoveries worldwide

ACTIVITY -OPTION-

Reread "The Arts and Entertainment" on page 111. Think about the sports, music, and movies you enjoy. Write an **essay** describing how the cultures of other countries influence your activities.

TERMS & NAMES

Explain the significance of each of the following:

1. immigrant
2. citizenship
3. democracy
4. political process
5. United States Constitution
6. Bill of Rights
7. factors of production
8. free enterprise/ market economy
9. value
10. globalization

REVIEW QUESTIONS

We the People *(pages 87–91)*

1. What are some reasons that people have immigrated to the United States?
2. What are some responsibilities of citizens of the United States?

A Constitutional Democracy *(pages 94–98)*

3. What were the goals of the early leaders when they wrote the United States Constitution?
4. What were the leaders attempting to do when they set up a system of checks and balances within the federal government?

The United States Economy *(pages 102–107)*

5. What are examples of wants that a government must fund?
6. How does each factor of production contribute to the making of a product?

United States Culture: Crossing Borders *(pages 110–113)*

7. What can you conclude from the fact that cultural values were directly stated in the U.S. Constitution?
8. If globalization continues, how will it affect the cultures of the world?

CRITICAL THINKING

Synthesizing

1. Using your completed chart from Reading Social Studies, p. 86, explain why the economy, form of government, and cultural values of the United States continue to attract so many immigrants each year.

Forming and Supporting Opinions

2. Martin Luther King, Jr., fought against laws he thought were unjust. How was this good citizenship? Explain.

Making Inferences

3. What were the major concerns of the leaders who wrote the U.S. Constitution and how did they address them?

Visual Summary

1 **We the People**
- The United States is made up of immigrants from many countries.
- U.S. citizens share many rights and responsibilities.

A Constitutional Democracy 2
- After the American colonists gained independence, they wrote a Constitution that created a limited government and protected their rights and freedoms.

The United States Economy 3
- The United States has a free enterprise/market economy.
- Because more countries have market economies, a global economy is developing with expanded trade among nations.

United States Culture: Crossing Borders 4
- Americans believe in strong values, many of which are protected by the U.S. Constitution.
- American culture has been shaped by many groups and now influences the cultures of other nations.

Use the map and your knowledge of world cultures and geography to answer questions 1 and 2.

Additional Test Practice, pp. S1–S33

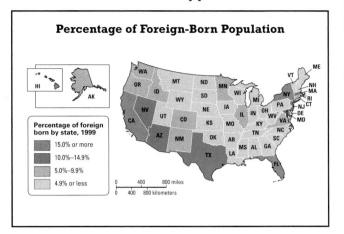

Percentage of Foreign-Born Population

Percentage of foreign born by state, 1999

- 15.0% or more
- 10.0%–14.9%
- 5.0%–9.9%
- 4.9% or less

0   400   800 miles
0   400   800 kilometers

1. Which states have the highest percentage of foreign-born people?

A. Alaska, Colorado, Oregon, Washington

B. Arizona, Maryland, Nevada, Texas

C. Arkansas, Iowa, Louisiana, Mississippi

D. California, Florida, Hawaii, New York

2. Where are most states with a high percentage of foreign-born people located?

A. On the coasts or borders

B. In the southeast region

C. In the central region

D. Only by the northern border

This quotation is from a presentation made to high school and middle school students. Use the quotation and your knowledge of world cultures and geography to answer question 3.

PRIMARY SOURCE

[Martin Luther King day] is America's celebration.
It is each of our individual's day of celebration.
It is a moment of rejoicing for all Americans.
It is a moment of reflection for all Americans.
It is a moment of renewal on our long diversity journey.
It is a moment of challenge for each of us.

  FRANK A. BLETHEN, Publisher, *The Seattle Times,* from a presentation on January 17, 2003

3. Which of the following best expresses the point of view of the passage?

A. The holiday can be both an individual and a group holiday.

B. The holiday contradicts the basic values of the U.S. Constitution.

C. The holiday is a time set aside only for celebration.

D. It is not necessary for all Americans to celebrate or observe the day.

TEST PRACTICE
CLASSZONE.COM

ALTERNATIVE ASSESSMENT

1. **WRITING ABOUT HISTORY**

The music of other cultures has influenced many of the forms of music enjoyed in the United States and many American musicians. Write a biography of a favorite musician of today or from the past.

- Research the musician to learn what musical influences shaped his or her work. Find out if these influences were from other cultures or times.
- If possible, include copies of photographs with captions to accompany your biography.

2. COOPERATIVE LEARNING

With a group of four to six classmates, think of a natural event such as a flood, drought, or storm that affected your community or your region of the country. Research the event and interview people who remember it. Create a display about the event, explaining its causes and its effects on the area. Share the responsibilities of researching, interviewing, and creating drawings, models, or diagrams.

INTEGRATED TECHNOLOGY

Doing Internet Research

Use the Internet, as well as other sources in the library, to learn about the Constitutional Convention. Write a report of your findings.

- You might research historic documents or biographies of the founding fathers to find information about process of creating the Constitution.
- In your research, find out what the specific concerns of the small and large states were and how they differed. Explore how a compromise was reached that allowed the convention to draft the Constitution.
- You might use a chart or graph to present information about the different proposals and the final compromise.

For Internet links to support this activity, go to

RESEARCH LINKS
CLASSZONE.COM

Canada Today

CANADA

ATLANTIC

PACIFIC OCEAN

PACIFIC OCEAN

OCEAN

INDIAN OCEAN

How does a country's geography influence its culture?

Region • In 1989, the Canadian Museum of Civilization opened in Hull, Quebec, on the banks of the Ottawa River. The museum celebrates the geographic and cultural diversity of Canada. Douglas Cardinal, an architect from Calgary, Alberta, and a descendant of the Canadian Blackfoot people, designed the two distinct buildings. He wanted them to reflect Canada's landforms.

The structures evoke the glaciers and rocky formations of the western Canadian Shield. The limestone from which the walls are made comes from the province of Manitoba. Totem poles carved from red cedar trees by First Nations people of British Columbia line the museum entrance.

What do you think?

♦ How are the varied landforms and resources of Canada represented in the museum?

♦ Describe some geographic features in the area where you live. Explain how they affect the traditions and activities of people in your community.

Region Hudson Bay, a huge body of water in northeast Canada, is home to ice floes nine months of the year. Nevertheless, the bay is open to shipping throughout the year.

BEFORE YOU READ

▶▶ *What Do You Know?*

Before you read this chapter, consider what you know about Canada. Have you ever read that Canada has the world's longest coastline? Did you know that Canada is an independent democracy with a constitution, yet it pledges loyalty to the British monarch? Perhaps you know that 60 percent of the National Hockey League's players are Canadian? Recall what you have learned about Canada from personal experience, television, and other classes. Think about how Canada is similar to the United States and how it is different.

▶▶ *What Do You Want to Know?*

Decide what you would like to know about Canada's history, government, economy, and culture. In your notebook, record what you hope to learn from this chapter.

Culture • The art of totem pole carving almost disappeared in the mid-1800s. Museums began to preserve totem poles in the 1850s. ▼

READ AND TAKE NOTES

Reading Strategy: Analyzing Causes and Effects To help you understand how geographic, historical, and cultural factors have influenced Canada's development, pay attention to causes and effects as you read Chapter 5. Notice that several factors may cause the same effect. Use the chart below to make connections between statements about geography, history, and culture and statements describing Canada today.

- Copy the chart into your notebook.
- On the chart, read statements describing issues and conditions in Canada today (effects).
- As you read the chapter, identify the effects of the listed causes and note them on the chart.

Culture • The 1893 Montreal Amateur Athletic Association was the first hockey team to win the Stanley Cup. ▲

Causes		Effects
Early settlers were from France and Britain, two nations that had conflicts.		
French-speaking Canadians have kept their own language and culture separate from the rest of the nation.	→	
The people of First Nations and other culture groups want to preserve their traditions.		
Cold climate, geographic barriers, and poor soil exist in northern parts of Canada.	→	
The Arctic Ocean and Hudson Bay are frozen for most of the year.	→	
Landforms such as the Rocky Mountains create transportation barriers.		

O Canada! Immigrant Roots

MAIN IDEA

Canada's population includes many groups of people from different lands who retain their cultural identities.

WHY IT MATTERS NOW

Knowing the history of the people of Canada helps in understanding Canada's policy of multiculturalism.

DATELINE

EXTRA

Place • Champlain has great hopes for the future of Quebec. ▲

QUEBEC, NEW FRANCE, JUNE 1609

New colonists have just arrived to join the first settlers of Quebec. Only French explorer Samuel de Champlain and 8 of the 32 men he led here survived their first winter in the new colony. Champlain chose this location that the Algonquins call Quebec, or the Narrows, after much searching.

After arriving last July, he and his men built houses, planted grain, and worked to encourage fur trading and friendly relations with the native people. Champlain has spent years traveling around New France and mapping and recording information about the seacoast and rivers.

Who Are the Canadians?

The people of Canada come from many countries—not just France. More than 50 ethnic groups make up the population. More than two-thirds of Canadians have European ancestry. About 40 percent have British roots and 27 percent share a French heritage. Other Canadians trace their families back to Germany, Italy, and Ukraine, as well as to nations in Africa and Asia. Less than 5 percent of all Canadians are people of the First Nations.

TAKING NOTES
Use your chart to take notes about Canada.

Causes	Effects
Early settlers were from enemy countries, France and Britian	
French-speaking Canadians have...	

The First Nations

People have lived in North America for at least 12,000 years. At times in the past, the levels of the oceans were as much as 300 feet lower than they are today. Then the narrow water passage between Asia and North America—the Bering Strait—became dry land. Small bands of people crossed this land bridge into North America and settled throughout North America and South America.

The Canadians of the **First Nations** are descendants of those first settlers from Asia. In the Arctic north, Inuit and other native people make up more than half the population. Large numbers of First Nations people, including Cree, Micmac, Abenaki, and Ojibwa, live in southern Canada near the United States border.

European Immigrants

The first major wave of European settlement began in the 1600s. Both Britain and France established colonies in what is now Canada. These two countries had a long history of conflict, and they continued their rivalry on the North American continent. Between 1754 and 1763, they fought the French and Indian War for control of North America.

BACKGROUND

The name *Canada* comes from *Kanata,* a First Nations Huron-Iroquois word that means "village."

Spotlight on CULTURE

Totem Poles—Carving History The Haida people in Canada's Queen Charlotte Islands and the Kwakiutl in central British Columbia have been skilled totem carvers for centuries. Early craftspeople believed that red cedar was a gift from the Great Spirit. They used simple tools to carve beautiful, detailed totem poles from these trees.

Totem poles, such as these in Stanley Park, Vancouver, display brightly painted animal figures, or totems. These include eagles, whales, grizzly bears, wolves, ravens, frogs, and halibut. Totems are symbols that tell stories, celebrate important events, and preserve the history of native clans. Totem poles have also been used as grave markers and monuments.

THINKING CRITICALLY

1. **Making Inferences**
   What do the totem poles tell you about the First Nations people's relationship with nature?

2. **Drawing Conclusions**
   What roles do totem poles play in native culture?

For more on totem poles, go to   **RESEARCH LINKS**
CLASSZONE.COM

France lost the war and surrendered most of its Canadian territory to Great Britain. However, many French settlers remained, and disputes continued between them and the fast-growing population of British settlers.

Canada and the United Kingdom

In 1791, the British government established itself in two areas in Canada. Upper Canada, now Ontario, had mostly British settlers. Lower Canada, now Quebec, remained largely French. Although hostilities continued between the two populations, in 1867 they were united as the Dominion of Canada, along with Nova Scotia and New Brunswick. Canada became a self-governing nation, although the British monarch remained its head of state.

In 1869, the Hudson's Bay Company sold land to Canada that later became the provinces of Manitoba, Alberta, and Saskatchewan. In 1871, British Columbia joined the Dominion, and Canada now reached to the Pacific Ocean. In 1931, with the enactment of the Statute of Westminster, Canada gained equal status with the United Kingdom and joined the Commonwealth of Nations. In 1982, the last legal connection between Canada and the British Parliament ended, although Canada remains a member of the Commonwealth.

Later Immigrants Most of Canada's early immigrants were English, Scottish, Irish, and French. After World War I, other Europeans arrived from countries such as Italy, Poland, and Ukraine. Most Italian immigrants settled in Toronto and Montreal. Most Ukrainians moved to the prairies of central Canada. After World War II, Germans and Dutch entered the country, settling primarily in Ontario and British Columbia. In the 1960s, new immigration laws allowed people to migrate from Africa, Latin America, Asia, and the Pacific Islands.

Culture • British General James Wolfe's troops defeated the French and captured Quebec in 1759 during the French and Indian War. Benjamin West's painting *The Death of General Wolfe* shows Wolfe's death at the end of the battle. ▲

Canadian Citizens and Citizenship

As Canadian citizens, those of English or French descent have retained their separate languages and identities. Other groups have also kept the traditions of their homelands after settling in Canada. To support these citizen groups, Canada has adopted an official policy of **multiculturalism**—an acceptance of many cultures instead of just one.

Reading
Social Studies

A. Drawing Inferences How might Canada's policy of multiculturalism lead to increased immigration?

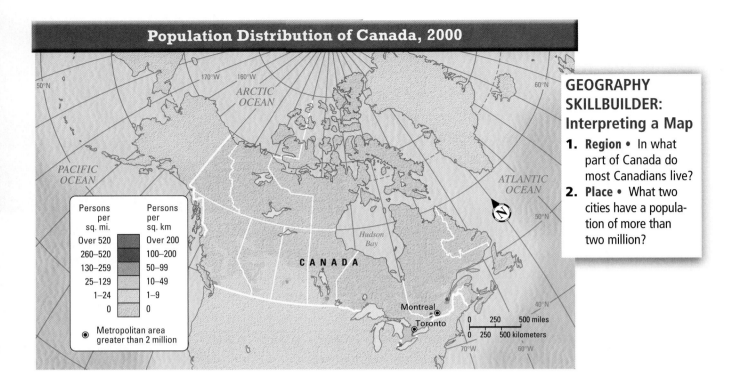

Population Distribution of Canada, 2000

Persons per sq. mi. | Persons per sq. km
Over 520 | Over 200
260–520 | 100–200
130–259 | 50–99
25–129 | 10–49
1–24 | 1–9
0 | 0

⊙ Metropolitan area greater than 2 million

GEOGRAPHY SKILLBUILDER: Interpreting a Map

1. **Region** • In what part of Canada do most Canadians live?
2. **Place** • What two cities have a population of more than two million?

Canadian citizens have many of the same rights and responsibilities as U.S. citizens. They must obey Canada's laws. They have the option of voting and participating in the political system. They are guaranteed freedom of religion, speech, and assembly, as well as equal protection and treatment for all under Canadian law.

Where Do Most Canadians Live?

While Canada's land area is second only to Russia's, its population is a relatively small 31 million people. Canadians often live where they find a favorable combination of geographic features and economic opportunities. Three-fourths of the population live in the cities and towns of southern Canada. In this region, the Great Lakes, the St. Lawrence Seaway, numerous rivers, and an excellent railway system provide convenient transportation for people and goods. Some Canadians live on farms in the central prairies and in port cities along the coasts. The northern regions of Canada are rugged and very cold. Few people live in those remote areas.

Reading **Social Studies**

B. Analyzing Motives What geographic and economic features attract people to settle in some parts of Canada?

Vancouver, Gateway to the Pacific Vancouver, British Columbia, is called Canada's "Gateway to the Pacific." As Canada's largest port, it trades heavily with Asian countries.

Thousands of Chinese from Hong Kong and many Japanese arrived in Canada at the end of the 20th century. Recent refugees have come from Vietnam, Laos, and Cambodia. **Refugees** are people who flee a country because of war, disaster, or persecution.

Toronto, City of Immigrants Toronto, Ontario's capital, is home to one-twelfth of Canada's population but contains one-fourth of its immigrants. More than 70,000 immigrants arrive each year from more than 100 countries in Asia, Europe, the West Indies, and North America. More than 40 percent of Toronto's population is foreign-born, and 10 percent arrived after 1991. Toronto's location, with access to the Atlantic Ocean and the United States, has helped it become a center of industry and international trade.

Place • Toronto is on the shore of Lake Ontario, the easternmost Great Lake. Toronto's skyline is highlighted by the CN Tower. ▲

SECTION ① ASSESSMENT

Terms & Names

1. Explain the significance of: (a) First Nation   (b) multiculturalism   (c) refugee

Using Graphics

2. Make a spider map like this one to record details about the people who settled in Canada.

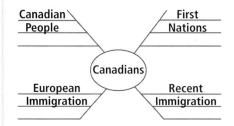

Canadian People — First Nations — Canadians — European Immigration — Recent Immigration

Main Ideas

3. (a) How did the first people reach North America? Who are their descendants?

(b) Describe the relationship between the British and Canada in the 1700s and the 1800s.

(c) What are some of the rights and responsibilities of Canadian citizens?

Critical Thinking

4. **Synthesizing**

How has the policy of multiculturalism benefited recent immigrants to Canada?

Think About

• the historic relations between the French and the English

• the many groups of immigrants and refugees in Canada

ACTIVITY -OPTION-   Choose one place in Canada where you might like to live. Look at the information in the Unit Atlas and in this section. Write and illustrate a **magazine article** about this location.

A Constitutional Monarchy

TERMS & NAMES
constitutional monarchy
Parliament
prime minister
Pierre Trudeau
separatist

MAIN IDEA
Canada is a democracy that protects the rights of individuals and of different cultures.

WHY IT MATTERS NOW
Canada's form of government has enabled the country to remain united despite conflicts among different groups of citizens.

DATELINE

NUNAVUT, CANADA, APRIL 1, 1999—The Inuit, the native people of Arctic Canada, have today been granted a separate territory in northern Canada. This historic day comes as a result of almost 25 years of negotiations with Canada's government. The Inuit argued that as a First Nations people, they have lived here for at least 4,000 years and have the right to govern their own land.

Today the Canadian government turned over 733,600 square miles of land that had been the eastern part of the Northwest Territories. Nunavut (NOO•nuh•voot)—which means "our land" in Inuktitut, the language of the Inuit—becomes the third territory of Canada. The capital is Iqaluit on Baffin Island.

Place • The Inuit build igloos out of blocks of snow to use as temporary winter homes. ▲

A Nation of Provinces and Territories

Other First Nations people also seek the self-government that the Inuit won. At this time, Canada remains a nation of ten provinces and three territories. The responsibilities of the central government include national defense, trade and banking, immigration, criminal law, and postal service. The provincial governments administer education, property rights, local government, hospitals, and provincial taxes. Territorial governments have fewer responsibilities but still enjoy limited self-government.

TAKING NOTES
Use your chart to take notes about Canada.

Causes	Effects
Early settlers were from enemy countries, France and Britian	
French-speaking Canadians have...	

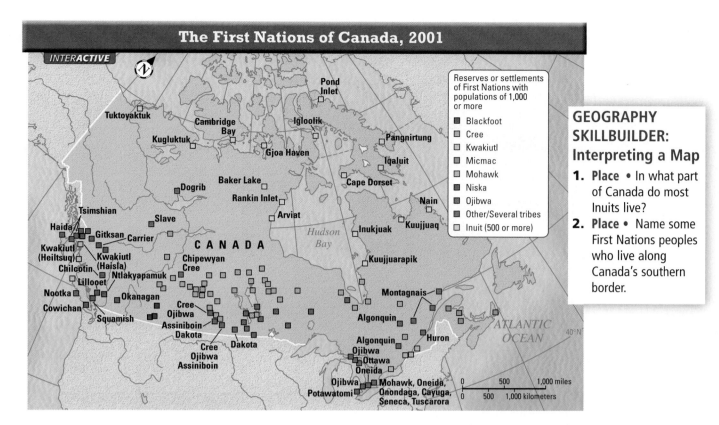

The First Nations of Canada, 2001

INTER**ACTIVE**

Tuktoyaktuk
Kugluktuk
Cambridge Bay
Gjoa Haven
Pond Inlet
Igloolik
Pangnirtung
Iqaluit
Cape Dorset
Baker Lake
Dogrib
Rankin Inlet
Arviat
Nain
Slave
Tsimshian
Haida
Gitksan
Carrier
Kwakiutl (Heiltsuq)
Kwakiutl (Haisla)
Chilcotin
Ntlakyapamuk
Lillooet
Nootka
Okanagan
Cowichan
Squamish
Chipewyan
Cree
Cree
Ojibwa
Assiniboin
Dakota
Cree
Dakota
Cree Ojibwa Assiniboin
Ojibwa Potawatomi
CANADA
Hudson Bay
Inukjuak
Kuujjuaq
Kuujjuarapik
Montagnais
Algonquin
Algonquin Ojibwa Ottawa Oneida
Huron
Mohawk, Oneida, Onondaga, Cayuga, Seneca, Tuscarora
ATLANTIC OCEAN
40°N

Reserves or settlements of First Nations with populations of 1,000 or more
- Blackfoot
- Cree
- Kwakiutl
- Micmac
- Mohawk
- Niska
- Ojibwa
- Other/Several tribes
- Inuit (500 or more)

0   500   1,000 miles
0   500   1,000 kilometers

GEOGRAPHY SKILLBUILDER: Interpreting a Map

1. **Place** • In what part of Canada do most Inuits live?
2. **Place** • Name some First Nations peoples who live along Canada's southern border.

Organization of Canada's Government

BACKGROUND
The prime minister and his cabinet are accountable to the members of the House of Commons. If they lose the support of the majority of members, they must resign, or ask the governor-general to dissolve Parliament and call an election.

Canada is a **constitutional monarchy**. It has a constitution to explain the powers of the government and owes allegiance to a monarch, a king or a queen. The Canadian government consists of the legislative and the judicial branches. Executive duties are within the legislature.

Head of State The British monarch is Canada's head of state. Since the queen or king does not live in Canada, she or he selects a governor-general as a representative. The monarch and the governor-general have little genuine power in Canadian government. They represent the historical traditions of Canada.

Legislature Canada's legislature, called **Parliament,** has two bodies, the House of Commons and the Senate. Together they determine Canadian laws and policies. Citizens elect members of the House of Commons. The leader of the party with the most members becomes the head of government, or **prime minister,** who runs the executive branch within the legislature. Senators are chosen by the prime minister from each of the ten provinces and three territories.

Reading
Social Studies

A. Comparing What are some of the powers of the prime minister, and how do these differ from those of the U.S. president?

Location • The Parliament Buildings in Ottawa, Canada's capital, house the legislature of the central government. ▼

Comparing the Canadian and U.S. Governments

Aspects of Government	Canada	United States
Type	Constitutional Monarchy (limited power)	Constitutional Republic (limited power)
Head of State	Monarch	President
Head of Government	Prime Minister	President
Legislature	Parliament	Congress
System	Federal (central and provinces)	Federal (central and states)

SKILLBUILDER: Reading a Chart

1. **Place** • Name three ways in which the government of Canada differs from that of the United States.
2. **Place** • How are the governments of Canada and the United States alike?

Judiciary Canada has both federal and provincial courts. The highest court is the federal Supreme Court. It is made up of the chief justice of Canada and eight other judges.

Vocabulary

judiciary: the judicial branch of government, the court system

Pierre Elliott Trudeau (1919–2000) From 1968 to 1979 and from 1980 to 1984, Pierre Trudeau was Canada's prime minister. Born in Montreal, Quebec, of French and Scottish ancestry, he grew up speaking both French and English. Despite his French-Canadian background, Trudeau successfully opposed Quebec's attempts to separate from Canada. He considered keeping Quebec a part of Canada one of his great achievements.

In 1982, Trudeau also helped enact a new Canadian constitution. At right, British Queen Elizabeth II signs a proclamation in 1982, making the new Canadian Constitution law, while Trudeau, seated, looks on. He worked to establish diplomatic relations with China and achieved Canada's complete independence from the British Parliament.

Equality and Justice

Canada is a democracy. Its government is responsible for protecting people's rights.

Civil Rights Prime Minister **Pierre Trudeau** led an effort to add a Charter of Rights and Freedoms to the Canadian Constitution in 1982. The Charter is similar to the U.S. Constitution's Bill of Rights. Among other rights, the Charter guarantees freedom of speech and freedom of religion. It protects every citizen's right to vote and to be assisted by a lawyer if arrested. It says that Canadians are free to live and work anywhere in Canada. The Charter also says that people have equal rights regardless of their race, religion, gender, age, or national origin.

Reading **Social Studies**

B. Analyzing Motives Why did Prime Minister Trudeau want a special document stating the rights of all Canadians?

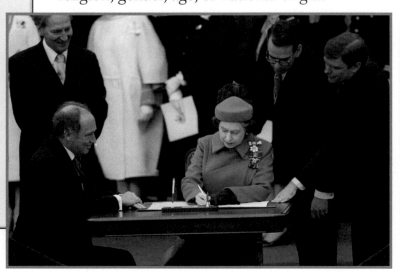

Many Cultures, Many Needs

Canada's people come from different cultures, and many wish to safeguard their special language and customs. Some French-speaking Canadians are **separatists,** or people who want the province of Quebec to become an independent country. In 1980 and in 1995, separatists asked for a vote on whether Quebec should become independent. Both times the issue was defeated, but the separatists promised to try again.

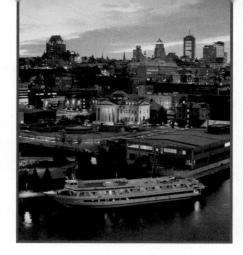

Place • Quebec City, overlooking the St. Lawrence River, is the capital of the province of Quebec and the center of French-Canadian culture. ▲

Quebec's Importance The federal government wants Quebec to remain part of Canada. Quebec is a major contributor to Canada's economy. Quebec is responsible for half of Canada's aerospace production, half of its information technology, and 38 percent of its high-tech industry. French culture is important in Canada's history and modern-day identity.

Laws Protecting Multiculturalism The Quebec provincial government has passed laws to preserve its citizens' French heritage. In an attempt to satisfy the separatists, Canada's federal government passed the Canadian Multicultural Act in 1988. This act guarantees the right of all Canadians to preserve their cultural heritage. Finding ways to maintain a unified country remains a critical issue in Canada today.

Reading
Social Studies

C. Finding Causes What led to the passage of the Multicultural Act of 1988?

SECTION 2 ASSESSMENT

Terms & Names

1. **Explain the significance of:** (a) constitutional monarchy (b) Parliament (c) prime minister
   (d) Pierre Trudeau (e) separatist

Using Graphics

2. Make a diagram like the one shown below. Add details to show how the Canadian government is organized.

Canada's Government	
Head of state	
Legislature	
Judiciary	

Main Ideas

3. (a) What are some similarities and differences between Canadian and U.S. governments?

   (b) Describe some of the rights guaranteed in the Charter of Rights and Freedoms.

   (c) What is the purpose of the Multicultural Act?

Critical Thinking

4. **Predict**

   What might happen if Quebec became a separate country?

   Think About

   ◆ Quebec's location
   ◆ Canada's multiculturalism
   ◆ economic impacts on Quebec and Canada

ACTIVITY -OPTION- Conduct research and create a **travel poster** to attract tourists to French-speaking Canada. Highlight the culture of Quebec.

Canada's Economy

TERMS & NAMES
industry
export
import
transportation corridor
transportation barrier

MAIN IDEA

Canada has a strong economy built on natural resources, a variety of industries, and good transportation.

WHY IT MATTERS NOW

Canada is a leader in the global economy.

DATELINE

DAWSON, YUKON TERRITORY, AUGUST 1898— Gold! That's the cry on the street here in Dawson. Just two years ago, this was a small, unknown town of 5,000 people. Then gold was discovered nearby on a branch of the Klondike River. The Klondike Gold Rush was on. People came here from all over the world hoping to strike it rich.

Now Dawson has more than 30,000 people crowding its streets. Most live in tents. Every day, thousands head up the creeks looking for gold. Most of these people haven't found any yet and never will. However, a few lucky prospectors have already made their fortunes.

Human-Environment Interaction •
Prospectors use gold dust to pay for merchandise in a store in the Yukon Territory. ▲

Contributors to the Economy

Canada is rich in natural resources, including gold. Europeans were first drawn to Canada by the abundant fishing and fur trading. In the 1800s, gold and other minerals were discovered. Today, most Canadians work in the service and manufacturing industries. Canada's skilled labor force, natural resources, and international trade all contribute to the country's economy.

TAKING NOTES

Use your chart to take notes about Canada.

Causes	Effects
Early settlers were from enemy countries, France and Britian	
French-speaking Canadians have...	

INTERACTIVE

GEOGRAPHY SKILLBUILDER: Interpreting a Map

1. **Human-Environment Interaction** • For what is most of Canada's land used?
2. **Region** • Where is most of Canada's commercial farming located?

Legend (land use):
- Manufacturing and trade
- Commercial farming
- Livestock raising
- Subsistence farming
- Nomadic herding
- Forestry
- Commercial fishing
- Hunting, fishing, and forestry
- Little or no economic activity

Resources:
- Coal
- Copper
- Fish
- Hydroelectric power
- Iron ore
- Lead
- Natural gas
- Nickel
- Petroleum
- Timber
- Uranium
- Zinc

Industry Based on Natural Resources A nation's resources are a source of wealth. The prairie provinces of central Canada have extensive grasslands and good soil, making this area an ideal place to raise beef cattle and grow wheat. On the rich farmlands along the St. Lawrence River, farmers harvest grains, vegetables, and fruit. People plant potatoes and raise dairy cattle on the east coast. The Grand Banks, located off the coast of Newfoundland, is one of the world's most abundant fisheries. The salmon caught off Canada's Pacific coast enrich that area's economy.

Much of Canada is covered in forests, making the timber industry important, especially in British Columbia. **Industry** refers to any area of economic activity. Mining in the northern territories yields iron ore, gold, silver, copper, and other metals.

Trade Canada's openness to trade has contributed to the growth of its economy. Today almost 80 percent of Canada's raw materials are shipped as exports. **Exports** are goods traded to other countries. Canada's main exports are wood and paper products, fuel, minerals, aluminum, wheat, and oil. These and manufactured goods are sold around the world.

BACKGROUND

The Grand Banks, first noted by explorer John Cabot in 1498, extends 350 miles north to south and 420 miles east to west.

Social Studies

A. Recognizing Important Details What are Canada's main exports?

Canada Today **129**

Canada and the United States share a valuable trade partnership. Most of Canada's exports go to the United States. Most of its **imports**, or goods brought into the country, are from the United States. In 1994, Canada, the United States, and Mexico signed the North American Free Trade Agreement, or NAFTA, which lowered trade barriers among the three countries.

Industry and the Economy

Canada's well-educated work force is important to its economy. Canadians work in all four types of industry seen in the chart shown below. Since World War II, Canada has shifted from a mostly rural economy to a major industrial and urban economy.

Types of Industry		
Primary Industries	Prepare and process raw materials, such as timber, wheat, and iron ore, so other companies or consumers can use them *Examples:* **farms; mining companies; logging companies**	
Secondary Industries	Manufacturing—turn raw materials into products that consumers or other businesses can use *Examples:* **bakeries; car manufacturers; furniture makers**	
Tertiary Industries	Service industries—do not make goods or consume goods; distributors—move goods from the manufacturer to another business or to consumers *Examples:* **wholesalers; transportation companies (truck, train, airplane, or ship); retailers of food, clothing, and other goods; health care; education; recreation; banking**	
Quaternary Industries	Pass on information *Examples:* **communication companies, such as Internet service providers and cable companies; financial, research, and other companies that gather and pass on information**	

Tertiary, or service, industries, such as health care, recreation, education, transportation, banking, and the government, occupy about two-thirds of Canada's work force. About 30 percent of Canadians work in secondary, or manufacturing, industries. One of Canada's main products is transportation equipment, including automobiles, trucks, subway cars, and airplanes. Food processing, especially meat and poultry processing, is an important industry in Canada as well. Canada also makes chemicals, medicines, machinery, metal products, steel, and paper.

Transportation

Transportation is a major Canadian industry. The ability to import and export goods and move them from place to place across Canada's vast land area affects many consumers and businesses.

Reading
Social Studies

B. Analyzing Effects Why are transportation corridors important to the development of industry?

Vocabulary

transcontinental: spanning or crossing a continent

Canada's geography both helps and hinders transportation. Canada has natural **transportation corridors**, or paths that make transportation easier. Rivers and coastal waters, sometimes combined with human-made canals and locks, provide convenient travel routes. The St. Lawrence Seaway, for example, allows oceangoing ships to travel between the Atlantic Ocean and the Great Lakes. Another important route is Canada's transcontinental railway system, which crosses the continent from coast to coast.

Canada also has **transportation barriers**, or geographic features that prevent or slow down transportation. In much of the north, snow and ice block travel by land or water. The Rocky Mountains in the west are another major obstacle. Industry develops slowly in regions where transportation is difficult.

Region • The Canadian Pacific Railway Company completed a transcontinental line from Montreal to a Vancouver suburb in 1885. ▲

SECTION 3 ASSESSMENT

Terms & Names

1. **Explain the significance of:** (a) industry (b) export (c) import (d) transportation corridor (e) transportation barrier

Using Graphics

2. Make a chart like the one shown below to list goods that might be produced in each area.

Prairie Provinces	St. Lawrence River Valley	East Coast	British Columbia	Northern Territories

Main Ideas

3. (a) What important factors have helped build Canada's economy?

   (b) Give an example of a primary, a secondary, a tertiary, and a quaternary industry.

   (c) What are some transportation corridors and barriers in Canada?

Critical Thinking

4. **Drawing Conclusions**

   Why do you think Canada and the United States have become such good trade partners?

   Think About
   • geographic location
   • their languages
   • their governments

ACTIVITY -OPTION- Imagine that you are prospecting for gold in Dawson during the Klondike Gold Rush. Write a **newspaper article** describing what you have brought with you, how you traveled there, and what the town is like.

A Multicultural Society

TERMS & NAMES
national identity
bilingual
Francophone

MAIN IDEA	WHY IT MATTERS NOW
Many immigrant groups have contributed to Canadian culture while preserving their own identities.	Canada's desire to safeguard its cultural diversity is one of its most serious challenges.

DATELINE

MONTREAL, CANADA, 1893—Score! The Montreal Amateur Athletic Association team is the best hockey team in Canada, and it has a silver trophy cup to prove it. Canada's governor-general, Sir Frederick Arthur, Lord Stanley of Preston, presented the award to "the championship hockey club of the Dominion of Canada."

Many Canadians love this sport. First played by the Micmac, a First Nations people in Nova Scotia, ice hockey has spread across Canada and south to the United States. Competition for Stanley's Cup will make the sport even more exciting.

Culture • The winning team poses with Lord Stanley's Cup, which was purchased for about $50. ▲

Canadian Identity

Hockey is one of many good things about living in Canada. From 1994 to 2000, the United Nations rated Canada the best of 175 countries in a survey that examines the health, education, and wealth of each country's citizens. Yet, Canadians still seek a **national identity,** or sense of belonging to a nation, to unite its many immigrant cultures.

TAKING NOTES
Use your chart to take notes about Canada.

Causes	Effects
Early settlers were from enemy countries, France and Britian.	
French-speaking Canadians have...	

Distribution of Bilingual Speakers, 2001

ARCTIC OCEAN

ATLANTIC OCEAN

Hudson Bay

CANADA

Percentage of population who speak English and French

- 50.0–70.3
- 35.0–49.9
- 20.0–34.9
- 10.0–19.9
- 5.0–9.9
- 0–4.9

0   250   500 miles
0   250   500 kilometers

GEOGRAPHY SKILLBUILDER: Interpreting a Map

1. **Culture** • What part of Canada has the highest percentage of people who speak both English and French?
2. **Culture** • Where in Canada do less than five percent of the people speak both English and French?

Languages Many Canadians are **bilingual,** which means they speak two languages. Look at this map to see where bilingual Canadians live. Canada has two official languages, English and French. Literature, official documents, road signs, newspapers, and television broadcasts are in both languages. The two languages are not exactly like those spoken in England, the United States, and France. **Francophones** are French-speaking people. Canadian French, based on the French of the 1800s, is pronounced differently from the French spoken in modern France.

Culture •
Business signs on a street in Quebec City reflect the strong influence of French culture. ▶

Canadian English uses some words, pronunciations, and spellings that differ from those used in the United States. For example, Canadians say *taps* and *serviettes* when people in the United States say *faucets* and *napkins*. For *about* and *house*, Canadians might say *aboot* and *hoos*. Many Canadians write *colour* for *color*, *theatre* for *theater*, and *cheque* for *check*. The nation's first prime minister, Sir John A. Macdonald, ordered that all official Canadian documents be written using standards set by dictionaries written in England.

Reading Social Studies

A. Synthesizing Why does Canada have two official languages?

Arts and Entertainment

Canada has rich traditions in the arts, actively supported by government funding. For example, the Canada Council for the Arts gives money to more than 8,400 artists and art organizations each year. Provincial governments also support regional arts programs.

Canadians read many of the same newspapers and magazines, and watch many of the same television shows and movies as do people in the United States. Canadian musicians, such as Neil Young, Joni Mitchell, Buffy Ste. Marie, Céline Dion, and Shania Twain, are popular in both countries. Comedian-actors Dan Aykroyd and Jim Carrey are also from Canada.

Vocabulary

provincial: of, or relating to, a province

Culture • The National Gallery of Canada in Ottawa is a visual arts museum that exhibits works by both Canadian and international artists. ◄

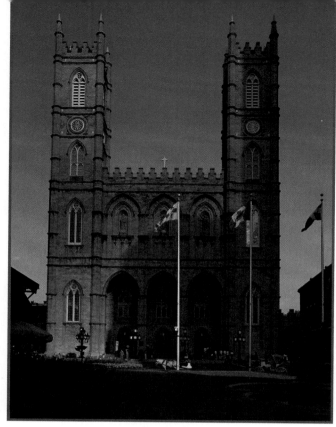

Culture • Notre-Dame was built in Montreal between 1824 and 1829. The architecture of the church—as well as the paintings, sculptures, and stained-glass windows inside—attracts many thousands of visitors each year. ◄

Religion

Christianity is widely practiced in Canada, but many other religions are followed as well, including Buddhism, Hinduism, Islam, and Judaism. Some religions are grounded in a spirituality based on respect for Earth and all forms of life. People of every cultural group are free to worship as they choose.

Culture Regions

BACKGROUND

Inuit culture has been greatly affected by contact with the modern world. However, some Inuit traditions have been preserved in their arts and crafts, dialects, and ways of living in Arctic Canada.

Most Canadian immigrants during the 1600s, 1700s, and 1800s were European. Recently, more people have arrived from Asia and South America. People who share the same language and background often settle in the same area. As a result, Canada has various culture regions, or areas where many people belonging to one cultural group live together.

Culture regions exist in different parts of Canada. Quebec is home to many French-speaking Canadians. In Nunavut more than 50 percent of the people are Inuit. Almost 16 percent of the population of Vancouver are Chinese, mostly from Hong Kong.

Connections to History

Raising the Maple Leaf A country's flag is an important national symbol. After 1763, when the United Kingdom won the French and Indian War, the British Royal Union Flag, or Union Jack, became Canada's flag. Efforts to design a new flag for Canada began in 1925. The Red Ensign, which had the Union Jack in its upper left corner and the Canadian coat of arms on its right side, was raised 20 years later.

In 1965, the Houses of Parliament adopted the Maple Leaf, which remains the flag of Canada today. The red background is a connection to the Red Ensign, and the maple leaf is Canada's national symbol.

Maple Leaf

Red Ensign

Union Jack

Getting different culture regions to agree on national issues is sometimes difficult. The adoption of the Maple Leaf as Canada's flag in 1965 was one successful effort to unite all Canadians.

A VOICE FROM CANADA

The flag is the symbol of the nation's unity, for it, beyond any doubt, represents all the citizens of Canada without distinction of race, language, belief or opinion.

—Speaker of the Senate Maurice Bourget

Conflict and Cooperation Languages, customs, and lifestyles differ among the cultural groups of Canada. Sometimes these differences lead to conflict. For example, in the second half of the 20th century, some Canadians thought that the thousands of Chinese immigrants settling in the Vancouver area would change Canadian culture through their language and customs.

In 1975, the government began reviewing immigration policy. Chinese groups in Vancouver organized a Chinese-Canadian conference. They asked for continued support of multiculturalism and that immigration laws remain open for all people. The concerned groups solved the problem through human rights laws.

Reading **Social Studies**

B. Analyzing Causes How do cultural differences cause conflicts among people?

SECTION 4 ASSESSMENT

Terms & Names
1. Explain the significance of: (a) national identity   (b) bilingual   (c) Francophone

Using Graphics

2. Make a spider map like the one shown below to illustrate how various groups contribute to making a unique Canadian culture.

Main Ideas

3. (a) What are the two main languages spoken in Canada?

   (b) How does Canada support its own arts and entertainment?

   (c) What do people living in culture regions have in common?

Critical Thinking

4. **Forming and Supporting Opinions**

   Do culture regions create more benefits or more disadvantages for Canada as a whole?

   Think About
   - existing and future conflicts
   - how different groups contribute to Canadian culture

ACTIVITY -OPTION-   With a partner, choose a culture region of Canada. Create a **mural** or **collage** to show characteristics of the culture.

Identifying Cause and Effect

▶▶ Defining the Skill

A cause is an event, a person, or an idea that brings about a result, or an effect. An effect is something that results from a cause. Understanding the relationship between cause and effect is key to understanding the world and its cultures.

▶▶ Applying the Skill

The following paragraph describes where most Canadians live. Use the strategies listed below to help you identify why Canadians live there.

How to Identify a Cause-and-Effect Relationship

Strategy ❶ Look for the cause of, or reason for, the cause-and-effect relationship. It might be suggested in the title and topic sentence. Ask yourself what happened and why it happened. Writers may indicate a cause-and-effect relationship by using words such as *thus, therefore, so,* and *as a result.* Use those words as clues.

Strategy ❷ Look for the results of the event or action. Ask yourself what happened as a result of the action. You have found the effect.

Strategy ❸ Remember that several causes can combine to create one event. Also remember that one cause can have several effects. Ask yourself if anything else helped to bring about the event. Ask yourself if there are any other results.

> ❶ WHERE CANADIANS LIVE
> ❷ Most of Canada's people live within 100 miles of the United States border. This heavily populated area covers only about 10 percent of the country. ❶ The mild climate in that part of the country makes living there more pleasant than living in the colder northern regions. ❸ People can find jobs more easily in the large cities located near the border. ❸ Many Americans who live in Canada can cross the border easily to visit family and friends.

Make a Diagram

Using a diagram can help you understand causes and effects. The diagram to the right shows what causes people in Canada to live close to the U.S. border and what effect is created.

| Mild climate |
| Better economic opportunities |
| Closeness to U.S. friends and family |

→ A majority of Canada's population live close to the U.S. border.

▶▶ Practicing the Skill

Turn to Chapter 5, "Canada Today," Section 3, "Canada's Economy," and make a diagram of the causes that have resulted in Canada's strong economy.

TERMS & NAMES

Explain the significance of each of the following:

1. multiculturalism
2. refugee
3. Parliament
4. prime minister
5. export
6. import
7. transportation corridor
8. transportation barrier
9. bilingual
10. Francophone

REVIEW QUESTIONS

O Canada! Immigrant Roots *(pages 119–123)*

1. How did the United Kingdom gain control of Canada?
2. What effects does the policy of multiculturalism have on Canada?

A Constitutional Monarchy *(pages 124–127)*

3. How is Canada's federal government organized?
4. How has Canada tried to satisfy the needs of its many culture groups?

Canada's Economy *(pages 128–131)*

5. How does Canada's wealth of natural resources contribute to its economy?
6. What are Canada's chief transportation corridors and barriers?

A Multicultural Society *(pages 132–136)*

7. How have the native languages of England and France changed in Canada?
8. What are some major culture groups of Canada?

CRITICAL THINKING

Analyzing Causes and Effects

1. Using your completed chart from Reading Social Studies, p. 118, describe some factors that influence where people settle in Canada.

Drawing Conclusions

2. Many people in Quebec wanted the province to separate from the rest of Canada. What in Prime Minister Pierre Trudeau's background made him effective in keeping Quebec part of Canada?

Making Inferences

3. How do you think the policy of multiculturalism affects the way Canadians of different cultures respond to one another?

Visual Summary

1 O Canada! Immigrant Roots

- The Canadian people have come from many countries.
- Canada is a very large country with a small population; most people settled in the southern part of the country.

2 A Constitutional Monarchy

- The Canadian government is a constitutional monarchy that is made up of two main branches: a legislative branch and a judicial branch.
- Canada has passed laws to protect the civil rights of its people and to support multiculturalism.

3 Canada's Economy

- Canada has many natural resources that contribute to its economy.
- Canada's most important trade partner is the United States.

4 A Multicultural Society

- Many cultural groups have helped to build the unique Canadian culture of today.

- The diverse cultures of the population create challenges in unifying Canada.

Use the map and your knowledge of world cultures and geography to answer questions 1 and 2.

Additional Test Practice, pp. S1–S33

1. In which province is Canada's capital city located?

A. British Columbia

B. Nova Scotia

C. Ontario

D. Quebec

2. Which province is located on the Pacific Coast?

A. British Columbia

B. Manitoba

C. New Brunswick

D. Newfoundland and Labrador

This excerpt is from an article about the hockey competition of the 2002 winter Olympics in Utah. Use the quotation and your knowledge of world cultures and geography to answer question 3.

PRIMARY SOURCE

Winning its first Olympic gold medal in 50 years in the sport it invented, Team Canada overwhelmed the United States, 5–2, with a crushing third period Sunday to complete the finest hockey tournament the world has ever seen. . . . There was a major difference that inspired Canada's killing-blow two-goal period: The Americans *wanted* to win but the Canadians *had* to win.

MICHAEL HUNT, *Wisconsin Journal Sentinel*

3. The passage supports which of the following observations?

A. The Canadian team's success was due to the poor performance of the Americans.

B. The Canadian team's national pride helped them overpower the U.S. team.

C. The Canadian team was bound to win because Canada had invented hockey.

D. The Canadian team's success was due to better physical training of its players.

TEST PRACTICE
CLASSZONE.COM

ALTERNATIVE ASSESSMENT

1. **WRITING ABOUT HISTORY**

Should the Canadian government provide support for the arts? Research this topic and write an editorial based on your findings.

• Using the Internet and the library, research government support for the arts, currently and in the past. You might also contact Canadian national museums and arts associations for information.

• Based on your research, decide whether government support is necessary, and if so, whether it should be increased or decreased. State your opinion and support it with facts from your research.

2. COOPERATIVE LEARNING

Work with a small group to prepare an interview for a public television broadcast on the topic of self-government for cultural groups. One member of your group can take the role of news moderator, and other members can each represent a different group. Together, brainstorm a list of cultural groups and prepare a set of interview questions. Individuals can do research to find out how the group views self-government.

INTEGRATED TECHNOLOGY

Doing Internet Research

Canada is a large country with diverse geographic regions. Choose one region, such as the Yukon Territory or the Maritime Provinces, and research what it is like to live there. Prepare a presentation of your findings.

• Use the Internet or other resources in the library to learn about the geography of your chosen region.

• Other sources of information might be Canadian museums and tourist bureaus.

• Focus your research on topics such as the region's weather, types of plants that grow there, kinds of jobs residents have, how tourists would travel around the region, and what tourists might see and do.

For Internet links to support this activity, go to

RESEARCH LINKS
CLASSZONE.COM

LATIN AMERICA

Place Machu Picchu is a complex of Inca ruins perched high in the Andes Mountains of Peru. The remains of the impressive granite structures were designated a UNESCO World Heritage Site in 1983.

MACHU PICCHU   LATIN AMERICA

INTEGRATED TECHNOLOGY

eEdition
- Interactive Maps
- Interactive Visuals

 VIDEO
Mexico: Rosita in Mexico

 INTERNET RESOURCES

Go to **classzone.com** for:
- Research Links
- Internet Activities
- Data Updates
- Unit Quiz
- Maps
- Test Practice
- Current Events
- Web Research Guide

Latin America: Physical

MEXICO

Baja California

Sierra Madre Occidental

Sierra Madre Oriental

Rio Grande

Gulf of California

Gulf of Mexico

Yucatán Peninsula

Orizaba
18,854 ft.
(5,747 m)

Popocatépetl
17,930 ft.
(5,465 m)

Tajumulco
13,844 ft.
(4,220 m)

BELIZE

CENTRAL AMERICA

HONDURAS

GUATEMALA

EL SALVADOR

NICARAGUA

COSTA RICA

Isthmus of Panama

Panama Canal

Barú
11,400 ft.
(3,475 m)

PANAMA

BAHAMAS

Greater Antilles

CUBA

JAMAICA

HAITI

DOMINICAN REPUBLIC

WEST INDIES

Caribbean Sea

Lesser Antilles

Netherlands Antilles

VENEZUELA

GUYANA

SURINAME

French Guiana (Fr.)

Llanos

Orinoco R.

Guiana Highlands

COLOMBIA

Negro R.

ECUADOR

AMAZON BASIN

Amazon R.

PERU

Madeira R.

ANDES

Lake Titicaca

BOLIVIA

SOUTH AMERICA

BRAZIL

Xingu R.

Araguaia R.

Tapajós R.

São Francisco R.

Mato Grosso Plateau

BRAZILIAN HIGHLANDS

Atacama Desert

PARAGUAY

Gran Chaco

Paraguay R.

Paraná R.

Mt. Aconcagua
22,831 ft.
(6,959 m)

ARGENTINA

URUGUAY

Uruguay R.

Pampas

Plata R.

CHILE

Patagonia

Tierra del Fuego

Falkland Is.

South Georgia I.

Cape Horn

ATLANTIC OCEAN

PACIFIC OCEAN

ATLANTIC OCEAN

Tropic of Cancer

20°N

Equator

0°

20°S

Tropic of Capricorn

40°S

N

Elevation

13,100 ft.	(4,000 m)
6,600 ft.	(2,000 m)
3,275 ft.	(1,000 m)
650 ft.	(200 m)
0 ft.	(0 m)

Below sea level

▲ Mountain peak

0   500   1,000 miles

0   500   1,000 kilometers

100°W   80°W   60°W   40°W

Elevation Profile: South America

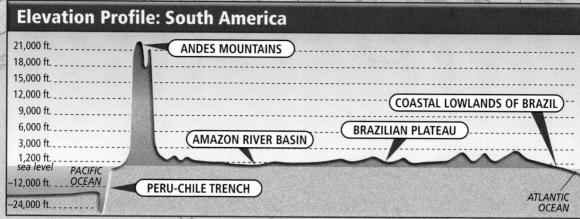

21,000 ft.
18,000 ft.
15,000 ft.
12,000 ft.
9,000 ft.
6,000 ft.
3,000 ft.
1,200 ft.
sea level
−12,000 ft.
−24,000 ft.

ANDES MOUNTAINS

COASTAL LOWLANDS OF BRAZIL

BRAZILIAN PLATEAU

AMAZON RIVER BASIN

PACIFIC OCEAN

PERU-CHILE TRENCH

ATLANTIC OCEAN

Latin America–United States Landmass and Population

Latin America

United States

LANDMASS

Latin America

7,981,950 square miles

Continental United States

3,165,630 square miles

POPULATION

Latin America
514,662,785

United States
281,421,906

= 50,000,000

FAST FACTS

✔ **HIGHEST MOUNTAIN:**
Mt. Anconcagua, 22,831 ft.

✔ **LONGEST RIVER:**
Amazon River, 3,900 mi. long

✔ **HIGHEST RECORDED TEMPERATURE:**
120°F, Rivadavia, Argentina,
December 11, 1905

✔ **LOWEST RECORDED TEMPERATURE:**
-27°F, Sarmiento, Argentina,
June 1, 1907

✔ **HIGHEST AVERAGE ANNUAL PRECIPITATION IN THE WORLD:**
Lloro, Colombia, 523.6 in.

✔ **LOWEST AVERAGE ANNUAL PRECIPITATION IN THE WORLD:**
Arica, Chile, 0.03 in.

GEOGRAPHY SKILLBUILDER: Interpreting Maps and Visuals
1. **Location** • The Isthmus of Panama separates what two bodies of water?
2. **Place** • What is the depth of the Peru-Chile Trench?

Latin America: Political

Legend:
- National boundary
- ★ National capital
- • Other city

0   500   1,000 miles
0   500   1,000 kilometers

**Places and labels on map:**

Tijuana
Ciudad Juárez
Chihuahua
Monterrey
Gulf of California
MEXICO
Guadalajara
— Tropic of Cancer —
20°N
México City
Córdoba
Puebla
Acapulco
Gulf of Mexico
Havana
BAHAMAS
CUBA
Cayman Is. (U.K.)
BELIZE
Belmopan
JAMAICA
Kingston
HAITI
Port-au-Prince
GUATEMALA
Guatemala City
HONDURAS
Tegucigalpa
San Salvador
NICARAGUA
EL SALVADOR
Managua
San José
COSTA RICA
PANAMA
Panama City
Caribbean Sea
Netherlands Antilles (Neth.)
Aruba (Neth.)
Caracas
Maracaibo
Mérida
Medellín
Bogotá
Cali
COLOMBIA
VENEZUELA
GUYANA
Georgetown
SURINAME
Paramaribo
Cayenne
French Guiana (Fr.)
0° — Equator —
Galápagos Is. (Ec.)
Quito
Guayaquil
ECUADOR
Manaus
Belém
Fortaleza
Recife
PACIFIC OCEAN
PERU
Lima
BOLIVIA
La Paz
Santa Cruz
Sucre
BRAZIL
Brasília
Goiânia
Belo Horizonte
Salvador
Rio de Janeiro
São Paulo
Curitiba
20°S
PARAGUAY
Asunción
Pôrto Alegre
N
Juan Fernández Is. (Chile)
Santiago
Rosario
Buenos Aires
ARGENTINA
URUGUAY
Montevideo
CHILE
40°S
ATLANTIC OCEAN
Falkland Is. (U.K.)
South Georgia I. (U.K.)

Inset (Caribbean):

Turks & Caicos (U.K.)
DOMINICAN REPUBLIC
Virgin Is. (U.S. & U.K.)
Anguilla (U.K.)
San Juan
ST. KITTS & NEVIS
ANTIGUA & BARBUDA
Santo Domingo
Puerto Rico (U.S.)
Guadeloupe (Fr.)
Montserrat (U.K.)
Martinique (Fr.)
DOMINICA
BARBADOS
ST. LUCIA
GRENADA
ST. VINCENT & THE GRENADINES
TRINIDAD & TOBAGO
Caribbean Sea
ATLANTIC OCEAN

100°W   80°W   60°W   40°W

City Populations of Latin America

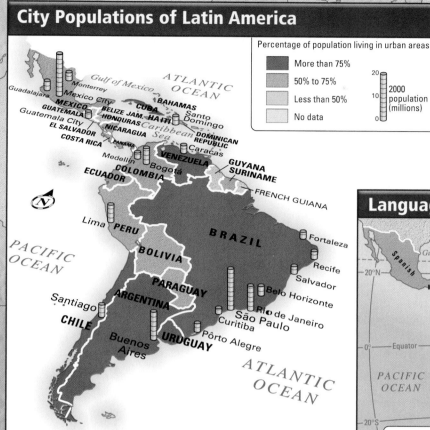

Percentage of population living in urban areas

- More than 75%
- 50% to 75%
- Less than 50%
- No data

20
10
0
2000 population (millions)

Languages of Latin America

- Indo-European
- Other languages
- **French** Spoken language

0   500   1,000 miles
0   500   1,000 kilometers

Fast Facts

✔ **LARGEST COUNTRY (in land area):** Brazil, 3,300,171 sq. mi.

✔ **SMALLEST COUNTRY (in land area):** Grenada, 120 sq. mi.

✔ **LARGEST CITY (population):** Mexico City, 18,131,000 (2000)

✔ **HIGHEST POPULATION DENSITY:** Barbados, 1,612 people per sq. mi.

✔ **LOWEST POPULATION DENSITY:** French Guiana, 5 people per sq. mi.

GEOGRAPHY SKILLBUILDER: Interpreting Maps and Visuals

1. **Location** • Which countries have no coastline?
2. **Region** • What language do most people in Brazil speak?

For updates on these statistics, go to

DATA UPDATE
CLASSZONE.COM

Country Flag	Country/Capital	Currency	Population (2001 estimate)	Life Expectancy (years)	Birthrate (per 1,000 pop.) (2000)
	Antigua and Barbuda St. John's	East Caribbean Dollar	67,000	70	20
	Argentina Buenos Aires	Peso	37,385,000	75	19
	Bahamas Nassau	Bahamian Dollar	298,000	71	20
	Barbados Bridgetown	Barbadian Dollar	275,000	73	14
	Belize Belmopan	Belizean Dollar	256,000	71	32
	Bolivia La Paz, Sucre	Boliviano	8,300,000	64	28
	Brazil Brasília	Real	174,469,000	63	19
	Chile Santiago	Chilean Peso	15,328,000	76	17
	Colombia Bogotá	Colombian Peso	40,349,000	70	23
	Costa Rica San José	Costa Rican Colon	3,773,000	76	21
	Cuba Havana	Peso	11,184,000	76	13
	Dominica Roseau	East Caribbean Dollar	71,000	73	18
	Dominican Republic Santo Domingo	Dominican Peso	8,581,000	73	25
	Ecuador Quito	U.S. Dollar and Sucre	13,184,000	71	27
	El Salvador San Salvador	Salvadoran Colon	6,238,000	70	29
	Grenada St. George's	East Caribbean Dollar	89,000	65	23
	Guatemala Guatemala City	Quetzal	12,974,000	66	35
	Guyana Georgetown	Guyanese Dollar	697,000	64	18

DATA FILE

Infant Mortality (per 1,000 live births) (2000)	Doctors (per 100,000 pop.) (1997–1998)	Literacy Rate (percentage) (1996–1998)	Passenger Cars (per 1,000 pop.) (1991–1998)	Total Area (square miles)	Map (not to scale)
20.0	114	90	207	171	
17.8	268	96	136	1,073,399	
17.8	152	98	245	5,386	
16.2	125	97	167	166	
30.8	55	93	10	8,867	
60.2	130	83	26	424,164	
33.8	127	85	84	3,300,171	
9.6	110	95	62	292,135	
23.2	116	91	31	440,831	
12.7	141	95	14	19,730	
7.7	530	96	2	42,804	
8.5	49	90	104	290	
40.8	216	82	14	18,704	
29.3	170	90	22	103,930	
27.2	107	71	6	8,124	
10.9	50	96	94	120	
45.0	93	56	9	42,042	
48.6	18	98	34	83,000	

Country Flag	Country/Capital	Currency	Population (2000 estimate)	Life Expectancy (years)	Birthrate (per 1,000 pop.) (2000)
	Haiti Port-au-Prince	Gourde	6,965,000	49	32
	Honduras Tegucigalpa	Lempira	6,406,000	70	33
	Jamaica Kingston	Jamaican Dollar	2,666,000	75	19
	Mexico Mexico City	New Peso	101,879,000	71	23
	Nicaragua Managua	Gold Cordoba	4,918,000	69	28
	Panama Panama City	Balboa	2,846,000	75	20
	Paraguay Asunción	Guarani	5,734,000	74	31
	Peru Lima	New Sol	27,484,000	70	24
	St. Kitts and Nevis Basseterre	East Caribbean Dollar	39,000	71	19
	St. Lucia Castries	East Caribbean Dollar	158,000	72	22
	St. Vincent and the Grenadines Kingstown	East Caribbean Dollar	116,000	72	18
	Suriname Paramaribo	Surinamese Guilder	434,000	71	21
	Trinidad and Tobago Port of Spain	Trinidad and Tobago Dollar	1,170,000	68	14
	Uruguay Montevideo	Uruguayan Peso	3,360,000	75	17
	Venezuela Caracas	Bolivar	23,917,000	73	21
	United States Washington, D.C.	Dollar	281,422,000	77	15

DATA FILE

Infant Mortality (per 1,000 live births) (2000)	Doctors (per 100,000 pop.) (1997–1998)	Literacy Rate (percentage) (1996–1998)	Passenger Cars (per 1,000 pop.) (1991–1998)	Total Area (square miles)	Map (not to scale)
96.3	8	45	5	10,714	
39.8	83	73	14	43,277	
13.4	140	85	17	4,244	
23.4	186	90	87	756,066	
38.7	86	66	16	50,464	
22.7	167	91	54	29,157	
35.3	110	92	14	157,048	
37.1	93	89	20	496,225	
16.9	117	90	130	104	
16.2	47	80	68	238	
14.6	88	82	44	150	
25.6	25	93	111	63,251	
18.3	79	98	107	1,978	
12.9	370	97	147	68,498	
25.5	236	91	68	352,144	
7.0	251	97	489	3,787,319	

GEOGRAPHY SKILLBUILDER: Interpreting a Chart

(Do not give United States as an answer.)
1. **Place** • Which countries have the highest life expectancy?
2. **Place** • Which country has the most cars per person?

CHAPTER 6

Latin America: Its Land and History

SECTION 1 Physical Geography

SECTION 2 Ancient Latin America

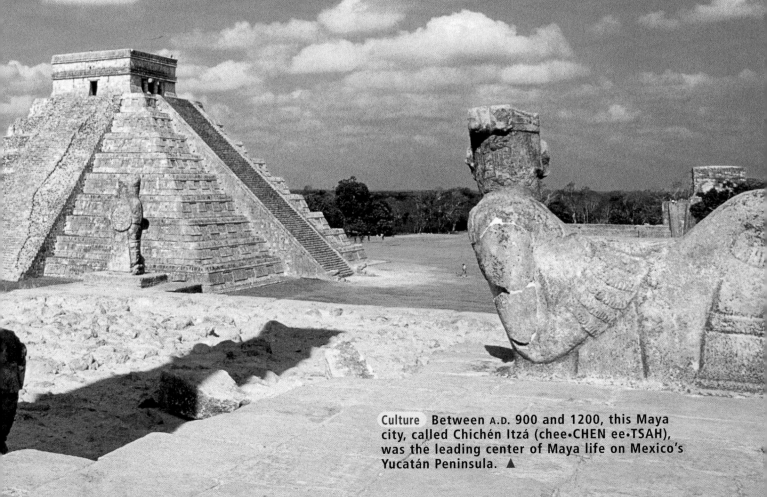

What conflicts arise when there is competition for a natural resource?

Human-Environment Interaction • About 50 percent of the world's rain forests are in Latin America, with 30 percent in Brazil alone. In Latin America, the rain forest is a natural resource that plays many different roles. It serves as a habitat for exotic plants and animals and a home to Native Americans. It is a moderator of the world climate and a destination for tourists. It also acts as a source of land that can be cleared and put to other uses, such as cattle ranching or logging.

What do you think?

♦ How might different groups want to use a rain forest as a resource? Think about the rain forest's inhabitants, tourists, environmentalists, and businesses.

♦ How might these different uses conflict with one another?

Culture Between A.D. 900 and 1200, this Maya city, called Chichén Itzá (chee•CHEN ee•TSAH), was the leading center of Maya life on Mexico's Yucatán Peninsula. ▲

READING SOCIAL STUDIES

BEFORE YOU READ

▶▶ *What Do You Know?*

Before you read the chapter, consider what you already know about the history and geography of Latin America. What countries make up Latin America? Does the region have well-known geographic features, such as mountains or rivers? You may have read folk tales from the ancient Maya, Aztec, and Inca civilizations. Think about what happened to these cultures and their people. Have you heard of the Aztec ruler Montezuma II?

▶▶ *What Do You Want to Know?*

Decide what else you want to know about Latin America. In your notebook, record what you hope to learn from this chapter.

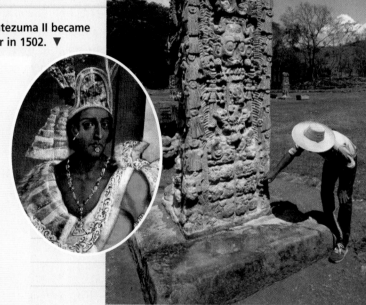

Culture • The Maya carved many stone monuments. ▼

Culture • Montezuma II became the Aztec ruler in 1502. ▼

READ AND TAKE NOTES

Reading Strategy: Comparing and Contrasting Comparing and contrasting can be a useful strategy for studying cultures. When you compare, you look for similarities. When you contrast, you look for differences. Use the chart shown here to compare and contrast the ancient civilizations of Latin America.

- Copy the chart into your notebook.

- As you read Section 2, take notes on the Maya, Aztec, and Inca.

- Write your notes under the appropriate headings.

	Maya	Aztec	Inca
Location			
Dates			
Achievements			
Reasons for Decline			

Latin America: Physical Geography

MAIN IDEA

Latin America's landforms, bodies of water, and climate offer a wide range of environments and resources.

WHY IT MATTERS NOW

Physical geography influences Latin America's cultures, offering them both resources and obstacles.

DATELINE

EXTRA

PUEBLA, MEXICO, DECEMBER 19, 2000

Yesterday, Mount Popocatépetl erupted, spewing out glowing five-foot-long rocks for miles in one of its largest eruptions in a thousand years. More than 30 million people live within sight of the volcano, and tens of thousands live close enough to be at risk when it erupts.

Government trucks drove through villages sounding warnings on speakers while church bells rang out the danger. In spite of the resulting damage, no one has been killed. However, authorities warn, a larger eruption could occur at any time.

Place • The Aztec named the volcano Popocatépetl, which means "smoking mountain." ▲

Defining Latin America

Latin America includes Mexico, Central America, the Caribbean, and South America. Because the languages of most of its colonizers—Spanish and Portuguese—are derived from Latin, Europeans later referred to the region's colonies as *Latin America*. Because the region is defined by a cultural connection, in this case language, it is called a culture region.

TAKING NOTES

Use your chart to take notes about Latin America.

	Maya	Aztec
Location		
Dates		

Mexico

Look at the map on page 155. Mexico is the farthest north of the Latin American countries. You can see that Mexico's major physical features include mountains, plateaus, and plains.

A Varied Landscape Mexico's two major mountain ranges share the name Sierra Madre (see·EHR·uh MAH·dray). Notice that in between the two ranges—the Sierra Madre Occidental and the Sierra Madre Oriental—sits Mexico's large central plateau. The vast northern stretches of the central plateau are desert.

Now look just south of the central plateau. There you will see Mexico's two highest mountain peaks, Orizaba (or·ih·ZAH·buh) and Popocatépetl (POH·puh·KAT·uh·PEHT·uhl). Both are volcanoes. Volcanic activity and earthquakes frequently plague Mexico—and many other parts of Latin America too. They are caused by the movement of five tectonic plates.

A Problem of Place At the southern end of the central plateau sits Mexico City, the world's second most populated city. Air pollution is severe there, and the city's location has contributed to this problem. The mountains surrounding the city to the east, south, and west trap automobile exhaust and other pollutants that the city's huge population generates.

An added problem of location for Mexico City is the ground on which it was built—a drained lakebed. The vibrations that earthquakes send through Earth grow much stronger and more damaging when they pass through the soft, loose soils of a lakebed, thus making Mexico City highly vulnerable to the effects of earthquakes.

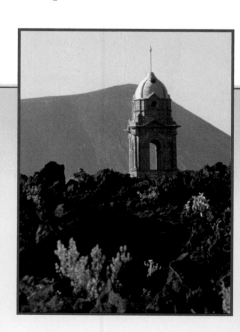

Eruption Disruption On February 20, 1943, something very strange happened in a cornfield in west-central Mexico. Before the eyes of a startled farmer, the land violently split open. Within 24 hours, a small, smoking cone had appeared—the tiny beginning of a mighty volcano called Paricutín (pah·REE·koo·TEEN). Scientists rushed to the area to watch the volcano being born. Within a year, a mountain stood in place of what had been farmland and a village.

While it was active, Paricutín rose to 10,400 feet above sea level. It poured lava over about a 10-square-mile area, burying streets and buildings, such as this nearby church. In 1952, it stopped erupting completely and became dormant. But the volcano that sprouted in a cornfield had given scientists a rare opportunity to study the life cycle of one of nature's most dramatic and dangerous features.

INTER*ACTIVE*

GEOGRAPHY SKILLBUILDER:
Interpreting a Map

1. Location • What is the tallest mountain in Central America?

2. Region • Which area of Mexico is almost entirely at sea level?

UNITED STATES

ATLANTIC OCEAN

Gulf of California

Sierra Madre Occidental

Central Plateau

Sierra Madre Oriental

Gulf Coastal Plain

Gulf of Mexico

Popocatépetl
17,802 ft.
(5,426 m.)

Pico de Orizaba
18,854 ft.
(5,747 m.)

Havana

Tropic of Cancer

Pico Duarte
10,417 ft.
(3,175 m.)

Paricutín
9,210 ft.
(2,808 m.)

Mexico City

Yucatán Peninsula

Pico Turquino
6,561 ft.
(2,000 m.)

Sierra Madre del Sur

Belmopan

Port-au-Prince

Santo Domingo

Tacaná
13,428 ft.
(4,093 m.)

Tegucigalpa

Caribbean Sea

Tajumulco
13,845 ft.
(4,220 m.)

Guatemala City

San Salvador

Managua

San José

Chirripó Grande
12,530 ft.
(3,819 m.)

Barú
11,400 ft.
(3,475 m.)

Panama City

Equator

Elevation

13,100 ft.	(4,000 m)
6,600 ft.	(2,000 m)
1,600 ft.	(500 m)
650 ft.	(200 m)
0 ft.	(0 m)
Below sea level	

▲ Mountain peak

⊛ National capital

0   250   500 miles
0   250   500 kilometers

SOUTH AMERICA

PACIFIC OCEAN

N

Central America and the Caribbean

Look at the physical map in the Unit Atlas. Central America is the mountainous landmass that forms a bridge between Mexico and South America. Now look to the east, and you will see island nations scattered throughout the Caribbean Sea.

Central America About 80 percent of Central America is hilly or mountainous, and most of it is covered with forests. Rain forests cover much of the lowlands. In the higher regions, deciduous trees cloak many of the slopes.

A string of more than 40 volcanoes lines 900 miles of Central America's Pacific coast, where two tectonic plates crash against each other. This is the most active group of volcanoes in North or South America. Earthquakes also occur frequently. They can completely destroy buildings, towns, and cities. They can also set landslides and mudslides in motion, sending land, houses, and people hurtling down the slopes.

The Caribbean Islands As you can see on the map (page 155), the Caribbean Islands lie to the east of Central America. Some of these islands, such as St. Kitts and Grenada, are actually the peaks of volcanic mountains rising from the ocean floor. Over thousands of years, the volcanoes erupted, spewing lava that cooled, hardened, and added to the mountains' height.

Other islands, such as the Bahamas, began as coral reefs. Coral is made of organisms that shed hard skeletons when they die. The skeletons pile up, and a reef, or ridge, develops. A coral reef that becomes an island usually encircles a volcanic island and then grows over it.

Vocabulary

deciduous: a tree that loses its leaves each year

Reading
Social Studies

A. Clarifying
What causes so many volcanoes and earthquakes in this region?

Place • Coral reefs form in lots of different colors. ▼

South America

Look at the map on page 142 of the Unit Atlas. You can see that the equator runs through Ecuador, Colombia, and Brazil. You can also see that only the Isthmus of Panama links South America to North America.

The Andes On the map, you can see the Andes mountain range, which stretches over 5,000 miles along South America's west coast. It is the longest continuous mountain range on Earth's surface. Mount Aconcagua (AK·uhn·KAH·gwuh) in Argentina is the highest peak in the Western Hemisphere.

Beyond the Andes Notice the central plains east of the Andes. The plains in southern South America are called the *Pampas*. South America's largest rivers begin in the Andes, drain the central plains, and then flow into the Atlantic Ocean. They include the Orinoco (AWR·uh·NOH·koh), the Paraná-Paraguay-Plata (PAR·uh· NAH-PAR·uh·gwy-PLAH·tuh), and the Amazon.

The Amazon In 2000, 22 people explored the Andes's rivers to confirm the source of the Amazon River, which had been discovered in 1971. The mighty river begins in the Peruvian Andes as a trickle of water. It then flows for nearly 4,000 miles to the Atlantic Ocean. No other river carries as much water to the sea. Along with more than 1,000 **tributaries,** which are rivers or streams that flow into a larger body of water, the Amazon drains water from Peru, Ecuador, Colombia, Bolivia, Venezuela, and Brazil.

The Amazon at Risk **Deforestation,** or the process of cutting and clearing away trees from a forest, has greatly affected the Amazon rain forest. In recent years, Amazon deforestation has provided timber and cleared land for cattle ranches.

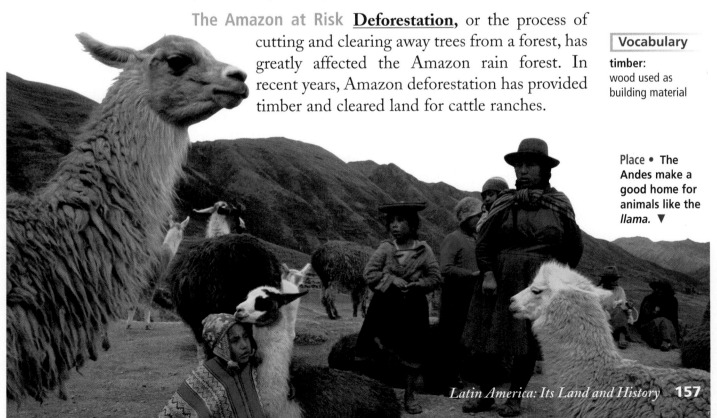

Place • The Andes make a good home for animals like the *llama.* ▼

Most plants release oxygen into the air and absorb carbon dioxide. By reducing the number of trees and plants, deforestation increases the amount of carbon dioxide in the air. Some scientists think the increase in carbon dioxide contributes to global warming because carbon dioxide traps warm air at Earth's surface.

Others worry that animals who find food in the rain forest may need to move—or may die out—when large areas of forest are cut down. The Native American tribes that inhabit the rain forest are also at risk of being squeezed out of the land they live on.

Climate

Latin America's climate varies greatly from area to area. It is influenced by elevation, location, wind patterns, and ocean currents.

The Tropical Zone A large portion of Latin America lies in the **Tropical Zone,** which, as you can see on the map below, is between the latitudes 23°27' north and 23°27' south. The Tropical Zone may be rainy or dry, but it is typically hot. Also, temperature is always lower at higher elevations, but in the Tropical Zone, all elevations are warmer than they are elsewhere.

Wind and Water The waters in the Caribbean Sea stay warm most of the year and heat the air over them. A warm wind then blows across the islands, keeping the climate warm even in the winter.

Reading
Social Studies

B. Drawing Conclusions
What aspect of the Tropical Zone's location on Earth causes it to be warmer than the other areas?

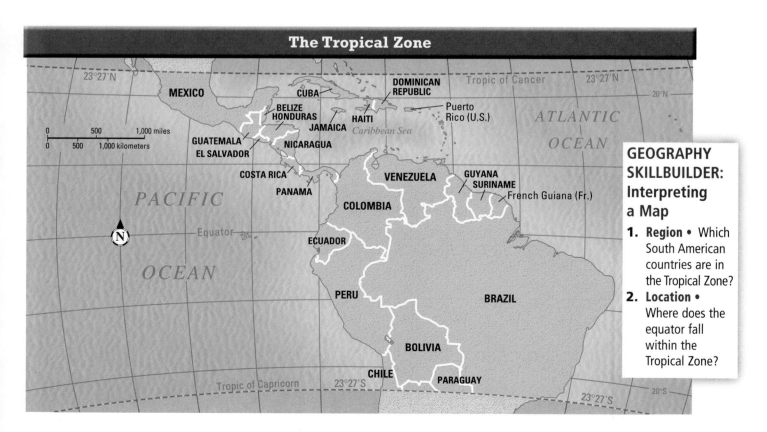

The Tropical Zone

GEOGRAPHY SKILLBUILDER: Interpreting a Map

1. **Region** • Which South American countries are in the Tropical Zone?

2. **Location** • Where does the equator fall within the Tropical Zone?

Normal Year	**El Niño Year**
Westerly trade winds	Westerly trade winds die out
Warm surface water	Warm surface water, warm air, and storms

SKILLBUILDER:
Interpreting a Diagram

1. What effect does the increased air pressure of *El Niño* have on the warm surface water of the Pacific?
2. What are the patterns of wind and water in a normal year?

El Niño At times, unusually high air pressure in the south Pacific causes certain winds over the ocean, called trade winds, to die out. Without the trade winds, the ocean's sun-warmed surface water flows eastward, toward North and South America. Because this typically occurs around Christmastime, people call the current **El Niño** (ehl NEE·nyaw). This term is Spanish for "the Christ child" because Christmas celebrates the birth of Jesus.

The warmer water of *El Niño* warms the air. Warmer air holds more water and so releases more rain when it cools. This added precipitation often causes heavy rains and flooding in Latin America and other parts of the eastern Pacific. At the same time, areas in the western Pacific, such as Indonesia, may have less rain than usual.

SECTION 1 ASSESSMENT

Terms & Names

1. Explain the significance of: **(a)** tributary   **(b)** deforestation   **(c)** Tropical Zone   **(d)** *El Niño*

Using Graphics

2. Use a chart like the one below to list the key physical features of each country or region.

Key Physical Features			
Mexico	Central America	The Caribbean Islands	South America

Main Ideas

3. **(a)** Name two types of natural disasters that occur frequently in Latin America.

(b) Describe two ways in which the Caribbean Islands formed.

(c) What happens when increased air pressure causes trade winds to lessen?

Critical Thinking

4. **Forming and Supporting Opinions**
Do you favor limiting the deforestation of the Amazon rain forest? Why? Why not?

Think About
* the economic benefits of timber production and cattle ranching
* the destruction of habitats
* the effects on the global environment

ACTIVITY -OPTION-   Look at the map on page 158 that shows the Tropical Zone. Make a **list** of all the Latin American countries that are wholly or partly in the Tropical Zone.

Ancient Latin America

TERMS & NAMES
hieroglyph
chinampa
Machu Picchu
Hernán Cortés
Montezuma II
Francisco Pizarro
Atahualpa
Columbian Exchange

MAIN IDEA	WHY IT MATTERS NOW
The ancient cultures of Latin America established civilizations in challenging geographic settings.	These cultures serve as models for how successful civilizations develop.

DATELINE

EL MIRADOR, GUATEMALA, 200 B.C.—In El Mirador today, a council of the city's leaders made a major announcement. Next month, construction will begin on a massive building complex for the city's center.

The plans include an enormous pyramid made of three smaller pyramids sitting atop a large stepped platform. The council expects to employ thousands of people to cut and carry the stone slabs that will be used to build the structure. The project is expected to take many months to complete.

Place • An artist made this drawing to show what El Mirador's three-part pyramid will look like. ▼

Ancient Civilizations of Latin America

Many ancient civilizations, such as the Egyptian, developed in river valleys and thrived there. The rivers provided water for both irrigation and transportation. In Latin America, however, some ancient civilizations flourished far from rivers. For example, the Maya of Mexico and Central America built cities in dense jungles. The Aztec of Mexico constructed their capital on a swampy island. The Inca of South America built cities high up in the Andes.

TAKING NOTES
Use your chart to take notes about Latin America.

	Maya	Aztec
Location		
Dates		

The Maya

In the areas that are today southern and eastern Mexico, western Honduras, Guatemala, El Salvador, and Belize, the ancient Maya built a widespread civilization. Small Maya communities existed as early as 1600 B.C. From A.D. 250 to A.D. 900, the Maya established one of Latin America's most important civilizations.

Maya Intellectual Advances The ancient Maya studied math and astronomy extensively. The Maya were among the first civilizations in the world known to understand the advanced mathematical concept of zero. They also had an intricate calendar system that included a 260-day calendar of sacred days, a 365-day calendar based on the sun's movement, and a calendar that measured the number of days that had passed since a fixed starting point.

The Maya established the best-developed written language in ancient Latin America. The basic units of the writing system were symbols called **hieroglyphs,** or glyphs. Each glyph represented a word or a syllable. The U.S. lawyer John Lloyd Stephens, while traveling through the Maya area in the 1800s, described his awe at seeing the glyphs and not being able to read them because no one had yet deciphered them.

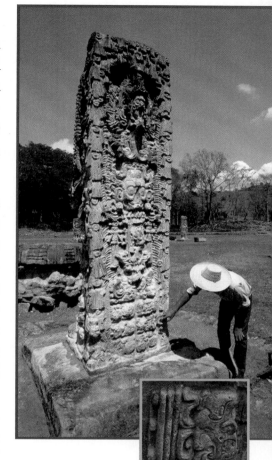

Culture • The Maya often carved hieroglyphs on stone monuments. ▲

Reading
Social Studies

A. Drawing Conclusions How does having a system of writing help a civilization survive?

> *A VOICE FROM LATIN AMERICA*
>
> These structures . . . these stones . . . standing as they do in the depths of a tropical forest, silent and solemn, strange in design, excellent in sculpture, rich in ornament . . . their whole history so entirely unknown, with hieroglyphics explaining all, but perfectly unintelligible.
>
> **John Lloyd Stephens**

Maya Agriculture Farming was essential to Maya life. Using a method called slash-and-burn agriculture, the Maya cut down and burned trees, planting crops in their place. After a few years, they let the forest grow back, so the soil could regain its nutrients. Later the area could again be cut, burned, and farmed. The Maya also built up ridges of farming land on floodplains. The floodplains were rich with nutrients, and the ridges kept the crops from getting too wet.

Colossal Olmec Heads Mexico's oldest known civilization is called the Olmec, which flourished from about 1200 to 600 B.C. The Olmec are famous for the colossal heads (like the one shown below) that they carved from a type of stone called basalt.

Thought to be portraits of Olmec rulers, some of these heads stand over nine feet tall. Each weighs thousands of pounds. All of Mexico's later Native American cultures were influenced by the Olmec. However, only the Olmec produced these giant stone monuments.

Culture • This stone carving honors the Aztec sun god, whose face is shown in the center. ▼

Decline of Maya Civilization Around A.D. 900, the Maya way of life began to change. For unknown reasons, the construction of massive temples and stone monuments stopped. Cities were abandoned. However, the Maya people did not disappear—they just spread out. More than 6 million Maya people still live in Guatemala, Belize, and southern Mexico and speak dialects based on the languages of their Maya ancestors.

The Aztec

Where modern Mexico City now stands, the waters of Lake Texcoco once lapped the shores of an island city called Tenochtitlán (teh·NOHCH·tee·TLAHN). With as many as 200,000 inhabitants, Tenochtitlán served as the capital of the Aztec Empire.

Aztec Origins The Aztec were composed of a number of tribes of wandering warriors. Of these, the Mexica (MEH·hee·KAH) were dominant. Mexico took its name from the Mexica. During the 1200s, the Aztec gradually grew in numbers and military strength until they controlled the region. They dominated until the early 1500s, when the Spanish conquered them.

Aztec Warfare and Religion The Aztec Empire centered on warfare. All able men, including priests, were expected to join the Aztec army, for two reasons. The first was to maintain a powerful empire, but the second was religious. The Aztec believed that anyone who died in battle had the great honor of dying for Huitzilopochtli (WEE·tsuh·loh·POHCH·tlee), the Aztec god of war.

Aztec Agriculture The Aztec held great power over their empire. One reason for their success was that the island location of their capital protected them from attack. However, much of the island was marsh, posing a major challenge to farming. The resourceful Aztec built floating gardens, called *chinampas* (chee·NAHM·pahs), on which they grew crops. First, they piled up plants from the water. Then they anchored these rafts between trunks of willow trees.

Willows

Crops

Mud

Plants

Human-Environment Interaction • This infographic shows how the Aztec built and farmed the *chinampas*. ▲

Finally, they heaped the lake's fertile mud on the piles to create plots for farming. The Aztec grew many crops, such as maize, beans, squash, avocados, tomatoes, peppers, and flowers. They also raised turkeys, ducks, geese, and dogs for food.

The Inca

Around 1400, high in the Andes of Peru, a group of people called the Inca rose up to conquer the people of the surrounding areas. From their capital, Cuzco, the Inca soon ruled a huge empire that included parts of what are now Colombia, Ecuador, Bolivia, northern Chile, and northwestern Argentina.

Inca Agriculture To farm on the steep mountainsides, the Inca built stone terraces. These gave the Inca large areas of flat land to farm. The terraces also helped prevent erosion of the soil. In the desert lands to the west, the Inca built irrigation canals to water their crops. Some of these canals spanned entire valleys. Because of terracing and irrigation, Inca farmers were able to grow crops such as potatoes, maize, and a grain called *quinoa*.

Andean Agriculture

Long before the rise of the Inca Empire, people living in the Andes had learned to farm the steep valley walls by building terraces into the sides of the mountains. They had also learned to build canals, many of them lined with stone, to carry water to their crops. The Inca improved and expanded the existing terraces and canals until they could feed 15 million people, with enough food left over to put away stores for three to seven years.

In the Andes, valley walls rise as high as 10,000 feet and temperatures can span a 55-degree range.

Inca canals stretched for miles. They were often lined and covered with stones. Some were cut through solid rock.

The Inca grew maize, hundreds of kinds of potatoes, and many other crops. Farmers had to plant crops adapted to many different climates because of the great variations in altitude and temperature.

The Inca had few farm tools. The most widely used was the *taclla,* or digging stick. It consisted of a pointed hardwood pole with a footrest for pushing the tool into the ground. Some *tacllas* had metal tips. The other main tools were hoes and clubs.

Workers directed by royal architects built stone retaining walls. Inside the walls, they placed layers of stone, clay, gravel, and topsoil. This combination allowed water to slowly work its way to lower terraces.

THINKING Critically

1. Analyzing Motives
Why did people living in the Andes need to build terraces and canals?

2. Recognizing Effects
What role did agriculture play in the building and maintenance of the Inca Empire?

Culture •
The Inca kept records by tying knots in a series of strings called *quipu* (KEE•poo). ◄

Communicating Across the Inca Empire Stone roads were a major technological feat of the Inca. These roads are still in use today. Having no written language or knowledge of the wheel, Inca rulers ordered roads built on which runners carried verbal messages to distant places. The runners worked in relay teams stationed along the roads. One runner told the message to the next. Messages could travel 150 miles a day along the stone roads. This system of communication was important to the Inca because their empire spread out over thousands of miles.

B. Recognizing Effects How did building stone roads improve the ability of the Inca rulers to control a large region?

Inca Stonework The Inca are known for their stonework. They erected many massive buildings, some with stones weighing as much as 200 tons. Wooden rollers were used to move these heavy stone blocks. The most remarkable of Inca stonework is the city of **Machu Picchu** (MAH•choo PEEK•choo), which still stands almost 8,000 feet above sea level. The walls of Machu Picchu were constructed so that they appear to emerge from the mountainsides. Around them, terraces connected by stairways run down the steep slopes. (See photograph on pages 140–141.)

Spotlight on CULTURE

Inca Weaving The Inca had no formal written language, but they used weaving as a means of representing ideas. Using wool sheared from llamas and alpacas, as well as many colorful plant dyes, the Inca wove images into the fabrics they wore and traded. Concepts related to the passing of seasons, agricultural practices, and history were all represented in the weavings. In Peru today, Edwin Sulca Lagos is famous for his Inca-inspired weavings. This one is covered in designs from the Inca calendar.

THINKING CRITICALLY

1. **Hypothesizing**
   What sorts of images might the Inca have used to convey concepts such as time or seasons?

2. **Identifying Problems**
   What risks did the Inca face by recording ideas only on fabric?

For more on Inca weaving, go to

RESEARCH LINKS
CLASSZONE.COM

The Spanish in Latin America

Until about 500 years ago, Latin America was populated solely by Native Americans. In the 1500s, the Spanish arrived in the region. One famous Spanish soldier, **Hernán Cortés** (ehr·NAHN kawr·TEHS), captured the Aztec ruler, **Montezuma II** (MAHN·tih·ZOO·muh), in 1519. He claimed the Aztec Empire for Spain in 1521 and renamed it New Spain. A decade later, another Spanish soldier, **Francisco Pizarro,** defeated the Inca ruler, **Atahualpa** (AH·tuh·WAHL·puh), and claimed Atahualpa's empire for Spain.

Culture •
Montezuma II was a great warrior who was feared throughout the Aztec Empire. ▲

Time of Change Once in control of Latin America, the Spanish enslaved many Native Americans and forced them to do labor, such as mining silver. The Spanish also worked hard to convert the Native Americans to Christianity.

Latin America and Spain also exchanged culture. Ships carrying Latin American goods sailed to Spain. The Spanish soon began growing corn, peppers, and tomatoes—crops they had never seen before. Manufactured products from Spain, especially textiles, were also shipped to Latin America. So were foods and animals, such as peaches and pigs. This trade was part of the **Columbian Exchange,** or the exchange of goods and ideas between European countries and their colonies in North and South America.

SECTION 2 ASSESSMENT

Terms & Names

1. Explain the significance of: (a) hieroglyph (b) *chinampa* (c) Machu Picchu (d) Hernán Cortés (e) Montezuma II (f) Francisco Pizarro (g) Atahualpa (h) Columbian Exchange

Using Graphics

2. Use a chart like the one below to list effects of the Spanish arriving in Latin America.

Effects of Spanish Arrival in Latin America	
1.	
2.	
3.	
4.	

Main Ideas

3. (a) Describe the writing system that the Maya developed.

   (b) How did the Inca pass important messages across great distances?

   (c) What was the Columbian Exchange and how did it work?

Critical Thinking

4. **Recognizing Effects**

   How did the Maya, Aztec, and Inca develop agricultural methods that responded to the environments in which they each lived?

   Think About
   * physical surroundings
   * available resources

ACTIVITY -OPTION-

Imagine you live in Tenochtitlán and have spent the day constructing *chinampas*. Write a **letter** to a friend describing the process.

Finding and Summarizing the Main Idea

▶▶ Defining the Skill

When you find and summarize the main idea, you restate the subject of a written passage in fewer words. You include only the main idea and the most important details. It is important to use your own words when summarizing.

▶▶ Applying the Skill

The passage to the right tells about the climate in Latin America. Use the strategies listed below to help you find the main idea and summarize a passage.

How to Summarize

Strategy ❶ Look for a topic sentence stating the main idea. This is often at the beginning of a section or paragraph. Briefly restate the main idea in your own words.

Strategy ❷ Include key facts, numbers, dates, amounts, or percentages from the text.

Strategy ❸ After writing your summary, review it to see that you have included the main idea and the most important details.

The Tropical Zone

❶ A large portion of Latin America lies within the Tropical Zone, ❷ which is the region between the latitudes 23°27' north and 23°27' south. ❷ The Tropical Zone may be rainy or dry, but it is typically hot. ❷ Also, temperature is always lower at higher elevations, but in the Tropical Zone, all elevations are warmer than they are elsewhere.

Write a Summary

You can write your summary in a paragraph. The paragraph below summarizes the passage you just read.

> ❸ Much of Latin America is in the Tropical Zone. This zone is between latitudes 23°27' north and 23°27' south. Usually, the Tropical Zone is hot. Also, the elevations in the Tropical Zone are warmer than the same elevations in other places.

▶▶ Practicing the Skill

Turn to page 161 in Chapter 6, Section 2, "Ancient Latin America." Read "Maya Agriculture," find the main idea, and write a paragraph summarizing the passage.

TERMS & NAMES

Explain the significance of each of the following:

1. tributary
2. deforestation
3. Tropical Zone
4. *El Niño*
5. hieroglyph
6. *chinampa*
7. Machu Picchu
8. Hernán Cortés
9. Montezuma II
10. Columbian Exchange

REVIEW QUESTIONS

Physical Geography *(pages 153–159)*

1. Describe two problems that Mexico City faces because of its location.
2. What two types of islands are found in the Caribbean?
3. Describe the climate in the Tropical Zone.
4. How have tectonic plates affected Latin America's physical geography? Give two examples.

Ancient Latin America *(pages 160–166)*

5. Explain the use of each of the three Maya calendars.
6. Why was warfare so important to the Aztec?
7. Describe two means of communication used by the Inca.
8. What types of changes took place in Latin America once the Spanish took control?

CRITICAL THINKING

Comparing

1. Using your completed chart from Reading Social Studies, p. 152, compare two ancient Latin American civilizations. List the similarities in the locations, dates, characteristics, achievements, and declines of the two civilizations.

Synthesizing

2. How are the farming methods of the Maya, the Aztec, and the Inca examples of people adapting to their environment?

Hypothesizing

3. Around A.D. 900, the Maya civilization—though not the people—began to disappear. What might have contributed to this decline?

Visual Summary

1 Physical Geography

- A variety of physical features, such as mountains and rivers, have impacted life in Latin America. Also, natural disasters, such as earthquakes and volcanic eruptions, occur frequently because of the region's location on five tectonic plates.
- The variations in Latin America's climate are caused by factors such as elevation, location, wind, and water.

2 Ancient Latin America

- The Maya, the Aztec, and the Inca all built major civilizations in Latin America.
- Each civilization developed creative solutions to problems presented by the physical geography around them.

Use the map and your knowledge of world cultures and geography to answer questions 1 and 2.

Additional Test Practice, pp. S1–S33

Original rain forest

Rain forest as of 2000

0   500   1,000 miles
0   500   1,000 kilometers

1. In what part of South America did no rain forest exist in 2000?

A. East

B. North

C. Northwest

D. South

2. What major trend does this map show?

A. The rain forests of South America are decreasing.

B. The rain forests of South America are increasing.

C. The rain forests of South America have not changed.

D. The rain forests of South America have disappeared.

This passage is from a speech that Prince Charles of the United Kingdom gave about tropical rain forests. Use the quotation and your knowledge of world cultures and geography to answer question 3.

PRIMARY SOURCE

It is not just those who depend directly on the tropical forests who suffer from deforestation, but the entire population of tropical forest countries. The forests assist in the regulation of local climate patterns, protecting watersheds, preventing floods, guaranteeing and controlling huge flows of life-giving water. Strip away the forests and there is, first, too much water . . . and then too little.

CHARLES, PRINCE OF WALES, from a speech given on February 6, 1990

3. Which of the following observations is supported by the passage?

A. Those who inhabit the tropical forest suffer the most from the effects of deforestation.

B. Efforts to save the tropical forest should be the sole responsibility of those people who live there.

C. The preservation of tropical forests will positively affect the entire country in which they exist.

D. Deforestation of the tropical forest has little effect on the climate of countries in the region.

TEST PRACTICE
CLASSZONE.COM

ALTERNATIVE ASSESSMENT

1. **WRITING ABOUT HISTORY**

The Columbian Exchange brought a sharing of both goods and ideas between European countries and the colonies in Latin America. Write a magazine article about the Columbian Exchange.

- Use the Internet and library resources to learn about the crops, goods, animals, and ideas that were sent in each direction across the Atlantic Ocean.

- Explain which trade items came from Latin America and which came from Europe. Describe how the new items were used in each region.

2. COOPERATIVE LEARNING

Both the Aztec and the Maya used two calendars—one with 260 days and one with 365 days. With a small group of classmates, research one of the Aztec or Mayan calendars. Find out how many months were in a year, how many days were in a month, and what the names of the months or days were. Then, together, create a calendar based on your findings.

INTEGRATED TECHNOLOGY

Doing Internet Research

The ancient cultures of Latin America were among the earliest civilizations. Research one of these ancient cultures—Aztec, Maya, or Inca—in order to prepare a report.

- Use the Internet or reference sources in the library to learn about one aspect of daily life, such as religion, trade, or warfare, in the culture you chose.

- You might find information about ancient ruins on Web sites.

- If possible, include illustrations with your report.

For Internet links to support this activity, go to

RESEARCH LINKS
CLASSZONE.COM

CHAPTER 7

Mexico Today

Place Mexico City's main plaza, the Zócalo, is the center of one of the world's largest cities.

FOCUS ON
GEOGRAPHY

How has Mexico's lack of farmable land shaped how people live?

Human-Environment Interaction • Only 12 percent of Mexico's land is arable—that is, farmable. The rest is too steep and rocky or too dry. Even the land that people can farm is not always very productive. Inconsistent rainfall, erosion, and pollution problems can pose serious challenges to farming. Also, some people do farm in mountainous regions, but planting and harvesting crops there can be very difficult.

What do you think?

♦ How do countries benefit economically from having a great deal of arable land?

♦ What challenges does Mexico face—in its economy and daily life—as a result of having little arable land?

READING SOCIAL STUDIES

BEFORE YOU READ

▶▶ *What Do You Know?*

Before you read the chapter, think about what you already know about Mexico. You may have read about the Aztec in another class. Do you know about any aspects of Mexico's culture today? Think about what you've heard on the news about Mexico—do you know who the president of Mexico is?

Culture • The Aztec feather shields were no match for Spanish armor. ▲

▶▶ *What Do You Want to Know?*

Decide what else you want to know about Mexico. In your notebook, record what you hope to learn from this chapter.

READ AND TAKE NOTES

Reading Strategy: Organizing Information
One effective way to organize information is with a time line. Time lines show events in sequence, or the order in which they happened. Making a time line for the events in this chapter will help you better understand what happened when.

- Copy the time line in your notebook.
- As you read the chapter, note the key events discussed in it.
- Write these events beside the appropriate dates on your time line.

Place • At the Ballet Folklórico, the culture of Mexico takes center stage. ▲

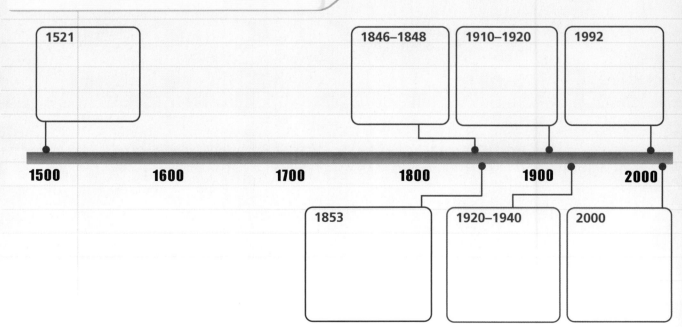

| 1521 | | 1846–1848 | 1910–1920 | 1992 |

| **1500** | **1600** | **1700** | **1800** | **1900** | **2000** |

| 1853 | | 1920–1940 | 2000 |

The Roots of Modern Mexico

TERMS & NAMES
peninsular
criollo
mestizo
encomienda
Father Miguel Hidalgo
Treaty of Guadalupe Hidalgo
Gadsden Purchase

MAIN IDEA

Modern Mexico arose from conflict and cooperation among Native American, African, and Spanish Mexicans.

WHY IT MATTERS NOW

The culture of Mexico today reflects the influences of and interactions among these groups.

DATELINE
EXTRA

TENOCHTITLÁN, AZTEC EMPIRE, 1519

Today, in the palace of the Aztec emperor Montezuma II, a Spanish explorer got a taste of something he is sure to remember. A treat enjoyed by both the Aztec and Maya, the drink, called *chocolatl*, is thick, smooth, and decidedly bitter. With no sugar added to sweeten it, this unusual drink is spiced with flavors such as chili pepper and vanilla.

Always served in liquid form, the drink is consumed by the Native Americans at a high rate. Emperor Montezuma II drinks up to 50 cups a day. The Spaniards hope to take the chocolate, as they call it, back to Europe—although they plan to find some way to help ease the bitter taste.

Region • Cacao seeds grow inside pods like this. ▲

The Arrival of the Spanish

The leader of the Spanish army that first landed on the shores of Mexico was Hernán Cortés. He hoped to win new lands for Spain, as well as gold and glory for himself.

Cortés reached the east coast of Mexico in 1519 with about 500 soldiers. He claimed the land for the king and queen of Spain. Quickly, however, he learned that the land was ruled by the powerful Aztec emperor Montezuma II.

TAKING NOTES

Use your time line to take notes about Mexico.

1500   1700

A Clash of Cultures

Montezuma II ruled an empire of between 5 and 6 million people. However, many of his Native American subjects wanted to be free. They helped the Spanish conquer the Aztec king. They did not expect that the Spanish would become their new rulers.

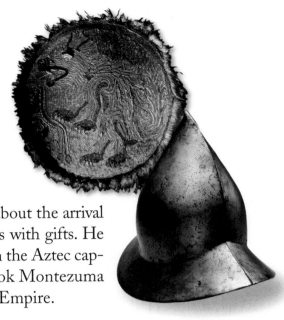

The First Encounter Montezuma II heard about the arrival of the Spanish, and soon he welcomed Cortés with gifts. He even allowed Cortés to stay in a royal palace in the Aztec capital, Tenochtitlán. Within a week, Cortés took Montezuma II prisoner—and took control of the Aztec Empire.

The Spanish Takeover Other Aztec leaders drove the Spanish from Tenochtitlán. However, during the fighting that followed, Montezuma II was killed. The Spanish then retook the city, greatly aided by their Native American allies. The Spanish also had an essential advantage over the Aztec: their weapons. The Aztec had only war clubs, spears, and arrows. The Spanish soldiers had steel swords, armor, guns, and cannons, as well as horses. The invading army destroyed Tenochtitlán street by street.

Culture • Aztec feather shields offered less protection than Spanish metal helmets and armor. ▲

Reading
Social Studies

A. Analyzing Motives Why did some Native Americans help the Spanish fight the Aztec?

The Founding of New Spain

The fall of Tenochtitlán in 1521 marked the end of the Aztec Empire and the beginning of Spanish rule in Mexico. The Spanish called their empire "New Spain," just as the English called their territory in North America "New England." Where Tenochtitlán had stood, the Spanish established Mexico City as their capital. Spain ruled Mexico for the next 300 years.

A New Way of Life The Spanish victory caused more than a change of rulers in Mexico. The Spanish introduced a different way of life to the region. They brought new animals, such as horses, cattle, sheep, and pigs. They also brought new trades, such as ironsmithing and shipbuilding. They brought a new religion as well—Christianity.

Connections to Science

Invisible Weapons Smallpox and other diseases from Europe killed millions of Native Americans between 1500 and 1900. Smallpox (germ cell shown below right) had long been widespread in Europe, and most Europeans were at least partly immune. Native Americans, however, had no immunity to it because it had never before existed in the Americas.

Within months of the Spanish soldiers' arrival in Mexico, many thousands of Native Americans got sick with smallpox (shown below) and died from it—including Montezuma II's successor. Smallpox proved far more deadly to Native Americans than Spanish swords and cannons.

Vocabulary

ironsmithing: making items out of iron

The Influence of the Church

Because the Catholic Church was powerful in Spain, it soon became powerful in New Spain. Catholic priests set up churches, schools, and hospitals. Sometimes Native Americans accepted Christianity willingly. Sometimes, though, they were forced to become Christian against their will.

A Cultural Blend Even though the Native Americans had to accept many new ways of life, the old ways were not lost entirely. For instance, an essential element of Native American cooking was the tortilla, a flat, round bread made from corn or flour. Tortillas are still made daily all over Mexico. As with food, many other aspects of the two cultures blended in the new Mexican culture.

Life in New Spain

BACKGROUND

The Iberian Peninsula consists of two countries—Portugal and Spain. (See the map of Europe on page 262.)

A new multilayered society developed in Mexico. The ruling class were Spanish officials who were born in Spain. They were called _**peninsulares**_ (peh·neen·soo·LAH·rehs) because they were from the Iberian Peninsula in Europe.

A second class were _**criollos**_ (kree·AW·yaws), people who were born in Mexico but whose parents were born in Spain. _Criollos_ were often wealthy and powerful, but they were not in as high a social class as the _peninsulares_.

A _**mestizo**_ (mehs·TEE·saw) is a person who is of Spanish and Native American ancestry. _Mestizos_ formed the third layer of New Spain's society.

Movement •
Mexicans today celebrate Catholic holy days that the Spanish established. This festival honors Our Lady of Guadalupe. ▼

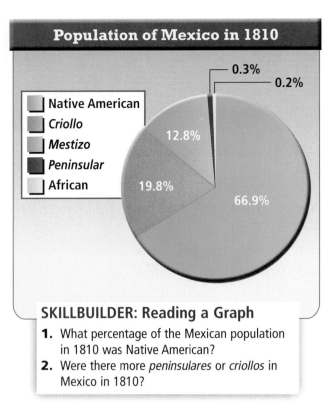

Population of Mexico in 1810

- Native American
- Criollo
- Mestizo
- Peninsular
- African

0.3%
0.2%
12.8%
19.8%
66.9%

SKILLBUILDER: Reading a Graph

1. What percentage of the Mexican population in 1810 was Native American?
2. Were there more *peninsulares* or *criollos* in Mexico in 1810?

A fourth group of people arrived in Mexico unwillingly—the enslaved Africans brought by European slave ships. African farming techniques, musical traditions, and crafts soon blended into the Mexican culture.

Encomienda New Spain's largest group was the Native Americans. They made up the bottom layer of society. The rulers of Spain set up in Mexico a system called **encomienda** (ehn·kaw·MYEHN·dah). Under this system, Spanish men were each given a Native American village to oversee. The villagers had to pay tribute—in goods, money, or labor—to this Spaniard. They were essentially enslaved. The results of their labor helped to make Spain rich. However, the villagers lived in poverty and hardship.

The War of Independence

Based on earlier European and American political writers, many Mexican religious and political leaders in the early 1800s were saying that Mexicans should be free to choose their own government. They argued that Mexico should be independent from Spain. The demand for Mexican independence grew stronger after 1808, when France conquered Spain.

A Cry for Freedom Then, before dawn on September 16, 1810, the farmers in the mountain village of Dolores heard their church bells ringing. At the church, their priest, **Father Miguel Hidalgo,** gave a fiery speech urging them to throw off Spanish rule. No one knows the exact text of the speech, but it is known as the *Grito de Dolores* (Cry of Dolores). Urged on by his words, a small army of Native Americans and *mestizos* marched with Father Hidalgo toward Mexico City. Along the way, thousands more joined them.

A Difficult Challenge Father Hidalgo's army had few weapons. Mostly, his men carried clubs and farm tools, such as sickles and axes. When they faced the government soldiers, the farmers were soon defeated. Father Hidalgo was captured and executed, but the revolution he had sparked did not die.

Reading **Social Studies**

B. Clarifying What ideas from other parts of the world did Mexicans agree with?

Vocabulary
sickle:
a blade used for cutting tall grass or grain

Independence at Last New leaders took Father Hidalgo's place. A few wealthy Spanish nobles and many *criollos* joined the fight for independence. The struggle lasted for 11 years. In 1821, the rebels finally overthrew the Spanish government, and Mexico became independent. However, the *peninsulares* and *criollos* still ruled the country. Native Americans and *mestizos* benefited little from independence from Spain.

War with the United States

In 1821, the new nation of Mexico was far larger than it is today. You can see on the map on page 178 that northern Mexico included much of what is now the Southwestern United States. Spanish explorers claimed this entire region in the 1500s and 1600s. Spanish and Mexican priests built missions there in the 1600s.

Desert and Distance Much of this land was desert. Travel was slow and communication difficult. Mexico was at war with Native Americans in this region, such as the Apache and the Comanche tribes. For all these reasons, few Mexicans settled there.

To encourage settlement, the Mexican government invited foreigners to move into these northern lands. Most of the newcomers were from the United States and still felt some loyalty to that country. By the 1830s, settlers in Texas from the United States greatly outnumbered those from Mexico.

Texas Independence In 1835, many settlers in Texas decided to break away from Mexico and rose in revolt. After several fierce battles, the Texans won their independence. They set up the Republic of Texas in 1836.

Most Texans wanted to become part of the United States. In 1845, the United States agreed, but Mexico and the United States could not agree where the boundary between Texas and Mexico should be. Each side claimed land that the other wanted.

The Mexican War In 1846, the dispute grew into a war. During the next two years, U.S. forces won control of northern Mexico; it was made official when Mexico was forced to sign the **Treaty of Guadalupe Hidalgo.**

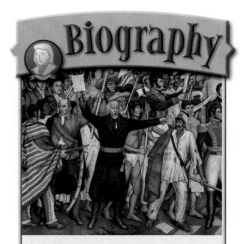

Biography

Father Hidalgo Father Miguel Hidalgo y Costilla, shown in the center of the illustration above, was born in 1753. He was a *criollo* who felt great sympathy for the Native Americans and *mestizos*. As a priest in the small village of Dolores, Father Hidalgo joined a secret group that fought for Mexico's independence.

Father Hidalgo is known as the Father of Mexican Independence. Every September 16, Mexicans shout slogans from the *Grito de Dolores* in celebration of their independence and Father Hidalgo.

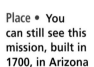

Place • **You can still see this mission, built in 1700, in Arizona today.** ▼

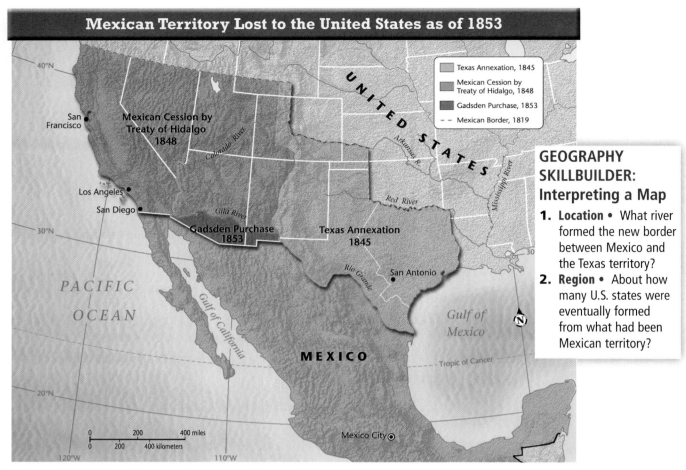

Mexican Territory Lost to the United States as of 1853

- Texas Annexation, 1845
- Mexican Cession by Treaty of Hidalgo, 1848
- Gadsden Purchase, 1853
- – – Mexican Border, 1819

Mexican Cession by Treaty of Hidalgo 1848

Gadsden Purchase 1853

Texas Annexation 1845

UNITED STATES

San Francisco

Los Angeles

San Diego

PACIFIC OCEAN

Colorado River

Gila River

Arkansas R.

Red River

Mississippi River

Rio Grande

San Antonio

Gulf of California

MEXICO

Gulf of Mexico

Tropic of Cancer

Mexico City

GEOGRAPHY SKILLBUILDER: Interpreting a Map

1. **Location** • What river formed the new border between Mexico and the Texas territory?
2. **Region** • About how many U.S. states were eventually formed from what had been Mexican territory?

A few years later, in 1853, the **Gadsden Purchase** gave the United States more of Mexico's northern land. The two countries have since made slight adjustments to the border, but they have not fought a war again.

SECTION 1 ASSESSMENT

Terms & Names

1. Explain the significance of:
   (a) *peninsular*   (b) *criollo*   (c) *mestizo*   (d) *encomienda*   (e) Father Miguel Hidalgo
   (f) Treaty of Guadalupe Hidalgo   (g) Gadsden Purchase

Using Graphics

2. Use a chart like this one to list the five social groups that made up New Spain and their characteristics.

Social Group	Characteristics

Main Ideas

3. (a) What advantages allowed Cortés's small army to conquer Mexico?

   (b) In what ways did Spanish rule change life in Mexico?

   (c) What were the results of the war between Mexico and the United States?

Critical Thinking

4. **Analyzing Causes**

   Why did Mexicans decide to fight for independence from Spain?

   Think About

   ◆ influential events around the world

   ◆ reasons for discontent among the *criollos, mestizos,* and Native Americans

ACTIVITY -OPTION- Reread the information about the first meeting of the Spanish and the Aztec. Write a **short story** describing the event from either the Spanish or Aztec viewpoint.

Government in Mexico: Revolution and Reform

SECTION 2

TERMS & NAMES
Benito Juárez
Francisco Madero
hacienda
Emiliano Zapata
ejido
Institutional Revolutionary Party
Vicente Fox

MAIN IDEA
Through periods of reform and revolution, Mexico struggled to establish a strong democratic national government.

WHY IT MATTERS NOW
Other countries, such as the United States, are more willing to work as partners with Mexico because its government is democratic.

DATELINE

QUERÉTARO, MEXICO, 1917—Amid the battles of the Mexican Revolution, politicians today took a step toward reforming the nation. After many weeks of discussion and debate, they produced a new constitution for Mexico. The document presents new approaches to issues such as education, landownership, and religion.

Perhaps this constitution will become a basis for a new and stable Mexican government. For now, though, the constant fighting among sides continues. The potential power of the constitution will be revealed only in time, as the government puts the document into action.

Location • President Venustiano Carranza organized the meetings that resulted in the 1917 constitution. ▲

A Struggle for Power

The constitution of 1917 was written as a response to the struggles of the previous century. During that time, Mexico spent many years fighting wars. In 1821, Mexico won its war for independence from Spain. Two decades later, Mexicans entered into and then lost a war with the United States over Texas, California, and other lands. During all these years, still another struggle was going on—a struggle for power within Mexico.

TAKING NOTES
Use your time line to take notes about Mexico.

1500   1700

In the years after independence, army leaders often took over Mexico's government. In some parts of the country, bandits attacked travelers. Elsewhere, Mexicans fought with Spanish landowners. Everywhere, a few people enjoyed great wealth, while many suffered in poverty.

Benito Juárez Brings Reform

By the 1850s, many Mexicans were eager for reform. They found a leader in **Benito Juárez,** a man who rose from poverty to become president of Mexico and a hero to his people. He became minister of justice in 1855, and he later became chief justice of the Supreme Court. In 1858, he gained the presidency, giving control of the Mexican government to the reformers.

Response to Reform The reformers wrote a new constitution for Mexico in 1857. For the first time, Mexicans had a bill of rights, promising them freedom of speech and equality under the law. The constitution of 1857 also ended slavery and forced labor. However, the new constitution did not promise freedom of religion. Nor did it make Catholicism Mexico's official religion, as many church leaders had hoped it would. The reformers also cut back the army's power in the government.

These reforms stirred up a storm of controversy. Church leaders, army leaders, and wealthy landowners were outraged. From 1858 to 1860, the War of Reform raged between the reformers and their opponents.

Culture • Benito Juárez was a Zapotec, one of the many Native American groups in Mexico. He grew up in a mountain village, studied law, and then went into politics. ▲

Foreign Intervention in Mexico The War of Reform left Mexico so weak—because of death, debt, and unemployment—that the country was an easy target for foreign takeover. Spain, Britain, and France sent troops into Mexico. In 1863, after more than a year of fighting, the French marched into Mexico City and established themselves in control of the country. They made a European nobleman named Maximilian emperor. Maximilian did not reign long. The Mexicans overthrew Maximilian and executed him in 1867.

Culture • Mexican forces fight their way to victory in an early battle against the French in 1862. ▼

An End to Reform That same year, Benito Juárez and the reformers returned to power. Juárez remained president until his death in 1872. Unfortunately, his successors cared about reform less than he had. Poverty and lack of education remained problems. A few rich families held most of the political and economic power. Not until the 20th century did a new wave of reform begin.

The Mexican Revolution

By 1910, the divisions between rich and poor in Mexico were huge. Just 800 families owned more than 90 percent of the farmland. Of Mexico's 15 million people, 10 million owned no land at all.

A Decade of War Once again, many Mexicans decided to fight for reforms. And once again, the struggle turned bloody. From 1910 to 1920, Mexico endured the Mexican Revolution.

The Revolution was a fight among many armies. Almost every part of Mexico had an army of rebels and reformers with particular goals. One of the first revolutionary leaders was a wealthy rancher named **Francisco Madero,** who became president in 1911. For Madero and his supporters, the key issue was free, honest elections. For others, however, the most important problem was landownership.

Region • During the Revolution, Francisco "Pancho" Villa was a famous leader in the north of Mexico. ▼

The Problem of Land Poor farmers wanted land of their own. They believed the government should give each farm family a few acres by breaking up the giant *haciendas.* A **hacienda** is a big farm or ranch, often as large as 40,000 or 50,000 acres. Much of the *hacienda* land had once belonged to village farmers. But a law passed in 1883 allowed some of the wealthiest ranch owners to easily take away land from the village farmers. During the 1880s and 1890s, the ranch owners took over millions of acres of land owned by village farmers, and that land became part of their *haciendas.*

Reading Social Studies

A. Analyzing Issues What sorts of concerns led Mexicans to fight in the Mexican Revolution?

Region • Like this one, many of Mexico's *haciendas* were situated on huge pieces of land. ▶

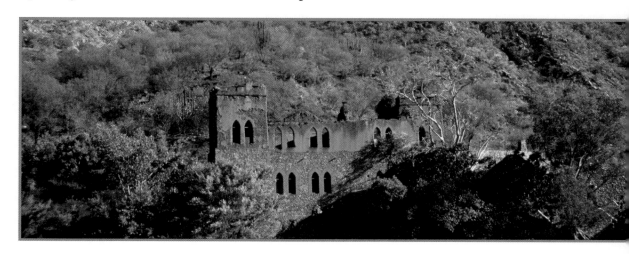

Emiliano Zapata was a legendary fighter for farmers' rights. With his famous motto—"Land and Liberty!"—Zapata gathered an army in the south of Mexico and urged farmers to join him.

A VOICE FROM MEXICO

Join me. . . . We want a much better president. Rise up with us because we don't like what the rich men pay us. It is not enough for us to eat and dress ourselves. I also want for everyone to have his piece of land so that he can plant and harvest corn, beans, and other crops. What do you say? Are you going to join us?

Emiliano Zapata

Connections to Citizenship

The Mexican Flag In the middle of Mexico's flag sits an eagle holding a snake in its mouth—a symbol from an Aztec legend about the founding of their capital, Tenochtitlán. The legend says that in the 1100s, the Aztec sun god told the Aztec to build a city on the spot where they saw an eagle with a snake in its mouth. When they saw just such an eagle in the middle of Lake Texcoco, they knew where to build their capital.

Each of the flag's red, white, and green stripes represents one of the "three guarantees" of the Mexican War of Independence. By flying a flag that combines a symbol from Aztec times with one from the period of independence, Mexico shows how important its roots are to its modern identity.

A Continuing Revolution

Over the course of a decade, dozens of large and small armies fought with one another. In 1913, Madero was murdered. The same fate befell Zapata in 1919. Between 1910 and 1920, more than 1 million Mexicans died in the battles of the Revolution. In 1920, a new government managed to make peace among the many armies. The fighting was over, but the Revolution—the effort to reform Mexico's government and economy— went on.

Answering Demands for Land In 1917, a new constitution was written, and one of its promises was to distribute land more equally among the people. Between 1920 and 1940, the government broke up many of the giant *haciendas*. Millions of acres were divided among small farmers or given to *ejidos*. An ***ejido*** (eh·HEE·daw) is a community farm owned by all the villagers together. Farmers were proud and happy to have their own land once again.

Reading Social Studies

B. Summarizing How did the 1917 constitution respond to concerns about landownership?

The Revolution in Politics The idea of the Revolution was so important and popular among new Mexicans that the most powerful political party called itself the party of the Revolution. Its name changed several times, but the word *revolution* was always part of it. Today, it is called the **Institutional Revolutionary Party** (Partido Revolucionario Institucional, or PRI). This party won every presidential election in Mexico from 1929 until 2000, with power passing peacefully from one president to the next.

Mexico's Government Today

December 1, 2000, was a historic occasion in Mexico. On that day, **Vicente Fox** became Mexico's new president. Fox was the first president in more than 70 years who did not belong to the PRI. Instead, he belonged to the National Action Party (Partido Acción Nacional, or PAN). The election of a president from a party other than the PRI confirmed that Mexico was entering a time of new political possibilities.

National Government Mexico's official name is Estados Unidos Mexicanos, or the United Mexican States. Thirty-one states make up the nation. Mexico is a democracy and a republic. All Mexicans who are 18 or older have the right to vote. The Mexican government has three branches. As in the United States, these branches are the executive, legislative, and judicial.

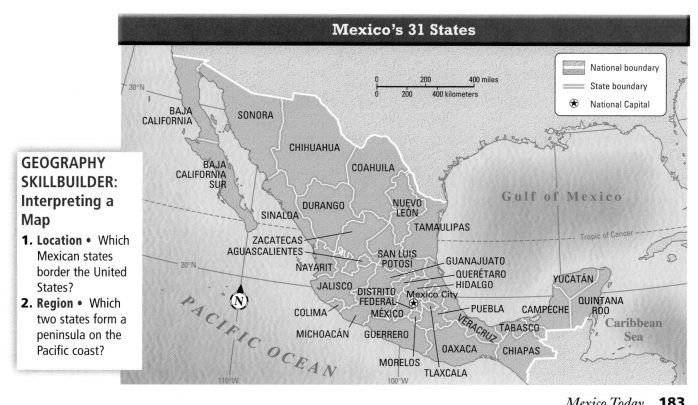

Mexico's 31 States

GEOGRAPHY SKILLBUILDER: Interpreting a Map

1. **Location** • Which Mexican states border the United States?
2. **Region** • Which two states form a peninsula on the Pacific coast?

State Government Like the United States, Mexico has a federal system of government, in which power is shared between the national government and state governments. Voters in each state elect a governor. Each state also has its own legislature that makes laws. However, the national government has some control over the state governments. For example, the president and the national Senate together can remove a state governor from office.

Local Government Most towns and villages depend on money from the national government. Therefore, a local government has less say in its town's affairs than the national government does. However, local governments do provide essential public services, such as maintaining sewer systems and public safety.

Region •
The Mexican government issues stamps that celebrate its people and achievements. ▶

SECTION 2 ASSESSMENT

Terms & Names
1. Explain the significance of:
   - (a) Benito Juárez
   - (b) Francisco Madero
   - (c) *hacienda*
   - (d) Emiliano Zapata
   - (e) *ejido*
   - (f) Institutional Revolutionary Party
   - (g) Vicente Fox

Using Graphics
2. Use a chart like this one to record details about each level of Mexico's government.

National	State	Local

Main Ideas
3. (a) What changes did reformers such as Benito Juárez help bring about in Mexico?

   (b) Why was the Mexican Revolution fought among many armies?

   (c) How did the Mexican government help farmers gain land of their own?

Critical Thinking
4. **Analyzing Points of View**

   How did different groups view the need for reform and change in Mexico during the years from 1850 to 1940?

   Think About
   - Juárez and the reformers
   - Madero and his supporters
   - the owners of the *haciendas*
   - Zapata and the small farmers

Think about a constitution's bill of rights. Write a **speech** explaining why a bill of rights is important to citizens.

Mexico's Changing Economy

TERMS & NAMES

Carlos Salinas
de Gortari
privatization
distribution
maquiladora
nationalize
PEMEX
tourism

MAIN IDEA

In the mid-1900s, the basis of Mexico's economy changed from farming to industry and tourism.

WHY IT MATTERS NOW

Mexico's successful expansion of its economy has helped the nation to prosper.

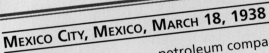

DATELINE

EXTRA

MEXICO CITY, MEXICO, MARCH 18, 1938

President Lázaro Cárdenas's radio address today established a new course for Mexico's economy. Speaking to the nation, the president announced that foreigners will no longer be allowed to control petroleum companies in Mexico.

The oil industry will now be run by the Mexican government itself. It is hoped that this change will boost both Mexico's economy and its national identity.

Human-Environment Interaction • The Mexican government will now own all oil-producing equipment, such as these oil wells in Veracruz. ▶

Farming in a Time of Change

The 1938 decision that the government would own Mexico's oil industry was made in an effort to expand Mexico's economy. The expansion was necessary because, from ancient times until the mid-1900s, most Mexicans worked in just one industry—farming. Since the 1950s, great numbers of Mexicans have left farming for other kinds of work. However, farming is still important to Mexico's economy.

TAKING NOTES
Use your time line to take notes about Mexico.

1500   1700

Human-Environment Interaction • At far left, a worker on a small Mexican farm carries crops on his back. At left, a private farm turns out hundreds of crates of produce at once. ◄

The Problems of Farming About one-fourth of Mexican workers are farmers. Many small farmers still work on the *ejidos,* or community farms, that were set up after the Revolution.

Although the *ejido* system gave land to many poor villagers, it did not lift them out of poverty. Farmers could not use the land as security for a bank loan because they did not really own their land—the *ejido* did. Without much money, they could not buy tractors, plows, or fertilizer. They had to continue to farm in the old ways, with hand tools on worn-out soil.

A New System In 1991, Mexican president **Carlos Salinas de Gortari** decided it was time to change the *ejido* system. Under Salinas's new laws, farmers could vote to divide their *ejido* into individual farms. Each farm family would have its own piece of land. The family could sell, rent, or trade its land. This process of replacing community ownership with individual, or private, ownership is called **privatization**.

The supporters of privatization hope that private farms will be able to grow more crops. Many of these farms are run like big businesses. Banks lend them money so they can afford to buy and use modern machinery. They can then grow the crops that Mexico sells to other countries, such as cotton, coffee, sugar cane, and strawberries.

Ejidos still make up about half the farmland in Mexico. This is partly because some farmers do not want to divide their *ejidos* into private farms. They worry that privatization might once again put most of the country's land into the hands of a few wealthy people.

Reading
Social Studies

A. Clarifying How does using land on an *ejido* differ from owning one's own land?

Region • In this Mexican factory, workers make car parts. ▲

The Growth of Business and Industry

During the mid-1900s, industry became a larger part of Mexico's economy because the Mexican government took steps to encourage its growth. For example, the government built new power plants to supply energy for factories. It also constructed homes for factory workers.

The Mexican government also helped new companies get started by lending them money from the national bank. Sometimes the government lowered taxes on businesses or helped companies pay back money they had borrowed.

Effects of Government Aid The new policies encouraged production. As a result, new factories sprang up that made products such as steel, chemicals, paper, soft drinks, and textiles. The Mexican government also promoted the building of highways, railroads, and airports to aid manufacturers in the distribution of goods. **Distribution** is the process of moving products to their markets.

Privatization of Business In the same way that it was privatizing farms, the Mexican government during the 1990s began to privatize businesses. It raised millions of dollars by selling businesses, such as banks, mines, and steel mills, to private companies. By 2000, only a few key industries—such as the oil industry—were still in government hands.

Foreign-Owned Businesses in Mexico During the 1990s, many of Mexico's fastest-growing factories were situated along its border with the United States. These factories are called *maquiladoras.* In Mexico, a **_maquiladora_** (mah·kee·lah·DAW·rah) is a factory that imports duty-free parts from the United States to make products that it then exports back across the border. The lack of a tax on the parts helps keep operating costs low. Also, most of Mexico's *maquiladoras* are owned by foreigners, who save money because wages are lower in Mexico than in countries such as the United States. Although the wages are not great, *maquiladoras* have provided hundreds of thousands of jobs in Mexico.

Vocabulary

duty-free: free of government-imposed taxes

Citizenship IN ACTION

Na Bolom Since 1951, an organization called Na Bolom (headquarters shown below) has tried to help maintain Mexico's national heritage. Na Bolom works with the Maya living in the southeastern part of Mexico to uphold their traditional ways of life while also developing their economic opportunities. The group also tries to protect the often-threatened resources of the surrounding environment, such as the rain forest.

NAFTA Giving tax breaks on trade items is also a goal of the North American Free Trade Agreement (NAFTA). NAFTA has reduced taxes on items traded among Mexico, the United States, and Canada. However, some Mexicans are not sure NAFTA is a good idea—they worry that having such close ties to the United States and Canada gives those countries too much influence over Mexico. Despite these concerns, Mexico has nearly doubled its trade with the United States and with Canada since NAFTA was approved in 1992.

Mexico's Rich Resources

Just as gold and silver drew the Spanish to Mexico in the 1500s, other minerals that are found there attract worldwide interest today. While Mexico produces more silver than any other country in the world, it also mines lead, zinc, graphite, sulfur, and copper.

The Booming Oil Industry By far the most important of Mexico's natural resources is petroleum, or oil. In 1938, the Mexican government decided to **nationalize,** or establish government control of, the oil industry. Today, when many other businesses have been privatized, the oil industry is still government owned. An agency called **PEMEX** (which stands for Petróleos Mexicanos, or Mexican Petroleum) runs the industry. PEMEX is Mexico's largest and most important company. Oil is Mexico's biggest export, and the United States is its largest buyer.

Reading
Social Studies

B. Contrasting How does nationalization differ from privatization?

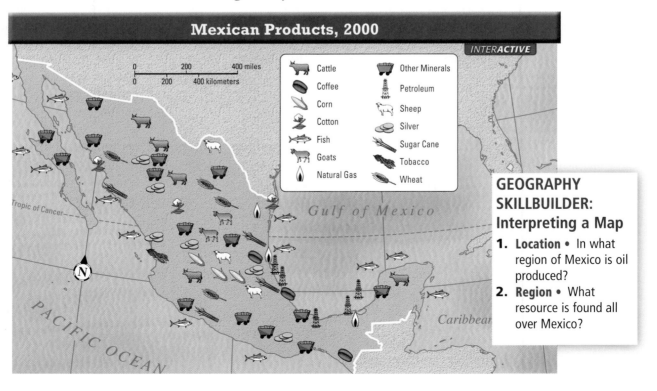

Mexican Products, 2000

INTER**ACTIVE**

Cattle	Other Minerals
Coffee	Petroleum
Corn	Sheep
Cotton	Silver
Fish	Sugar Cane
Goats	Tobacco
Natural Gas	Wheat

GEOGRAPHY SKILLBUILDER: Interpreting a Map

1. **Location** • In what region of Mexico is oil produced?
2. **Region** • What resource is found all over Mexico?

Tourism Is Big Business

Mexico's second-largest business is tourism. **Tourism** is the business of helping people travel on vacations. Tourists come to Mexico to enjoy its warm weather and its sunny beaches. Many people also visit the ancient Native American ruins. Visitors admire art in Mexico City's spectacular museums. They also shop for fine silver jewelry, weavings, wood carvings, and other handicrafts.

Place •
Tourists who travel to Santa Catalina Island, off western Mexico, can see rattleless rattlesnakes, which live nowhere else on Earth. ▲

Economic Effects of Tourism A popular tourist place in Mexico is Cancún, on the country's southeastern coast. The story of Cancún shows the effect tourism has had on Mexico's economy.

Until 1970, Cancún was a small Maya village of about 100 people. Its shoreline had white sand beaches and palm trees. The weather was sunny almost every day. In 1970, the Mexican government decided Cancún was an ideal place for a holiday resort. Working together, the government and private businesses built an airport, new roads, and skyscraper hotels.

Today, more than 2.5 million people from all over the world visit Cancún's resorts each year. Because of the tourism boom, the once tiny village has become a city with about 500,000 people.

SECTION 3 ASSESSMENT

Terms & Names

1. Explain the significance of: (a) Carlos Salinas de Gortari   (b) privatization   (c) distribution   (d) *maquiladora*
   (e) nationalize   (f) PEMEX   (g) tourism

Using Graphics

2. Use a chart like this one to take notes on four important parts of Mexico's economy.

Mexico's Economy	
Farming	
Industry	
Mining	
Tourism	

Main Ideas

3. (a) How has privatization changed the *ejido* system?

   (b) What part has Mexico's government played in the growth of industry?

   (c) How does tourism contribute to Mexico's economy?

Critical Thinking

4. **Forming and Supporting Opinions**

   Do you think the privatization of farmland in Mexico has been a positive step for Mexico's farmers? Why or why not?

   Think About
   - the concerns of some *ejido* farmers
   - farmers' need to modernize
   - Mexico's history of land reform

ACTIVITY -OPTION-   Draw a **flow chart** that shows the process by which goods are produced and distributed by a *maquiladora*.

Mexico's Culture Today

TERMS & NAMES
Diego Rivera
Frida Kahlo
Octavio Paz
rural
urban
Day of the Dead
fiesta

MAIN IDEA	WHY IT MATTERS NOW
Modern Mexican culture reflects a blending of Native American and Spanish heritages, as well as many new elements.	Cultures change over time, but understanding their histories can help you better understand their characteristics today.

DATELINE

GUADALAJARA, MEXICO, NOVEMBER 2, 2000—The streets of Guadalajara today buzzed with activity. Families strolled into cemeteries with armfuls of brightly colored flowers to lay on the gravesites of their relatives.

While eating picnics of spicy meat dishes, egg bread, and sugary desserts, family members shared favorite stories about their departed loved ones. In performing these and other customs, which mix Christian and Aztec traditions, they celebrated the Day of the Dead in typical Mexican fashion.

Culture • This gravesite is decorated for the Day of the Dead. ▲

Mexico's Blend of Cultures

Mexican culture today reflects the same pattern seen in the Day of the Dead celebrations—a mixing of traditions. This mix includes three main cultures. The first two, Native American and Spanish, have long histories. The third, modern Mexican, results from the natural changes Mexicans have gone through over time.

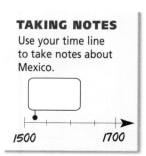

TAKING NOTES
Use your time line to take notes about Mexico.

1500   1700

Culture in Architecture A plaza near the center of Mexico City symbolizes the traditions that have come together in Mexico. At the center of this Plaza of Three Cultures stand the stone ruins of the Aztec marketplace. Nearby, a Spanish Catholic church borders the plaza. Beyond the plaza, skyscrapers rise against the sky and stand as landmarks of modern Mexico.

Culture in Other Forms of Art Just as Mexico's architecture reveals the multiple layers of its culture, so do other art forms. A series of historical murals decorates the walkways of the National Palace in Mexico City. Painted by **Diego Rivera,** one of Mexico's most celebrated 20th-century artists, these murals depict scenes from the Aztec Empire, New Spain, and the Mexican Revolution. Rivera's wife, **Frida Kahlo** (FREE·duh KAH·loh), is another favorite Mexican painter. After being injured badly in a bus accident, Kahlo painted many famous self-portraits from her bed.

Mexican literature also echoes the country's three cultural traditions. **Octavio Paz,** who won the Nobel Prize in literature in 1990, often writes about the connections between elements of Mexico's past.

Life in the City

About one of every five Mexicans lives in Mexico City. Thousands of people move there each year, hoping to work in factories or attend one of the city's universities or colleges. While Mexico City is by far the largest city in the country, many other cities and towns are growing quickly. Like Mexico City, they offer a blend of opportunities and problems.

Place • Aztec ruins, Spanish colonial architecture, and modern high-rises share space in the Plaza of Three Cultures. ▼

Mexico's Urban-Rural Population Distribution

29.3%

70.7%

1910

25.8%

74.2%

1999

Urban
Rural

SKILLBUILDER: Reading a Graph

1. What percentage of Mexico's population was urban in 1910? in 1999?
2. What does this tell you about changes that have taken place in Mexican society?

A Lively Capital With more than 18 million inhabitants, Mexico City is the second-largest city in the world, after Tokyo, Japan. It is also the cultural center of Mexico. The great marble Palace of Fine Arts houses the national opera, theater, and symphony. It is also home to the famous Ballet Folklórico, a group that performs spectacular dances based on Mexican traditions.

The Cost of Growth Growth has, however, created problems. Streets are jammed with traffic. Car exhaust creates a blanket of smog over the city. The government has responded to the pollution problem in a number of ways. One solution was to free taxi drivers from paying taxes on their vehicles if they drive cars that pollute less.

Spotlight on CULTURE

Culture • The dancers in Ballet Folklórico wear detailed, bright costumes. ▶

As is true in most large cities, a noticeable gap exists between the lives of Mexico City's rich and poor citizens. While luxurious homes and fine shopping centers line some streets, many people also live in poverty.

Life in the Countryside

In the smaller villages and farming towns, much of Mexico's older way of life still goes on. At the center of each village is a plaza, where people gather to talk and visit with neighbors. Most people speak Spanish, but many also speak Native American languages, such as those of the Aztec and Maya.

Each village sets aside one day a week as market day. People gather in the plaza to buy, sell, or trade food, clothing, and other goods. Farmers come in from surrounding areas, bringing vegetables and handicrafts. The scent of freshly baked *tortillas* and *frijoles*, or beans, fills the air.

Poverty in the Countryside Mexico's **rural** areas—those in the countryside—face the serious problem of poverty. Some homes have only one room and a dirt floor. Farmhouses may lack electricity and running water. These hardships have driven many rural Mexicans to seek jobs in **urban,** or city, settings.

Education is also more limited in the rural areas than in the urban ones. Without education, it is especially hard for people to escape poverty.

Mexican Muralist After the Mexican Revolution, artist Diego Rivera (1886–1957) painted a series of famous murals on the walls of the National Palace in Mexico City. Rivera wanted to use his art to remind Mexicans of the important events in their country's past. This mural shows a typical day in the Aztec capital, Tenochtitlán—now Mexico City.

THINKING CRITICALLY

1. **Synthesizing**
   What aspects of Aztec society was Rivera celebrating in this mural?

2. **Recognizing Details**
   Identify three activities depicted in the mural.

For more on Diego Rivera, go to

RESEARCH LINKS
CLASSZONE.COM

Our Lady of Guadalupe In 1531, many Mexicans believe, Mary, the mother of Jesus, appeared to Juan Diego, a Native American man, in the Villa de Guadalupe Hidalgo. Mary asked Juan Diego to carry some roses in his cloak to the local bishop. Amazingly, Juan Diego found that roses were blooming even in winter on a harsh, rocky hillside. More astonishingly, when he opened his cloak, Juan Diego saw on it an image of Mary.

Many Mexicans saw these events as miraculous. They began calling Mary "Our Lady of Guadalupe" (shown at right). She was so loved that Father Hidalgo carried a banner with her image to rally support for independence. Mexicans still regard her as their protector.

Holidays

September 16 is Mexico's Independence Day. To celebrate, Mexicans reenact Father Hidalgo's call in 1810 to rise up against Spanish rule. Then people watch fireworks, dance, and play music in the streets late into the night.

Another major holiday has a somber name— the **Day of the Dead.** Nevertheless, Mexicans see it as a joyful time. They set aside November 1 and 2 to remember and honor their loved ones who have died. They decorate the graves with candles and flowers. Bakeries sell loaves of bread shaped like bones, and many stores sell small candy skulls. Relatives gather for meals at the cemeteries.

At least once a year, each village or town celebrates a **fiesta.** A fiesta is a holiday with parades, games, and feasts. It usually takes place on a saint's day—a day set aside by the Catholic Church to honor the memory of a holy person. While these days have religious origins, they are also celebrated as big neighborhood parties.

SECTION 4 ASSESSMENT

Terms & Names
1. Explain the significance of:　(a) Diego Rivera　(b) Frida Kahlo　(c) Octavio Paz　(d) rural　(e) urban　(f) Day of the Dead　(g) fiesta

Using Graphics

2. Use a chart like this one to list the positive and negative features of living in urban or in rural Mexico.

	Positive Features	Negative Features
Rural Mexico		
Urban Mexico		

Main Ideas

3. (a) What three traditions mix in Mexico's culture today?

(b) Why is Mexico City growing so rapidly? What are the effects of that growth?

(c) Describe some of Mexico's holidays.

Critical Thinking

4. Comparing

Do you see any similarities between the mix of cultural traditions in Mexico and the mix in the United States? What are they?

Think About

• forms of art, music, dance, and architecture

• languages spoken

• holidays celebrated

ACTIVITY -OPTION- Imagine that you are traveling through Mexico. Write a **journal entry** describing what you saw and did in its cities and towns.

Reading a Graph

▶▶ Defining the Skill

Graphs use pictures and symbols, along with words, to show information. There are many different kinds of graphs. Bar graphs, line graphs, and pie graphs are the most common. Bar graphs compare numbers or sets of numbers. The length or height of each bar shows a quantity. It is easy to compare different categories using a bar graph.

▶▶ Applying the Skill

The bar graph to the right shows the number of Mexican state governors who belong to each political party. Use the strategies listed below to help you interpret the graph.

How to Read a Graph

Strategy ❶ Read the title to identify the main idea of the graph.

Strategy ❷ Read the vertical axis (the one that goes up and down) on the left side of the graph. This one shows the number of state governors. Each bar represents the number of Mexican state governors who were members of a particular political party.

Strategy ❸ Read the horizontal axis (the one that runs across the bottom of the graph). This one shows the three political parties of Mexico's governors in 2000.

Strategy ❹ Summarize the information given in each part of the graph. Use the title to help you focus on what information the graph is presenting.

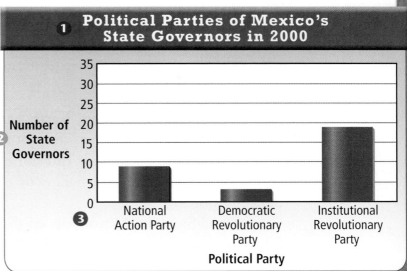

❶ Political Parties of Mexico's State Governors in 2000

❷ Number of State Governors

❸ National Action Party — Democratic Revolutionary Party — Institutional Revolutionary Party

Political Party

Write a Summary

Writing a summary will help you understand the information in the graph. The paragraph to the right summarizes the information from the bar graph.

❹ In the year 2000, the state governors in Mexico belonged to three different political parties. The majority belonged to the Institutional Revolutionary Party. The next largest group was the National Action Party, and the smallest number of governors belonged to the Democratic Revolutionary Party. This shows that the Institutional Revolutionary Party was probably the most powerful party in Mexico.

▶▶ Practicing the Skill

Turn to page 176 in Chapter 7, Section 1, "The Roots of Modern Mexico." Look at the graph entitled "Population of Mexico in 1810," and write a paragraph summarizing what you learned from it.

How Quetzalcoatl Brought Music to the World

THIS MEXICAN FOLK TALE was first written down as a poem in Nahuatl (NAH•WAHT•uhl), the language of the Aztec, in the 1500s. The myth on which it is based may be a thousand years older. It was passed by word of mouth from one storyteller to another for centuries.

1. A name of Tezcatlipoca (tehs•KAH•tlee•POH•kah), a powerful Aztec god.

2. The quetzal is a bird that lives in the rain forests of southern Mexico and Central America. *Coatl* means "serpent" in Nahuatl.

When time began, Earth had no music. Brooks did not babble, and birds did not sing. This, however, does not mean that music did not exist. High in the heavens in the Palace of the Sun, musicians of every sort filled the air with dazzling notes.

The god Smoking Mirror[1] envied this music, and he knew that the Sun would never share his prized possession with Earth. Therefore, Smoking Mirror lifted his voice to the air and shouted in every valley and cave for his friend Quetzalcoatl,[2] the feathered serpent who was also Lord of the Winds.

At a distance just beyond the horizon, Quetzalcoatl slumbered in silence. At the sound of Smoking Mirror's call, Quetzalcoatl slowly opened one eye and muttered with a sigh, "What does Smoking Mirror want now? Just as I find a dream, he finds a problem." With that being said, he whirled his serpent body 'round and stormed toward Smoking Mirror's ringing voice.

When Quetzalcoatl reached Smoking Mirror, he asked, "What is the matter now?" Smoking Mirror replied, "This morning, as I walked upon the bright and brilliant Earth that the two of us created, I realized that it is incomplete."

Quetzalcoatl responded doubtfully, "That is not so! There are beautiful creeks and colorful birds in the world! Don't you smell the fragrance of the rose or feel the soft grass beneath your feet?"

"I do," responded Smoking Mirror, "but there is no music! Earth cannot sing its joy when there is no music. That is why I must ask you to go to the Palace of the Sun and return with musicians who are able to spread music across Earth."

"The musicians are faithful servants of the Sun," replied Quetzalcoatl. "They will never leave him." Smoking Mirror remained silent. After a while, the silence began to bother Quetzalcoatl, and he realized the importance of music. So up he went, through the blue smoke of the sky, to the Palace of the Sun.

The Sun saw the Lord of the Winds coming and told his musicians that they must be very quiet, or the feathered serpent would carry them away to the dark and silent Earth. As Quetzalcoatl reached the palace, the glorious music stopped, and the musicians turned their instruments away from the feathered serpent.

But with his command over the wind, Quetzalcoatl brought forth fierce storm clouds that blocked the radiance of the Sun. He then produced his own light as a guide for the frightened musicians. Mistaking the serpent's light for the light of the Sun, the musicians stepped into Quetzalcoatl's embrace. The feathered serpent gently floated the musicians to Earth.

When the musicians saw Smoking Mirror, they knew instantly that they had been tricked. What they saw, however, was not the horrible place described by the Sun. Instead, Earth was full of wondrous colors and activity. It was still within reach of the Sun's warming rays. The musicians then embarked on journeys throughout the world. On their way, they taught the birds to sing, the brooks to babble, the leaves to rustle, and the people to make music of their very own.

Reading
THE LITERATURE

What words and phrases give the reader a sense of Quetzalcoatl's personality? How does the author convey Quetzalcoatl's attitude toward the task Smoking Mirror gives him?

Thinking About
THE LITERATURE

What does this folk tale suggest about the role of music in Aztec society? Why might this folk tale be popular in Mexico today?

Writing About
THE LITERATURE

Write a dialogue involving the musicians, Quetzalcoatl, and the Sun, in which Quetzalcoatl tries to persuade the musicians to come with him to Earth and the Sun urges them to stay. As a class, compare and contrast the arguments each side makes.

Further Reading To learn about more Mexican stories, read *The Tree Is Older Than You Are*, edited by Naomi Shihab Nye.

Explain the significance of each of the following:

1. *criollo*
2. *mestizo*
3. Father Miguel Hidalgo
4. Treaty of Guadalupe Hidalgo
5. Benito Juárez
6. *hacienda*
7. *maquiladora*
8. PEMEX
9. Diego Rivera
10. fiesta

REVIEW QUESTIONS

The Roots of Modern Mexico *(pages 173–178)*

1. Why did Cortés need the help of some Native Americans to defeat Montezuma II?
2. How was Mexico's War of Independence connected to events elsewhere in the world at that time?

Government in Mexico: Revolution and Reform *(pages 179–184)*

3. What concerns did Mexicans in the 1800s and 1900s have about land ownership?
4. What was unique about Mexico's presidential election in 2000?

Mexico's Changing Economy *(pages 185–189)*

5. Why has the *ejido* system been unsuccessful at ending poverty for many villagers?
6. What is the role of oil in Mexico's economy?

Mexico's Culture Today *(pages 190–194)*

7. What are some of the problems caused by Mexico City's rapid growth?
8. What event do Mexicans celebrate every September 16?

CRITICAL THINKING

Sequencing Events

1. Using your completed time line from Reading Social Studies, p. 172, list the points in Mexico's history when the nation's government changed drastically.

Forming and Supporting Opinions

2. Do you think the Mexican government's decision in the 1990s to privatize farming and business was a good one? Explain.

Hypothesizing

3. Modern artists, such as Diego Rivera and Octavio Paz, have used images from both Mexico's past and its present in their works. What do you think this says about the way Mexicans today view their nation's history?

Visual Summary

1 The Roots of Modern Mexico

- From 1810 to 1821, Mexico fought for and gained independence from Spain.

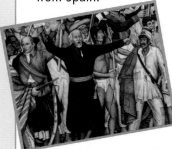

2 Government in Mexico: Revolution and Reform

- The Mexican Revolution (1910–1920) established a new government.
- Today, the government of Mexico is a federal republic.

3 Mexico's Changing Economy

- Farming is still an important part of Mexico's economy, but today its top businesses are oil production and tourism.

4 Mexico's Culture Today

- Mexico's culture combines its Native American and Spanish pasts with new elements.
- Mexico's holidays and arts show the influence of its history.

Use the map and your knowledge of world cultures and geography to answer questions 1 and 2.

Additional Test Practice, pp. S1–S33

1. What are the most common uses of land in the northern region of Mexico?

A. Forest, livestock grazing, unproductive

B. Farmed land, forest, livestock grazing

C. Livestock grazing, mining, unproductive

D. Farmed land, livestock grazing, unproductive

2. Where does more farming occur in Mexico?

A. Along the southern border

B. In the northern half

C. In the southern half

D. On the western peninsula

The following quotation about the painter Diego Rivera is from a news interview. Use the quotation and your knowledge of world cultures and geography to answer question 3.

PRIMARY SOURCE

When people think of Mexico, when people close their eyes and think of Mexico, most of the time, you imagine a world similar to that described by Diego Rivera in his paintings.

> **GREGORIO LUKE,** interview on *NewsHour with Jim Lehrer,* July 15, 1999

3. The passage supports which of the following points of view?

A. Rivera's paintings have little connection to Mexico.

B. Diego Rivera has captured the spirit of Mexico in his paintings.

C. Rivera has painted aspects of Mexico in a realistic style.

D. If you see Diego Rivera's paintings, you don't need to go to Mexico.

TEST PRACTICE
CLASSZONE.COM

ALTERNATIVE ASSESSMENT

1. WRITING ABOUT HISTORY

Mexico City is the second largest city in the world and the cultural center of Mexico. Imagine that you are a travel consultant and create a guide for visitors to Mexico City.

• Use the Internet and the library to learn about the museums and cultural institutions, such as the opera, theater, symphony, and ballet. You might also contact the Mexican tourist bureau for information.

• Design a guide that would inform visitors to the city about these institutions. Write a description of each. Include illustrations and captions.

2. COOPERATIVE LEARNING

Work with a group of classmates to create a news show about the experience of Mexicans during the Mexican Revolution. Choose a specific year and a specific location as the focus of your news show. Group members can take the roles of anchor, reporter, or interviewee.

INTEGRATED TECHNOLOGY

Doing Internet Research

The varied climates in Mexico affect the way people live and the type of work they do. Use the Internet to research the climate in one region of Mexico.

• Research online and print encyclopedias, atlases, and almanacs to learn about the climate of the region you chose.

• Find out how the climate in that particular region affects the way of life of the people there.

• Include maps or graphs that visually support the information in your report.

For Internet links to support this activity, go to

RESEARCH LINKS
CLASSZONE.COM

CHAPTER

8

Central America and the Caribbean Islands

PACIFIC
OCEAN

ATLANTIC

PACIFIC
OCEAN

**CENTRAL AMERICA
AND THE CARIBBEAN
ISLANDS**

OCEAN

INDIAN
OCEAN

N

Why do the Caribbean Islands attract so many tourists?

Place • Thousands of people from all over the world travel to the Caribbean Islands each year. They may stay in Aruba, Tobago, the Bahamas, or any of the other islands. Wherever they go, tourists are sure to find long sandy beaches, clear blue water, and towering volcanic mountains.

Grenada (shown above) is a favorite destination, with its crater lakes, waterfalls, fragrant spice trees, and rain forests. Off its shores, coral reefs offer divers a glimpse at many underwater plants and animals. The climate stays comfortable all year, with steady breezes and temperatures ranging from 75°F to 87°F.

What do you think?

♦ What features of the Caribbean's physical geography attract tourists?

♦ Why does the Caribbean's climate draw tourists there all year?

Region Community markets, such as this one in Chichicastenango (CHEE•chee•cahs•tay•NAHN•goh), Guatemala, exist throughout Central America as places to sell goods and mingle with neighbors.

201

READING SOCIAL STUDIES

BEFORE YOU READ

▶▶ *What Do You Know?*

Before you read the chapter, think about what you already know about Central America and the Caribbean Islands. You may have heard Caribbean music like reggae. Perhaps you have seen colorful woven cloth from Central America. Do you know where the Panama Canal is? Have you heard of Fidel Castro?

▶▶ *What Do You Want to Know?*

Decide what else you want to know about Central America and the Caribbean Islands. In your notebook, record what you hope to learn from this chapter.

Place • **This painting shows people working on a Caribbean sugar cane plantation.** ▲

READ AND TAKE NOTES

Reading Strategy: Identifying Problems and Solutions Identifying problems and solutions is a useful strategy for increasing your understanding of what you read. You can make a chart that lists issues. In the chart, identify the problems with those issues and the solutions to the problems to better understand the issues.

- Copy the chart into your notebook.

- As you read the chapter, look for issues related to government and economy.

- Record the problems and solutions involved in each issue on your chart.

Culture • Cubans celebrate a holiday called Carnival. ◀

Issues	Problems	Solutions
Colonization (1492–1800s)		
The Panama Canal (1903–1914)		
Spanish-American War (1898)		
Dictatorships		
Economic Development		
U.S./Cuba Relations		
Civil War in Guatemala		

Establishing Independence

TERMS & NAMES
West Indies
dependency
mulatto
ladino
dictator

MAIN IDEA

Central America and the Caribbean Islands have struggled to become independent nations with democratic governments.

WHY IT MATTERS NOW

The quest for democracy continues in Central America and the Caribbean, as it does elsewhere in the world today.

DATELINE EXTRA

ST. DOMINGUE, CARIBBEAN ISLANDS, 1803

Word has arrived from France that François Dominique Toussaint L'Ouverture died there recently. He was taken to France last year to be imprisoned after leading the slave rebellion here in St. Domingue. The rebellion was so successful that St. Domingue seems just days away from declaring its independence once and for all.

Toussaint was given the nickname L'Ouverture, which means "opening" in French, because he always found an opening in enemy lines. His success in leading the rebellion is staggering when one realizes that his army of former slaves, mostly uneducated, defeated, in turn, the French, the British, and the Spanish.

Culture • Toussaint has become a hero to many. ▲

Central America and the Caribbean

Central America includes seven nations—Belize, Guatemala, Honduras, El Salvador, Nicaragua, Costa Rica, and Panama. Its neighbors—St. Domingue, now called Haiti, and the other islands of the Caribbean—are known as the **West Indies**. They include 13 nations and 11 dependencies. A **dependency** is a place that is governed by or closely connected with another country. For example, Puerto Rico is a dependency of the United States.

TAKING NOTES

Use your chart to take notes about Central America and the Caribbean.

Issues	Problems	Solutions
Colonization		
Panama Canal		

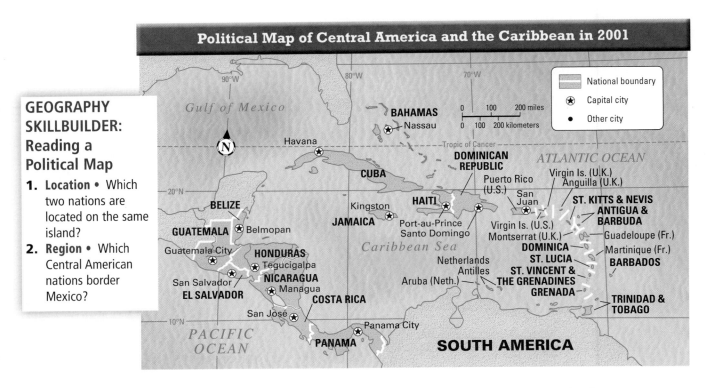

Political Map of Central America and the Caribbean in 2001

Legend:
- National boundary
- ⊛ Capital city
- • Other city

Map labels: Gulf of Mexico, Havana, BAHAMAS, Nassau, Tropic of Cancer, DOMINICAN REPUBLIC, ATLANTIC OCEAN, CUBA, Puerto Rico (U.S.), Virgin Is. (U.K.), Anguilla (U.K.), BELIZE, Kingston, HAITI, San Juan, ST. KITTS & NEVIS, ANTIGUA & BARBUDA, GUATEMALA, Belmopan, JAMAICA, Port-au-Prince, Santo Domingo, Virgin Is. (U.S.), Montserrat (U.K.), Guadeloupe (Fr.), Guatemala City, HONDURAS, Tegucigalpa, Caribbean Sea, DOMINICA, Martinique (Fr.), ST. LUCIA, BARBADOS, San Salvador, NICARAGUA, Netherlands Antilles, ST. VINCENT & THE GRENADINES, EL SALVADOR, Managua, Aruba (Neth.), GRENADA, COSTA RICA, TRINIDAD & TOBAGO, San José, Panama City, PACIFIC OCEAN, PANAMA, SOUTH AMERICA

GEOGRAPHY SKILLBUILDER: Reading a Political Map

1. **Location** • Which two nations are located on the same island?
2. **Region** • Which Central American nations border Mexico?

Peoples of the Caribbean When Christopher Columbus reached the West Indies in 1492, about 750,000 Native Americans lived there. The Europeans who took over forced Native Americans to work on plantations and in mines. The harsh labor, plus European diseases unknown in the Americas, killed many Native Americans. Others died in battles with the Europeans. Within a few years, nearly all the Native Americans on the islands had died.

Without Native Americans to use for labor, European rulers looked for a new source of workers. By the 1520s, the Spanish began bringing shiploads of enslaved Africans to the West Indies. Other European nations joined in the slave trade. From the 1500s to the mid-1800s, about 10 million enslaved Africans arrived in the West Indies. As a result, many people in the Caribbean today are **mulattos** (mu·LAT·ohz), or people who have African and European ancestry. Few Caribbean people have Native American ancestry.

BACKGROUND

About 75 million people live in Central America and the Caribbean today.

Region • Like this man, many Caribbean people are of African descent. ▼

Central American People In Central America, the situation for the Native Americans was different. When the Spanish arrived in 1501, many Native Americans withdrew to the inland mountains and thus survived what proved to be a deadly encounter with the Spanish elsewhere. Today, one-fifth of Central Americans are Native Americans.

Reading Social Studies

A. **Finding Causes** How did geography help the Native Americans in Central America survive the arrival of Europeans?

The slave ships also arrived in Central America, bringing Africans to the region. Africans from the Caribbean also migrated to the area. As the years passed, the Spanish, Native Americans, and Africans intermarried. Those people with mixed European and Native American ancestry are called *ladinos* (luh•DEE•naws), and they make up about two-thirds of Central America's population today.

Region • Central Americans today reflect the region's rich mix of cultures and people. ▲

From Colonies to Independence

From the 1500s to the 1800s, European nations ruled Central America and the West Indies as colonies. These differed from the dependencies of today. Usually, a dependency is free to break off its connection to the other country, but a colony must either win its independence or be granted it.

The Lure of Gold and Sugar Spain was the first European country to colonize this region. Soon, however, the French, Dutch, and English set up their own colonies in the islands. While they found the gold they were looking for, they also found another source of wealth—sugar. Soon many of the islands were home to sugar plantations. Most of the workers who grew and cut the sugar cane were enslaved.

Becoming Independent By the 1800s, the people of Central America and the Caribbean Islands began to demand their independence. In 1804, the French colony of St. Domingue became the first nation in the region to win independence.

BACKGROUND

After independence, St. Domingue took a new name—Haiti (HAY•tee).

Other nations soon followed St. Domingue's example. In 1821, Guatemala, Honduras, Costa Rica, and Nicaragua declared independence from Spain. At first they united, but since 1839, they have existed as separate nations.

Relations with the United States

The United States of America is the largest neighbor of Central America and the West Indies. U.S. policies have long played a part in shaping the region's history.

Reggae After the Caribbean island of Jamaica gained independence from Britain in 1962, musicians such as Bob Marley (shown below) developed a new style of music called reggae (REHG•ay). Today, reggae is popular around the world. It is known for its political messages.

With their lyrics, the early reggae singers commented on social and economic problems. Reggae is enjoyed both for pleasure and for its ability to let the poor and the oppressed make their voices heard. Music has played a similar role in many cultures throughout history.

The Panama Canal Until the early 1900s, people who wanted to travel from one side of North or South America to the other had two choices. They could make the long, dangerous trip by land or sail all the way around South America. Because the Isthmus of Panama is about 40 miles wide, by 1900, first France, then the United States were eager to build a canal across it to connect the two oceans.

At that time, Panama was part of the South American nation of Colombia. The United States tried to buy from Colombia a strip of land on the isthmus. Colombia refused, and so the United States urged the people of Panama to break away. Soon, Panama did revolt. After establishing its own country in 1903, Panama agreed to lease the United States land to build a canal. The canal opened in 1914 and soon became one of the most important transportation routes in the world. Now ships only had to sail the 50 miles from one end of the canal to the other.

Human-Environment Interaction • By using the Panama Canal, ships save 2,000 to 8,000 miles, depending on where they start and end their trips. ▲

The Spanish-American War Long after Central America broke free of Spanish rule, Spain continued to control Cuba and Puerto Rico. During the late 1800s, the islanders there rebelled many times but were not able to gain independence.

In 1898, the United States declared war on Spain. It did so partly because it wanted to help the people of Cuba and Puerto Rico gain freedom from Spain. However, the United States also wanted to protect the many sugar cane plantations that U.S. businesses owned on the islands. By the end of the war, which lasted less than a year, Spain had lost its last colonies in the Americas. Puerto Rico became a U.S. dependency, a territory under the control of another nation. Cuba became an independent country, but the U.S. military set up bases there and kept tight control over the country.

Reading Social Studies

B. Recognizing Effects How did world affairs in the late 1800s affect the Caribbean?

Place • The United States controlled the Panama Canal and the land around it until December 31, 1999, when control passed to Panama. ▶

Dictatorships and Democracy

Independence did not necessarily bring freedom to the people of Central America and the West Indies. Only Costa Rica has been a democracy since the beginning of the 20th century.

Dictatorships Nearly all the other countries have spent many years under the rule of dictators. A **dictator** is a person who has complete control over a country's government. At times, dictators ruled Guatemala, Honduras, Panama, El Salvador, Haiti, and the Dominican Republic. Dictators often used violence to grab and keep power.

Hopes for Democracy Most countries in Central America and the West Indies now have democratically elected governments. The people of these countries removed most of their dictators, one by one. For example, in 1990, Nicaraguans replaced dictatorial rule by electing Violetta Barrios de Chamorro (vee·oh·LE·tuh BA·ree·ohs day chah·MOH·roh) as president. However, elected leaders sometimes refuse to give up power, thus becoming dictators. Sometimes, elections are not run fairly. Nevertheless, freedom is more widespread than it was 50 years ago.

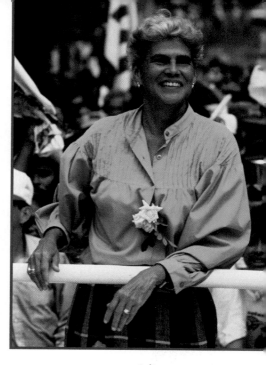

Culture •
Nicaragua's first female president, Violetta Barrios de Chamorro, governed from 1990 to 1996. ▲

SECTION 1 ASSESSMENT

Terms & Names

1. Explain the significance of:
   (a) West Indies
   (b) dependency
   (c) mulatto
   (d) *ladino*
   (e) dictator

Using Graphics

2. Use a chart like this one to note the effects Europeans had on the Native American populations in Central America and the Caribbean.

In Central America	In the Caribbean

Main Ideas

3. (a) Why are there more Native Americans in Central America today than in the Caribbean?

   (b) Describe the difference between dependencies and colonies.

   (c) List two reasons why the United States declared war on Spain.

Critical Thinking

4. **Identifying Problems**

   Why have some countries in Central America and the Caribbean had trouble establishing democracies?

   Think About

   • the region's history of being controlled by other countries and dictatorship

   • the powers and resources of dictators

ACTIVITY -OPTION- Imagine you lived on the island that became Haiti in 1804. Write a short **biography** of your island's hero, François Dominique Toussaint L'Ouverture.

Building Economies and Cultures

MAIN IDEA	WHY IT MATTERS NOW
The economies and cultures of this region reflect both the colonial past and efforts to modernize.	Though small in size, the region exports its culture and products to the United States and beyond.

◁ Back ▷ Forward ✕ Stop ⇄ Refresh 🏠 Home

Address: ▸ go

DATELINE

TEGUCIGALPA, HONDURAS, 1998—
A devastating hurricane hit Central America this week, reminding people that live here of the dangers of having an economy based mainly on agriculture. In addition to about 10,000 deaths, Honduras faces the loss of 70 percent of its crops to the hurricane's ferocious winds.

For example, the banana industry, which brings in $200 million for Hondurans each year, was nearly wiped out. Honduran president Carlos Roberto Flores Facusse described the horrific results of Hurricane Mitch: "In 72 hours, we saw what took as much as 50 years to build... destroyed."

Human-Environment Interaction • Many houses have been destroyed by Hurricane Mitch. ▲

The Economies of the Caribbean Islands

In the Caribbean, the economies of most islands have depended on growing one or two crops to sell to other countries. However, the islanders have also worked hard to create new businesses as well as new industries.

TAKING NOTES
Use your chart to take notes about Central America and the Caribbean.

Issues	Problems	Solutions
Colonization		
Panama Canal		

The Colonial Period For most of the colonial period, the Caribbean Islands focused mainly on one industry—growing **sugar cane**. From the 1600s to the 1800s, most islanders worked on sugar cane plantations. In the early years, the majority of these workers were enslaved. Even after slavery ended by the late 1800s, most workers owned no land of their own. Instead, they planted, tended, and cut sugar cane on plantations owned by the wealthy.

During the colonial period, most of the islands traded only with their ruling countries. Cuba, for example, sold its sugar to Spain and bought goods from Spain in return. But after the colonial period ended, many of the islands traded mostly with the United States.

Single-Product Economies Sugar was so valuable that plantation owners raised few other crops. Most did not even grow food. Many of the islands had to buy almost all their food from other countries. A country that depends on just one product for almost all its jobs and income has a **single-product economy**.

Economies Must Change A single-product economy can be unstable—if something happens to that single product, the country's economy will be ruined. By the late 1800s, the sugar business in the West Indies was in trouble. People raising sugar cane in other parts of the world offered the West Indies fierce competition. Steam-powered machines allowed these foreigners to process sugar cane at lower prices. The people of the West Indies had to find new ways to make a living.

The islanders found they needed to diversify their economies. To **diversify** an economy means to invest in a variety of industries. People began to raise other crops, such as pineapples and bananas. Industries, such as textiles, medical supplies, and electronic equipment, also developed in the Caribbean.

Reading **Social Studies**

A. Analyzing Issues Why did production of sugar elsewhere in the world affect the economies of the Caribbean?

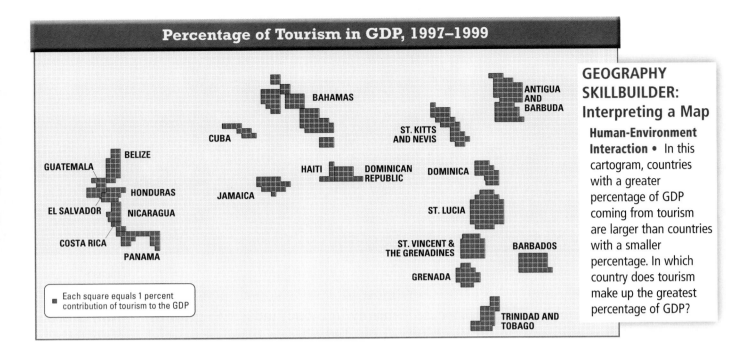

Percentage of Tourism in GDP, 1997–1999

BAHAMAS

ANTIGUA AND BARBUDA

CUBA

ST. KITTS AND NEVIS

GUATEMALA

BELIZE

HAITI

DOMINICAN REPUBLIC

DOMINICA

HONDURAS

JAMAICA

EL SALVADOR

NICARAGUA

ST. LUCIA

COSTA RICA

ST. VINCENT & THE GRENADINES

BARBADOS

PANAMA

GRENADA

TRINIDAD AND TOBAGO

■ Each square equals 1 percent contribution of tourism to the GDP

GEOGRAPHY SKILLBUILDER: Interpreting a Map

Human-Environment Interaction • In this cartogram, countries with a greater percentage of GDP coming from tourism are larger than countries with a smaller percentage. In which country does tourism make up the greatest percentage of GDP?

Citizenship IN ACTION

María Elena Cuadra Movement
In Central America, poverty and unemployment are widespread. In Nicaragua, many women take jobs in factories, like the one shown here, under poor conditions and for low wages.

Since 1994, the María Elena Cuadra Movement of Working and Unemployed Women (MEC) has been working to improve the position of women at work and in the home. MEC protects workers' rights, trains women in new skills, and lends money to women to start their own small businesses.

Tourism Takes Hold One of the most important industries in the Caribbean Islands is tourism. With warm weather and beautiful beaches, the islands attract tourists from around the world. About 8 million tourists flock there each year. On some of the smaller islands, such as Antigua, tourism is now the major industry.

The Economies of Central America

After the Spanish Central American countries became independent in the 1820s, they wanted to increase their trade with other nations. To do so, they needed to develop exports. During the 1800s, several Central American countries began to produce coffee. Soon it became an important export crop for Costa Rica, Guatemala, Honduras, El Salvador, and Nicaragua. In exchange for their exports, Central American countries purchased imports from other parts of the world.

The United States Steps In In the late 1800s, a major new export business got started in Central America. U.S.-based United Fruit Company (UFCO) set up huge banana plantations in the hot, wet lowlands of Central America.

UFCO did a huge amount of business, and bananas became another important Central American product.

Two Crops Are Not Enough The Central American economies grew to depend on bananas and coffee. Whenever the price of these items on the world market fell, Central Americans faced hardship. Like the Caribbean islanders, Central Americans wanted to diversify their economies.

Reading
Social Studies

B. Making Inferences
What are some factors that would cause the price of a product on the world market to fall?

Central American countries have worked to build more factories. Costa Rica, for example, has factories that make machinery, furniture, cloth, and medicine. The countries of the region have also developed tourism as an industry. Visitors arrive by the thousands in Guatemala to see the spectacular ruins of Maya temples. As different businesses grow, Central Americans will not be as dependent on agriculture as they were in the past.

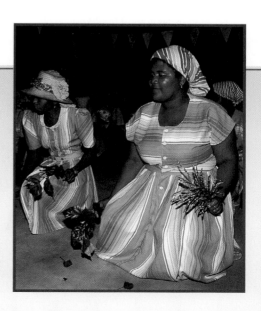

Region •
Coffee grows well in the cool highlands of Central America. ▲

Caribbean Cultures

Each country in the Caribbean has its own particular way of life. Native American, African, and European influences blend differently from place to place.

Languages In the Caribbean, people speak a variety of languages. These reflect the area's history. Look at page 145 of the Unit Atlas to see which languages are spoken in which areas.

Religions Roman Catholicism is the most widespread religion in the West Indies. However, many islanders practice religions that have African influences. In Haiti, elements of Catholic and African religious practices combine in the religion known as voodoo.

Strange but TRUE

A Language Lives On When Europeans arrived on the Caribbean island of St. Vincent in 1635, they encountered a startling mystery. The women of St. Vincent spoke one language, and the men spoke another.

Originally, they all spoke the Arawak language. However, when speakers of the Carib language attacked the Arawak-speaking islands, most of the Arawak-speaking men were killed. Only the female Arawak speakers survived.

The Arawakan women continued to speak their language, while the conquering men spoke the Carib language. Today, the language inherited from the Arawakan women is called Garífuna. Like the woman at the right, 30,000 people living on the Caribbean coast of Central America still speak it.

Central America and the Caribbean Islands **211**

In Cuba, Yoruba beliefs from Africa combine with Catholic beliefs in the religion called Santeria. In Trinidad, the Shango religion blends Catholic, Baptist, and West African beliefs.

Music Music, too, shows a blending of cultures. From Cuban salsa to Jamaican reggae, much Caribbean music combines African and European styles to make something completely new. The rap music that is popular in the United States also has Caribbean roots. Some of the first rappers to perform in the United States introduced to this country the Jamaican technique of mixing together tracks from different songs.

Central American Cultures

The countries of Central America share a common history. In their cultures, the Native American and Spanish heritages blend.

Languages Look again at the map on page 145. You can see that in most of Central America, people speak Spanish. Central Americans also speak about 80 Native American languages, nearly half of which are Maya languages.

Merengue Dancing is a popular pastime in Latin America. One of the favorite dances (and the national dance of the Dominican Republic) is the merengue (*shown below*). This dance form originated in the neighboring nations of Haiti and the Dominican Republic. It is known for its unique dance step, called a sliding step, in which the dancer always rests his or her weight on the same foot. People commonly explain this step with one of two legends. One legend says that enslaved people developed the step while chained to one another at the leg. Another legend has it that a Dominican war hero, wounded in the leg during a revolt, designed the step. Whatever the true story behind the dance, the merengue did arise as a folk dance in rural areas. Later it became a favorite of ballroom dancers.

THINKING CRITICALLY

1. **Drawing Conclusions**
   What do the two legends about the origins of the merengue's sliding step tell you about the significance of dancing in Latin American culture?

2. **Synthesizing**
   What different roles do you think dancing can play in a culture?

For more on the merengue, go to

RESEARCH LINKS
CLASSZONE.COM

Religions Catholicism is the most widespread religion in Central America. In recent years, however, millions of Central Americans have become Protestants and Mormons. Also, some ancient Maya religious beliefs still thrive. An example is the companion spirit. Maya people today believe that when a person is born, so is an animal. That animal, the companion spirit, lives through the same experiences as the person does. A person usually learns about his or her companion spirit in dreams.

Crafts Many Central American towns are known for their crafts, such as weaving, embroidery, pottery, silversmithing, and basketmaking. Many of the styles and methods used originated with ancient Native Americans. For example, many weavers use a backstrap loom—a 2,000-year-old device consisting of threads that are attached to a fixed post or tree on one end and a belt on the other end.

Culture • By wearing the belt around her waist, the weaver stretches the threads tight to weave on them. ▲

SECTION ② ASSESSMENT

Terms & Names

1. Explain the significance of: (a) sugar cane (b) single-product economy (c) diversify

Using Graphics

2. Use a chart like this one to check off the languages spoken in each region, country, or island mentioned in the text.

	Guatemala	Haiti
Native American		
Spanish		
French		
English		

Main Ideas

3. (a) List some ways in which sugar production affected the lives of Caribbean people.

   (b) How have Central American countries diversified their economies?

   (c) How do the religions in Central America and the Caribbean reflect the regions' histories?

Critical Thinking

4. **Forming and Supporting Opinions**
   How do you think the success of a foreign-owned company affects a country?

   Think About
   - the importance of UFCO's product to Central American economies
   - the jobs created by a successful company
   - who receives the company's profits

ACTIVITY -OPTION- A country with a single-product economy risks losing a great deal if that product fails. Make a **chart** of the factors that put the country in this risky position but that it cannot control.

Reading a Political Map

▶▶ Defining the Skill

Political maps show the boundaries of nations and other political areas, such as dependencies. Lines show these boundaries. Often political maps also show capitals and other cities.

▶▶ Applying the Skill

The political map at right shows the nations of Central America. Use the strategies listed below to identify the information shown on the map.

How to Read a Political Map

Strategy ❶ Read the title. It tells you which region's political areas are being represented.

Strategy ❷ Read the key. It tells you what each symbol stands for. This key shows boundaries between nations, national capitals, and other cities.

Strategy ❸ Read the scale. It tells you how many miles or kilometers each inch represents.

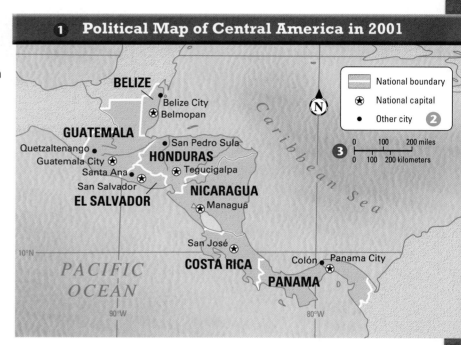

❶ Political Map of Central America in 2001

Key:
- National boundary
- ❂ National capital ❷
- • Other city

❸ 0 100 200 miles / 0 100 200 kilometers

Make a Chart

A chart can help you organize information given on maps. The chart below organizes information about the map you just studied.

▶▶ Practicing the Skill

Turn to Chapter 8, Section 1, "Establishing Independence." Study the political map of Central America and the Caribbean on page 204. Make a chart listing the nations of the Caribbean and the capitals that are shown on the map.

Central America		
Countries	Capitals	Other Cities
Guatemala	Guatemala City	Quetzaltenango
Belize	Belmopan	Belize City
Honduras	Tegucigalpa	San Pedro Sula
El Salvador	San Salvador	Santa Ana
Nicaragua	Managua	
Costa Rica	San José	
Panama	Panama City	Colón

Cuba Today

TERMS & NAMES
José Martí
Fidel Castro
Communism
malnutrition
Carnival

MAIN IDEA

After Cuba became independent, the country was ruled by a series of dictators. Since 1959, revolutionary leader Fidel Castro has ruled the nation.

WHY IT MATTERS NOW

At the turn of the century, Cuba was the only Communist country in the Western Hemisphere.

DATELINE

SIERRA MAESTRA, CUBA, 1956—Word has leaked out that revolutionary leader Fidel Castro has returned to Cuba. Three years ago, he received a 15-year prison sentence for leading an attack on the government. He was released early, a year ago, at which time he fled to Mexico to organize a group of revolutionaries.

Sources say that he and about 80 of his followers have returned to Cuba, though many of them were killed or captured upon arrival. The rest are hiding out in the Sierra Maestra, mountains in southeastern Cuba. People have been speculating about what kind of revolution may develop now that Castro is back in Cuba.

Place • While hiding deep in the Sierra Maestra, Castro is organizing his followers for revolution. ▲

Independence and Revolution

Long after Mexico and Central America gained independence, Cuba, the largest island in the Caribbean, still suffered Spanish rule. In 1895, Cubans led by **José Martí** continued fighting for the nation's independence. Three years later, the Spanish-American War reached the island. By the end of the war, Cuba had gained its independence from Spain. However, the United States maintained great influence over the nation.

TAKING NOTES
Use your chart to take notes about Central America and the Caribbean.

Issues	Problems	Solutions
Colonization		
Panama Canal		

U.S. Ties to Cuba Before the Spanish-American War, the United States wanted to add Cuba to the nation. After the Spanish-American War ended, the United States appointed a military governor for Cuba. From 1899 to 1902, the U.S. Army stayed in Cuba to keep peace and help set up a new government. Most Cubans resented the U.S. presence. However, during these years, Cubans and U.S. soldiers did build many needed roads, bridges, and public schools.

In 1902, the U.S. Army withdrew from Cuba, which then became independent. However, the United States insisted that it still had the right to send soldiers to Cuba any time. The U.S. Navy also kept a large base for its ships at Guantánamo Bay.

Time of Dictatorship After independence, Cuba had a series of leaders. Some were elected, and some took power by force. Most governed as dictators. Cuba's dictators were careful to stay friendly with the United States. They welcomed U.S. businesses and tourists. Havana, Cuba's capital, offered tourists luxury hotels and casinos. Most Cubans, however, remained poor.

Revolution Takes Hold Time and again, Cubans protested against the dictators. In the 1950s, Cubans who were angry at the government found a leader for their cause. He was a young lawyer named **Fidel Castro.** Born in 1927 to a wealthy family, Castro was known for being a dynamic speaker. In college, he developed a deep interest in politics. By late 1956, Castro and a few followers had established headquarters for their revolution in the mountains of southeastern Cuba.

Reading **Social Studies**

A. Drawing Conclusions If Cubans resented the U.S. presence in Cuba, why did their dictators stay friendly with the United States?

Culture • The two extremes of life in Cuba are apparent in this contrast of one of Havana's fancy hotels with one Cuban's simple dwelling. ▼

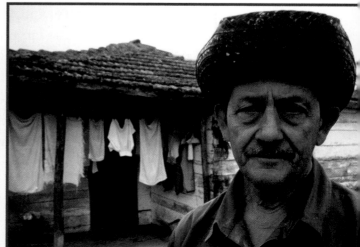

A few at a time, Cubans began to join Castro's small army. The rebel army won several battles against government troops. As the revolution grew stronger, Cuba's dictator, Fulgencio Batista (fool·HEHN·see·oh buh·TEES·tuh), fled the country on January 1, 1959. On January 8, 1959, Castro and his followers marched triumphantly into Havana. More than half a million Cubans greeted them joyfully. In a speech to the crowds, Castro promised that Cuba would have no more dictators.

The revolution had succeeded. Castro became the new commander-in-chief of Cuba's army. By July 1959, he had taken full control of Cuba's government.

A VOICE FROM CUBA

We cannot ever become dictators. Those who do not have the people with them must resort to being dictators. We have the love of the people, and because of that love, we will never turn away from our principles.

Fidel Castro

Cuba in the Cold War Castro took power in Cuba during the Cold War—a period of conflict between the United States and the Soviet Union. Castro needed the friendship of a powerful country. The Soviet Union was eager to have Cuba as an ally. It proved its interest in the smaller country by engaging in large-scale trade with Cuba as well as providing Cuba with weapons. This attention helped Castro choose to side with the Soviet Union in the Cold War.

Cuba Becomes a Communist Country The Soviet Union practiced an economic and political system known as **Communism.** Under this system, the government plans and controls a country's economy—in effect, the government owns the country's farms, factories, and businesses. Soon, Castro began to adopt Communist policies for Cuba's economy. His government took over the big sugar cane plantations, many of which had been owned by U.S. companies. His government then took over U.S. banks, oil refineries, and other businesses on the island.

Human-Environment Interaction • One of Castro's Communist policies was to take government control of farms, such as this one. ▼

In return, the United States cut off all trade with Cuba. Cubans could no longer sell their huge sugar crop to the United States. Instead, the Soviet Union bought Cuba's sugar. The Soviet government also sent weapons, farm machinery, food, and money to Cuba. In 1961, Castro declared that he and Cuba were Communist.

Castro as Dictator While the poor usually supported Castro's policies, many wealthier Cubans did not. They were particularly upset when he redistributed land so that no family or farm owned more than a certain amount. Castro also imprisoned people who spoke out against him. As a result, Cubans who opposed Castro began to flee to the United States and other countries. Over the years, hundreds of thousands of people left Cuba.

Castro has kept a tight hold on power for more than 40 years. Without ever being elected, he has remained head of state. His government has controlled all newspapers and radio and television stations. No one has been allowed to criticize his actions or the government. Despite his 1959 promise, Castro became a dictator.

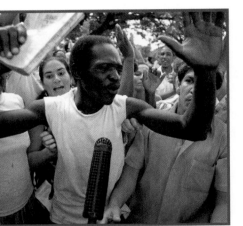

Place • In recent years, Cubans like these have continued to protest Castro's policies. ▲

Reading
Social Studies

B. Clarifying
What actions did Castro take that went against his 1959 promise?

Cuba's Economy

Since the Cuban revolution, the Cuban economy has changed in many ways. Since the collapse of the Soviet Union in 1991, Cuba has struggled to maintain its Communist way of life without Soviet aid.

Sugar and the Economy Sugar is Cuba's most important product in the world economy. The yearly sugar cane harvest is a key event for Cuba's economy. Once, workers with machetes cut the tough canes by hand. Then, with Soviet help, Castro's government bought huge machines to cut most of the cane. The cane harvest grew to record size.

While the Soviet Union was powerful, it traded oil, grain, and machinery with Cuba for sugar. Most of these products were worth more than sugar, so the Soviet Union was, in large part, supporting Cuba's economy.

Vocabulary
machete: large, wide-bladed knife

Living in Cuba

As with the economy, ways of life in Cuba have been greatly affected by Communism. Both education and health care reflect these changes.

Culture • These Cuban children sing their national anthem together at school. ▲

Education After the revolution, Cuba's government set up many new schools. In the 1960s, teachers and even school-children went into small villages to teach those who could not read or write. Many older people who had never had the chance to go to school learned to read for the first time.

Today, Cuban children must go to public school from ages 6 to 12. They can choose whether to continue their education after that. All schools are free, including college. Besides their academic subjects, students must take classes that teach Communist beliefs.

Health Care Like education, all health care in Cuba is paid for by the government. Cuba's health care system is probably the largest in Latin America. Every small village has a clinic.

However, Cuba had economic problems in the 1990s that affected both education and health care. Lack of fuel for buses and cars prevented some children from getting to school.

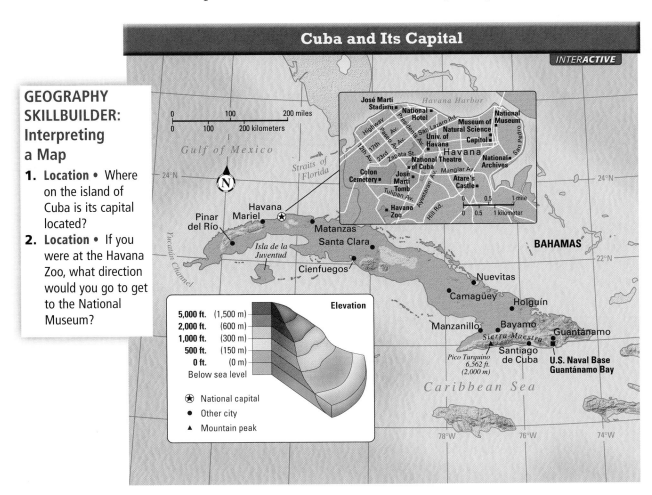

Cuba and Its Capital

INTERACTIVE

GEOGRAPHY SKILLBUILDER: Interpreting a Map

1. **Location** • Where on the island of Cuba is its capital located?
2. **Location** • If you were at the Havana Zoo, what direction would you go to get to the National Museum?

Food shortages caused malnutrition. **Malnutrition** is poor health due to a lack of eating the right kinds of food. It often causes sickness. From the 1960s to the 1980s, Cuba had almost wiped out malnutrition. Since 1990, malnutrition has again become a problem in Cuba.

Culture • During Carnival, the air fills with the lively music played by musicians such as these drummers. ▲

Arts, Sports, and Holidays

Both Castro's government and earlier dictators have placed strict limits on what artists, writers, and filmmakers may say in their work. As a result, some Cubans have fled to other countries in search of greater freedom of expression.

However, some art forms thrive in Cuba. Music is part of everyday life there. The unique sound of Cuban music combines African drums and Spanish guitars. Each different style and rhythm has its own name—son, mambo, cha-cha, rumba, salsa.

Sports are also popular in Cuba. The nation's favorite sport is baseball. Cuba's baseball team won a gold medal at the Olympics in 1996.

A favorite Cuban holiday, **Carnival,** takes place each year at the end of July. Cities and villages celebrate the end of the sugar harvest with festivals filled with music and dancing.

SECTION 3 ASSESSMENT

Terms & Names

1. Explain the significance of:
   (a) José Martí   (b) Fidel Castro   (c) Communism
   (d) malnutrition   (e) Carnival

Using Graphics

2. Use a diagram like this one to show the stages Cuba's government has gone through.

| Fight for independence | → | | → | | → |

Main Ideas

3. (a) What U.S. actions caused Cubans to resent the United States?

   (b) Describe how Fidel Castro instituted Communism in Cuba.

   (c) How was the Cuban economy once dependent on the Soviet Union?

Critical Thinking

4. **Drawing Conclusions**

   Why might some Cubans think Castro has helped their nation and others think he has hurt it?

   Think About

   ◆ Cuba's possible trade partners
   ◆ Cuba's health care system
   ◆ Cuba's education policies

ACTIVITY -OPTION-   Reread the sections about the U.S. ties to Cuba. Then make a **poster** displaying information about the relationship.

Guatemala Today

SECTION 4

TERMS & NAMES
Rafael Carrera
Jacobo Arbenz Guzmán
departamento

MAIN IDEA

The establishment of a stable government in Guatemala has been a struggle, causing much suffering along the way.

WHY IT MATTERS NOW

Guatemala's increased stability has improved its relationship with its neighbors, such as the United States.

◁ Back ▷ Forward ✗ Stop ⇄ Refresh ⌂ Home

Address: ▸ go

DATELINE

GUATEMALA CITY, GUATEMALA, DECEMBER 28, 1996
Tonight, Guatemala City is celebrating. However, the festivities don't mark a holiday or a party. They are, instead, signs of the historic action that will take place here tomorrow.

Guatemala's leaders will join their opponents in signing a peace agreement that will end a civil war that killed more than 100,000 Guatemalans over the past four decades. Finally, hopes for peace have arrived in the country that has suffered through Latin America's longest-lasting and most deadly civil war.

Place • **Many Guatemalans expressed relief and appreciation when they heard about the peace agreement.** ▶

History of Government

In 1821, along with three other Central American states, Guatemala gained independence from Spain. It broke from the other states in 1839 to become the nation we know today. Between 1821 and 1839, peasants in the mountains had staged revolts against the government. In 1837, an uneducated farmer, **Rafael Carrera** (rah·fy·EHL kuh·REHR·uh), led a revolt and emerged as a new leader for Guatemala. In 1854, he took over the presidency, which he held until his death in 1865.

TAKING NOTES
Use your chart to take notes about Central America and the Caribbean.

Issues	Problems	Solutions
Colonization		
Panama Canal		

From Dictatorial Rule to Reforms After Carrera died, a steady flow of dictators filled Guatemala's presidency. In 1944, a set of military officers revolted and won control of the nation. One of these officers, **Jacobo Arbenz Guzmán** (YAH·koh·boh AHR·bayns gooz·MAHN), saw the need for social reforms in Guatemala. When he became president in 1951, Guzmán decided to develop a market economy and raise Guatemala's standard of living. Guzmán also redistributed 1.5 million acres of land to 100,000 families. As in Mexico, the goal of redistributing land was to give many more people access to land that they could farm.

Place • Born in 1913, Jacobo Arbenz Guzmán was president of Guatemala from 1951 to 1954. ▲

U.S. Ties to Guatemala Serious opposition to Guzmán's redistribution program arose in the United States. Both United Fruit Company and the U.S. government owned much land in Guatemala. Guzmán established a policy of giving farmers any land that was not already being used. Eighty-five percent of UFCO's land in Guatemala was unused. Thus, UFCO was at great risk of losing that land.

The United States Steps In The United States took action in 1954. Accusing Guzmán of supporting Communism—a political system that the United States believed threatened national safety—the U.S. Central Intelligence Agency (CIA) supported an invasion of Guatemala's capital, Guatemala City. A Guatemalan colonel, Carlos Castillo Armas (CAR·lohs kah·STEE·yoh AR·mahs), led the attack. A frightened Guzmán quickly gave in. A new government, backed by the United States, took control of Guatemala.

Place • Rebel forces in Guatemala have included thousands of *ladinos* and Maya people. ▼

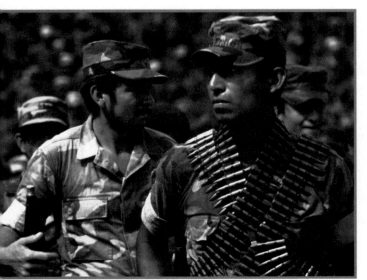

Civil War Takes Hold After 1954, Guatemala's government was ruled mainly by military officers. During much of this era, a civil war raged between government forces and rebels who opposed the government. Many people who expressed disagreement with government policy were murdered. More than 100,000 Guatemalans were killed or kidnapped before a peace agreement was reached in 1996.

Reading
Social Studies

A. Synthesizing Given the opposition to the new government after Guzmán's overthrow, do you think it continued social reforms?

Guatemala's Government Today

Guatemala's current constitution was written in 1985. It established the nation's government as a democratic republic with three branches. They are executive, legislative, and judicial.

Government's Three Branches A president heads Guatemala's executive branch. He or she is elected by the people every four years and may not be reelected. The president appoints a cabinet, or a group of advisers, to carry out the government's work.

Location •
Since the 1930s, Guatemala City's National Palace has housed the government's offices. ▲

Guatemala's legislative branch is called Congress. It has 113 members who are elected to four-year terms. Guatemala's Congress is unicameral, or has one chamber. Members of Congress may be reelected.

Guatemala's judicial branch has different levels of courts, somewhat like the United States. Unlike U.S. Supreme Court justices, whom the President appoints to serve for as long as they choose, Guatemala's Supreme Court judges are elected to five-year terms.

State and Local Governments Guatemala is a federal republic, so the national government shares power with state and local governments. Governors head Guatemala's 22 states, called *departamentos* (deh·pahr·tah·MEHN·taws). The president appoints each of the governors. Mayors elected by popular vote oversee the city governments.

Guatemala's Economy

At the turn of the century, Guatemala had the largest gross domestic product (GDP) in Central America. It also had the fastest growing GDP in the region.

Agriculture Guatemala's dominant industry is agriculture, which employs more than half of its work force. The nation's economy largely relies on the export of agricultural products. Since 1870, coffee has been Guatemala's leading export. Other agricultural exports include sugar, a spice called cardamom, and bananas.

Banana production began in the early 1900s, when U.S. companies built banana plantations in Guatemala. These fruit companies also developed railroads, ports, and communication systems in order to transport the bananas to foreign markets.

Other Parts of the Economy Guatemala also relies on manufacturing to bring in money. Food, beverages, and clothing are among its manufactured goods. These goods are sold both within Guatemala and as exports to other countries. While other Central American nations purchase many of Guatemala's manufactured goods, the United States purchases more of Guatemala's exports than any other country does.

In past years, Guatemala's economy has boomed with the sale of both textiles and clothing. Also, new nontraditional agricultural products, such as cut flowers and winter fruits, are selling quite well on the international market. Tourism is also a strong industry in Guatemala, which is home to many ancient Maya ruins.

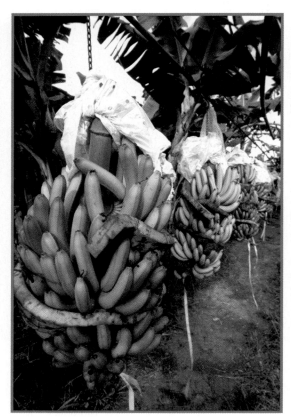

Human-Environment Interaction • Bananas are produced in mass quantity on Guatemala's many banana plantations. ▲

Reading
Social Studies

B. Clarifying
Does Guatemala have a single-product economy? Why or why not?

Place •
Standing nearly 150 feet high, this Maya temple at Tikal is one of Guatemala's major tourist attractions. ▼

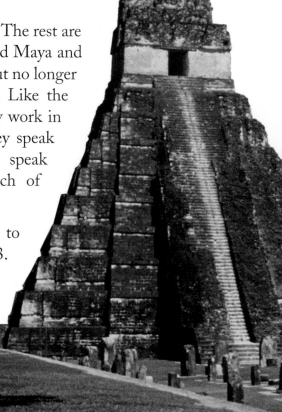

Living in Guatemala

More than half of Guatemala's people are Maya. The rest are *ladinos*. In Guatemala, *ladinos* are either of mixed Maya and Spanish ancestry, or they are of Maya ancestry but no longer practice Maya ways or speak Maya languages. Like the ancient Maya, most of Guatemala's Maya today work in agriculture and live in small rural villages. They speak Maya languages, though many of them also speak Spanish. They wear traditional clothing, much of which they weave by hand.

Education Guatemalan children are required to attend school from the age of 7 through 13. However, about one-third do not. Most of these children live in rural areas that have no schools. Only 15 percent of Guatemalans attend high school.

Culture • This Guatemalan woman sells many traditional Maya handwoven cloths. ▲

Two Sides of Guatemala Daily life in Guatemala is a matter of extremes. On the one hand, rural Guatemalans have few of the comforts that North Americans take for granted, such as indoor bathrooms, running water, and electricity. Outside the cities, most homes are very small, and many have dirt floors.

On the other hand, urban Guatemalans live in modern homes, attend schools and universities, and go to theaters, museums, and restaurants. Many of the cultural influences in the cities, such as movies, restaurant chains, clothing styles, magazines, cars, and television programs, come from foreign countries. The cultural influences in the rural areas are much more local in origin.

SECTION 4 ASSESSMENT

Terms & Names
1. Explain the significance of: (a) Rafael Carrera   (b) Jacobo Arbenz Guzmán   (c) *departamento*

Using Graphics
2. Use a table like this one to keep track of the sequence of events in Guatemala's history.

Year	Event
1837	
1839	
1944	
1951	
1954	
1985	
1996	

Main Ideas
3. (a) Why did the United States feel threatened when Jacobo Arbenz Guzmán established his policy of land redistribution?

(b) After 1954, how did the Guatemalan government treat people who expressed disagreement with its policies?

(c) What is Guatemala's leading export?

Critical Thinking
4. **Synthesizing**

What is the impact of having a powerful nation, such as the United States, be the largest purchaser of Guatemala's exports?

Think About
- the role of exports in Guatemala's economy
- U.S. interventions in Guatemala

ACTIVITY -OPTION-   Write a **paragraph** explaining three facts about Guatemala that you did not know before you read this section.

TERMS & NAMES

Explain the significance of each of the following:

1. West Indies
2. dependency
3. mulatto
4. *ladino*
5. dictator
6. single-product economy
7. diversify
8. Fidel Castro
9. Communism
10. Rafael Carrera

REVIEW QUESTIONS

Establishing Independence *(pages 203–207)*

1. Why did the United States want to build the Panama Canal?
2. What event freed the Caribbean Islands from Spanish rule?

Building Economies and Cultures *(pages 208–213)*

3. What risk did Caribbean islanders face by having single-product economies?
4. What two crops did Central American economies depend on before the countries diversified their economies?

Cuba Today *(pages 215–220)*

5. Why did hundreds of thousands of people flee from Cuba to the United States after Castro took over?
6. How did Cuba's relationship with the Soviet Union affect Cuba?

Guatemala Today *(pages 221–225)*

7. Why did Jacobo Arbenz Guzmán's program of land redistribution upset people in the United States?
8. What are the cultural backgrounds of Guatemala's *ladinos?*

CRITICAL THINKING

Identifying Problems and Solutions

1. Using your completed chart from Reading Social Studies, p. 202, choose one issue, such as dictatorship or colonization, and summarize the problems with it. Then summarize the solutions to the problems.

Drawing Conclusions

2. How do you think Fidel Castro's control of newspapers and television and radio stations has helped keep him in power?

Contrasting

3. Contrast the fates of Native Americans in the Caribbean Islands and in Central America after Europeans took over.

Visual Summary

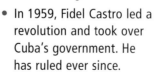

1 Establishing Independence

- People in Central America and the Caribbean fought first for independence and then for democracy.
- Central America's people are mostly *ladinos* and Native Americans, while the Caribbean's are largely of African or European descent.

2 Building Economies and Cultures

- The countries of the region had to diversify their economies so they would be more stable.
- The region's languages, religions, and music were influenced by the cultures of the colonizers, the enslaved Africans, and the Native Americans.

3 Cuba Today

- In 1959, Fidel Castro led a revolution and took over Cuba's government. He has ruled ever since.
- Throughout the 1900s, both the United States and the Soviet Union influenced events in Cuba.

4 Guatemala Today

- After decades of struggle, Guatemala's government has become more stable.
- Guatemala's economy relies heavily on agriculture, especially coffee production.
- More than half of Guatemala's people are Maya. The rest are *ladinos.*

Use the map and your knowledge of world cultures and geography to answer questions 1 and 2.

Additional Test Practice, pp. S1–S33

1. What natural features most likely attract tourists to Belize?

   A. Mountains

   B. Cities

   C. Lakes

   D. Hot springs

2. What human-made features might attract tourists to Belize?

   A. Mountains

   B. Maya ruins

   C. Coral reefs

   D. Rivers

The following passage is from the acceptance speech that President Oscar Arias of Costa Rica gave when he received the Nobel Peace Prize. Use the quotation and your knowledge of world cultures and geography to answer question 3.

PRIMARY SOURCE

Peace is not a matter of prizes or trophies. It is not the product of a victory or command. It has no finishing line, no final deadline, no fixed definition of achievement.

Peace is a never-ending process, the work of many decisions by many people in many countries. It is an attitude, a way of life, a way of solving problems and resolving conflicts. . . . It requires us to live and work together.

OSCAR ARIAS, acceptance speech, December 10, 1987

3. Which of the following statements most accurately restates Arias's belief about peace?

   A. Leaders like Arias are the only people who can help to bring about world peace.

   B. Now that Arias has received the Nobel Prize, he can stop working for peace.

   C. Peace has been achieved whenever a country is not presently fighting a war.

   D. Individual people can help create peace by the choices they make every day.

TEST PRACTICE
CLASSZONE.COM

ALTERNATIVE ASSESSMENT

1. WRITING ABOUT HISTORY

Imagine that you have traveled to one of the Caribbean islands, such as Grenada or Jamaica. Write a letter to a friend describing what you saw.

• Using the Internet or library resources, research the island. You might find books about the island in the travel section of the library.

• In your letter, describe scenery and the sights you visited, any special events you attended, and what you enjoyed most about the island. Include photographs or illustrations of special sights or experiences.

2. COOPERATIVE LEARNING

With a group of classmates, create a bulletin board about one of the countries in the Caribbean or Central America. Describe the climate, list the natural resources, and include information about the cities, politics, and the economy. Include maps, charts, and illustrations. Share the tasks of researching, writing, and creating the display with the members of your group.

INTEGRATED TECHNOLOGY

Doing Internet Research

The cultures of Central America and the Caribbean are rich and varied. Use the Internet to research the culture of one country, such as Belize or Cuba, to prepare a presentation.

• Use the Internet or resources in the library to learn about the culture of your chosen country.

• Learn about the art, music, religion, and other traditions of that country. Find out how its people have preserved cultural traditions of the past.

• Include copies of photographs or create your own drawings to include in your presentation.

For Internet links to support this activity, go to

RESEARCH LINKS
CLASSZONE.COM

CHAPTER 9

South America

ATLANTIC

PACIFIC

OCEAN

PACIFIC

OCEAN

OCEAN

INDIAN
OCEAN

SOUTH
AMERICA

OCEAN

Location The Amazon River winds eastward from the Andes through South America for nearly 4,000 miles.

228

How has movement from rural to urban areas affected South America?

Movement • Some of the largest and fastest-growing cities in the world are in South America—for example, São Paulo, Brazil, and Buenos Aires, Argentina. Since the mid-1900s, people have been moving from rural to urban areas. Today, three-quarters of all South Americans live in cities.

Although cities often offer more jobs, they also have serious drawbacks. For example, not everyone in South America's cities can find jobs. Others cannot find housing. In some cities, such as Rio de Janeiro, Brazil, some people live in extreme poverty. Because of problems like these, many people, including professionals such as teachers and doctors, have left South America for the United States and other countries that may offer better opportunities.

What do you think?

◆ Why do South Americans leave the countryside and move to cities?

◆ How might South America change when skilled professionals, such as doctors, move to other countries?

READING SOCIAL STUDIES

BEFORE YOU READ

▶▶ What Do You Know?

Before you read the chapter, consider what you already know about South America. What do you know about the region's history? What do you know about its role in the world's economy and culture? In particular, what do you know about Brazil and Peru? You may know that Brazil is famous for its successes in soccer. Think about what else you have read or seen on the news or in sports reports. Also consider connections to your own life: Have you ever heard music from South America, such as salsa?

▶▶ What Do You Want to Know?

Decide what else you want to know about South America. In your notebook, record what you hope to learn from this chapter.

Region • This Andean girl plays the region's music, called *huayno*. ▲

READ AND TAKE NOTES

Reading Strategy: Making Generalizations
Making generalizations is a useful strategy for understanding themes in social studies. A generalization is a conclusion supported by facts. Use the chart of generalizations below to better understand events and situations in South America.

- Copy the chart into your notebook.
- As you read the chapter, look for facts that support each generalization. Examples may be found in more than one section of the chapter.
- Beside each generalization, record the facts that support it.

Place • People crowd the streets of São Paulo in Brazil. ▲

Generalizations	Facts
Independence led to different types of governments in South America.	
South American countries are trying to cooperate with one another and with the United States.	
Geography and politics affect the economies of South America.	
Urban growth presents serious problems for some South American countries.	
South America's different cultures contribute to world culture.	

Establishing Independence

MAIN IDEA

After 300 years of rule by Spain and Portugal, South Americans won independence and established their own nations.

WHY IT MATTERS NOW

Because the United States has close economic and political ties with South America, it is important to understand the history of the region.

DATELINE

EXTRA

CAJAMARCA, THE ANDES, 1533

Word has just arrived that the Inca ruler, Atahualpa, was executed by a small group of Spanish adventurers. A few weeks ago, Atahualpa's messengers informed him that the Spanish were coming. Atahualpa commanded 30,000 warriors and saw no reason to worry. However, the Spanish, with cannons and guns, killed around 4,000 of Atahualpa's guards and then captured the Inca king. Atahualpa tried to buy his freedom, offering the Spanish a stack of gold 9 feet high in a room measuring 17 feet by 22 feet. The Spanish accepted the gold—and then executed Atahualpa anyway. Now many fear for the future of the Inca Empire.

Culture • The portrait on the left shows Atahualpa, while the one on the right shows Pizarro. ▲

Europeans Arrive in South America

In 1531, Spanish explorer Francisco Pizarro landed on the coast of what is now the South American country of Peru. He had with him horses, guns, cannons, and about 200 soldiers. His forces began the long climb up into the Andes Mountains, following the Inca road that led to the city of Cajamarca (KAH•hah•MAHR•kah).

TAKING NOTES

Use your chart to take notes about South America.

Generalizations	Facts
Independence led to different types of governments in South America.	
South American countries are trying to cooperate...	

Europeans Establish Control When Pizarro first encountered the Inca, he found a kingdom weakened by a bitter civil war. Pizarro quickly captured and executed the Inca ruler, Atahualpa. The Inca Empire soon fell under Spanish control.

Meanwhile, Portugal had claimed what is now Brazil, and so the Portuguese began to settle the region. However, dense rain forests prevented much exploration of the region's interior. The Portuguese therefore built most of their settlements along the Atlantic Coast.

Colonial South America Many Spanish and Portuguese settlers soon made their way to South America. As happened throughout the New World, the arrival of the Europeans led to the deaths of many Native Americans. Millions died from disease or overwork. As the Native American population shrank, the Europeans imported enslaved Africans to work mainly on the large sugar cane plantations in Brazil.

For nearly 300 years, Europeans ruled much of South America. Spain and Portugal between them claimed most of the land. Ships loaded with South American silver, gold, and sugar regularly sailed to these two countries. Both, especially Spain, grew enormously wealthy from their South American colonies.

European Colonizers of South America, 1500s

Portugal
Great Britain
France
Netherlands
Spain

0   500   1,000 miles
0   500   1,000 kilometers

GEOGRAPHY SKILLBUILDER:
Interpreting a Map
1. **Region** • What countries, other than Spain and Portugal, established colonies in South America?
2. **Place** • Which country controlled the smallest area of South America?

Independence

In the early 1800s, Spain and Portugal were still taking most of the wealth out of the South American colonies. People of Spanish or Portuguese descent born in South America wanted to share in the political and economic power. They were encouraged by the American Revolution in 1776 and the French Revolution

Key Independence Days in South America

| Feb.12, 1818 Chile | July 28, 1821 Peru | Sept. 7, 1822 Brazil |

1820   1825

1815   1830

Dec. 17, 1819 Gran Colombia   Aug. 6, 1825 Bolivia

SKILLBUILDER: Reading a Time Line

1. For each country on the time line, what event occurred on the date given?
2. On what day did Brazil achieve independence?

in 1789. At the same time, the *mestizos* and mulattos wanted to bring about change because they were often treated no better than slaves. South Americans soon decided to fight for independence.

Gaining Independence Beginning in 1810, two generals led a series of wars for independence. One was **Simón Bolívar** (see·MOHN boh·LEE·var), whose leadership freed the northern parts of South America. The other was **José de San Martín** (san mahr·TEEN). He was responsible for defeating Spanish forces in the south. By 1825, nearly all of Spanish South America was independent.

Meanwhile, Brazil gained its independence without a major war. When the French general Napoleon Bonaparte invaded Portugal in 1807, the Portuguese royal family fled to Brazil. After Napoleon's later defeat, the Portuguese king returned to Portugal in 1821. He left his son Pedro to be regent of Brazil. When the Brazilians demanded their freedom in 1822, Pedro agreed. Brazil then named Pedro its emperor.

Reading **Social Studies**

A. Recognizing Important Details How did Brazil gain its independence differently from other South American countries?

Biography

Simón Bolívar Simón Bolívar (shown at right) was born in Caracas, Venezuela, in 1783. As a teenager, Bolívar lived in Spain. He was influenced by the European Enlightenment and the philosophers Voltaire and Rousseau. A dream of freedom and independence for Hispanic America stirred Bolívar's soul, and he returned to South America.

Bolívar became a leader of the revolution in Venezuela in 1810. His clever military tactics led to victory over the Spanish and the creation of

the republic of Gran Colombia, which included what are now Colombia, Panama, Venezuela, and Ecuador. Bolívar became president of Gran Colombia and continued fighting farther south. Victorious there, he soon became the president of Peru and Bolivia, which was named for him. Because of his role in gaining South American independence from Spain, Bolívar is often called "the Liberator." He died in Colombia in 1830.

South America **233**

Governments of South America

However, South America's new independence did not lead to a stable, fair society, as revolutionary leaders had hoped. These leaders had little experience in government. Many of them wanted to establish constitutions that set limits on the powers of government. Doing this would allow citizens to participate in government.

Place • General Augusto Pinochet (pee·noh·CHEHT) ruled Chile as a military dictator from 1974 to 1990. ▲

Unlimited Governments However, wealthy citizens and former Spanish officials in South America wanted to keep their property and power. They did not want all citizens to have a say in government. To maintain order and to protect their interests, the powerful often gave control of the government to the military. This frequently resulted in unlimited governments, in which one person or one group held total power. In other cases, military leaders used their armies to take over limited governments in South America. By the 1990s, however, the majority of governments in South America were democratic.

BACKGROUND

A small group of people, usually military, who join together to seize government power is called a *junta* (HUN·tuh).

South American Cooperation Simón Bolívar tried to create a united South America—a nation of states like the United States. Although he was not successful, in the late 1800s the U.S. government began encouraging Pan-American unity. *Pan* means "all," so **Pan-American** means "all of the Americas."

In 1948, Latin American nations joined with the United States to form the **Organization of American States** (OAS). The OAS promotes economic cooperation, social justice, and the equality of all people. It encourages democracy within its member nations. For example, OAS officials observe elections to make sure they are run fairly. The organization also helps settle conflicts among its members. In 1979, the OAS established a special court to protect human rights in its member countries.

The countries of South America will probably never join together in the way that Simón Bolívar envisioned. They are, however, working together to achieve justice and a better life for all their people.

Region • An OAS official and a U.S. government official are shown here using a map of South America to discuss Pan-American issues. ▼

Reading
Social Studies

B. Analyzing Motives Why do you think the United States wanted to establish Pan-American ties?

The People of South America

Until the 1800s, immigrants to South America came mostly from Spain and Portugal. During the 1880s, South America attracted many more European immigrants.

Region • Welsh settlers started sheep ranches in South America, while Swiss immigrants in Brazil developed the cheese industry. ▼

Immigrants Influence Society The new immigrants helped build South America's economy by establishing a variety of industries. Also, as all immigrants do, they brought their own customs to their new home. For example, the British introduced the game of football (which people in the United States call soccer), and it quickly became a popular sport across South America.

South America's Population Today There are many ethnic groups within South America's population—Native Americans, descendants of Europeans or of enslaved Africans, and people of mixed ancestry. Some of these groups live in particular regions, while others are more widespread. For example, many Africans live in the tropical lowlands where their enslaved ancestors worked. Native Americans make up a large part of the population in the Andean nations of Peru, Bolivia, and Ecuador. The majority of South Americans, however, are either *mestizos* or mulattos.

SECTION 1 ASSESSMENT

Terms & Names

1. Explain the significance of:
   (a) Simón Bolívar
   (b) José de San Martín
   (c) Pan-American
   (d) Organization of American States

Using Graphics

2. Use a chart like this one to list the contributions to South America's history made by the four main groups from which the people of South America are descended.

Group	Contributions
Native Americans	
European Colonists	
Enslaved Africans	
Other Immigrants	

Main Ideas

3. (a) From what South American products did European nations profit?

   (b) How has South America's population changed since the 1500s?

   (c) What challenges have many South American governments faced in recent years?

Critical Thinking

4. **Synthesizing**

   What challenges do you think South Americans faced in their fights for independence?

   Think About
   - differences in wealth between the colonial rulers and the general population
   - who held political power
   - living conditions

ACTIVITY -OPTION- Imagine you work for the OAS. Make a **poster** that highlights the benefits the organization offers its members.

Explore the Mysteries of Chichén Itzá

You are a movie director making a documentary film called *Mysteries of the Maya*. You are shooting your film at the ruins of Chichén Itzá, a city of stone deep in the jungle of Mexico's Yucatán Peninsula. Many things about the Maya culture are still a mystery. You want to inform your audience about Chichén Itzá, but you also want to make them feel the mood of the place— awesome and mysterious.

COOPERATIVE LEARNING On these pages you will find challenges that you and your crew will face in making the documentary. Working with your crew, decide which one of these problems you will solve. Divide the work among crew members. Look for helpful information in the Data File. Keep in mind that you will present your solution to the class.

LANGUAGE ARTS CHALLENGE

"As darkness falls, colored lights play on the buildings . . ."

While your film crew visits Chichén Itzá, you are awed by the nighttime "light and sound show." As darkness falls, colored lights play on the buildings, and a narrator tells the Maya's story. How can you include this scene in your film? How can you convey the mood of this site to a TV audience? Choose one of these options. Use the Data File for help.

ACTIVITIES

1. Write a brief (60-second) promotional advertisement to be shown during TV station breaks. Include sketches or descriptions of photographs or art you will use in the commercial. If possible, think of background music, too.
2. As a member of the film crew, write a journal entry describing your experiences at the light and sound show.

CHICHÉN ITZÁ

* **City was founded by Maya** about sixth century A.D.

* The name, which means **"mouth of the wells of Itzá,"** refers to the site's two deep natural wells, or cenotes. The Itzá were a Maya group.

* One **cenote** supplied water. The other, about 200 feet across, was sacred to the rain god. Human sacrifices, mostly young people, were thrown into it, along with gold and jade ornaments.

* The Maya had many gods. **Chac** was the rain god. Kukulcan was pictured as a feathered serpent.

* Major buildings—**Pyramid of Kukulcan** (El Castillo), **Temple of the Warriors, Great Ball Court**— were built about A.D. 900–1200.

* City was abandoned about A.D. 1450.

TEMPLE OF KUKULCAN/ EL CASTILLO ("THE CASTLE")

* Four-sided pyramid represents the **Maya calendar** in several ways.

* Four steep stairways, with 91 steps each, climb each side of the pyramid. Including the top platform, the **steps total 365.** There are 18 flat platforms—the number of months in the Maya calendar.

* At the **spring and fall equinoxes,** sunlight falls on one staircase in a pattern that looks like a serpent creeping down the pyramid.

To learn more about Chichén Itzá, visit

RESEARCH LINKS
CLASSZONE.COM

SCIENCE CHALLENGE

"El Castillo, the pyramid of the serpent god"

From the top of El Castillo, the pyramid of the serpent god Kukulcan, you can see the stone ruins and the jungle surrounding them. This great temple-pyramid is the heart of Chichén Itzá. Maya priests, who were also scientists, studied the skies and made an accurate calendar. This pyramid reflects their knowledge of astronomy. How will your film explain this knowledge? Use one of these options to present information. Look in the Data File for help.

ACTIVITIES

1. Draw a diagram of El Castillo. Write a speech in which the film's narrator uses the diagram to explain the significance of the pyramid's structure and location.
2. Draw a storyboard to show what happens at El Castillo during the spring equinox.

Activity Wrap-Up

As a group, review the way you solved the challenge you chose. Organize your solution and present it to the class.

Building Economies and Cultures

TERMS & NAMES
free-trade zone
economic indicator
urbanization

MAIN IDEA

While South America's countries work to overcome challenges to their economies, their cultures flourish.

WHY IT MATTERS NOW

Cultural elements from South America, such as music, literature, and dance, are popular around the world.

DATELINE

BOGOTÁ, COLOMBIA, SEPTEMBER 9, 2000— All over Bogotá, people are talking about last week's meeting in Brazil's capital, Brasília. It marked the first-ever meeting of the presidents of South America's 12 nations.

Many people here say that holding this meeting in Brazil's capital indicates that Brazil is going to take a leadership role in the region. As one Colombian official in Bogotá said: "We have serious economic and political problems here. Brazil, the biggest and richest nation in South America, needs to exercise leadership." Indeed, it seems that Brazil has decided to do just that.

Region • Brazil's president, Fernando Henrique Cardoso, sponsored the 12-nation meeting. ▲

Geography and Trade in South America

Many South American nations have found that working together results in greater economic opportunity. Partly this is because they face similar challenges and possibilities. A common factor influencing many of the region's economies is geography. South America's physical geography presents the region with both transportation barriers and transportation corridors.

TAKING NOTES

Use your chart to take notes about South America.

Generalizations	Facts
Independence led to different types of governments in South America.	
South American countries are trying to cooperate . . .	

Barriers South America's transportation barriers have interfered with trade and contacts with other cultures. For example, Portuguese explorers had trouble penetrating the dense Amazon rain forest. Because of this, they built their settlements along the coastline. Today, rain forests and rugged regions such as the Andes still prevent easy travel across the continent.

Corridors South America also has transportation corridors, such as the Amazon River system. Before the Europeans arrived, Native Americans canoed along the Amazon and its tributaries. Today, oceangoing vessels enter the Amazon system on Brazil's north coast. They carry goods such as food, clothing, and tools. They bring back lumber, rubber, animal skins, Brazil nuts, and other raw materials for shipment overseas.

Movement • Ships like this one can carry goods inland on the Amazon for more than 2,000 miles. ▲

Spotlight on CULTURE

Gabriela Mistral Chilean poet Gabriela Mistral (1889–1957; shown at right) used poetry to express her deep feelings for the people and land of South America, as in this poem, "Chilean Earth." She particularly loved children, and their rhymes and lullabies influenced her writing.

South Americans and people around the world greatly admire Mistral's work. As the first South American to win the Nobel Prize in Literature, she became a symbol of the hopes and dreams of a whole continent.

THINKING CRITICALLY

1. **Drawing Conclusions**
   What about Chile does Mistral celebrate in this poem?

2. **Forming and Supporting Opinions**
   Why do you think Mistral's poetry inspired South Americans?

For more on Gabriela Mistral, go to

RESEARCH LINKS
CLASSZONE.COM

Chilean Earth

We dance on Chilean earth
more beautiful than Lia and Raquel:
the earth that kneads men,
their lips and hearts without bitterness.

The land most green with orchards,
the land most blond with grain,
the land most red with grapevines,
how sweetly it brushes our feet!

Its dust molded our cheeks,
Its rivers, our laughter,
and it kisses our feet with a melody
that makes my mother sigh.
For the sake of its beauty,
we want to light up the fields with song.
It is free,
and for freedom we want
to bathe its face in music.

Tomorrow we will open its rocks;
we will create vineyards and orchards;
tomorrow we will exalt its people.
Today we need only to dance!

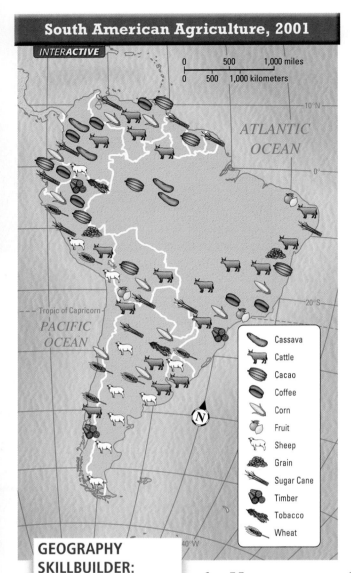

INTERACTIVE

ATLANTIC OCEAN

PACIFIC OCEAN

Tropic of Capricorn

10°N

0°

20°S

40°W

Cassava	
Cattle	
Cacao	
Coffee	
Corn	
Fruit	
Sheep	
Grain	
Sugar Cane	
Timber	
Tobacco	
Wheat	

GEOGRAPHY SKILLBUILDER: Interpreting a Map

1. **Place** • Name an agricultural product from southern South America.
2. **Region** • Name an agricultural product that is produced in many parts of South America.

Products and Industries of South America

The rich natural resources of South America include abundant minerals and fertile land. However, few South American countries have fully developed their natural resources.

Mineral Resources Under the surface of South America's land lie many precious minerals—including gold, iron ore, lead, petroleum, tin, and copper. Many South American countries mine these minerals for export. For example, Chile mostly mines copper, Bolivia has a great amount of tin, and Colombia supplies the world with emeralds.

Agricultural Products South America is not only rich in mineral resources, but it also boasts some of the largest farms in the world. These farms produce goods for export, such as beef, grain, sugar, wool, bananas, and coffee. However, most of South America's farms are small. On these farms, individual farmers struggle to grow even enough food to feed their families. Many poor farmers have given up and moved to cities, hoping to find jobs there.

Manufacturing The most important South American industrial countries are Venezuela, Chile, Argentina, and Brazil. In fact, Brazil is one of the most important industrial nations in the world. It manufactures enough cars and trucks to supply the entire continent. Brazil also manufactures computers, televisions, and airplanes. In other South American countries, manufactured goods include shoes, furniture, beverages, and textiles.

Economic Cooperation Lack of funding prevents many South American countries from developing manufacturing. To improve their economies, countries may cooperate economically. For example, in 1994, the heads of 34 North and South American countries met in Miami, Florida, at the first Summit of the Americas.

Reading **Social Studies**

A. Contrasting How do South America's small farms and large farms differ?

BACKGROUND

The countries continued to develop the idea of a Free-Trade Zone of the Americas at additional Summit of the Americas meetings in 1998 and in 2001.

Reading
Social Studies

B. Making Inferences How do you think a high literacy rate can help boost a country's economy?

There, they agreed to create the huge Free-Trade Zone of the Americas, which would include almost every country in North and South America by the year 2005. In a **free-trade zone,** people and goods move across borders without being taxed. Many South Americans are confident that the Free-Trade Zone of the Americas will lead to greater prosperity in the region.

Economic Indicators Economic cooperation among nations can be challenging if some economies are strong and others are weak. Differences can be measured by **economic indicators,** statistics that show how a country's economy is doing. The literacy rate shows the percentage of a country's people who can read and write at an elementary school level. Life expectancy, or the average age to which people in a country live, gives clues about a country's health care and nutrition.

Country	Literacy Rate	Life Expectancy
Argentina	96%	75 years
Bolivia	83%	64 years
Brazil	85%	63 years
Chile	95%	76 years
Colombia	91%	70 years
Ecuador	90%	71 years
Guyana	98%	64 years
Paraguay	92%	74 years
Peru	89%	70 years
Suriname	93%	71 years
Uruguay	97%	75 years
Venezuela	91%	73 years

SKILLBUILDER: Interpreting a Chart

1. Which nation has the highest literacy rate? Which has the lowest?
2. What is the life expectancy in Brazil?

Daily Life in South America

As with all regions, South America is home to both urban and rural areas. Many of the urban areas are enormous. City populations include some very wealthy people and many middle-class people who work in government or business. Millions more, however, live in extreme poverty. Nevertheless, South Americans enjoy a proud tradition of music and literature.

The Urban Setting For the past 50 years or so, South America has experienced major **urbanization,** meaning that many people have moved from the countryside to cities. Multiple factors caused this movement to occur. For example, the growth of manufacturing created more jobs in cities. At the same time, many rural people lived in poverty, without enough land to support their families. The promise of jobs, schools, and health services drew them to cities.

Today, several South American cities rank among the largest in the world. In 2000, São Paulo (sown POW·loh) in Brazil was home to nearly 18 million people, and Buenos Aires (BWAY·nos AIR·ays) in Argentina had nearly 13 million people.

Houses cannot be built quickly enough to keep up with the growing number of people. Large slums surround South America's biggest cities. In these areas, people live in shacks of cardboard, wood scraps, or tin. They often have no electricity or running water.

The Arts Despite the terrible poverty of millions, the arts in South America have thrived. The region's literature is admired throughout the world. The Nobel Prize in Literature has been given to three South Americans—Chilean poets Gabriela Mistral (mih·STRAHL) and Pablo Neruda (neh·ROO·duh), and Colombian novelist Gabriel García Márquez (gar·SEE·uh MAR·kez). Many South American poets and writers express their unique cultural heritage in their work. South American novelists also founded a literary style, magical realism, in which everyday reality mixes with fantasy.

Region •
Peruvians play *huayno* on flutes like the one this girl is using. ▲

Music, too, is an important part of the culture of South America. The traditional music of the Andean regions, called *huayno*, is played on flutes and drums. Some forms of music, such as salsa, have African roots. As more and more South Americans move to urban areas, musicians there are combining the traditional musical styles with rock and other popular types of music from Europe and North America.

SECTION 2 ASSESSMENT

Terms & Names
1. Explain the significance of: (a) free-trade zone   (b) economic indicator   (c) urbanization

Using Graphics

2. Use a spider map like this one to show six factors that have influenced South America's economic progress.

South America's Economic Progress

Main Ideas

3. (a) Name one geographic feature that is a transportation barrier and one that is a transportation corridor.

(b) List five of South America's important natural resources.

(c) Name the three South Americans who have won the Nobel Prize in Literature.

Critical Thinking

4. **Identifying Problems**

What challenges do South American countries face in building strong economies?

Think About
  ◆ physical geography
  ◆ the needs of a rapidly growing population
  ◆ the effects of urbanization

ACTIVITY -OPTION-   Look at the physical map of South America on page 142. Write a short **description** of a way to overcome one of South America's transportation barriers.

Brazil Today

TERMS & NAMES
inflation
São Paulo
Rio de Janeiro
Brasília
Carnival

MAIN IDEA	WHY IT MATTERS NOW
As the largest country in South America, Brazil has achieved economic success while facing challenges such as unemployment.	Brazil's huge land area, population, and economic success enable it to influence its neighbors in South America and North America.

DATELINE

RIO DE JANEIRO, BRAZIL, DECEMBER 30, 2001—Preparations are almost complete for the New Year's Eve celebration tomorrow. Shop owners are sold out of the small blue and white boats that worshipers of the sea goddess Iemanjá will set adrift on the sea. They will fill the boats with offerings to the goddess in hopes that she will bless them with a good fishing season.

Millions of people will also throw flowers into the water. If the flowers drift back to shore, Iemanjá is not happy with the offering. If the flowers drift out to sea, the people can expect to have a good year.

Culture • These residents of Rio de Janeiro get ready to set their boat off to greet Iemanjá. ▲

Brazil: Regional Leader

Almost anything that happens in Brazil is newsworthy—because Brazil is the largest country in South America, covering almost half the continent. Its population of 172 million is close in size to the combined population of all the other South American countries. Brazil's gross domestic product is larger than that of any other South American country.

TAKING NOTES

Use your chart to take notes about South America.

Generalizations	Facts
Independence led to different types of governments in South America.	
South American countries are trying to cooperate…	

The Government of Brazil

After gaining independence from Portugal in 1822, Brazil was ruled by a series of emperors. In 1889, Brazil became a constitutional republic. Beginning in 1930, a series of dictators and military leaders ruled Brazil. Democratic government was restored in 1985. Power today is shared by a president, an elected congress, and a court system.

The Economy of Brazil

Brazil has the largest economy in South America. The country's gross domestic product is nearly twice that of Argentina, which is the next largest economy in South America.

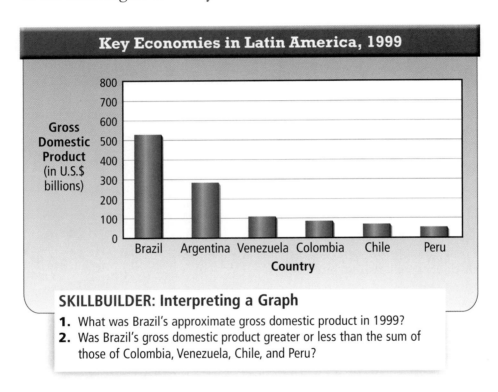

Key Economies in Latin America, 1999

SKILLBUILDER: Interpreting a Graph

1. What was Brazil's approximate gross domestic product in 1999?
2. Was Brazil's gross domestic product greater or less than the sum of those of Colombia, Venezuela, Chile, and Peru?

The Growth of Industry In Brazil, the government controls or influences certain industries to help the economy grow. For example, in the 1950s, the government promoted the building of automobile factories to cut down on the number of cars imported into Brazil. By the late 1980s, Brazil was building more than 1 million vehicles a year, enough to export some to other countries.

Agricultural Production In the world, Brazil is second only to the United States in exporting crops. When it comes to coffee, Brazil produces more than any other country in the world. Brazil is also a leading producer of oranges, bananas, and corn.

Unemployment and Inflation Even though Brazil's economy is the strongest in Latin America, many Brazilians are unemployed. Unemployment results when not enough businesses hire workers, or when workers do not have the education or training they need for the jobs available. Even those who have jobs may face hard times, especially due to inflation. **Inflation** is a general increase in the price of goods or services. It occurs when goods or services are in great demand, allowing producers to charge higher prices for them. The combination of unemployment and inflation has led to much poverty in Brazil.

Place • Automobile plants supply Brazil with many cars, like these parked in a plant lot, for export each year. ▲

Reading
Social Studies

A. Synthesizing How would inflation pose challenges even to people who do have jobs?

The People of Brazil

When explorers from Portugal arrived in Brazil in 1500, as many as 5 million Native Americans lived there. During the 1500s, the Portuguese established large sugar cane plantations in northeastern Brazil. At first they enslaved Native Americans to work on the plantations. Soon, however, many Native Americans died of disease. The plantation owners then turned to Africa for labor. Eventually, Brazil brought over more enslaved Africans than any other North or South American country.

Today, Native Americans make up less than 1 percent of Brazil's population. In northeastern Brazil, most people have African ancestors, while many people in Brazil have both European and African ancestors.

BACKGROUND

Of the 10 million to 15 million enslaved Africans brought to North and South America, more than 3.5 million ended up in Brazil.

Can Cars Run on Sugar? Brazil's first major export was sugar made from sugar cane (shown at right). However, the plentiful sugar cane isn't just used to make sugar. Today, Brazilians use sugar cane to produce ethanol. Like gasoline, ethanol is a fuel used to run cars.

Nearly half of the cars sold in Brazil run on a gasoline-ethanol mix. Thousands run on ethanol alone. Producing ethanol from sugar cane makes good use of an abundant resource and creates more jobs in the sugar cane industry. Also, its production is less harmful to the environment than is gasoline's.

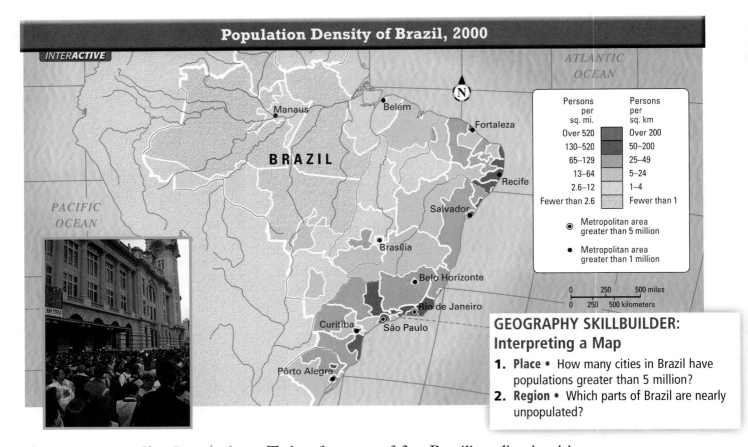

Population Density of Brazil, 2000

INTER**ACTIVE**

Persons per sq. mi.	Persons per sq. km
Over 520	Over 200
130–520	50–200
65–129	25–49
13–64	5–24
2.6–12	1–4
Fewer than 2.6	Fewer than 1

◉ Metropolitan area greater than 5 million

● Metropolitan area greater than 1 million

0   250   500 miles
0   250   500 kilometers

GEOGRAPHY SKILLBUILDER:
Interpreting a Map
1. **Place** • How many cities in Brazil have populations greater than 5 million?
2. **Region** • Which parts of Brazil are nearly unpopulated?

Place • The overcrowding of Brazil's cities, such as São Paulo, has put many stresses on the nation. ▲

City Populations Today, four out of five Brazilians live in cities. Brazil's two largest cities, **São Paulo** and **Rio de Janeiro,** are growing quickly. In 2000, São Paulo's population was close to 18 million. At the rate it is growing, the population will be more than 20 million in 2015. The national population is also increasing rapidly. In 1999, Brazil's population was almost 172 million. If current trends continue, by 2025 it could reach 210 million.

Because of much crowding along Brazil's Atlantic coast, the government wanted people to move into Brazil's vast interior. In 1956, it decided to create a new capital, **Brasília,** 600 miles inland. Now, like every other city in Brazil, Brasília has problems with overcrowding.

Reading
Social Studies

B. Hypothesizing What problems can rapid population growth cause?

The Culture of Brazil

Brazil's lively culture is a blend of influences from the many cultural groups that have come to Brazil over the centuries. Brazil's music, foods, and religious practices reflect that blend.

A Rich Mix Brazilian languages, religions, and musical traditions all reflect the multiple roots of Brazil's culture. For example, Brazil's official language is Portuguese. Included in Brazilian Portuguese, however, are many words from Tupi-Guarani (TOO•pee-GWAH•ruh•NEE), the language of Native Americans from the interior of northern Brazil.

As for religion, most Brazilians are Catholic, the religion brought to Brazil by the Portuguese. However, the number of non-Catholics is increasing. In 1940, only 5 percent of Brazilians were not Catholic. In 2000, non-Catholics had risen to 20 percent of the population because immigrants and missionaries had brought other religions to Brazil. Even so, more Catholics live in Brazil than in any other country in the world.

In addition, African religions still thrive in Brazil. For example, many people worship the African sea goddess Iemanjá. African influences can also be heard in Brazilian music, such as samba, which is based on African rhythms.

Holidays A Brazilian holiday called **Carnival** highlights the country's cultural diversity. This famous festival occurs during the four days before Lent. Carnival includes huge parades and street parties. In Rio de Janeiro, groups of African Brazilians perform samba dances. The dancers wear elaborate costumes of feathers and brightly colored, sparkling cloth.

BACKGROUND

In Christianity, Lent is the 40-day period before Easter.

Sports Brazilian football, called soccer in the United States, is a sport that most of the country gets excited about. Brazil is often a finalist in the World Cup, the sport's world championship competition. Brazilians enjoy watching professional football; millions of them also enjoy playing the game.

SECTION 3 ASSESSMENT

Terms & Names
1. Explain the significance of:
   - (a) inflation
   - (b) São Paulo
   - (c) Rio de Janeiro
   - (d) Brasília
   - (e) Carnival

Using Graphics
2. Use a chart like this one to record key facts about Brazil's geography, history, government, economy, and culture.

Geography	History	Government	Economy	Culture

Main Ideas
3. (a) Why can Brazil be described as an "economic giant"?

   (b) Where do most people in Brazil live today?

   (c) Why did the Brazilian government move the capital inland to Brasília?

Critical Thinking
4. **Drawing Conclusions**

   Why do you think Brazil's economy is the most successful in South America?

   Think About
   - the government's role in the economy
   - natural resources
   - population size

Write a **speech** about the different groups that have influenced Brazilian culture. Include descriptions of each group's contributions.

The Legacy of Latin America

Food

People the world over have developed a taste for foods that originated in Latin America. Chile peppers, tomatoes, sweet potatoes, corn, and chocolate are just a few of the Latin American foods regularly found in kitchens and restaurants around the globe.

Natural Rubber

Ancient Latin Americans were the first to make use of natural rubber. Harvested from trees of the genus *Hevea*, native to Brazil, natural rubber is used around the world for everything from erasers to tires for racecars, airplanes, and trucks. The Maya invented chewing gum more than 1,000 years ago. They chewed a rubberlike substance called chicle (CHIHK•uhl), which is made from the sap of the sapodilla tree. Natural chicle was used to make chewing gum in the United States until the 1940s, when it was replaced with artificial ingredients.

Cowboys

Pioneers in the southwestern United States first learned many of the skills of cattle ranching from *vaqueros* (vah•KEH•rohs), Mexican cowboys working on Texas cattle ranches. The *vaqueros* showed the newcomers how to use lariats, saddles, spurs, and branding irons.

Language

Some of the words we use every day come from Spanish or from Native American languages. Examples are *coyote, patio, tomato, cocoa, cafeteria, canyon, corral, chile, lariat, lasso, rodeo,* and *stampede.*

stam·pede (stăm-pēd´) *n.* **1.** A sudden frenzied rush of panic-stricken animals. **2.** A sudden headlong rush or flight of a crowd of people. **3.** A mass impulsive action: *a stampede of support for the candidate. v.* **-ped·ed, -ped·ing, -pedes** —*tr.* **1.** To cause (a herd of animals) to flee in panic. **2.** To cause (a crowd of people) to act on mass impulse. —*intr.* **1.** To flee in a headlong rush. **2.** To act on mass impulse. [Spanish *estampida,* uproar, stampede, from Provençal, from *estampir,* to stamp, of Germanic origin.] —**stam·ped´er** *n.*

Life-Saving Medicines

Native peoples in Latin America, especially in the Amazon rain forest, have been sharing their knowledge of medicinal plants for centuries—to the world's benefit. Two important contributions to modern medicine have been quinine, used to cure malaria, and curare, used to fight serious nerve diseases, such as multiple sclerosis.

Quinine ▲

Find Out More About It!

Study the text and photos on these pages to learn about inventions, creations, and contributions that have come from Latin America. Then choose the item that interests you the most and do research in the library or on the Internet to learn more about it. Use the information you gather to create a poster that celebrates the contribution.

RESEARCH LINKS
CLASSZONE.COM

Peru Today

TERMS & NAMES
oasis
guerrilla warfare
Alberto Fujimori
Quechua

MAIN IDEA

Peru's physical features and its unstable governments have posed challenges to the development of its economy and its people.

WHY IT MATTERS NOW

Peru's economic problems also affect its trading partners, including the United States.

DATELINE

CHINCHA ISLANDS, PERU, 1842— Officials recently announced a major new source of prosperity for Peru. Dried sea-bird droppings, called guano, are now being exported around the world to be used as plant fertilizer.

The idea of using guano as fertilizer came from ancient Inca farmers. Recently, scientific research has confirmed that guano is rich in phosphates and nitrates, which help plants to grow. Fertilizer companies in Britain and other countries are now paying huge sums of money for the right to dig guano from Peru.

Human-Environment Interaction • Guano comes from a number of sea birds, including cormorants like this one. ▲

The Land of Peru

Though Peru is rich in resources, such as guano, variations in its physical geography also present problems. Three types of landforms exist in Peru: mountains, rain forest, and desert. Each type has its own special characteristics, but all three are transportation barriers rather than transportation corridors. Traveling from one part of Peru to another is not easy.

TAKING NOTES
Use your chart to take notes about South America.

Generalizations	Facts
Independence led to different types of governments in South America.	
South American countries are trying to cooperate...	

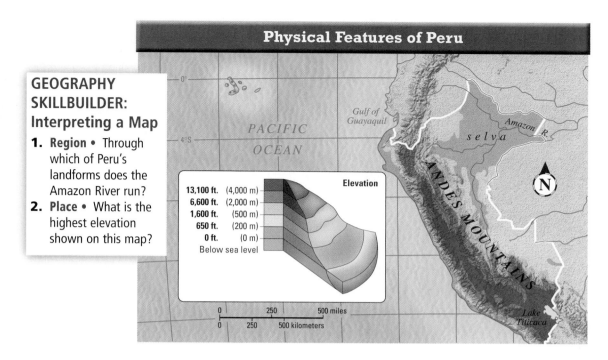

Physical Features of Peru

GEOGRAPHY SKILLBUILDER: Interpreting a Map

1. **Region** • Through which of Peru's landforms does the Amazon River run?
2. **Place** • What is the highest elevation shown on this map?

PACIFIC OCEAN

Gulf of Guayaquil

selva

Amazon R.

ANDES MOUNTAINS

Lake Titicaca

Elevation

13,100 ft. (4,000 m)
6,600 ft. (2,000 m)
1,600 ft. (500 m)
650 ft. (200 m)
0 ft. (0 m)
Below sea level

0   250   500 miles
0   250   500 kilometers

Three Types of Landforms Look at the map above. You can see that the Andes Mountains run the entire length of Peru, dividing the country in two. In places, the mountains are so steep that they are practically impassable. Notice that off the eastern slopes of the Andes stretches rain forest, which is called selva in Spanish. Now look to the west of the Andes, along the Pacific coast. Here the northern stretches of Chile's Atacama Desert reach into Peru. Most of Peru's cities, large farms, and factories are located in the desert, in or near oases. An **oasis** is a fertile region in a desert that formed around a river or spring.

Reading
Social Studies

A. Clarifying Why do you think Peru's cities are located in the desert rather than in other environments?

The Economy of Peru

Peru has many resources, but it also has many problems. The country's harsh geography affects its economy. For example, the cold, rocky highlands and the cool, dry desert cover so much area that there is not enough arable land to feed the growing population.

Place • Because of cold currents in the Pacific Ocean, Peru's desert has an average summer temperature of only 73°F. ▶

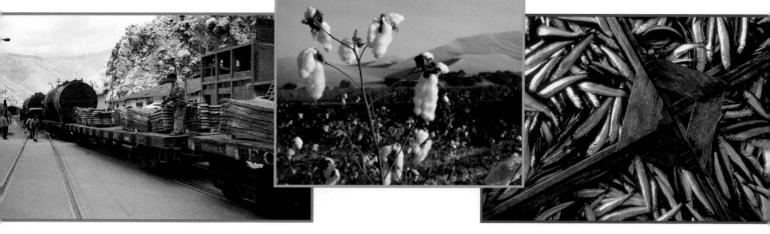

Place • At left, a freight train transports copper ingots through Peru. At center, cotton plants grow in Ica, Peru. ▲

Place • Many crates of anchovies are sold in Peru each year. ▲

Agriculture Like many other countries, Peru must import certain foods. These include grains, vegetable oils, and some meats, many of which come from the United States. However, Peruvians do grow sugar cane, cotton, and coffee for export. Also, southern Peru has a large dairy industry that serves markets both in Peru and beyond. Meats from cattle, sheep, alpaca, and goats are also processed and distributed within the country.

Fishing The cold waters along the Pacific Coast are fine fishing grounds. Sardines and anchovies are the most important fish in the Peruvian catch. They are dried and made into fishmeal, which is sold as feed for livestock throughout the world.

Mining Peru is an important supplier of metals such as silver, copper, and bismuth. It also contains oil and gold deposits. However, the richest deposits of minerals in the country exist in dense rain forests and at elevations of over 12,000 feet. Because it is difficult to mine in these locations, Peru's mineral resources have not brought the country the great wealth that they could.

The Government of Peru

Peru declared itself independent of Spain in 1821. The nation was not completely free, however, until December of 1824, when Simón Bolívar finally drove out the Spanish. Following independence, Peru's military leaders began fighting one another. Struggles between military and civilian leaders continued until late in the 20th century.

Guerrilla Warfare Perhaps the greatest struggle in Peru's modern history arose in the early 1980s. At that time, Communist groups rose up to fight against the democracy that they felt was failing Peru. The most powerful of these groups was Sendero Luminoso (sen·DAIR·oh loo·mih·NOH·soh), or Shining Path.

BACKGROUND

Although in Spanish *guerrilla* is pronounced geh-REE-yuh, in English it is pronounced like the word *gorilla*. The word is Spanish for "small-scale war."

Sendero Luminoso fought for changes using **guerrilla warfare,** or nontraditional military tactics characterized by small groups using surprise attacks. The military responded, and many citizens died in the crossfire. Until Sendero Luminoso's leader, Abimael Guzmán Reynoso (ah·bee·mah·EHL gooz·MAHN ray·NAW·saw), was imprisoned in 1992, the civil war continued.

Government in Crisis The 1990s did not bring better times to Peru. From 1990 to 2000, **Alberto Fujimori,** the son of Japanese immigrants, was president. At first, many of Peru's poor rural people supported him. By May 2000, however, he and his officials were accused of corruption. Many resignations followed, and in November, Fujimori abandoned the presidency and fled to Japan. The new president, Alejandro Toledo (al·eh·HAHN·droh toh·LAY·doh), faced the challenge of trying to win back the trust of Peruvians after the government scandals.

Peruvian People and Culture

Today, more Native Americans live in Peru than in any other South American country. Forty-five percent of Peru's people are Native Americans—the descendants of the Inca. Many of these people are **Quechua** (KEHCH·wuh), people who live in the Andes highlands and speak the Inca language Quechua. Along with Spanish, Quechua is one of Peru's official languages. Many people in the highlands speak the language of another Native American group, the Aymara (EYE·mah·RAH). The Inca conquered the Aymara in the 15th century, but the language lived on.

After Native Americans, *mestizos* are Peru's next largest group. Peru's population also includes people with European, African, and Asian ancestors.

Urban and Rural Life Most of Peru's people live in cities or towns. Lima is Peru's capital and its biggest city, with about 7 million people. Lima has grown very quickly, which poses some severe problems. At the dawn of the 21st century, many neighborhoods lacked basic city services, such as electricity, running water, and public transportation.

B. Drawing Conclusions
How do you think the violence and corruption in government affected people's daily lives in Peru?

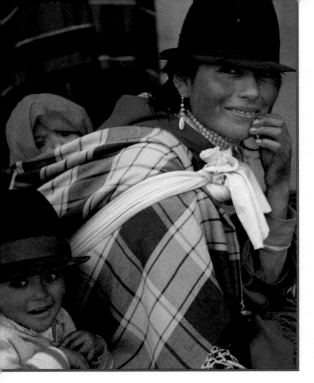

Many of Peru's rural farmers are very poor. They farm such small plots of land that often they cannot grow enough to feed their families. These rural people, who are mainly Native Americans, often move to the cities in search of a better life. However, many have little education and cannot speak Spanish, making it hard to find work.

Religion Peru's religions reflect multiple cultural traditions. Catholicism is the national religion of Peru, and more than 90 percent of Peruvians are Catholic. However, many Inca religious practices also still exist. At times, the Inca and Catholic customs mix. For example, some villages honor Catholic saints with traditional Inca festivals.

Region • Like this mother and daughter, many Quechua live in the Andes of Ecuador, Peru, and Bolivia. ▲

Literature The literature of Peru reveals modern themes as well as traditional ones. Peru's most famous living novelist, Mario Vargas Llosa (MAHR·yoh VAHR·guhs YOH·suh), is known for his belief that a novel should represent life to the fullest. César Vallejo (SAY·sar vuh·YAY·hoh), a *mestizo*, is Peru's most famous poet and is considered one of the world's best Spanish-language poets. His poetry describes what life is like for Peru's Native Americans and tells about suffering and struggles that all people may face.

SECTION 4 ASSESSMENT

Terms & Names

1. Explain the significance of: (a) oasis   (b) guerrilla warfare   (c) Alberto Fujimori   (d) Quechua

Using Graphics

2. Use a chart like this one to list the products generated by each of Peru's industries.

Industry	Products
Agriculture	
Fishing	
Mining	

Main Ideas

3. (a) Describe the three types of landforms in Peru.

   (b) Describe the challenges facing Peru's economy.

   (c) Which group makes up the largest part of Peru's population?

Critical Thinking

4. **Forming and Supporting Opinions**

   Why did Peru's guerrillas use violence to bring about change? Were they right to do so? Explain.

   Think About
   - reasons for discontent in Peru
   - the history of democracy in Peru
   - other possible methods of demanding change

ACTIVITY -OPTION- Imagine you live in Peru. Write a **short story** describing your daily life, including what you do for work and for recreation.

Reading a Time Line

▶▶ Defining the Skill

A time line is a visual list of dates and events shown in the order in which they occurred. Time lines can be horizontal or vertical. On horizontal time lines, the earliest date is on the left. On vertical time lines, the earliest date is usually at the top.

▶▶ Applying the Skill

The time line below shows the dates of expeditions to explore the Amazon River. Use the strategies listed below to help you read the time line.

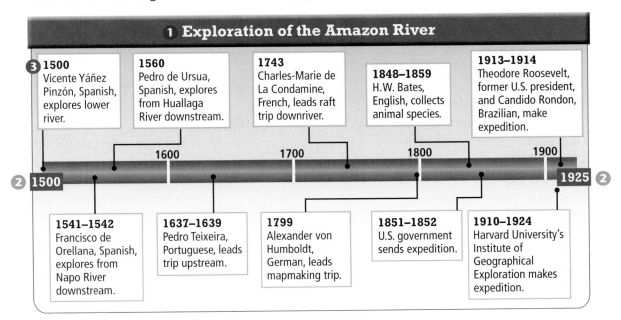

❶ Exploration of the Amazon River

❸ 1500
Vicente Yáñez Pinzón, Spanish, explores lower river.

1560
Pedro de Ursua, Spanish, explores from Huallaga River downstream.

1743
Charles-Marie de La Condamine, French, leads raft trip downriver.

1848–1859
H.W. Bates, English, collects animal species.

1913–1914
Theodore Roosevelt, former U.S. president, and Candido Rondon, Brazilian, make expedition.

1600   1700   1800   1900

❷ 1500   **1925 ❷**

1541–1542
Francisco de Orellana, Spanish, explores from Napo River downstream.

1637–1639
Pedro Teixeira, Portuguese, leads trip upstream.

1799
Alexander von Humboldt, German, leads mapmaking trip.

1851–1852
U.S. government sends expedition.

1910–1924
Harvard University's Institute of Geographical Exploration makes expedition.

How to Read a Time Line

Strategy ❶ Read the title. It will tell you the main idea of the time line.

Strategy ❷ Read the dates at the beginning and the end of the time line. These will show the period of time that the time line covers.

Strategy ❸ Read the dates and events in order, beginning with the earliest one. Think about how each event may have influenced later events. Take note of which nations were involved in each expedition.

Strategy ❹ Summarize the main idea of the time line. Remember that the title will help you focus on the main idea.

Write a Summary

Writing a summary can help you understand the information shown on a time line. The summary to the right states the time period covered and the main idea of the time line.

▶▶ Practicing the Skill

Turn to page 233 in Chapter 9, Section 1. Look at the time line entitled "Key Independence Days in South America," and write a paragraph summarizing what you learned from it.

> **❹** The time line covers the period between 1500 and 1925. During that period of time, people from Europe and the United States explored the Amazon River. The time line shows that on their expeditions, people explored the river, made maps, and collected animal species.

TERMS & NAMES

Explain the significance of each of the following:

1. Simón Bolívar
2. Pan-American
3. free-trade zone
4. urbanization
5. São Paulo
6. Brasília
7. Carnival
8. oasis
9. guerrilla warfare
10. Quechua

REVIEW QUESTIONS

Establishing Independence *(pages 231–235)*

1. What caused the death of so many Native Americans after the arrival of the Europeans in South America?
2. How did many South American nations end up with unlimited governments after independence?

Building Economies and Cultures *(pages 238–242)*

3. List three of South America's major natural resources.
4. Why have so many people moved to South America's cities in the past 50 years?

Brazil Today *(pages 243–247)*

5. What are two causes of unemployment in Brazil?
6. Why did the government of Brazil build the city of Brasília?

Peru Today *(pages 250–254)*

7. Describe the three types of landforms that make up Peru.
8. How does the Native American population in Peru compare in size with the Native American populations elsewhere in South America?

CRITICAL THINKING

Making Generalizations

1. Using your completed chart from Reading Social Studies, p. 230, write a paragraph explaining the facts that support one generalization about South America.

Contrasting

2. Brazil and Venezuela both gained independence from European countries. How did the road to freedom for Brazil contrast with that of Venezuela?

Synthesizing

3. When South American nations form trade blocs, how is that different from uniting politically?

Visual Summary

Establishing Independence

1

- After 300 years of colonial rule, the countries of South America gained independence.
- South America's population today reflects the arrival of immigrants from Europe, Africa, and Asia.

Building Economies and Cultures

2

- Geographic features and growing populations have challenged economic progress in South America.
- The countries of the region work together to benefit all of their economies.

Brazil Today

3

- Brazil is South America's largest and most economically successful country.
- Despite economic success, Brazil still faces unemployment and inflation.

Peru Today

4

- Peru's physical geography hinders the development of its economy.
- Peru has suffered many political problems, such as guerrilla warfare and corrupt government.

Use the map and your knowledge of world cultures and geography to answer questions 1 and 2.

Additional Test Practice, pp. S1–S33

1900   1950   2000

- City with population greater than 1 million

1. How many South American cities had populations over 1 million in 1950?

A. 0

B. 5

C. 9

D. 12

2. How many more South American cities had populations over 1 million in 2000 than in 1950?

A. 5

B. 16

C. 21

D. 26

In the following passage, Daniel Munduruku describes learning the ancient myths of his people. Use the quotation and your knowledge of world cultures and geography to answer question 3.

PRIMARY SOURCE

When I was a five-year-old boy, my grandfather would sit me on his lap and. . . tell the stories that explained the origins of our people and the vision of the universe. . . . . Now . . . I realize that those ancient myths say what cannot be said. They are pure poetry, and through them I see how an identity can be created in the oral tradition.

DANIEL MUNDURUKU, *Tales of the Amazon, How the Munduruku Indians Live*

3. According to the passage, in what way is storytelling important to the Munduruku culture?

A. The stories preserve the beliefs and identity of the Munduruku.

B. Telling stories is a way for grandparents to be close to young children.

C. The stories are an example of the art of the Munduruku culture.

D. The stories are important to the Munduruku if they are written down.

TEST PRACTICE
CLASSZONE.COM

ALTERNATIVE ASSESSMENT

1. **WRITING ABOUT HISTORY**

If you were a passenger in an expedition flying over Peru, you would be able to see the long coastline, mountains, rain forests, and desert. Imagine that you are such traveler, and write a journal entry about what you see from your flight.

- Use the Internet or reference sources in the library to research the geography of Peru.
- In your journal entry, describe the varied landforms you see. Include descriptive details, as well as your personal impressions of the views.

2. COOPERATIVE LEARNING

With a group of classmates, decide on a problem that your country faces, such as overcrowding. Then, plan a new city to help solve the problem. Describe how the city would be organized, what services would be provided for the people, and where to locate homes, businesses, and parks. Create a map of your new city with illustrations of important buildings and a list of key services that the city provides.

INTEGRATED TECHNOLOGY

Doing Internet Research

Many useful products are harvested from the rain forest. Use the Internet to research one product, such as a medicinal plant, and find out how it is used in different parts of the world.

- Using the Internet or books and periodicals in the library, find out about your product.
- Focus your research on how the product is harvested, transported, and used worldwide.
- Create a presentation of your findings. Include visuals such as maps, charts, graphs, or illustrations to support your findings.

For Internet links to support this activity, go to

RESEARCH LINKS
CLASSZONE.COM

UNIT 4

Place Completed in A.D. 80, the Colosseum in Rome, Italy, held 50,000 spectators. There they watched battles between gladiators, among other contests. The Colosseum is the largest structure that survives from the Roman Empire.

EUROPE, RUSSIA, AND THE INDEPENDENT REPUBLICS

THE COLOSSEUM

PACIFIC OCEAN

PACIFIC OCEAN

ATLANTIC OCEAN

EUROPE, RUSSIA, AND THE INDEPENDENT REPUBLICS

INTEGRATED TECHNOLOGY

eEdition
- Interactive Maps
- Interactive Visuals

 VIDEO
France: Raphaël in Brittany

INTERNET RESOURCES

Go to **classzone.com** for:
- Research Links
- Internet Activities
- Data Updates
- Unit Quiz
- Maps
- Test Practice
- Current Events
- Web Research Guide

ARCTIC OCEAN

Franz Josef
Land

Svalbard

Novaya Zemlya

Kara Sea

Barents Sea

Norwegian Sea

Arctic Circle

ICELAND

SWEDEN

FINLAND

Dvina R.

West

Central
Siberian
Plateau

NORWAY

RUSSIA

Siberian

Jutland

ESTONIA

Volga R.

Kama R.

Plain

Yenisey R.

Angara R.

North
Sea

DENMARK

LATVIA

LITHUANIA

RUS.

Central
Russian
Upland

Ob R.

U
R
A
L

M
O
U
N
T
A
I
N
S

Ob R.

Irtysh R.

Sayan Mts.

IRELAND

UNITED
KINGDOM

NETH.

GERMANY

POLAND

BELARUS

UKRAINE

Don R.

BEL.

LUX.

Rhine R.

CZECH R.

SLOVAKIA

Dnieper R.

KAZAKHSTAN

ATLANTIC
OCEAN

FRANCE

SWITZ.

Mt. Blanc
15,771 ft.
(4,807 m)

ALPS

AUS.

SLO.

HUNGARY

CRO.

BOS. & H.

ROMANIA

Danube R.

MOLDOVA

Mt. Elbrus
18,510 ft.
(5,642 m)

Caucasus

Aral
Sea

UZBEKISTAN

KYRGYZSTAN

Pyrenees

Corsica

ITALY

YUGO.

MAC.

BULGARIA

Black Sea

GEORGIA

Caspian
Sea

TURKMENISTAN

TAJIKISTAN

Douro R.

Iberian
Peninsula

Sardinia

ALB.

Mt. Etna
10,902 ft.
(3,323 m)

GREECE

ARMENIA

AZERBAIJAN

PORTUGAL

SPAIN

Sicily

Crete

Mediterranean Sea

N

0   500   1,000 miles
0   500   1,000 kilometers

Climates of Europe, Russia, and the Independent Republics

ARCTIC OCEAN

ARCTIC OCEAN

Arctic Circle

ATLANTIC
OCEAN

PACIFIC
OCEAN

Black Sea

Mediterranean Sea

N

0   1,000   2,000 miles
0   1,000   2,000 kilometers

	Desert		Humid continental
	Semiarid		Subarctic
	Mediterranean		Tundra
	Marine west coast		Highland
	Humid subtropical		

Europe, Russia, and the Independent Republics: Physical

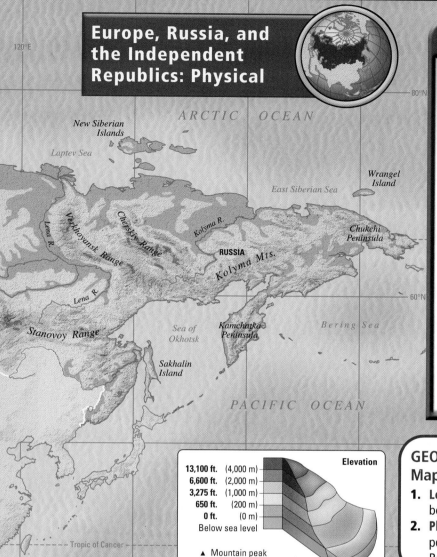

ARCTIC OCEAN

New Siberian Islands

Laptev Sea

Wrangel Island

East Siberian Sea

Verkhoyansk Range

Lena R.

Chersky Range

Kolyma R.

Chukchi Peninsula

RUSSIA

Kolyma Mts.

Lena R.

Stanovoy Range

Sea of Okhotsk

Kamchatka Peninsula

Bering Sea

Sakhalin Island

PACIFIC OCEAN

Tropic of Cancer

FAST FACTS

✓ **LONG COASTLINE:**
The coastline of Europe alone is 24,000 miles long. Earth measures 24,902 miles around at the Equator.

✓ **BELOW SEA LEVEL:**
Almost a third of the Netherlands and a large portion of the land by the Caspian Sea are below sea level.

✓ **HIGHEST MOUNTAIN:**
Mt. Elbrus in Russia, 18,510 ft.

✓ **DEEPEST LAKE:**
Lake Baikal, 5,714 ft. deep

✓ **LARGEST INLAND SEA:**
Caspian Sea, 149,200 sq. mi.

✓ **LONGEST RIVER:**
Volga River, 2,193 mi.

Elevation

13,100 ft.	(4,000 m)
6,600 ft.	(2,000 m)
3,275 ft.	(1,000 m)
650 ft.	(200 m)
0 ft.	(0 m)
Below sea level	

▲ Mountain peak

GEOGRAPHY SKILLBUILDER: Interpreting Maps and Visuals

1. **Location** • Which countries have mountains at their borders?
2. **Place** • About how many times larger is the population of Europe, Russia, and the Independent Republics than that of the United States?

Europe, Russia, and the Independent Republics– United States Landmass and Population

Europe, Russia, and the Independent Republics

United States

LANDMASS

Europe, Russia, and the Independent Republics

10,489,029 square miles

Continental United States

3,165,630 square miles

POPULATION

Europe, Russia, and the Independent Republics
654,628,000

United States
281,421,906

👤 = 50,000,000

ARCTIC OCEAN

Svalbard (Nor.)

Franz Josef Land

Severnaya Zemlya

Nowaja Zemlya

Kara Sea

Barents Sea

ICELAND
Reykjavik

Murmansk

Arkhangelsk

R U S S I A

Norilsk

Norwegian Sea

Arctic Circle

SWEDEN

FINLAND

Trondheim

Tampere

Dvina R.

Ob R.

Yenisey R.

NORWAY
Bergen
Oslo

Stockholm

Helsinki

St. Petersburg

ESTONIA

LATVIA

LITHUANIA

Perm

Yekaterinburg

Ob R.

Angara R.

Göteborg

North Sea

DENMARK
Copenhagen

Minsk

Moscow
Nizhniy
Novgorod

Kazan

Volga R.

Kama R.

Ufa

Chelyabinsk

Omsk

Novosibirsk

Krasnoyarsk

Glasgow Edinburgh
Belfast

BEL.

NETH.

BELARUS

Togliatti
Samara

Irkutsk

Dublin
IRELAND

UNITED
KINGDOM
London

Amsterdam
Berlin

Warsaw

Kiev

Kharkiv

Don R.

Volgograd

Astana

Semey

Brussels

GERMANY

POLAND

UKRAINE

MOLDOVA

Donetsk

ATLANTIC OCEAN

Paris
LUX.

CZECH R.

Bern

AUS.

SLOVAKIA

HUNGARY

ROMANIA

Odessa

Rostov

Krasnodar

Astrakhan

KAZAKHSTAN

Bishkek

Almaty

Nantes

SWITZ.

SLO.

CRO.

Belgrade

Bucharest

Aral Sea

Bordeaux
FRANCE

Milan

ITALY

BOS. & H.

Sarajevo

YUGO.

Sofia

BULGARIA

Black Sea

GEORGIA
Tbilisi

Baku

Caspian Sea

UZBEKISTAN

KYRGYZSTAN

Marseille
Corsica
Rome

MAC.

ARMENIA
Yerevan

Tashkent

TAJIKISTAN

PORTUGAL

Douro R.

Madrid

Barcelona

Naples

ALB.

GREECE

AZERBAIJAN

TURKMENISTAN
Ashgabat

Dushanbe

Lisbon

SPAIN
Seville

Sardinia

Tirane

Sicily

Athens

Crete

Mediterranean Sea

Population Density of Europe, Russia, and the Independent Republics

ARCTIC OCEAN

ARCTIC OCEAN

Arctic Circle

ATLANTIC OCEAN

PACIFIC OCEAN

Black Sea

Mediterranean Sea

ATLANTIC OCEAN

Equator

Persons per sq. mi.	Persons per sq. km
Over 520	Over 200
260–520	100–200
130–259	50–99
25–129	10–49
1–24	1–9
0	0

0   1,000   2,000 miles
0   1,000   2,000 kilometers

Europe, Russia, and the Independent Republics: Political

New Siberian Islands

Laptev Sea

Lena R.

Kolyma R.

RUSSIA

Yakutsk

Lena R.

East Siberian Sea

Wrangel Island

Sea of Okhotsk

Bering Sea

Sakhalin Island

Petropavlovsk-Kamchatskiy

Khabarovsk

Vladivostok

PACIFIC OCEAN

Tropic of Cancer

National boundary
National capital
Other city

0   500   1,000 miles
0   500 1,000 kilometers

FAST FACTS

SMALLEST COUNTRY IN THE WORLD: Vatican City, less than 0.2 sq. mi.

LARGEST COUNTRY IN THE WORLD: Russia, 6,592,800 sq. mi.

LONGEST ROAD TUNNEL: Oslo, Norway, 15.3 mi. long

OLDEST PAINTINGS: Cave paintings near Verona, Italy, at 32,000 to 37,000 years of age

GEOGRAPHY SKILLBUILDER: Interpreting Maps and Visuals

1. **Location** • Name two countries that do not have seaports.
2. **Movement** • What route would you take to drive from Paris to Bern?

Road Map of Selected European Countries

Paris — A4 — A4 — N104
A11 A10 A5 Troyes A31 A35 GERMANY A5
Orléans A6 A31
A10 FRANCE A38 Dijon A36 A3
A71 A39 A5 A1 A2
A5 Bern SWITZERLAND
A6 A1 Lausanne
A40 Geneva A12
A72 Lyon Chambéry ITALY

0   25   50 miles
0   25   50 kilometers

National capital
Other city
Major road

For updates on these statistics, go to

DATA UPDATE
CLASSZONE.COM

Country Flag	Country/Capital	Currency	Population (2001 estimate)	Life Expectancy (years)	Birthrate (per 1,000 pop.) (2000)
	Albania Tiranë	Lek	3,510,000	71	19
	Andorra Andorra la Vella	French Franc	68,000	83	11
	Armenia Yerevan	Dram	3,336,000	75	10
	Austria Vienna	Euro*	8,151,000	78	10
	Azerbaijan Baku	Manat	7,771,000	70	15
	Belarus Minsk	Ruble	10,350,000	68	9
	Belgium Brussels	Euro*	10,259,000	78	11
	Bosnia-Herzegovina Sarajevo	Conv. Mark	3,922,000	73	13
	Bulgaria Sofia	Lev	7,707,000	71	8
	Croatia Zagreb	Kuna	4,334,000	73	11
	Czech Republic Prague	Koruna	10,264,000	75	9
	Denmark Copenhagen	Danish Krone	5,353,000	77	12
	Estonia Tallinn	Kroon	1,423,000	70	8
	Finland Helsinki	Euro*	5,176,000	78	11
	France Paris	Euro*	59,551,000	79	13
	Georgia Tbilisi	Lavi	4,989,000	73	9
	Germany Berlin	Euro*	83,029,000	77	9

*On January 1, 2002, the euro became the common currency for 12 of the member nations of the European Union.

DATA FILE

Infant Mortality (per 1,000 live births) (2000)	Doctors (per 100,000 pop.) (1990–1998)	Literacy Rate (percentage) (1991–1998)	Passenger Cars (per 1,000 pop.) (1996–1997)	Total Area (square miles)	Map (not to scale)
41.3	129	83	10 (1990)	11,100	
6.4	253	100	552	174	
41.0	316	98	2	11,506	
4.9	302	100	468	32,378	
83.0	360	99	36	33,436	
15.0	443	100	111	80,154	
5.6	395	99	434	11,787	
25.2	143	86	23	19,741	
14.9	345	98	202	42,822	
8.2	229	98	160	21,830	
4.6	303	99	428	30,448	
4.7	290	100	339	16,637	
13.0	297	99	294	17,413	
4.2	299	100	378	130,560	
4.8	303	99	437	212,934	
53.0	436	99	80	26,911	
4.7	350	100	504	137,830	

Country Flag	Country/Capital	Currency	Population (2001 estimate)	Life Expectancy (years)	Birthrate (per 1,000 pop.) (2000)	
	Greece Athens	Euro*	10,624,000	78	10	
	Hungary Budapest	Forint	10,106,000	71	9	
	Iceland Reykjavik	Krona	278,000	80	15	
	Ireland Dublin	Euro*	3,841,000	76	15	
	Italy Rome	Euro*	57,680,000	78	9	
	Kazakhstan Astana	Tenge	16,731,000	65	14	
	Kyrgyzstan Bishkek	Som	4,753,000	67	22	
	Latvia Riga	Lat	2,385,000	70	8	
	Liechtenstein Vaduz	Swiss Franc	33,000	73	14	
	Lithuania Vilnius	Litas	3,611,000	72	10	
	Luxembourg Luxembourg	Euro*	443,000	77	13	
	Macedonia Skopje	Denar	2,046,000	73	15	
	Malta Valletta	Lira	395,000	77	12	
	Moldova Chisinau	Leu	4,432,000	67	11	
	Monaco Monaco	French Franc	32,000	79	20	
	Netherlands Amsterdam	Euro*	15,981,000	78	13	
	Norway Oslo	Krone	4,503,000	79	13	
	Poland Warsaw	Zloty	38,634,000	74	10	

*On January 1, 2002, the euro became the common currency for 12 of the member nations of the European Union.

DATA FILE

Infant Mortality (per 1,000 live births) (2000)	Doctors (per 100,000 pop.) (1990–1998)	Literacy Rate (percentage) (1991–1998)	Passenger Cars (per 1,000 pop.) (1996–1997)	Total Area (square miles)	Map (not to scale)
6.7	392	97	223	50,950	
8.9	357	99	222	35,919	
4.0	326	100	489	39,768	
6.2	219	100	292	27,135	
5.5	554	98	540	116,320	
59.0	353	99	61	1,048,300	
77.0	301	97	32	76,641	
16.0	282	100	174	24,595	
5.1	100	100	592 (1993)	62	
15.0	395	100	242	25,174	
5.0	272	100	515	999	
16.3	204	89	132	9,927	
5.3	261	91	321	124	
43.0	400 (1995)	99	46	13,012	
5.9	664	100	548	0.6	
5.0	251	100	372	16,033	
4.0	413	100	399	125,050	
8.9	236	99	195	124,807	

Country Flag	Country/Capital	Currency	Population (2001 estimate)	Life Expectancy (years)	Birthrate (per 1,000 pop.) (2000)
	Portugal Lisbon	Euro*	10,066,000	76	11
	Romania Bucharest	Leu	22,364,000	70	11
	Russia Moscow	Ruble	145,470,000	67	8
	San Marino San Marino	Italian Lira	27,000	80	11
	Slovakia Bratislava	Koruna	5,415,000	73	11
	Slovenia Ljubljana	Tolar	1,930,000	75	9
	Spain Madrid	Euro*	40,038,000	78	9
	Sweden Stockholm	Krona	8,875,000	80	10
	Switzerland Bern	Franc	7,283,000	80	11
	Tajikistan Dushanbe	Ruble	6,579,000	68	21
	Turkmenistan Ashgabat	Manat	4,603,000	66	21
	Ukraine Kiev	Hryvnya	48,760,000	68	8
	United Kingdom London	Pound	59,648,000	77	12
	Uzbekistan Tashkent	Som	25,155,000	69	23
	Vatican City Vatican City	Vatican Lira/Italian Lira	870 (2000)	N/A	N/A
	Yugoslavia Belgrade	New Dinar	10,677,000	73	11
	United States Washington, D.C.	Dollar	281,422,000	77	15

*On January 1, 2002, the euro became the common currency for 12 of the member nations of the European Union.

DATA FILE

Infant Mortality (per 1,000 live births) (2000)	Doctors (per 100,000 pop.) (1990–1998)	Literacy Rate (percentage) (1991–1998)	Passenger Cars (per 1,000 pop.) (1996–1997)	Total Area (square miles)	Map (not to scale)
6.0	312	91	295	35,514	
20.5	184	98	106	92,042	
20.0	421	100	120	6,592,812	
8.8	252	99	955	23	
8.8	353	100	185	18,923	
5.2	228	99	343	7,819	
5.7	424	97	384	195,363	
3.5	311	100	417	173,730	
4.8	323	100	460	15,942	
117.0	201	99	31	55,251	
73.0	300 (1997)	98	N/A	188,455	
22.0	299	100	97	233,089	
5.7	164	100	434	94,548	
72.0	309	88	37	173,591	
N/A	N/A	100	N/A	0.17	
10.4	203	98	173	39,448	
7.0	251	97	489	3,787,319	

GEOGRAPHY SKILLBUILDER: Interpreting a Chart
1. Place • Which country in the region has the highest life expectancy?
2. Place • How many fewer cars per thousand people does Greece have than Germany?

CHAPTER 10

Western Europe: Its Land and Early History

EUROPE

ATLANTIC

PACIFIC OCEAN

PACIFIC

OCEAN

INDIAN OCEAN

OCEAN

(Region) Many European cities show their history in their architecture. In Segovia, Spain, an ancient Roman aqueduct lies below the walls of a castle built in the Middle Ages.

How does the Gulf Stream affect the climate of Europe?

Region • The Gulf Stream is a strong ocean current that flows from the Gulf of Mexico across the Atlantic Ocean to Europe. It carries warm water and warm, moist air, which contribute to Europe's mild climate. The Gulf Stream warms the water of some Northern European ports, allowing them to remain open in the winter when they might otherwise be frozen. Palm trees even grow in Scotland, which is as far north as southern Alaska!

What do you think?

◆ In what other ways, such as tourism, might Europe benefit from the Gulf Stream?

◆ How might a region's mild climate help its economy?

BEFORE YOU READ

▶▶ *What Do You Know?*

Before you read the chapter, think about what you already know about Europe. What are some of its geographical features? What do you know about its early history? Have you ever read myths from ancient Greece or ancient Rome? Have you ever heard of Julius Caesar or Hercules? What do you know about knights and castles from the Middle Ages?

▶▶ *What Do You Want to Know?*

Decide what you want to know about these early periods of European history. Record your questions in your notebook before you read this chapter.

Region • Ancient Greece made important contributions in literature, philosophy, and architecture. ▼

READ AND TAKE NOTES

Reading Strategy: Categorizing One way to make sense of what you read is to categorize, or sort, information. Making a chart to categorize the information in this chapter will help you to understand the contributions made by early European cultures.

- Copy the chart below into your notebook.
- As you read, look for information relating to the categories of social structure, architecture, religion, and arts and sciences.
- Write your notes under the appropriate headings.

Region • The Middle Ages saw the rise of the Catholic Church and the growth of a middle class. ▲

Region • Ancient Rome made its mark in government, law, and engineering. ▲

Time Period	Social Structure	Architecture	Religion	Arts and Sciences
Ancient Greece				
Ancient Rome				
Middle Ages				

A Land of Varied Riches

TERMS & NAMES
Mediterranean Sea
peninsula
fjord
Ural Mountains
plain

MAIN IDEA

Europe is a continent with varied geographic features, abundant natural resources, and a climate that can support agriculture.

WHY IT MATTERS NOW

The development of Europe's diverse cultures has been shaped by the continent's diverse geography.

DATELINE

EXTRA

LONDON, ENGLAND, MAY 6, 1994

Rough waters have always made the English Channel, which separates England and France, difficult to cross. Now, however, you can travel under the water! Today, a tunnel nicknamed "the Chunnel" opens, allowing high-speed trains to travel between London and Paris in about three hours. The Chunnel—short for Channel Tunnel—was carved through chalky earth under the sea floor and took seven years to build. It is the largest European construction project of the 20th century.

Movement • Eurostar trains make the 31-mile trip under the English Channel in only 20 minutes. ▲

England
Chunnel
English Channel
France

ation • The Channel nel connects England France. ▲

The Geography of Europe

Today, cars, airplanes, and trains are common forms of high-speed transportation across Europe. Before the 19th century, however, the fastest form of transportation was to travel by water—on top of it, rather than under it.

TAKING NOTES
Use your chart to take notes about Western Europe.

Time Period	Social Structure	Architecture
Ancient Greece		
Ancient Rome		

Waterways Look at the map of Europe on page 277. Water surrounds the continent to the north, south, and west. The southern coast of Europe borders the warm waters of the **Mediterranean Sea.** Europe also has many rivers. The highly traveled Rhine and Danube rivers are two of the most important. The Volga, which flows nearly 2,200 miles through western Russia, is the continent's longest. For hundreds of years, these and other waterways have been home to boats and barges carrying people and goods inland across great distances.

Landforms Several large **peninsulas,** or bodies of land surrounded by water on three sides, form the European continent. In Northern Europe, the Scandinavian Peninsula is home to Norway and Sweden. Along the jagged shoreline of this peninsula are beautiful fjords (fyawrdz). A **fjord** is a long, narrow, deep inlet of the sea located between steep cliffs. In Western Europe, the Iberian Peninsula includes Portugal and Spain. The Iberian Peninsula is separated from the rest of the continent by a mountain range called the Pyrenees (PEER·uh·NEEZ). The entire continent of Europe, itself surrounded by water on three sides, is a giant peninsula.

Reading
Social Studies

A. Clarifying Why were waterways important for the movement of people and goods?

BACKGROUND

Europe can be divided into four areas: Western Europe, Northern Europe, Eastern Europe, and Russia and its neighboring countries.

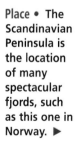

Place • The Scandinavian Peninsula is the location of many spectacular fjords, such as this one in Norway. ▶

Place • The Alps remain snowcapped year-round. ▶

Reading
Social Studies

B. Clarifying
What natural landform separates Europe from Asia?

Mountain ranges, including the towering Alps, also stretch across much of the continent. Along Europe's eastern border, the **Ural Mountains** (YUR·uhl) divide the continent from Asia. The many mountain ranges of Europe separated groups of people from one another as they settled the land thousands of years ago. This is one of the reasons why different cultures developed across the continent.

The Great European Plain Not all of Europe is mountainous. A vast region called the Great European Plain stretches from the coast of France to the Ural Mountains. A **plain** is a large, flat area of land, usually without many trees. The Great European Plain is the location of some of the world's richest farmland. Ancient trading centers attracted many people to this area, which today includes some of the largest cities in Europe—Paris, Berlin, Warsaw, and Moscow.

Climate

Vocabulary

Gulf Stream:
a warm ocean current that flows northeast from the Gulf of Mexico through the Atlantic Ocean.

Although the Gulf Stream brings warm air and water to Europe, the winters are still severe in the mountains and in the far north. In some of these areas, cold winds blow southward from the Arctic Circle and make the average temperature fall below 0°F in January. The Alps and the Pyrenees, however, protect the European countries along the Mediterranean Sea from these chilling winds. In these warmer parts of southern Europe, the average temperature in January stays above 50°F.

The summers in the south are usually hot and dry, with an average July temperature around 80°F. This makes the Mediterranean coast a popular vacation spot. Elsewhere in Europe, in all but the coldest areas of the mountains and the far north, the average July temperature ranges from 50°F to 70°F.

Natural Resources

Europe has a large variety of natural resources, including minerals. The rich coal deposits of Germany's Ruhr (rur) Valley region have helped to make that area one of the world's major industrial centers. Russia and Ukraine have large deposits of iron ore, which is used to make iron for automobiles and countless other products.

Region • Western Europe benefits from a varied landscape rich in natural resources. ▼

Land Use in Europe Today

INTER**ACTIVE**

Legend:
- Forest
- Orchards and vineyards
- Dairy land and fodder crops
- Rye and potatoes
- Wheat
- Upland grazing
- Unused land
- Urban and industrial

ATLANTIC OCEAN

North Sea

Baltic Sea

Bay of Biscay

Adriatic Sea

Mediterranean Sea

Black Sea

Arctic Circle

GEOGRAPHY SKILLBUILDER: Interpreting a Map

1. **Place** • What are the three most common uses of land in Europe?
2. **Location** • Where is the majority of unused land?

Vocabulary

precipitation: moisture, including rain, snow, and hail, that falls to the ground

Europe also has rich soil and plentiful rainfall. The average precipitation for the Great European Plain, for example, is between 20 and 40 inches per year. The map above shows the agricultural uses of the land, highlighting the major crops. Notice that few parts of the continent are too cold or too hot and dry to support some form of agriculture. These characteristics have made Europe a world leader in crop production.

SECTION 1 ASSESSMENT

Terms & Names

1. **Explain the significance of:**
   (a) Mediterranean Sea (b) peninsula (c) fjord
   (d) Ural Mountains (e) plain

Using Graphics

2. Use a spider map like this one to list the different geographic features of Europe, and give a few specific examples of each.

Peninsula

Main Ideas

3. (a) How does the Gulf Stream affect the climate of Europe?
   (b) What separates Europe from Asia?
   (c) How do waterways, such as rivers and seas, strengthen trade in Europe?

Critical Thinking

4. **Recognizing Effects**

   How did Europe's many mountain ranges affect its development?

   Think About
   - climate
   - trade and travel
   - the separation of groups of people

ACTIVITY -OPTION-

Reread the information about the Chunnel. Write a **short story** in which you imagine what it might have been like to work on the Chunnel's construction.

Ancient Greece

TERMS & NAMES
city-state
polis
Aegean Sea
oligarchy
Athens
philosopher
Aristotle
Alexander the Great

MAIN IDEA

The ancient Greeks developed a complex society, with remarkable achievements in the arts, sciences, and government.

WHY IT MATTERS NOW

The achievements of the ancient Greeks continue to influence culture, science, and politics in the world today.

DATELINE

ATHENS, GREECE, FEBRUARY 2, 1997— Five years after construction workers began building the new Athens subway, artifacts from ancient Greek civilization are still being discovered. When completed, the new subway will reduce traffic and air pollution in the capital. Historians and archaeologists, however, have been the first to benefit from this massive public works project.

Workers have discovered statues, coins, jewelry, and gravesites from ancient Greece. Recently, workers digging the foundation for a downtown Athens station found an ancient dog collar decorated with gemstones. Local officials have promised to create permanent displays of some artifacts in stations throughout the new subway system.

Place • Building the subway in Athens led to spectacular discoveries of ancient artifacts. ▲

The Land and Early History of Greece

The Greek Peninsula is mountainous, which made travel by land difficult for early settlers. Most of the rocky land also contains poor soil and few large trees, but settlers were able to cultivate the soil to grow olives and grapes. The greatest natural resource of the peninsula is the water that surrounds it. The ancient Greeks depended on these seas for fishing and trade, and they became excellent sailors.

TAKING NOTES

Use your chart to take notes about Western Europe.

Time Period	Social Structure	Archi-tecture
Ancient Greece		
Ancient Rome		

The Formation of City-States As the ancient Greek population grew, people created city-states. A **city-state** included a central city, called a **polis,** and surrounding villages. Each ancient Greek city-state had its own laws and form of government. The city-states were united by a common language, shared religious beliefs, and a similar way of life.

The Growth of Colonies By the mid-eighth century B.C., the Greeks were leaving the peninsula in search of better land and greater opportunities for trade. During the next 200 years, they built dozens of communities on the islands and coastline of the **Aegean Sea** (ih·JEE·uhn). Some Greeks settled as far away as modern-day Spain and North Africa.

Once established, these distant Greek communities traded with each other and with those communities on the Greek Peninsula. This made a great variety of goods available to the ancient Greeks, including wheat for bread, timber for building boats, and iron ore for making strong tools and weapons.

Connections to Language

Metropolis When ancient Greeks moved away from a large polis to a distant community, they referred to their former city-state as their metropolis. In Greek, this means "mother-city." Today, we use the word *metropolis* to mean any large urban area, such as Los Angeles, London, Tokyo, or Athens (*shown below*).

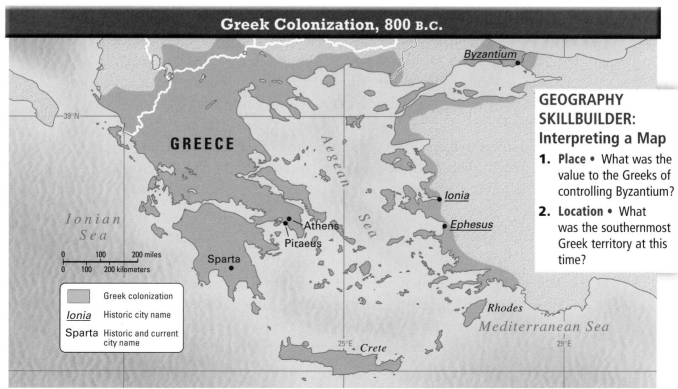

Greek Colonization, 800 B.C.

GREECE

Ionian Sea

Aegean Sea

Byzantium

Ionia

Ephesus

Athens
Piraeus

Sparta

Rhodes

Mediterranean Sea

Crete

0 100 200 miles
0 100 200 kilometers

Greek colonization
Ionia Historic city name
Sparta Historic and current city name

GEOGRAPHY SKILLBUILDER: Interpreting a Map

1. **Place** • What was the value to the Greeks of controlling Byzantium?

2. **Location** • What was the southernmost Greek territory at this time?

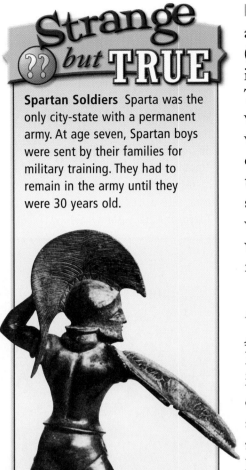
Individual Forms of Government Some ancient Greek city-states were oligarchies (AHL·ih·GAHR·kees). An **oligarchy** is a system in which a few powerful, wealthy individuals rule. The word *oligarchy* comes from an ancient Greek word meaning "rule by the few." Other city-states were ruled by a tyrant, a single person who took control of the government against the wishes of the community. Still other ancient Greek city-states developed an early form of democracy. The word *democracy* comes from an ancient Greek word meaning "rule by the people." In a democracy, citizens take part in the government.

Athens and Sparta

Athens, centrally located on the Greek Peninsula, was one of the largest and most important ancient Greek city-states. By the end of the sixth century B.C., Athens had developed a democratic form of government. Athenian citizens took part in political debates and voted on laws, but not everyone who lived in Athens enjoyed these rights. Participation in government was limited to free, adult males whose fathers had been citizens of Athens. Women, slaves, and foreign residents could not take part in government.

Athens's chief rival among the other Greek city-states was Sparta. Located in the southernmost part of the Greek Peninsula, Sparta was an oligarchy. It was ruled by two kings, who were supported by other officials. Sparta, like Athens, had a powerful army. Each city-state's army helped protect it from slave rebellions, guard against attack by rival city-states, and defend it from possible foreign invaders.

Learning and the Arts

In 480 B.C., the Persians, who controlled a large empire to the east, tried to conquer the Greek Peninsula. Several Greek city-states, including Athens and Sparta, joined forces to defeat the Persians. In the years following this victory, the ancient Greeks made remarkable achievements in literature, learning, and architecture.

Reading
Social Studies

A. Comparing Compare the three forms of government most common in ancient Greek city-states.

BACKGROUND

After the defeat of Persia, Athens became the most powerful Greek city-state. The most important Athenian leader of the time was Pericles (PEHR·ih·KLEEZ), who lived from c. 495 to 429 B.C.

Literature To honor their gods and goddesses, the ancient Greeks created myths and wrote poems and plays. Some of the greatest Greek plays were written during the fifth century B.C. During that time, the playwrights Aeschylus (EHS·kuh·luhs), Sophocles (SAHF·uh·KLEEZ), and Euripides (yu·RIHP·ih·DEEZ) wrote tragedies, which are serious plays that end unhappily. Many of these stories have been the basis for modern films and operas.

In addition to using the gods as characters, ancient Greek playwrights sometimes poked fun at important citizens, including generals and politicians. Aristophanes (ar·ih·STAHF·uh·NEEZ) was a popular writer of comedies of this type.

Philosophy Ancient Greece was the birthplace of some of the finest thinkers of the ancient world. Socrates (SAHK·ruh·TEEZ) was an important philosopher of the fifth century B.C. A **philosopher** studies and thinks about why the world is the way it is. Socrates studied and taught about friendship, knowledge, and justice. Another great philosopher, Plato (PLAY·toh), was a student of Socrates who studied and taught about human behavior, government, mathematics, and astronomy.

The ancient Greek philosopher Heraclitus (HEHR·uh·KLY·tuhs) wrote the following lines.

A VOICE FROM ANCIENT GREECE

One cannot step twice into the same river, for the water into which you first stepped has flowed on.

Heraclitus

Many people continue to study and write about the same philosophical questions that these, and other, ancient Greek philosophers explored.

The WORLD'S HERITAGE

Ancient Greek Architecture
Ancient Greek builders created some of the world's most impressive works of architecture. They built several beautiful temples atop the Acropolis (uh·KRAHP·uh·lihs) in Athens, shown at right. The most famous of the temples is the Parthenon (PAHR·thuh·nahn).

In the United States and elsewhere, government buildings, such as courthouses and post offices, have been built similar in style to the Parthenon. This use of ancient architecture echoes the democratic ideals of ancient Greece.

Region • In this mosaic Alexander the Great is shown riding into battle on his beloved horse, Bucephalus (byoo•SEHF•ah•luhs). ▲

Biography

Aristotle At the age of 17, Aristotle (384–322 B.C.) began studying philosophy with Plato. After Plato died, Aristotle received his most important assignment—to teach Alexander, the teenage son of King Philip II of Macedonia.

After teaching Alexander, Aristotle returned to Athens. There he taught and wrote about poetry, government, and astronomy. He started a famous school called the Lyceum (ly•SEE•uhm). Aristotle also collected and studied plants and animals. The work of this brilliant philosopher continues to greatly influence scientists and philosophers today.

The Spread of Greek Culture The city-states of ancient Greece were constantly at war with one another. By the fourth century B.C., this fighting had weakened their ability to defend themselves against foreign invaders. In 338 B.C., King Philip II of Macedonia conquered the land. After Philip died, his son, Alexander—who had been taught by **Aristotle**—took control.

Alexander the Great was an excellent military leader, and his armies conquered vast new territories. As Alexander's empire expanded, Greek culture, language, and ideas were spread throughout the Mediterranean region and as far east as modern-day India. Upon Alexander's death, however, his leading generals fought for control of his territory and divided it among themselves. This marked the end of one of the great empires of the ancient world.

SECTION 2 ASSESSMENT

Terms & Names

1. Explain the significance of:
   (a) city-state (b) polis (c) Aegean Sea (d) oligarchy
   (e) Athens (f) philosopher (g) Aristotle (h) Alexander the Great

Using Graphics

2. Use a chart like this one to list and describe the ancient Greek achievements in government, literature, and architecture.

Government	Literature	Architecture

Main Ideas

3. (a) Why were the surrounding areas of water an important natural resource of the Greek Peninsula?

   (b) Which people were allowed to participate in the government of ancient Athens?

   (c) How did Alexander the Great help to spread Greek culture?

Critical Thinking

4. **Summarizing**

   Why was the fifth century B.C. a remarkable time in ancient Greek history?

   Think About
   • warfare
   • leaders
   • literature and philosophy

ACTIVITY
-OPTION-
Reread the information about the individual forms of government common in ancient Greece. Present an **oral report** to the class that compares and contrasts two of the forms.

Making a Generalization

▶▶ Defining the Skill

To make generalizations means to make broad judgments based on information. When you make generalizations, you should gather information from several sources.

▶▶ Applying the Skill

The following three passages contain different information on the government of ancient Athens. Use the strategies listed below to make a generalization about Athenian government based on the passages.

How to Make a Generalization

Strategy ❶ Look for all the information that the sources have in common. These three sources all explain about Athenian government.

Strategy ❷ Form a generalization that describes ancient Athenian government in a way that all three sources would support. State your generalization in a sentence.

Make a Chart

Using a chart can help you make generalizations. The chart below shows how the information you just read can be used to generalize about the government of ancient Athens.

❶ Athenian citizens took part in political debates and voted on laws, but not everyone who lived in Athens enjoyed these rights. Participation in government was limited to free, adult males whose fathers had been citizens in Athens.

—*World Cultures and Geography*

In return for playing their parts as soldiers or sailors, ❶ ordinary Athenians insisted on controlling the government.

—*Encyclopaedia Britannica*

Unlike representative democracies or republics, in which one man is elected to speak for many, Athens was a true ❶ democracy: every citizen spoke for himself.

—*Classical Greece*

▶▶ Practicing the Skill

Turn to Chapter 10, Section 2, "Ancient Greece." Read the sections on literature and philosophy. Also read about ancient Greek writings in an encyclopedia, a library book, or on the Internet. Then make a chart like the one above to form a generalization about the importance of knowledge and learning to the ancient Greeks.

Ancient Rome

TERMS & NAMES
republic
Senate
patrician
plebeian
Julius Caesar
empire
Augustus
Constantine

MAIN IDEA

The ancient Romans made important contributions to government, law, and engineering.

WHY IT MATTERS NOW

The cultural achievements of the Romans continue to influence the art, architecture, and literature of today.

DATELINE

EXTRA

ROME, 295 B.C.

Yet another Roman road was completed today! Rome is famous for its vast network of roadways. Repairing old roads and adding new ones keeps Roman engineers busy. Construction is time-consuming because the lengthy roads, which are paved with large stones, must be carefully planned. However, the benefits are worth the effort.

The roads connect the great city to distant lands under Roman rule. These roadways also enable the army to move quickly. These days, it seems that almost all roads lead to Rome. In fact, when this massive undertaking is finished, Roman roads will stretch for tens of thousands of miles across the land.

Location • All roads lead to Rome—including the Via Appia (VEE•uh APP•ee•uh) shown here. ▲

The Beginnings of Ancient Rome

Ancient Rome began as a group of villages located along the banks of the Tiber River in what is now Italy. There, early settlers herded sheep and grew wheat, olives, and grapes. Around 750 B.C., these villages united to form the city of Rome.

TAKING NOTES

Use your chart to take notes about Western Europe.

Time Period	Social Structure	Architecture
Ancient Greece		
Ancient Rome		

The Formation of the Roman Republic For more than 200 years, kings ruled Rome. Then, in 509 B.C., Rome became a republic. A **republic** is a nation in which power belongs to the citizens, who govern themselves through elected representatives.

The Senate The Roman **Senate** was an assembly of elected representatives. It was the single most powerful ruling body of the Roman Republic. Each year, the Senate selected two leaders, called consuls, to head the government and the military.

BACKGROUND

In ancient Rome, a senator held his position for life.

Patricians At first, most of the people elected to the Senate were patricians (puh·TRIHSH·uhns). In ancient Rome, a **patrician** was a member of a wealthy, landowning family who claimed to be able to trace its roots back to the founding of Rome. The patricians also controlled the law, since they were the only citizens who were allowed to be judges.

Plebeians An ordinary, working male citizen of ancient Rome—such as a farmer or craftsperson—was called a **plebeian** (plih·BEE·uhn). Plebeians had the right to vote, but they could not hold public office until 287 B.C., when they gained equality with patricians.

The Expansion of the Roman World

Over hundreds of years, Rome grew into a mighty city. By the third century B.C., Rome ruled most of the Italian Peninsula. This gave Rome control of the central Mediterranean.

The city-state of Carthage, which ruled North Africa and southern Spain, controlled the western Mediterranean. To take control over this area as well, Rome fought Carthage and eventually won.

As Rome's population grew, its army also expanded in size and strength. Under the leadership of ambitious generals, Rome's highly trained soldiers set out to conquer new territories one by one.

Strange but TRUE

Roman Law It may be hard to believe, but in the early Roman Republic, laws were not written down. Only the patrician judges knew what the laws were. This meant that judges usually ruled in favor of fellow patricians and against plebeians.

The plebeians grew tired of unfair treatment and demanded that the judges create a written code of laws that applied to all Roman citizens. This code, called the Law of the Twelve Tables, was written around 450 B.C. It formed the foundation of Roman law.

ATLANTIC
OCEAN

GAUL

SPAIN

AFRICA

Rome
ITALY

Adriatic Sea

Carthage

SICILY

GREECE

Black Sea

Mediterranean Sea

EGYPT

509 B.C.
241 B.C.
146 B.C.
• Major city

N

0   250   500 miles
0   250   500 kilometers

GEOGRAPHY SKILLBUILDER: Interpreting a Map

1. **Location** • Around which body of water was Roman control located in 146 B.C.?
2. **Region** • When was Roman control at its greatest?

As Rome's control over its neighbors expanded, its culture and language continued to spread into Spain and Greece. By the end of the second century B.C., the Romans ruled most of the land surrounding the Mediterranean Sea. The ancient Romans even called the Mediterranean *mare nostrum* (MAH•ray NOH•struhm), which means "our sea."

Region • Once in power, Julius Caesar had his likeness stamped on coins such as this one. ▼

From Republic to Empire

As the Roman Republic grew, its citizens became a more and more diverse group of people. Many Romans practiced different religions and followed different customs, but they were united by a common system of government and law. In the middle of the first century B.C., however, Rome's form of government changed.

The End of the Roman Republic Julius Caesar, a successful Roman general and famous speaker, was the governor of the territory called Gaul. By conquering nearby territories to expand the land under his control, he increased both his power and his reputation. The Roman Senate feared that Caesar might become too powerful, and they ordered him to resign. Caesar, however, had other ideas.

BACKGROUND

Ancient Gaul included the lands that are modern-day France, Belgium, and parts of northern Italy.

Rather than resign, Caesar fought a long, fierce battle for control of the Roman Republic. In 45 B.C., he finally triumphed and returned to Rome. Caesar eventually became dictator of the Roman world. A dictator is a person who holds total control over a government. Caesar's rule marked the end of the Roman Republic.

The Beginning of the Roman Empire Julius Caesar had great plans to reorganize the way ancient Rome was governed, but his rule was cut short. On March 15, 44 B.C., a group of senators, angered by Caesar's plans and power, stabbed him to death on the floor of the Roman Senate. A civil war then erupted that lasted for several years.

Reading
Social Studies

A. Recognizing Important Details How many years separated the rules of Julius Caesar and Augustus?

In 27 B.C., Caesar's adopted son, Octavian, was named the first emperor of Rome. This marks the official beginning of the Roman Empire. An **empire** is a nation or group of territories ruled by a single, powerful leader, or emperor. As emperor, Octavian took the name **Augustus.**

The Augustan Age Augustus ruled the Roman Empire for more than 40 years. During this time, called the Augustan Age, the empire continued to expand. To help protect the enormous amount of land under his control, Augustus sent military forces along its borders, which now extended northward to the Rhine and Danube rivers.

Region • Sculptures of Augustus were sent all over the Roman Empire to let people know what their leader looked like. ▲

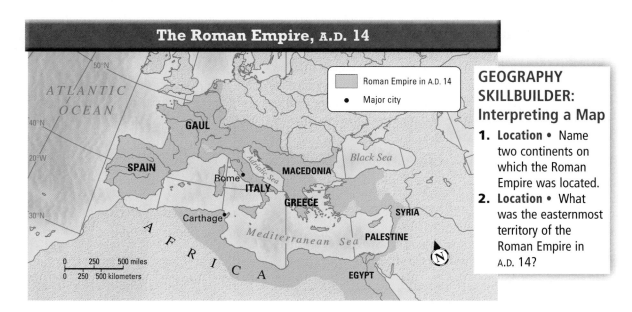

The Roman Empire, A.D. 14

Roman Empire in A.D. 14
• Major city

ATLANTIC OCEAN

GAUL

SPAIN

Rome
ITALY

Carthage

Adriatic Sea

MACEDONIA

GREECE

Black Sea

SYRIA

PALESTINE

Mediterranean Sea

A F R I C A

EGYPT

50°N
40°N
20°W
30°N

0   250   500 miles
0   250   500 kilometers

N

GEOGRAPHY SKILLBUILDER: Interpreting a Map

1. **Location** • Name two continents on which the Roman Empire was located.
2. **Location** • What was the easternmost territory of the Roman Empire in A.D. 14?

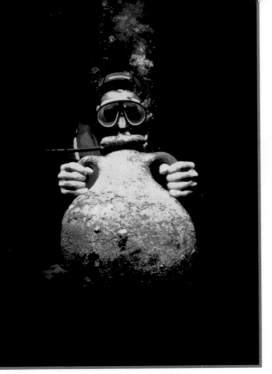

While the Roman army kept peace, architects and engineers built many new public buildings. Trade increased, with olive oil, wine, pottery, marble, and grain being shipped all across the Mediterranean. Lighthouses were constructed, too, to help ships find their way into port.

Vocabulary

marble:
a hard, smooth stone, often white in color

The Augustan Age was also a time of great Roman literature. One of the most famous works of the age is the *Aeneid* (ih·NEE·ud). This long poem tells the story of Rome's founding. Augustus himself asked the famous poet Virgil to write it. This period of peace and cultural growth that Augustus created in the Roman Empire was called the "Pax Romana" (pahks roh·MAH·nah). The Pax Romana, or Roman Peace, lasted for 200 years.

Region • A diver holds an artifact from an ancient Roman shipwreck in the Mediterranean Sea. ▲

Spotlight on CULTURE

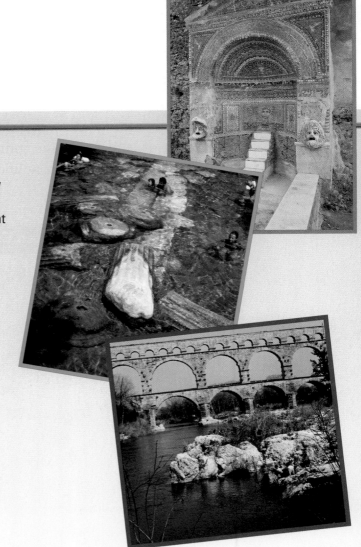

Architecture Various inventions helped the Roman Empire grow and prosper. In addition to buildings and roads, Roman architects and engineers constructed water systems called aqueducts. Ancient aqueducts were raised tunnels that carried fresh water over long distances.

Built throughout the empire, aqueducts poured millions of gallons of water into Rome and other cities every day. They supplied clean water to private homes, fountains, and public baths. Today, some ancient Roman aqueducts still stand in France, Spain, and even on the outskirts of Rome itself.

THINKING CRITICALLY
1. Analyzing Motives
   Why did Romans want a way to transport water?

2. Hypothesizing
   Do you think the Roman Empire would have grown so large and prosperous without the aqueducts?

For more on Roman architecture, go to

RESEARCH LINKS
CLASSZONE.COM

The Rise of Christianity

Reading Social Studies

B. Making Inferences How do you think the Roman Empire indirectly helped the spread of Christianity?

In the years following the death of Augustus in A.D. 14, a new religion from the Middle East began to take hold in the rest of the Mediterranean world: Christianity. At first, this religion became popular mainly in the eastern half of the Roman Empire. Many followers there preached about its teachings. Christianity spread along the transportation network constructed by the Romans. By the third century A.D., this religion had spread throughout the empire.

Most earlier Roman leaders had tolerated the different religions practiced throughout the empire. Christians, however, were viewed with suspicion and suffered persecution as early as A.D. 64. Roman leaders and people of other religions even blamed the Christians for natural disasters. Many Christians during this time were punished or killed for their beliefs.

Region • Constantine (died A.D. 337) was the first Christian emperor of Rome. ▼

The First Christian Emperor

Things changed when **Constantine** became emperor of Rome in A.D. 306. In A.D. 312, before a battle, Constantine claimed to have had a vision of a cross in the sky. The emperor promised that if he won the battle, he would become a Christian. Constantine was victorious, and the next year he fulfilled his promise. Christianity became the official religion of the Roman Empire. Today, Christianity has nearly two billion followers worldwide.

SECTION 3 ASSESSMENT

Terms & Names

1. Explain the significance of:
   (a) republic
   (b) Senate
   (c) patrician
   (d) plebeian
   (e) Julius Caesar
   (f) empire
   (g) Augustus
   (h) Constantine

Using Graphics

2. Use a chart like this one to outline the achievements of ancient Rome's Augustan Age.

Achievement	Effects

Main Ideas

3. (a) On what waterway is the city of Rome located?

   (b) What helped to unite the many different citizens of the Roman Republic?

   (c) How did Christianity spread throughout the Roman Empire?

Critical Thinking

4. **Drawing Conclusions**

   Why was ancient Rome able to control most of the land surrounding the Mediterranean Sea?

   Think About

   • the location of the Italian Peninsula

   • Rome's army

   • Rome's wars with Carthage

ACTIVITY -OPTION- Review the information about the beginnings of ancient Rome. Create a **chart** that compares the two important classes of Roman society: patricians and plebeians.

Time of Change: The Middle Ages

TERMS & NAMES
medieval
Charlemagne
feudalism
manorialism
guild
Magna Carta

MAIN IDEA

The Middle Ages was a time of great change in Western Europe.

WHY IT MATTERS NOW

Some developments that occurred during the Middle Ages continue to affect life in Europe today.

DATELINE

ROME, A.D. 476—A Germanic tribe called the Visigoths has attacked our city of Rome and overthrown the emperor, Romulus Augustulus. The Roman army—no longer as large or as well organized as it was during the height of the empire—was unable to fight off the invaders.

After looting the great city, fierce bands of warriors and bandits have continued raiding towns and villages throughout Western Europe. They are stealing jewels and money, killing both people and animals, and even seizing control of entire territories. The Roman Empire seems to have breathed its last breath.

Region • Visigoth artifacts, like these saddle buckles, were found near Rome. ▲

Western Europe in Collapse

As the Roman Empire collapsed in the fifth century, more and more people fled to the countryside to escape invaders from the north and east. Eventually, there was no central government to maintain roads, public buildings, or water systems. Most towns and cities in Western Europe shrank or were totally abandoned. Long-distance travel became unsafe, and trade less common.

TAKING NOTES
Use your chart to take notes about Western Europe.

Time Period	Social Structure	Architecture
Ancient Greece		
Ancient Rome		

Reading
Social Studies

A. Clarifying
Who provided
leadership during
the Middle Ages?

The Beginning of the Medieval Era The period of history between the fall of the Roman Empire and the beginning of the modern world is called the Middle Ages, or **medieval** (MEE·dee·EE·vuhl) era. During this time, many of the advances and inventions of the ancient world were lost. Without a strong central government, many Europeans turned to military leaders and the Roman Catholic Church for leadership and support.

Charlemagne and the Christian Church

Among the most famous military leaders was the Germanic King Charlemagne (SHAHR·luh·mayn). In the late 700s, **Charlemagne,** or Charles the Great, worked to bring political order to the northwestern fringes of what had been the Roman Empire. This great warrior not only fought to increase the size of his kingdom, he also worked to improve life for those who lived there.

A New Roman Emperor Eventually, news of Charlemagne's accomplishments spread to Rome. Although the old empire was gone, Rome was now the center of the Catholic Church. The Pope recognized that joining forces with Charlemagne might bring greater power to the Church.

In 800, the Pope crowned Charlemagne as the new Holy Roman Emperor. During Charlemagne's rule, education improved, the government became stronger, and Catholicism spread. But after Charlemagne's death, Western Europe was once again without a strong political leader.

Region •
Charlemagne
established
order and
supported
education and
culture for a
brief period
in the early
Middle Ages. ▲

The Role of the Church

Throughout Western Europe in medieval times, each community was centered around a church. The church offered religious services, established orphanages, and helped care for the poor, sick, and elderly. They also hosted feasts, festivals, and other celebrations. As communities grew, their members often donated money and labor to build new and larger churches.

Monks and Nuns Some people chose to dedicate their lives to serving God and the Church. These religious people were called monks and nuns. Monks were men who devoted their time to praying, studying, and copying and decorating holy books by hand. Monks lived in communities called monasteries. Many monasteries became important centers of learning in medieval society.

Women who served the Church were called nuns. In the Middle Ages, it was common for a woman to become a nun after her husband died. Nuns prayed, sewed, taught young girls, cared for the poor, and also copied and decorated books. They lived in secluded communities called convents.

Two Medieval Systems

During the Middle Ages, almost all the land was owned by powerful nobles—lords, kings, and high church officials. The central government was not very strong. The nobles sometimes even controlled the king and constantly fought among themselves. To protect their lands and position, nobles developed a system known as feudalism.

The Feudal System <u>Feudalism</u> was a system of political ties in which the nobles, such as kings, gave out land to less powerful nobles, such as knights. In return for the land, the noble, called a vassal, made a vow to provide various services to the lord. The most important was to furnish his lord with knights, foot soldiers, and arms for battle.

The parcel of land granted to a vassal by his lord was called a fief (feef). The center of the lord's fief was the manor, which consisted of a large house or castle, surrounding farmland, villages, and a church. A fief might also include several other manors or castles belonging to the fief-owner's vassals.

The Bayeux Tapestry This famous work of art depicts the invasion of England by William the Conqueror in 1066. The Bayeux (by•YOO) Tapestry is a series of scenes from the point of view of the invaders, who came from Normandy. Normandy is a part of what is now France. The work is an important source of information about not only the conquest of England, but also medieval armor, clothing, and other aspects of culture.

Although called a tapestry, the work is really an embroidered strip of linen about 230 feet long. It includes captions in Latin. The Bayeux Tapestry was probably made by nuns in England about 1092.

Manorialism On the manor, peasants lived and farmed, but they usually did not own the land they lived on. In exchange for their lord's protection, the peasants contributed their labor and a certain amount of the food they raised. Some peasants, known as serfs, actually belonged to the fief on which they lived. They were not slaves, but they were not free to leave the land without the permission of the lord. This system, in which the lord received food and work in exchange for his protection, is known as **manorialism**.

Medieval Ways of Life

Medieval nobles had more power than the peasants. However, the difference in the standard of living between the very rich and the very poor was not as great as the difference today.

Castle Life The manor houses or castles may have been large, but they were built more for defense than for comfort. Thick stone walls and few windows made the rooms cold, damp, and dark. Fires added warmth but made the air smoky. Medieval noble families may have slept on feather mattresses, but lice and other pests were a constant annoyance. Most castles did not have indoor plumbing.

Peasant Life Peasants lived outside the castle walls in small dwellings, often with dirt floors and straw roofs. They owned little furniture and slept on straw mattresses. It was common for peasant families to keep their farm animals inside their homes.

Peasants often worked two or three days a week for their lord, harvesting crops and repairing roads and bridges. The rest of the week they farmed their own small plots. Many days were religious festivals during which no one worked.

The Growth of Medieval Towns

By the middle of the 11th century, life was improving for many people in Western Europe. New farming methods increased the supply of food and shortened the time it took to harvest crops. Fewer farmers were needed, and workers began to leave the countryside in search of other opportunities. People moved back into towns or formed new ones that grew into booming centers of trade. The population increased, and more and more people owned property or started businesses.

Guilds As competition among local businesspeople grew, tradespeople and craftspeople created their own guilds, or business associations. Similar to modern trade unions, a **guild** protected workers' rights, set wages and prices, and settled disputes. Membership in a guild was also a common requirement for citizens who sought one of the few elective public offices.

B. Analyzing Motives Why did people create guilds?

The Late Middle Ages

Over time, the towns of the late Middle Ages grew in size, power, and wealth. The citizens of these towns began to establish local governments and to elect leaders.

Governments Challenge the Church The Pope insisted that he had supreme authority over all the Christian lands. Kings and other government leaders, however, did not agree that the Pope was more powerful than they were. This is an issue that continues to be discussed today.

The Magna Carta The rulers of Western Europe also struggled for power with members of the nobility. In England, nobles rebelled against King John. In 1215, the nobles forced the English king to sign a document called the **Magna Carta** (MAG·nuh KAHR·tuh), or Great Charter. This document limited the king's power and gave the nobles a larger role in the government.

Region • High taxes and failures on the battlefield made King John one of the most hated kings of England. ▼

Region • The Magna Carta influenced the creators of the U.S. Constitution. ▲

SECTION 4 ASSESSMENT

Terms & Names
1. Explain the significance of:

   (a) medieval   (b) Charlemagne   (c) feudalism

   (d) manorialism   (e) guild   (f) Magna Carta

Using Graphics
2. Use a flow chart like this one to show how Europe changed over four time periods: A.D. 476, the 800s, the mid-1000s, and the 1200s.

```
┌──────────┐
│   476    │
└──────────┘
     ↓
┌──────────┐
│          │
└──────────┘
     ↓
┌──────────┐
│  800s    │
└──────────┘
     ↓
```

Main Ideas
3. (a) Why is this era of European history called the Middle Ages?

   (b) Describe the role of the Church in medieval society.

   (c) How did manorialism help both nobles and peasants?

Critical Thinking
4. **Contrasting**

   How did life differ for nobles and peasants under feudalism?

Think About
- where they lived
- what they ate
- how they did their work

ACTIVITY -OPTION-   Review the information about serfs. Write a series of short **journal entries** describing what a week in the life of a serf might have been like during the Middle Ages.

TERMS & NAMES

Explain the significance of each of the following:

1. peninsula
2. plain
3. city-state
4. Aegean Sea
5. Athens
6. republic
7. empire
8. Constantine
9. feudalism
10. Magna Carta

REVIEW QUESTIONS

A Land of Varied Riches *(pages 273–277)*

1. What is special about Europe's physical environment?
2. Why is the Great European Plain an important region?

Ancient Greece *(pages 278–282)*

3. What helped to unite the separate city-states of ancient Greece?
4. What caused the people of Athens to join forces with their rival city-state, Sparta, in 480 B.C.?

Ancient Rome *(pages 284–289)*

5. Why did the ancient Romans call the Mediterranean Sea "our sea"?
6. Why did the Roman Senate ask Julius Caesar to resign?

Time of Change: The Middle Ages *(pages 290–295)*

7. Why did the people turn to the Roman Catholic Church for leadership and support during the Middle Ages?
8. What contributed to the growth of towns during the Middle Ages?

CRITICAL THINKING

Recognizing Effects

1. Using your completed chart from Reading Social Studies, p. 272, identify changes in art, culture, religion, and social structure from the time of ancient Rome to the Middle Ages.

Hypothesizing

2. Many myths and plays of ancient Greece have been the basis for modern films and dramas. What does this indicate about these ancient stories and characters?

Analyzing Causes

3. How did the long, peaceful reign of Augustus help to promote architecture, literature, and art in the Roman Empire?

Visual Summary

 A Land of Varied Riches

- The rich natural resources and varied geography of Europe helped to shape its development.

Ancient Greece

- The ancient Greeks developed a complex society and system of government.
- The achievements of the ancient Greeks in architecture, literature, and philosophy had a lasting impact on the world.

Ancient Rome

- Under strong leadership, ancient Rome experienced a time of great growth.
- Ancient Rome's contributions to government, engineering, and literature influenced Western culture.

Time of Change: The Middle Ages

- The social order and government of the Middle Ages transformed Europe into a modern society.

Use the map and your knowledge of world cultures and geography to answer questions 1 and 2.

Additional Test Practice, pp. S1–S33

1. What bodies of water does the Gulf Stream flow through on the way to Europe?

   A. Atlantic Ocean and Gulf of Mexico

   B. Atlantic Ocean and Tropic of Cancer

   C. Atlantic Ocean and West Indies

   D. Gulf of Mexico and Tropic of Cancer

2. Which of the following regions do you think is most directly affected by the Gulf Stream?

   A. Africa

   B. Central America

   C. Europe

   D. South America

The following passage is from a biography of Julius Caesar. Use the quotation and your knowledge of world cultures and geography to answer question 3.

PRIMARY SOURCE

The conspirators who murdered Julius Caesar . . . failed miserably to destroy him. Though they killed his body, they could not extinguish his spirit, his vision for Rome's future. . . . Many plebes [common people] . . . and soldiers saw him as their champion. And his bloody death unleashed the pent-up distrust and anger they felt for the . . . ruling class.

DON NARDO, *Julius Caesar*

3. The passage supports which of the following observations?

   A. Caesar's assassination was celebrated by the masses in Rome.

   B. Caesar's energy and his hopes for Rome lived on in spite of his death.

   C. The soldiers joined with the conspirators to remove Caesar from power.

   D. The death of Caesar signaled the end to his vision for Rome.

TEST PRACTICE
CLASSZONE.COM

ALTERNATIVE ASSESSMENT

1. WRITING ABOUT HISTORY

TThe Pope crowned Charlemagne as the Holy Roman Emperor in 800. Research this event and write a biography of Charlemagne in which you focus on his reign as emperor.

- Use the Internet or library resources to research Charlemagne and his impact on political, economic, and religious life in Europe.

- As a biographer, focus on the facts and important details you found in your research. Also, include your impressions of his reign.

2. COOPERATIVE LEARNING

Work with a small group of classmates to design and create a playbill for a Greek tragedy. Your playbill, or program for the audience, should include a cover illustration, a list of the characters, a summary of the story, and information about the playwright. Group members can share the responsibilities of researching, writing, and illustrating the playbill.

INTEGRATED TECHNOLOGY

Doing Internet Research

Different regions of Europe contain different natural resources. Focus on one European region, such as the Ruhr Valley, the Mediterranean Sea, or the independent republics of Eastern Europe. Use the Internet to research the region and its natural resources.

- Use the Internet, as well print encyclopedias, atlases, and other reference books to learn about the region.

- Focus your research on the natural resources found there, how they contributed to the region's development, and how the region has developed in modern times.

- Organize your findings into a report. Include a map that shows the region and its resources.

For Internet links to support this activity, go to

RESEARCH LINKS
CLASSZONE.COM

CHAPTER 11

The Growth of New Ideas

How can trade spread disease?

Movement • In 1347, an epidemic of bubonic plague (boo•BAHN•ihk playg) hit Europe. This plague, also called the Black Death, started in Asia. Caravans and trading ships carried it to port cities on the Mediterranean Sea. The plague spread from Sicily to the Italian Peninsula and then to France, Spain, and England.

The Black Death was carried by fleas that infected both rats and humans. Rats did not die from the plague. Instead, they served as hosts, or carriers, for the disease. By 1349, the horrors of the epidemic reached Switzerland, Austria, and Hungary. Later, it even reached as far north and east as Scandinavia and Russia. Historians estimate that this plague killed one out of every three persons in Europe.

What do you think?

♦ Why might the plague have reached Italy before it spread to England?

♦ How do you think the Black Death might have affected the economy of Europe?

Place The Cape of Saint Vincent is at the southwest tip of Portugal, jutting into the Atlantic Ocean. This was the location of Prince Henry's School of Navigation, where Portuguese sailors learned ways to explore the oceans of the world.

299

BEFORE YOU READ

▶▶ *What Do You Know?*

Do you know who first sailed around the world? Do you know that Leonardo da Vinci drew plans for a helicopter 400 years before it was actually built? Think of other discoveries, inventions, events, and famous people. What do you think life was like for common people during this time? Think about movies you have seen, books you have read, and what you have learned in other classes about the Renaissance, the Industrial Revolution, and political revolutions in France, Russia, and the United States.

▶▶ *What Do You Want to Know?*

Decide what you know about changes in the West from the Renaissance into the 1800s. In your notebook, record what you hope to learn from this chapter.

READ AND TAKE NOTES

Reading Strategy: Categorizing One way to make sense of what you read is to categorize ideas. Categorizing means sorting information by certain traits, ideas, or characteristics. Use the chart below to categorize details about the topics covered in this chapter.

- Copy the chart into your notebook.
- As you read each section, look for information about ideas, people, and events.
- Record key details in each category.

Movement • New tools and inventions contributed to social and political changes. Some improvements include the astrolabe (above), the steam engine (left), and movable type (below). ◀

Influences	New Ideas	People/Achievements	Events/Effects
The Renaissance			
European Exploration and Conquest			
Scientific and Industrial Revolutions			
Political Revolutions			
The Russian Empire			

Renaissance Connections

TERMS & NAMES
Crusades
Renaissance
Florence
Leonardo da Vinci
William Shakespeare
Reformation
Martin Luther
Protestant

MAIN IDEA

The rebirth of art, literature, and ideas during the Renaissance changed European society.

WHY IT MATTERS NOW

Many accomplishments of the Renaissance are high points of Western culture and continue to inspire artists, writers, and thinkers of today.

DATELINE

EXTRA

PARIS, FRANCE, 1269

Paris is buzzing with activity as thousands of European soldiers assemble here. This is the starting-off point for the eighth Crusade, which has nearly a thousand miles to travel. King Louis IX of France, who is in command, is confident that his armies can restore European power over the Holy Land.

Since the Crusades began in 1096, the Christians have fought against the Muslims and founded four states in the eastern Mediterranean. European power has weakened since then. However, King Louis's army looks ready to recapture the lost territory for Christianity.

Movement • Crusaders will make their way toward the Holy Land. ▲

Europeans Encounter New Cultures

The **Crusades**—a series of expeditions from the 11th to the 13th centuries by Western European Christians to capture the Holy Lands from Muslims—greatly changed life in Western Europe. The Crusades opened up trade routes, linking Western Europe with southwestern Asia and North Africa. They also helped Europeans rediscover the ideas of ancient Greece and Rome.

TAKING NOTES
Use your chart to take notes about people and ideas.

Influences	New Ideas	People/ Achievements
The Renaissance		
European Exploration		

0 50 100 miles
0 50 100 kilometers

Milan
Venice
Mantua
Genoa
Pisa
Florence
I T A L Y
Adriatic Sea
Corsica
42°N
Rome
N
Sardinia
Naples
Tyrrhenian Sea
40°N
Sicily
Mediterranean Sea
38°N
12°E   14°E   16°E   18°E

Florence
Genoa
Milan
Kingdom of the Two Sicilies
Papal States
Venice

GEOGRAPHY SKILLBUILDER:
Interpreting a Map

1. **Location •** Which city-state does not have access to water?
2. **Location •** Which city-state was in the best position to trade by land and sea with Asia?

Over time, this interest in the ancient world sparked a new era of creativity and learning in Western Europe. This cultural era, which lasted from the 14th to the 16th century, is called the **Renaissance**.

The Rebirth of Europe

The Renaissance began on the Italian Peninsula in the mid-14th century. During this time, many artists, architects, writers, and scholars created works of great importance. These included beautiful paintings, large sculptures, impressive buildings, and thought-provoking literature. As new ideas and achievements spread across the continent of Europe, they changed the way people viewed themselves and the world.

The Italian City-States In the 14th century, the Italian Peninsula was divided into many independent city-states. Some of these city-states, such as **Florence,** were bustling centers of banking, trade, and manufacturing.

BACKGROUND

After Rome fell, many achievements of ancient times were lost. Many books and manuscripts, however, were preserved by Muslim and Christian scholars.

Region • Florence, once a wealthy city-state, remains an important economic and cultural center. The Duomo, shown here, is a symbol of the city's Renaissance past. ▼

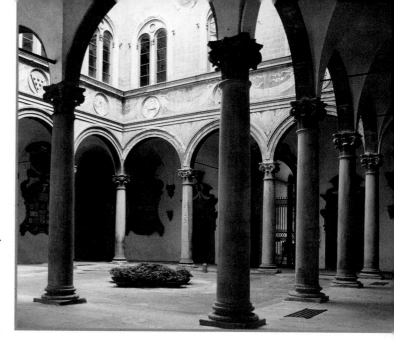

Region • The wealthy merchants in Italy built large palaces, called palazzos, such as Florence's Palazzo Medici shown here. ▶

The wealthy businesspeople who lived in these city-states were members of a new class of aristocrats. Unlike the nobles of the feudal system, these aristocrats lived in cities, and their wealth came from money and goods rather than from the lands they owned.

A Changing View of the World Religion was important to people's daily life during the Renaissance, but many wealthy Europeans began to turn increased attention to the material comforts of life.

New wealth allowed aristocratic families to build large homes for themselves in the city centers, decorating them with luxurious objects. They ate expensive food and dressed in fine clothes and jewels, often acquired as a result of the expanded trade routes. Aristocrats also placed increased emphasis on education and the arts.

Learning and the Arts Flourish

Wealthy citizens were proud of their city-states and often became generous patrons. A patron gave artists and scholars money and, sometimes, a place to live and work. They hired architects and designers to improve local churches, to design grand new buildings, and to create public sculptures and fountains. As one Italian city-state made additions and improvements, others competed to outdo it.

Biography

The Medici Family Among the most famous patrons of the Renaissance were the Medici (MEHD•uh•chee). They were a wealthy family of bankers and merchants. In fact, they were the most powerful leaders of Florence from the early 1400s until the 18th century.

Along with Lorenzo, pictured below, the Medici family included famous princes and dukes, two queens, and four popes. Throughout the 15th and 16th centuries, the Medici supported many artists, including Botticelli, Michelangelo, and Raphael. Today, Florence is still filled with important works of art made possible by the Medici.

Culture •
Leonardo da Vinci completed the painting *La Belle Ferronnière* in 1495. ▲

As part of the competition to improve the appearance and status of their individual city-states, patrons wanted to attract the brightest and best-known scholars and poets of the time. Patrons believed that the contributions of these individuals would, in turn, add to the greatness of their city-states and attract more wealth.

The Visual Arts: New Subjects and Methods Most medieval art was based on religious subjects. Painters and sculptors of the early Renaissance created religious art too, but they also began to depict other subjects. Some made portraits for wealthy patrons. Others created works showing historical scenes or mythological stories.

Leonardo da Vinci One of the most famous artists and scientists of the Renaissance was **Leonardo da Vinci** (lee·uh·NAHR·doh duh VIHN·chee) (1452–1519). Among his best-known paintings are the *Mona Lisa,* a portrait of a young woman with a mysterious smile, and *The Last Supper.* Da Vinci was more than just a talented painter, however.

Throughout his life, da Vinci observed the world around him. He studied the flow of water, the flight of birds, and the workings of the human body. Da Vinci, who became a skilled engineer, scientist, and inventor, filled notebooks with thousands of sketches of his discoveries and inventions. He even drew ideas for flying machines, parachutes, and submarines—hundreds of years before they were built.

Reading
Social Studies

A. Contrasting
How did the subject matter of Renaissance art differ from medieval art?

Connections to Math

Perspective During the Renaissance, artists began to use a technique called linear perspective. Linear perspective is a system of using lines to create the illusion of depth and distance. In the drawing below, notice how the perspective lines move toward a single point in the distance, giving the picture depth.

The Northern Renaissance

As the new Renaissance ideas about religion and art spread to Northern Europe, they inspired artists and writers working there. The Dutch scholar and philosopher Desiderius Erasmus (ih·RAS·muhs) (1466–1536), for example, criticized the church for its wealth and poked fun at its officials. During the late 16th and early 17th centuries, another writer—the Englishman **William Shakespeare**—wrote a series of popular stage plays. Many of his works, including *Romeo and Juliet* and *Macbeth,* are still read and performed around the world.

The Reformation

BACKGROUND

In 1516, the English writer Thomas More published a famous book called *Utopia*. It describes the author's idea of a perfect society. Today, the word "utopia" is used to describe any ideal place.

Roman Catholicism was still the most powerful religion in Western Europe. Some of the views of the northern Renaissance writers and scholars, however, were in conflict with the Roman Catholic Church. These new ideas would eventually lead to the **Reformation,** a 16th-century movement to change church practices.

Martin Luther The German monk **Martin Luther** (1483–1546) was one of the most important critics of the church. The wealth and corruption of many church officials disturbed him. Luther also spoke out against the church's policy of selling indulgences—the practice of forgiving sins in exchange for money.

In 1517, Luther wrote 95 theses, or statements of belief, attacking the sale of indulgences and other church practices. Copies were printed and handed out throughout Western Europe. After this, Luther was excommunicated, or cast out and no longer recognized as a member of a church, and went into hiding. While in hiding, he translated the Bible from Latin into German so that all literate, German-speaking people could read it. Under Luther's leadership, many Europeans began to challenge the practices of the Roman Catholic Church.

The Printing Press Until the Renaissance, each copy of a book had to be written by hand— usually by monks or nuns. A Renaissance invention, however, changed that forever. Around 1450, a German printer named Johann Gutenberg (Yoh•HAHN GOO•tuhn•BERG) began to use a method of printing with movable type. This meant that multiple copies of books, such as this Bible, could be printed quickly and less expensively.

Although many Renaissance books dealt with religious subjects, printers also published plays, poetry, works of philosophy and science, and tales of travel and adventure. As greater numbers of books were published, more and more Europeans learned to read.

For more on the printing press, go to

CLASSZONE.COM

THINKING CRITICALLY

1. **Recognizing Effects**
   What were three effects of the invention of Gutenberg's printing press?

2. **Synthesizing**
   Before the printing press, who produced the books?

A Conflict over Religious Beliefs

Reading
Social Studies

B. Clarifying How did Protestants get their name?

Luther's followers were called **Protestants** because they protested events at an assembly that ended the church's tolerance of their beliefs. Many people in Western Europe still supported the church, however. This conflict led to religious wars that ended in 1555. At that time, the Peace of Augsburg declared that German rulers could decide the official religion of their own state.

The Spread of Protestant Ideas By 1600, Protestantism had spread to England and the Scandinavian Peninsula. Protestants pushed to expand education for more Europeans. They did this because being able to read meant being able to study the Bible. They also encouraged translation of the Bible into the native language of each country.

The Counter Reformation The Roman Catholic Church responded to Protestantism by launching its own movement in the mid-16th century. As part of this movement, called the Counter Reformation, the church stopped selling indulgences. It also created a new religious order called the Society of Jesus, or the Jesuits. Jesuit missionaries and scholars worked to spread Catholic ideas across Europe, to Asia, and to the lands of the "new world" across the Atlantic Ocean.

Region •
Martin Luther's writings and actions changed Christianity forever. ▲

SECTION 1 ASSESSMENT

Terms & Names

1. Explain the significance of:
  (a) Crusades   (b) Renaissance   (c) Florence   (d) Leonardo da Vinci
  (e) William Shakespeare   (f) Reformation   (g) Martin Luther   (h) Protestants

Using Graphics

2. Use a spider map like this one to chart the characteristics and accomplishments of the Renaissance.

Renaissance Accomplishments

Main Ideas

3. (a) Where and when did the Renaissance begin?

  (b) In what ways were the wealthy Europeans of the Renaissance different from the wealthy Europeans of feudal times?

  (c) What was the Counter Reformation?

Critical Thinking

4. Hypothesizing

Why do you think Protestantism spread so quickly in Northern Europe?

Think About

- new methods of printing
- the ideas of the northern Renaissance
- the work of Martin Luther

ACTIVITY -OPTION-   Write a **letter** to an imagined patron asking for support to create a project—such as a public sculpture, park, fountain, or building—to beautify your community.

Traders, Explorers, and Colonists

TERMS & NAMES
Prince Henry the Navigator
Christopher Columbus
Ferdinand Magellan
circumnavigate
imperialism

MAIN IDEA

European trade and exploration changed the lives of many people on both sides of the Atlantic.

WHY IT MATTERS NOW

Today, citizens of the Americas continue to feel the effects of European exploration and colonization.

DATELINE

SAGRES, PORTUGAL, 1421—
Portugal's Prince Henry may not have journeyed to sea, but he has earned a well-deserved nickname: "The Navigator." He has organized expeditions of sailors to explore the west coast of Africa. Five years ago, Henry also founded a School of Navigation. It is here in Sagres, at Portugal's southwestern tip, which juts into the Atlantic Ocean.

Astronomers, geographers, and mathematicians gather here to study and teach new methods of traveling across the seas. They plan expeditions using the latest maps, tools, and information about the winds and currents of the Atlantic Ocean. Sometimes the scholars add to their knowledge by talking with sea captains about their voyages.

Movement • Prince Henry of Portugal founded the School of Navigation. ▲

Trade Between Europe and Asia

For centuries before the Renaissance, European traders traveled back and forth across the Mediterranean. Merchants commonly journeyed from southern Europe to North Africa and to the eastern Mediterranean. Spices were one of the most important items traded at this time.

TAKING NOTES
Use your chart to take notes about people and ideas.

Influences	New Ideas	People/ Achievements
The Renaissance		
European Exploration		

The Spice Trade Spices were in great demand by Europeans. Before refrigeration, meat and fish spoiled quickly. To help preserve food and to improve its flavor, people used spices such as pepper, cinnamon, nutmeg, and cloves. These spices came from Asia.

For centuries, Italian merchants from Genoa and Venice controlled the spice trade. They sailed to ports in the eastern Mediterranean, where they would purchase spices and other goods from traders who had traveled across Asia. The Italian merchants would then bring these goods back to Europe.

The Possibility of Great Wealth Transporting goods across these great distances was costly. Everyone along the way had to be paid and wanted to earn a profit. By the time the spices reached Europe, they had to be sold at extremely high prices.

European merchants knew that if they could trade directly with people in Asia, they could make enormous profits. In the 15th century, Europeans began to search for a new route to Asia.

BACKGROUND

In addition to spices, European countries traded for precious metals, which they used to make coins. Metals such as gold and silver were scarce in Europe.

Leaders in Exploration

The small country of Portugal is at the westernmost part of the European continent. Portuguese sailors had navigated the waters of the Atlantic Ocean for centuries. As shown on the map below, they traveled down the west coast of Africa and as far west into the Atlantic as Madeira, the Azores, and the Canary Islands.

Exploring the African Coast In the early 1400s, Portugal's **Prince Henry the Navigator** decided to send explorers farther down the coast of Africa. He believed that if explorers could find a way around Africa, it might be a shortcut to Asia. Portuguese explorers returned home from these expeditions with gold dust, ivory, and more knowledge of navigation. By the time Henry died in 1460, the Portuguese had ventured around the great bulge of western Africa to present-day Sierra Leone.

Portuguese Explorers, 1400s

← Dias 1487–1488
← da Gama 1497–1498

GEOGRAPHY SKILLBUILDER:
Interpreting a Map

1. **Movement** • Which explorer reached Asia?
2. **Location** • Which continent was most explored by the Portuguese?

The Race Around Africa Bold Portuguese explorers continued to push farther down the African coast. Finally, in 1488, Bartolomeu Dias (BAHR·too·loo·MAY·oo DEE·uhsh) rounded the southern tip of Africa. The Portuguese named the tip the Cape of Good Hope.

Less than ten years later, Vasco da Gama (vas·KOH deh GAH·muh) led a sea expedition all the way to Asia. Da Gama and his crew traveled for 317 days and 13,500 miles before reaching the coast of India. They were the first Europeans to discover a sea route to Asia. Now, the riches of Asia could be brought directly to Europe. After setting up trading posts along the coast of the Indian Ocean, Portugal ruled these waterways.

Europe Enters a New Age

Portugal was not the only European country to understand that whoever controlled trade with Asia would have great power and wealth. Spain and England quickly entered the race to find a direct sea route of their own.

Christopher Columbus Some explorers believed that the shortest way to Asia was to sail west across the Atlantic Ocean. Queen Isabella of Spain agreed to fund an expedition across the Atlantic.

In August 1492, an Italian named **Christopher Columbus** and 90 crew members left Spain aboard three ships—the *Santa Maria*, the *Pinta*, and the *Niña*. The Atlantic Ocean proved to be wider than maps of the time suggested. On October 12, after weeks at sea, the crew spotted land. Although Columbus thought he had found Asia, they were off the coast of an island in the Caribbean. This was still a great distance from their spice-rich destination.

Ferdinand Magellan In 1519, Spain funded an expedition for the Portuguese explorer **Ferdinand Magellan** (muh·JEHL·uhn). Magellan left Spain with five ships and more than 200 sailors. As they traveled west, the crew battled violent storms and rough seas. Food was in short supply, and starving sailors ate rats and sawdust. Some died of disease.

Reading Social Studies

A. Recognizing Important Details What continent did Columbus reach, and where did he think he was?

Connections to Science

New Ships In the early 15th century, Portuguese shipbuilders designed a sturdy ship called a caravel, pictured below. Built for exploration and trade, the caravel was small and had a narrow body. This helped the ship to cut through waves and to travel in shallow water.

The caravel also used a combination of square and triangular sails. These made sailing easier against strong, shifting winds.

Movement • Sailors figured their ship's position with the astrolabe. It measured the position of the sun and stars in relation to the horizon. ▼

By the time Magellan and his ships reached the Philippines in Asia, the sailors had spent 18 long months at sea. Then, during a battle there, Magellan and several crew members were killed. The expedition returned to Spain after a three-year journey. Only one boat and 18 crew members succeeded. They had to **circumnavigate,** or sail completely around, the world.

Reading Social Studies

B. Identifying Problems What were the main problems faced by Magellan and his crew?

John Cabot King Henry VII of England did not want Portugal and Spain to claim all the riches of Asia. He funded a voyage by Italian-born Giovanni Caboto, called John Cabot by the English, who believed that a northern route across the Atlantic Ocean might be a shortcut to Asia.

Aboard one small ship, Cabot and 18 crew members sailed west from England in May 1497. When they reached land the following month, Cabot thought they had found Asia. Most likely, they landed in present-day Newfoundland in Canada.

The Outcomes of Exploration

The kings and queens of Europe sent explorers in search of a direct trade route to Asia. These expeditions, however, turned out to have unexpected results.

A Clash of Cultures European countries founded many new colonies along the coastal areas of Africa and North and South America. This practice of one country controlling the government and economy of another country or territory is called **imperialism.** These conquered lands were already home to large, self-ruling populations. They had their own cultural traditions. After the arrival of the Europeans, the lives of these indigenous peoples would never be the same.

Vocabulary
indigenous: born and living in a place, rather than having come from somewhere else

Religious Conversion The European monarchs were Christians. They had strong religious beliefs, and they sent missionaries and other religious officials to help convert conquered peoples to Christianity. The European rulers also hoped that these new converts would help Christianity overcome other powerful religions, especially Islam.

The Spread of Diseases Without knowing it, the European explorers and colonists carried diseases with them, including smallpox, malaria, and measles. These diseases were unknown in the Americas, and killed tens of thousands of people there.

Columbus, Cabot, and Magellan, 1492–1522

INTERACTIVE

GEOGRAPHY SKILLBUILDER: Interpreting a Map
1. **Movement** • Which explorer traveled in the Pacific Islands?
2. **Location** • What continent did John Cabot reach?

Slavery European explorations also led to an expanding slave trade. The Portuguese purchased West Coast African people to work as slaves back in Portugal, where the work force had been reduced by plague. In other colonized areas, such as Mexico and parts of South America, Europeans forced conquered peoples to work the land where they lived. For hundreds of years, Africans and conquered peoples of the Americas would be forced to work under horrible conditions.

SECTION 2 ASSESSMENT

Terms & Names

1. Explain the significance of:
   (a) Prince Henry the Navigator
   (b) Christopher Columbus
   (c) Ferdinand Magellan
   (d) circumnavigate
   (e) imperialism

Using Graphics

2. Use a chart like this one to compare characteristics of the voyages of Christopher Columbus and Vasco da Gama.

Columbus's Voyage	Da Gama's Voyage

Main Ideas

3. (a) Why were spices so important to Europeans?

   (b) Why did Europeans want to find a new route to Asia?

   (c) Name three ways in which European exploration affected the indigenous peoples of North and South America.

Critical Thinking

4. **Making Inferences**

   Why do you think the Portuguese became leaders of European exploration?

   Think About

   • the location of Portugal
   • early Portuguese voyages
   • Prince Henry and his School of Navigation

ACTIVITY -OPTION- Reread the information about Magellan's voyage around the world. Write a **journal entry** describing the events of the voyage from the point of view of a crew member.

Researching Topics on the Internet

▶▶ Defining the Skill

The Internet is a computer network that connects libraries, museums, universities, government agencies, businesses, news organizations, and private individuals all over the world. Each location on the Internet has a home page with its own address, or URL (universal resource locator). With a computer connected to the Internet, you can reach the home pages of many organizations and services. The international collection of home pages, known as the World Wide Web, is an excellent source of up-to-date information about the regions and countries of the world.

▶▶ Applying the Skill

The Web page shown below is the European Reading Room at the Library of Congress Web site. Use the strategies listed below to help you understand how to research topics on the Internet.

How to Research Topics on the Internet

Strategy ❶ Once on the Internet, go directly to the Web page. For example, type http://www.loc.gov/rr/european/extlinks.html in the box at the top of the Web browser and press ENTER. The Web page will appear on your screen.

Strategy ❷ Explore the European Reading Room links. Click any of the links to find more information about a subject. These links take you to other Web sites.

Strategy ❸ Always confirm information you have found on the Internet. The Web sites of universities, government agencies, museums, and trustworthy news organizations are more reliable than others. You can often find information about a site's creator by looking for copyright information or reviewing the home page.

▶▶ Practicing the Skill

Turn to Chapter 11, Section 1, "Renaissance Connections." Reread the section and make a list of topics you would like to research.

For Internet links to support this activity, go to

RESEARCH LINKS
CLASSZONE.COM

The Age of Revolution

TERMS & NAMES
Scientific Revolution
Industrial Revolution
labor force
capitalism
French Revolution
Reign of Terror
Napoleon Bonaparte

MAIN IDEA

Scientific, industrial, and political revolutions transformed European society.

WHY IT MATTERS NOW

European revolutions in science, technology, and politics helped to create modern societies throughout the world.

DATELINE

EXTRA

LEIPZIG, GERMANY, APRIL 1839

A new era in German history has begun. The Leipzig-Dresden railway is open for business. Although short rail lines have been in service for a few years, this is the first long-distance railway in this part of Europe.

The steam locomotive that powers the German train was made in England. It is the latest improvement to

George Stephenson's "Rocket" train, which set a speed record of 30 mph in 1829. Already, this new form of transportation is changing Europe. The railroads are attracting many passengers and are also ideal for hauling goods. It seems that wherever new train stations are built, growth and prosperity soon follow.

Region ● Leipzig's railway will now take passengers all the way to Dresden. ▲

Changes in Science and Industry

The steam-powered locomotive was only one in a long line of technological improvements made in Europe since the 1600s. In fact, scientists and inventors made so many discoveries during these years that Europe experienced both a scientific and an industrial revolution. These periods of great change would help to create modern societies.

TAKING NOTES

Use your chart to take notes about people and ideas.

Influences	New Ideas	People/ Achievements
The Renaissance		
European Exploration		

The Scientific Revolution In the 16th and 17th centuries, scientific discoveries changed the way Europeans looked at the world. This led to the **Scientific Revolution**.

In Italy, Galileo Galilei (GAL·uh·LEE·oh GAL·uh·LAY) (1564–1642) studied the stars and planets using a new invention called the telescope. Later in Holland, Antoni van Leeuwenhoek (LAY·vuhn·huk) (1632–1723) used a microscope to explore an unknown world found in a drop of water. The Swedish botanist Carolus Linnaeus (lih·NEE·uhs) (1707–1778) even developed a system to name and classify all living things on Earth.

Culture •
In 1610, Galileo used his telescope to observe that Jupiter had moons. ▲

The Industrial Revolution Many inventions of the Scientific Revolution began to change the way people worked all across Europe. Machines performed jobs that once had been done by humans and animals. This brought about such great change that it led to a revolution in the way goods were produced: the **Industrial Revolution**.

Machines were grouped together to make products in large factories. Early factories were built in the countryside near streams and rivers so that they could be powered by water. By the late 1700s, however, new steam engines were used to power the machinery. More and more factories could now be built in cities. People, in turn, moved from the countryside to the cities in search of work.

Reading
Social Studies

A. Finding Causes How did the Scientific Revolution lead to the Industrial Revolution?

The Workshop of the World

The Industrial Revolution began in England in the late 1700s. The first English factories made textiles, or cloth. The steam-powered machines of the textile industry produced large amounts of goods quickly and cheaply. So many factories were built in England that the country earned the nickname "The Workshop of the World."

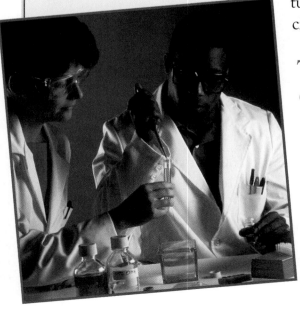

BACKGROUND

In the 1850s, laws were finally passed to help protect women and children from long hours and harsh working conditions.

Hard Work for Low Pay The Industrial Revolution created a need for workers, or a **labor force,** in cities. The workers who ran the textile machines made up part of this labor force. Most workers could earn more income in cities than on farms, but life could be hard. Factory laborers worked long hours and received low pay. In fact, many families often sent their children to work to help create more income.

In 1838, women and children made up more than 75 percent of all textile factory workers. Children as young as seven were forced to work 12 hours a day, six days a week.

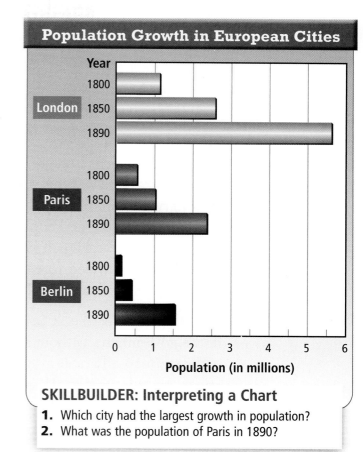

Population Growth in European Cities

SKILLBUILDER: Interpreting a Chart

1. Which city had the largest growth in population?
2. What was the population of Paris in 1890?

The Spread of Industrialization

The textile industry in 18th-century England was one step in the development of an economic system called **capitalism.** In this system, factories and other businesses that make and sell goods are privately owned. Private business owners make decisions about what goods to produce. They sell these goods at a price that will earn a profit.

Industrialization spread from England to other countries, including Germany, France, Belgium, and the United States. Cities in these countries grew rapidly and became more crowded and dirtier. Diseases, such as cholera (KAHL·uhr·uh) and typhoid (TY·foyd) fever, spread. Smoke from factories blackened city skies, and pollution fouled the rivers.

Place •
Factories, like this one in Sheffield, England, were found throughout Western Europe by the mid-19th century. ▶

The French Revolution

Along with changes in science, technology, and the economy came new ideas about government. In the late 18th century, many ordinary citizens began to fight for more political rights.

Ripe for Political Change By the 1780s, the French government was deeply in debt because of bad investments and the costs of waging wars. Life was miserable for the common working people. Poor harvests combined with increased population had led to food shortages and hunger. People were forced to pay heavy taxes. At the same time, the French king, Louis XVI, and his queen, Marie Antoinette, continued to enjoy an expensive life at court, entertaining themselves and the French nobility.

Storming the Bastille The citizens of France demanded changes in the government, without success. Then, on July 14, 1789, angry mobs stormed a Paris prison called the Bastille (ba•STEEL). The attack on this prison, which reflected the royal family's power, became symbolic of the **French Revolution**.

Revolts spread from Paris to the countryside, and poor and angry workers burned the homes of the nobility. By 1791, France had a new constitution that made all French citizens equal under the law.

Reading
Social Studies

B. Analyzing Motives
Why did the French citizens demand a new government?

Region • The storming of the Bastille remains a symbol of the French Revolution. ▼

BACKGROUND

Until the French Revolution, the guillotine was only used to execute nobles. It was considered the most humane type of execution.

The French Republic In 1792, France became a republic. King Louis XVI was found guilty of treason, or betraying one's country. In 1793, he and Marie Antoinette were sentenced to death. They were beheaded on the guillotine (GIHL·uh·teen).

Still, France was not at peace. The new revolutionary leaders refused to tolerate any disagreement. Between 1793 and 1794, these new leaders executed 17,000 people. This period of bloodshed became known as the **Reign of Terror**.

Napoleon French leaders continued to struggle for power until 1799, when General **Napoleon Bonaparte** (nuh·POH·lee·uhn BOH·nuh·PAHRT) took control. The French Revolution and the disorder that followed were finally over.

However, the new sense of equality brought about by the Revolution stirred feelings of nationalism among the French. Nationalism is pride in and loyalty to one's nation. Soon, the citizens of other European nations began to fight for more political power. Slowly, they, too, won more rights.

Region • Napoleon Bonaparte crowned himself emperor of France in 1804. He led France to victory in what became known as the Napoleonic Wars. ▲

SECTION 3 ASSESSMENT

Terms & Names

1. Explain the significance of:
   (a) Scientific Revolution
   (b) Industrial Revolution
   (c) labor force
   (d) capitalism
   (e) French Revolution
   (f) Reign of Terror
   (g) Napoleon Bonaparte

Using Graphics

2. Use a chart like this one to list some of the scientific, industrial, and political changes that occurred during the Age of Revolution.

Scientific Changes	Industrial Changes	Political Changes

Main Ideas

3. (a) Describe at least three inventions or discoveries of the Scientific Revolution.

   (b) How did the Industrial Revolution change the way people in Europe worked?

   (c) What changes occurred in France after the French Revolution?

Critical Thinking

4. **Recognizing Effects**

   How did industrialization change the cities to which it spread?

   Think About
   - population
   - diseases
   - the environment

Reread the section about the French Revolution. Write a **poem** or **lyrics** for a folk song that describe the events from the point of view of a common citizen or a member of the royal family.

The Russian Empire

TERMS & NAMES
czar
Ivan the Terrible
Peter the Great
Catherine the Great
Russian Revolution

MAIN IDEA

Strong leaders built Russia into a large empire, but the country's citizens had few rights and struggled with poverty.

WHY IT MATTERS NOW

Russia has had a great influence on world politics and is experiencing a period of great change.

DATELINE

MOSCOW, RUSSIA, 1560—Today, the most magnificent church in Moscow opened with a grand celebration. The Cathedral of St. Basil has ten domes—each one unique. The massive structure, built of bricks and white stone, is decorated with brilliant colors.

Ivan IV built this cathedral to celebrate his victory eight years ago over the Tatars (TAH•tuhrz). These Turkish people who live in Central Asia have long threatened Russia's security.

The victory also added the lands of the Tatars, including their capital at Kazan, to our growing empire. Russians everywhere should be proud of Moscow's new church and of the victory it symbolizes.

Place • Ivan IV has honored a Russian victory over the Tatars with the construction of St. Basil's Cathedral. ▲

Russia Rules Itself

Russia, geographically the world's largest nation, is located in both Europe and Asia. It takes up large parts of both continents, and both continents have helped shape its history.

Mongols from eastern Asia conquered Russia in the 13th century and ruled it for about 200 years. During the 15th century, Russia broke free of Mongol rule. At this time, the most important Russian city was Moscow, located in the west.

TAKING NOTES
Use your chart to take notes about people and ideas.

Influences	New Ideas	People/ Achievements
The Renaissance		
European Exploration		

Reading Social Studies

A. Clarifying Why did the Russian people give Ivan IV the nickname Ivan the Terrible?

The First Czars of Russia In 1547, a 16-year-old leader in Moscow was crowned the first **czar** (zahr), or emperor, of modern Russia. His official title was Ivan IV, but the people nicknamed him **Ivan the Terrible**. Ivan was known for his cruelty, especially toward those he viewed as Russia's enemies. During his rule of 37 years, the country was constantly at war.

During the reigns of Ivan the Terrible and the czars who followed him, Russia had an unlimited government. This is a form of government in which a single ruler holds all the power. The people have no say in how the country is run.

Conflicts at Home The first Russian czars were often in conflict with the Russian nobles, who possessed much land and wealth. The czars viewed the nobles as a threat to their control over the people. Ivan the Terrible ordered his soldiers to murder Russian nobles and church leaders who opposed him.

The poor farmers, or peasants, of Russia also suffered under the first czars. New laws forced the peasants to become serfs, who had to remain on the farms where they worked.

Region • Ivan the Terrible is said to have worn this fur-trimmed crown at his coronation in 1547. ▲

The Expansion of Russia

In addition to strengthening their control over the Russian people, the czars wanted to gain new territory. Throughout the 17th and 18th centuries, rulers such as Peter the Great and Catherine the Great conquered neighboring lands.

A Window on the West An intelligent man with big ideas for his country, **Peter the Great** ruled Russia from 1682 to 1725. After defeating Sweden in war and winning land along the Baltic Sea, Peter built a port city called St. Petersburg. This city, which Peter saw as Russia's "window on the west," became the new capital.

BACKGROUND

In 1721, Peter the Great changed his title from *czar* to *emperor,* a title that he thought sounded more European.

One of Peter's goals was to have closer ties with Western Europe. He hoped to use the ideas and inventions of the Scientific Revolution to modernize and strengthen Russia. During his rule, Peter reformed the army and the government and built new schools. He even ordered Russians to dress like Europeans and to shave off their beards. Peter's reforms made Russia stronger, but they did not improve life for Russian peasants.

Movement • Peter the Great brought to Russia many of the improvements of the Scientific and Industrial Revolutions. ▲

The Expansion of Russia, 1584–1796

ARCTIC OCEAN

NORWAY
SWEDEN
FINLAND
AUSTRIA
HUNGARY
POLAND
St. Petersburg
Archangel
Novgorod
Kiev
Moscow
Kazan
Constantinople
OTTOMAN EMPIRE
Astrakhan
Tomsk
SIBERIA
MANCHURIA
MONGOLIA

Baltic Sea
Dniester R.
Dnieper R.
Don R.
Volga R.
URAL MOUNTAINS
Ob R.
Yenisey R.
Lena R.
Black Sea
Caspian Sea
CAUCASUS MTS.

Russia in 1584
Russia in 1725
Russia in 1796

0   500   1,000 miles
0   500   1,000 kilometers

> **GEOGRAPHY SKILLBUILDER:**
> **Interpreting a Map**
> 1. **Location •** What body of water did Russia gain access to in 1796?
> 2. **Place •** When did Russia gain the most land?

A Great Empress **Catherine the Great** took control of Russia in 1762 and ruled until her death in 1796. Catherine added vast new lands to the empire, including the present-day countries of Ukraine (yoo•KRAYN) and Belarus (behl•uh•ROOS). Like Peter the Great, Catherine borrowed many ideas from Western Europe. She started new schools and encouraged art, science, and literature. Catherine also built new towns and expanded trade.

During Catherine's reign, Russia became one of Europe's most powerful nations. The lives of the peasants, however, remained miserable. Catherine thought about freeing them, but she knew the nobles would oppose her. When the peasants rebelled in the 1770s, Catherine crushed their uprising.

Movement • Catherine the Great continued Peter the Great's practice of bringing the ideas of Western Europe to Russia. ▼

A Divided Russia

In the 19th century, Russia remained a divided nation. Most people were poor peasants, and most of the wealth belonged to the nobles. This division would lead to conflict and eventually to a political revolution.

The Nobles Many Russian nobles sent their children to be educated in Germany and France. In fact, many noble families spoke French at home, speaking Russian only to their servants. The Western Europeans introduced many new ideas to the Russian nobles, among them the idea that a nation's government should reflect the wishes of its citizens.

BACKGROUND

Catherine the Great was born in Germany. She came to Russia at 15 to marry the heir to the throne, Peter III. He was a weak ruler, however, and Catherine, supported by the army and the people, overthrew him.

Many Russian nobles were army officers or government officials. Most supported the czar and were proud of Russia's growing power. In 1825, one group of nobles tried to replace the government. Their attempt to gain more power failed.

The Serfs In the 19th century, the Russian serfs still had no land or money of their own. They worked on farms owned by others and received little help from the Russian government.

In 1861, Alexander II decided to end serfdom in Russia. He hoped that freeing the serfs would help his country compete with Western Europe. The serfs had to pay a heavy tax, though, and the land they were given was often not good for farming. Most former serfs felt that they had gained very little.

Bloody Sunday The serfs were not the only unhappy Russians. Many university students, artists, and writers believed that the government's treatment of the serfs was unfair. Some joined groups that tried to overthrow the government. In addition, workers in Russia's cities complained about low pay and poor working conditions.

In 1905, a group of workers marched to the royal palace in St. Petersburg with a list of demands. Government troops shot many of them. News of the events of this "Bloody Sunday" spread across Russia, making people even angrier with the government and czar.

BACKGROUND

In the 1850s, Russia fought the Crimean War against Turkey. Two of Turkey's allies were Britain and France. When Russia lost, Alexander II thought this proved that his country was still far less advanced than Western European nations.

CULTURE

The Hermitage Museum One of the world's largest art museums is the Hermitage in St. Petersburg. It contains many works of art, including French, Spanish, and British paintings. Part of the collection is in the Winter Palace, a former royal residence.

Both Peter the Great and Catherine the Great collected European art. On a trip to Amsterdam in 1716, Peter bought paintings by the famous Dutch artist Rembrandt. About 50 years later, Catherine bought more than 200 works of art when she visited Germany. These royal collections became part of the Hermitage when it opened as a public museum in 1852.

THINKING CRITICALLY

1. **Analyzing Motives**
   Why did Peter the Great and Catherine the Great collect art from Western Europe?

2. **Making Inferences**
   Why do you think the works of art were displayed in a museum?

For more on the Hermitage Museum, go to

RESEARCH LINKS
CLASSZONE.COM

The End of the Russian Empire

In 1914, World War I began. Nicholas II—a quiet, shy man who did not want war—ruled Russia, but he failed to keep his country out of the battle. Russia, whose allies included the United Kingdom and France, suffered terrible losses fighting Germany and its allies.

Reading
Social Studies

B. Analyzing Motives Why did Russian workers strike?

During World War I, there were food shortages in the cities and workers went on strike. Russian revolutionaries organized the workers against the czar. Even the Russian army turned against their ruler, and in 1917, Nicholas was forced to give up power. This overturning of the Russian monarchy is known as the **Russian Revolution.**

Nicholas II and the royal family (the Romanovs) were imprisoned by the revolutionaries. On July 17, 1918, they were all shot to death. This execution ended more than 300 years of rule by the Romanov family and nearly 400 years of czarist rule.

Rasputin One of the most influential people at the court of Czar Nicholas II was Rasputin. He came from Siberia in eastern Russia and was a self-styled holy man. Crown prince Alexis suffered from the disease hemophilia, and no doctor in Russia could cure him. Rasputin seemed to mysteriously heal the boy, gaining favor with Nicholas's wife, Czarina Alexandra. However, in 1916, Russian nobles killed Rasputin out of fear of the considerable power and influence the monk had.

SECTION 4 ASSESSMENT

Terms & Names
1. **Explain the significance of:**
   (a) czar
   (b) Ivan the Terrible
   (c) Peter the Great
   (d) Catherine the Great
   (e) Russian Revolution

Using Graphics
2. Use a chart like this one to describe three characteristics of czars of Russia.

Ivan the Terrible	Peter the Great	Catherine the Great	Nicholas II

Main Ideas
3. (a) What effects did an unlimited government have on Russian peasants?
   (b) How did Peter the Great help reform Russia?
   (c) Alexander II ended serfdom in 1861, but this did little to help the serfs. Why?

Critical Thinking
4. **Finding Causes**
   What events led to the Russian Revolution?

Think About
- the life of the serfs
- Bloody Sunday
- the events of World War I

ACTIVITY -OPTION- Look at the map on page 320 that shows the expansion of Russia. Write a brief **summary** to describe how the Russian nation grew from the 1500s to 1800.

INTER**ACTIVE**

James Watt's Double-Action Steam Engine

Amid the excitement of the Industrial Revolution, James Watt (1736–1819), a Scottish inventor, patented a new steam engine. Steam power had been used for many years, but Watt's invention was an improved, double-action steam engine. This system, in which the steam pushes from both sides of the piston rather than from just one, enhanced efficiency and increased power. Watt's invention helped to advance manufacturing and transportation and influenced later inventions. Watt's double-action steam engine was one of the most important inventions of the Industrial Revolution.

How the Engine Works

Steam from the **boiler** enters the **piston cylinder**. The pressure of the steam pushes the **piston** to one side, moving the **piston rod**. When the piston reaches the end of the stroke, the **slide valve** shifts the steam to the other side of the piston, forcing it back and releasing the steam it compresses as exhaust.

❶ As water is converted to steam, its volume increases 1,600 percent.

❷ When the steam enters the piston cylinder, it forces the piston rod to one side.

❸ As the piston reaches the end of its stroke, the slide valve channels steam to the other side of the piston.

❹ The piston rod is pushed back, forcing the "old" steam out as exhaust.

Action 1   Slide valve   Boiler

Piston rod

❶

❷

Piston   Piston cylinder

| Key: | Steam | Exhaust |

Action 2   Slide valve

❸

❹

THINKING Critically

1. Drawing Conclusions
How did the steam engine help power the Industrial Revolution?

2. Recognizing Effects
How did Watt's steam engine change the lives of working people?

TERMS & NAMES

Explain the significance of each of the following:

1. Renaissance
2. Leonardo da Vinci
3. Reformation
4. Ferdinand Magellan
5. circumnavigate
6. imperialism
7. Industrial Revolution
8. Napoleon Bonaparte
9. Peter the Great
10. Russian Revolution

REVIEW QUESTIONS

Renaissance Connections *(pages 301–306)*

1. How did the subjects chosen by artists change during the Renaissance?
2. Why were the followers of Martin Luther called Protestants?

Traders, Explorers, and Colonists *(pages 307–311)*

3. Why were spices from Asia so expensive when sold in Europe?
4. What did Portuguese explorers bring back from their expeditions to western Africa?

The Age of Revolutions *(pages 313–317)*

5. When and where did the Industrial Revolution begin?
6. What conditions in France during the 1780s led to the French Revolution?

The Russian Empire *(pages 318–322)*

7. How did Ivan the Terrible earn his nickname?
8. What ideas did Catherine the Great borrow from Western Europe?

CRITICAL THINKING

Finding Causes

1. Using your completed chart from Reading Social Studies, p. 300, list the events that led to the growth of cities during the Industrial Revolution.

Recognizing Effects

2. What were the effects of the Crusades on life in Western Europe?

Analyzing Causes

3. In 19th-century Russia, the lives of poor citizens were very different from those of wealthy citizens. How do you think this division led to political revolution?

Visual Summary

1 Renaissance Connections

- European society was transformed by the art, literature, and ideas of the Renaissance.
- The accomplishments of this period are an important part of Western culture.

2 Traders, Explorers, and Colonists

- People on both sides of the Atlantic were changed by the voyages of the European explorers.
- European exploration led to colonization and to the slave trade.

3 The Age of Revolution

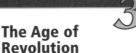

- The Age of Revolution resulted in great changes in European society, industry, and politics.
- These changes were felt around the world.

4 The Russian Empire

- Many citizens of the Russian Empire were deprived of their rights.
- Today, Russia is a large nation experiencing great change.

Use the map and your knowledge of geography to answer questions 1 and 2.

Additional Test Practice, pp. S1–S33

1. Judging from the arrows on the map, how might the plague have spread?

   A. mostly from north to south

   B. through the center of Eastern Europe

   C. along trade routes out of Italy

   D. in a circular pattern

2. According to the map, which body of water did the plague cross as it spread through Europe?

   A. Adriatic Sea

   B. Atlantic Ocean

   C. Black Sea

   D. North Sea

The following passage is from a biography of Leonardo da Vinci. Use the quotation and your knowledge of world cultures and geography to answer question 3.

Although we have called Leonardo a scientist, it is not a title he would have understood. The word "scientist" was not used before 1840. Leonardo did, however, use the word "science." To him it meant knowledge proved true by experience. He contrasted it with "speculation," by which he meant guesswork not proved by experience.

STEWART ROSS, *Leonardo da Vinci*

3. What did Leonardo da Vinci consider the basis of science?

   A. guesses

   B. experience

   C. dedication

   D. speculations

TEST PRACTICE
CLASSZONE.COM

ALTERNATIVE ASSESSMENT

1. WRITING ABOUT HISTORY

Imagine that you are a film maker. Write a proposal for a documentary film about Leonardo da Vinci and one of his inventions. In your proposal, describe the invention, tell how it works, and explain how da Vinci came up with the idea. Remember that the purpose of your documentary is to inform and entertain the viewer.

• Research the Internet or library books about Leonardo da Vinci to find an interesting invention.

• If possible, include a copy of da Vinci's sketch or a photograph of the invention.

2. COOPERATIVE LEARNING

With a group of three or four classmates, research the voyage of Ferdinand Magellan, the first explorer to lead an expedition that sailed around the world. Then prepare a presentation for your class. Group members can share the responsibilities of finding out who funded the trip, what hardships the sailors faced, and what eventually happened to Magellan. One member can create a map of Magellan's route.

INTEGRATED TECHNOLOGY

Doing Internet Research

The Scientific Revolution changed the way people viewed the world. Use the Internet to research one discovery or invention of a great scientist of the time, such as Galileo Galilei.

• Using the Internet, as well as other library resources, find out about the discovery or invention. You might find information in a biography of the scientist.

• Another source of information might be a science museum.

• Create a poster to explain your findings. Include a diagram or other illustration of the scientific discovery. Explain how the discovery or invention has affected life in modern times.

For Internet links to support this activity, go to

RESEARCH LINKS
CLASSZONE.COM

CHAPTER 12

Europe: War and Change

SECTION 1   European Empires

SECTION 2   Europe at War

SECTION 3   The Soviet Union

EUROPE AND THE FORMER SOVIET UNION

PACIFIC OCEAN

PACIFIC OCEAN

ATLANTIC OCEAN

INDIAN OCEAN

N

Place Berlin's Kaiser Wilhelm Memorial Church remains semi-destroyed as a monument to World War II. Germany has since rebuilt its cities. It is once again an important part of Europe's economy, politics, and culture.

Nach Destination / Destination

9 h 10	LONDON-WATERLOO	
9 h 16	LILLE EUROPE CALAIS	
9 h 25	AMIENS AB...	
9 h 34	ORRY CHAN...	
10 19	LONDON-WATERLOO	

FOCUS ON GEOGRAPHY

How has Europe's small landmass affected its history?

Place • The continent of Europe is home to more than 40 countries. Yet, it is approximately the same size as the United States. Since many European nations share borders with several other countries, Europeans often speak three or more languages. Across Europe, approximately 50 languages are spoken.

Europe is densely populated. In fact, the continent has almost three times as many people as the United States. So many people, living so close together, has sometimes led to competition and warfare over land and resources.

What do you think?

♦ How might the differences among Europeans cause conflict?

♦ How might the closeness of so many countries help to unite Europe?

READING SOCIAL STUDIES

BEFORE YOU READ

▶▶ *What Do You Know?*

Do you know that during World War I, armies trained dogs to guard supplies and assist soldiers? What do you know about World War I and World War II? Have you ever seen a movie or read a book about either conflict? What do you hear in the news about current events in Europe? Think about how events in Europe in the past century might have contributed to life there today.

▶▶ *What Do You Want to Know?*

Decide what you know about Europe's history in the 1900s and what it is like there today. In your notebook, record what you hope to learn from this chapter.

Region • The image of the hammer and sickle became the symbol of the Soviet Union. ▲

READ AND TAKE NOTES

Reading Strategy: Analyzing Causes and Effects
Analyzing causes and effects is an essential skill for understanding what you read in social studies, because events are caused by other events or situations. This sequence is called a chain of events. Understanding which causes lead to which events is essential in understanding history and other areas of social studies. Use the chart below to show causes and effects discussed in Chapter 12.

- Copy the chart into your notebook.
- As you read, record causes and effects for each event.

Region • During World War I, armies trained dogs to assist them. ▲

Causes	Event	Effects
	World War I	
	World War II	
	Growth of Soviet Union	

European Empires

TERMS & NAMES
nationalism
colonialism
Austria-Hungary
dual monarchy

MAIN IDEA

The beginning of the 20th century was a time of change in Europe, as feelings of nationalism began to take hold.

WHY IT MATTERS NOW

Feelings of nationalism continue to lead to conflicts that change the map of Europe.

DATELINE

NORWAY, SEPTEMBER 1905

It could have been war in the Scandinavian Peninsula. The armies of Norway and Sweden had begun preparations.

Instead, Sweden ended the crisis peacefully by granting Norway independence. Norway had been under Swedish control since 1814. Although Norway ran its own affairs within the country, Sweden set foreign policy and controlled Norway's international shipping and trade.

Prince Charles of Denmark has been invited to become king of Norway. The Norwegians will vote to approve their new leader. If chosen, he will become King Haakon VII.

The king's role will be largely ceremonial. His chief task will be to help unite the newly independent people of Norway.

Region • Prince Charles of Denmark, pictured here with his family, hopes to become King Haakon VII of Norway.

The Spread of Nationalism

Norway's independence from Sweden was a sign of new ideas that were sweeping across Europe at the time. During the late 19th and early 20th centuries, **nationalism,** or strong pride in one's nation or ethnic group, influenced the feelings of many Europeans. An ethnic group includes people with similar languages and traditions, but who are not necessarily ruled by a common government.

TAKING NOTES

Use your chart to take notes about war and change in Europe.

Causes	Event	Effects
	World War I	
	World War II	

Constitutional Monarchies In part, the spread of nationalism was fueled by the fact that more Europeans than ever before could vote. For centuries, many monarchs had unlimited power. In country after country, however, citizens demanded the right to elect lawmakers who would limit their monarch's authority. This kind of government is called a constitutional monarchy. A constitutional monarchy not only has a king or queen, but also a ruling body of elected officials. The United Kingdom is one example of a constitutional monarchy.

Reading Social Studies

A. Contrasting How does a constitutional monarchy differ from a democracy?

By 1900, many countries in Western Europe had become constitutional monarchies. Citizens of these countries strongly supported the governments that they helped to elect. When one country threatened another, most citizens were willing to go to war to defend their homeland.

The Defense of Colonial Empires At the beginning of the 20th century, many Western European countries—including France, Italy, the United Kingdom, Germany, and even tiny Belgium—had colonies in Asia and Africa. Colonies supplied the raw materials that the ruling countries needed to produce goods in their factories back home. Asian and African colonies, sometimes larger than the ruling country, were also important markets for manufactured goods.

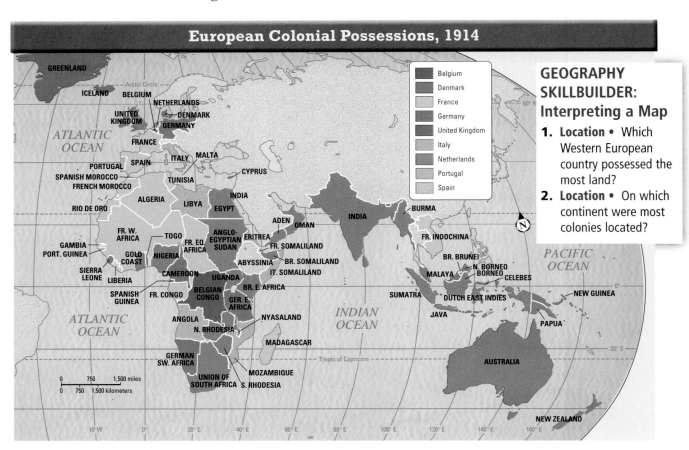

European Colonial Possessions, 1914

Legend:
- Belgium
- Denmark
- France
- Germany
- United Kingdom
- Italy
- Netherlands
- Portugal
- Spain

GEOGRAPHY SKILLBUILDER: Interpreting a Map

1. **Location** • Which Western European country possessed the most land?
2. **Location** • On which continent were most colonies located?

Location • In 1914, the United Kingdom could truthfully state that the sun never set on the British Empire. ◀

During this period of **colonialism,** Western European nations spent much of their wealth on building strong armies and navies. Their military forces helped to defend borders at home as well as colonies in other parts of the world. Colonies were so important that the ruling countries sometimes fought one another for control of them. They also struggled to extend their territories.

Spotlight on CULTURE

The Ballets Russes Begun in Paris, France, in 1909, the Ballets Russes (ba•LAY ROOS) was a dance company under the direction of the Russian producer Sergey Diaghilev (dee•AH•guh•LEHF). It was a critical and commercial success, and it spread artistic ideas.

Talented dancers and choreographers, such as Nijinsky, worked for Diaghilev. Famous composers—including Claude Debussy (duh•BYOO•see) and Igor Stravinsky—wrote music for performances. Pablo Picasso, Marc Chagall, and other great artists designed the sets. The Ballets Russes continued until Diaghilev's death in 1929.

THINKING CRITICALLY
1. Synthesizing
How did the Ballets Russes benefit the European art and theater communities?

2. Clarifying
How was the Ballets Russes more than a collection of dancers, musicians, and artists?

For more on the Ballets Russes, go to

RESEARCH LINKS
CLASSZONE.COM

Austria-Hungary, 1900

GEOGRAPHY SKILLBUILDER: Interpreting a Map

1. **Location** • Name three countries that bordered Austria-Hungary.
2. **Region** • What was the capital of Austria-Hungary?

Austria-Hungary By the end of the 19th century, most nations of Western and Northern Europe had become industrialized. The majority of Eastern Europe, including Russia, remained agricultural. These Eastern European countries imported most of their manufactured goods from Western and Northern Europe.

The largest empire in Eastern Europe in 1900 was **Austria-Hungary.** The empire was a **dual monarchy**, in which one ruler governs two nations. As you can see in the map above, Austria-Hungary also included parts of many other present-day countries, including Romania, the Czech Republic, and portions of Poland.

Reading **Social Studies**

B. Making Inferences Why do you think governing a dual monarchy was difficult?

SECTION 1 ASSESSMENT

Terms & Names

1. **Explain the significance of:**
   (a) nationalism
   (b) colonialism
   (c) Austria-Hungary
   (d) dual monarchy

Using Graphics

2. Look at the map on page 330 that shows European colonial territories. Use a chart like the one below to list the major colonial powers and their colonies.

Nation	Locations of Colonies

Main Ideas

3. (a) Identify one reason for the spread of nationalism in Europe.

   (b) Why did Western European nations spend much of their wealth on armies and navies?

   (c) How did the nations of Eastern Europe differ from those of Western and Northern Europe at the end of the 19th century?

Critical Thinking

4. **Drawing Conclusions**

   Why were their colonies so important to European nations?

   Think About
   - land and people
   - competition among nations
   - the production and sale of goods

ACTIVITY -OPTION- Reread the information about the Ballets Russes. Write an **outline** of a story or book that might be a good choice for a ballet. Explain your choice.

Europe at War

TERMS & NAMES
World War I
alliance
Adolf Hitler
fascism
Holocaust
World War II
NATO

MAIN IDEA

During the first half of the 20th century, European countries fought each other over land, wealth, and ideals.

WHY IT MATTERS NOW

The changes brought about by the two world wars continue to affect Europe today.

DATELINE

SARAJEVO, BOSNIA-HERZEGOVINA, JUNE 28, 1914—Today, Archduke of Austria-Hungary Franz Ferdinand and his wife, Duchess Sophie, were murdered as they drove through Sarajevo. A nineteen-year-old Serb, Gavrilo Princip, jumped on the Archduke's automobile and fired two shots. The first killed the Duchess. The second killed the Archduke, who was next in line to be emperor of Austria-Hungary.

The Serbians have protested against Austria-Hungary since 1908, when the empire took over Bosnia and Herzegovina (BAHZ•nee•uh HEHRT•suh•GOH•VEE•nuh). Princip has been arrested.

Region • Archduke Franz Ferdinand and his wife, Duchess Sophie, were fatally shot in Sarajevo. ▲

The World at War

Because of the murder of Archduke Franz Ferdinand in 1914, the emperor of Austria-Hungary declared war on Serbia. When Russia sent troops to defend Serbia, Germany declared war on Russia. Russia supported Serbia because both Russians and Serbians share a similar ethnic background—they are both Slavic peoples. This was the beginning of **World War I**.

TAKING NOTES
Use your chart to take notes about war and change in Europe.

Causes	Event	Effects
	World War I	
	World War II	

World War I Alliances (1914–1918)

THE CENTRAL POWERS	THE ALLIES
Austria-Hungary	Russia (dropped out in 1917)
Germany	France
Turkey (Ottoman Empire)	United Kingdom
Bulgaria	Italy (joined 1915)
	United States (joined 1917)

Place • World War I was primarily fought in trenches, which were dug by the armies for better defense. ▲

World War I Alliances European rulers wanted other leaders to think twice before declaring war on their countries. To help defend themselves, several countries joined alliances (uh·LY·uhn·sez). An **alliance** is an agreement among people or nations to unite for a common cause. Each member of an alliance agrees to help the other members in case one of them is attacked.

When Germany joined the war to support Austria-Hungary, France came in on the side of Russia. Germany then invaded Belgium, which was neutral, to attack France. Because Great Britain had promised to protect Belgium, it, too, declared war on Germany. After German submarines sank four American merchant ships, the United States joined the side of Russia, France, and Great Britain.

The chart above shows the major powers on both sides of World War I. Italy had originally been allied with Germany and Austria-Hungary but joined the Allies after the war began. Russia dropped out of the war completely after the revolution in that country in 1917.

SKILLBUILDER:
Interpreting a Political Cartoon
1. What does the artist mean by naming the figure "Progress"?
2. Why is the man wearing a gas mask?

Reading
Social Studies

A. Recognizing Important Details Why did Great Britain enter World War I?

World War I was costly in terms of human life. When it was over, nearly 22 million civilians and soldiers on both sides were dead. The Allies had won, and Europe had been devastated.

Europe After World War I

More people were killed during World War I than during all the wars of the 19th century combined. Afterward, people in many countries on both sides of the costly war—and even those not directly involved—were poor, homeless, and without work.

The Allies blamed Germany for much of the killing and damage during the war. In 1919, Germany and the Allies signed the Treaty of Versailles (vuhr·SY).

Strange but TRUE

War Dogs During World War I, dogs were trained to guard ammunition, to detect mines, and to carry messages. Dogs even helped to search for the wounded.

War dogs saved many lives. They were especially helpful in forested areas and at night. These dogs are wearing protective masks to keep them safe from poison gas attacks.

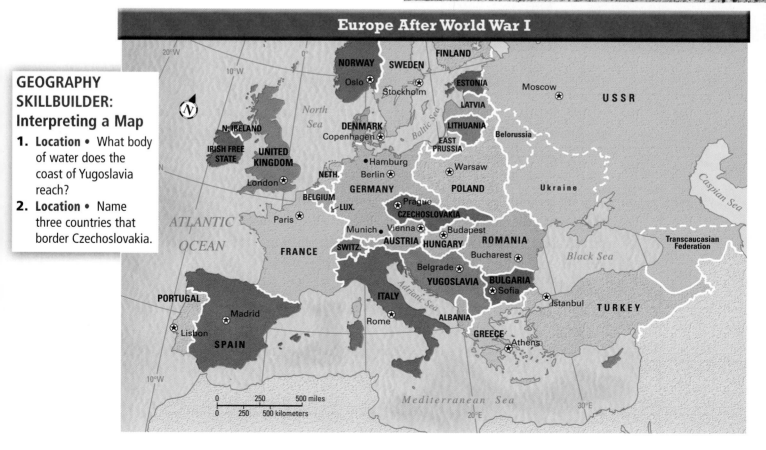

Europe After World War I

GEOGRAPHY SKILLBUILDER: Interpreting a Map

1. **Location** • What body of water does the coast of Yugoslavia reach?
2. **Location** • Name three countries that border Czechoslovakia.

The Treaty of Versailles demanded that Germany be punished by being forced to pay for the damage done to the Allied countries. Germany was also made to give up valuable territory.

A New Map of Europe Additional treaties during the following year also altered the political boundaries of many European countries. As the map on page 335 shows, Austria-Hungary was divided as a result of the war, becoming two separate countries. This allowed several Eastern European ethnic groups that had been part of Austria-Hungary to gain their independence.

World War II

By the 1930s, Germany was still paying for the damage done to the Allied countries during World War I. The German economy was in ruins, and the Germans greatly wished to rebuild their own country. In 1933, citizens elected **Adolf Hitler** and the National Socialist, or Nazi, Party. The Nazi Party believed in fascism. **Fascism** (FASH·IHZ·uhm) is a philosophy that supports a strong, central government controlled by the military and led by a powerful dictator. People believed that this new leader would help Germany recover.

World War II Alliances (1939–1945)

THE AXIS POWERS
Germany
Italy
Japan

THE ALLIES
United Kingdom
France
(until June 1940)
Soviet Union
(formerly "Russia")
United States
(joined in 1941)

Reading
Social Studies

B. Finding Causes
What conditions led Germans to find hope in Adolf Hitler?

BACKGROUND
Like Germany, Italy was also ruled by a fascist dictator after World War I: Benito Mussolini (1883–1945).

Hitler and the Nazi Party Fascists practiced an extreme form of patriotism and nationalism. Fascists also had racist beliefs.

In the 1930s, Hitler unjustly blamed the Jewish citizens of Germany, among other specific groups, for the country's problems. His Nazi followers seized Jewish property and began to send Jews, along with disabled people, political opponents, and others, to concentration camps. During this **Holocaust,** millions of people were deliberately killed, and others starved or died from disease.

In 1934, Hitler took command of the armed forces. Then, in 1939, Hitler's army invaded Poland. **World War II** had begun. By June 1940, Hitler's army had swept through Western Europe, conquering Belgium, the Netherlands, Luxembourg, France, Denmark, and Norway. A year later, Germany invaded the Soviet Union.

WWII Alliances The chart on page 336 shows the major powers on both sides of World War II. As in World War I, the United States at first tried to stay out of the conflict but entered the war after Japan bombed U.S. military bases at Pearl Harbor in Hawaii on December 7, 1941.

Europe After World War II

World War II turned much of Europe into a battleground. By the end of the war, the United States, France, and the United Kingdom occupied Western Europe. The Soviet Union occupied Eastern Europe, including the eastern part of Germany.

Once peace was established, the western allies helped to set up free governments in Western Europe. In 1949, the countries of Western Europe joined Canada and the United States to form a defense alliance called **NATO** (NAY·toh). The members of this alliance, whose name stands for North Atlantic Treaty Organization, agreed to defend one another if they were attacked by the Soviet Union or any other country. Without a common enemy, political differences quickly separated the Soviet Union from Western Europe and the United States.

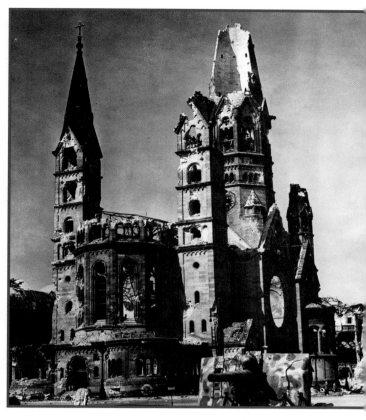

Place • The Kaiser Wilhelm Memorial Church in Berlin was nearly destroyed by Allied bombs. The ruins still stand today as a World War II monument. See pages 326–327. ▲

Biography

Anne Frank In July 1942, during World War II, Anne Frank and her family went into hiding in Amsterdam—a city in the Netherlands. The Frank family were Jewish and were afraid they would be sent to a concentration camp. Anne was only thirteen.

For two years, Anne, her father, mother, sister, and four other people lived in rooms in an attic. Their rooms were sealed off from the rest of the building. While in hiding, Anne kept a diary. Although the family was discovered and Anne died in a concentration camp, her diary was eventually published. Today, this famous book—translated into many languages and the basis for a play and a film—lives on.

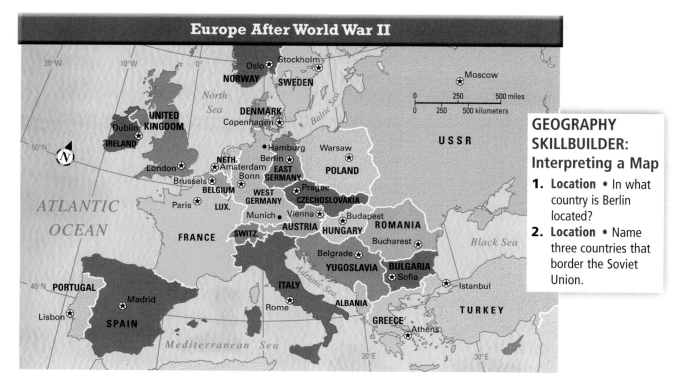

Europe After World War II

GEOGRAPHY SKILLBUILDER:
Interpreting a Map
1. **Location** • In what country is Berlin located?
2. **Location** • Name three countries that border the Soviet Union.

The Marshall Plan United States Secretary of State George C. Marshall created the Economic Cooperation Act of 1948, also known as the Marshall Plan. This plan provided U.S. aid—agricultural, industrial, and financial—to countries of Western Europe. The Marshall Plan greatly benefited war-torn Europe. It may also have prevented economic depression or political instability.

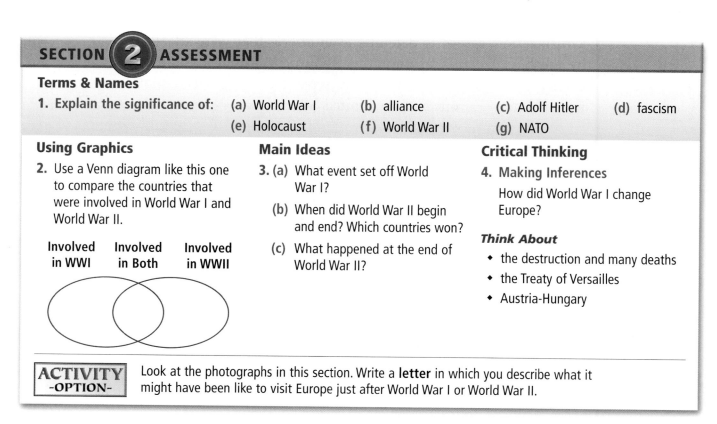

SECTION 2 ASSESSMENT

Terms & Names
1. **Explain the significance of:**
   (a) World War I   (b) alliance   (c) Adolf Hitler   (d) fascism
   (e) Holocaust   (f) World War II   (g) NATO

Using Graphics
2. Use a Venn diagram like this one to compare the countries that were involved in World War I and World War II.

Involved in WWI   Involved in Both   Involved in WWII

Main Ideas
3. (a) What event set off World War I?
   (b) When did World War II begin and end? Which countries won?
   (c) What happened at the end of World War II?

Critical Thinking
4. **Making Inferences**
   How did World War I change Europe?

Think About
 • the destruction and many deaths
 • the Treaty of Versailles
 • Austria-Hungary

ACTIVITY -OPTION- Look at the photographs in this section. Write a **letter** in which you describe what it might have been like to visit Europe just after World War I or World War II.

Reading a Political Cartoon

▶▶ Defining the Skill

Political cartoons—also known as editorial cartoons—express an opinion about a serious subject. A political cartoonist uses symbols, familiar objects, and people to make his or her point quickly and visually. Sometimes the caption and words in the cartoon help to clarify the meaning. Although a cartoonist may use humor to make a point, political cartoons are not always funny.

▶▶ Applying the Skill

This political cartoon was created in the period between World War I and World War II. However, Europeans were already concerned about developments in Germany.

How to Read a Political Cartoon

Strategy ❶ Read the cartoon's title and any other words. For example, some cartoons have labels, captions, and thought balloons. Then study the cartoon as a whole.

Strategy ❷ If the cartoon has people in it, are they famous? Sometimes the cartoonist wants to comment on a famous person, such as a world leader. Look for symbols or details in the cartoon. For example, in this cartoon a German soldier is climbing out of the Versailles Treaty. Think about the relationships between the words and the images.

Strategy ❸ Summarize the cartoonist's message. What is the cartoonist's point of view about the subject? What does this cartoonist think was the cause of Hitler's rise to power?

❶ THE SOURCE

Make a Chart

A chart can help you to analyze the information in a political cartoon. Once you understand the cartoon's elements, you can summarize its meaning. Use a chart such as this one to help you organize the information.

Important Words	Hitler Party; Versailles Treaty
Important Symbols/Images	German soldier with "Hitler Party" on his helmet crawling out of the Versailles Treaty that officially ended World War I.
Summary ❸	The terms of the Versailles Treaty led to the rise of Hitler's party in Germany; Hitler's party, symbolized by a soldier, is war-like and threatens Europe.

▶▶ Practicing the Skill

Study the political cartoon in Chapter 12, Section 2, on page 334. Make a chart similar to the one above in which you list the important parts of the cartoon and write a summary of the cartoon's message.

Fionn Mac Cumhail
and the
Giant's Causeway [1]

FIONN MAC CUMHAIL, more commonly known as Finn MacCool, is a familiar figure in Irish folk tales. He first appears in the ancient Celtic tales known as the Fenian cycle. In the following story, retold by Una Leavy, Fionn is portrayed as a clever giant, hard at work with the Fianna, his band of Irish warriors. They begin to build a bridge from Ireland to Scotland, because, as the boastful Fionn says, "There are giants over there that I'm longing to conquer." Plans suddenly change, however, and Fionn must go home.

1. The Giant's Causeway, which takes its name from this legend, is a striking natural rock formation on the coast of Ireland.

2. The region of Ireland where Fionn and the Fianna are building their bridge to Scotland. It is the location of the actual Giant's Causeway.

Fionn Mac Cumhail and the Fianna worked quickly on the bridge, splitting stones into splendid pillars and columns. Further and further they stretched out into the ocean. From time to time, there came a distant rumble. "Is it thunder?" asked the Fianna, but they went on working. Then one of their spies came ashore. "I've just been to Scotland!" he said. "There's a huge giant there called Fathach Mór. He's doing long jumps—you can hear the thumping. He has a magic little finger with the strength of ten men! He's in training for the long jump to Antrim." [2]

Fionn's face paled. "The strength of ten men!" he thought. "I'll never fight him. He'll squash me into a pancake." But he could not admit that he was nervous, so he said to the Fianna, "I've just had a message from Bláithín, my wife. I must go home at once—you can all take a holiday."

He set off by himself and never did a man travel faster. Bláithín was surprised to see him. "And is the great causeway finished already?" she asked.

"No indeed," replied Fionn.

"What's the matter?" Bláithín asked. So Fionn told her.

"What will I do, Bláithín?" he asked. "There's the strength of ten men in his magic little finger. He'll squish me into a jelly!"

Bláithín laughed. "Just leave him to me. Stoke up the fire and fetch me the sack of flour. Then go outside and find nine flat stones." Fionn did as he was told. Bláithín worked all night making ten oatcakes. In each she put a large flat stone, all except the last. This one she marked with her thumbprint. "Go and cut down some wood," she said. "You must make an enormous cradle."

Fionn worked all morning. The cradle was just finished when there was a mighty rumble and the dishes shook.

"It's him," squealed Fionn.

"Don't worry!" said Bláithín. "Put on this bonnet. Now into the cradle and leave me to do the talking."

"Does Fionn Mac Cumhail live here?" boomed a great voice above her.

"He does," said Bláithín, "though he's away at the moment. He's gone to capture the giant, Fathach Mór."

"I'm Fathach Mór!" bellowed the giant. "I've been searching for Fionn everywhere."

"Did you ever see Fionn?" she asked. "Sure you're only a baby compared with him. He'll be home shortly and you can see for yourself. But now that you're here, would you do me a favor? The well has run dry and Fionn was supposed to lift up the mountain this morning. There's spring water underneath it. Do you think you could get me some?"

"Of course," shouted the giant as he scooped out a hole in the mountain, the size of a crater.

Fionn shook with fear in the cradle and even Bláithín turned pale. But she thanked the giant and invited him in. "Though you and Fionn are enemies, you are still a guest," she said. "Have some fresh bread." And she put the oatcakes before him. Fathach Mór began to eat. Almost at once he gave a piercing yell and spat out two teeth.

"What kind of bread is this?" he screeched. "I've broken my teeth on it."

"How can you say such a thing?" asked Bláithín. "Even the child in the cradle eats them!" And she gave Fionn the cake with the thumbprint. Fathach looked at the cradle. "Whose child is that?" he asked in wonder.

"That's Fionn's son," said Bláithín.

"And how old is he?" he asked then.

"Just ten months," replied Bláithín.

"Can he talk?" asked the giant.

"Not yet, but you should hear him roar!" At once, Fionn began to yell.

"Quick, quick," cried Bláithín. "Let him suck your little finger. If Fionn comes home and hears him, he'll be in such a temper. With an anxious glance at the door, the giant gave Fionn his finger. Fionn bit off the giant's magic little finger. Screeching, the giant bolted from the house. Fionn leaped from the cradle in bib and bonnet and danced his Bláithín round the kitchen.

Reading
THE LITERATURE

Before reading this story, how did you expect Fionn Mac Cumhail to act? Did you expect him to be the hero of the story? Who is? How does the character solve the problem in the story? What skills are used to solve it?

Thinking About
THE LITERATURE

In many European myths and legends, the heroes are powerful and fearless. How does Fionn act in this story? What words does the author use to make clear Fionn's attitude toward the danger he faces? How does he differ from other legendary figures that you have read about?

Writing About
THE LITERATURE

Often, myths are created in order to answer questions about or explain mysteries in the world. This legend explains why the causeway was never finished. How might the story about Fionn be different if the causeway had been finished?

About the Author

Una Leavy, the author of *Irish Fairy Tales & Legends,* is an Irish writer who lives with her husband and children in County Mayo, Ireland.

Further Reading *The Names upon the Harp* by Marie Heaney recounts myths and legends of early Irish literature, including the stories about Fionn Mac Cumhail that make up the Fenian cycle.

The Soviet Union

TERMS & NAMES
Iron Curtain
puppet government
one-party system
Joseph Stalin
collective farm
Warsaw Pact
Cold War

MAIN IDEA	WHY IT MATTERS NOW
After World War II, the Soviet Union was the most powerful country in Europe, but life for most Soviet citizens was difficult.	Russia, the former Soviet Union, remains powerful and is currently experiencing great change.

DATELINE — EXTRA

WARSAW, POLAND, MAY 14, 1955

Today, the Soviet Union and most Eastern European countries announced that they have signed the Warsaw Treaty of Friendship, Cooperation, and Mutual Assistance. The members of this alliance agree to offer military defense to one another for a period of 20 years.

Yugoslavia is the only country in Eastern Europe that did not sign the agreement.

The new treaty, also called the Warsaw Pact, allows the Soviet Union to keep troops in the countries that are located between the Soviet Union and Western Europe. The Warsaw Pact is a response to the formation of NATO, an alliance that Western European countries joined six years ago.

Region • Warsaw hosted Eastern European officials who signed a military alliance here in the Palace of Culture. ▲

East Against West

After World War II, political differences divided the Soviet-controlled countries of Eastern Europe from those of Western Europe. These differences gave rise to an invisible wall known as the **Iron Curtain.** While there was no actual curtain, people of the East were restricted from traveling outside of their countries. Westerners who wished to visit the East also faced restrictions.

TAKING NOTES
Use your chart to take notes about war and change in Europe.

Causes	Event	Effects
	World War I	
	World War II	

The Strongest Nation in Europe The Union of Soviet Socialist Republics, or USSR, was the official name of the Soviet Union. It included 15 republics, of which Russia was the largest. The Soviet Union entered World War II in 1941, when Germany invaded its borders. German troops destroyed much of the western Soviet Union and killed millions of people. This invasion brought the Soviet Union close to collapse. However, with the defeat of Germany, the Soviet Union rose to become the strongest nation in Europe.

Region •
The hammer and sickle became the symbol of Soviet Communism. The tools represent the unity of the peasants (sickle) with the workers (hammer). ▲

Communism After World War II, the Soviet Union established Communist governments in Eastern Europe. The Soviets made sure—either by politics or by force—that these new Eastern European governments were loyal to the Soviet Union.

Soviet Control of Eastern Europe The Soviet Union controlled the countries of Eastern Europe through puppet governments. A **puppet government** is one that does what it is told by an outside force. In this case, the Eastern European governments followed orders from Soviet leaders in Moscow.

Most Eastern Europeans did have the chance to vote, but they had only one political party to choose from: the Communist Party. All other parties were outlawed. This meant that there was only one candidate to choose from for each government position. This is an example of a **one-party system.** Soviet citizens could not complain about the government. In fact, they could be jailed for expressing any view that the Soviet leaders did not like.

Reading
Social Studies

A. Making Inferences
How do you think the Soviet Union enforced a one-party system in Eastern Europe?

Movement • The government-controlled factories in the Soviet Union did not produce enough of certain items. When goods that were often in short supply—such as bread and shoes—finally became available, people had to wait in long lines to buy them. ◄

Joseph Stalin

Region • Joseph Stalin ruled the Soviet Union from 1928 to 1953. ▲

Joseph Stalin (STAH·lihn) (1879–1953) ruled the Soviet Union during World War II. Stalin took power after the death of Vladimir Lenin. Lenin was a Communist leader who had helped overthrow the czar and ruled the Soviet Union from 1917 until his death in 1924. The name Stalin is related to the Russian word for "steel." Stalin was greatly feared, and his rule was indeed as tough as steel. He controlled the government until his death.

The Five-Year Plans Under Stalin, the government controlled every aspect of Soviet life. Stalin hoped to strengthen the country with his five-year plans, which were sets of economic goals. For example, Stalin ordered many new factories to be built. The Soviet government decided where and what types of factories to build, how many goods to produce, and how to distribute them. These decisions were based on the Communist theory that this would benefit the most people.

Region • The Soviet government managed the factories while citizens provided the actual labor. ◀

ARCTIC OCEAN

FINLAND
SWEDEN
NORWAY
60°N
North Sea
W. GERMANY   DEN.
UNITED KINGDOM   E. GERMANY
IRELAND   NETH.   POLAND
BELG.
CZECH.
FRANCE   AUS. HUNG.
SWITZ.
YUGO.   ROMANIA
PORTUGAL
ITALY   BULG.   Black Sea
ALB.
SPAIN
GREECE   TURKEY
Mediterranean Sea
Baltic Sea

AFRICA

GEOGRAPHY SKILLBUILDER: Interpreting a Map

1. **Region** • Which countries were behind the Iron Curtain but not in the Soviet Union?
2. **Location** • What was the westernmost country in the Warsaw Pact?

The Iron Curtain and the Warsaw Pact Nations, 1955

INTERACTIVE

ARCTIC OCEAN

N

SIBERIA

Lena R.

Yenisey R.

UNION OF SOVIET SOCIALIST REPUBLICS

Ob R.

Volga R.

Caspian Sea

PACIFIC OCEAN

ASIA

ARABIA

| 0 | | 1,000 | | 2,000 miles |
| 0 | 1,000 | | 2,000 kilometers | |

Legend:
- Soviet Union
- Warsaw Pact members
- Western European Nations
- Iron Curtain

140°E

Soviet Agriculture Stalin also hoped to strengthen the Soviet Union by controlling the country's agriculture. During the 1930s, peasants were forced to move to collective farms. A **collective farm** was government-owned and employed large numbers of workers. All the crops produced by the collective farms were distributed by the government. Sometimes farm workers did not receive enough food to feed themselves and their families.

Region • Similar to urban factory workers, Russian peasants labored on government-controlled collective farms. ▼

The Secret Police Stalin used his secret police to get rid of citizens he did not trust. The secret police arrested those who did not support the Soviet government. Suspects were transported to slave-labor camps in Siberia. Millions of men and women were sent to this remote and bitterly cold region of northeastern Russia. Many never returned home.

The Cold War

From 1941 to 1945, the United Kingdom, the United States, and the Soviet Union shared a goal: to defeat the Axis Powers. They became allies to make that happen. Once the war ended, however, these countries no longer had a common enemy—and had little reason to work together. Most Western European countries were constitutional monarchies or democracies, and most Eastern European countries had Communist, largely Soviet-controlled, governments.

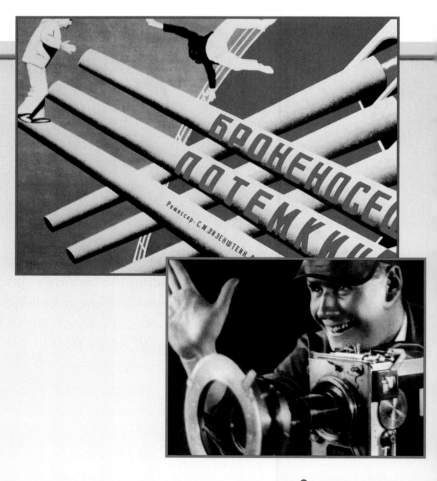

Soviet Film The Russian director Sergey Eisenstein (EYE•zen•stine) (1898–1948), bottom right, made only six movies, but they are among the most important works in film history. The silent film *Battleship Potemkin* (1925), whose poster is to the right, is one of Eisenstein's most famous. It is about a mutiny at sea. The director's use of close-ups and his method of combining short scenes changed the way films were made all over the world.

Just before the start of World War II, Eisenstein made the film *Alexander Nevsky* (1938). It tells the story of a historic battle that the Russians won against German-speaking invaders in the 1200s. This film became very popular during World War II, which it seemed to foreshadow.

THINKING CRITICALLY

1. Clarifying
What influenced Eisenstein to direct war films?

2. Synthesizing
What did Eisenstein want to show about the relationship between Russians and Germans?

For more on Sergey Eisenstein, go to

RESEARCH LINKS
CLASSZONE.COM

Region • The Brandenburg Gate was a part of the Berlin Wall that separated East Berlin from West Berlin. ◄

The members of NATO and the nations in the **Warsaw Pact**—the alliance of Eastern European countries behind the Iron Curtain—refused to trade or cooperate with each other. The countries never actually fought, so this period of political noncooperation is called the **Cold War.** Both sides in the Cold War were hesitant to start a war that would involve the use of newly developed nuclear weapons, which could cause destruction on a global scale.

Reading
Social Studies

B. Comparing
Compare the Soviet Union's fears in the Cold War with those of the United States and Western Europe.

The United States and Western Europe feared that the Soviet Union would influence other countries to become Communist. At the same time, the Soviet Union wanted to protect itself against invasion. This led the countries on either side of the Iron Curtain to view and treat each other as possible threats. The tense international situation caused by the Cold War would continue for almost 40 years.

SECTION 3 ASSESSMENT

Terms & Names

1. Explain the significance of:
   (a) Iron Curtain (b) puppet government (c) one-party system (d) Joseph Stalin
   (e) collective farm (f) Warsaw Pact (g) Cold War

Using Graphics

2. Use a chart like this one to describe three elements of Joseph Stalin's rule of the Soviet Union.

Five-Year Plans	Agriculture	Secret Police

Main Ideas

3. (a) What happened to the Soviet Union during World War II?

   (b) How did the governments of most Western and Eastern European countries differ?

   (c) How did Joseph Stalin rule the Soviet Union?

Critical Thinking

4. **Analyzing Motives**

   Why do you think the Soviet Union wanted to control the countries of Eastern Europe?

   Think About
   • the events of World War II
   • the location of the Eastern European countries
   • the governments of the Soviet Union and Western Europe

ACTIVITY -OPTION- Reread the information about the secret police. Write a dramatic **scene** in which the main character is sent to a labor camp in Siberia.

TERMS & NAMES

Explain the significance of each of the following:

1. nationalism
2. colonialism
3. World War I
4. alliance
5. World War II
6. NATO
7. Adolf Hitler
8. Warsaw Pact
9. Iron Curtain
10. Cold War

REVIEW QUESTIONS

European Empires *(pages 329–332)*

1. What was the largest empire in Eastern Europe in 1900?
2. What is one reason why European nations built up their military?

Europe at War *(pages 333–338)*

3. Why did European countries join alliances?
4. What did the Treaty of Versailles require Germany to do?
5. What country did Germany invade to begin World War II?

The Soviet Union *(pages 342–347)*

6. Why did most Eastern European voters have only one political party to choose from?
7. How did the Iron Curtain affect the lives of Eastern Europeans?
8. Why were both sides in the Cold War hesitant to start a war?

CRITICAL THINKING

Identifying Problems

1. Using your completed chart from Reading Social Studies, p. 328, list some of the causes and effects of World Wars I and II.

Making Inferences

2. Why might a citizen who has helped elect a government be more willing to fight to defend it?

Hypothesizing

3. How do you think Soviet peasants felt about collective farms? Why?

Visual Summary

European Empires

- In early-20th-century Europe, feelings of nationalism arose.
- Western European nations ruled colonial empires.

1

2

Europe at War

- Due to a complex set of alliances, most of Europe was drawn into World War I.
- The Treaty of Versailles set the stage for an even more widespread conflict—World War II.

The Soviet Union

3

- After World War II, the Soviet Union was very powerful.
- However, life was difficult for many Soviet citizens.

Use the map and your knowledge of geography to answer questions 1 and 2.

Additional Test Practice, pp. S1–S33

1. Which areas of Europe are the least densely populated?

A. The area just south of the North Sea

B. Areas on the Atlantic Coast

C. Areas along the Mediterranean Sea

D. Areas near the Arctic Circle

2. Judging from this map, why do you think some areas are more densely populated than others?

A. Many people tend to move to mountainous regions.

B. Many people tend to settle in cities near coasts or rivers.

C. Many people tend to avoid living on peninsulas.

D. Many people like to live on islands because of the fishing.

The excerpt is from a famous speech that Winston Churchill gave during the Cold War. Use the quotation and your knowledge of world cultures and geography to answer question 3.

PRIMARY SOURCE

From Stettin in the Baltic to Trieste in the Adriatic, an iron curtain has descended across the Continent. Behind that line lie all the capitals of the ancient states of Central and Eastern Europe. . . . All these famous cities and the populations around them lie in what I might call the Soviet sphere, and all are subject, in one form or another, not only to Soviet influence but to a very high and in some cases increasing measure of control from Moscow.

WINSTON CHURCHILL,
"Iron Curtain" speech, Fulton, Missouri

3. According to the passage, what threat did the iron curtain provide?

A. The Communist Soviet Union controlled the region behind the iron curtain.

B. Famine and disease threatened countries in Central and Eastern Europe.

C. Hitler and his forces wanted to reconquer the region behind the iron curtain.

D. A barrier prevented people from visiting the cities of Central and Eastern Europe

TEST PRACTICE
CLASSZONE.COM

ALTERNATIVE ASSESSMENT

1. 📝 **WRITING ABOUT HISTORY**

Imagine that you are a government official from a European nation living in one of the nation's colonies in Asia or Africa. Write a letter to your family telling them what life in the colony is like in the year 1900.

• Use the Internet or the library to research one of the European colonies in Asia or Africa.

• In your letter, identify the colony and describe its location. Include information about the colony's climate, geography, culture, and people. Describe your country's plans for the colony.

2. COOPERATIVE LEARNING

With a small group, design a monument to commemorate an event in 20th-century Europe, such as a particular battle from World War I, the Holocaust, or World War II. Share the responsibilities of researching the event, designing the monument, and presenting it to your class. In your presentation, provide some background information and suggest a permanent location for your monument.

INTEGRATED/TECHNOLOGY

Doing Internet Research

Countries such as Switzerland and Sweden were not directly involved in World War I or World War II. Use the Internet to research one of the neutral countries and include your findings in a report.

• Use the Internet and other library resources to identify a country that wasn't directly involved in the wars.

• Another source of information might be a historical museum or archive.

• Look for information about the country's government and economy in the first half of the 20th century, how the country was affected by the wars, and what life was like for its citizens.

For Internet links to support this activity, go to

RESEARCH LINKS
CLASSZONE.COM

CHAPTER 13

Modern Europe

ATLANTIC OCEAN

PACIFIC OCEAN

PACIFIC OCEAN

OCEAN

INDIAN OCEAN

EUROPE AND RUSSIA

Movement High-speed trains, like this one in France, make travel in Europe very convenient.

FOCUS ON **GEOGRAPHY**

How are the new republics of Eastern Europe using natural resources to build their economies?

Human-Environment Interaction • Natural resources are often an important part of a nation's economy. When the Soviet Union broke up in 1991, the newly independent nations of Eastern Europe chose to develop market economies.

In Ukraine, which is rich in coal and iron, mining and manufacturing are major industries. (Ukraine once had vast petroleum and natural gas resources, but heavy production used up much of them.) Estonia, Latvia, and Lithuania have large forests and good farmland. Estonia is also rich in oil shale, which it uses to make electricity.

What do you think?

♦ How do natural resources affect the types of goods a country produces?

♦ Why is it important for countries to use natural resources carefully?

TGV

BEFORE YOU READ

▶▶ *What Do You Know?*

Before you read the chapter, think about what you already know about Europe. Do you have family, friends, or neighbors who were born in Europe? Have you read books, such as the Harry Potter series, that take place in Europe? Think about what you have seen or heard about Italy, England, France, or Germany in the news, during sporting events, and in your other classes.

▶▶ *What Do You Want to Know?*

Decide what you know about Europe today. Then, in your notebook, record what you hope to learn from this chapter.

Region • Euros are the most visible symbol of economic unity in Europe. ▲

READ AND TAKE NOTES

Reading Strategy: Comparing Comparing is a useful strategy for understanding how events change societies. As you read this chapter, compare Eastern Europe under Communism with Eastern Europe after Communism. Use the chart below to take notes.

- Copy the chart into your notebook.
- As you read, notice how government, economics, and culture differ under the old and new systems.
- After you read each section, record key ideas on your chart.

Place • Some Christians in Ukraine dye Easter eggs brilliant colors. ▲

Aspect	Under Communism	After Communism
Government		
Economy		
Culture		

Eastern Europe Under Communism

TERMS & NAMES
propaganda
private property rights
Nikita Khrushchev
deposed
détente

MAIN IDEA

The Communist government of the Soviet Union controlled the lives of its citizens.

WHY IT MATTERS NOW

Today, many republics of the former Soviet Union have become independent nations.

DATELINE

EXTRA

THE KREMLIN, MOSCOW, APRIL 12, 1961

A 27-year-old Soviet pilot has become the first person to travel into space. Soviet officials proudly announced today that cosmonaut Yuri Gagarin had orbited Earth in 1 hour and 29 minutes.

His 4.75-ton spacecraft, *Vostok I*, flew at a maximum altitude of 187 miles above the planet. Its top speed was 18,000 miles per hour.

Gagarin graduated from the Soviet Air Force cadet school just four years ago. He is the son of a carpenter and began to study flying while in college. Gagarin's space flight puts the Soviet Union a giant step ahead of the United States in the space race.

Movement • Yuri Gagarin becomes the first human in space. ▶

Soviet Culture

The Soviet space program of the 1950s and 1960s brought international attention to that country. Daily life for citizens of the Soviet Union and of the Eastern European countries under its control, however, was difficult. Most people were poor and had little, if any, say in their government.

TAKING NOTES
Use your chart to take notes about modern Europe.

Aspect	Under Communism	After Communism
Government		
Economy		

Strange but TRUE ??

Space Dogs Four years before Yuri Gagarin blasted into space, a Russian dog orbited the planet. Her name was Laika (LY•kuh), which means "Barker." Laika, pictured below, was launched into space on *Sputnik 2* in November 1957. The Soviets did not then have the ability to bring a spacecraft down safely, and Laika lived in space for only a few days.

In August 1960, however, the Russians sent two other dogs into space. Named Belka and Strelka, they were the first living creatures to go into space and return safely to Earth.

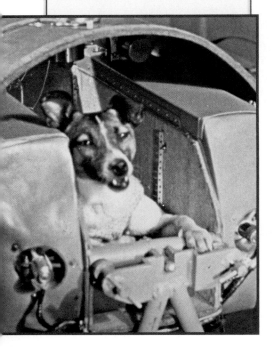

Creating a National Identity The Soviet government was fearful that some ethnic groups might want to break away from the Soviet Union. To keep this from happening, Soviet leaders tried to create a strong national identity. They wanted people in the republic of Latvia, for example, to think of themselves as Soviets, not as Latvians.

To help achieve its goals, the Soviet government created and distributed **propaganda** (PRAHP•uh•GAN•duh), or material designed to spread certain beliefs. Soviet propaganda included pamphlets, posters, artwork, statues, songs, and films. It praised the Soviet Union, its leaders, and Communism.

Soviet Control of Daily Life To prevent different ethnic groups from identifying with their individual cultures rather than with the Soviet Union, the Soviet government outlawed many cultural celebrations. It destroyed churches and other religious buildings and killed thousands of religious leaders. The members of many ethnic groups were not allowed to speak their native languages or celebrate certain holidays.

The Soviet government also controlled communications media, such as newspapers, books, and radio. This meant that most Soviet citizens could not learn much about other nations around the world.

Literature and the Arts The works of many writers, poets, and other artists who lived during the Soviet era often were banned or censored. Soviet artists were forced to join government-run unions. These unions told artists what kinds of works they could create. Artists who disobeyed were punished. Some were imprisoned or even killed.

Region • This statue, a form of propaganda, displays the Soviet belief in the unity of the worker (hammer) and the farmer (sickle). ▼

Ethnic and Cultural Groups of the Soviet Union, c. 1950

ARCTIC OCEAN

RUSSIA
ESTONIA
LITHUANIA
LATVIA
BYELORUSSIA
MOLDAVIA
UKRAINE
RUSSIA
GEORGIA
ARMENIA
AZERBAIJAN
KAZAKHSTAN
UZBEKISTAN
TURKMENIA
KIRGHIZIA
TAJIKISTAN

Bering Sea

Arctic Circle
Baltic Sea
Black Sea
Caspian Sea

0   250   500 miles
0 250 500 kilometers

Caucasian peoples
Indo-European peoples
Uralic and Altaic peoples
Sparsely populated

GEOGRAPHY SKILLBUILDER: Interpreting a Map
1. **Place** • Where in the Soviet Union do most Uralic and Altaic people live?
2. **Region** • What is the most common ethnicity of the Soviet Union?

Sports The leaders of the Soviet Union wanted their country to be seen as equal to, if not better than, other powerful nations. One way to achieve this goal was to become a strong competitor in the Olympics and in other international sports competitions.

The Soviet government supported its top athletes and provided for all their basic needs. It even hired and paid for the coaches and paid for all training. The hockey teams and gymnasts of the Soviet Union were among the best in the world.

The Soviet Economy

In addition to controlling the governments of the Soviet Union and of those Eastern European countries under its influence, Soviet leaders also ran the economy. When the Soviets installed Communist governments in Eastern Europe after World War II, they promised to improve industry and to bring new wealth to be shared among all citizens. This did not happen.

Government Control Communism in the Soviet Union did not support **private property rights,** or the right of individuals to own land or an industry. The Soviets wanted all major industries to be owned by the government rather than by private citizens. So the government took over factories, railroads, and businesses.

Region • Romanian gymnasts, like Nadia Comaneci, won medals at the Olympics. ▼

Modern Europe **355**

The Soviet government decided what would be produced, how it would be produced, and who would get what was produced. These choices were made based on Soviet interests, not on the interests of the republics or of individuals. Communist countries of Eastern Europe were often unable to meet the needs—including bread, meat, and clothing—of their citizens.

Reading **Social Studies**

A. Clarifying Who benefited most from Soviet industry?

Attempts at Change

Starting in the 1950s, Eastern Europeans began to demand more goods of better quality. They also wanted changes in the government. In 1956, Hungary and Poland tried to free their governments and economies from Soviet control. But the Communist army put an end to these attempts at change.

Khrushchev From 1958 until 1964, **Nikita Khrushchev** (KRUSH·chehf) ruled the Soviet Union. During this period, called "The Thaw," writers and other citizens began to have greater freedoms. Khrushchev even visited the United States in 1959, but the thaw in the Cold War did not last. In 1964, with the Soviet economy growing weaker, Khrushchev was **deposed,** or removed from power.

Spotlight on CULTURE

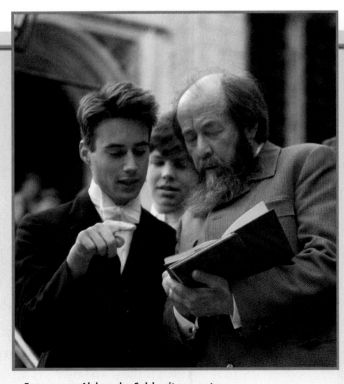

Solzhenitsyn In 1945, army officer Aleksandr Solzhenitsyn (SOHL·zhuh·NEET·sihn), far right, called the Soviet leader Joseph Stalin "the boss." For this, he was sentenced to eight years in slave-labor camps. Later, Solzhenitsyn wrote books about his experiences in those camps. He also wrote a letter against censorship. The government called him a traitor, and in 1969 it forced Solzhenitsyn to leave the writers' union. Five years later, Solzhenitsyn left the country.

Although Solzhenitsyn's works were banned, many Soviet citizens read them in secret. Copies of his and other banned books were passed from person to person across the nation. Through such writings, Soviet citizens learned many things that the government had tried to hide from them.

THINKING CRITICALLY

1. **Analyzing Motives** Why would the Soviet government stop people from reading Solzhenitsyn's books?

2. **Comparing** Compare the censorship of literature in the Soviet Union with censorship in the United States.

For more on Aleksandar Solzhenitsyn, go to

RESEARCH LINKS
CLASSZONE.COM

Reading Social Studies

B. Recognizing Important Details How did the Soviet Union maintain control over other Eastern European nations?

The Prague Spring In January 1968 in Czechoslovakia, Alexander Dubček (DOOB•chek) became the First Secretary of the Czechoslovak Communist Party. His attempts to lessen the Soviet Union's control over Czechoslovakia led to a period of improvement called the "Prague Spring." Czech citizens enjoyed greater freedoms, including more contact with Western Europe. In August of that year, however, the Soviet Union sent troops to force a return to strict Communist control. Dubček was later replaced, and Soviet controls were back in place.

Place • Nikita Khrushchev, the son of a miner and grandson of a peasant, lessened government control of Soviet citizens. ▲

Détente The member nations of NATO, which were concerned about starting an all-out war with the Soviet Union, were unable to stop the Soviet control of Eastern Europe. In the 1970s, however, leaders of the Soviet Union and the United States began to have more contact with each other. This led to a period of **détente** (day•TAHNT), or lessening tension, between the members of NATO and the Warsaw Pact nations.

Region • Citizens of Czechoslovakia protested Soviet control in 1968. ◄

Place • The old city of Dubrovnik is in Croatia, a part of the former Yugoslavia, which was a Communist country in Eastern Europe. ▶

Economic Crisis By the 1980s, economic conditions in the Soviet Union and in those countries under its control had still not improved. Even after détente, the Soviet government continued to spend most of its money on the armed forces and nuclear weapons. In addition, people who lived in the non-Russian republics of the Soviet Union now wanted more control over their own affairs. Many citizens began to reject the Soviet economic system, but the Soviet leaders refused to give up any of their power or control.

SECTION 1 ASSESSMENT

Terms & Names

1. Explain the significance of: (a) propaganda   (b) private property rights   (c) Nikita Khrushchev   (d) deposed   (e) détente

Using Graphics

2. Use a chart like this one to list and describe major aspects of Soviet culture.

Aspects of Soviet Culture

Main Ideas

3. (a) Why did Soviet leaders try to create a strong national identity?

   (b) What began to happen in Eastern Europe in the 1950s?

   (c) Describe the significance of the "Prague Spring."

Critical Thinking

4. **Analyzing Motives**

   Why do you think the works of many writers, poets, and artists were banned or censored during the Soviet era?

   Think About

   • what Soviet citizens learned from Solzhenitsyn's works

   • the government's use of propaganda

   • what life was like for most Soviet citizens

ACTIVITY -OPTION- Reread the information under "Literature and the Arts" and the Spotlight on Culture feature. Write a **speech** for or against censorship in the arts.

Using an Electronic Card Catalog

▶▶ Defining the Skill

To find books, magazines, or other sources of information in a library, you may use an electronic card catalog. This catalog is a computerized search program on the Internet that lists every book, periodical, or other resource found in the library. You can search for resources in the catalog in four ways: by title, by author, by subject, and by keyword. Once you have typed in your search information, the catalog will give you a list of every resource that matches it. This is called bibliographic information. You can use an electronic card catalog to build a bibliography, or a list of books, on the topic you are researching.

▶▶ Applying the Skill

The screen below shows the results of an electronic search for information about the Danube River. To use the information on the screen, follow the strategies listed below.

How to Use an Electronic Card Catalog

Strategy ❶ To begin your search, choose Subject, Title, Author, or Keyword. The student doing this search chose "Subject" and then typed in "Danube River."

Strategy ❷ Based on your search, the catalog will give you a list of records that match that subject. You must then select one of the records to view the details about the resource. The catalog will then give you a screen like the one to the right. This detailed record lists the author, title, and information about where and when the resource was published, and by whom.

Strategy ❸ Locate the call number for the book. The call number indicates the section in the library where you will find the book. You can also find out if the book is available in the library you are using. If not, it may be available in another library in the network.

▶▶ Practicing the Skill

Review the text in Chapter 13, Section 1 to find a topic that interests you, such as Yuri Gagarin. Use the Subject search on an electronic card catalog to find information about your topic. Make a bibliography about the subject. Organize your bibliography alphabetically by author. For each book you list, also include the title, city, publisher, and date of publication.

Eastern Europe and Russia

TERMS & NAMES
Mikhail Gorbachev
parliamentary republic
coalition government
ethnic cleansing
Duma

MAIN IDEA

After the breakup of the Soviet Union, many former Soviet republics and countries of Eastern Europe became independent.

WHY IT MATTERS NOW

Nations once under Soviet rule are taking steps toward new economies and democratic governments.

DATELINE

THE KREMLIN, MOSCOW, 1988—To reduce military spending, the Soviet Union has begun removing large numbers of troops and arms from Eastern Europe. This latest news is just one of many changes in the Soviet government since Mikhail Gorbachev (GAWR•buh•chawf) came to power three years ago.

Although Gorbachev believes in the ideals of the Soviet system, he thinks that change is necessary to help solve the country's economic and political problems. Since 1985 Gorbachev has reduced Cold War tensions with the United States. At home in the Soviet Union, he has allowed more political and economic freedom.

Region • Mikhail Gorbachev leads the Soviet Union toward a freer society. ▲

The Breakup of the Soviet Union

Mikhail Gorbachev's reforms did not solve the problems of the Soviet Union. The economy continued to get worse. When Gorbachev did not force the countries of Eastern Europe to remain Communist, this further displeased many Communists.

TAKING NOTES
Use your chart to take notes about modern Europe.

Aspect	Under Communism	After Communism
Government		
Economy		

Vocabulary

coup d'état:
the overthrow of
a government,
usually by a small
group in a position
of power; often
shortened to "coup"

In 1991, a group of more traditional Soviet leaders tried to take over the Soviet government. Thousands of people opposed this coup d'état (KOO•day•TAH), and the coup failed. Then, one by one, the Soviet republics declared independence. The Warsaw Pact was dissolved. By the end of 1991, the Soviet Union no longer existed. The huge country had become 15 different nations.

Modern Eastern Europe

Each former Soviet republic set up its own non-Communist government. The countries of Eastern Europe that had been under Soviet control held democratic elections, and many wrote or revised their constitutions.

BACKGROUND

The Central Asian Soviet republics were mostly Muslim. These republics are now the countries of Kazakhstan, Turkmenistan, Uzbekistan, Kyrgyzstan, and Tajikistan.

In some countries, such as the Czech Republic, former Communists were banned from important government posts. In other countries, such as Bulgaria, the former Communists reorganized themselves into a new political party and have won elections. Many different ethnic groups also tried to create new states within a nation or to reestablish old states that had not existed in many years.

Parliamentary Republics Today, most of the countries of Eastern Europe are parliamentary republics. A **parliamentary republic** is a form of government led by the head of the political party with the most members in parliament. The head of government, usually a prime minister, proposes the programs that the government will undertake. Most of these countries also have a president who has ceremonial, rather than political, duties.

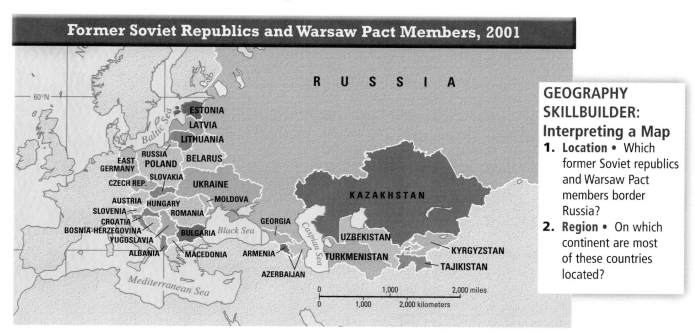

Former Soviet Republics and Warsaw Pact Members, 2001

GEOGRAPHY SKILLBUILDER: Interpreting a Map

1. **Location** • Which former Soviet republics and Warsaw Pact members border Russia?
2. **Region** • On which continent are most of these countries located?

In some countries, small political parties have joined forces to work together to form a government. This is called a **coalition government.**

New Economies Under Soviet rule, Eastern Europe struggled economically and its people's freedoms were severely restricted. Although Eastern Europeans gained their freedom, they also faced problems such as inflation and unemployment.

Eastern Europe's countries are changing from command economies to free-market economies. Some countries, such as Slovakia, made this change slowly. Others, such as Poland, reformed their economic system and achieved economic success.

Many former Soviet republics, which did not quickly reform their economic systems, are in bad economic shape. Some of these nations are terribly poor. Struggles for power have led to violence and sometimes civil war. Pollution from the Soviet era threatens people's health. Still, some republics, including Ukraine, Latvia, Lithuania, and Estonia, are making progress as independent nations.

Defense After the breakup of the Soviet Union, Eastern European nations no longer looked to the Soviet government to defend them. Many wanted to become members of NATO. Belonging to NATO would help assure them of protection in case of invasion.

Reading
Social Studies

A. Comparing
Compare a command economy with a free-market economy.

Spotlight on CULTURE

Easter in Ukraine In Ukraine, most Christians belong to the Orthodox Church. These Ukrainians are known for the special way in which they celebrate the Easter holiday. They create beautiful Easter eggs, which are dyed bright colors and covered with intricate designs. These eggs are so beautiful that people around the world collect them.

Ukrainians also bake a special bread for Easter. They decorate it with designs made from pieces of dough. Families bring the bread and other foods to church to be blessed on Easter. Then they eat the foods for the holiday feast.

THINKING CRITICALLY

1. **Analyzing Issues**
   Why were Ukrainian Easter eggs not common during the Soviet era?

2. **Comparing**
   How do your family's holiday customs compare with Ukrainian customs?

For more on Easter in Ukraine, go to **RESEARCH LINKS**
CLASSZONE.COM

In 1999 three new members joined NATO: Poland, Hungary, and the Czech Republic. In 2001 Bulgaria, Romania, Slovakia, Slovenia, and the Baltic states were also working to become NATO members.

War in the Balkan Peninsula

Since the late 1980s, much of Eastern Europe has been a place of turmoil and struggle. Yugoslavia, one of the countries located on Europe's Balkan Peninsula, has experienced terrible wars, extreme hardships, and great change.

Under Tito After World War II, Yugoslavia came under Marshal Tito's (TEE•toh) dictatorship. Tito controlled all the country's many different ethnic groups, which included Serbs, Croats, and Muslims. His rule continued until his death in 1980. Slobodan Milošević (sloh•boh•DON muh•LAW•shuh•vich) became Yugoslavia's president in 1989, after years of political turmoil.

Milosevic Slobodan Milošević, a Serb, wanted the Serbs to rule Yugoslavia. The Serbs in Bosnia began fighting the Croats and Muslims living there. The Bosnian Serbs murdered many Muslims so that Serbs would be in the majority. The Serbs called these killings of members of minority ethnic groups **ethnic cleansing**. Finally, NATO attacked the Bosnian Serbs and ended the war.

Connections to Science

Pollution Soviet leaders thought that industry would improve life for everyone. Developing industry was so important that the Soviet government did not worry about pollution. Few laws were passed to protect the environment.

In the 1970s and 1980s there was not enough money to modernize industry or to reduce pollution. Some areas also could not afford proper sewage systems or recycling plants. Today, Eastern Europe has some of the worst pollution problems on the continent.

The Balkan States, 1991 and 2001

	National boundaries, 2001
	Yugoslavia, 1991
	Autonomous province boundaries, 2001
⊛	National capital

AUSTRIA
HUNGARY
Slovenia
Croatia
Vojvodina
YUGOSLAVIA
Belgrade
ROMANIA
Bosnia and Herzegovina
Serbia
SAN MARINO
Adriatic Sea
Montenegro
ITALY
Kosovo
BULGARIA
Macedonia
ALBANIA
GREECE

0   100   200 miles
0   100   200 kilometers

12°E   18°E

GEOGRAPHY SKILLBUILDER: Interpreting a Map
1. **Location** • Which Balkan state borders Greece?
2. **Region** • How many countries developed from Yugoslavia?

In 1995 the Serbs, Croats, and Muslims of Bosnia signed a peace treaty. In 1999 Milošević began using ethnic cleansing against the Albanians in Kosovo, a region of Serbia. NATO launched an air war against Yugoslavia that ended with the defeat of the Serbs. In 2000, public protests led to Milošević's removal. He was subsequently arrested and tried for war crimes by the United Nations.

Modern Russia

Life in Russia has improved since the breakup of the Soviet Union. Russian citizens can elect their own leaders. They enjoy more freedom of speech. New businesses have sprung up, and some Russians have become wealthy.

Unfortunately, Russia still faces serious problems. Many leaders are dishonest. The nation has been slow to reform its economic system. Most of the nation's new wealth has gone to a small number of people, so that many Russians remain poor. The crime rate has grown tremendously. The government has also fought a war against Chechnya (CHECH·nee·yah), a region of Russia that wants to become independent.

Russian Culture The fall of communism helped most Russians to follow their cultural practices more freely. Russians gained the freedom to practice the religion of their choice. They can also buy and read the great works of Russian literature that once were banned. At the beginning of the 21st century, writers and other artists also have far more freedom to express themselves.

New magazines and newspapers are being published. Even new history books are being written. For the first time in decades, these publications are telling more of the truth about the Soviet Union.

Russia's Government Russia has a democratic form of government. The president is elected by the people. The people also elect members of the **Duma** (DOO·muh), which is part of the legislature.

Russian Icons A special feature of Russian Orthodox churches is their beautiful religious paintings called icons (EYE·kahns). Russian icons usually depict biblical figures and scenes. They often decorate every corner of a church.

The greatest Russian icon painter was Andrei Rublev (AHN·dray ruhb·LYAWF). He worked in the late 1300s and early 1400s. Rublev's paintings, one of which is shown below, are brightly colored and highlighted in gold. His work influenced many later painters, and today he is considered one of the world's great religious artists.

Reading
Social Studies

B. Identifying Problems What are the main problems that face Russia today?

BACKGROUND

One of the most popular pastimes in Russia is the game of chess. In fact, many of the world's greatest chess players, such as Boris Spassky, have been Russian.

Russia's Natural Resources Today

INTERACTIVE

Legend:
- Forest
- Grassland
- Desert
- Tundra
- Farmland
- Fishing
- Natural gas
- Coal
- Oil
- Iron
- Gold
- Lead

ARCTIC OCEAN

Bering Sea

Sea of Okhotsk

R U S S I A

0   250   500 miles
0   250   500 kilometers

GEOGRAPHY SKILLBUILDER: Interpreting a Map

1. **Human-Environment Interaction** • Name three of Russia's more common natural resources.

2. **Place** • What is the most common type of land in Russia?

Democracy is still new to the Russian people. Some citizens are working to improve the system to reduce corruption and to ensure that everyone receives fair treatment. Even the thought of changing the government is new to most Russians. Under the Soviets, people had to accept things the way they were.

BACKGROUND

Russian highways are in poor condition. Also, many rivers and major ports are closed by ice in the winter. As a result, most Russian goods are transported by railroad.

Resources and Industry The map above shows Russia's major natural resources. The country is one of the world's largest producers of oil. Russia also contains the world's largest forests. Its trees are made into lumber, paper, and other wood products.

Russian factories produce steel from iron ore. Other factories use that steel to make tractors and other large machines. Since Russian ships can reach both the Pacific and Atlantic oceans, Russia also has a large fishing industry.

Economics Following the lead of Eastern European countries, Russia has been moving toward a free-market economy. Citizens can own land, and foreign companies are encouraged to do business in Russia. These changes have given many Russians more opportunities, but they have also brought difficulties.

Connections to Language

The Russian Language More than 150 million people speak Russian. It is related to other Slavic languages of Eastern Europe, including Polish, Serbian, and Bulgarian.

Russian is written using the Cyrillic (suh•RIHL•ihk) alphabet, which has 33 characters.

Many of the newly independent republics are now returning to the Latin alphabet, used to write English and most other languages of the Western world. The major powers in the world economy base their languages on the Latin alphabet, making communication easier with other countries.

Hello
Привет

Place • Forestry is a major industry in Russia. These harvested logs are being floated downriver to be processed. ▶

Prices are no longer controlled by the government. This means that companies can charge a price that is high enough for them to make a profit. At the beginning of the 21st century, however, people's wages have not risen as fast as prices. Many people cannot afford to buy new products.

Some Russians have done well in the new economy. On the other hand, people with less education and less access to power have not done as well. Also, today most new businesses and jobs are in the cities, which means that people in small towns have fewer job opportunities.

SECTION 2 ASSESSMENT

Terms & Names
1. **Explain the significance of:** (a) Mikhail Gorbachev (b) parliamentary republic (c) coalition government
   (d) ethnic cleansing (e) Duma

Using Graphics
2. Use a flow chart like this one to outline the changes in Eastern Europe and Russia from 1988 through 2000.

   ```
   1988:
     ↓
   
     ↓
   
   ```

Main Ideas
3. (a) What happened to the governments of the former Soviet republics after independence?

   (b) How have the economies of Eastern European countries changed now that those countries are free?

   (c) In what ways has life in Russia improved since the breakup of the Soviet Union?

Critical Thinking
4. **Making Inferences**

   Why do you think many Eastern European countries would like to join NATO?

   Think About
   - what happened to the Warsaw Pact
   - the economies of Eastern Europe
   - the relationship between Eastern Europe and Russia

ACTIVITY -OPTION- Reread the information in the Spotlight on Culture feature. Write a short, personal **essay** that describes a special family, school, neighborhood, or holiday celebration in which you participated.

The European Union

TERMS & NAMES
European Union
currency
euro
tariff
standard of living
Court of Human Rights

MAIN IDEA
Europeans want to maintain a high quality of life for all citizens while preserving their unique cultures.

WHY IT MATTERS NOW
A prosperous and culturally diverse Europe provides goods and markets for the rest of the world.

| Back | Forward | Stop | Refresh | Home |

Address: ▸go

DATELINE

WESTERN EUROPE, DECEMBER 2001—Starting next month, people in many Western European nations will begin trading their old bills and coins for euros—the new money of the European Union (EU). The design of the bills, below, is the same for all EU members.

The design of the euro coins, however, will be different. Individual countries are minting their own. As shown here, one side has a standard euro design. The other side has national symbols that relate to each country. In 1996, artists and sculptors from all over Europe entered a contest to design the coins. The winner was Luc Luycx (lewk lowx) from Belgium.

Region • Euros reached the European market in January 2002. ▲

Western Europe Today

Today, in Western Europe, all national leaders share their power with elected lawmakers. Citizens take part in government by voting and through membership in a variety of political parties. The Unit Atlas on pages 260–269 shows modern Europe.

TAKING NOTES
Use your chart to take notes about modern Europe.

Aspect	Under Communism	After Communism
Government		
Economy		

The European Union Many countries of Western Europe belong to a group called the **European Union** (EU). At first, countries joined the EU to encourage trade. This economic group, however, is becoming a loose political union.

Many former Communist countries of Eastern Europe want to join the Union too. They know that membership will help them economically and politically. Eastern European countries, however, cannot automatically join the EU. Many must first make legal, economic, and environmental improvements. The EU has agreed to include them over time. With a possible membership of more than 20 nations by 2003, the EU may be the best hope for European peace and prosperity.

Regional Governments In Western Europe, each nation also has regional governments, similar to those of individual states in the United States. Regional governments are demanding—and receiving—greater power. As a result, many people in Western Europe enjoy increased self-rule and participation in the political process.

BACKGROUND

In 2001, the EU gave initial approval to the Czech Republic, Estonia, Hungary, Poland, and Slovenia to join in the near future.

Region • The headquarters of the European Central Bank is located in Frankfurt, Germany. ◄

EU Economies

BACKGROUND

Some EU nations, including the United Kingdom and Denmark, have not agreed to give up their existing currency.

Traditionally, each European nation has had its own **currency,** or system of money. The EU is meant to make international trade much simpler. With more Europeans using the **euro,** the currency of the EU, currency no longer has to be exchanged every time a payment crosses a border.

Improved Trade To encourage trade, members have also done away with tariffs on the goods they trade with one another. A **tariff** is a duty or fee that must be paid on imported or exported goods, making them more expensive. EU members have lifted border controls as well. This means that goods, services, and people flow freely among these member nations.

Another goal of the EU is to achieve economic equality among its members. To reach this goal, EU members are sharing their wealth. Poorer countries such as Ireland receive money to help them build businesses.

Reading Social Studies

A. Clarifying How would improved trade raise the standard of living?

A Higher Standard of Living Member nations hope that increased trade and shared wealth will help give all citizens of the EU a high standard of living. A person's **standard of living,** or quality of life, is based on the availability of goods and services.

People who have a high standard of living have enough food and housing, good transportation and communications, and access to schools and health care. They also have a high rate of literacy, meaning that most adults are able to read.

Additional Benefits The members of the EU are helping the countries of Eastern Europe to raise their environmental standards. They are willing to pay up to 75 percent of the cost for a new waste treatment system in Romania, for example. The program includes recycling centers for paper, glass, and plastics. It will clean up and close old dumping grounds, which were leaking pollution into the ground water.

Connections to Economics

Tourism For many European nations, tourism is an important part of the economy. In fact, the continent represents about 60 percent of the world's tourist market. Visitors come to enjoy Europe's climate, historic sites, museums, and food.

Popular destinations include Spain, Italy, Austria, and the United Kingdom. France, below, is the most visited country in the world. In 1999 it hosted more than 73 million tourists.

The EU also runs programs that train people for jobs. As citizens of a member nation, people are not limited to a job in their own country. They may work in any part of the EU. They can even vote in local elections wherever they live. In addition, the Council of Europe's **Court of Human Rights** protects the rights of all its citizens in whichever member country they live.

Cultural Diversity

Although many European nations are part of the EU, they still have their own distinct cultural traditions. These traditions may include different languages, unique foods, certain ways of doing business, and even special games and celebrations. Many of these traditions developed over hundreds of years.

Some nations are a mix of several cultures. In Belgium, for example, Flemings live in the north and speak Dutch. Another major group, the Walloons, lives in the south. They speak French. A third group of German-speaking Belgians lives in the eastern part of the country. Many Belgian cities include people from all three groups.

City Life Many of the world's famous and exciting cities are located in Western Europe. London, Madrid, Paris, Amsterdam, and Rome are just a few of the major centers for the arts, business, and learning. These cities are centuries old, and Europeans work hard to preserve them.

Europeans also take pride in the conveniences that their cities offer. Most major urban areas have excellent public transportation, including subways, buses, and trains. Sidewalk cafés are also popular, where people come to meet friends, eat, and relax.

Reading
Social Studies

B. Identifying Problems What are the main problems facing the European Union?

Region • Many Europeans center their social lives around urban sidewalk cafés, such as this one in Italy. ▼

Region • Quaint small European villages are popular tourist attractions. ▶

BACKGROUND

Many European families cannot make a living on a small farm. The government may offer support to such families, to help preserve the nation's rural culture.

Country Life European cities have much to offer, but the countryside is also popular—especially for vacationers. The Italian region of Tuscany (TUHS·kuh·nee) and the French region of Provence (pruh·VAHNS) are two of the best-known examples of the many beautiful rural areas.

Small European villages may have only a café, a grocery store, a post office, a town square, and a collection of houses. Many families who live in such areas have been farming or raising animals on the same land for generations. Some even live in houses that their families have owned for hundreds of years.

SECTION 3 ASSESSMENT

Terms & Names

1. **Explain the significance of:**
   - (a) European Union (EU)
   - (b) currency
   - (c) euro
   - (d) tariff
   - (e) standard of living
   - (f) Court of Human Rights

Using Graphics

2. Use a chart like this one to compare aspects of city life and country life in Europe.

City Life	Country Life

Main Ideas

3. (a) Describe the importance of the new shared currency that is based on the euro.

   (b) Can any European country automatically join the EU? Why or why not?

   (c) List at least two benefits, other than a shared currency, for countries that are members of the EU.

Critical Thinking

4. **Synthesizing**

   Why may the EU be the best hope for European peace and prosperity?

   Think About
   - the number of member countries
   - the goals of the EU
   - modern European conflicts

ACTIVITY -OPTION- Choose one photograph from this section that shows a place in Europe. Write a **postcard** or **e-mail** to a friend or family member as if you were there. What sights and sounds will you describe?

900 1910 1920 1930 1940 1950 1960 1970
990 2000

1700 1710 1720 1730 1740 1750 1760 1780
1800 1810 1820 1830 1840 1850 1860 1870
1890 1900 1910 1920 1930 1940 1950 1960
1980 1990 2000

Linking Past and Present

The Legacy of Europe

Movable Type

Before Johann Gutenberg (1400–1468) invented the printing press in Germany, European monks copied books by hand. Movable type made it possible to print multiple copies of books quickly, allowing people access to them. The printing process advanced greatly in the 1930s. By the mid-1940s, printed works included complex illustrations and color. Today, people create text and images and print them directly from their computers.

Early printing press ▲

Nitroglycerin

For almost 20 years, Alfred Nobel (1833–1896), shown at left, worked on developing a way to safely contain and ignite nitroglycerin, a powerful explosive. Eventually, chemists and doctors realized that nitroglycerin widens blood vessels and can be used to treat patients with heart conditions. Given in tablet, patch, or oral-spray form, nitroglycerin has saved countless lives.

Architecture

The White House in Washington, D.C., is one of many buildings in the United States that has been influenced by Roman architecture. Roman buildings often featured vaulted domes, columns, and large interior spaces. This type of architecture has influenced other buildings in the United States, including many banks and courthouses.

Democracy

Around 500 B.C., several Greek city-states established democracies, replacing their single-ruler governments. The word *democracy* derives from two Greek words: *demos,* meaning "people," and *kratos,* meaning "power." Today, the idea of rule by the people is found around the world, from the United States to France to India.

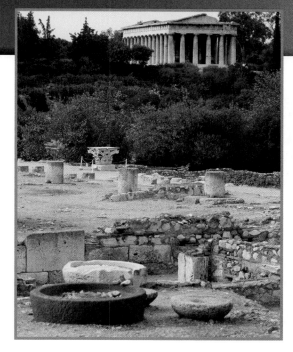

The agora, or marketplace, of ancient Athens was often the scene of political activities. ▲

Find Out More About It!

Study the text and photos on these pages to learn about inventions, creations, and contributions that have come from Europe. Then choose the item that interests you the most and use the library or the Internet to learn more about it. Use the information you gather to create a poster celebrating the contribution.

RESEARCH LINKS
CLASSZONE.COM

Yacht ▼

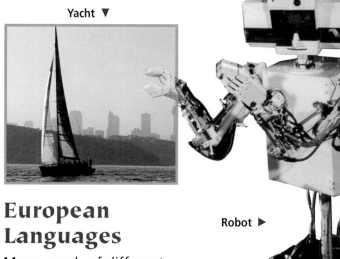

European Languages

Many words of different European languages have made their way into English. For example, the word *dinner* is actually French in origin. As English people traveled and settled around the world, they borrowed words from such European languages as German, Spanish, and Norwegian to use in their everyday communication. Examples of some of these words we use today are *kindergarten* (German), *dinner* (French), *yacht* (Dutch), *corridor* (Italian), *vanilla* (Spanish), *flamingo* (Portuguese), *robot* (Czech), and *ski* (Norwegian).

Robot ▶

Flamingo ▶

ASSESSMENT

TERMS & NAMES

Explain the significance of each of the following:

1. propaganda
2. Nikita Khrushchev
3. détente
4. Mikhail Gorbachev
5. ethnic cleansing
6. Duma
7. currency
8. euro
9. tariff
10. standard of living

REVIEW QUESTIONS

Eastern Europe Under Communism *(pages 353–358)*

1. Why did the Soviet government outlaw many cultural celebrations?
2. Explain why most Soviet citizens learned little about other nations around the world.
3. How did the Soviet Union maintain control over Eastern European countries?

Eastern Europe and Russia *(pages 360–366)*

4. How did the Soviet Union change during 1991?
5. List at least three of Russia's major natural resources.

The European Union *(pages 367–371)*

6. What is the importance of the European Union (EU)?
7. Name one benefit of being a member of the EU.
8. Identify at least three of Europe's major centers of the arts, business, and learning.

CRITICAL THINKING

Comparing

1. Using your completed chart from Reading Social Studies, p. 352, compare Eastern Europe under Communism with Eastern Europe after Communism.

Summarizing

2. Outline the changes to the Russian economy since the breakup of the Soviet Union.

Recognizing Important Details

3. What types of changes must Eastern European countries make in order to join the EU?

Visual Summary

Eastern Europe Under Communism

1

- The Soviet Union's communist government controlled the lives of its citizens.
- Under Nikita Khrushchev, citizens began to have greater freedom.

2

Eastern Europe and Russia

- Today, independent nations once under Soviet rule are taking steps toward new economies and greater freedom.

The European Union

3

- Many European countries are members of an economic and political alliance called the European Union (EU).

Use the map and your knowledge of geography to answer questions 1 and 2.

Additional Test Practice, pp. S1–S33

1. Which of the following countries has the greatest variety of power resources?

   A. Estonia

   B. Latvia

   C. Lithuania

   D. Ukraine

2. If you were a dairy farmer, in which country would you probably live?

   A. Belarus

   B. Lithuania

   C. Russia

   D. Ukraine

In the following passage, Mikhail Gorbachev explains his reasons for reforming the Soviet economy. Use the quotation and your knowledge of world cultures and geography to answer question 3.

PRIMARY SOURCE

The country began to lose momentum. Economic failures became more frequent. Difficulties began to accumulate and deteriorate, and unresolved problems to multiply. . . . Analyzing the situation, we first discovered a slowing economic growth. In the last fifteen years the national income growth rates had declined by more than a half.

MIKHAIL GORBACHEV, *Perestroika*

3. According to Gorbachev, what difficulty did the Soviet economy face?

   A. Jobs were being eliminated.

   B. Prices were rapidly rising.

   C. Growth rates were declining.

   D. Factories were being closed.

TEST PRACTICE
CLASSZONE.COM

ALTERNATIVE ASSESSMENT

1. WRITING ABOUT HISTORY

During "The Thaw" in the Soviet Union (1958–1964), people gained many freedoms. Research these freedoms and find out how these changes affected the lives of average citizens in the Soviet Union. Then write a journal entry that might have been written by a citizen after he or she experienced one of these freedoms for the first time. Share your entry with the class.

2. COOPERATIVE LEARNING

When the Soviet Union broke apart into 15 nations, each country had to set up a new government. In a group of three to five classmates, create a government and constitution. Assign each group member a role in the new government, such as a representative or president. Outline the responsibilities of each member. Work together to write a brief constitution for your government including sections that outline basic rights, freedoms, and responsibilities of citizens.

INTEGRATED TECHNOLOGY

Doing Internet Research

Use the Internet and library resources to research the economy of any one of the Balkan states. Write a short report of your findings. List the Web sites that you used to prepare your report.

- Specifically look for information about the types of industry that exist in that state as well as any economic problems the state might face.

- Include graphs or charts that show the state's major imports and exports.

For Internet links to support this activity, go to

RESEARCH LINKS
CLASSZONE.COM

CHAPTER 14

Europe Today

Place London's Piccadilly Circus is an intersection of major roads, with an Underground, or subway, stop at the center. Piccadilly Circus is a popular tourist attraction and shopping district.

UNDERGROUND

SWEDEN

POLAND

UNITED KINGDOM

GERMANY

FRANCE

ATLANTIC

PACIFIC

PACIFIC OCEAN

OCEAN

INDIAN OCEAN

OCEAN

Why is it important for Europeans to protect their seas?

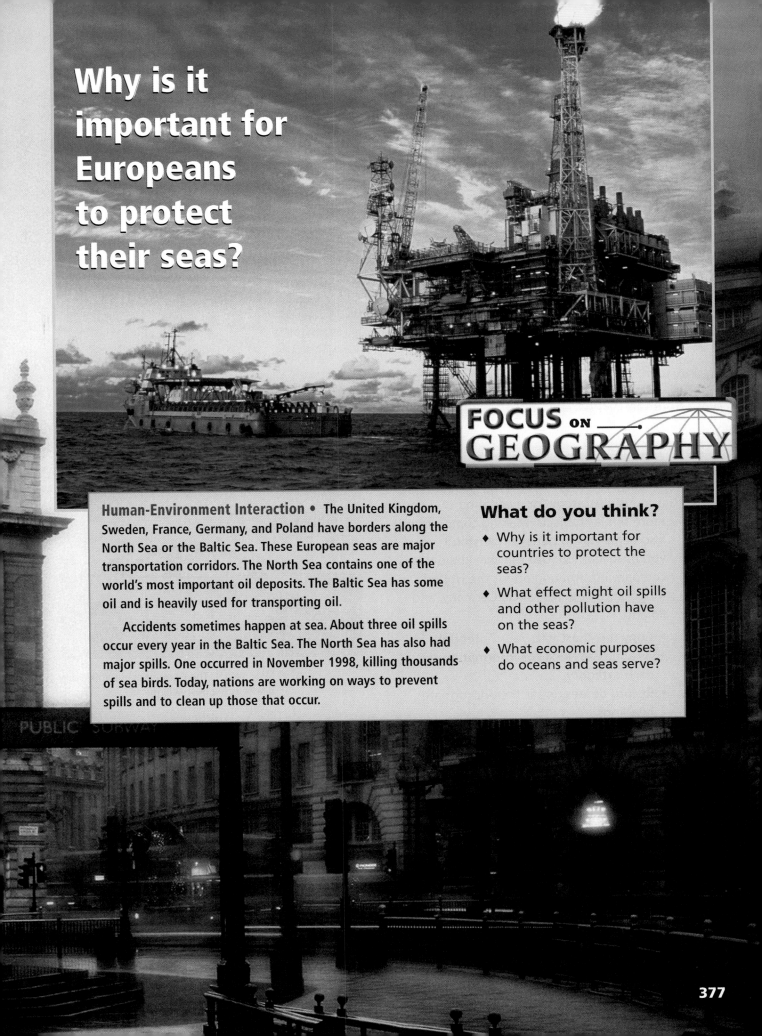

FOCUS ON GEOGRAPHY

Human-Environment Interaction • The United Kingdom, Sweden, France, Germany, and Poland have borders along the North Sea or the Baltic Sea. These European seas are major transportation corridors. The North Sea contains one of the world's most important oil deposits. The Baltic Sea has some oil and is heavily used for transporting oil.

Accidents sometimes happen at sea. About three oil spills occur every year in the Baltic Sea. The North Sea has also had major spills. One occurred in November 1998, killing thousands of sea birds. Today, nations are working on ways to prevent spills and to clean up those that occur.

What do you think?

- ♦ Why is it important for countries to protect the seas?
- ♦ What effect might oil spills and other pollution have on the seas?
- ♦ What economic purposes do oceans and seas serve?

BEFORE YOU READ

▶▶ *What Do You Know?*

Did you know that from the end of WW II until 1990, Germany was two separate countries and Poland was controlled by the Soviet Union? Do you have relatives or friends who come from the United Kingdom, Sweden, France, Germany, or Poland? Have you ever seen the Queen of England or the Pope, who is from Poland, on television? Have you heard of the Nobel Prize, which is awarded in Sweden? Think about what you have learned in other classes, what you have read, and what you have heard or seen in the news about these countries.

▶▶ *What Do You Want to Know?*

Consider what you know about the countries covered in Chapter 14. In your notebook, record what you hope to learn from this chapter.

Region • Sweden's Nobel Prize honors great achievements worldwide. ▲

READ AND TAKE NOTES

Reading Strategy: Comparing Comparing is a useful strategy for evaluating two or more similar subjects. Making comparisons also helps you to better understand what you have learned. Use the chart below to compare information about the United Kingdom, Sweden, France, Germany, and Poland.

- Copy the chart into your notebook.
- As you read, look for information for each category.
- Record details under the appropriate headings.

Movement • The German-made Volkswagen Beetle is the best-selling car ever. ▲

Country	Physical Geography	Government	Economy	Culture	Interesting Facts
United Kingdom					
Sweden					
France					
Germany					
Poland					

The United Kingdom

SECTION 1

TERMS & NAMES
London
secede
Good Friday
  Accord
Charles Dickens

MAIN IDEA

The United Kingdom is a small nation in Western Europe with a history of colonization.

WHY IT MATTERS NOW

British economic, political, and cultural traditions have influenced nations around the world.

DATELINE

BARCELONA, SPAIN, MAY 30, 1999

They did it! Manchester United won the triple crown of soccer. The British fans here are going wild, and their excitement is easy to understand. Manchester United is only the third soccer team to win its league championship, cup titles, and the Champions League final.

Football, or "soccer" as Americans call it, is the world's most popular sport. The British invented a form of the game, called "mob football," in the 1300s. Back then, the playing field was the size of a small town, and there might have been as many as 500 players. A set of rules for the game was developed in 1863. Today, football is the national pastime in the United Kingdom.

Region • Manchester United celebrates after winning soccer's triple crown. ▲

A Kingdom of Four Political Regions

The United Kingdom is a small island nation of Western Europe. Its culture has had an enormous impact on the world. The nation's official name is the United Kingdom of Great Britain and Northern Ireland. **London,** located in southeastern England, is the capital.

TAKING NOTES

Use your chart to take notes about Europe today.

Country	Physical Geography	Government
United Kingdom		
Sweden		

United Kingdom

England

Scotland

Wales

Northern Ireland

Four different political regions make up the United Kingdom: Scotland, England, Wales, and Northern Ireland (see the map below). The British monarchy has ruled over the four regions for hundreds of years.

National Government Today, the government of the United Kingdom is a constitutional monarchy. The British monarch is a symbol of power rather than an actual ruler. The power to govern belongs to Parliament, which is the national lawmaking body.

The British Parliament has two parts. The House of Lords is made up of nobles. Elected representatives make up the House of Commons. The House of Commons is the more powerful of the two houses.

The prime minister leads the government. He or she is usually the leader of the political party that wins the most seats in the House of Commons. The other political parties go into "opposition," which means their role is to question government policies.

Regional Government in Great Britain Recently, the national government of the United Kingdom has returned some self-rule to some regions of Great Britain. In the late 1990s, voters in Wales approved plans for their own assembly, or body of lawmakers. Also at this time, the Scots voted to create their own parliament. Both Wales's assembly and Scotland's parliament met for the first time in 1999.

Vocabulary

monarchy: government by king or queen

Reading
Social Studies

A. Clarifying
Who is the head of government in the United Kingdom?

The United Kingdom Today

INTER**ACTIVE**

NORTH ATLANTIC OCEAN

NORWAY

Shetland Islands

0   50   100 miles
0   50   100 kilometers

Orkney Islands

Hebrides

Highlands

Moray Firth

Inverness

SCOTLAND *Dee* • Aberdeen

Grampian Mts.

Dundee *Firth of Forth*

North Sea

Clyde • Edinburgh

Glasgow *Tweed*

Cheviot Hills

Londonderry •

Carlisle

NORTHERN IRELAND • Belfast

Isle of Man

Cumbrian Mts.

Durham

Irish Sea

Swale

THE PENNINES

Bradford • Leeds *Humber River*

Dublin ⊛ Manchester • Sheffield

Liverpool *Dee*

IRELAND *Cardigan Bay*

ENGLAND

Cambrian Mts.

• Birmingham

Severn

Cork •

Wye

WALES • Oxford

St. George's Channel

Cotswold Hills

Cardiff

London • Canterbury

Thames *Strait of Dover*

Dover

Southampton

Celtic Sea

Plymouth

Isle of Wight

English Channel

FRANCE

NETH.

GERMANY

BELGIUM

LUX.

Legend:
— National boundary
--- Regional boundary
⊛ National capital
• Other city

GEOGRAPHY SKILLBUILDER: Interpreting a Map

1. **Location •** Which region of the United Kingdom is on a different island?
2. **Location •** Which body of water separates the United Kingdom from France?

BACKGROUND

The roots of division in Northern Ireland go back to at least the 1600s, when English and Scottish colonists settled there. These Protestant settlers took over the lands of Irish Catholics.

Governing Northern Ireland Throughout the 20th century, there were conflicts in Northern Ireland between Irish Catholic nationalists and Irish Protestants who supported the government of the United Kingdom. In fact, during the 1960s, many Irish Catholics wanted Northern Ireland to **secede,** or withdraw from, the United Kingdom. They hoped to unite Northern Ireland with the Republic of Ireland. Irish Protestants—a majority in the region—generally wanted to remain part of the United Kingdom.

In 1969, riots broke out, and the British government sent in troops to stop them. Violence between groups of Protestants and Catholics continued for almost 30 years. In 1998, representatives from both sides signed the **Good Friday Accord**. This agreement set up the Northern Ireland Assembly, which represents both Catholic and Protestant voters. For this government to succeed in Northern Ireland, however, the former enemies will need to work together.

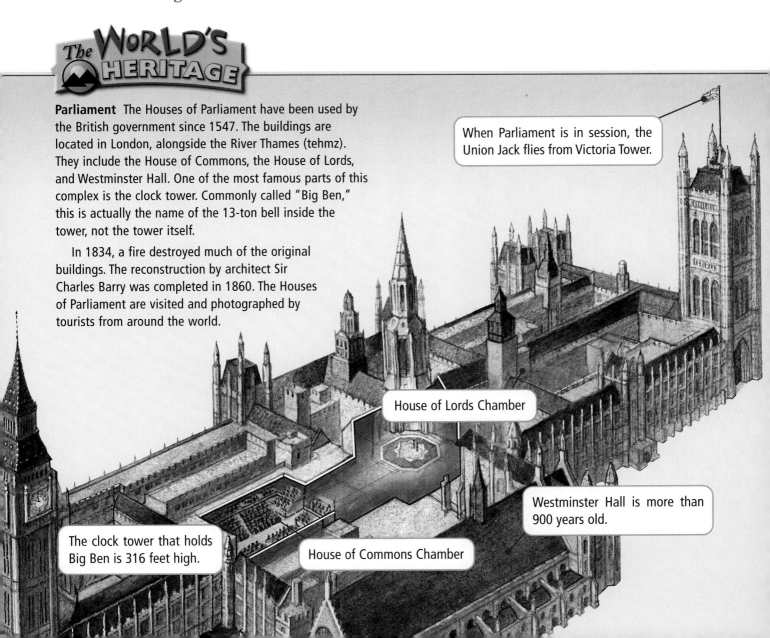

The WORLD'S HERITAGE

Parliament The Houses of Parliament have been used by the British government since 1547. The buildings are located in London, alongside the River Thames (tehmz). They include the House of Commons, the House of Lords, and Westminster Hall. One of the most famous parts of this complex is the clock tower. Commonly called "Big Ben," this is actually the name of the 13-ton bell inside the tower, not the tower itself.

In 1834, a fire destroyed much of the original buildings. The reconstruction by architect Sir Charles Barry was completed in 1860. The Houses of Parliament are visited and photographed by tourists from around the world.

When Parliament is in session, the Union Jack flies from Victoria Tower.

House of Lords Chamber

Westminster Hall is more than 900 years old.

The clock tower that holds Big Ben is 316 feet high.

House of Commons Chamber

Region •
London's New
Globe Theater
is a replica of
the 17th-century
playhouse that
originally
hosted William
Shakespeare's
works. ◄

Cultural Heritage

The United Kingdom has a rich cultural heritage that includes the great Renaissance playwright William Shakespeare. With a long history as an imperial power, the nation has been exporting its culture around the world for hundreds of years. For example, India, Canada, and other former British colonies modeled their governments on the British parliamentary system. British culture has also set trends in sports, music, and literature.

Music British music influenced the early music of Canada and the United States, both former British colonies. One British tune long familiar to people in the United States is "God Save the Queen." You probably know it as "My Country, 'Tis of Thee." Several countries have put the words of their national anthems to this traditional British melody.

During the 1960s, many British musical groups—including the Beatles and the Rolling Stones—dominated music charts around the world. In later decades, other British singers, including Elton John, Sting, and Dido, became popular favorites.

Literature The best-known cultural export of the United Kingdom, aside from the English language itself, may be literature. In the 19th century, Mary Shelley dreamed up Frankenstein's monster, and Sir Arthur Conan Doyle first wrote about Sherlock Holmes. Another popular author of the time was **Charles Dickens** (1812–1870), who wrote *Oliver Twist* and *A Christmas Carol*.

Region • In the
early 1960s, the
Beatles became
wildly popular,
not only in the
United Kingdom,
but also around
the world. ▼

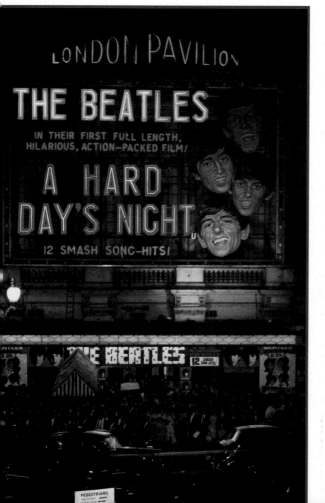

Reading
Social Studies

B. Recognizing
Important
Details Why
was the United
Kingdom able to
spread British
culture across
the world?

Two gifted British writers of the 20th century are Virginia Woolf and George Orwell. Modern British authors have also given the world many popular stories for young people. They include C. S. Lewis, who wrote *The Chronicles of Narnia*, and J. K. Rowling, who created the Harry Potter books.

Region • J. K. Rowling's Harry Potter books have captured the imaginations of children worldwide. ▲

The British Economy

The United Kingdom is an important trading and financial center. Many British citizens also make their living in mining and manufacturing. Factories in the United Kingdom turn out a variety of products ranging from china to sports cars. The nation has plenty of coal, natural gas, and oil to fuel its factories, but it has few other natural resources.

The need for imported goods makes trade another major industry of the United Kingdom. The nation imports many raw materials used in manufacturing. It also imports food, because the farms of this nation produce only enough to feed about two-thirds of its large population.

SECTION 1 ASSESSMENT

Terms & Names

1. Explain the significance of:
   (a) London
   (b) secede
   (c) Good Friday Accord
   (d) Charles Dickens

Using Graphics

2. Use a chart like this one to describe the major aspects of the United Kingdom's modern government, economy, and culture.

Modern United Kingdom	
Government	
Economy	
Culture	

Main Ideas

3. (a) Identify the four regions that make up the United Kingdom.

   (b) What role does the British monarch play in the government of the modern United Kingdom?

   (c) What impact has the culture of the United Kingdom had on its colonies and on other parts of the world?

Critical Thinking

4. **Analyzing Issues**

   Why do you think the conflict in Northern Ireland is so difficult to resolve?

   Think About
   - differences in religious beliefs
   - recent changes in British regional governments
   - the long period of continued violence

ACTIVITY -OPTION- Reread the information about British football from the "Dateline" feature that opens the section. Write a **description** of a sport that interests you.

Sweden

TERMS & NAMES
Riksdag
ombudsman
armed neutrality
hydroelectricity
acid rain
skerry

MAIN IDEA

Sweden offers its people a high standard of living, although it also faces environmental problems.

WHY IT MATTERS NOW

Modern Sweden is dealing with environmental issues that affect many countries around the world.

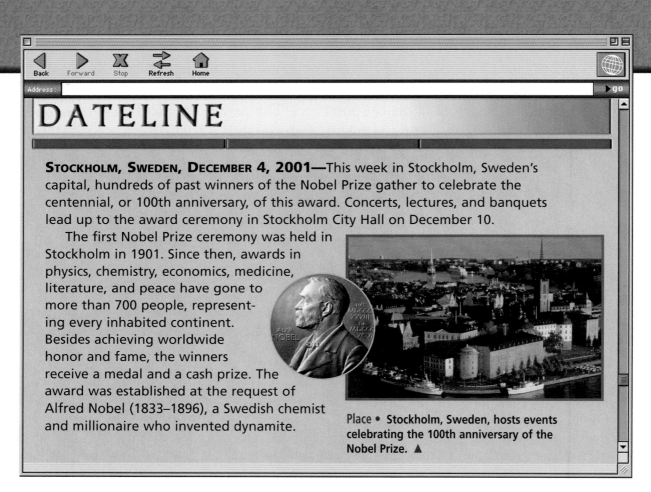

| Back | Forward | Stop | Refresh | Home |

Address: ▶ go

DATELINE

STOCKHOLM, SWEDEN, DECEMBER 4, 2001—This week in Stockholm, Sweden's capital, hundreds of past winners of the Nobel Prize gather to celebrate the centennial, or 100th anniversary, of this award. Concerts, lectures, and banquets lead up to the award ceremony in Stockholm City Hall on December 10.

The first Nobel Prize ceremony was held in Stockholm in 1901. Since then, awards in physics, chemistry, economics, medicine, literature, and peace have gone to more than 700 people, representing every inhabited continent. Besides achieving worldwide honor and fame, the winners receive a medal and a cash prize. The award was established at the request of Alfred Nobel (1833–1896), a Swedish chemist and millionaire who invented dynamite.

Place • Stockholm, Sweden, hosts events celebrating the 100th anniversary of the Nobel Prize. ▲

Sweden's Government

Home of the Nobel Prize, Sweden shares the Scandinavian Peninsula with Norway in Northern Europe (see the map on page 385). The country is a constitutional monarchy; the Swedish monarch has only ceremonial powers and cannot make laws. Instead, the people elect representatives to four-year terms in the Swedish parliament, called the **Riksdag** (REEKS·DAHG).

TAKING NOTES
Use your chart to take notes about Europe today.

Country	Physical Geography	Government
United Kingdom		
Sweden		

The Riksdag The 349 members of the Riksdag nominate Sweden's prime minister. They also appoint ombudsmen. **Ombudsmen** are officials who protect citizens' rights and make sure that the Swedish courts and civil service follow the law.

Swedish citizens vote to determine how many members of each political party serve in the Riksdag. Before 1976, the Social Democratic Labour Party had been in power for nearly 44 years. Today, the Swedish government includes four other parties.

Region •
Women are active in Swedish government. ▶

Foreign Policy Since World War I, Sweden's foreign policy has been one of **armed neutrality**. This means that in times of war, the country has its own military forces but does not take sides in other nations' conflicts.

Even during peacetime, the Swedish government tries not to form military alliances. Unless Sweden is directly attacked, it will not become involved in war. The country is a strong supporter of the United Nations.

Reading
Social Studies

A. Synthesizing
How does Sweden's neutrality affect its foreign relations?

The Economy and the Environment

Privately owned businesses and international trade are important to Sweden's economy. It exports many goods, including metals, minerals, and wood. Engineering and communications are major industries. The automobile industry also provides many jobs.

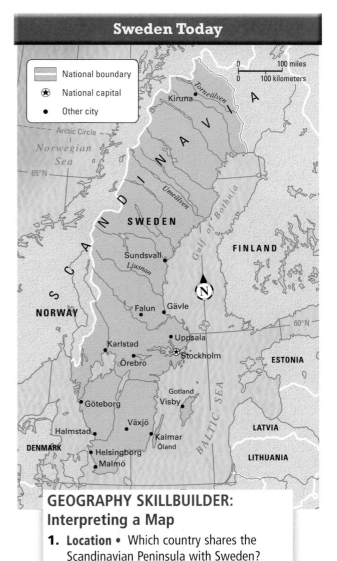

Sweden Today

National boundary
★ National capital
• Other city

0   100 miles
0   100 kilometers

Norwegian Sea
Arctic Circle
65°N
Kiruna
Torneälven
SCANDINAVIA
Umeälven
SWEDEN
Sundsvall
Ljusnan
FINLAND
Gulf of Bothnia
NORWAY
Falun   Gävle
60°N
Karlstad
Uppsala
Örebro
Stockholm
ESTONIA
Göteborg
Gotland
Visby
BALTIC SEA
Halmstad
Växjö
Kalmar
Öland
LATVIA
DENMARK
Helsingborg
Malmö
LITHUANIA

GEOGRAPHY SKILLBUILDER:
Interpreting a Map

1. **Location** • Which country shares the Scandinavian Peninsula with Sweden?
2. **Region** • What is the national capital of Sweden?

The Swedish Labor Force After World War II, many Swedes left their towns and villages to find work in the large cities in the south. Today, more than 80 percent of the population lives in these urban areas. Much of Sweden's labor force is highly educated and enjoys a high standard of living.

Power Sources **Hydroelectricity,** or power generated by water, is the main source of electrical power in Sweden. Nuclear power is also widely used. The Swedish government is looking into other, safer sources of energy, which include solar- and wind-powered energy.

Place • Many in Sweden's highly educated labor force work in the high-tech and engineering industries. ▲

Acid Rain Sweden and its neighboring countries share similar environmental problems. One of the most severe problems is **acid rain.** Acid rain occurs when air pollutants come back to Earth in the form of precipitation. These pollutants may soon poison many trees throughout the region. Sweden and neighboring countries are working to clean up the environment by trying to control air pollutants produced by cars and factories.

Reading
Social Studies

B. Clarifying What causes acid rain?

Daily Life and Culture

Culturally and ethnically, Sweden is primarily a homogeneous country. Ninety percent of the population are native to Sweden and are members of the Lutheran Church of Sweden. The majority of people speak Swedish.

Since World War II, immigrants from Turkey, Greece, and other countries have brought some cultural diversity to Sweden's population. Today, about one in nine people living in Sweden is an immigrant or the child of an immigrant.

Vocabulary

homogeneous: the same throughout

Region • December 13 is St. Lucia's Day, one of Sweden's most important Christian holidays. ▼

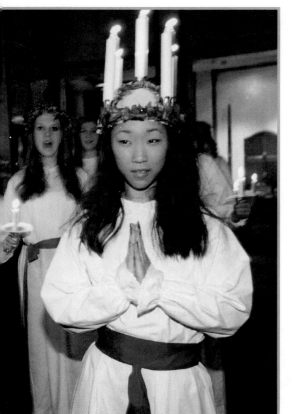

Recreation Workers in Sweden have many benefits, including long vacations. The Swedes love taking time to enjoy both winter and summer sports. Sweden, with its cold weather and many hills and mountains, is a great place for cross-country and downhill skiing. Skating, hockey, and ice fishing are also popular.

Place • Sweden's cold winters have made downhill and cross-country skiing popular. ▶

Many small islands, called **skerries,** dot the Swedish coast. In the summer, many people visit these islands to hike, camp, and fish. Tennis, soccer, and outdoor performances such as concerts are popular as well.

Contributions to World Culture Sweden is well-known for its contributions to drama, literature, and film. The late 19th-century and early 20th-century plays of August Strindberg are produced all over the world. Astrid Lindgren's children's books, including *Pippi Longstocking* (1945), still delight readers everywhere. Ingmar Bergman is famous for the many great films he directed.

SECTION 2 ASSESSMENT

Terms & Names
1. Explain the significance of:
   - (a) Riksdag
   - (b) ombudsman
   - (c) armed neutrality
   - (d) hydroelectricity
   - (e) acid rain
   - (f) skerry

Using Graphics
2. Use a spider map like this one to outline the major aspects of Sweden's government, economy, and culture.

Main Ideas
3. (a) On which European peninsula is Sweden located? What other country shares this peninsula?

   (b) What happened to the Swedish labor force after World War II?

   (c) How has immigration since World War II changed the population of Sweden?

Critical Thinking
4. **Evaluating Decisions**

   What do you think might be the advantages and disadvantages of armed neutrality for Sweden?

Think About
   - Sweden's location
   - the damage and expense of war
   - the benefits of alliances

ACTIVITY -OPTION- Reread the "Dateline" feature at the beginning of this section. Write a short **description** of which category you would like to earn a Nobel Prize in and why.

Spend a Day in Renaissance Florence

You are a traveler visiting Florence, Italy, in the year 1505. It is exciting to be here now. All over Europe, people have heard about the Renaissance, or cultural rebirth, that is taking place in this beautiful city. Artists, architects, writers, and scientists are turning out brilliant work. In the day you spend here, you want to learn about this new cultural movement. You want to be able to tell people at home about Renaissance Florence.

COOPERATIVE LEARNING On these pages are challenges you will encounter as you tour Renaissance Florence. Working with a small group, choose one of these challenges to solve. Divide the work among group members. Look for helpful information in the Data File. Keep in mind that you will present your solution to the class.

LANGUAGE ARTS CHALLENGE

"Florence is home to brilliant artists and writers."

Why did the Renaissance start here? Florence is home to brilliant artists and writers. Successful merchants and craftworkers, along with several powerful families, have made the city rich. Many wealthy people are patrons, or sponsors, of artists' work. You are curious about the people of Florence. Who are the leading figures? What is life like here? Choose one of these options to discover the answers. Use the Data File for help.

ACTIVITIES

1. Choose one major figure who lived in Florence during the Renaissance and research his or her life. Then write a short first-person monologue in which, speaking as that person, you describe your life and work.

2. Imagine you are an ordinary young Florentine living in 1505—for example, a goldsmith's apprentice. Write journal entries for a week in your life.

SCIENCE CHALLENGE

"Its red-tiled dome soars above most other buildings."

The people of Florence are proud of their cathedral, known as the Duomo ("dome" in Italian). Its red-tiled dome soars above most other buildings. People say that its architect used new techniques to build the dome. What discoveries have Renaissance scientists made? How important is science in this cultural movement? Use one of these options to present information. Look in the Data File for help.

ACTIVITIES

1. Draw a cross-section diagram of the dome of the Duomo, designed by Filippo Brunelleschi. Be able to demonstrate how a dome like this is supported.
2. Prepare to interview Brunelleschi about his ideas and inventions. Research his life and work, and create a list of questions to ask him.

Activity Wrap-Up

As a group, review your solution to the challenge you selected. Then present your solution to the class.

LANDMARKS OF RENAISSANCE FLORENCE

- Florence is built on both sides of the **Arno River**. Its population during the Renaissance was about 100,000. Most of the famous buildings are on the right bank. Besides its artists, Renaissance Florence was known for its craftworkers, such as goldsmiths and leatherworkers.

- The **Duomo** stands on the Piazza del Duomo, an open square. In 1418, Filippo Brunelleschi won a contest to build a dome over the unfinished church. He invented new methods and machines to build it. As in earlier domes, vaults or pointed arches support the dome. Brunelleschi added a circular support wall, called a drum, to build it higher.

- The **Ponte Vecchio** ("Old Bridge"), built in 1345, is one of several bridges across the Arno River. Shops, especially those of goldsmiths, line both sides of the bridge.

- The **Pitti Palace**, built in 1458, is on the left bank of the river.

MAJOR FIGURES OF THE RENAISSANCE

- **Filippo Brunelleschi** (1377–1446), architect of the Duomo and the Pitti Palace.

- **Dante** (1265–1321), poet, author of *Divine Comedy.* Dante pioneered the usage of everyday language, instead of Latin, in literature.

- **Isabella d'Este** (1474–1539), noblewoman and patron of many artists.

- **Leonardo da Vinci** (1452–1519), painter, sculptor, engineer, scientist.

- **Michelangelo** (1475–1564), sculptor, painter, architect; sculptor of *David* (1504).

- **Raphael** (1483–1520), painter and architect.

To learn more about Renaissance Florence, go to

RESEARCH LINKS
CLASSZONE.COM

France

TERMS & NAMES
Charles de Gaulle
French Resistance
Jean Monnet
socialism
European Community
impressionism

MAIN IDEA

France was ruined politically and economically by World War II but has since made a full recovery.

WHY IT MATTERS NOW

France is an important member of the European Union and continues to influence the world's economy and cultures.

DATELINE

EXTRA

PARIS, FRANCE, AUGUST 26, 1944

Paris is free! The church bells are still ringing from yesterday's celebrations. After four long years of German control, Paris finally has been liberated. General Charles de Gaulle returned from the United Kingdom yesterday and celebrated the liberation by leading a parade from the Arc de Triomphe to Notre Dame Cathedral.

The liberation of Paris is the result of a two-and-a-half-month advance of Allied forces from the beaches of Normandy in northern France. The French Resistance in Paris began disrupting the German occupiers on August 19, and yesterday, the French army entered Paris.

Region • The liberation of Paris is a significant symbolic victory for the Allies. ▲

The Fifth Republic

During World War II, **Charles de Gaulle** (1890–1970) was a general in the French army. After Germany conquered France in 1940, de Gaulle fled to the United Kingdom. There, he became the leader of the French in exile and stayed in contact with the French Resistance. The **French Resistance** established communications for the Allied war effort, spied on German activity, and sometimes assassinated high-ranking German officers.

TAKING NOTES
Use your chart to take notes about Europe today.

Country	Physical Geography	Government
United Kingdom		
Sweden		

France Today

UNITED KINGDOM

★ National capital
● Other city

English Channel

Calais • Dunkerque
Lille • BELGIUM
Cherbourg • Amiens • Arras
Le Havre • Rouen
Caen • *Seine* Paris ★ Reims • Metz • Nancy
Brest • Chartres • Troyes
Rennes • Le Mans • Orléans • *Loire*
Nantes • Tours • Dijon • Besançon
La Rochelle • Bourges • Clermont-Ferrand • Vichy • Lyon
Limoges • *Rhône*
St.-Étienne • Grenoble
Dordogne
Bordeaux • FRANCE
Garonne • Nîmes • Avignon • Nice
Bayonne • Montpellier • Cannes
Toulouse • Toulon • Calvi
Lourdes • Narbonne • Marseille
Carcassonne • Perpignan • Ajaccio • Bastia

LUXEMBOURG
GERMANY
Strasbourg
Mulhouse
SWITZERLAND
ITALY
MONACO

Bay of Biscay

45°N

SPAIN

ANDORRA

Mediterranean Sea

0   100   200 miles
0   100   200 kilometers

3°E   6°E

GEOGRAPHY SKILLBUILDER:
Interpreting a Map
1. **Location** • Name three countries that border France.
2. **Location** • Which bodies of water does France have access to?

On December 21, 1958, Charles de Gaulle was elected president of France. He reorganized the French constitution and instituted the Fifth Republic of France.

The Government of the Fifth Republic France is a parliamentary republic. Governmental power is split between the president and parliament. The president is elected by the public to a seven-year term; beginning in 2002, the president will serve a five-year term. The president's primary responsibilities are to act as guardian of the constitution and to ensure proper functioning of other authorities.

Parliament has two parts: the Senate and the National Assembly. The president chooses a prime minister, who heads parliament and is largely responsible for the internal workings of the government. The French government is very active in the country's economy.

A Centralized Economy

World War II left France poor and in need of rebuilding. The National Planning Board, established by **Jean Monnet** (moh•NAY) in 1946, launched a series of five-year plans to modernize France and set economic goals for the country.

Reading
Social Studies

A. Comparing Compare the term and role of the president of France with the president of the United States.

Connections to History

Lascaux Cave Paintings On September 12, 1940, while hiking in the hills of Lascaux (lah•SKOH) near the town of Montignac in southern France, four teenage boys discovered ancient cave paintings. They found the caves after their dog fell in a hole in the ground.

Henri Breuil (broy), one of the first archaeologists on the scene, counted more than 600 images of horses (shown here), deer, and bison. The cave paintings are about 17,000 years old, making them some of the oldest works of art yet discovered.

The result of these plans was a mixed economy, with both public and private sectors. The French government nationalized, or took over, major banks; insurance companies; the electric, coal, and steel industries; schools; universities; hospitals; railroads; airlines; and even an automobile company.

This nationalization of industry is a form of socialism. **Socialism** is an economic system in which some businesses and industries are controlled by the government. The government also provides many health and welfare benefits, such as health care, housing, and unemployment insurance. However, today the French government is slowly placing more of the economy under the control of private companies.

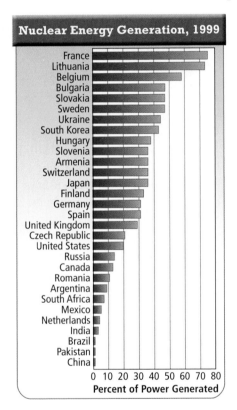

Nuclear Energy Generation, 1999

France
Lithuania
Belgium
Bulgaria
Slovakia
Sweden
Ukraine
South Korea
Hungary
Slovenia
Armenia
Switzerland
Japan
Finland
Germany
Spain
United Kingdom
Czech Republic
United States
Russia
Canada
Romania
Argentina
South Africa
Mexico
Netherlands
India
Brazil
Pakistan
China

0 10 20 30 40 50 60 70 80
Percent of Power Generated

Region • Nuclear power plants are a common sight in the French countryside. ▼

Energy The French economy grew rapidly after 1946, and the country's industry was powered mainly by coal, oil, and gas. When worldwide oil prices rose in the 1970s, the French economy suffered. In the 1980s, France turned to nuclear power so that its economy would be less dependent on oil. Today France draws 75 percent of its power from nuclear energy, a higher percentage than any other nation in the world.

Most famous for its wines, France also exports grains, automobiles, electrical machinery, and chemicals. Although only about 7 percent of the labor force works on farms, France exports more agricultural products than any other nation in the European Community.

The **European Community** is an association developed after World War II to promote economic unity among the countries of Western Europe. Its success gave rise to greater unity, both politically and economically, in the European Union.

Reading
Social Studies

B. Analyzing Motives Why does France produce a large amount of nuclear energy?

BACKGROUND

Tourism is a major industry in France. The country hosts more than 70 million visitors annually, making it the most visited country in the world.

The Culture of Paris

Paris, the capital city of France, is famous for its contributions to world culture, most especially in the arts. Nicknamed "City of Light," Paris has long been an intellectual and artistic center.

Edouard Manet (muh·NAY) (1832–1883) helped influence one of the most important art movements of modern times, impressionism. **Impressionism** is an art style that uses light to create an impression of a scene rather than a strictly realistic picture. Manet inspired such artists as Claude Monet (moh·NAY), Pierre Renoir (ruhn·WAHR), and Paul Cézanne (say·ZAHN). This group of artists worked together in Paris and shared their thoughts and opinions of art.

Paris's Musée d'Orsay and the Louvre (loove) house two of the greatest collections of fine art in the world. The School of Fine Arts leads a tradition of education and art instruction that has produced artists such as Pierre Bonnard (baw·NAHR) (1867–1947) and Balthus (1908–2001).

Region • Monet and his family often modeled for Manet, as in this 1874 painting, *Monet Working on His Boat in Argenteuil.* ▲

Literature France has a rich tradition of literature as well. Marcel Proust, who wrote *Remembrance of Things Past*, was an influential writer in the early 20th century. Other significant writers include Albert Camus (kah·MOO), who wrote *The Stranger*, and Simone de Beauvoir (boh·VWAHR), author of *The Mandarins*.

SECTION 3 ASSESSMENT

Terms & Names

1. Explain the significance of:
   (a) Charles de Gaulle
   (b) French Resistance
   (c) Jean Monnet
   (d) socialism
   (e) European Community
   (f) impressionism

Using Graphics

2. Use a chart like this one to list the major aspects of French government, economy, and culture.

	Major Aspects
Government	
Economy	
Culture	

Main Ideas

3. (a) What role does the French government play in the country's economy?

   (b) What is France's primary source of power?

   (c) Name three contributions of French culture to the world.

Critical Thinking

4. Clarifying

   How was the liberation of Paris a symbolic victory?

   Think About

   • the actions of the French Resistance

   • the cultural life of Paris

ACTIVITY -OPTION- Reread the text on Manet. Draw an impressionist **portrait** of a classmate, friend, or family member.

Germany

MAIN IDEA

Germany has overcome many obstacles to become both a unified and a modern nation.

WHY IT MATTERS NOW

Germany has helped to shape recent European history and contemporary Western culture.

DATELINE

BERLIN, GERMANY, OCTOBER 3, 1990— It is just past midnight. Church bells are ringing, fireworks are exploding, bands are playing, and the streets are filled with celebrating Germans. At midnight, the treaty to reunite East and West Germany became official. Germany is whole once more!

Just a year ago, the Berlin Wall—a 103-mile-long barrier of concrete and barbed wire—still separated East and West Berlin. Constructed in 1961, the Wall kept East Germans from escaping from their Communist government to democratic West Germany. Then, in 1989, as the Communist government weakened, the Wall came down.

Location • Germans celebrate unification in front of the Reichstag, the seat of the federal government. ▲

A Divided Germany

Today, the reunified nation of Germany is one of the largest countries in Europe. When World War II ended in 1945, however, Germany was divided. United States, French, and British soldiers occupied the new West German nation, and Soviet soldiers occupied the new East Germany.

TAKING NOTES
Use your chart to take notes about Europe today.

Country	Physical Geography	Government
United Kingdom		
Sweden		

West Germany The United States helped West Germany set up a democratic government. In part, the United States supported the new nation because it was located between the Communist countries of Eastern Europe and the rest of Western Europe.

With the help of U.S. loans, West Germany experienced a so-called economic miracle. In 20 years, it rebuilt its factories and became one of the world's richest nations. Its economy later became the driving force behind the European Union.

East Germany In contrast to West Germany, East Germany remained poor. Most East Germans saw West Germany, and Western Europe in general, as a place where people had better lives. East Germany's Communist government, however, discouraged contact between east and west.

By 1989, the Soviet Union's control of Eastern Europe was weakening. Hungary, a Soviet ally, relaxed control over its borders with Western Europe. East Germans began crossing the Hungarian border into Austria and eventually made their way into West Germany. After the **Berlin Wall** came down in 1989, more East Germans fled to West Germany.

BACKGROUND

Although Berlin was inside East Germany, it had a large free zone defended by the Allies. The Berlin Wall separated the two parts of the city: East Berlin and West Berlin.

Germany Today

GEOGRAPHY SKILLBUILDER: Interpreting a Map

1. **Location** • Which country is nearest to Germany's national capital?
2. **Place** • Which was larger, East or West Germany?

Region • The new Volkswagen Beetle is typical of German car design, known for its simplicity and style. The first Volkswagen was designed by Ferdinand Porsche (POOR·sheh) in 1934. ▲

Reunified Germany

Since the 1990 **reunification,** or the reuniting of East and West Germany, the German government has spent billions of dollars rebuilding the eastern part of the country. The effort has included roads, factories, housing, and hospitals. The city of Berlin, once again the nation's capital, was also rebuilt. The newly reunified nation also restored the Reichstag (RYK·shtahg), where the Federal Assembly meets.

However, reunification has also caused tensions between "Ossies" (OSS·eez) and "Wessies" (VEHSS·eez). Many Ossies complain about the lack of jobs and the cost of housing. Many Wessies complain about paying taxes to rebuild the nation and to help support the former East Germans.

Reading
Social Studies

Clarifying Why did East Germany need to be rebuilt and not West Germany?

Vocabulary

Ossies:
former East Germans

Wessies:
former West Germans

German Culture

Germany's rich cultural traditions may help to unite its people, who are especially proud of their music and literature. Germans are also famous for designing high-quality products, such as cars, electronic appliances, and other complex machinery.

Music Three of Germany's best-known composers are Johann Sebastian Bach (bahck) (1685–1750), George Frederick Handel (HAHN·duhl) (1685–1759), and **Ludwig van Beethoven** (LOOD·vig vahn BAY·TOH·vuhn) (1770–1827). Their music is still performed and recorded all over the world. German composer Richard Wagner (VAHG·nuhr) (1813–1883) wrote many operas, including a series based on German myths and legends known as the Ring Cycle.

Biography

Beethoven Perhaps the best-loved German composer is Ludwig van Beethoven. Beethoven began to lose his hearing when he was in his 20s. By the time he was 50, he was almost deaf.

Beethoven refused to let his deafness stop him from creating music, however. "I will grapple with Fate, it shall not overcome me," he wrote. In 1824, he finished his Ninth Symphony, which ends with a section containing the well-known "Ode to Joy." An orchestra played this same symphony at an open-air concert during the destruction of the Berlin Wall.

Place •
Half-timber architecture, shown here, is common throughout Germany. ▲

BACKGROUND

More than 100 million people around the world speak German.

Literature One of the greatest writers in the German language was **Rainer Maria Rilke** (RIHL·kuh) (1875–1926). His poems, which are still admired and studied today, were a way for Rilke to communicate his feelings and experiences.

Other important 20th-century German authors include Günter Grass (grahs) (b. 1927) and Thomas Mann (man) (1875–1955). Grass has written about the horrors of World War II, the setting for his novel *The Tin Drum.* Both writers were awarded the Nobel Prize in Literature—Mann in 1929 and Grass in 1999.

SECTION 4 ASSESSMENT

Terms & Names

1. Explain the significance of:
   (a) Berlin Wall
   (b) reunification
   (c) Ludwig van Beethoven
   (d) Rainer Maria Rilke

Using Graphics

2. Use a chart like this one to compare aspects of Germany before and after reunification.

Before Reunification	After Reunification

Main Ideas

3. (a) Describe the economic miracle that occurred in West Germany.

   (b) Why has there been tension between the Ossies and the Wessies?

   (c) On what projects has Germany spent billions of dollars since 1990?

Critical Thinking

4. **Synthesizing**

   What makes Germany an important European country?

   Think About

   ♦ its location

   ♦ its size

   ♦ its role in modern history

ACTIVITY -OPTION- Reread the "Dateline" feature at the beginning of the section. Write a **short story** describing what it might have been like to celebrate the reunification of Germany in 1990.

Making an Outline

►► Defining the Skill

Before writing a research report, you must decide on your topic and then gather information about it. When you have all of the information you need, then you begin to organize it. One way of organizing your information before writing the report is to make an outline. An outline lists the main ideas in the order in which they will appear in the report. It also organizes the main ideas and supporting details according to their importance. The form of every outline is the same. Main ideas are listed on the left and labeled with capital Roman numerals. Supporting ideas are indented and labeled with capital letters. Supporting details are indented farther and labeled with numerals.

►► Applying the Skill

The outline to the right is for a biography of Marie Curie, one of the great physicists of all time. Use the strategies listed below to help you learn how to make an outline.

How to Make an Outline

Strategy ❶ Read the main ideas of this report. They are labeled with capital Roman numerals. Each main idea will need at least one paragraph.

Strategy ❷ Read the supporting ideas for each main idea. These are labeled with capital letters. Notice that some of the main ideas require more supporting ideas than others.

Strategy ❸ Read the supporting details that are included in this outline. These are labeled with numerals. The writer of this outline did not include the supporting details for some of the supporting ideas. It is not necessary to include every piece of information that you have. An outline is intended merely as a guide for you to follow as you write the report.

Strategy ❹ A report can be organized in different ways. This biography is organized chronologically, that is, according to time. It starts with Curie's birth and ends with her legacy after death. The outline follows the order of events in her life. A report can be organized in other ways, such as comparing and contrasting or according to advantages and disadvantages. The outline should clearly reflect the way the report is organized.

❶ I. Who Was She?
   A. Polish-born physicist
❷   B. Birth and early life
   C. Schooling
      1. In secret in Poland (women were not allowed to enter
❸   higher education)
      2. In France at the Sorbonne
❹   a. license of physical sciences, 1893
        b. license of mathematical sciences, 1894
II. The Physicist
   A. Life and work with husband, Pierre Curie
      1. Discoveries
        a. polonium, summer 1898
        b. radium, fall 1898
      2. Nobel Prize in Physics, 1903
        a. shared with Henri Becquerel
        b. Marie was the first woman to ever be awarded
         a Nobel Prize
   B. Her own accomplishments
      1. Became the first female professor at the Sorbonne
        a. took over Pierre's position after his death, 1906
      2. Her research on radioactivity was published, 1910
      3. Nobel Prize in Chemistry, 1911

►► Practicing the Skill

Look through Chapter 14 and find a topic that interests you. Gather information about that topic, and then write an outline for a report about that topic. Be sure to use the correct outline form.

Poland

TERMS & NAMES
Solidarity
Lech Walesa
Czeslaw Milosz
censorship
dissident

MAIN IDEA

Poland has gone through the difficulties of establishing a new democratic government and a new economic system.

WHY IT MATTERS NOW

Poland is an excellent example of the success that has been achieved by the newly independent Eastern European nations.

DATELINE

GDAŃSK, POLAND, 1980

In response to recent increases in food prices, many strikes have broken out across Poland. Today's strikes are much larger than the strikes that occurred in 1976. The shipyards in Gdańsk have 17,000 striking workers. One of the strikers' demands is the right to form labor unions. The recent strikes are yet another sign of the country's weakening economy, which has continued to decline over the past decade. Poland's attempts to improve its economic health by borrowing money from other nations have not helped, as the government is unable to repay those loans.

Place • Polish workers protest poor conditions under the Communist government. ▲

Political and Economic Struggles

The strikes and riots of the 1970s and 1980s were not the first actions Polish citizens took against their government. In 1956, Polish workers had rioted to protest their low wages.

In fact, there have been political and economic struggles in Poland since World War II ended in 1945. At that time, Communists took over the government and set strict wage and price controls.

TAKING NOTES
Use your chart to take notes about Europe today.

Country	Physical Geography	Government
United Kingdom		
Sweden		

Poland Today

GEOGRAPHY SKILLBUILDER: Interpreting a Map

1. **Location** • Name a port city in Poland.
2. **Location** • How many different countries border Poland?

Solidarity In 1980, labor unions throughout Poland joined an organization called **Solidarity.** This trade union was led by **Lech Walesa** (LEK wah·LEHN·suh), an electrical worker from the shipyards of Gdańsk (guh·DAHNSK).

In the beginning, Solidarity's goals were to increase pay and improve working conditions. Before long, however, the organization set its sights on bigger goals. In late 1981, members of Solidarity were calling for free elections and an end to Communist rule. Even though Solidarity had about 10 million members, the government fought back. It suspended the organization, cracked down on protesters, and arrested thousands of members, including Walesa.

BACKGROUND

Poland's capital and largest city is Warsaw. The nation's citizens are called Poles.

Region • In 1980, Solidarity leader Lech Walesa gained the support of labor unions. Ten years later, he became Poland's president. ◄

Region • Poland's senate helps ensure that all the country's citizens have representation. ◄

A Free Poland

In the late 1980s, economic conditions continued to worsen in Poland. The government asked Solidarity leaders to help them solve the country's economic difficulties. Finally, the Communists agreed to Solidarity's demand for free elections.

When the elections were held in 1989, many Solidarity candidates were elected, and the Communists lost power. In 1990, Lech Walesa became the president of a free Poland.

A New Constitution Today, Poland is a parliamentary republic. The country approved a new constitution in 1997. This constitution guarantees civil rights such as free speech. It also helps to balance the powers held by the president, the prime minister, and parliament.

Parliament Poland's parliament is made up of two houses. The upper house, or senate, has 100 members. The lower house, which has 460 members, chooses the prime minister. Usually, as in the United Kingdom, the prime minister is a member of the largest party or alliance of parties within parliament.

A number of seats in parliament are reserved for representatives of the small German and Ukrainian ethnic groups in Poland. In this way, all Polish citizens are ensured a voice in their government.

A Changing Economy

Besides a new government, the Poles have also had to deal with a changing economy. In 1990, Poland's new democratic government quickly switched from a command economy to a free market economy. Prices were no longer controlled by the government, and trade suddenly faced international competition.

Reading
Social Studies

A. Recognizing Important Details What led to free elections in Poland?

BACKGROUND

The Polish president, who is elected every five years, is the head of state.

Inflation Although Polish shops were able to sell goods that had not been available before, prices rose quickly—by almost 80 percent. With this inflation, or a continual rise in prices, people's wages could not keep up with the cost of goods.

Many Polish companies, which could not compete with high-quality foreign goods, went out of business. This, in turn, resulted in high unemployment. As more and more people lost their jobs, Poland's overall standard of living fell.

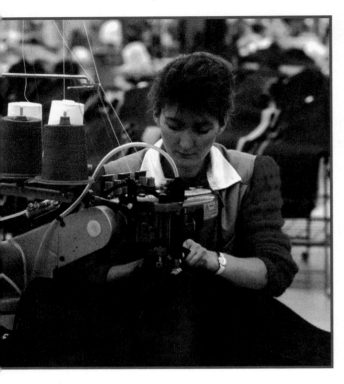

Region • With Poland's economy on the rise, unemployment has decreased. ▲

An Improving Economy In time, new Polish businesses found success, giving more people work. Inflation started to drop. By 1999, inflation was down to around 7 percent. By 2000, Poland no longer needed the economic aid it had been receiving from the United States.

One way to measure the strength of a country's economy is to look at consumer spending. Between 1995 and 2000, Poles bought new cars at a high rate of half a million each year. Today, Poland has 2 million small and medium-sized businesses. The success of these small businesses is another sign of Poland's healthy economy.

Poland's Culture

The history of Poland has been one of ups and downs. In the 1500s and 1600s, Poland was a large and powerful kingdom. By 1795, Russia, Prussia, and Austria had taken control of its land, and Poland ceased to exist as an independent country. Poland did not become a republic until 1918, after World War I. Throughout the centuries, however, Poland has had a rich culture.

Literature Polish literature is full of accounts of struggles for national independence and stories about glorious kingdoms won and lost by heroic patriots.

One of Poland's best-known writers of recent times is **Czeslaw Milosz** (CHEH•slawv MEE•LAWSH) (b. 1911). Milosz published his first book of poems in the 1930s. After World War II, he worked as a diplomat in the United States and then France.

BACKGROUND

A famous Polish general and patriot, Thaddeus Kosciusko (KAHS•ee•UHS•koh), fought on the side of the colonists during the American Revolution.

Milosz, who became a professor at the University of California at Berkeley, won the Nobel Prize in Literature in 1980.

Reading
Social Studies

B. Analyzing Motives Why did the Communist government control the media?

Censorship Under Communist rule, the Polish media were controlled by the government. The government decided what the media could and could not say. It outlawed any information that did not support and praise the accomplishments of Communism. As a result of this **censorship,** many writers could not publish their works. Some of them became dissidents. A **dissident** is a person who openly disagrees with a government's policies.

Place • In 1978, Poland's pride was greatly boosted when Polish-born John Paul II was elected pope. He was the first non-Italian to be elected pope in 456 years. ▲

Supporting the Arts In order to help Polish writers, the government now allows publications printed in Poland to be sold tax-free. To help Polish actors, screenwriters, and directors, movie theaters are repaid their costs for showing Polish movies. Public-sponsored television stations are supported not only by free-market advertising but also by fees the public pays to own television sets.

SECTION 5 ASSESSMENT

Terms & Names

1. Explain the significance of:
   (a) Solidarity
   (b) Lech Walesa
   (c) Czeslaw Milosz
   (d) censorship
   (e) dissident

Using Graphics

2. Use a chart like this one to compare and contrast one aspect of Poland with the same aspect of the United Kingdom, Sweden, France, or Germany.

Poland	Other Country

Main Ideas

3. (a) How did the Polish government respond to Solidarity's goals?

   (b) What was the outcome of Poland's free election in the late 1980s?

   (c) Describe the recent changes in the economy of Poland.

Critical Thinking

4. **Summarizing**

   How would you describe what life was like in Poland before the changes of 1990?

   Think About
   • strikes and riots
   • the Communist government
   • censorship

ACTIVITY -OPTION- Reread the information about Solidarity. Write a short **speech** that might have been given to gain support for the organization in the 1980s.

TERMS & NAMES

Explain the significance of each of the following:

1. London
2. Good Friday Accord
3. armed neutrality
4. hydroelectricity
5. Charles de Gaulle
6. socialism
7. Berlin Wall
8. reunification
9. censorship
10. dissident

REVIEW QUESTIONS

The United Kingdom *(pages 379–383)*

1. What are the two houses that form the British Parliament? Which is more powerful?
2. Why is it necessary for the United Kingdom to import foods and other goods?

Sweden *(pages 384–387)*

3. What role do ombudsmen play in the Swedish government?
4. Why is Sweden an excellent place for skiing?

France *(pages 390–393)*

5. What is France's main source of energy?
6. Identify at least three Impressionist painters.

Germany *(pages 394–397)*

7. What role did the United States government play in West Germany after World War II?
8. Identify at least three famous German composers.

Poland *(pages 399–403)*

9. Why is Lech Walesa important to modern Poland?
10. Describe the new constitution that Poland approved in 1997.

CRITICAL THINKING

Comparing

1. Using your completed chart from Reading Social Studies, p. 378, compare the governments and economies of the United Kingdom, Sweden, France, Germany, and Poland.

Hypothesizing

2. One of Sweden's severe environmental problems is acid rain. Why might it be difficult for a country to solve this problem?

Making Inferences

3. Why do you think it was important to the United States that West Germany have a democratic government?

Visual Summary

The United Kingdom *1*

- British economic, political, and cultural traditions have influenced nations around the world.

2 **Sweden**

- Sweden offers its people a high standard of living.
- Sweden is dealing with environmental issues such as nuclear power and acid rain.

France

- France has made a speedy recovery from World War II.

3

Germany *4*

- Germany has overcome many obstacles to become a unified and modern nation.

Poland *5*

- Poland is an example of the success made possible by the recent independence of Eastern European nations.

Use the map and your knowledge of geography to answer questions 1 and 2.

Additional Test Practice, pp. S1–S33

1. Which of these cities has an airport but is not a capital?

A. Birmingham

B. Paris

C. Stockholm

D. Wroclaw

2. If a ship is traveling along a major shipping line between Liverpool and Göteborg, what seaport would it pass?

A. Gdansk

B. Lille

C. Southhampton

D. Stockholm

The following excerpt is from a speech about Lech Walesa when he won the Nobel Peace Prize in 1983. Use the quotation and your knowledge of world cultures and geography to answer question 3.

PRIMARY SOURCE

He was faced with overwhelming difficulties; the choice of strategy was not easy. The goal was clear enough; the workers' right to organize and the right to negotiate with the country's officials on the workers' social and economic situation. But which of the many available paths would lead him to this goal? . . . Walesa's chosen strategy was that of peace and negotiation.

EGIL AARVIK, excerpt of presentation speech

3. What peaceful strategy did Walesa use to achieve his goal?

A. opposing Communists

B. negotiating with officials

C. facing overwhelming difficulties

D. choosing a clear path

TEST PRACTICE
CLASSZONE.COM

ALTERNATIVE ASSESSMENT

1. **WRITING ABOUT HISTORY**

On November 9, 1989, the Berlin Wall was torn down, and East and West Germany were reunited. Write a headline and a feature article that might have appeared in a newspaper the next day. Include historic information about the wall. Conduct research to find quotes from people who were present at the event and include several of them in your article. Share your article with the class.

2. COOPERATIVE LEARNING

Many festivals and holidays are celebrated in the United Kingdom, Sweden, France, Germany, and Poland. Working in a small group, create a presentation about one of these. Work together to research the meaning of the holiday or festival you choose, when it is celebrated, and the foods and activities associated with it. Decide what form your presentation will take and divide the tasks needed to complete the project.

INTEGRATED TECHNOLOGY

Doing Internet Research

Use the Internet or other library resources to research the life and work of a well-known artist, author, or poet from the United Kingdom, Sweden, France, Germany, or Poland. Prepare a presentation of your findings.

• You might research biographies of the person and collections of his or her work.

• In your research, find out what was historically or socially significant about your subject's writing or artwork.

• Include a copy of the person's artwork or an excerpt from his or her writing.

For Internet links to support this activity, go to

RESEARCH LINKS
CLASSZONE.COM

The Attack: September 11, 2001

Terrorism is the use of violence against people or property to force changes in societies or governments. Acts of terrorism are not new. Throughout history, individuals and groups have used terror tactics to achieve political or social goals.

In recent decades, however, terrorist groups have carried out increasingly destructive and high-profile attacks. The growing threat of terrorism has caused many people to feel vulnerable and afraid. However, it also has prompted action from many nations, including the United States.

Many of the terrorist activities of the late 20th century occurred far from U.S. soil. As a result, most Americans felt safe from such violence. All that changed, however, on the morning of September 11, 2001.

A Surprise Strike

As the nation began another workday, 19 terrorists hijacked four airplanes heading from East Coast airports to California. The hijackers crashed two of the jets into the twin towers of the World Trade Center in New York City. They slammed a third plane into the Pentagon outside Washington, D.C. The fourth plane crashed into an empty field in Pennsylvania after passengers apparently fought the hijackers.

The attacks destroyed the World Trade Center and badly damaged a section of the Pentagon. In all, some 3,000 people died. Life for Americans would never be the same after that day. Before, most U.S. citizens viewed terrorism as something that happened in other countries. Now they knew it could happen on their soil as well.

Officials soon learned that those responsible for the attacks were part of a largely Islamic terrorist network known as al-Qaeda. Observers, including many Muslims, accuse al-Qaeda of preaching a false and extreme form of Islam. Its members believe, among other things, that the United States and other Western nations are evil.

U.S. president George W. Bush vowed to hunt down all those responsible for the attacks. In addition, he called for a greater international effort to combat global terrorism. "This battle will take time and resolve," the president declared. "But make no mistake about it: we will win."

Securing the Nation

As the Bush Administration began its campaign against terrorism, it

Flight Path of the Hijacked Airliners, September 11, 2001

also sought to prevent any further attacks on America. In October 2001, the president signed into law the USA Patriot Act. The law gave the federal government a broad range of new powers to strengthen national security.

The new law enabled officials to detain foreigners suspected of terrorism for up to seven days without charging them with a crime. Officials could also monitor all phone and Internet use by suspects, and prosecute terrorist crimes without any time restrictions or limitations.

In addition, the government created a new cabinet position, the Department of Homeland Security, to coordinate national efforts against terrorism. President Bush named former Pennsylvania governor Tom Ridge as the first Secretary of Homeland Security.

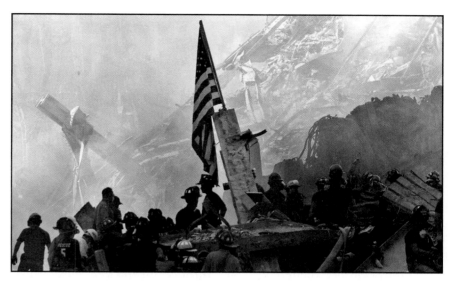

Underneath a U.S. flag posted amid the rubble of the World Trade Center, rescue workers search for survivors of the attack.

Some critics charged that a number of the government's new anti-terrorism measures violated people's civil rights. Supporters countered that occasionally limiting some civil liberties was justified in the name of greater national security.

The federal government also stepped in to ensure greater security at the nation's airports. The September 11 attacks had originated at several airports, with four hijackings occurring at nearly the same time. In November 2001, President Bush signed the Aviation and Transportation Security Act into law. The law put the federal government in charge of airport security. Before, individual airports had been responsible for security. The new law created a federal security force to inspect passengers and carry-on bags. It also required the screening of checked baggage.

While the September 11 attacks shook the United States, they also strengthened the nation's unity and resolve. In 2003, officials approved plans to rebuild on the World Trade Center site and construct a memorial. Meanwhile, the country has grown more unified as Americans recognize the need to stand together against terrorism.

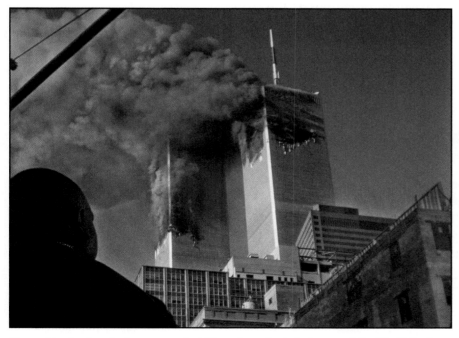

Stunned bystanders look on as smoke billows from the twin towers of the World Trade Center moments after an airplane slammed into each one.

Fighting Back

The attack against the United States on September 11, 2001, represented the single most deadly act of terrorism in modern history. By that time, however, few regions of the world had been spared from terrorist attacks. Today, America and other nations are responding to terrorism in a variety of ways.

The Rise of Terrorism

The problem of modern international terrorism first gained world attention during the 1972 Summer Olympic Games in Munich, Germany. Members of a Palestinian terrorist group killed two Israeli athletes and took nine others hostage. Five of the terrorists, all the hostages, and a police officer were later killed in a bloody gun battle.

Since then, terrorist activities have occurred across the globe. In Europe, the Irish Republican Army (IRA) used terrorist tactics for decades against Britain. The IRA has long opposed British control of Northern Ireland. Since 1998, the two sides have been working toward a peaceful solution to their conflict. In South America, a group known as the Shining Path terrorized the residents of Peru throughout the late 20th century. The group sought to overthrow the government and establish a Communist state.

Africa, too, has seen its share of terrorism. Groups belonging to the al-Qaeda terrorist organization operated in many African countries. Indeed, officials have linked several major attacks against U.S. facilities in Africa to al-Qaeda. In 1998, for example, bombings at the U.S. embassies in Kenya and Tanzania left more than 200 dead and 5,000 injured.

Most terrorists work in a similar way: targeting high profile events or crowded places where people normally feel safe. They include such places as subway stations, bus stops, restaurants, or shopping malls. Terrorists choose these spots carefully in order to gain the most attention and to achieve the highest level of intimidation.

Terrorists use bullets and bombs as their main weapons. In recent years, however, some terrorist groups have used biological and chemical agents in their attacks. These actions involve the release of bacteria or poisonous gas into the air. Gas was the weapon of choice for a radical Japanese religious cult, Aum Shinrikyo. In 1995, cult members released sarin, a deadly nerve gas, in subway stations in Tokyo. Twelve people were killed and more than 5,700 injured. The possibility of this type of terrorism is particularly worrisome, because biochemical agents are relatively easy to acquire.

Terrorism: A Global Problem

PLACE	YEAR	EVENT
Munich, Germany	1972	Palestinians take Israeli hostages at Summer Olympics; hostages and terrorists die in gun battle with police
Beirut, Lebanon	1983	Terrorists detonate truck bomb at U.S. marine barracks, killing 241
Tokyo, Japan	1995	Religious extremists release lethal gas into subway stations, killing 12 and injuring thousands
Omagh, Northern Ireland	1998	Faction of Irish Republican Army sets off car bomb, killing 29
Moscow, Russia	2002	Rebels from Chechnya seize a crowded theater; rescue effort leaves more than 100 hostages and all the terrorists dead

Hunting Down Terrorists

Most governments have adopted an aggressive approach to tracking down and punishing terrorist groups. This approach includes spying on the groups to gather information on membership and future plans. It also includes striking back harshly after a terrorist attack, even to the point of assassinating known terrorist leaders.

Another approach that governments use is to make it more difficult for terrorists to act. This involves eliminating a terrorist group's source of funding. President Bush issued an executive order freezing the U.S. assets of alleged terrorist organizations as well as various groups accused of supporting terrorism. President Bush asked other nations to freeze such assets as well. By the spring of 2002, the White House reported, the United States and other countries had blocked nearly $80 million in alleged terrorist assets.

Battling al-Qaeda

In one of the more aggressive responses to terrorism, the United States quickly took military action against those it held responsible for the September 11 attacks.

U.S. officials had determined that members of the al-Qaeda terrorist group had carried out the assault under the direction of the group's leader, Osama bin Laden. Bin Laden was a Saudi Arabian millionaire who lived in Afghanistan. He directed his terrorist activities under the protection of the country's extreme Islamic government, known as the Taliban.

The United States demanded that the Taliban turn over bin Laden. The Taliban refused. In October 2001, U.S. forces began bombing Taliban air defenses, airfields, and command centers. They also struck numerous al-Qaeda training camps. On the ground, the United States provided assistance to rebel groups opposed to the Taliban. By December, the United States had driven the Taliban from power and severely weakened the al-Qaeda network. However, as of 2003, Osama bin Laden was still believed to be at large.

Osama bin Laden delivers a videotaped message from a hidden location shortly after the U.S.-led strikes against Afghanistan began.

Troops battling the Taliban in Afghanistan await transport by helicopter.

The War in Iraq

In the ongoing battle against terrorism, the United States confronted the leader of Iraq, Saddam Hussein. The longtime dictator had concerned the world community for years. During the 1980s, Hussein had used chemical weapons to put down a rebellion in his own country. In 1990, he had invaded neighboring Kuwait—only to be pushed back by a U.S.-led military effort. In light of such history, many viewed Hussein as an increasing threat to peace and stability in the world. As a result, the Bush Administration led an effort in early 2003 to remove Hussein from power.

The Path to War

One of the main concerns about Saddam Hussein was his possible development of so-called weapons of mass destruction. These are weapons that can kill large numbers of people. They include chemical and biological agents as well as nuclear devices.

Bowing to world pressure, Hussein allowed inspectors from the United Nations to search Iraq for such outlawed weapons. Some investigators, however, insisted that the Iraqis were not fully cooperating with the inspections.

U.S. and British officials soon threatened to use to force to disarm Iraq. During his State of the Union address in January 2003, President Bush declared Hussein too great a threat to ignore in an age of increased terrorism. Reminding Americans of the September 11 attacks, Bush stated, "Imagine those 19 hijackers with other weapons and other plans—this time armed by Saddam Hussein. It would take one vial, one canister, one crate slipped into this country to bring a day of horror like none we have ever known. We will do every-thing in our power to make sure that day never comes."

Operation Iraqi Freedom

In the months that followed, the UN Security Council debated what action to take. Some countries, such as France and Germany, called for letting the inspectors continue searching for weapons. British prime minister Tony Blair, however, accused the Iraqis of "deception and evasion" and insisted inspections would never work.

On March 17, President Bush gave Saddam Hussein and his top aides 48 hours to leave the country or face a military strike. The Iraqi leader refused. On March 19, a coalition led by the United States and Britain launched air strikes in and around the Iraqi capital, Baghdad. The next day, coalition forces marched into Iraq though Kuwait. The invasion of Iraq to remove Saddam Hussein, known as Operation Iraqi Freedom, had begun.

The military operation met with strong opposition from numerous countries. Russian president Vladimir Putin claimed the invasion could "in no way be justified." He and others criticized the policy of attacking a nation to prevent it from future misdeeds. U.S. and British officials, however, argued that they would not wait for Hussein to strike first.

As coalition troops marched north to Baghdad, they met pockets of stiff resistance and engaged in fierce fighting in several southern cities. Meanwhile, coalition forces parachuted into northern Iraq and began moving south toward the capital city. By early April, Baghdad had fallen and the regime of Saddam Hussein had collapsed. After less than four weeks of fighting, the coalition had won the war.

U.S. Army Specialist Shoshana Johnson was one of several Americans held prisoner and eventually released during the war in Iraq.

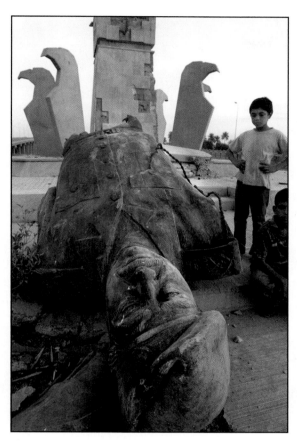

As the regime of Saddam Hussein collapsed, statues of the dictator toppled.

The Struggle Continues

Despite the coalition victory, much work remained in Iraq. The United States installed a civil administrator, retired diplomat L. Paul Bremer, to help oversee the rebuilding of the nation. With the help of Bremer and others, the Iraqis established their own interim government several months after the war. The new governing body went to work creating a constitution and planning democratic elections.

Meanwhile, numerous U.S. troops had to remain behind to help maintain order and battle pockets of fighters loyal to Saddam Hussein. As for the defeated dictator, intelligence officials searched for clues of his whereabouts. The former Iraqi leader disappeared toward the end of the war, and it was unclear whether he had died or escaped.

Finally, the United States and Britain came under increasing fire for failing to find any weapons of mass destruction in the months after the conflict ended. U.S. and British officials insisted that it would be only a matter of time before they found Hussein's deadly arsenal.

Despite the unresolved issues, coalition leaders declared the defeat of Saddam Hussein to be a victory for global security. In a post-war speech to U.S. troops aboard the aircraft carrier USS Abraham Lincoln, President Bush urged the world community to keep moving forward in its battle against terrorism. "We do not know the day of final victory, but we have seen the turning of the tide," declared the president. "No act of the terrorists will change our purpose, or weaken our resolve, or alter their fate. Their cause is lost. Free nations will press on to victory."

President George W. Bush and British prime minister Tony Blair stood together throughout the war.

Special Report Assessment

1. Main Ideas

a. What steps did the U.S. government take to make the nation more secure after the attacks on September 11, 2001?

b. Why did the United States take military action against the Taliban in Afghanistan?

c. What was the result of Operation Iraqi Freedom?

2. Critical Thinking

Analyzing Issues Is it important for the U.S. government to respect people's civil rights as it wages a war against terrorism? Why or why not?

THINK ABOUT
- what steps are necessary to protect the nation
- a government that grows too powerful

World Cultures AND GEOGRAPHY

Skillbuilder Handbook

Table of Contents

1.1 Summarizing

Defining the Skill

When you **summarize,** you restate a paragraph, passage, or chapter in fewer words. You include only the main ideas and most important details. It is important to use your own words when summarizing.

Applying the Skill

The passage below describes the origins of several state names in the United States. Use the strategies listed below to help you summarize the passage.

How to Summarize

Strategy ❶ Look for topic sentences stating the main idea or ideas. These are often at the beginning of a section or paragraph. Briefly restate each main idea—in your own words.

Strategy ❷ Include key facts and any names, dates, numbers, amounts, or percentages from the text.

Strategy ❸ After writing your summary, review it to see that you have included only the most important details.

STATES' NAMES

❶ The name of a state often comes from that state's geography. For example, ❷ the name for Montana comes from a Latin word that means "mountainous."

❶ Other states are named after people who were in power at the time the area was explored or settled. Present-day Louisiana was explored by a Frenchman named La Salle. ❷ He named the area Louisiana after the French king at the time, Louis XIV. The state of ❷ Georgia was named after King George II of England, who granted the right to start the colony.

❶ Still other states get their names from Native American tribes living in the area when Europeans arrived. ❷ Arkansas, Alabama, and Massachusetts were named for the Native American tribes living there.

Write a Summary

You should be able to write your summary in a short paragraph. The paragraph at right summarizes the passage you just read.

 The names of states in the United States often came from geographical features, the names of people in power, or the names of Native American tribes.

Practicing the Skill

Turn to Chapter 4, Section 2, "A Constitutional Democracy." Read "Three Branches of Government" and write a paragraph summarizing the passage.

1.2 Taking Notes

Defining the Skill

When you **take notes,** you write down the important ideas and details of a paragraph, passage, or chapter. A chart or an outline can help you organize your notes to use in the future.

Applying the Skill

The following passage describes the vegetation regions of North and South America. Use the strategies listed below to help you take notes on the passage.

How to Take and Organize Notes

Strategy 1 Look at the title to find the main topic of the passage.

Strategy 2 Identify the main ideas and details of the passage. Then summarize the main idea and details in your notes.

Strategy 3 Identify key terms and define them. The term *vegetation region* is shown in boldface type and underlined; both techniques signal that it is a key term

Strategy 4 In your notes, use abbreviations to save time and space. You can abbreviate words such as *north (n.), south (s.),* and *United States (U.S.)* to save time and space.

---

1 VEGETATION OF NORTH AND SOUTH AMERICA

2 North and South America have similar **3** vegetation regions. Some of these are are **2** deserts, tropical rain forests, forests, and grasslands. Both North and South America have deserts, which are very dry. **2** The Painted Desert in the United States and the Patagonia area of Argentina are examples of deserts.

A large percentage of the world's tropical rain forests lie in South America and southern North America. **2** The Amazon region in Brazil has the largest tropical rain forest in the world.

2 North America has many more forests than South America does. Both continents have grasslands. **2** The central part of North America is a type of grassland called prairie.

Make a Chart

Making a chart can help you take notes on a passage. The chart below contains notes from the passage you just read.

2 Item	Notes
1. **3** vegetation region	an area of land that has similar plants
a. desert	Painted in **4** N. America; Patagonia in **4** S. America
b. tropical rain forest	Amazon region in Brazil largest in world
c. forest	**4** N. America has more than **4** S. America
d. grassland	central **4** N. America type of grassland called prairie

Practicing the Skill

Turn to Chapter 1, Section 1, "The World at Your Fingertips." Read "History and Geography" and use a chart to take notes on the passage.

1.3 Sequencing Events

Defining the Skill

Sequence is the order in which events follow one another. By being able to follow the sequence of events through history, you can get an accurate sense of the relationship among events.

Applying the Skill

The following passage shows the sequence of events that led to the American Civil War. Use the strategies listed below to help you follow the sequence of events.

How to Find the Sequence of Events

Strategy 1 Look for specific dates provided in the text. The dates may not always read from earliest to latest, so be sure to match an event with the date.

Strategy 2 Look for clues about time that allow you to order events according to sequence. Words and phrases such as *day, week, month,* or *year* may help to sequence the events.

> **THE CIVIL WAR BEGINS**
>
> On **1** December 20, 1860, South Carolina became the first state to secede, or leave the Union. Many other states followed. In **2** February of the following year, these states united to form the Confederate States of America, also known as the Confederacy. Soon afterward, Confederate soldiers began seizing federal forts. By the time that Lincoln was sworn in as president on **1** March 4, 1861, only four southern forts remained in Union hands. The most important was Fort Sumter, on an island in Charleston harbor.
>
> On the morning of **1** April 12, Confederate cannons began firing on Fort Sumter. The war between North and South had begun.

Make a Time Line

Making a time line can help you sequence events. The time line below shows the sequence of events in the passage you just read.

December 20, 1860: South Carolina leaves the Union.

February 1861: Confederacy formed.

March 4, 1861: Lincoln sworn in as president.

April 12, 1861: Confederacy attacks Fort Sumter. Civil War begins.

Practicing the Skill

Turn to Chapter 11, Section 2, "Traders, Explorers, and Colonists." Read "Leaders in Exploration" and "Europe Enters a New Age," then make a time line showing the sequence of events in those two passages.

1.4 Finding Main Ideas

Defining the Skill

The **main idea** is a statement that summarizes the subject of a speech, an article, a section of a book, or a paragraph. Main ideas can be stated or unstated. The main idea of a paragraph is often stated in the first or last sentence. If it is the first sentence, it is followed by sentences that support that main idea. If it is the last sentence, the details build up to the main idea. To find an unstated idea, you must use the details of the paragraph as clues.

Applying the Skill

The following paragraph describes the Taino, some of the first Native Americans to see European explorers. Use the strategies listed below to help you identify the main idea.

How to Find the Main Idea

Strategy ① Identify what you think may be the stated main idea. Check the first and last sentences of the paragraph to see if either could be the stated main idea.

Strategy ② Identify details that support the main idea. Some details explain that idea. Others give examples of what is stated in the main idea.

> ### DECLINE OF THE TAINO
>
> ① The Taino were some of the first people in the western hemisphere to see European explorers, and the meeting nearly destroyed them. Christopher Columbus landed in what is now the West Indies in 1492. He thought he had found India, so he called the Taino people he found there "Indians." The Europeans were looking for gold. ② They enslaved the Taino, forcing them to work long hours in mines or in other dangerous jobs. ② Many Taino died because of this treatment. ② Others died from diseases the Europeans unknowingly brought with them. ② By the mid-1500s, almost all of the Taino had been destroyed. However, some survived. The Taino still exist today.

Make a Chart

Making a chart can help you identify the main idea and details in a passage or paragraph. The chart below identifies the main idea and details in the paragraph you just read.

Main Idea: Meeting Europeans led to the near destruction of the Taino.

Detail: The Europeans enslaved the Taino and made them mine for gold.
Detail: Many Taino died from the hard work.
Detail: Other Taino died from diseases brought by the Europeans.
Detail: Almost all the Taino were destroyed by the mid-1500s.

Practicing the Skill

Turn to Chapter 6, Section 2, "Ancient Latin America." Read "The Spanish in Latin America" and create a chart that identifies the main idea and the supporting details.

1.5 Categorizing

Defining the Skill

To **categorize** is to sort people, objects, ideas, or other information into groups, called categories. Historians categorize information to help them identify and understand patterns in historical events.

Applying the Skill

The following passage discusses the involvement of various countries in World War II. Use the strategies listed below to help you categorize information.

How to Categorize

Strategy 1 First, decide what kind of information needs to be categorized. Decide what the passage is about and how that information can be sorted into categories. For example, look at the different ways countries reacted to World War II.

Strategy 2 Then find out what the categories will be. To find how countries reacted to the war, look for clue words such as *in response, some, other,* and *both.*

Strategy 3 Once you have chosen the categories, sort information into them. Which countries were Axis Powers? Which were Allies? What about the ones who were conquered and those who never fought at all?

> ## WORLD WAR II ALLIANCES
>
> **1** During World War II, most countries around the world had to choose which side to take in the conflict. Some countries were conquered so quickly that they could not join either side. **2** *Others* chose to remain neutral. **2** Italy and Japan joined with Germany to form the Axis Powers. In 1939, Germany began the war by conquering Poland. **2** *In response,* Great Britain and France (the first two Allied Powers) declared war on Germany. Germany quickly conquered many countries, including Denmark, Norway, the Netherlands, Belgium, and France. **2** During 1941, *both* the Soviet Union and the United States entered the war on the Allied side. **2** Sweden and Switzerland remained neutral during the war.

Make a Chart

Making a chart can help you categorize information. You should have one more column than you have categories. The chart below shows how the information from the passage you just read can be categorized.

3 Name of Alliance	Axis	Allied Powers	Neutral
Countries	• Germany • Japan • Italy	• Great Britain • France • Soviet Union • United States	• Sweden • Switzerland

Practicing the Skill

Turn to Chapter 14, Section 4, "Germany." Read "A Divided Germany" and make a chart in which you categorize the changes that took place in Germany after World War II.

1.6 Making Public Speeches

Defining the Skill

A speech is a talk given in public to an audience. Some speeches are given to persuade the audience to think or act in a certain way, or to support a cause. You can learn how to **make public speeches** effectively by analyzing great speeches in history.

Applying the Skill

The following is a part of the Gettysburg Address given by Abraham Lincoln in 1863 to dedicate a cemetery on the Civil War battlefield at Gettysburg. Use the strategies listed below to help you analyze Lincoln's speech and prepare a speech of your own.

How to Analyze and Prepare a Speech

Strategy ❶ Choose one central idea or theme and organize your speech to support it. Lincoln organized his speech around the idea of giving meaning to the deaths of American soldiers.

Strategy ❷ Use words or images that will win over your audience. Lincoln said the dead soldiers had given the living a task—to help the nation "have a new birth of freedom."

Strategy ❸ Repeat words or images to drive home your main point—as if it is the "hook" of a pop song. Lincoln repeats the word *here,* to emphasize the idea that the new freedom will begin here, in a place of sacrifice and death. It all starts "here."

GETTYSBURG ADDRESS

The world will little note, nor long remember what we say ❸ here, but it can never forget what they did ❸ here. ❶ It is for us the living, rather, to be dedicated ❸ here to the unfinished work which they who fought ❸ here have thus far so nobly advanced. It is rather for us to be ❸ here dedicated to the great task remaining before us—that from these honored dead we take increased devotion to that cause for which they gave the last full measure of devotion—that we ❸ here highly resolve that these dead shall not have died in vain— ❷ that this nation, under God, shall have a new birth of freedom—and that government of the people, by the people, for the people, shall not perish from the earth.

Make an Outline

Making an outline like the one to the right will help you make an effective public speech.

Practicing the Skill

Turn to Chapter 3, Section 2, "A Rich Diversity in Climate and Resources." Read the section, especially the quote from John F. Kennedy on page 79, and use the quote as the subject for your speech. First, make an outline like the one to the right to organize your ideas. Then write your speech. Next, practice giving your speech. Make it a three-minute speech.

Title: Gettysburg Address

I. Introduce Theme: The living will give meaning to these soldiers' deaths.
  A. Those who fought will never be forgotten.
  B. It is job of the living to complete the task for which the soldiers died—preserving the government and spreading freedom.

II. Repeat theme: Here we dedicate ourselves to the task
  A. We take up the cause from those who gave their lives for it.
  B. We resolve that the soldiers will not have died in vain.

III. Conclude: Here there will be a new birth of freedom.

2.1 Analyzing Points of View

Defining the Skill

Analyzing points of view means looking closely at a person's arguments to understand the reasons behind that person's beliefs. The goal of analyzing a point of view is to understand different thoughts, opinions, and beliefs about a topic.

Applying the Skill

The following passage describes the difference between Native American and European attitudes about land use. Use the strategies below to help you analyze the points of view.

How to Analyze Points of View

Strategy ❶ Look for statements that show you a particular point of view on an issue. For example, Native Americans believed land should be preserved for the future. European colonists believed land could be owned and changed as desired.

Strategy ❷ Think about why different people or groups held a particular point of view. Ask yourself what they valued. What were they trying to gain or to protect? What were they willing to sacrifice?

Strategy ❸ Write a summary that explains why different groups of people might have taken different positions on this issue.

> **LAND USE**
>
> Native Americans and Europeans had many conflicts because of differing ideas about land use. ❶ Most Native Americans believed that land must be preserved for future generations. They believed the present generation had the right to use land for hunting and farming. However, no one had the right to buy or sell land. Also, no one should ever damage or destroy land.
>
> In contrast, Europeans had a long history of taming wilderness and owning land. As a result, ❶ Europeans believed that they could buy land, sell it, and alter it. For example, if they wished to mine for gold underground, they could destroy landscape as they dug the mine. ❶ Europeans used land to make money.

Make a Diagram

Using a diagram can help you analyze points of view. The diagram below analyzes the different points of view of the Native Americans and the European colonists in the passage you just read.

❷ *Native Americans*
- *preserved land for the future*
- *used land to provide for present needs*
- *wanted to protect the heritage of their descendants*

❷ *Colonists*
- *tradition of taming wilderness and owning land*
- *bought and sold land; changed and sometimes harmed it*
- *wanted to make money*

❸ *Native Americans wanted to preserve the land. They did so because they valued their heritage. The colonists bought land, sold it, and changed it. They did so because they valued making money*

Practicing the Skill

Turn to Chapter 5, Section 2, "A Constitutional Monarchy." Read "Many Cultures, Many Needs" about the disagreement between separatists and nationalists regarding Quebec's independence. Make a diagram to analyze their different points of view.

2.2 Comparing and Contrasting

Defining the Skill

Comparing means looking at the similarities and differences between two or more things. **Contrasting** means examining only the differences between them. Historians compare and contrast events, personalities, behaviors, beliefs, and situations in order to understand them.

Applying the Skill

The following passage describes the states of Alaska and Texas. Use the strategies below to help you compare and contrast these two states.

How to Compare and Contrast

Strategy ❶ Look for two aspects of the subject that can be compared and contrasted. This passage compares Alaska and Texas, the two largest states in the United States.

Strategy ❷ To contrast, look for clue words that show how two things differ. Clue words include *however, but, on the other hand, while,* and *yet.*

Strategy ❸ To find similarities, look for clue words indicating that two things are alike. Clue words include *both, together, alike,* and *similarly.*

TWO BIG STATES

❶ Texas and Alaska are ❸ *alike* in being the two largest states in the United States, ❷ *but* they have little else in common. Alaska is more than twice as large as Texas. ❷ *However,* Texas has about 30 times the population of Alaska. Because of their size, ❸ *both* states have a variety of climate zones, ❷ *yet* Texas is generally warmer than Alaska. One reason for this is that Alaska lies much further north. More than 30 percent of Alaska's land is within the Arctic Circle. Texas has very fertile soil and more farms than any other state, ❷ *while* agriculture is a small part of Alaska's economy. Finally, Texas became a state more than 100 years before Alaska did.

Make a Venn Diagram

Making a Venn diagram will help you identify similarities and differences between two things. In the overlapping area, list characteristics shared by both subjects. Then, in the separate ovals, list the characteristics of each subject not shared by the other. This Venn diagram compares and contrasts Texas and Alaska.

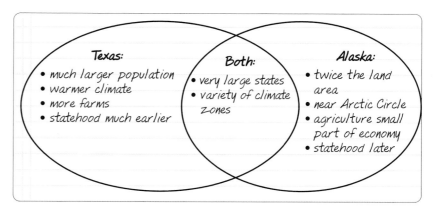

Texas:
- much larger population
- warmer climate
- more farms
- statehood much earlier

Both:
- very large states
- variety of climate zones

Alaska:
- twice the land area
- near Arctic Circle
- agriculture small part of economy
- statehood later

Practicing the Skill

Turn to Chapter 7, Section 2, "Government in Mexico: Revolution and Reform." Read "Mexico's Government Today" and make a Venn diagram showing the similarities and differences between Mexico's government and that of the United States.

2.3 Analyzing Causes; Recognizing Effects

Defining the Skill

A **cause** is an action in history that makes something happen. An **effect** is the historical event that is the result of the cause. A single event may have several causes. It is also possible for one cause to result in several effects. Historians identify cause-and-effect relationships to help them understand why historical events took place.

Applying the Skill

The following paragraph describes events that caused changes in the way of life of the ancient Maya people of Central America. Use the strategies below to help you identify the cause-and-effect relationships.

How to Analyze Causes and Recognize Effects

Strategy ① Ask why an action took place. Ask yourself a question about the title and topic sentence, such as, "What caused Maya civilization to decline?"

Strategy ② Look for effects. Ask yourself, "What happened?" (the effect). Then ask, "Why did it happen?" (the cause). For example, "What caused the Maya to abandon their cities?"

Strategy ③ Look for clue words that signal causes, such as *cause*, *contributed*, and *led to*.

> **① DECLINE OF MAYA CIVILIZATION**
>
> ① The civilization of the Maya went into a mysterious decline around A.D. 900. ② Maya cities in the southern lowlands were abandoned, trade ceased, and the huge stone pyramids of the Maya fell into ruin. No one really understands what happened to the Maya, but there are many theories.
>
> ③ Some believe that a change in climate *caused* the decline of Maya civilization. Three long droughts between 810 and 910 meant that there was not enough water for Maya crops. ② As a result, the Maya abandoned their cities. ③ Other researchers believe that additional problems *contributed* to the crisis. They include overpopulation and warfare among the Maya nobility.

Make a Diagram

Using a diagram can help you understand causes and effects. The diagram below shows two causes and an effect for the passage you just read.

Cause: Three long droughts occurred between 810 and 910.

Cause: Other problems such as overpopulation and warfare among the Maya nobility developed.

Effect: Maya civilization declined.

Practicing the Skill

Turn to Chapter 3, Section 2, "A Rich Diversity in Climate and Resources." Read Connections to History, "The Dust Bowl Disaster" and make a diagram about the causes and effects of the drought on the Great Plains during the 1930s.

2.4 Making Inferences

Defining the Skill

Inferences are ideas that the author has not directly stated. **Making inferences** involves reading between the lines to interpret the information you read. You can make inferences by studying what is stated and using your common sense and previous knowledge.

Applying the Skill

The passage below explains what we know about the early Native Americans who built gigantic mounds of earth for ceremonial purposes. Use the strategies below to help you make inferences from the passage.

How to Make Inferences

Strategy ❶ Read to find statements of facts and ideas. Knowing the facts will give you a good basis for making inferences.

Strategy ❷ Use your knowledge, logic, and common sense to make inferences that are based on facts. Ask yourself, "What does the author want me to understand?" For example, from the facts about how the earth for the mounds was transported, you can make the inference that building the mounds was incredibly hard work and took a very long time. See other inferences in the chart below.

> ### THE MOUND BUILDERS
>
> Early Native American people built gigantic mounds of earth for ceremonial purposes. ❶ The people who built the mounds did not have wheeled vehicles or pack animals to transport the earth. The mounds are made of hundreds of tons of earth. Some mounds appear to have been used as burial plots. ❶ Many Indian artifacts were found buried in those mounds. Other giant mounds served as platforms for temples. ❶ Still other mounds seem to have been symbolic. For example, the Great Serpent Mound in Ohio is shaped like a giant snake.

Make a Chart

Making a chart will help you organize information and make logical inferences. The chart below organizes information from the passage you just read.

❶ Stated Facts and Ideas	❷ Inferences
The Mound Builders did not have wheeled vehicles or pack animals to transport the earth. The mounds contain hundreds of tons of earth.	Building the mounds was incredibly difficult and time-consuming work, as the builders had to carry the earth by hand.
Artifacts were found buried in the mounds.	Native Americans buried objects with their dead.
Some mounds were symbolic, such as the Great Serpent Mound.	The serpent may have been important in their religion.

Practicing the Skill

Turn to Chapter 3, Section 1, "From Coast to Coast." Read Strange but True, "Quakes Shake Central U.S. Lands" and use a chart like the one above to make inferences about earthquakes in the United States.

2.5 Making Decisions

Defining the Skill

Making decisions involves choosing between two or more options, or courses of action. In most cases, decisions have consequences, or results. Sometimes decisions may lead to new problems. By understanding how historical figures made decisions, you can learn how to improve your own decision-making skills.

Applying the Skill

The passage below explains the decision British Prime Minister Chamberlain faced when Germany threatened aggression in 1938. Use the strategies below to analyze his decision.

How to Make Decisions

Strategy 1 Identify a decision that needs to be made. Think about what factors make the decision difficult.

Strategy 2 Identify possible consequences of the decision. Remember that there can be more than one consequence to a decision.

Strategy 3 Identify the decision that was made.

Strategy 4 Identify actual consequences that resulted from the decision.

> ### PEACE OR WAR?
>
> In 1938, German leader Adolf Hitler demanded a part of Czechoslovakia where mostly Germans lived. **1** British Prime Minister Neville Chamberlain had to decide how to respond to that aggression. **2** He could threaten to go to war, but he feared that Britain was not ready. **2** If he gave Germany the region, he might avoid war, but he would be setting a bad example by giving in to a dictator. **3** Along with the French leader, Chamberlain decided to give Germany what it demanded. In exchange, Hitler promised not to take any more land in Europe. **4** Six months later, Germany took the rest of Czechoslovakia and later invaded Poland.

Make a Flow Chart

A flow chart can help you identify the process of making a decision. The flow chart below shows the decision-making process in the passage you just read.

1 Decision to Be Made: How should Chamberlain handle German aggression? Should he give Hitler what he wants or fight against it?

2 Possible Consequences: Go to war and risk losing because his country is not ready.

2 Possible Consequences: Give Hitler what he wants and risk setting a bad example.

3 Decision Made: Give Hitler and Germany part of Czechoslovakia

4 Actual Consequence: Hitler broke his word and invaded Czechoslovakia and Poland. Britain had to fight a war with Germany anyway.

Practicing the Skill

Turn to Chapter 13, Section 2, "Eastern Europe and Russia." Read "The Breakup of the Soviet Union" and make a flow chart to identify Gorbachev's decision and its consequences as described in the section.

2.6 Recognizing Propaganda

Defining the Skill

Propaganda is communication that aims to influence people's opinions, emotions, or actions. Propaganda is not always factual. Rather, it uses one-sided language or striking symbols to sway people's emotions. Modern advertising often uses propaganda. By thinking critically, you will avoid being swayed by propaganda.

Applying the Skill

The following political cartoon from World War I shows an immigrant being exposed as an "enemy alien." Use the strategies listed below to help you understand how the cartoon works as propaganda.

How to Recognize Propaganda

Strategy ❶ Identify the aim, or purpose, of the cartoon. Point out the subject and explain the point of view.

Strategy ❷ Identify those images in the cartoon that viewers might respond to emotionally and identify the emotions.

Strategy ❸ Think critically about the cartoon. What facts has the cartoon ignored?

Stripped! By J. H. Cassel

Make a Chart

Making a chart will help you think critically about a piece of propaganda. The chart below summarizes the information about the anti-immigrant cartoon.

❶	Identify Purpose	The cartoon shows "an enemy alien" being exposed by the U.S. government.
❷	Identify Emotions	The cartoonist uses the man's posture to suggest he is sneaky and has something to hide. The cartoonist also shows him trying to hide under a "cloak" of patriotism—the U.S. flag.
❸	Think Critically	Some viewers may conclude that all recent immigrants are enemy aliens, when probably only a tiny minority were helping the enemy during World War I.

Practicing the Skill

Turn to Chapter 13, Section 1, "Eastern Europe Under Communism." Read "Soviet Culture," paying special attention to the photograph on page 354. Use a chart like the one above to think critically about the statue shown in the photograph as an example of propaganda.

2.7 Identifying Facts and Opinions

Defining the Skill

Facts are events, dates, statistics, or statements that can be proved to be true. Opinions are judgments, beliefs, and feelings. By identifying facts and opinions, you will be able to think critically when a person is trying to influence your own opinion.

Applying the Skill

The following passage tells about a man named John Henry, who became a legend in American folklore. Use the strategies listed below to distinguish facts from opinions.

How to Recognize Facts and Opinions

Strategy ❶ Look for specific information that can be proved or checked for accuracy.

Strategy ❷ Look for assertions, claims, and judgments that express opinions. In this case the author gives a direct opinion about the stories told of John Henry.

Strategy ❸ Think about whether statements can be checked for accuracy. Then, identify the facts and opinions in a chart.

> ### JOHN HENRY: MAN AND MYTH
>
> ❶ John Henry was an African American who worked for the railroads in the late 1800s. His job was to lay down track for the trains. Many famous stories have been written about John Henry, and the most famous is the one about his race against the steam drill. ❶ The first written version of the story dates from 1900.
>
> According to the tale, John was helping dig out the Big Bend Tunnel, when someone started using a steam-powered drill. John Henry was the strongest man on the job, so he raced the drill to see whether he could dig faster than a machine. John Henry won the race, but he died soon after. ❷ This legend may be the most interesting story in U.S. history.

Make a Chart

The chart below analyzes the facts and opinions from the passage above.

Statement	❸ Can It Be Proved?	❸ Fact or Opinion
John Henry worked for the railroads in the 1800s.	Yes. Check newspapers and other historical documents.	Fact
The first version of the story dates from 1900.	Yes. Check the date of the actual written version of the story.	Fact
The legend of John Henry's race against the steam-powered drill may be the most interesting story in American history.	No. This is the opinion of the author; other stories may be just as interesting.	Opinion

Practicing the Skill

Turn to Chapter 3, Section 2, "A Rich Diversity in Climate and Resources," and read the section entitled "Neighbors and Leaders." Make a chart in which you analyze key statements to determine whether they are facts or opinions.

2.8 Forming and Supporting Opinions

Defining the Skill

When you form **opinions,** you interpret and judge the importance of events and people in history. You should always **support your opinions** with facts, examples, and quotes.

Applying the Skill

The following passage describes the unification of Europe. Use the strategies listed below to form and support your opinions about the topic.

How to Recognize Facts and Opinions

Strategy ① Look for important information about the subject. Information can include facts, quotations, and examples.

Strategy ② Form an opinion about the subject by asking yourself questions about the information. For example, how important was the subject? How does it relate to similar subjects in your own experience?

Strategy ③ Support your opinions with facts, quotations, and examples. If the facts do not support the opinion, then rewrite your opinion so that it is supported by the facts.

UNIFYING EUROPE

In 1951, six nations—Belgium, France, Italy, Luxembourg, the Netherlands, and West Germany—placed their coal and steel industries under the control of one group. Six years later, the same countries formed an organization called the European Economic Community, or Common Market. ① This made trade easier among member countries. By 1995, 15 European countries were members of what is now called the European Union (EU).

① The European Union has passed laws to clean up the environment. Through the EU, nations have shared scientific information and new technology. ① They have also combined police forces to fight crime.

Make a Chart

Making a chart can help you organize your opinions and supporting facts. The following chart summarizes one possible opinion about the unification of Europe.

② Opinion	The establishment of the European Union has been good for Europe.
③ Facts	The Common Market made trade easier.
	The EU passed laws to clean up the environment.
	EU nations have shared scientific information and new technology.
	EU nations work together to fight crime.

Practicing the Skill

Turn to Chapter 8, Section 3, "Cuba Today." Read "Living in Cuba," and form your own opinion about the Cuban way of life. Make a chart like the one above to summarize your opinion and the supporting facts and examples.

2.9 Identifying and Solving Problems

Defining the Skill

Identifying problems means finding and understanding the difficulties faced by a particular group of people during a certain time. **Solving problems** means understanding how people tried to remedy those problems. By studying how people solved problems in the past, you can learn ways to solve problems today.

Applying the Skill

The following paragraph describes the problems that resulted when women tried to gain equality. Use the strategies listed below to learn how women responded.

How to Identify Problems and Solutions

Strategy ① Look for the difficulties or problems caused by the situation.

Strategy ② Consider how the problem affected people or groups with different points of view. For example, the main problem described here is how to increase job opportunities for women.

Strategy ③ Look for the solutions that people or groups employed to deal with the problem. Think about whether the solution was a good one for people or groups with differing points of view.

> ### JOB OPPORTUNITIES FOR WOMEN
>
> ① In the mid-20th century women had limited job opportunities. In 1950, only 30 percent of women worked outside the home. By 1960, that number had risen to about 40 percent. Women working outside the home faced several obstacles.
>
> ② For example, the jobs traditionally open to women were in areas like clerical work. Such jobs paid poorly and offered few chances to advance. ② Many men were unwilling to share power with women. ③ In the 1970s, women demanded more rights. They began to move into "blue collar" jobs, such as construction work. ③ Other women gained the education to move into professions like law. By 2000, women were working in every field.

Make a Chart

Making a chart will help you identify and organize information about problems and solutions. The chart below shows problems and solutions included in the passage you just read.

① Problem	② Differing Points of View	③ Solution
In the mid-20th century, there were limited job opportunities for women.	Women wanted jobs with better pay and opportunity to advance. Men did not want to share power.	Women demanded rights. Women gained education. In time, women were working in every field.

Practicing the Skill

Turn to Chapter 12, Section 1, "European Empires." Read "The Spread of Nationalism." Then make a chart that summarizes the problems faced by the monarchies of Europe and their citizens and the solutions they agreed on.

2.10 Evaluating

Defining the Skill

To **evaluate** is to make a judgment about something. Historians evaluate the actions of people in history. One way to do this is to examine both the positives and the negatives of a historical action, then decide which is stronger—the positive or the negative.

Applying the Skill

The following passage describes President Franklin Roosevelt's attempts to pull the United States out of the Great Depression. Use the strategies listed below to evaluate how successful he was.

How to Evaluate

Strategy ① Before you evaluate a person's actions, first determine what that person was trying to do. In this case, think about what Roosevelt wanted to accomplish.

Strategy ② Look for statements that show the positive, or successful, results of his actions. For example, did he achieve his goals?

Strategy ③ Also look for statements that show the negative, or unsuccessful, results of his actions. Did he fail to achieve something he tried to do?

Strategy ④ Write an overall evaluation of the person's actions.

> ### THE NEW DEAL
>
> ① As U.S. president, Franklin Roosevelt wanted to lift the country out of the Great Depression. He called his policies the New Deal. ② Roosevelt used government resources to create jobs. He said, "People who are hungry and out of a job are the stuff of which dictatorships are made." ② He created the Public Works Administration to build roads and bridges and the Civilian Conservation Corps to create parks. The idea was to put people back to work, so they would spend money and help the economy. ③ Roosevelt's New Deal did not end the Depression, but it gave people hope—and the people re-elected Roosevelt three times.

Make a Diagram for Evaluating

Using a diagram can help you evaluate. List the positives and negatives of the historical person's actions and decisions. Then make an overall judgment. The diagram below shows how the information from the passage you just read can be diagrammed.

② *Positive Results:*
- *Unemployed people went back to work*
- *Roads and bridges were built and parks were created*

③ *Negative Results:*
- *In spite of his efforts, the Great Depression continued*

④ *Evaluation:*
Roosevelt was successful because he improved people's lives, and the people showed their appreciation by re-electing him three times.

Practicing the Skill

Turn to Chapter 2, Section 2, "A Rich Diversity in Climate and Resources." Read "Neighbors and Leaders," and make a diagram in which you evaluate U.S. and Canadian cooperation.

2.11 Making Generalizations

Defining the Skill

To **make generalizations** means to make broad judgments based on information. When you make generalizations, you should gather information from several sources.

Applying the Skill

The following three passages contain ideas on America as a melting pot of different cultures. Use the strategies listed below to make a generalization about these ideas.

How to Make Generalizations

Strategy ① Look for information that the sources have in common. These three sources all look at the relationship of immigrants to the United States.

Strategy ② Form a generalization that describes this relationship in a way that all three sources would agree with. State your generalization in a sentence.

> ### THE MELTING POT
>
> At the turn of the century, ① many native-born Americans thought of their country as a melting pot, a mixture of people of different cultures and races who blended together by abandoning their native languages and customs.
>
> —*The Americans*
>
> ① A nation, like a tree, does not thrive well till it is engrafted with a foreign stock.
>
> —*Journals* (Emerson, 1823)
>
> ① The United States has often been called a *melting pot*. But in other ways, U.S. society is an example of *cultural pluralism.* . . . That is, large numbers of its people have retained features of the cultures of their ancestors.
>
> —*World Book Encyclopedia*

Make a Chart

Using a chart can help you make generalizations. The chart below shows how the information you just read can be used to generalize about the contributions of immigrants.

① Many Americans saw America as a place where different cultures blended into one culture.

① America is like a tree that is made stronger by foreign groups coming in.

② Generalization: Whether blending into the melting pot or preserving their separate cultures, immigrants help to make America a great country.

① America is a place where different people come together to form common bonds while also retaining their own cultures.

Practicing the Skill

Turn to Chapter 7, Section 1, "The Roots of Modern Mexico." Read "Life in New Spain," and study the graph on page 176. Also read Biography, "Father Hidalgo" on page 177. Use a chart like the one above to make a generalization about the class system in Mexico.

3.1 Interpreting Time Lines

Defining the Skill

A **time line** is a visual list of events and dates shown in the order in which they occurred. Time lines can be horizontal or vertical. On horizontal time lines, the earliest date is on the left. On vertical time lines, the earliest date is often at the top.

Applying the Skill

The time line below lists dates and events associated with the Civil Rights Movement in the United States. Use the strategies listed below to help you interpret the information.

How to Read a Time Line

Strategy ❶ Read the dates at the beginning and end of the time line. These will show the period of history that is covered. The time line to the right is a vertical time line. It shows the sequence of events from top to bottom instead of from left to right.

Strategy ❷ Read the dates and events in sequential order, beginning with the earliest one. Pay particular attention to how the entries relate to each other. Think about whether earlier events influenced later events.

Strategy ❸ Summarize the focus, or main idea, of the time line. Try to write a main idea sentence that describes the time line.

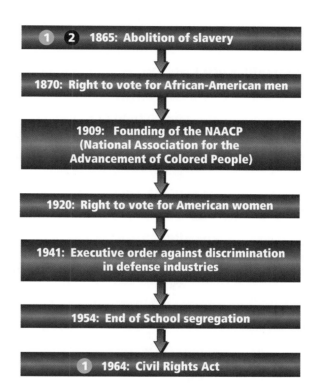

❶ ❷ **1865: Abolition of slavery**

1870: Right to vote for African-American men

1909: Founding of the NAACP (National Association for the Advancement of Colored People)

1920: Right to vote for American women

1941: Executive order against discrimination in defense industries

1954: End of School segregation

❶ **1964: Civil Rights Act**

Write a Summary

Writing a summary can help you understand information shown on a time line. The summary to the right states the main idea of the time line and tells how the events are related.

❸ *Although slavery was abolished in 1865, gaining civil rights was a long and gradual process for African Americans. It involved the passage of amendments granting them the vote, an executive order against discrimination during World War II, and the Civil Rights Act of 1964.*

Practicing the Skill

Turn to Chapter 9, page 233, and write a summary of the information shown on the time line.

4.1 Using an Electronic Card Catalog

Defining the Skill

An **electronic card catalog** is a library's computerized search program that will help you locate books and other materials in the library. You can search the catalog by entering a book title, an author's name, or a subject of interest to you. The electronic card catalog also provides basic information about each book (author, title, publisher, and date of publication). You can use an electronic card catalog to create a bibliography (a list of books) on any topic that interests you.

Applying the Skill

The screen shown below is from an electronic search for information about the Amazon River. Use the strategies listed below to help you use the information on the screen.

How to Use an Electronic Card Catalog

Strategy ❶ Begin searching by choosing either subject, title, or author, depending on the topic of your search. For this search, the user chose "Subject" and typed in the words "Amazon River."

Strategy ❷ Once you have selected a book from the results of your search, identify the author, title, city, publisher, and date of publication.

Strategy ❸ Look for any special features in the book. This book is illustrated, and it includes maps, bibliographical references, and an index.

Strategy ❹ Locate the call number for the book. The call number indicates the section in the library where you will find the book. You can also find out if the book is available in the library you are using. If not, it may be in another library in the network.

```
Search Request:
❶ Subject          Title          Author
   ─────────────────────────────────────────────
   Find  Options  Locations  Backup  Startover  Help

❷ Barter, James.  The Amazon.  San Diego: Lucent
   Books, ©2003.
      ❷ AUTHOR:    Barter, James
      ❷  TITLE:    The Amazon/James Barter.
      ❷ PUBLISHED: San Diego: Lucent Books, ©2003.
      ❸ PAGING:    112p.: ill., maps; 24 cm.
         SERIES:   Rivers of the World
      ❸ NOTES:     Includes bibliographical
                   references (p. 100-104) and index.
   ❹ CALL NUMBER:  J 981.1 BA
```

Practicing the Skill

Turn to Chapter 5, "Canada Today," and find a topic that interests you, such as the First Nations of northern Canada, the cultural conflicts in Quebec, the history of the St. Lawrence Seaway, or the design of Canada's flag. Use the SUBJECT search on an electronic card catalog to find information about your topic. Make a bibliography of books about the subject. Be sure to include the author, title, city, publisher, and date of publication for all the books in your bibliography.

4.2 Creating a Database

Defining the Skill

A **database** is a collection of data, or information, that is organized so that you can find and retrieve information on a specific topic quickly and easily. Once a computerized database is set up, you can search it to find specific information without going through the entire database. The database will provide a list of all information in the database related to your topic. Learning how to use a database will help you learn how to create one.

Applying the Skill

The chart below is a database for famous mountains in the Western Hemisphere. Use the strategies listed below to help you understand and use the database.

How to Create a Database

Strategy ❶ Identify the topic of the database. The keywords, or most important words, in this title are "Mountains" and "Western Hemisphere." These words were used to begin the research for this database.

Strategy ❷ Identify the kind of data you need to enter in your database. These will be the column headings of your database. The key words "Mountain," "Location," "Height," and "Interesting Facts" were chosen to focus the research.

Strategy ❸ Identify the entries included under each heading.

Strategy ❹ Use the database to help you find information quickly. For example, in this database you could search for "Volcanoes" to find a list of famous mountains that are also volcanoes.

❶ FAMOUS MOUNTAINS OF THE WESTERN HEMISPHERE			
❷ MOUNTAIN	LOCATION	HEIGHT ABOVE SEA LEVEL (FEET)	INTERESTING FACTS
❸ Aconcagua	Argentina	22,834	Tallest mountain in Western Hemisphere
Cotopaxi	Ecuador	19,347	❹ One of tallest active volcanoes
Logan	Canada	19,524	Tallest mountain in Canada
Mauna Kea	Hawaii	13,796	Tallest mountain in world from ocean floor to peak
Mauna Loa	Hawaii	13,677	❹ Largest volcano in the world
McKinley	Alaska	20,320	Tallest mountain in North America
Orizaba	Mexico	18,700	Tallest mountain in Mexico
Shasta	California	14,162	Well-known twin peaks

Practicing the Skill

Create a database of Central and South American countries that shows the name of each country, its location, its land area, and its population. Use the information on pages 146–149 "Data File" to provide the data. Use a format like the one above for your database.

4.3 Using the Internet

Defining the Skill

The **Internet** is a computer network that connects to universities, libraries, news organizations, government agencies, businesses, and private individuals throughout the world. Each location on the Internet has a home page with its own address, or URL (Universal Resource Locator). With a computer connected to the Internet, you can reach the home pages of many organizations and services. The international collection of home pages, known as the World Wide Web, is a good source of up-to-date information about current events as well as research on subjects in geography.

Applying the Skill

The Web page below shows helpful links for Unit 1 of *World Cultures and Geography*. Use the strategies listed below to help you understand how to use the Web page.

How to Use the Internet

Strategy ➊ Go directly to a Web page. For example, type http://www.classzone.com/books/wc_survey/ in the box at the top of the screen and press ENTER (or RETURN). The Web page will appear on your screen. Then click on the link for Unit 1. A new web page will appear. Find the link for research links. Click on it and you will go to a third web page. Finally, click on the link for *Web sites on the world* and it will take you to the screen shown here.

Strategy ➋ Explore the links on the right side of the screen. Click on any one of the links to find out more about a specific subject. These links take you to other pages on this Web site. Some pages include links to related information that can be found at other places on the Internet.

Strategy ➌ When using the Internet for research, you should confirm the information you find. Web sites set up by universities, government agencies, and reputable news sources are more reliable than other sources. You can often find information about the creator of a site by looking for copyright information.

Practicing the Skill

Turn to Chapter 23, Section 1, "Physical Geography." Read the section and make a list of thematic maps you would like to research. If you have Internet access, go to classzone.com. There you will find links that provide more information about the topics in the section.

4.4 Creating a Multimedia Presentation

Defining the Skill

Movies, CD-ROMs, television, and computer software are different kinds of media. To **create a multimedia presentation,** you need to collect information in different media and organize them into one presentation.

Applying the Skill

The illustration below shows students using computers to create a multimedia presentation. Use the strategies listed below to help you create your own multimedia presentation.

How to Create a Multimedia Presentation

Strategy ❶ Identify the topic of your presentation and decide which media are best for an effective presentation. For example, you may want to use video or photographic images to show the impressive architecture of medieval castles Or, you may want to use CDs or audiotapes to provide music or to make sounds that go with your presentations, like the sound of a drawbridge closing.

Strategy ❷ Research the topic in a variety of sources. Images, text, props, and background music should reflect the region and the historical period of your topic.

Strategy ❸ Write the script for the presentation and then record it using a microphone and audiotape. You could use a narrator and characters' voices to tell the story. Primary sources are an excellent source for script material.

Strategy ❹ Videotape the presentation or create it on your computer. Having the presentation as a file on your computer will preserve it for future viewing and allow you to show it to different groups of people.

Practicing the Skill

Turn to Chapter 10, "Western Europe: Its Land and Early History." Choose a topic from the chapter and use the strategies listed above to create a multimedia presentation about it.

Glossary

A

absolute location *n.* the exact spot on Earth where a place is found. (p. 36)

acid rain *n.* rain or snow that carries air pollutants to Earth. (p. 386)

Aegean (ih•JEE•uhn) **Sea** *n.* a branch of the Mediterranean Sea that is located between Greece and Turkey. (p. 279)

alliance (uh•LY•uhns) *n.* an agreement among people or nations to unite for a common cause and to help any alliance member that is attacked. (p. 334)

Anasazi *n.* a group of Native Americans who developed a complex civilization in the U.S. Southwest. (p. 88)

armed neutrality *n.* a policy by which a country maintains military forces but does not take sides in the conflicts of other nations. (p. 385)

Athens *n.* the capital of Greece and once one of the most important ancient Greek city-states. (p. 280)

Austria-Hungary *n.* in the 1900s, a dual monarchy in which the Hapsburg emperor ruled both Austria and Hungary. (p. 332)

B

Berlin Wall *n.* a wire-and-concrete wall that divided Germany's East Berlin and West Berlin from 1961 to 1989. (p. 395)

bilingual *adj.* able to speak two languages. (p. 133)

Bill of Rights *n.* ten amendments to the U.S. Constitution that list specific freedoms guaranteed to every U.S. citizen. (p. 96)

Brasília *n.* the capital of Brazil. (p. 246)

C

capitalism *n.* an economic system in which the factories and businesses that make and sell goods are privately owned and the owners make the decisions about what goods to produce. (p. 315)

Carnival *n.* a Cuban holiday that celebrates the end of the harvest each year in July. (p. 220); *n.* a Brazilian holiday that occurs during the four days before Lent. (p. 247)

cartographer *n.* a person who makes maps. (p. 45)

censorship *n.* the outlawing of materials that contain certain information. (p. 403)

chinampa (chee•NAHM•pah) *n.* a floating garden on which the Aztec grew crops. (p. 162)

circumnavigate *v.* to sail completely around. (p. 310)

citizen *n.* a legal member of a country. (p. 20)

citizenship *n.* the status of a citizen, which includes certain duties and rights. (p. 91)

city-state *n.* a central city and its surrounding villages, which together follow the same law, have one form of government, and share language, religious beliefs, and ways of life. (p. 279)

climate *n.* the typical weather of a region over a long time. (p. 75)

coalition government *n.* a government formed by political parties joining together. (p. 362)

Cold War *n.* after World War II, a period of political noncooperation between the members of NATO and the Warsaw Pact nations, during which these countries refused to trade or cooperate with each other. (p. 347)

collective farm *n.* a government-owned farm that employs large numbers of workers, often in Communist countries. (p. 345)

colonialism *n.* a system by which a country maintains colonies outside its borders. (p. 331)

Columbian Exchange *n.* the exchange of goods between Europe and its colonies in North and South America. (p. 166)

Communism *n.* an economic and political system in which property is owned collectively and labor is organized in a way that is supposed to benefit all people. (p. 217)

competition *n.* the rivalry among businesses to sell the most goods to consumers and make the greatest profit. (p. 106)

constitutional amendment *n.* a formal change or addition to the U.S. Constitution. (p. 96)

constitutional monarchy *n.* a government ruled by a king or queen whose power is determined by the nation's constitution and laws. (p. 125)

consumer *n.* a person who uses goods or services. (p. 105)

continent *n.* a landmass above water on earth. (p. 35)

Court of Human Rights *n.* the Council of Europe's court that protects the rights of all citizens in whichever of its member countries they live. (p. 370)

criollo (kree•AW•yaw) *n.* a person born in Mexico whose parents were born in Spain. (p. 175)

Crusades *n.* a series of military expeditions led by Western European Christians in the 11th, 12th, and 13th centuries to reclaim control of the Holy Lands from the Muslims. (p. 301)

culture *n.* the beliefs, customs, laws, art, and ways of living that a group of people share. (p. 21)

culture region *n.* an area of the world in which many people share similar beliefs, history, and languages. (p. 24)

culture trait *n.* the food, clothing, technology, beliefs, language, and tools that the people of a culture share. (p. 21)

currency *n.* money used as a form of exchange. (p. 369)

czar (zahr) *n.* in Russia, an emperor. (p. 319)

D

Day of the Dead *n.* a Mexican holiday, on November 1 and 2, for honoring loved ones who have died. (p. 194)

deforestation *n.* the process of cutting and clearing away trees from a forest. (p. 157)

democracy *n.* a government that receives its power from the people. (p. 91)

departamento (deh•pahr•tah•MEHN•taw) *n.* a Guatemalan state. (p. 223)

dependency *n.* a place governed by or closely connected with a country that it is not officially part of. (p. 203)

deposed *v.* removed from power. (p. 356)

détente (day•TAHNT) *n.* a relaxing of tensions between nations. (p. 357)

dictator *n.* a person who has complete control over a country's government. (p. 207)

dissident *n.* a person who openly disagrees with a government's policies. (p. 403)

distribution *n.* the process of moving products to their markets. (p. 187)

diversify *v.* to conduct business activities in a variety of industries. (p. 209)

dual monarchy *n.* a form of government in which one ruler governs two nations. (p. 332)

Duma (DOO•muh) *n.* one of the two houses of the Russian legislature. (p. 364)

E

economic indicator *n.* a measure that shows how a country's economy is doing. (p. 241)

economics *n.* the study of how resources are managed in the production, exchange, and use of goods and services. (p. 20)

economy *n.* the system by which business owners in a region use productive resources to provide goods and services that satisfy people's wants. (p. 79)

ejido (eh•HEE•daw) *n.* in Mexico, a community farm owned by the people of a village together. (p. 182)

El Niño (ehl NEE•nyaw) *n.* a current in the Pacific Ocean that results from changes in air pressure and that causes changes in weather patterns. (p. 159)

empire *n.* a nation or group of territories ruled by an emperor. (p. 287)

encomienda (ehn•kaw•MYEHN•dah) *n.* a system that the rulers of Spain established in Mexico, under which Spanish men received a Native American village to oversee and gain tribute from. (p. 176)

equal opportunity *n.* a guarantee that government and private institutions will not discriminate against people on the basis of factors such as race, religion, age, gender, or disability. (p. 90)

erosion *n.* the process by which environmental factors, such as wind, rivers, and rain, wear away soil and stone. (p. 74)

ethnic cleansing *n.* the organized killing of members of an ethnic group or groups. (p. 363)

euro *n.* the common unit of currency used by European Union countries. (p. 369)

European Community *n.* an association developed after World War II to promote economic unity among the countries of Western Europe. (p. 392)

European Union (EU) *n.* an economic and political grouping of countries in Western Europe. (p. 368)

export *n.* a product traded with or sold to another country. (p. 129)

F

factor of production *n.* one of the elements needed for production of goods or services to occur. (p. 103)

fascism (FASH•IHZ•uhm) *n.* a political philosophy that promotes a strong, central government controlled by the military and led by a powerful dictator. (p. 336)

federal government *n.* a national government. (p. 96)

feudalism *n.* in medieval Europe, a political and economic system in which lords gave land to less powerful nobles, called vassals, in return for which the vassals agreed to provide various services to the lords. (p. 292)

fiesta *n.* a holiday celebrated by a village or town, with events such as parades, games, and feasts. (p. 194)

First Nations *n.* in Canada, a group of descendants of the first settlers of North America, who came from Asia. (p. 120)

fjord (fyawrd) *n.* a long, narrow, deep inlet of the sea located between steep cliffs. (p. 274)

Florence *n.* a city in Italy that was a bustling center of banking, trade, and manufacturing during the 14th century. (p. 302)

Francophone *n.* a French-speaking person. (p. 133)

free enterprise/market economy *n.* an economy that allows business owners to compete in the market with little government interference. (p. 105)

free-trade zone *n.* an area in which goods can move across borders without being taxed. (p. 241)

French Resistance *n.* an anti-German movement in France during World War II. (p. 390)

French Revolution *n.* a revolution that began on July 14, 1789, and that led to France's becoming a republic. (p. 316)

G

Gadsden Purchase *n.* the 1853 purchase by the United States of a piece of land from northern Mexico. (p. 178)

GDP *n.* gross domestic product, or the total value of the goods and services produced in a country during a given time period. (p. 104)

geography *n.* the study of people, places, and the environment. (p. 18)

glacier *n.* a thick sheet of ice that moves slowly across land. (p. 73)

globalization *n.* the spreading of an idea, product, or technology around the world. (p. 111)

Good Friday Accord *n.* an agreement signed in 1998 by Ireland's Protestants and Catholics that established the Northern Ireland Assembly to represent voters from both groups. (p. 381)

government *n.* the people and groups within a society that have the authority to make laws, to make sure they are carried out, and to settle disagreements about them. (p. 19)

guerrilla warfare *n.* nontraditional military tactics by small groups involving surprise attacks. (p. 253)

guild *n.* a business association created by people working in the same industry to protect their common interests and maintain standards within the industry. (p. 294)

H

hacienda *n.* in Spanish-speaking countries, a big farm or ranch. (p. 181)

hieroglyph *n.* a picture or symbol used in hieroglyphics. (p. 161)

history *n.* a record of the past. (p. 18)

Holocaust *n.* the organized killing of European Jews and others by the Nazis during World War II. (p. 336)

hydroelectricity *n.* electrical power generated by water. (p. 386)

I

immigrant *n.* a person who comes to a country to take up residence. (p. 88)

imperialism *n.* the practice of one country's controlling the government and economy of another country or territory. (p. 310)

import *n.* a product brought into a country through trade or sale. (p. 130)

impressionism *n.* a style of art that creates an impression of a scene rather than a strictly realistic picture. (p. 393)

Industrial Revolution *n.* a period of change beginning in the late 18th century, during which goods began to be manufactured by power-driven machines. (p. 314)

industry *n.* any area of economic activity. (p. 129)

inflation *n.* a continuing increase in the price of goods and services, or a continuing decrease in the capability of money to buy goods and services. (p. 245)

Institutional Revolutionary Party *n.* the most powerful political party in Mexico from the 1920s to 2000, which won every presidential election during that time. (p. 183)

interdependence *n.* the economic, political, and social dependence of culture regions on one another. (p. 26)

Iron Curtain *n.* a political barrier that isolated the peoples of Eastern Europe after World War II, restricting their ability to travel outside the region. (p. 342)

L

labor force *n.* a pool of available workers. (p. 315)

ladino (lah•DEE•noh) *n.* a person of mixed European and Native American ancestry. (p. 205)

landform *n.* a feature of Earth's surface, such as a mountain, valley, or plateau. (p. 73)

latitude *n.* a measure of distance north or south of the equator. (p. 36)

limited government *n.* government in which the powers of the leaders are limited. (p. 95)

London *n.* the capital of England. (p. 379)

longitude *n.* a measure of distance east or west of a line called the prime meridian. (p. 36)

M

Machu Picchu (MAH•choo PEEK•choo) *n.* an ancient stone city built by the Inca. (p. 165)

Magna Carta (MAG•nuh KAHR•tuh) *n.* a document signed by England's King John in 1215 that guaranteed English people basic rights. (p. 295)

malnutrition *n.* poor nutrition, usually from not eating the right foods, which can result in poor health. (p. 220)

manorialism *n.* a social system in which peasants worked on a lord's land and supplied him with food in exchange for his protection of them. (p. 293)

map projection *n.* one of the different ways of showing Earth's curved surface on a flat map. (p. 47)

maquiladora (mah•kee•lah•DAW•rah) *n.* in Mexico, a factory that imports duty-free parts from the United States to make products that it then exports back across the border. (p. 187)

market economy See **free enterprise/ market economy.**

medieval (MEE•dee•EE•vuhl) *adj.* relating to the period of history between the fall of the Roman Empire and the beginning of the modern world, often dated from 476 to 1453. (p. 291)

Mediterranean Sea *n.* an inland sea that borders Europe, Southwest Asia, and Africa. (p. 274)

mestizo (mehs•TEE•saw) *n.* a person of mixed European and Native American ancestry. (p. 175)

migrate *v.* to move from one area in order to settle in another. (p. 38)

mulatto (mu•LAT•oh) *n.* a person of mixed African and European ancestry. (p. 204)

multiculturalism *n.* an acceptance of many cultures instead of just one. (p. 121)

N

national identity *n.* a sense of belonging to a nation. (p. 132)

nationalism *n.* strong pride in one's nation or ethnic group. (p. 329)

nationalize *v.* to establish government control of a service or industry. (p. 188)

NATO (NAY•toh) *n.* the North Atlantic Treaty Organization, a defense alliance formed in 1949, with the countries of Western Europe, Canada, and the United States agreeing to defend one another if attacked. (p. 337)

O

oasis *n.* a region in a desert that is fertile because it is near a river or spring. (p. 251)

oligarchy (AHL•ih•GAHR•kee) *n.* a government in which a few powerful individuals rule. (p. 280)

ombudsman *n.* a Swedish official who protects citizens' rights and ensures that the courts and civil service follow the law. (p. 385)

one-party system *n.* a system in which there is only one political party and only one candidate to choose from for each government position. (p. 343)

Organization of American States (OAS) *n.* an organization of the nations of the Americas that encourages democracy and promotes economic cooperation, social justice, and the equality of all people. (p. 234)

P

Pan-American *adj.* relating to all of the Americas. (p. 234)

Parliament *n.* Canada's national lawmaking body. (p. 125)

parliamentary republic *n.* a republic whose head of government, usually a prime minister, is the leader of the political party that has the most members in the parliament. (p. 361)

patrician (puh•TRIHSH•uhn) *n.* in ancient Rome, a member of a wealthy, landowning family that claimed to be able to trace its roots back to the founding of Rome. (p. 285)

patriotism *n.* love for one's country. (p. 91)

PEMEX *n. Petróleos Mexicanos,* or "Mexican Petroleum," a government agency that runs the oil industry in Mexico. (p. 188)

peninsula *n.* a body of land surrounded by water on three sides. (p. 274)

peninsular (peh•neen•soo•LAHR) *n.* a person who was born in Spain but who lived in Mexico after the Spanish took control. (p. 175)

philosopher *n.* a person who studies and thinks about why the world is the way it is. (p. 281)

plain *n.* a large flat area of land that usually does not have many trees. (p. 275)

plebeian (plih•BEE•uhn) *n.* a common citizen of ancient Rome. (p. 285)

polis *n.* the central city of a city-state. (p. 279)

political process *n.* legal activities through which a citizen influences public policy. (p. 91)

precipitation *n.* moisture that falls to Earth, such as rain or snow. (p. 75)

prime minister *n.* in a parliamentary democracy, the leader of the cabinet and often also of the executive branch. (p. 125)

private property rights *n.* the right of individuals to own land or industry. (p. 355)

privatization *n.* the process of replacing community ownership with individual, or private, ownership. (p. 186)

profit *n.* the money that remains after the costs of producing a product are paid. (p. 105)

propaganda (PRAHP•uh•GAN•duh) *n.* material designed to spread certain beliefs. (p. 354)

Protestant *n.* a member of a Christian church based on the principles of the Reformation. (p. 306)

puppet government *n.* a government that is controlled by an outside force. (p. 343)

Q

Quechua (KEHCH•wuh) *n.* people who live in the Andes highlands and speak the Inca language Quechua. (p. 253)

R

Reformation *n.* a 16th-century movement to change practices within the Roman Catholic Church. (p. 305)

refugee *n.* a person who flees a country because of war, disaster, or persecution. (p. 122)

Reign of Terror *n.* the period between 1793 and 1794 during which France's new leaders executed thousands of its citizens. (p. 317)

relative location *n.* the location of one place in relation to other places. (p. 37)

Renaissance *n.* an era of creativity and learning in Western Europe from the 14th century to the 16th century. (p. 302)

republic *n.* a form of government in which people rule through elected representatives. (p. 285)

reunification *n.* the uniting again of parts. (p. 396)

Riksdag (RIHKS•DAHG) *n.* Sweden's parliament. (p. 384)

Rio de Janeiro *n.* a city in Brazil. (p. 246)

river system *n.* a network that includes a major river and its tributaries. (p. 74)

rural *adj.* of the countryside. (p. 193)

Russian Revolution *n.* the 1917 revolution that removed the Russian monarchy from power after it had ruled for 400 years. (p. 322)

S

São Paulo *n.* a city in Brazil. (p. 246)

scarcity *n.* a word economists use to describe the conflict between people's desires and limited resources. (p. 20)

Scientific Revolution *n.* a period of great scientific change and discovery during the 16th and 17th centuries. (p. 314)

secede *v.* to withdraw from a political union, such as a nation. (p. 381)

Senate *n.* the assembly of elected representatives that was the most powerful ruling body of the Roman Republic. (p. 285)

separatist *n.* a person who wants to separate from a body to which he or she belongs, such as a church or nation. (p. 127)

single-product economy *n.* an economy that depends on just one product for the majority of its income. (p. 209)

skerry *n.* a small island. (p. 387)

socialism *n.* an economic system in which businesses and industries are owned collectively or by the government. (p. 392)

Solidarity *n.* a trade union in Poland that originally aimed to increase pay and improve working conditions and that later opposed Communism. (p. 400)

standard of living *n.* a measure of quality of life. (p. 369)

sugar cane *n.* a plant from which sugar is made. (p. 209)

T

tariff *n.* a fee imposed by a government on imported or exported goods. (p. 369)

technology *n.* tools and equipment made through scientific discoveries. (p. 112)

thematic map *n.* a map that focuses on a specific idea or theme. (p. 46)

tourism *n.* the business of helping people travel on vacations. (p. 189)

transportation barrier *n.* a geographic feature that prevents or slows transportation. (p. 131)

transportation corridor *n.* a path that makes transportation easier. (p. 131)

Treaty of Guadalupe Hidalgo *n.* a treaty that the United States forced Mexico to sign in 1848, giving Mexico's northern lands to the United States. (p. 177)

tributary *n.* a stream or river that flows into a larger river. (p. 157)

Tropical Zone *n.* the region of the world that lies between the latitudes 23°27' north and 23°27' south. (p. 158)

U

United States Constitution *n.* the document that is the foundation for all U.S. laws and the framework for the U.S. government. (p. 94)

unlimited government *n.* a government in which the leaders have almost absolute power. (p. 95)

Ural (YUR•uhl) **Mountains** *n.* a mountain range that divides Europe from Asia. (p. 275)

urban *adj.* of the city. (p. 193)

urbanization *n.* the movement of people from the countryside to cities. (p. 241)

V

value *n.* a principle or ideal by which people live. (p. 110)

vegetation *n.* plant life, such as trees, plants, and grasses. (p. 75)

W

Warsaw Pact *n.* a treaty signed in 1955 that established an alliance among the Soviet Union, Albania, Bulgaria, Czechoslovakia, East Germany, Hungary, Poland, and Romania. (p. 347)

weather *n.* the state of Earth's atmosphere at a given time and place. (p. 75)

West Indies *n.* the Caribbean Islands. (p. 203)

World War I *n.* a war fought from 1914 to 1918 between the Allies (Russia, France, the United Kingdom, Italy, and the United States) and the Central Powers (Austria-Hungary, Germany, Turkey, and Bulgaria). (p. 333)

World War II *n.* a war fought from 1939 to 1945 between the Axis powers (Germany Italy, and Japan) and the Allies (the United Kingdom, France, the Soviet Union, and the United States). (p. 336)

Spanish Glossary

A

absolute location [ubicación absoluta] *s.* lugar exacto donde se halla un lugar en la Tierra. (pág. 36)

acid rain [lluvia ácida] *s.* lluvia o nieve que lleva sustancias contaminantes a la Tierra. (pág. 386)

Aegean (ih•JEE•uhn) **Sea** [mar Egeo] *s.* parte del Mar Mediterráneo ubicada entre Grecia y Turquía. (pág. 279)

alliance (uh•LY•uhns) [alianza] *s.* acuerdo de unión entre pueblos o naciones por una causa común y de ayuda mutua en caso de que uno sea atacado. (pág. 334)

Anasazi [anasazi] *s.* grupo de indígenas que desarrollaron una cultura compleja en el sudoeste de Estados Unidos. (pág. 88)

armed neutrality [neutralidad armada] *s.* política mediante la cual un país mantiene fuerzas armadas pero no participa en conflictos de otras naciones. (pág. 385)

Athens [Atenas] *s.* capital de Grecia y una de las ciudades-estado más importantes de la antigua Grecia. (pág. 280)

Austria-Hungary [Austria-Hungría] *s.* monarquía dual mediante la cual a comienzos del siglo XX el emperador de la dinastía de los Hasburgo gobernó Austria y Hungría. (pág. 332)

B

Berlin Wall [Muro de Berlín] *s.* pared de cemento y alambre que desde 1961 a 1989 dividía la parte este de Berlín de la parte oeste. (pág. 395)

bilingual [bilingüe] *adj.* que puede hablar dos idiomas. (pág. 133)

Bill of Rights [Declaración de Derechos] *s.* las diez enmiendas a la Constitución de los Estados Unidos que enumeran libertades específicas garantizadas a todos los ciudadanos estadounidenses. (pág. 96)

C

capitalism [capitalismo] *s.* sistema económico en el cual las empresas y comercios que fabrican y venden productos y mercancías son de propiedad privada; los dueños de dichas empresas y comercios deciden lo que desean producir y vender. (pág. 315)

Carnival [carnaval] *s.* feriado cubano que celebra cada año el fin de la cosecha en el mes de julio. (pág. 220); *s.* feriado brasileño de cuatro días anterior al comienzo de la cuaresma. (pág. 247)

cartographer [cartógrafo] *s.* persona que hace mapas. (pág. 45)

censorship [censura] *s.* prohibición de materiales que contienen cierta información. (pág. 403)

chinampa (chee•NAHM•pah) *s.* huerta flotante en la que los aztecas sembraban sus cultivos. (pág. 162)

circumnavigate [circunnavegar] *v.* dar la vuelta alrededor de algo en una nave. (pág. 310)

citizen [ciudadano] *s.* habitante legal de un país. (pág. 20)

citizenship [ciudadanía] *s.* estado de un ciudadano que incluye derechos y obligaciones. (pág. 91)

city-state [ciudad estado] *s.* ciudad central y sus aldeas aledañas que acatan las mismas leyes, tienen una sola forma de gobierno y comparten una lengua, creencias religiosas y estilos de vida. (pág. 279)

climate [clima] *s.* condición típica de la atmósfera en determinada región. (pág. 75)

coalition government [gobierno de coalición] *s.* gobierno formado por la unión de partidos políticos. (pág. 362)

Cold War [Guerra Fría] *s.* período político posterior a la Segunda Guerra Mundial, caracterizado por la falta de cooperación y relaciones comerciales entre los países miembros de la OTAN y las naciones del Pacto de Varsovia. (pág. 347)

collective farm [granja colectiva] *s.* granja que pertenece al gobierno, que emplea a gran número de trabajadores generalmente en países comunistas. (pág. 345)

colonialism [colonialismo] *s.* sistema mediante el cual un país mantiene colonias en otras partes del mundo. (pág. 331)

Columbian Exchange [intercambio colombino] *s.* intercambio de mercancías entre Europa y sus colonias en América. (pág. 166)

Communism [comunismo] *s.* sistema político y económico en el cual la propiedad es colectiva y la actividad laboral es organizada de manera de beneficiar a todos los individuos. (pág. 217)

competition [competencia] *s.* rivalidad entre empresas por vender la mayor cantidad de productos y mercaderías a los consumidores y por obtener el mayor beneficio. (pág. 106)

constitutional amendment [enmienda constitucional] *s.* cambio formal a la constitución de los Estados Unidos. (pág. 96)

constitutional monarchy [monarquía constitucional] *s.* gobierno encabezado por un rey o reina, cuyo poder está determinado por la constitución y leyes de la nación. (pág. 125)

consumer [consumidor] *s.* persona que usa productos o servicios. (pág. 105)

continent [continente] *s.* masa continental sobre agua en la Tierra. (pág. 35)

Court of Human Rights [Corte de Derechos Humanos] *s.* corte que protege los derechos de ciudadanos que habiten en países miembros. (pág. 370)

criollo (kree•AW•yaw) *s.* persona nacida en México cuyos padres provienen de España. (pág. 175)

Crusades [las cruzadas] *s.* serie de expediciones militares dirigidas por cristianos de Europa occidental en los siglos XI, XII y XIII, para apoderarse de nuevo de las Tierras Santas, en poder de los musulmanes. (pág. 301)

culture [cultura] *s.* conjunto de creencias, costumbres, leyes, formas artísticas y de vida compartidas por un grupo de personas. (pág. 21)

culture region [región cultural] *s.* territorio donde muchas personas comparten creencias, historia y lenguas similares. (pág. 24)

culture trait [característica cultural] *s.* alimento, vestimenta, tecnología, creencia, lengua u otro elemento compartido por un pueblo o cultura. (pág. 21)

currency [moneda] *s.* sistema que sirve para medir el valor de las cosas que se intercambian. (pág. 369)

czar (zahr) [zar] *s.* emperador ruso. (pág. 319)

D

Day of the Dead [Día de los Muertos] *s.* feriado mexicano del 1 al 2 de noviembre en honor a los seres queridos que han muerto. (pág. 194)

deforestation [deforestación] *s.* proceso mediante el cual se cortan árboles y se van eliminando bosques. (pág. 157)

democracy [democracia] *s.* sistema de gobierno mediante el cual los gobernantes reciben el poder del pueblo. (pág. 91)

departamento (deh•pahr•tah•MEHN•taw) *s.* nombre que reciben los estados en Guatemala. (pág. 223)

dependency [territorio dependiente] *s.* lugar gobernado o que está estrechamente conectado con un país del cual no forma parte. (pág. 203)

deposed [depuesto] *v.* removido del poder. (pág. 356)

détente (day•TAHNT) [distensión] *s.* disminución de la tensión entre países. (pág. 357)

dictator [dictador] *s.* persona que tiene el control absoluto del gobierno de un país. (pág. 207)

fiesta *s.* feriado celebrado por una comunidad o pueblo, con desfiles, juegos y banquetes. (pág. 194)

First Nation [Primera Nación] *s.* nombre que reciben en Canadá los descendientes de los primeros pobladores en Norteamérica que provenían de Asia. (pág. 120)

fjord (fyawrd) [fiordo] *s.* entrada larga y estrecha del mar formada entre acantilados abruptos. (pág. 274)

Florence [Florencia] *s.* ciudad italiana que durante el siglo XIV mantuvo una dinámica actividad bancaria, comercial y manufacturera. (pág. 302)

Francophone [francófono] *s.* persona que habla francés. (pág. 133)

free enterprise/market economy [librecambismo/economía de libre mercado] *s.* economía que permite a empresarios y comerciantes competir en el mercado con poca interferencia del gobierno. (pág. 105)

free-trade zone [zona de libre comercio] *s.* área en la que tanto personas como mercaderías pueden circular más allá de las fronteras sin que esta actividad sea gravada con impuestos. (pág. 241)

French Resistance [Resistencia francesa] *s.* en Francia, un movimiento antialemán durante la Segunda Guerra Mundial. (pág. 390)

French Revolution [Revolución francesa] *s.* revolución que comenzó el 14 de julio de 1789 y tuvo como resultado la conversión de Francia en una república. (pág. 316)

G

Gadsden Purchase [Compra de Gadsden] *s.* compra mediante la cual los Estados Unidos adquirieron en 1853 parte del territorio del norte de México. (pág. 178)

GDP [PIB, Producto Interno Bruto] *s.* valor total de los productos y servicios producidos en un país durante un período determinado. (pág. 104)

geography [geografía] *s.* estudio de los pueblos, lugares y el medio ambiente. (pág. 18)

glacier [glaciar] *s.* espesas formaciones de hielo que se mueven lentamente por la tierra. (pág. 73)

globalization [globalización] *s.* difusión de una idea, producto o tecnología por todo el mundo. (pág. 111)

Good Friday Accord [Acuerdo del Viernes Santo] *s.* acuerdo firmado por los protestantes y católicos de Irlanda del Norte que estableció la Asamblea de Irlanda del Norte, asamblea esta que representa a los votantes de ambos grupos. (pág. 381)

government [gobierno] *s.* los individuos y grupos en una sociedad que tienen la autoridad de crear leyes y hacerlas cumplir, y de resolver desacuerdos que puedan surgir con respecto a ellas. (pág. 19)

guerrilla warfare [guerrilla] *s.* tácticas militares no tradicionales llevadas a cabo por grupos pequeños que realizan ataques sorpresivos. (pág. 253)

guild [gremio] *s.* asociación creada por personas que trabajan en una misma industria, con el fin de proteger sus intereses comunes y mantener ciertos criterios y principios aplicables a la industria. (pág. 294)

H

hacienda *s.* en países hispanos, finca o granja de gran tamaño. (pág. 181)

hieroglyph [jeroglífico] *s.* dibujo y símbolo de la escritura jeroglífica. (pág. 161)

history [historia] *s.* un registro de los acontecimientos del pasado. (pág. 18)

Holocuast [Holocausto] *s.* matanza sistemática (genocidio) de los judíos europeos y otros por el partido nazi durante la Segunda Guerra Mundial. (pág. 336)

hydroelectricity [electricidad hidráulica] *s.* energía eléctrica producida por el agua. (pág. 386)

market economy Ver **free enterprise.**

medieval (MEE•dee•EE•vuhl) [medieval] *adj.* que pertenece al período de la historia comprendido entre la caída del Imperio romano y el comienzo del mundo moderno, aproximadamente desde 476 a 1453. (pág. 291)

Mediterranean Sea [mar Mediterráneo] *s.* mar interno que bordea Europa, el sudoeste de Asia y África. (pág. 274)

mestizo s. persona de descendencia mixta, con sangre europea e indígena. (pág. 175)

migrate [migrar] *v.* irse de un área para establecerse en otra. (pág. 38)

mulatto [mulato] *s.* persona con descendencia mixta, de sangre europea y africana. (pág. 204)

multiculturalism [multiculturalismo] *s.* la aceptación de muchas culturas en vez de una solamente. (pág. 121)

N

national identity [identidad nacional] *s.* sentimiento de pertenencia a una nación. (pág. 132)

nationalism [nacionalismo] *s.* intenso orgullo por el país o grupo étnico propio. (pág. 329)

nationalize [nacionalizar] *v.* pasar al control gubernamental un servicio o industria. (pág. 188)

NATO (NAY•toh) [OTAN, Organización del Tratado del Atlántico Norte] *s.* alianza de defensa que agrupa a los países de Europa occidental, Canadá y Estados Unidos, que acuerdan la defensa común en caso de ataque. (pág. 337)

O

oasis [oasis] *s.* región fértil en un desierto que se formó alrededor de un río o manantial. (pág. 251)

oligarchy (AHL•ih•GAHR•kee) [oligarquía] *s.* gobierno de sólo unos pocos individuos poderosos. (pág. 280)

ombudsman [defensor del pueblo] *s.* funcionario del gobierno sueco que protege los derechos de los ciudadanos y asegura que los tribunales y la administración pública cumplan con la ley. (pág. 385)

one-party system [sistema monopartidista] *s.* sistema donde sólo se puede votar por un partido político y por un candidato para cada puesto de gobierno. (pág. 343)

Organization of American States (OAS) [OEA, Organización de los Estados Americanos] *s.* organización de todas las naciones americanas, que promueve la democracia y la cooperación económica, la justicia social y la igualdad entre los pueblos. (pág. 234)

P

Pan-American [panamericano] *adj.* relativo a todas las Américas. (pág. 234)

Parliament [Parlamento] *s.* cuerpo legislativo nacional de Canadá. (pág. 125)

parliamentary republic [república parlamentaria] *s.* república cuyo jefe de estado, en general un primer ministro, es el líder del partido político que tiene la mayoría de representantes en el parlamento. (pág. 361)

patrician (puh•TRIHSH•uhn) [patricio] *s.* miembro de familia adinerada y hacendada en la antigua Roma, que afirmaba que sus orígenes se remontan a la época de la fundación de Roma. (pág. 285)

patriotism [patriotismo] *s.* amor por el país propio. (pág. 91)

PEMEX *s.* Petróleos Mexicanos, agencia gubernamental que administra la industria petrolera en México. (pág. 188)

peninsula [península] *s.* territorio rodeado de agua en tres de sus lados. (pág. 274)

peninsular s. persona que nació en España pero vivió en México luego de la conquista de los españoles. (pág. 175)

philosopher [filósofo] *s.* persona que estudia y piensa sobre el mundo y su naturaleza. (pág. 281)

plain [llanura] *s.* superficie extensa y plana que suele no tener muchos árboles. (pág. 275)

plebeian (plih•BEE•uhn) [plebeyo] *s.* ciudadano corriente (sin título de nobleza) en la antigua Roma. (pág. 285)

polis [polis] *s.* ciudad central de una ciudad estado. (pág. 279)

political process [proceso político] *s.* actividades permitidas por la ley mediante las cuales el ciudadano influye en las políticas públicas. (pág. 91)

precipitation [precipitación] *s.* humedad como la lluvia o la nieve que cae a la Tierra. (pág. 75)

prime minister [primer ministro] *s.* en una democracia parlamentaria, líder del gabinete y frecuentemente de la administración ejecutiva. (pág. 125)

private property rights [derechos de propiedad privada] *s.* derechos individuales de ser propietario de bienes raíces, campos o industrias. (pág. 355)

privatization [privatización] *s.* proceso mediante el cual la propiedad que pertenece a la comunidad se convierte en propiedad privada o individual. (pág. 186)

profit [ganancia] *s.* dinero que sobra luego de pagar el costo de producir un producto. (pág. 105)

propaganda (PRAHP•uh•GAN•duh) [propaganda] *s.* material cuyo objetivo es difundir ciertas creencias. (pág. 354)

Protestant [protestante] *s.* miembro de una iglesia cristiana fundada de acuerdo a los principis de la Reforma. (pág. 306)

puppet government [gobierno títere] *s.* gobierno que hace lo que le indica un poder exterior. (pág. 343)

Q

Quechua (KEHCH•wuh) *s.* habitante de los Andes que habla una lengua inca del mismo nombre. (pág. 253)

R

Reformation [Reforma] *s.* movimiento del siglo XVI que se propuso cambiar las prácticas de la Iglesia Católica. (pág. 305)

refugee [refugiado] *s.* persona que huye de un país a raíz de una guerra, catástrofe, o porque es objeto de persecuciones. (pág. 122)

Reign of Terror [reino del Terror] *s.* período comprendido entre 1793 y 1794 durante el cual las nuevas autoridades en Francia ejecutaron miles de ciudadanos. (pág. 317)

relative location [ubicación relativa] *s.* ubicación de un lugar en relación con otros. (pág. 37)

Renaissance *s.* período de creatividad y de aprendizaje en Europa occidental entre los siglos XIV y XVI. (pág. 302)

republic [república] *s.* forma de gobierno controlado por sus cuidadanos a través de representates elegidos por los cuidadanos. (pág. 285)

reunification [reunificación] *s.* acción de unificar nuevamente las partes. (pág. 396)

Riksdag (RIHKS•DAHG) *s.* parlamento sueco. (pág. 384)

Rio de Janeiro *s.* ciudad brasileña. (pág. 246)

river system [sistema fluvial] *s.* que incluye ríos principales y sus tributarios. (pág. 74)

rural [rural] *adj.* que pertenece al campo. (pág. 193)

Russian Revolution [Revolución rusa] *s.* revolución de 1917 que eliminó la monarquía rusa del poder luego de 400 años de vigencia. (pág. 322)

S

São Paulo [San Pablo] *s.* ciudad brasileña. (pág. 246)

scarcity [escasez] *s.* palabra usada por los economistas para describir el conflicto que existe entre el deseo de los seres humanos y los recursos limitados para satisfacerlo. (pág. 20)

Scientific Revolution [Revolución científica] *s.* período de grandes cambios científicos y descubrimientos durante los siglos XVI a XVII. (pág. 314)

secede [separarse] *v.* independizarse de una unidad política, como una nación. (pág. 381)

Senate [Senado] *s.* asamblea más poderosa de la República romana, cuyos representantes eran elegidos. (pág. 285)

separatist [separatista] *s.* persona que desea separarse del cuerpo al que pertenece, como la iglesia o la nación. (pág. 127)

single-product economy [economía de un solo producto] *s.* economía cuya mayor parte de los ingresos depende de un solo producto. (pág. 209)

skerry [arrecife] *s.* islote. (pág. 387)

socialism [socialismo] *s.* sistema económico en donde algunos negocios e industrias le pertenecen a una cooperativa o al gobierno. (pág. 392)

Solidarity [Solidaridad] *s.* sindicato polaco cuya finalidad inicial fue aumentar el salario, mejorar las condiciones laborales de los trabajadores y luego oponerse al Comunismo. (pág. 400)

standard of living [nivel de vida] *s.* forma de medir la calidad de vida. (pág. 369)

sugar cane [caña de azúcar] *s.* planta de la que se extrae el azúcar. (pág. 209)

T

tariff [arancel aduanero] *s.* tarifa o suma de dinero impuesto por el gobierno en productos que se importan o exportan. (pág. 369)

technology [tecnología] *s.* herramientas o equipos que se crean a partir de ciertos descubrimientos. (pág. 112)

thematic map [mapa temático] *s.* mapa que se centra en una idea o tema particular. (pág. 46)

tourism [turismo] *s.* industria que estimula a la gente a viajar por placer. (pág. 189)

transportation barrier [barrera al transporte] *s.* obstáculo que impide el transporte o lo disminuye. (pág. 131)

transportation corridor [vía de transporte] *s.* camino que facilita el transporte. (pág. 131)

Treaty of Guadalupe Hidalgo [Tratado de Guadalupe Hidalgo] *s.* tratado que Estados Unidos exigió a México que firmara en 1848, mediante el cual México cedió a Estados Unidos su territorio en el norte. (pág. 177)

tributary [tributario] *s.* arroyo o río que confluye en otro río de mayor caudal. (pág. 157)

Tropical Zone [Zona Tropical] *s.* región del mundo comprendida entre las latitudes 23°27' al norte y 23°27' al sur. (pág. 158)

U

United States Constitution [Constitución de Estados Unidos] *s.* documento que fundamenta todas las leyes del gobierno de Estados Unidos y constituye su marco jurídico. (pág. 94)

unlimited government [gobierno ilimitado] *s.* gobierno en el que las autoridades ejercen la mayor parte del poder. (pág. 95)

Ural (YUR•uhl) **Mountains** [Montes Urales] *s.* cadena montañosa que divide Europa de Asia. (pág. 275)

urban [urbano] *adj.* que pertenece a la ciudad. (pág. 193)

urbanization [urbanización] *s.* movimiento de personas del campo a la ciudad. (pág. 241)

V

value [valor] *s.* principio e ideal básico de las personas. (pág. 110)

vegetation [vegetación] *s.* conjunto de plantas, arbustos, árboles y hierbas. (pág. 75)

W

Warsaw Pact [Pacto de Varsovia] *s.* tratado firmado en 1955 que estableció una alianza entre la Unión Soviética, Albania, Bulgaria, Checoslovaquia, Alemania Oriental, Hungría, Polonia y Rumania. (pág. 347)

weather [tiempo] *s.* estado atmosférico cercano a la Tierra en un momento y lugar determinados. (pág. 75)

West Indies [Indias Occidentales/las Antillas] *s.* islas del Caribe. (pág. 203)

World War I [Primera Guerra Mundial] *s.* guerra de 1914 a 1918 entre los aliados (Rusia, Francia, el Reino Unido, Italia y los Estados Unidos) y las potencias centrales (Imperio autro-húngaro, Alemania, Turquía y Bulgaria). (pág. 333)

World War II [Segunda Guerra Mundial] *s.* guerra de 1939 a 1945 entre las potencias del Eje (Alemania, Italia y Japón) y los aliados (el Reino Unido, Francia, la Unión Soviética y los Estados Unidos). (pág. 336)

Index

An *i* preceding a page reference in italics indicates that there is an illustration, and usually text information as well, on that page. An *m* or a *c* preceding an italic page reference indicates a map or a chart, as well as text information on that page.

Acknowledgments

Text Credits

Chapter 1, pages 28–29: "How Thunder and Earthquake Made Ocean," from *Keepers of the Earth: Native American Stories and Environmental Activities for Children* by Michael J. Caduto and Joseph Bruchac. Copyright © 1988, 1989 Michael J. Caduto and Joseph Bruchac. Reprinted by permission of Fulcrum Publishing.

Chapter 3, page 83: Excerpts from *The Dust Bowl: Men, Dust, and the Depression* by Paul Bonnifield. Copyright © 1979 by the University of New Mexico Press. Reprinted by permission of the University of New Mexico Press.

Chapter 4, page 100: "Coney" from *Subway Swinger* by Virginia Schonborg, copyright © 1970 by Virginia Schonborg. Used by permission of HarperCollins Publishers.

Chapter 4, page 100: "Knoxville, Tennessee" from *Black Feeling, Black Talk, Black Judgment* by Nikki Giovanni. Copyright 1968, 1970 by Nikki Giovanni. Reprinted by permission of HarperCollins Publishers Inc.

page 101: "Scenic" from *Collected Poems, 1953–1993* by John Updike, copyright © 1993 by John Updike. Used by permission of Alfred A. Knopf, a division of Random House, Inc.

Chapter 4, page 115: Excerpt from "Diversity: The American Journey" by Frank A. Blethen, *Seattle Times* Publisher and CEO. Reprinted by permission of the author.

Chapter 5, page 139: Excerpt from "Canadian Bakin': Nation ends 50 years of hockey frustrations" by Michael Hunt, *Milwaukee Journal Sentinel.* Reprinted by permission of the Milwaukee Journal Sentinel.

Chapter 7, page 199: Excerpt from interview from the *NewsHour with Jim Lehrer,* July 15, 1999. Copyright © 1999 by NewsHour. Reprinted by permission of NewsHour.

Chapter 8, page 227: Excerpt from "Nobel Accceptance Speech" by Oscar Arias Sánchez. Copyright © The Nobel Foundation. Reprinted by permission of The Nobel Foundation.

Chapter 9, page 239: "Chilean Earth" from *A Gabriela Mistral Reader,* translation copyright 1993 by Maria Giachetti. Reprinted by permission of White Pine Press.

page 249: Copyright © 2000 by Houghton Mifflin Company, Reproduced by permission from *The American Heritage Dictionary of the English Language, Fourth Edition.*

Chapter 10, page 281: Quote by Herakleitos, translated by Guy Davenport, from *7 Greeks,* copyright © 1995 by Guy Davenport. Reprinted by Sales Territory: U.S./Canadian rights only.

Chapter 12, page 340: "The Giant's Causeway" from *Irish Fairy Tales and Legends* retold by Una Leavy. Copyright © 1996 by The Watts Publishing Group Ltd.

Chapter 12, page 349: Excerpt from *Blood, Toil, Tears and Sweat* by Winston Churchill. Reproduced with permission of Curtis Brown Ltd., London, on behalf of the Estate of Sir Winston S. Churchill. Copyright © the Estate of Sir Winston S. Churchill.

Chapter 14, page 405: Excerpt from "Presentation Speech" by Egil Aarvik. Copyright © The Nobel Foundation. Reprinted by permission of The Nobel Foundation.

Art Credits

Beverly Doyle 28; John Edwards Studio 81; Ken Goldammer 12; Nenad Jakesevic 163, 164, 168, 381, 404; Rich McMahon 44, 323; Gary Overacre 340–341; Matthew Pippin xiv, 236–237. All other artwork created by Publicom, Inc.

Map Credits

This product contains proprietary property of **MAPQUEST.COM** Unauthorized use, including copying, of this product is expressly prohibited.

Photography Credits

Cover NASA; (See page 14 for full credits.); **vii** *left* Terry Wild Studio; *bottom* Copyright © Panoramic Images; *top* D. Robert and Lorri Franz/Corbis; *right* Copyright © SuperStock; **viii** *top* Michel Zabe/Art Resource, New York; *center* AFP/Corbis; *bottom* Staffan Widstand/Corbis; **ix** *top left* Erich Lessing/Art Resource, New York; *bottom left* Dave Bartruff/Corbis; *bottom right* Hulton|Archive/Getty Images; *top* Erich Lessing/Art Resource, New York; *top right* Reunion des Musées Nationaux/Art Resource, New York; *center right* Scott Gilchrist/Archivision.com; **x** *top left* S. Bavister/Robert Harding Picture Library; *bottom left* John Noble/Corbis; *bottom* John Launois/Black Star Publishing/PictureQuest; *bottom right* AFP/Corbis; *top* Copyright © Brannhage/Premium/Panoramic Images; **S12** Reprinted with the permission of the *St. Louis Post Dispatch,* 2002; **S13** The Granger Collection, New York; **S26** Kevin Schafer/Corbis; **S29** The Granger Collection, New York; **S30–31** Stephanie Maze/Corbis; **S32** Mary Evans Picture Library.

UNIT ONE

2–3 NASA; **4** *bottom right* NOAA; *left* © Roger Ressmeyer/Corbis; *top right* Science Museum/Science and Society Picture Library, London.

Chapter 1

14 *top left* Brian A. Vikander/Corbis; *top center* Owen Franken/Corbis; *bottom left* Tim Thompson/Corbis; *center left* Kevin Schafer/Corbis; *bottom center* Maria Taglienti/The Image Bank/GettyImages; *center right* James A. Sugar/Corbis; *bottom right* Nicholas deVore III/Photographers Aspen/PictureQuest; *top right* Dean Conger/Corbis; **15** *top* John Callahan/Stone/GettyImages; *bottom left* The Purcell Team/Corbis; *center left* Helen Norman/Corbis; *center* Nik Wheeler/Corbis; *bottom center* Dennis Degnan/Corbis; *center right* Neil Rabinowitz/Corbis; *bottom right* Martin Rogers/Corbis; **16** *top* Copyright © Jim West; *bottom* K. Gilham/Robert Harding Picture Library; **17** *top* The Image Bank/Getty Images; *bottom* The Military Picture Library/Corbis; **18** *bottom* © Roger Ressmeyer/Corbis; *top* Skjold Photographs; **19** *left* © Franz-Marc Frei/Corbis; *right* © Peter Turnley/Corbis; *center* © Owen Franken/Corbis; **20** *right* Copyright © Jim West; *left* © Reuters NewMedia Inc./Corbis; **21** © Ed Reinke/AP/Wide World Photos; **22** Joseph Sohm/ Visions of America, LLC/PictureQuest; **23** *bottom* Joe Sohm, Chromosohm/Stock Connection/ PictureQuest; *top* Scott Teven/Stock Connection/ PictureQuest; **24** *right* The Granger Collection, New York; **26** *left* © Neil Rabinowitz/Corbis; *right* © Dave G. Houser/Corbis; *center* © Roman Soumar/Corbis; **28–29** Illustration © Bill Cigliano **30** *bottom left* Picture Finders/eStock Photography/PictureQuest.

Chapter 2

32–33 © David Hardy/Photo Researchers, Inc.; **33** Dagli Orti/Biblioteca Nacionale Marciana Venice/The Art Archive; **34** *top* © Stuart Franklin/Magnum Photos; *bottom* © Francis E. Caldwell, Affordable Photo; **35** *left* The Granger Collection, New York; **36** Schafer and Hill/Stone/GettyImages; **37** *top* © Francis E. Caldwell, Affordable Photo; *bottom* Digital Image © 1996 Corbis; Original image courtesy of NASA/CORBIS; **38** © Thonig/Premium Stock/PictureQuest; **39** David Muench/ Stone/GettyImages; **42** *left* © Bettmann/Corbis; *top right* © Victoria & Albert Museum, London/Art Resource, NY; *bottom right* The Art Archive/India Office Library; **43** *bottom* Austrian Archives/Corbis; *top right* The Granger Collection, New York; **45** *right* The Granger Collection, New York; **46** Illustration © Bill Cigliano; **47** Library of Congress, Prints and Photographs Division; **50** David Muench/Stone/GettyImages; **51** NASA.

UNIT TWO

52–53 Copyright © Panoramic Images.

Chapter 3

66–67 Paul A. Souders/Corbis; **67** *top* James Randklev/Corbis; **68** *bottom* Michael Melford/The Image Bank/ GettyImages; *top* Raymond Gehman/Corbis; **69** *right* Corbis; *left* Pat O'Hara/Corbis; **70** Michael Melford/The Image Bank/GettyImages; **71** *top* D. Robert and Lorri Franz/Corbis; *center* Bettmann/Corbis; *bottom* Bettmann/ Corbis; **72** *right* Paul A. Souders/Corbis; *left* Copyright © Didier Dorval/Masterfile; **73** M. L. Fuller and the U. S. Geological Society; **74** Paul A. Souders/Corbis; **75** Copyright © F. Hoffman/The Image Works; **76** Bettmann/Corbis; **78** *top* Raymond Gehman/Corbis; *bottom* Phillip Gould/Corbis; **79** David Reed/AP/Wide World Photos; **82** *right* David Reed/AP/Wide World Photos; *left* Corbis.

Chapter 4

84–85 Copyright © Tom Jelen/Panoramic Images; **85** *bottom right* Dennis Brack/Black Star Publishing/PictureQuest; *top left* Reuters NewMedia Inc./Corbis; *bottom left* Ed Kashi/Corbis; *top center* Copyright © Marianne Barcellona/ Time Pix; *center* Reuters NewMedia Inc./Corbis; *bottom center* Copyright © David Lassman/The Image Works; *top right* AFP/Corbis; **86** *top* The Granger Collection, New York; *bottom* Reuters NewMedia Inc./Corbis; **87** The Granger Collection, New York; **88** *bottom* Copyright © Nancy Richmond/The Image Works; *top* The Granger Collection, New York; **89** The Granger Collection, New York; **90** Reuters NewMedia Inc./Corbis; **92** *top left* NASA; *bottom right* European Space Agency; **93** *bottom right* European Space Agency; **93–94** NASA The Everett Collection; **94** The Everett Collection; **95** Art Resource, New York; **96** *bottom* Copyright © Topham/The Image Works; *top* The Granger Collection, New York; **100** *top* Tony Freeman; *bottom* Copyright © Rafael Macia/Photo Researchers; **101** *bottom* Copyright © Jim Corwin/Photo Researchers; **102** Copyright © Norbert Schwerine/The Image Works; **103** Teri Bloom; **104** *bottom* U.S. Treasury Department; **105** Kevin R. Morris/Bohemian Nomad PictureMakers/Corbis; **106** Copyright © Monika Graff/The Image Works; **108** *top* Corbis; *center* Spencer Grant III/Stock Boston/PictureQuest; *bottom* Paul A. Souders/Corbis; **109** *bottom right* Culver Pictures; *top* Archive Photos/PictureQuest; *bottom left* Farrell Greham/Corbis; *center* Michael S. Yamashita/Corbis; **110** Tom Vano/Index Stock Imagery/PictureQuest; **111** *right* Terry Wild Studio; *left* William Folsom/Words and Pictures/PictureQuest; **114** *left* The Granger Collection, New York; *right* Terry Wild Studio; *center* The Everett Collection.

Chapter 5

116–117 Copyright © First Light/Panoramic Images; 117 *top* Canadian Museum of Civilization, image number S93–2826; 118 *top* Kevin R. Morris/Corbis; *bottom* Hockey Hall of Fame; 119 *all* The Granger Collection, New York; 120 Kevin R. Morris/Corbis; 121 Private Collection/Phillips, Fine Art Auctioneers, New York/The Bridgeman Art Library; 123 *top* Copyright © James Schwabel/Panoramic Images; 124 Copyright © SuperStock; 125 Copyright © Bill Brooks/Masterfile; 126 Ron Poling/Canadian Press/AP/Wide World Photos; 127 Yves Marcoux/Stone/GettyImages; 128 Bettmann/Corbis; 131 The Granger Collection, New York; 132 Hockey Hall of Fame; 133 Copyright © J. A. Kraulis/Masterfile; 134 Lee Snider/Corbis; 135 Archivision.com; 138 *top left* Copyright © James Schwabel/Panoramic Images; *bottom left* Copyright © Bill Brooks/Masterfile; *top right* The Granger Collection, New York; *bottom right* Copyright © J. A. Kraulis/Masterfile.

UNIT THREE

140–141 Bill Pogue/Stone/GettyImages.

Chapter 6

150–151 Cosmo Condina/Stone/GettyImages; 151 *top* Kevin Schafer/Corbis; 152 *right* Richard A. Cooke/Corbis; *left* Archivo Iconografico, S. A./Corbis; 153 AFP/Corbis; 154 Danny Lehman/Corbis; 156 *top* Guido A. Rossi/The Image Bank/GettyImages; *bottom* Stephen Frink/Corbis; 157 Galen Rowell/Corbis; 160 *left* Lara Fox; *right* After Hansen 1990: II. Drawn by TW Rutledge. Used by permission; 161 *top* Richard A. Cooke/Corbis; *bottom* Copyright © Craig Lovell/Painet; 162 *top* Mireille Vautier/Woodfin Camp/PictureQuest; *bottom* Michel Zabe/Art Resource, New York; 165 *bottom* Edwin Sulca Lagos; *top* Werner Forman Archive/Art Resource, New York; 166 Archivo Iconografico, S. A./Corbis; 168 *center left* Kevin Schafer/Corbis; *top left* Guido A. Rossi/The Image Bank/GettyImages; *bottom right* Werner Forman Archive/Art Resource, New York.

Chapter 7

170–171 Robert Frerck/Stone/GettyImages; 171 *top* R.G.K. Photography/Stone/GettyImages; 172 *top* Erich Lessing/Art Resource, New York; *center* Cabacete [Helmet] (c. 1480). Private collection. Photograph courtesy of the Cleveland (Ohio) Museum of Art; *bottom* Danny Lehman/Corbis; 173 *right* The Granger Collection, New York; *left* Richard T. Nowitz/Corbis; 174 *bottom center* Copyright © SPL/Custom Medical Stock Photography; *bottom left* The Granger Collection, New York; *top left* Erich Lessing/Art Resource, New York; *top right* Cabacete [Helmet] (c. 1480). Private collection. Photograph courtesy of the Cleveland (Ohio) Museum of Art; 175 David Hiser/Stone/GettyImages; 177 *top* Schalkwijk/Art Resource, New York; *bottom* Greg Probst/Corbis; 179 *left* PhotoDisc/GettyImages; *right* Bettmann/Corbis; 180 *top* Bettmann/Corbis; *bottom* The Granger Collection, New York; 181 *center* Bettmann/Corbis; *bottom* Tom Bean/Corbis; 184 Latin Focus.com; 185 J. P. Courau/D. Donne Bryant Stock Photography; 186 *left* Annie GriffithsBelt/Corbis; *right* Robert Frerck/Stone/GettyImages; 187 *top* Danny Lehman; *bottom* Jose Welbers/Latin Focus.com; 189 ZSSD/Latin Focus.com; 190 *right* Kal Muller/Woodfin Camp/PictureQuest; *left* Copyright © Erwin Nielsen/Painet; 191 Peter Menzel/Stock Boston/PictureQuest; 192 Schalkwijk/Art Resource, New York; 193 Danny Lehman/Corbis; 194 Charles and Josette Lenars/Corbis; 196 *top* Cosmo Condina/Stone/GettyImages; *bottom* Copyright © Bernard Neuwirtch/Painet; 197 Gary S. Withey/Bruce Coleman/Picture Quest; 198 *top right* Annie Griffiths Belt/Corbis; *bottom right* Danny Lehman/Corbis; *bottom left* Schalkwijk/Art Resource, New York.

Chapter 8

200–201 Copyright © Michel Frigan/Film Works Inc.; 201 *top* Dave G. Houser/Corbis; 202 *bottom* Reuters NewMedia Inc./Corbis; *top right* Copyright © Topham/The Image Works; 203 Copyright © The Image Works; 204 James Strachan/Stone/GettyImages; 205 *center Ladino* Reuters NewMedia Inc./Corbis; *bottom Ladino* Reuters NewMedia Inc./Corbis; *top Ladino* Martin Rogers/Corbis; *bottom right* Archive Photos/PictureQuest; 206 Jeff Greenberg/eStock Photography/PictureQuest; 207 Bill Gentile/Corbis; 208 AFP/Corbis; 209 Copyright © Topham/The Image Works; 210 AFP/Corbis; 211 *top* Bill Ross/Corbis; *bottom* Copyright © Rob Crandall/StockBoston; 212 Suzanne Murphy-Larronde; 213 Nik Wheeler/Corbis; 215 Sovfoto/Eastfoto/PictureQuest; 216 *center left* Bettmann/Corbis; *bottom left* Richard Bickel/Corbis; *bottom right* Latin Focus.com; 217 Latin Focus.com; 218 AFP/Corbis; 219 Copyright © Marge George/Spectrum Stock; 220 Reuters NewMedia Inc./Corbis; 221 Scott Sandy/AP/Wide World Photos; 222 *top* Latin Focus.com; *bottom* Cindy Karp/Black Star Publishing/PictureQuest; 223 Jan Butchofsky-Houser/Corbis; 224 *top* Martin Rogers/Corbis; *bottom* World Pictures/eStock Photography/PictureQuest; 225 Jan Butchofsky-Houser/Corbis; 226 *bottom left* Copyright © The Image Works; *top* Suzanne Murphy-Larronde; *bottom center* Sovfoto/Eastfoto/PictureQuest; *bottom right* Jan Butchofsky-Houser/Corbis.

Chapter 9

228–229 Layne Kennedy/Corbis; 229 *top* Eye Ubiquitous/Corbis; 230 *bottom* David Wolf; *top* Steve Vidler/ eStock Photography/PictureQuest; 231 *all* The Granger Collection, New York; 233 Christie's Images/Corbis; 234 *top* AFP/Corbis; *bottom* Bettmann/Corbis; 235 *bottom* Latin Focus.com; *top* Richard Hamilton Smith/Corbis; 238 Reuters NewMedia Inc./Corbis; 239 *top* Victor Englebert; *bottom* Corbis; 242 Steve Vidler/eStock Photography/ PictureQuest; 243 Copyright © Larry Luxner/Luxner News; 245 *bottom* Tim Page/Corbis; *top* Copyright © Les Stone/The Image Works; 246 David Wolf; 247 *top* Reuters NewMedia Inc./Corbis; *bottom* Bettmann/Corbis; 248 *top* Macduff Everton/Corbis; *bottom* AFP/Corbis; 249 *top* Dagli Orti/National History Museum Mexico City/ The Art Archive; *bottom* Garden Picture Library; 250 Latin Focus.com; 251 Cory Langley; 252 *right* Richard Hamilton Smith/Corbis; *left* Victor Engelbert; *center* Charles and Josette Lenars/Corbis; 253 Victor Engelbert; 254 Staffan Widstrand/Corbis; 256 *bottom left* Christie's Images/Corbis; *bottom center* Victor Engelbert; *top* David Wolf; *bottom right* Staffan Widstrand/Corbis.

UNIT FOUR

258–259 Stuart Dee/The Image Bank/GettyImages.

Chapter 10

270–271 Copyright © James L. Stanfield/National Geographic Society Image Collection; 271 *top* Robert Harding Picture Library; 272 *top* Sef/Art Resource, New York; *bottom left, bottom right* Erich Lessing/Art Resource, New York; 273 Bill Ross/Corbis; 274 Arnulf Husmo/Stone/GettyImages; 275 Walter Bibikow/Index Stock Imagery/PictureQuest; 276 *top left* Jonathan Blair/Corbis; *top right* Eye Ubiquitous/Corbis; *bottom* Johan Elzenga/Stone/GettyImages; 278 *all* Greek Culture Ministry/AP/Wide World Photos; 279 HorreeZirkzee Produk/Corbis; 280 Foto Marburg/ Art Resource, New York; 281 Sef/Art Resource, New York; 282 *left* Nimatallah/Art Resource, New York; *right* Scala/Art Resource, New York; 284 Copyright © Macduff Everton/The Image Works; 285 Erich Lessing/Art Resource, New York; 286 Giraudon/Art Resource, New York; 287 Erich Lessing/Art Resource, New York; 288 *top left* Jeff Rotman; *center* Scala/Art Resource, New York; *bottom right* O. Alamany and E. Vicens/Corbis; *bottom center* Bettmann/Corbis; 289 Erich Lessing/Art Resource, New York; 290 Art Resource, New York; 291 Reunion des Musées Nationaux/Art Resource, New York; 292 Catherine Karnow/Corbis; *spread* Musée de la Tapisserre, Bayoux, France/The Bridgeman Art Library; 293 *top* Jose Fuste Raga/eStockPhotography/PictureQuest; 294 Erich Lessing/ Art Resource, New York; 295 *right* Dept. of the Environment, London/The Bridgeman Art Library; *left* The Granger Collection, New York; 296 *top left* Sef/Art Resource, New York; *bottom* Erich Lessing/Art Resource, New York; *top right* Jose Fuste Raga/eStockPhotography/PictureQuest.

Chapter 11

298–299 Bruno Barbey/Magnum/PictureQuest; 299 *top* The Granger Collection, New York; *center* Leonard L. T. Phodes/Animals Animals; 300 *center* Mary Evans Picture Library; *top* Reunion des Musées Nationaux/Art Resource, New York; *bottom* The Pierpont Morgan Library/Art Resource, New York; 301 The Granger Collection, New York; 302 Alinari/Art Resource, New York; 303 *top* Scott Gilchrist/Archivision.com; *bottom* Palazzo Medici- Riccardi, Florence, Italy/The Bridgeman Art Library; 304 *bottom* Scala/Art Resource, New York; *top* Reunion des Musées Nationaux/Art Resource, New York; 305 The Pierpont Morgan Library/Art Resource, New York; 306 Corbis; 307 Giraudon/Art Resource, New York; 309 North Wind Pictures; 310 Reunion des Musées Nationaux/Art Resource, New York; 313 AKG London; 314 *center* Scala/Art Resource, New York; *top* NASA; *bottom* Copyright © Will & Deni McIntyre/Photo Researchers; 315 The Granger Collection, New York; 316 Hulton-Deutsch Collection/ Corbis; 317 Victoria & Albert Museum, London/Art Resource, New York; 318 *right* © Courtesy of the Estate of Ruskin Spear/Private Collection/Phillips, Fine Art Auctioneers, New York/The Bridgeman Art Library; *left* Giraudon/ Art Resource, New York; 319 *top* Scala/Art Resource, New York; *bottom* Roger Tidman/Corbis; 320 Erich Lessing/ Art Resource, New York; 321 Chuck Nacke/Woodfin Camp/PictureQuest; 322 Hulton-Deutsch Collection/Corbis; 324 *top left* North Wind Pictures; *bottom left* Alinari/Art Resource, New York; *bottom right* Hulton-Deutsch Collection/Corbis; *top right* © Courtesy of the Estate of Ruskin Spear/Private Collection/Phillips, Fine Art Auctioneers, New York/The Bridgeman Art Library; 325 The Library of Congress Website.

Chapter 12

326–327 Michael S. Yamashita/Corbis; 327 *top* Owen Franken/Corbis; 328 *top* Ralph White/Corbis; *bottom* Hulton|Archive/Getty Images; 329 Hulton|Archive/Getty Images; 331 *bottom* Hulton|Archive/Getty Images; *center* Gianni Dagli Orti/Corbis; *top* Mark Rykoff/Rykoff Collection/Corbis; 333 *right* Bettmann/Corbis; *left* Hulton|Archive/ Getty Images; 334 *top* Hulton|Archive/Getty Images; *bottom* Art Young; 335 Hulton|Archive/Getty Images; 337 *bottom* Hulton|Archive/Getty Images; *top* Hulton-Deutsch Collection/Corbis; 339 Reprinted with the permission of the *St. Louis Post Dispatch,* 2002; 342 Paul Almasy/Corbis; 343 *bottom* Sovfoto/Eastfoto/PictureQuest; *top* Ralph White/Corbis; 344 *bottom* Hulton|Archive/Getty Images; *top* Sovfoto/Eastfoto/PictureQuest; 345 Culver Pictures; 346 *bottom* Hulton|Archive/Getty Images; *center* The Kobal Collection; 347 Dave Bartruff/Corbis; 348 *right* Sovfoto/

Eastfoto/PictureQuest; *left* Hulton|Archive/Getty Images; *center* Hulton-Deutsch Collection/Corbis; **349** Mandeville Special Collections at UCSD.

Chapter 13

350–351 Copyright © Brannhage/Premium/Panoramic Images; **351** *top* Sovfoto/Eastfoto; **352** *top* Premium Stock/Corbis; *bottom* Craig Aurness/Corbis; **353** Mark Rykoff/Corbis; **354** *left* NASA/AP/Wide World Photos; *right* Sovfoto/Eastfoto; **355** Copyright © Giuliano Bevilacqua/TimePix; **356** Bryn Colton/Corbis; **357** *top* Bettmann/ Corbis; *bottom* AP/Wide World Photos; **358** Bojan Brecelj/Corbis; **360** David and Peter Turnley/Corbis; **362** Craig Aurness/Corbis; **363** Copyright © Bios (F. Gilson)/Peter Arnold; **364** Scala/Art Resource, New York; **366** Sovfoto/ Eastfoto/PictureQuest; **367** *bottom* Hoa Qui/Index Stock Imagery/PictureQuest; *top* Premium Stock/Corbis; **368** AFP/Corbis; **369** Mike Mazzaschi/Stock Boston/PictureQuest; **370** S. Bavister/Robert Harding Picture Library; **371** Copyright © Malcolm S. Kirk/Peter Arnold; **372** *bottom* John Neubauer/Photo Edit/PictureQuest; *top right* Underwood & Underwood/Corbis; *top left* Bettmann/Corbis; **373** *top* Wolfgang Kaehler/Corbis; *left* Paul A. Souders/ Corbis; *center* Roger Ressmeyer/Corbis; *bottom right* Academy of Natural Sciences of Philadelphia/Corbis; **374** *left* Bettmann/Corbis; *right* Premium Stock/Corbis; *center* David and Peter Turnley/Corbis.

Chapter 14

376–377 Alan Thornton/Stone/GettyImages; **377** *top* Mark A. Leman/Stone/GettyImages; **378** *top* Ted Spiegel/ Corbis; *bottom* www.carpix.net; **379** *bottom right* Michael Neveux/Corbis; *center* AFP/Corbis; **382** *bottom* John Launois/Black Star Publishing/PictureQuest; *top* Copyright © Julian Nieman/Collections; **383** AFP/Corbis; **384** *right* Nik Wheeler/Corbis; *left* Ted Spiegel/Corbis; **385** Hans T. Dahlskog/Pressens Bild; **386** *bottom* AFP/Corbis; *top* Alex Farnsworth/The Image Works; **387** John Noble/Corbis; **388–389** Museo de Firenze Com'era, Florence, Italy/ The Bridgeman Art Library; **390** *right* Bettmann/Corbis; *left* Corbis; **391** Bettmann/Corbis; **392** Robert Estall/Corbis; **393** Art Resource, New York; **394** *right* AFP/Corbis; *left* Thomas Hoepker/Magnum/PictureQuest; **396** *bottom center* Erich Lessing/Art Resource, New York; *top* www.carpix.net; *bottom right* Josef Karl Stieler/Archivo Iconografico, S. A./Corbis; **397** Carmen Redondo/Corbis; **399** Chuck Fishman/Contact Press Images/PictureQuest; **400** Bettmann/ Corbis; **401** Dennis Chamberlain/Black Star Publishing/PictureQuest; **402** Steven Weinberg/Stone/GettyImages; **403** Vittoriano Rastelli/Corbis; **404** *top left* Copyright © Alex Farnsworth/The Image Works; *top right* Thomas Hoepker/Magnum/PictureQuest; *bottom right* Bettmann/Corbis; *center* Corbis.

Special Report

407 *top* AP/Wide World Photos; *bottom* AP/Wide World Photos; **409** *top* AP/Wide World Photos; *bottom* AP/Wide World Photos; **410** AP/Wide World Photos; **411** *left* © Mario Tama/Getty Images; *right* © Reuters NewMedia Inc./Corbis.